# Allied Coastal Forces

# Allied
# Coastal
# Forces
## of World War II

**Volume I:**
**Fairmile designs and**
**US submarine chasers**

## John Lambert
## Al Ross

CONWAY

MARITIME PRESS

*Frontispiece: A typical scene at HMS* Hornet,
*Gosport, in June 1944; MGB 317 is coming in – a C*
*type of the 1st Flotilla. HDMLs (1391 outboard)*
*and other Cs, including 330, are moored in the*
*stream. The D boats alongside are units of the 55th*
*MTB Flotilla ('Shark's Teeth'), showing the*
*cluttered upper deck of the period.*
Imperial War Museum

© John Lambert and Al Ross, 1990

First published in Great Britain 1990 by
Conway Maritime Press Limited
24 Bride Lane, Fleet Street
London EC4Y 8DR

*British Library Cataloguing-in-Publication Data*
Lambert, John
  Allied coastal forces of World War II
  Vol. 1, Fairmile designs and US submarine chasers
  1. Allied navies. Military equipment, 1939–1945
  I. Title   II. Ross, Al
  623.825

  ISBN 0–85177–519–5

Designed by John Mitchell
Typeset by Inforum Typesetting, Portsmouth
Printed and bound by The Bath Press, Bath

# Contents

# Foreword

As National President of the Coastal Forces Veterans Association, it gives me great pleasure to recommend this first volume of John Lambert's detailed account of all the craft in which we served. I know that it has been a labour of great love for him; nevertheless a glance at the contents is enough to show one that a great deal of thought and careful work has gone into the preparation of all the details and all the drawings – it really is a *tour de force*.

The Fairmile boats with which this book is largely concerned – the A and B Class MLs, the C Class MGBs and the D Class MTBs and MGBs – formed a considerable part of the Coastal Forces organisation, and served in all theatres of the war. This book, giving details of all the boats and their armaments, also explains the organisation of their production, and sets out their service and achievements. It will be of permanent value to all historians of the Coastal Forces.

The next volume of John Lambert's trilogy will cover the Vosper 70ft MTBs, and this will be of the greatest interest to me, since I spent almost all my seagoing time with Coastal Forces in Vosper boats (and then served in the Vosper company for twenty-one years after I was invalided out of the Royal Navy). It would also have been of greatest interest to my illustrious predecessor as CFVA President. The great Peter Dickens spent all his time in MTBs commanding the 21st Flotilla of Vosper 70ft boats.

The final volume will take care of the British Power Boat 70ft MTBs/MGBs, of which the 71ft 6in MGBs, which began to come into service early in 1942 under Robert Hichens, were superbly successful boats.

John Lambert has done us all a great service.

**Commander Christopher W Dreyer**
**DSO, DSC, RN (Rtd), President CFVA**

# Author's note

I have been researching the subject of this book for a number of years. The idea was first mooted about six years ago, in correspondence between myself and Dr Al Ross of Bangor, Maine, USA. We share the same interests (producing accurate detailed drawings of small warships), both served in our nations' respective navies (neither of us in Coastal Forces, as it happens), and we have both produced books and many articles. The object of this joint venture is to describe in detail the vessels, armament and equipment used by the Allied Coastal Forces during World War II.

Dr Ross and I have exchanged ideas frequently and freely since about 1983, and I was able to visit him in the United States in the summer of 1987. We discussed the project in great detail and exchanged drawings and photographs, and I returned to my side of the 'pond' with many new ideas and much new information that I wished to include.

Originally our research was to have been published in one large volume in the spring of 1988, but the amount of work involved and the amount of information obtained quickly exceeded by far the scope of my provisional synopsis of May 1986. With a great many subjects drawn, we felt jointly that the whole project would be better presented as three smaller, though still substantial, books.

Much thought has gone into the content of each book, and each will add to an overall picture of Allied Coastal Forces. Each will deal with a particular design, company or class of warship, with details of selected weapons systems in use on those units (though common to many types), main engines and other equipment. The layout is based upon the Conway Anatomy of the Ship series, adapted to cover greater and more varied subject matter.

The decision to cover the Fairmile Marine Company in this first book, along with a wooden United States Submarine Chaser design, was mine. One of the reasons for this is that the Fairmile organisation seems to represent a particularly coherent subject. These books are about the vessels built and how they developed, and in the case of the Fairmile boats the initial development was completed without the benefit of war experience; the A and B classes went straight into service. This contrasts directly with the process outlined in Book 2, which will describe pre-war Vosper

ideas and show their evolution during hostilities.

Despite a great deal of research, however, much remains obscure. I have never found trials reports or 'ship's covers' for Fairmile boats – it would seem that none exist. I have checked through the mass of original drawings held at the National Maritime Museum archives at Woolwich, and found little that was new to me. There was nothing at all on the A, C or F classes. Nevertheless, the Fairmile methods of construction are well shown in the drawings that I have obtained, from a variety of both official and unofficial sources, of the well-known B type.

The Coastal Forces Veterans Association has been an excellent source of information. I have been in correspondence with more than eighty members over the years, many of whom have been kind enough to record thoughts and memories of their vessels, as well as provide details of the armament and equipment of the period.

I am grateful to many, many individuals who have assisted me in my research (their names are listed in the Acknowledgements). A number of Fairmile drawings have been provided from private sources, and I have been able to borrow a copy of the *Fairmile ML Engineering Handbook*. In the case of the A and C classes, I have been able to provide only a general arrangement layout and construction from the MoD (Navy) lists, but I have been able to follow the development of the types with help from Mr Geoffrey Hudson, CFVA's historian, and other members.

Eton College has provided additional facts about the founder of Fairmile, and the Public Record Office and the Naval Historical Branch have provided additional background information. The ships and weapons are the meat of this study, however, and I am grateful to be able to record the wartime efforts of the draughtsmen of the period.

The vast majority of the drawings shown here are available on large sheets, in some cases with several sheets per subject (the Fairmile B requires nine). Copies of these may be purchased from two outlets: David MacGregor Plans, 99 Lonsdale Road, London, SW13 9DA; and Marine Modelling Monthly, Traplet Publications Limited, Traplet House, Severn Drive, Upton-on-Severn, Worcestershire WR8 0SL.

# Acknowledgements

A great many people, both here and abroad, have assisted with this project over the past five years. I have met many, and spoken on the telephone or have been in correspondence with many more, which has added to my depth of knowledge. Without their help this volume would perhaps not be as comprehensive as it is. Their names are shown in no order of precedence.

My thanks first are due to the Coastal Forces Veterans Association officers and members of the executive committee, to their president, Commander Christopher W Dreyer DSO, DSC, RN (Rtd), to Len Bridge, their secretary, and to Geoffrey M Hudson, their honorary historian; many other members are listed below.

Other sources include: Leslie Brown of Vosper Thornycroft; Robert Tough of Tough Brothers; Len 'Rover' Reynolds (author of *Gunboat 658*); Sandie Armstrong of Brixham; Graham 'Dave' Davis and Dave Fricker, both of the Medusa Project; RG Morley C Eng, MI Mech E; DK Brown RCNC; OA Goulden (author of *From Trombay to Changi*); George Sidney Selman MRINA; Edwin 'Bert' West, late of Fairmile; Alain Rainville of the Public Archives in Ottowa; Alan Francis of the Naval Historical Branch; William 'Bill' Hollick C Eng, FI Mech E; The World Ship Society; Petty Officer (Diver) P McCabe; the staff of the Draught Room and the Brass Foundry of the National Maritime Museum; the Photographic Library of the Imperial War Museum; and Priddy's Hard Naval Armament Museum.

Others with whom I have corresponded on one or more occasions are: Bertie Beavis, AA Beven, John Boscott, John Buckley, George Burrows, Donald A Campbell, Cedric Cannon, Ken Cassells of New Zealand, LD Conquest, Bill Darracott, J Davies, PR Davis, A Disney, GL Dooley, Alex Dowling, Ralph Eastwood, Ray Ellis, GO Evans, KS Fisher, GA Flamank, JR Fletcher, 'Spike' Gill, Bill Hall, FGH Hawkins, Dorrien L Hill, George Hobbs, Ron Hobbs, Len Hughes, DEJ Hunt, CW Jamson, Errol W Keenan, James Kinross, George Lay, H Maxwell Lewis, Edwin Mayer, GS Mizon, Bob Morgan, Guy Moss, Peter I Munnock, Bob Parker, Douglas E Pigg, RV Price, P Redhead, Eileen J Robertson, KD Ross, Ernest Scott, Frank R Shaw, John D Smale, 'Mac' Macdonald Spencer, Leslie J Sprigg JP, HW Tomlinson, CH Turner, Charles Turner, Roy Tyldesley, Ken Upperton, Hal Venables of Australia, Sir Nigel Vernon Bt, Oscar de Ville, Cecil Watkins of Australia, Joe Welch, Dr RTC Worsley of Canada, AE Wouton, and Peter Wyllie.

My thanks to you all.

Finally, my thanks to Sheila, who read through my masses of bumph, made some light of my thoughts and retyped everything, with some spelling improvements.

# Abbreviations

| | |
|---|---|
| ASL | Air Safety Launch |
| ASR | Air/Sea Rescue |
| BU | Broken up |
| CT | Controlled Target |
| CTL | Constructive Total Loss |
| DCTB | Distant Controlled Target Boat |
| DY | Dockyard |
| FC | Fleet Craft (Harbour Service) |
| FDB | Fast Despatch Boat |
| FF | Free French |
| HO | Handed over |
| HSL | Harbour Service Launch |
| LRRC | Long Range Rescue Craft (RAF) |
| MAC | Motor Attendant Craft (for M/S) |
| ML(A) | ML (Air Service) |
| MSU | Mediterranean Survey Unit |
| PO | Paid off |
| RAF | Royal Air Force |
| RAN | Royal Australian Navy |
| RCB | Remote Controlled (Target) Boat |
| RCN | Royal Canadian Navy |
| RIN | Royal Indian Navy |
| RML | Rescue Motor Launch |
| R Neth N | Royal Netherlands Navy |
| RNN | Royal Norwegian Navy |
| RNVR | Royal Naval Volunteer Reserve |
| RPN | Royal Pakistan Navy |
| SAN | South African Navy |
| SC | Surface Craft |
| SCC | Sea Cadet Corps |
| SML | Survey Motor Launch |
| STT | Ship Target Trials |
| TC | Training Craft |
| USN | United States Navy |
| WD | War Department (RASC) |

# The Fairmile Marine Company

This book is concerned principally with the well known wooden warships that stemmed from the Fairmile Marine Company of Cobham, Surrey. To the best of my knowledge the idea of mass-producing wooden minor warships in time of war was the unique idea of one man, Fairmile's founder. Each type was designed and built in kit form, to be assembled at a multitude of small shipyards both at home and abroad, while at the same time freeing the few specialist producers such as Vosper, White and the British Power Boat Co to continue the construction of more specialist high-speed craft. The Fairmile designs also used basic materials, and relied on many new, non-naval industries to provide materials without interfering in the flow of products from those specialist manufacturers.

During World War I, the increasing success of German submarine attacks on shipping by torpedo, and an increase of minelaying in home waters, forced the Royal Navy to seek a method of combatting this threat. It led to a demand for large numbers of anti-submarine motor launches to reduce the threat of coastal attacks. With British industry fully committed, there was no additional production available, and the required numbers could not be found from home sources.

In the spring of 1915 an Admiralty delegation visited the United States and selected the Electric Launch Company (Elco) of Bayonne, New Jersey, to construct fifty wooden anti-submarine launches for the Royal Navy (MLs 1–50), with the Standard Motor Construction Company to build the engines. The British contract was signed on 9 April 1915, with the delivery of the first twenty-five, consigned through Canadian Vickers, promised for 30 November. Soon after the first vessels were completed, on 8 June, the Admiralty ordered a further 500 (MLs 51–550). All were to be ready for delivery by 15 November 1916. (Elso is still proud of this achievement –550 boats in 488 days.)

These Elco boats were designed by Irwin Chase, and their construction was supervised by Henry Sutphen, both men being active between the wars and much involved in the Elco PT boat programme of World War II.

The Admiralty required a speed of 19 knots fully loaded, with an endurance of 800 nautical miles at full speed (1000 miles at 15 knots, or 2100 miles at 11 knots). They were to be capable of keeping station in rough weather, but, because they could not cross the Atlantic under their own power, they were to be of a size capable of being shipped as deck cargo. As first designed, their length (overall) was 75ft, but after completion of the first few this was increased to 80ft. Powered by two six-cylinder Standard Motors petrol engines, they also carried a 4.5kW generator. The total fuel allowed a radius of action of about 750 nautical miles at 19 knots. On trials (before being armed) their speeds varied from 19.25 to almost 21 knots. They displaced some 42 tons and on their arrival in the UK were armed with a single 3-pounder gun, or on occasion a .303in Lewis gun as well. As they had entered service prior to the introduction of the depth charge, they were fitted with a number of primitive anti-submarine devices. These included towed explosive paravanes and small 14lb bombs attached to 4ft 6in long handles, and, ultimately, ten D type depth charges, which were dropped over the side.

While these boats provided a measure of anti-submarine defence, it was found that in truth they were not well suited to the weather conditions prevailing off the British coastline, being wet in any seaway, rather lively and somewhat uncomfortable. By 1916, with a number in service, the Royal Navy was committed to the craft, but considered them too small. It was felt that a boat of 100–120ft in length would have been more suitable. Soon after the hostilities ended they were sold out of service. These vessels were to help stimulate the imagination of the founder of the Fairmile organisation.

Noel Macklin (actually Albert Noel Campbell Macklin) was born on 28 October 1886, the son of Charles Campbell Macklin, a barrister, and Leslie Cordery. The son of a well-to-do family, Noel attended Lee's School at Forest Row. He went to Eton in September 1899 (Broadbent's House – where he is said to have kept a lion cub!), leaving at Christmas 1901. He later became a big game hunter, a first-class rifle shot and photographer. He decided to exploit these interests commercially, and produced a remarkable film on African wildlife, which he showed at the Stoll Opera House. The start of the 1914–18 War intervened in his commercial activities, however, and he joined up. Macklin served in France during the first year, but was wounded and invalided out as a captain in the Royal Horse Artillery (RHA) in 1915. After convalescing, he became a lieutenant in the RNVR and served with the Dover Patrol from 1916 to 1918. This experience was no doubt formative to his activities in the later conflict.

Between the wars Macklin interested himself in flying, yachting and motor-car racing and engaged in a variety of commercial projects, with varying success. His interest in ballooning resulted in aerial advertising. Cadmium plating and bottling oxygen also caught his attention, while his interest in motor-cars resulted in the building of the Silver Hawk and the Invicta, which secured a number of world records but little or no profit. In 1933 he found a winner in the anglicised version of the Hudson car, called the Railton, designed by Reid Railton and built by the Fairmile Engineering Company. In this venture the chassis and engine were standard, and the customer chose his own coachwork. (There is still a thriving interest in this prestige car through an owners club, and some were used by the Metropolitan Police as plain-clothes police cars.)

When it became obvious that war was impending, the versatile Macklin reviewed the ways in which he could contribute to the war effort, and considered various possibilities from aircraft to boats.

The urgent need for anti-submarine vessels occurred to him after reading an article by Vice-Admiral CV Usborne, CB, CMG, and with his typical instant grasp of the requirements he immediately sought expert advice on design and method of construction, the engine power required and the possible sources of supply of materials and engines. Within days, the Fairmile Marine Company was in being and the services of a prominent naval architect secured. Admiral Usborne was asked to act as naval adviser. Macklin already had first-class engineers and technical staff associated with his car-building activities, which were carried out in the sheds behind his house, 'The Cottage', at Fairmile, Cobham.

It was from these premises that the whole of the vast Fairmile organisation was to be run. The result of Macklin's activities was the design of a motor launch, subsequently to be known as the Fairmile A type, of between 50 and 60 tons displacement, 110ft long and propelled by three Hall-Scott Defender petrol engines, each of 600hp, giving a maximum speed of 25 knots. The hull form was based upon the fishery protection boat *Vaila*, but the Admiralty declined to place an order. Macklin was convinced that the idea was sound, and that the type would be required in considerable numbers if war broke out. He decided to proceed with the construction of a prototype – ML 100, as she was later numbered –

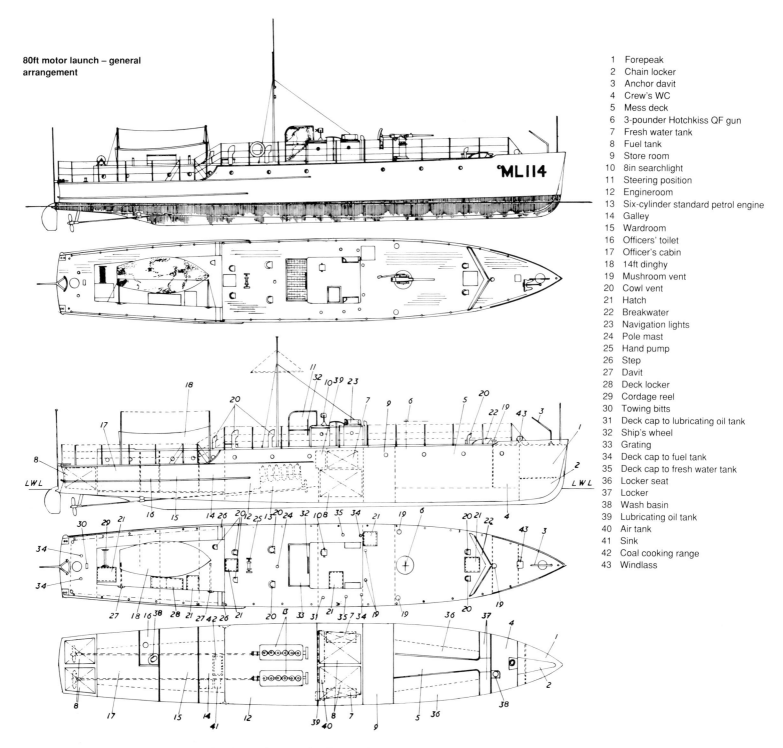

80ft motor launch – general arrangement

ML114

and ordered her to be built at Woodnut's yard at Bembridge on the Isle of Wight. The work proceeded at some speed, and the vessel was half built when it became evident that war was indeed imminent. The Admiralty had second thoughts, decided that the new method of construction was sound, and placed a covering order for the new design on 27 July 1939, some two months before war was declared. This order was followed by another soon after the declaration of war, when on 22 September the Admiralty ordered a further eleven A types and thirteen of a new Admiralty design, the Fairmile B type.

On receipt of the revised contract, Macklin realised that he did not have the required capital to order more material, and in discussion with the Admiralty came to the remarkable arrangement that the Fairmile Company should carry on business under an agency agreement, thus virtually becoming an Admiralty Department, yet should retain its original name and receive firm contracts from the Director of Navy Contracts. Macklin received a lump sum for his

interest, and a substantial salary as chairman and managing director of the company, but before concluding the arrangement he made it quite clear that he would not be bound by Civil Service procedure. His staff then were virtually paid civil servants, but retained their commercial interests. They made purchases and carried out business generally to the company's advantage, but no profit was made and overheads covering design, planning, supervision, handling and spare-parts service were kept below 4 per cent. These arrangements were not fully understood by some Admiralty departments and contractors, and some resentment existed for a time, due mainly to the apparent freedom with which the Fairmile organisation operated.

The staff amounted to approximately 550 people, with a variety of skills and imbued with an enthusiasm to get the job done depsite official red tape. Without this enthusiasm, stemming from Macklin himself, the success of the company would have been impossible.

In accordance with his undertaking not to impinge on other

Admiralty programmes, Macklin made arrangements for the supply of required items through the most unlikely contacts, a great many with no previous Admiralty or nautical experience. A linoleum manufacturer turned all the propeller shafting, wire netting manufacturers produced rudders, a bell foundry cast propellers and a well known radiator manufacturer started a prosperous fuel and oil tank division.

The main job of cutting the material for the hulls was entrusted to the works of Alfred Lockhart Ltd, at Brentford. This was done on a very economical basis indeed, and there was little or no waste beyond the sawdust. All the Fairmile designs, from the A type through the B, C and D to the H and the one-off F type were laid off in the Lockhart lofts and the templates prepared there, including those required for the armour plating (when fitted). The templates were periodically checked for close accuracy.

For each new design, mock-ups were made at the Lockhart works of deckhouses and bridges, for approval by the service departments concerned. Each new development and request was fed into the production lines with minimum fuss. The average monthly consumption of timber was as follows:

| | |
|---|---|
| Mahogany | 50,000cu ft |
| Pitch pine and BC pine | 30,000cu ft |
| English oak | 5000cu ft |
| Teak and iroko | 8000cu ft |
| English elm | 2000cu ft |
| Canadian rock elm | 1000cu ft |
| Silver spruce | 4000cu ft |

Effective co-operation was received from members of the Timber Control Office staff handling the supplies. The acquisition of logs suitable for keel sections was always difficult due to the required size; on occasion, when they were received from locations which had suffered bombing raids, pieces of metal were embedded in them – an annoying state of affairs at a time when the supply of broad bandsaws was particularly difficult.

The acquisition of mahogany for planking in adequate quantities was a problem, too, as the daily consumption of planking and decking was about 1000 cubic feet. Timber which failed to pass inspection for use as planking was utilised in the making of furniture for boats. The planking section also handled divisional bulkhead and cabin sole material.

Wood for stringers was also a problem to acquire in sufficient lengths – many were therefore made with scarfed joints, various types of resin glue being employed (see the Fairmile B class construction drawings).

When the production of a new Fairmile type was contemplated, the Timber Control Office and Lockhart staff collaborated to decide on a construction for which the requisite timbers would be available in sufficient quantities. Each type went straight into full production; by the time the prototype had been finished, many others were approaching completion and any initial mistakes would have meant a serious delay in production and waste of materials.

Short cuts were taken in equipping for changes in operational duties. A system of steel strips, suitably drilled and tapped, allowed a variety of special armaments to be fitted with limited notice, such as American torpedo tubes removed from some of the fifty ex-American destroyers acquired early in the war, or the 18in or 21in British-design tubes fitted to the later Fairmile Ds when used for minelaying later in the war. The A type was easily adapted, using the same system, when used for minelaying.

The joinery was prefabricated down to the smallest item, and was designed to use up rejected wood and off-cuts from the hull parts. Each type of craft required at least 100 different joinery items

per boat, with the D class requiring over 200. Each item was delivered complete with fittings and battens for hull attachment.

The delivery of ML parts was ultimately divided into six 15-ton lorry loads per boat. They were so arranged to supply the parts or kits in the correct order for building, at intervals based on actual building times. A record was kept showing the required delivery date of any part for any boat. In addition to sets of parts for new boats, many orders for replacements for battle damage or sea damage had to be supplied.

The Lockhart yard also held the central stores to which all parts connected with the hulls were delivered, and the kits made up for despatch to the boatbuilders at home and abroad. It was fortunate indeed that the yard was not subject to enemy air attack, although a number of subsidiary stores had been established around the country. These parts were manufactured in prefabricated sections by furniture producers at factories far from the sea, such as the Mullard Company (now MFI), Gee, Parker Knoll and Heals, as well as piano makers and manufacturers of greenhouses and garden furniture.

Hardware, including engines (supplied under Lend-Lease from the USA) were stored in No 4 Store, built within the perimeter of the old motor racing track at Brooklands.

The different designs will be described more fully below, but briefly the A type MLs were severely criticised for a number of reasons, though they served a useful purpose. Besides the type's yeoman service as a minelayer in home waters, the production of the A type showed that the Fairmile scheme worked well and could produce boats in large numbers very rapidly and cheaply. It was practical and could adapt to modifications brought about through war experience.

Anticipating future demand for a general-purpose vessel, the Admiralty instructed Fairmile to proceed with the construction of MLs with a round bilge form, designed and tank-tested by the Admiralty, with the company to arrange the framing to suit their prefabricating methods. I have noted above that the first thirteen of these, the B types, were ordered at the same time as the repeat As. The hull, though originally designed to accept three engines, was fitted with two 600hp Hall-Scott Defenders, the loss of speed being accepted in order to allow half as many boats again from the limited supply of these engines from the USA.

The B type design proved to be thoroughly sound and produced a very versatile craft, capable of a multitude of uses in every theatre of war. Special training programmes were introduced to get them into service as soon as possible, and they were soon constructed worldwide, as shown below.

In late 1940, despite the criticism of the A type, it was decided to build more hulls powered by three main engines, this time the more powerful supercharged Hall-Scott Defender of 900hp. These vessels, the C type, were fitted as motor gunboats, and twenty-four were built for use in convoy escort work, mainly on the East Coast. As their designed speed was only 26 knots, it was recognised that they would be ineffectual against the German E-boat, and the Admiralty therefore had to prepare a different design, as the standard Vosper short boats did not carry sufficient firepower to destroy them, and in heavy seas could not sustain the necessary high speed.

Fortunately, more powerful engines were now available in the shape of the American 1250hp Packard petrol engine, and the Admiralty had already developed the lines and model-tested a hard chine hull of a size suitable to take four of the new engines. Proceeding as with the design of the B type, Fairmile worked on the D type combined MGB/MTB in March 1941. The first boat, MGB 601, built by Tough Bros on the Thames at Teddington, ran trials in February 1942. As they were first ordered as MLs, the first group were listed as gunboats, but then two 21in torpedo tubes were added. Later units had four 18in tubes and minelaying equipment. Later still a number were converted and built as long-range air-sea rescue craft; these, too, are fully described below. The D class proved to be the most heavily armed craft in coastal forces worldwide, apart from the steam gunboats which were produced in very limited numbers and constructed of steel.

Large numbers of experiments were carried out on Fairmile craft in addition to the vast production programme, and some of these are mentioned below. Perhaps the most notable were trials with the variable-pitch propeller and the Bristol air-cooled radial engine. Many trials were carried out with the former; the culminating triumph, albeit expensive, was the linking of the throttle control of a supercharged engine to the pitch mechanism of the propeller, such that, whatever the revolutions, load and sea conditions, the propeller pitch adjusted itself so that the main engines did not overboost.

To increase the speed of the overloaded D type, which could just make 31 knots with its powerful armament and increased displacement, the company considered the 1750hp Bristol Centaurus engine (later fitted to the Hawker Sea Fury aircraft). As this was in very limited supply, and not immediately available for trials, Fairmile decided as an interim measure to use the 1350hp Hercules to assess the problems of an air-cooled installation, with the intention of replacing it when the larger unit became available. The arrangements were successful despite the problems associated with the large air intakes and exhausts, which took up considerable deck area, for the large volume of cooling air required; the fan itself required over 400hp. The more powerful engines did not materialise, but Bristol later built a private-venture design powered by the Centaurus after the war; this, however, failed to arouse sufficient interest from the Admiralty to result in a purchase. Despite a search of the Fairmile drawings collection, I have been unable to come up with even a G/A drawing of this vessel, although one photograph of the F type, of which there are very few, is included below.

In the United Kingdom, Fairmile craft were built on 140 slipways in 45 yards, most of which were very small indeed. Many had to be extended, and slipways and boatyard facilities supplemented by Fairmile before construction of new boats could commence. It is worth noting that, from Fairmile's own figures for the number of boats built per annum, per slip, of the principal boatbuilders in the UK, the Royal Dockyards were rated lowest. These were each permitted to build a few vessels, presumably simply to allow them some insight into Fairmile methods. Fairmile also accummulated a large quantity of hand-held electric tools for loan to small shipyards to facilitate the assembly work. The work itself was overseen by the company's own foremen, and the Fairmile transport division organised all deliveries of material. Urgent demands were met by a squad of motor cycle despatch riders and a fleet of forty small cars, while larger equipment and the bulky sets of prefabricated parts were delivered by Fairmile lorries.

In all, 883 new boats were built, 703 in the UK, while 180 boat sets of parts were shipped abroad for construction worldwide (see the lists below). In 1941 one boat was completed every 36 hours. Average building times were as follows: A type, 22 weeks; B type, 24.8 weeks; C type, 29 weeks; D type, 43.3 weeks. The H type Landing Craft–Infantry was also designed and constructed using Fairmile methods. In addition a large number of 45ft Motor Fishing Vessels (MFVs) and Harbour Service Launches (HSLs) were built by the company.

A total tonnage of 66,636 tons was built, involving 2560 cubic feet of timber, 207,505,000 fastenings, 418 miles of piping, 2,207 miles of wiring and 309,050 gallons of paint. (This total includes fifty of the H type landing craft.)

## UK Ports at which Fairmile boats were built

| Portsmouth area | | Chatham area | |
|---|---|---|---|
| St Helens, Isle of Wight | 7 | Lowestoft | 13 |
| Lymington, Hants | 4 | Teddington, Middx | 2 |
| Southampton | 8 | Brightlingsea | 4 |
| Littlehampton, Sussex | 4 | Grimsby Docks | 2 |
| Bournemouth | 2 | TOTAL | 21 |
| Sarisbury Green, Hants | 4 | | |
| Shoreham-by-Sea, Sussex | 8 | Clyde area | |
| TOTAL | 37 | Rosneath, Dumbarton | 9 |
| | | Sandbank, Argyll | 6 |
| Devonport area | | Renfrew | 8 |
| Bangor, North Wales | 4 | Tarbert, Argyll | 2 |
| Looe, Cornwall | 13 | TOTAL | 25 |
| Teignmouth, Devon | 4 | | |
| Brixham, Devon | 2 | Forth area | |
| Plymouth | 4 | St Monace, Fife | 8 |
| Hamworthy, Dorset | 6 | Inverness | 4 |
| TOTAL | 33 | TOTAL | 12 |

Note: 17 boats unallocated

To deal with the maintenance of craft in service, the Fairmile company evolved a service offering replacement parts within 24 hours (in the UK), often anticipating a vessel's return to base. For engine overhaul and servicing of components, a local firm of motor engineers, well known in connection with motor racing, was employed. Fairmile also set up a training establishment for ERAs and motor mechanics, as well as issuing the *Fairmile Motor Launch Engineering Handbook* in February 1941, which detailed the various engineering systems and running routines, and gave much useful information.

Unlike the Packard engines, the Hall-Scott engines were always in short supply, and bottlenecks were avoided only because of the very great reliability of the engine, provided that maintenance was carried out.

In 1944 Noel Macklin was knighted for his services and awarded a substantial sum of money, which nevertheless can only have been partial compensation for the loss of profits which the company might have made, had it retained its commercial status.

When hostilities ended, with large numbers of D types being made ready for service against the Japanese, the gigantic task of disposing of the numerous Coastal Forces craft and the vast quantity of engines, installation equipment and spares which had accumulated was entrusted to Sir Noel, who was appointed the Director of Small Craft Disposals at the Admiralty 1945–46. He died on 10 November 1946.

An officer who knew him well paid a fitting tribute:

> The most impressive moment I can remember, in connection with Macklin, was during a large conference attended by much top 'brass', including several Admirals and Departmental heads. Macklin had been confined to an invalid chair owing to his failing health, but as he was wheeled into the conference, which had been in progress for some time, everyone stood, as a unanimous, instinctive compliment to real presence in this frail invalid.

The Department of Small Craft Disposals was closed down in 1947. The Fairmile designs, still in use worldwide as houseboats and pleasure craft, survive in small numbers. Fairmile (Marine Consultants) Ltd remained for a long time at Cobham, Surrey, but finally closed down in about 1984.

# Equipment and training organisations

The Director of Naval Stores received the completion schedule for Fairmile launches with some apparent alarm on 30 December 1939:

> It is understood that 145 Motor A/S Launches of the Fairmile type have now been ordered, the first of which, ML 100, proceeds on trials in January 1940, the remainder completing twenty-five by the end of May, and then at a rate of twenty a month.

He was obviously concerned about the organisation of stores required, and was provided with a specification by Fairmile. The boatbuilders would supply the anchor and chain cable gear, 12ft dinghy, fire extinguishers (both fitted and portable), compass equipment and navigational lanterns. The Admiralty had to supply the lifefloat (pattern 20), lifejackets, Asdic gear and W/T gear. The contractors would supply the necessary consumable stores for the trials, and the only additional items required from the Admiralty would be signalling flags, binoculars, a portable electric signalling lantern and an Aldis lantern, a ship's log, and clocks or watches.

The DNS was aware that no provision had been made to boatbuilders for forms or special stores lists for the new craft, and he requested that arrangements be made as early as possible for the contracts for the 145 boats to include the provision of those forms in accordance with the usual practice.

He also observed that, as the boats were to be distributed around the coast, it would be necessary for stocks of Naval stores to be maintained at various dockyards and bases. He proposed that the establishment to be drawn up should include (in the same manner as that for MTBs) an allowance of stores for the base for each six boats attached. The maintenance of these stocks of special stores would depend in the first instance on the preparation of the form D.127b, and that it was essential for those forms to be provided to the boatbuilders at a very early date.

On 16 January 1940 proposals for equipping and training crews of MLs were outlined. It was foreseen that the delivery of Fairmile boats from the builders would be as follows: January (1), March (1), April (3), May (12), and thereafter about 20 per month. The organisation for equipment and training would therefore need to be in working order by mid-April 1940 (that is, within three months). A Motor Launch Section would therefore be established at each of the three home ports (Portsmouth, Chatham and Devonport) under a Commander (Motor Launches). His duties would be the formation and training of crews, the equipping of the boats, and their trials. It was proposed that at each port there should be one Fairmile manned with an active-service crew as soon as possible, so the first three to be completed were earmarked for that duty. Each Cdr-ML would also require a small permanent staff to assist him.

The first engine room crews were to receive preliminary training at the Fairmile Company's works at Cobham, for which a detailed training scheme had been prepared on Form N.603/40. Antisubmarine (A/S) ratings were to receive preliminary training at HMS *Osprey* at Portland, and when training was complete, both engine room and A/S ratings were to proceed to the appropriate home port, where they would be formed with the officers and remaining ratings into a crew, and would carry out training in a Fairmile under the Cdr (ML). When training was completed to his satisfaction the whole crew would transfer with its officers to the building yard to join its designated boat.

It was proposed that the Fairmile Company should provide a skilled coxswain and engine room rating to navigate the boat and

deliver it to one of the three home ports. The crew of the boat would be aboard to assist and to gain experience, but would not be in charge. Two immediate problems that arose from this proposal were the questions of who would be responsible for any loss which might occur during the passage, and who would provide the essential victuals and navigating stores.

On arrival at the home port, the boat was to be equipped under the general supervision of the Cdr (ML). The major items to be fitted would be the Asdic oscillator, the 3-pounder gun and the anti-aircraft Lewis guns. Stores, too, would have to be embarked. The Dockyard Department had been approached informally as to how this work could be undertaken, and it was understood that the equipment could be fitted as convenient by the dockyards or by local contractors within easy reach of the naval depot (each boat had to be slipped or docked to fit the Asdic oscillator).

Trials of the boat would then be conducted under the supervision of the Cdr (ML), though in the interest of speed of delivery it was considered desirable in some cases to arrange for trials to be carried out on passage to or off the home port before the boat was equipped. After trials and the fitting of weapons and equipment, it might be necessary for the boat to proceed to Portland to work up anti-submarine efficiency before going to its operational station, although this point required investigation.

It was noted that, for the purposes of equipping, the three Commanders (Motor Launches) could come conveniently under the proposed Boat Section of the DNE, then under consideration. It was also noted that the proposed organisation could easily be adapted to training crews and equipping future types of boat.

Forward planning had shown that thirty-seven Fairmiles were to be built in Scotland, and of those, twenty-five were to come from the Clyde area and twelve from the vicinity of the Forth. In addition, it was probable that a considerable number of the local defence (HDML) and minesweeping boats (Motor Minesweepers) then under consideration would be built in Scotland; therefore it was thought desirable to set up a similar organisation in the North Clyde area.

The formation and training of crews for these boats would continue to be undertaken at southern ports. It was considered preferable, however, for the work of equipping to be carried out by a selected firm on the Clyde, at which stores and equipment could be collected. Boats could subsequently proceed to the new antisubmarine school at Campbeltown to work up. It had been ascertained that all types of boat (A and B types) could pass through the Caledonian Canal, but not through the Forth-Clyde Canal.

On the same day, the Deputy Controller circulated copies of the proposed training schemes to all heads of departments in the Admiralty at Bath. The next day he added these further thoughts:

> It was understood that the crew of a boat of the Fairmile type consisted of two officers, two Chief or Petty Officers and eight ratings. It was presumed that the Director of Naval Construction would have an Overseer at each building yard who would demand all the necessary Naval stores for fitting in place on board.

He also suggested that the Department of Naval Engineering and the Director of Supply should prepare a standard establishment of naval stores for these vessels, showing what stores were required for fitting in place. It was further suggested that the remainder of the stores should be boxed in sets by the storing yards and sent by rail to the overseer, each box marked 'Commissioning Naval Stores for Fairmile Boat No . . .' or 'Job No . . .' He also asked that the Engineer Overseer arrange locally for each boat to be filled up with fuel and lubricating oil before it left the fitting-out port, and suggested that the Department of Victualling should lay down a scale of mess traps, cooking and other gear, and loan clothing, and forward these items to the overseers, boxed up and marked 'Victualling Stores for Fairmile Boat No . . .' or 'Job No . . .'

The Deputy Controller observed that it was difficult to make any suggestion for the supply of provisions as it was not yet known what arrangements there would be on board the vessels for stowage, or what system would be adopted finally for the victualling of crews. The best solution appeared to be that, as the crews were being sent up as a unit from a home port, the ratings should be given a suitable advance of victualling allowance before they left, so that they could buy and take with them service provisions if desired, and also obtain fresh meat, vegetables and bread at the fitting-out port. The only stores necessary to send from the victualling yards appeared to be rum and a reserve stock of corned beef and biscuit, which could be sent with the mess traps. His final comment was that perhaps 'the establishment for MTBs would be suitable'.

Further reports followed, proposing additional requirements for the storage arrangements for the Fairmile boats, on N.S. 07044/39. Definite information was still required on the stores being provided by the boatbuilders; unless Admiralty departments could furnish that information from specifications or contracts, it was proposed that a representative should visit the Fairmile Company in order to obtain the necessary particulars.

An Establishment of Naval Stores would be required, showing:

(1) Stores required at builder's works;
(2) Stores to be placed on board after delivery of the boats;
(3) Base stores (on the presumption that the boats would be allocated to bases on completion).

This establishment could no doubt be largely modelled on the establishment for MTBs already prepared (a copy of the establishments for MTBs 1–19 was enclosed with the report).

Spare gear lists – Form D.320b – were to be prepared by the boatbuilders in conjunction with overseers, as for MTBs, Fast Motor Boats, and similar vessels. Special stores lists – Form D.127b – were to be prepared by the boatbuilders in conjunction with the Overseers and HMS *Vernon* and *Osprey*. The quantities estimated to be required should indicate:

(1) Those to be carried in the individual boats.
(2) The quantities estimated to be required for a period of 12 months for six boats, to be maintained in Depot Ships or at bases as may be decided.

The Director of Victualling (Bath) replied on 2 February:

Victualling – When the boats are in commission the crew will probably receive victualling allowance; this is the practice in MTBs and similar vessels.

It was presumed that, until the crews actually joined their boats, they would be on subsistence or Provision Allowance as they were not likely to be in a position to use service provisions. As soon as they joined their boat for passage to the home port, they could be placed on Victualling Allowance and use the service provisions which had been sent up to the boat, with the fresh provisions obtained at the fitting-out port. Arrangements would have to be made for the latter to be paid for as a charge to the Crown and

issued to the crew at service issuing prices.

The report continued that the existing establishments for Motor Minesweepers would appear suitable for the MLs. It was proposed that the depots from which the crews were sent should be instructed to arrange with the victualling yard for mess gear and loan clothing according to those scales to be sent to the vessels at the building yards either with or in advance of the crew. The authorities at the home port to which the first vessel proceeded would be asked to report whether any modification in those scales was necessary after some experience had been gained.

The following representatives were present at a Deputy Controller's meeting held on 15 February 1940:

| | |
|---|---|
| For the Controller | Captain E M Evans Lombe |
| Director of Anti-Submarine Warfare | Captain P F Cooper<br>Lt Cdr E Welman |
| Director of Training & Staff Duties | Commander P W Brock |
| Naval Assistant to Second Sea Lord | Lt Cdr W A Dye |
| Director of Personal Services | Commander R Buxton |
| Captain A/S HMS *Osprey* | Commander H Falcon-Stewart |
| Captain MTBs HMS *Hornet* | Captain P Maurice |
| Director of Naval Construction | Mr W J Holt |
| Director of Naval Equipment | Commander P G Stewart |
| Director of Torpedoes & Mining | Commander P Skelton |
| Director of Naval Ordnance | Commander G Oswald |
| Director of Signal Division | Lt Cdr C Bonham-Carter |
| Engineer-in-Chief | Commander (E) N Dalton |
| Director of Dockyards | Mr A Partridge |
| Director of Armament Supply | Mr D Todd |
| Director of Contracts | Mr A T Larter |

The proposed scheme for training crews and for equipping Fairmile Motor Launches was circulated with the agenda, and the Deputy Controller described briefly the requirements.

It was agreed that four organisations should be set up for training crews and equipping MLs. Three of those, at Portsmouth, Plymouth and Chatham, would undertake both training crews and equipping MLs; the fourth, on the Clyde, would undertake equipping only.

The Deputy Controller asked if four officers of captain or commander rank would be available to take charge of those organisations, but it was observed that it would be necessary to accept retired officers, though these were available. He suggested that the officer appointed to Portsmouth should be senior in rank, preferably a captain, and should be the central authority for the development of Motor Launches, and the representative of A/S weapons agreed with the proposal.

Captain Evans Lombe outlined the programme of Motor Launch delivery and the dates by which it would be necessary for the organisation to be in operation.

It was agreed that captains and commanders (ML) should be appointed to *Hornet* (additional) on 1 April 1940, for one week's experience with one of the early MLs, carrying out trials, and thereafter proceeding to their duties on 8 April.

It was also agreed that captains and commanders (ML) at the home ports should come under the administration of the Commodores, RN Barracks. The officer appointed on the Clyde would report to the Flag Officer-in-Charge, Glasgow.

*ML 136 in December 1940 and newly commissioned –*
*a posed training shot in chilly Scotland, with the crew*
*closed up at action stations. She was fitted with a*
*3-pounder, Holman projector and two twin .303in*
*Lewis guns, and carried twelve depth charges. She*
*was engaged in the ML training programme.*
Imperial War Museum

Captain Evans Lombe outlined the duties to be undertaken by those appointed. They comprised:

(1) Formation of crews
(2) Training of crews
(3) Equipping of MLs
(4) Trials of MLs

The question was raised whether the Clyde (where no training would take place) would require as large a staff as the other bases, but it was considered that a large staff would be necessary as the number of boats for equipping and trials would be greater at the Clyde base than at the other ports.

It was agreed that the following staff would be required by each captain or commander (ML):

one lieutenant-commander, RNVR;
one lieutenant, RNVR;
one sub-lieutenant, RNVR (Special Electrical Branch);
two lieutenant-commanders or lieutenants (E), RNVR;
one petty officer, Higher Gunnery Rating;
one petty officer, LTO;
two ERAs (war entry);
one writer (WRNS).

The representative of the Engineer-in-Chief stated that it would be necessary for four of the eight engineer officers and four of the eight ERAs to undergo some preliminary training. This was agreed, and it was agreed that the eight should undertake training at Fairmile, Cobham, Surrey, starting on 19 March 1940. On 1 April they would join *Hornet* for a further week's training, finally taking up their duties with the Commanders (ML) on 8 April, when the remainder of the staff would join.

It was emphasised that an adequate number of MLs for training purposes was required if full advantage was to be taken of the production programme. This was agreed, and it was proposed that

the first six units to complete would be allotted to training duties and disposed one each at Portsmouth, Plymouth and Chatham and three at the A/S school, HMS *Osprey*. At a later stage, three more would be allocated for similar duties at the A/S school at Campbeltown.

Captain Evans Lombe pointed out that it was necessary to make special arrangements to form the crews, equip and carry out trials of ML 100 and ML 101 before the main scheme was in operation. The CO of HMS *Hornet* stated that he could undertake to supervise this, and that there was an immediate need for the new CO to join ML 100. It was therefore agreed that this should be undertaken, and the crew appointed as soon as possible (by crash draft). At the same time, arrangements were to be made to appoint the crew to *Hornet* (additional) for ML 101 on 14 March, thereafter proceeding on 22 March to join the boat at the yard of Messrs J R Silver Ltd, Roseneath, Dumbarton. Arrangements were also made to equip ML 101 at Vosper, Portsmouth, and to co-ordinate the provision of the necessary stores to enable ML 101 to be transferred from the Clyde to Portsmouth.

Further proposals agreed at the meeting were that the training and equipping procedure should conform generally to that laid down in CPFO 100/40; that each ML should commission at the builder's yard after inspection and the arrival of the crew; and that the CO should be responsible for the safe navigation of the ML from the builder's yard to the equipping port, though this arrangement should in no way absolve the Fairmile Company from their responsibility for the satisfactory completion of all sea trials and final acceptance trials on arrival at the equipping port. It was also agreed that the representatives of the Fairmile Company should be on board for the passage from the builder's yard to the equipping port as advisers, and that they should be victualled from naval sources for the passage. Finally, it was agreed that the passage of MLs unarmed from the builder's yard to the equipping port could be accepted, except that MLs built on the East Coast should carry their Lewis guns and pedestals.

Problems, however, were encountered. It was noted that the Dockyards were unable to undertake the additional work required in the programme, and that this work would therefore best be carried out by contract. It was proposed that arrangements should be made for one firm, conveniently close to the naval depots, to undertake the equipping of MLs at the rate of about one per week, and for two firms on the Clyde, preferably close together, to undertake similar work at the rate of one ML every five days between them. The DNC agreed to report to the Deputy Controller as soon as possible the names of suitable firms.

After discussion between representatives of the technical departments, it was agreed that items of equipment should be fitted and provided on MLs as follows:

*At the builder's yard*
3-pounder gun pedestal
Ammunition stowage between decks
Asdic gear (minus oscillator)
Wireless (radio) gear
Anchor and chain gear
Dinghy
Depth charge release gear, complete
Hand and foam fire extinguishers
Compasses
Navigation lanterns
Lifefloats (MTB pattern)
Airvelope life jackets
Signalling flags
Binoculars

Portable electric signalling lantern and Aldis lantern
Ship's log
Clocks and watches, other than the trip clock on the
  instrument board
One pair of .303in Lewis guns, two pedestals and LG
  ammunition (for MLs built on the East Coast only)

*At the equipping yard*
3-pounder gun and mounting
Outfit of 3-pounder ammunition
Fireworks
Depth charges
Asdic oscillator
One pair of .303in Lewis guns, two pedestals and LG
  ammunition (for MLs other than those built on the
  East Coast)

Captain Evans Lombe outlined the proposed scheme for carrying out trials and pointed out that, if engines and hulls could be
accepted on arrival off the equipping port, it would result in the
early release of the Fairmile Company's representative to fetch
another ML. However, it was agreed that, after the trials of the first
boats and subject to the arrangements proving satisfactory in practice, Commanders (ML) should have discretion to carry out trials
of engines and hulls on arrival. The Engineer Officer stated that the
EO on the staff would be the accepting authority for the engines
and that the equipment trials of guns, depth charges, wireless
equipment and asdic gear should be carried out, where available,
by the local technical schools, or, where these were not available, by
the local gunnery, torpedo, signal and A/S equipping organisation.

The Deputy Controller pointed out that the delay which might
arise in carrying out rough-weather trials in the first boat, ML 100,
might delay the programme unnecessarily, and suggested that these
trials might be carried out in a later ML. This was agreed, as was
the proposal that the CO of *Hornet* should have discretion to decide
whether the trials were carried out in ML 100 or 101 (both type A
Fairmiles).

The final agreements provided for the laying down and provision
of stores, mess gear and loan clothing, including a list of items to be
issued at the builder's yard. Lists of stores and victuals at the
equipping yard, and lists of base stores, spare gear and special
stores, were also agreed.

Discussion also took place on the storage of ammunition, stores
and equipment destined for MLs equipping on the Clyde, the provision of charts and navigational publications, and the arrangements for compass correction on MLs before they sailed from the
builder's yard to the equipping port.

In accordance with paragraph 18 of the minutes of the Deputy
Controller's meeting held on 15 February, a further meeting was
convened at the Spa Hotel, Bath, on 4 March to discuss the points
enumerated. The following representatives attended:

| | |
|---|---|
| For DNE | Captain H A C Dick, DDNE |
| DNE Department | Commander R G Stewart |
| | Lt Cdr J Mulock |
| D of V | Mr LeMarie |
| D of S | Mr A C Blick |
| | Mr W Smith |
| DNC | Mr W J Holt |
| E-in-C | Lt Cdr S Jackman |
| DSD | Lt Cdr Johnston |
| DEE | Mr G Jenkins |
| Fairmile Marine Co | Mr G Skentlebury |

Lists of stores supplied by the Fairmile Marine Company were
provided. The naval stores supplied from the Establishment of
Naval Stores was agreed by the departments concerned, but the
Director of Supply pointed out that amendments might be in order
when the trials of ML 100 were finalised, though he would go
ahead provisionally with the agreed establishment.

The Director of Victualling agreed that all mess gear and loan
clothing should be sent direct to the builder's yard. Victualling
stores were to provide lists of provisions for 14 days direct to the
builder's yard.

There was some concern about naval stores, as they were considered insufficient for the passage of the boat from the builder's
yard to the equipping port, in view of the fact that Fairmile was not
supplying navigating stores and other equipment considered
necessary. The Stores representative stated that he would prefer all
the stores listed to be sent to the builder's yard. Although he con-
curred that at first sight the transportation was excessive, he argued
that in fact the outstanding items were only small in number.

The Fairmile Company agreed to supply the Engineer-in-Chief
with a list of special tools and equipment required for the American
Hall-Scott petrol engines. Again, these were to be updated after the
trials of ML 101.

Mr Holt pointed out that, owing to the large number of small
yards involved, it would be impossible to provide an overseer at
each yard, and consequently the yards would have to be under the
supervision of an Area Overseer. The number of small yards also
meant that a delay was probable if the usual system of supply were
followed, and it was agreed that, as a special case, such stores as
were required were to be supplied to the builders and equipping
yards from the storing yard directly on the instructions of the Admiralty departments concerned, who would be guided by the weekly report of progress passed on by the Fairmile Company. Fairmile,
in turn, agreed to make arrangements for the security of those
stores with the shipbuilders concerned.

Thus, the whole organisation to provide new craft to the fleet, in
ever increasing numbers, was set up in a very short time. On 21
February all proposals were approved and passed to the
Commanders-in-Chief, Portsmouth, Western Approaches, The
Nore and Rosyth, with copies to the C-in-C, Home Fleet, the Flag
Officer-in-Charge, Glasgow, the Flag Officer-in-Charge, Green-
ock, the Commodores, RN Barracks, Portsmouth, Devonport and
Chatham, the Commanding Officer, HMS *Hornet* and the Captain
A/S, HMS *Osprey*.

The report read:

> Their Lordships have approved the following scheme
> for the equipping, trials and training of crews for 145
> Motor Launches (Fairmile type) for the construction of
> which orders have been placed. These vessels, to be
> designated MLs 100–244, are being built by mass-
> production methods, the hulls being fabricated at a cen-
> tral factory and the components distributed to a num-
> ber of yacht-building firms for assembling. The main
> characteristics are as follows:
> Length 110ft; beam 18ft; draft 6ft; displacement
>   75 tons.
> Armament: one 3-pounder, one pair AA Lewis guns,
>   twelve depth charges.
> Asdic fitted.
> Speed: 21 knots with petrol-driven Hall-Scott engines.
> Approximate endurance: 1000 miles at 11 knots,
>   500 miles at 15 knots, 300 miles at 20 knots.
>
> MLs 112 and onwards will embody certain modifica-

tions to hull form and general arrangements.

The remainder of the five-page report outlined the arrangements previously agreed. On 18 March a follow-up report stated:

> With reference to Admiralty letter S.F.07203/40 dated 29 February 1940, approval has been given for the following firms to undertake the work of equipping Motor Launches (Fairmile type):
>
> | | |
> |---|---|
> | Portsmouth | Messrs Vosper Ltd |
> | Plymouth | Messrs Mashford Ltd, of Cremyll |
> | Chatham | Messrs Doust Ltd, of Rochester |
> | Clyde | Messrs Alex Robertson Ltd, of Sandbanks, Holy Loch |
> | | Messrs Morris & Lorimer Ltd, of Sandbanks, Holy Loch |

A revised schedule showing the building yard, estimated completion date and ports for training the crews and equipping the first twenty-five MLs was also enclosed.

As will be seen, the main characteristics prescribed above represented a very general and rather loose description of the actual boats. The A type could just make 25 knots, but the range specified was very optimistic. The B type, 2ft longer but with only two engines, could make 20 knots maximum, but had an endurance of 1500 miles at 12 knots.

Thus the vast organisation for the building and equipping of Fairmile boats, and training personnel, was established, and, in the event, even more boats were built than was at first envisaged. Later reports show the trend. One dated January 1941 shows the wide-ranging construction of both Fairmile Bs (still called the 110ft type) and the 72ft local defence type (HDML) designed by the Admiralty:

> Approval has now been given for an increase in the number of 110ft Fairmile and 72ft MLs to be built abroad. This approval involves no increase in the existing approved programme of MLs given in Section 17 Part II of the Controller's New Construction List of 12 November 1940, but simply constitutes an increase in the number of these vessels which will be constructed abroad within the present total number approved.
>
> The building programme as it stands to date is as follows:
>
> | | 110ft type | 72ft type |
> |---|---|---|
> | Singapore | 4 | 4 |
> | Rangoon | 2 | – |
> | Hong Kong | 2 | – |
> | India | 4 | – |
> | Durban | – | 1 |
> | TOTALS: | 12 | 5 |

Dealing first with the question of the 72ft type, five now remain to be ordered of the 1940–41 programme. C-in-C East Indies has reported in his 0814Z/15/10 a capacity to build four at Mombasa. In Admiralty Out Message 1307/27, C-in-C East Indies has been informed that it is intended to order four of these craft and requested to report names of firms who will construct them.

> DNC to forward full sets of drawings and specifications to NOIC Kilindini, Mombasa.
> DNC to place orders when names of firms are known.
> DNE to co-ordinate question of supply of engines, armaments and fittings.

*Note*: One more ML of this type remains to be ordered from the approved 1940–41 programme. This ML will be built abroad and further instructions will be issued when the place for building is decided.

The report continued in the same vein for the 100ft Fairmile type. There was a total requirement for eighty-four of these vessels abroad, of which ten were already ordered and two were allocated to Rangoon. Thus, the future requirement at the time of the report was seventy-two units. This raised the question of whether it would be necessary later to reduce the rate at which MLs were built in the United Kingdom.

There was a requirement for twelve Fairmile Bs at Alexandria, and investigation was undertaken into the possibility of shipping eight. Action had been taken to dispatch sets of drawings and specifications (one set by Air Mail, seven sets by the Cape route, and another seven sets through the Mediterranean route).

Eight Fairmile Bs were to be built in East Africa, two of them at Dar-es-Salaam, and another eight in Indian waters. The Government of India was to be approached on the matter of expanding the Indian building programme from the four MLs then ordered to eight, on the basis that nineteen such vessels had originally been offered.

Construction of thirty-two MLs was required in the Singapore area, although at the time the Singapore yards were fully committed, and all the available building berths were occupied. There was a requirement for twelve at Hong Kong, and if no berths were available, an approximate date was required when further building could be undertaken. Additional 105ft wooden minesweepers were also required.

Further signals were sent at the same time regarding additional MLs: four at Simonstown, four at Bermuda and four at Kingston, Jamaica. It was also noted that:

> Depth charges Mark VII and stores for the eight Fairmile MLs building at Alexandria will be available from local stocks. For the four 72ft LDMLs building at Mombasa and two Fairmiles at Dar-es-Salaam, supply will be arranged from Trincomalee. Three-pounder guns, machine guns and rifles, with ammunition, will be sent at the same time as the mountings. It is requested DNE will say when they are to be shipped.

This, then, gives some small indication of the huge organisation that was required to provide the training and back-up resources for Fairmile boats. The paperwork involved was vast, and the armament in particular hard to find, but problems were overcome and the ships joined the fleet worldwide.

# The Fairmile A type motor launch

The Fairmile A type was designed before war was declared, by Norman Hart, on the instructions of Noel Macklin. The hull form was based on that of the fishery protection boat *Vaila*, but no armament was indicated in the original proposal.

When the Admiralty declined to place an order, Macklin, convinced that his ideas for mass-production were sound, and that wooden motor launches would indeed be required in some numbers, undertook to have her built himself. She was ordered on 27 July 1939 from Woodnutt's boatyard in St Helens, across from Bembridge on the Isle of Wight. Her keel was laid on 29 October.

While the prototype was still incomplete (and thus before sea trials had begun), the Admiralty had a change of heart. A severe shortage of anti-submarine motor launches was acknowledged. The Admiralty ordered twenty-four A type motor launches on 22 September 1939, soon after war was declared. Only after trials of the B had proven it to be far superior was the order for the A type reduced to twelve units.

Despite the rapid implementation of a vast training programme, to add these new craft to the operational fleet, ML 100 was not accepted until 19 May 1940, to be followed by her close sister ML 101 nine days later. (In fact ML 101 completed on 21 March, two months earlier, but was not accepted until steering problems were resolved.)

No official records exist, but part of the reason for the late commissioning of ML 100 was the fact that, as built originally, she had only a single rudder on the centreline; this can be verified from her original general arrangement drawings. It was found on sea trials that such a centre, skeg-supported rudder gave a very poor turning circle, especially in a triple-screwed vessel (which any big ship naval architect could have pointed out). ML 100 was modified by fitting two small balanced rudders in the wake of the two wing propellers, which improved matters, although not greatly. The centreline skeg, supporting the centre screw shaft, was also reduced. The design still had too much lateral stability, and the As apparently remained very difficult to manoeuvre at slow speed, and not much better even at speed.

The Coastal Forces Veterans Association official historian, Geoffrey Hudson, suggests that certain As had only two Hall-Scott engines fitted on completion, presumably due to non-delivery of engines from the USA. This was rectified as soon as possible when supply improved, or at least by the first refit period.

The twelve units were, with two exceptions, all constructed at different British yards, which accounts for slight differences within the class. (Woodnutt built two, 100 and 102, and James A Silver Ltd of Rosneath constructed Nos 101 and 111.) Notable were differences in the bridge layout. The original design specified a small 'monkey's island' behind and above the very roomy wheelhouse, with a compass for the officer of the watch to con the ship simply via a voicepipe to the ship's wheel and telegraph below. (Engine revolutions were also voicepiped to the engineroom). Later, larger and grander conning positions were fitted, with an upper, or second, ship's wheel, telegraphs, engine throttles, and much more sophisticated controls.

*ML 106 minus funnel exhaust and fitted as a minelayer. She has a 3-pounder forward, twin .303in Lewis guns (covered) on the port side only, a Holman projector, twin .5in Vickers MGs on a Mark IV mounting aft and six ground mines. Note the IFF on the after bridge bulkhead. Imperial War Museum*

*ML 103 off Dover, mid to late 1941. She has been
rearmed as a minelayer, with six ground mines, a
3-pounder gun aft, twin .303in Lewis guns on the port
side only, a PAC rocket on the wheelhouse roof, a
Holman projector and two depth charges. Note the
short mainmast – was this to enable her to get into the
WWI submarine pens at Dover?*
Imperial War Museum

Armament, too, changed dramatically during the service life of
the A type. As built, they carried a single 3-pounder aft, backed up
by paired .303in Lewis guns or stripped Lewis guns in the anti-
aircraft role. A Holman projector was fitted early on, right aft on
the port side, and then amidships on later units. Twelve depth
charges were carried and a fixed asdic (sonar) was fitted when built
(although not shown on the drawings of the period).

In service the A type's fuel capacity, and therefore range, was
found wanting, particularly in the type's designed role as a coastal
convoy escort vessel. Indeed, the drawings show small cylindrical
fuel tanks, which in fact could have been made larger, and oval in
section. Despite their poor manoeuvrability and limited range –
only 600 nautical miles at half speed, 12 knots – the A type vessels
were reasonable sea boats.

By approximately 1941 (the exact date is obscure), the majority
of the class were converted to minelayers (three were already war
losses from mines). They were fitted with racks or mine chutes for
the stowage of six cylindrical ground mines or nine spherical moored mines, a decision which proved to be crucial. For this role, the
3-pounder gun was resited forward of the bridge, though before
she was fully converted for this role ML 103 was still carrying her
3-pounder aft, with twin .303in Lewis guns forward and two PAC
(parachute and cable projectors) one each side of the wheelhouse
roof, while carrying six ground mines.

Early boats were fitted with a main and mizzen mast, but this was

soon changed to a single mainmast, sited just abaft the bridge. Soon
after their change of duty to minelayers, most (if not all) were
modified by having the prominent funnel removed to reduce topweight. When the funnel was removed, 'dumbflow' silencers were
fitted, the engines exhausting through the sides. (Silencers were
used only when proceeding at under 10 knots.) When the A types
were refitted for this role, the asdic gear was removed. The opportunity was also taken to improve the close-range armament. The
Holman projector was resited over the engineroom, with a twin
0.5in Vickers machine gun on a Mark IV mounting aft. By late
1943, the close-range weapons systems had been updated again. A
single 20mm Oerlikon was mounted where the funnel had been,
with a twin Oerlikon on a Mark IX (manual) mounting aft. Chemical smoke apparatus and ordinary smoke canisters were standard
fittings.

It is interesting to note that when the Admiralty approved the
order for the original design – without any offensive armament –
the construction progress of this, the Fairmile prototype, was kept
under close scrutiny by Admiralty departments. The hull was constructed of African mahogany planking, and the ring frames of 1in
birch plywood were approximately 4ft 6in apart, with four intermediate bent timbers. With the three petrol engines and three
shafts, the potential of the design was good, with a top speed of
about 25 knots flat out, or 22 knots at 1800 rpm continuous. But
fuel stowage was only 1200 gallons in the six tanks, about half that
required for the type's designed role. Accommodation was provided for two officers, two petty officers and twelve ratings, although this was increased as armament was added. The original
units displaced some 50 tons (which increased, and would have
increased further if larger fuel tanks had been fitted), and it seems
that trials were not run at full load displacement.

Due to the hardchine hull form, the As were very resistant at
cruising speed, and the bow was inclined both to throw up a light
spray and to pound in a seaway. The accommodation, too, was

awkward in its layout. The inherent difficulties of maneouvring the A type in close company on convoy escort duty, particularly at night, must have caused many headaches on the bridge. These problems contributed to the decision to fit most of the A types for minelaying.

By 1942 the majority were fitted for minelaying with taut-wire measuring gear, and engaged in minelaying sorties off the French, Belgian and Dutch coasts.

In a memorandum dated 2 November 1942, Vice-Admiral HD Pridham-Wippell sent a top secret note to Dover Command, where the A type MLs were based:

(1) Their Lordships have noted that some seventeen enemy ships have been sunk or damaged in the minefields laid during the last fifteen months by the minelaying motor launches working from Dover.

(2) This represents a casualty rate of one ship for approximately every eight mines laid, which, having regard to the nature of the area, the comparative scarcity of suitable targets and the indirect effects achieved, Their Lordships consider a very satisfactory record.

(3) This recognition of the fine work carried out by the minelaying motor launches is well deserved, and is to be promulgated to all concerned.

(Admiralty Letter MOD 2140/42 of 30/10/42)

Not all the class were similarly modified, however, at least not at first. ML 107 was fitted for 'cloak and dagger' work, with a small motorboat ranged on her upper deck. She had an extended 'monkey's island' bridge and, like the others, had her 3-pounder moved to the focs'l. Aft, her 20mm gun was deleted, and instead a derrick for lifting the boat was stepped where the 3-pounder had been mounted, with the small motorboat settled in chocks just forward of it. The motorboat was a 12 to 14ft dinghy, clinker built, with a highly unreliable Stuart-Turner petrol engine, made even more temperamental by having been swamped and sunk at least once.

ML 107 was the NID/SOE boat (Naval Intelligence Division/

*ML 106 as an A/S escort in 1946. She is fitted with a 3-pounder forward, a 2in rocket flare projector and both single and twin 20mm mountings. A Y gun and two CSAs are fitted aft, just forward of the dinghy.* Author's collection

*Opposite: Fairmile As of the 50th ML Flotilla, circa 1941. Outboard is ML 103 with ground-influence mines. The inboard unit is carrying nine Mark XIX moored mines with a chalked OK on each. Note the twinned .303in Lewis guns plus the stripped Lewis carried on 103. The CSA and smoke floats are visible, but both units retain their Holmans.* Imperial War Museum

Special Operations Executive) based on the Helford River. She was apparently selected for that task due to an incident at her launch. She was constructed by Sussex Shipbuilders at Shoreham-by-Sea, and when completing the vessel the builders managed only to half-launch the hull, leaving her after end hung out over the rapidly falling tide in the Arun ditch; she consequently strained by hogging, if not breaking her back. This was resolved by jacking her up and hastily bolting on steel plates to her keelson. Chronic slowness during service was an inevitable result.

The stump derrick itself had no stays but a couple of simple, single-part manilla guys of about 1½in. The whip was about ¾in flexible steel wire, hoisted by a geared drum and pawl on the derrick post. She also had modified accommodation, providing a separate captain's cabin in addition to the separate POs' quarters and wardroom. She returned to minelaying duties later.

By 1945 the remaining As were scheduled for refit as anti-submarine escorts (another – ML 103 – had been sunk by a mine in August 1942) and they were to be rearmed with a 3-pounder forward, two 2in rocket flare launchers, a single 20mm where the funnel had been, a twin 20mm further aft, plus depth charges and a Y gun and type 291U radar. With the war's end, however, they were soon in reserve, and by the autumn of 1947 the remaining eight units were all sold out of service.

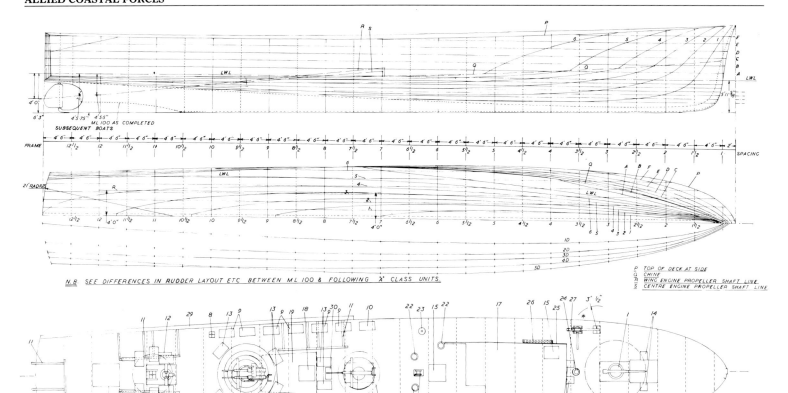

N.B. SEE DIFFERENCES IN RUDDER LAYOUT ETC BETWEEN ML 100 & FOLLOWING 'A' CLASS UNITS.

P  TOP OF DECK AT SIDE
Q  CHINE
R  WING ENGINE PROPELLER SHAFT LINE
S  CENTRE ENGINE PROPELLER SHAFT LINE

**Fairmile A escort vessel armament layout**

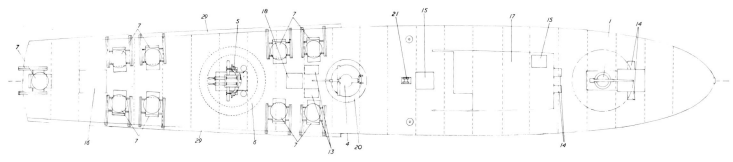

**Fairmile A minelayer with moored mines**

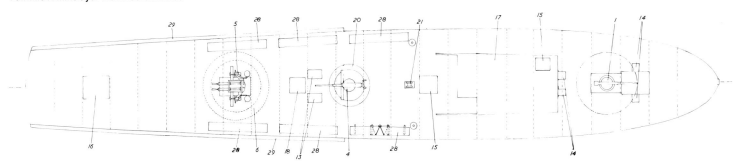

**Fairmile A minelayer with ground mines**

| | | | |
|---|---|---|---|
| 1 3-pounder gun on Mark I mounting | mounting was fitted in lieu of Mark IV mounting | 15 Hatch | 24 Stove funnel uptake |
| 2 Y gun | 7 Mark XIX or XVII moored mine | 16 Main hatch | 25 2ft 6in high brass blast screen |
| 3 Twin 20mm Oerlikon on Mark IX mounting | 8 Depth charge crane spigot | 17 Wheelhouse | 26 2in rocket flare stowage |
| 4 Single 20mm Oerlikon on Mark IV or VIIA mounting | 9 Depth charge | 18 Engineroom hatch | 27 Single 2in rocket flare projector |
| 5 Twin .5in Vickers MGs on Mark IV mounting | 10 Additional depth charge | 19 Portable engine hatch | 28 Mark IX, M Mark III or M Mark V ground mine |
| 6 Position of bandstand when 2-pounder Rolls-Royce Mark XIV | 11 Moored mine seating | 20 Stepped gun platform | 29 Additional rubber |
| | 12 Depth charge arbor | 21 Mast | 30 Fireworks tank |
| | 13 20mm Oerlikon ready use locker | 22 .303in readyuse buckets | 31 Pedestal for twin .303 Lewis guns |
| | 14 3-pounder ready use rack | 23 Pedestal for twin .303in Vickers GO guns | * Relative position of asdic dome |

**Above and opposite: Fairmile A lines**

*ML 100 flying the white ensign aft, in commission but still fitting out. She has two masts and a 3-pounder gun aft, but no depth charges yet. She was the prototype Fairmile design.* Imperial War Museum

1   Outer decking, ⁹⁄₁₆in teak
2   Inner decking, ½in mahogany
3   Frames and bulkheads, 1in plywood
4   Stringer 1¾in × 3in Canadian rock elm
5   Face pieces to butt hard on floor
6   Keel (pitch pine or British Columbia pine)
7   Inner planking, ½in mahogany
8   Outer planking ¾in mahogany
9   Bottom fashion frame (pitch pine)
10  Inner planking ⅝in mahogany
11  Outer planking ¾in mahogany
12  Top fashion frame (pitch pine)
13  Top lodging knee 1in plywood
14  Engine bearer, two thicknesses of ¾in plywood
15  Transom planking, double diagonal planks of ¾in teak
16  Transom timbers, 5in × 1½ pitch pine

17  Facing piece, 1½in sided Canadian rock elm
18  Rubber (Canadian rock elm)
19  Beam shelf (pitch pine)
20  Shelf pad (English oak)
21  Wedge
22  Hog (Canadian rock elm)
23  Floors, 2in SD × 4in Mld English oak
24  Stringer No 1
25  Stringer No 2
26  Stringer No 3
27  Stringer No 4
28  Stringer No 5
29  Chine pad (English oak)
30  Chine apron (Canadian rock elm)
31  Chine filling (Canadian rock elm)
32  Shelf (pitch pine)
33  Chine bone (Canadian rock elm)
34  Lower lodging knee (2in sided English oak)
35  Shelf (pitch pine)

**Fairmile A typical constructional sections**

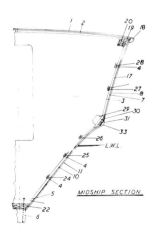

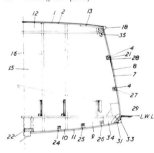

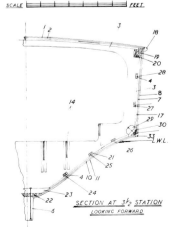

## Fairmile A class data

**Pennant nos**   100 to 111
**Designed by**   Norman Hart
**Built by a total of ten firms.**
**Construction**   Hard chine prefabricated double diagonal mahogany hull. Plywood frames, hull sub-divided into nine watertight compartments. Two underslung rudders.
**Dimensions**   Length overall 110ft 0in, beam 17ft 5in, draught 4ft 6in forward, 6ft 6in aft, freeboard amidships 5ft 11in.
**Displacement**   As designed, 57 tons, but increased as armament was added.
**Machinery**   Three Hall-Scott petrol engines of 600hp each. Funnel exhaust (later deleted). Auxiliary lighting engine Stuart 24-volt.
**Speed**   25 knots at 2200rpm maximum, 22 knots at 1800rpm continuous.
**Endurance**   600 miles at 12 knots.
**Fuel capacity**   1200 gallons.
**Heating and cooking**   Paraffin, later changed to coal to avoid condensation.
**Wheelhouse and steering**   Hydraulic steering originally fitted inside wheelhouse; this was later changed to Reid positive steering. Bridge steering was added later.
**Communications**   Radio (W/T), asdic – removed when units were rearmed, and one radar set and echo sounding set were fitted. CSA smoke apparatus.
**Crew**   Two officers, fourteen men.

*ML 100 modified for minelaying, seen here in late 1941. Her funnel has been removed and a twin .5in on a manual Mark IV mounting fitted amidships.* Imperial War Museum

ML 100 as an anti-submarine motor launch, armed with one Hotchkiss 3-pounder
Mark 1, two .303in Lewis guns and twelve depth charges, as completed.

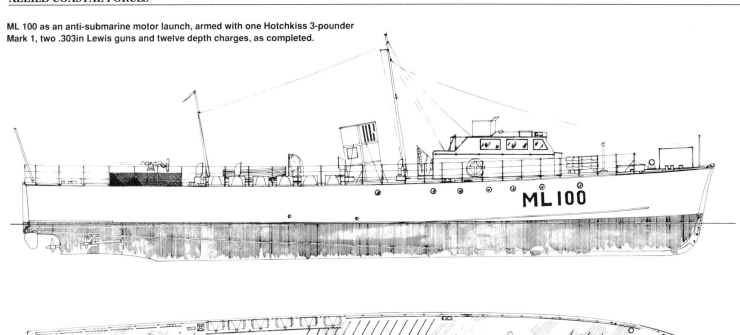

ML 100 internal profile

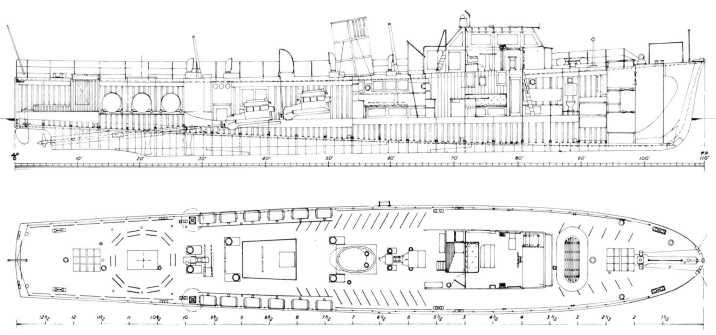

ML 100 deck plan

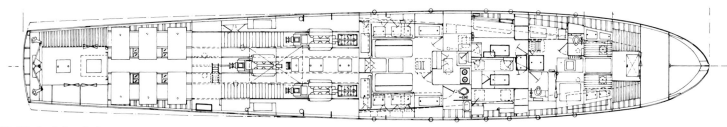

ML 100 plan below deck

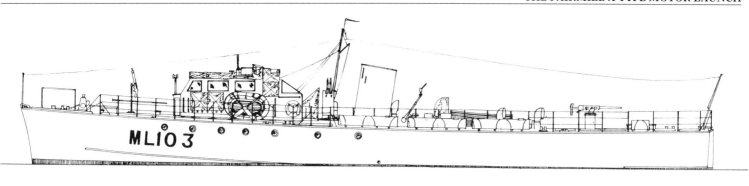

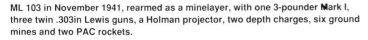

ML 103 in November 1941, rearmed as a minelayer, with one 3-pounder Mark I, three twin .303in Lewis guns, a Holman projector, two depth charges, six ground mines and two PAC rockets.

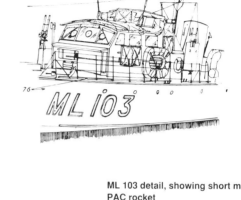

Below: ML 106 in May 1945 as an escort vessel, armed with one 3-pounder Mark I, two twin .303 in Vickers GO machine guns, one single 20mm Oerlikon Mark I (hand elevating), one twin 20mm Oerlikon Mark IX, one Y gun, four depth charges, two smoke floats and two 2in rocket flare projectors.

ML 103 detail, showing short mast and PAC rocket

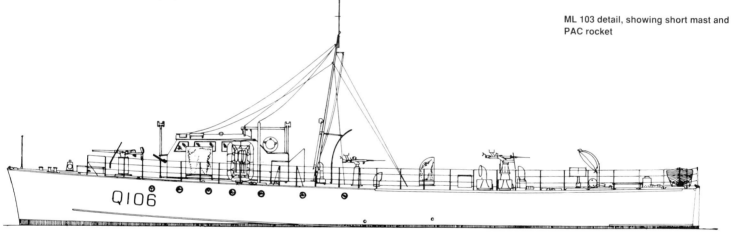

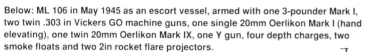

# Construction list

| No | Builder | Completed | Fate |
|---|---|---|---|
| **1 ordered 27.7.39 (under construction)** | | | |
| ML 100 | 10 | 19. 5.40 | Sold 10.47 |
| **24 ordered 22.9.39 (11 Fairmile A type and 13 Fairmile B type** | | | |
| ML 101 | 8 | 28. 5.40 | Sold 11.47 = *Firebird* |
| ML 102 | 10 | 15. 6.40 | Sold 8.47 = yacht *Carlyle* |
| ML 103 | 2 | 28. 6.40 | Mined 24.8.42 in the Dover Straits |
| ML 104 | 4 | 28. 6.40 | Sold 1947 |
| ML 105 | 3 | 8. 7.40 | Sold 5.46 |
| ML 106 | 7 | 5. 7.40 | Sold 1.47 |
| ML 107 | 9 | 30. 6.40 | Sold 8.47 |
| ML 108 | 5 | 4. 7.40 | Mined 5.9.43 in the Channel |
| ML 109 | 6 | 1. 8.40 | Mined 30.10.40 off the Humber |
| ML 110 | 1 | 24. 7.40 | Sold 8.47 |
| ML 111 | 8 | 27. 7.40 | Mined 25.11.40 off the Humber |

**Codes for builders**

1 Aldous Successors Ltd, Brightlingsea
2 Brook Marine Ltd, Oulton Broad, nr Lowestoft
3 Frank Curtis Ltd, Looe, Cornwall
4 A M Dickie & Sons, Bangor (North Wales) and Tarbert (Argyllshire)
5 James N Miller & Sons, East Shore, St Monance
6 William Osbourne Ltd, Littlehampton, Sussex
7 Alex Robertson (Yachtbuilders) & Sons Ltd, Sandbank, Argyllshire
8 James A Silver Ltd, Rosneath, Dumbartonshire
9 Sussex Shipbuilding Co Ltd, Shoreham-by-Sea
10 Woodnut & Co Ltd, Bembridge, Isle of Wight

**Fairmile A watertight subdivision and compartments, as designed**

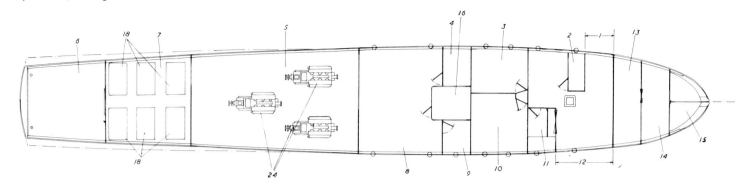

**Internal profile, as designed**

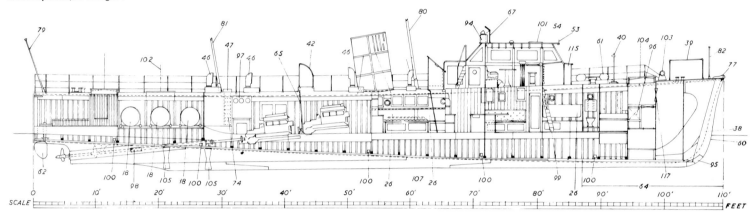

1 Tank space
2 Petty officers' WC
3 Petty officers' cabin (2)
4 Radio room
5 Motor room
6 After stores
7 Fuel stowage space
8 Crew messdeck
9 Crew's WC
10 Officer's cabin (2)
11 Officers' WC
12 Asdic and tank compartment
13 Stores
14 Chain space
15 Fore peak
16 Galley
17 Closed stowage space
18 Fuel tank (200gal)
19 Key board
20 Double door locker
21 Work bench
22 Locker (ML 100 only)
23 Fire extinguisher
24 Hall-Scott petrol engines
25 Main batteries
26 Folding cot berth
27 Shelf
28 Locker and seat
29 Wash hand basin
30 Galley stove
31 Floor hatch
32 Folding-leaf table
33 Officers' dresser
34 Wardrobe
35 Asdic
36 Asdic batteries (ML 100 only)

37 Rifle rack
38 Plywood stempiece
39 Handrail
40 .303in Lewis gun mounting
41 Crew's companionway
42 Companion to motor room
43 Rudder post deck plate (ML 100 only)
44 5in dia mushroom vent
45 Fuel tank filling cap
46 10in ventilator box
47 Motor room escape hatch
48 Wine locker
49 Hatch to cabin
50 Radio aerial lead in
51 Depth charge release gear
52 Deck plate for 4in handpump
53 Metal sight finger
54 Armoured deckhouse roof
55 Housing for COR anchor
56 Deck filling plate for generator set
57 Lubricating oil tank (ML 100 only)
58 Stowage for two petrol cans
59 5in dia mushroom vent
60 16 gauge copper nosing
61 Carley float
62 Twin rudder (ML 100 only)
63 Twin rudder steering gear (ML 100 only)
64 22ft 6in to centreline of asdic
65 Galvanised ladder
66 Chart locker
67 Wood dodger
68 Windlass pad
69 Ventilator trunk
70 Fuel tank sounding deck plate

71 A/S batteries (ML 101–111)
72 A/S generator set (later MLs)
73 All stanchions aft of this point to hinge
74 Motor room escape ladder to hinge up on underside of deck
75 ³⁄₁₆in chain guard in way of ladder with spring hook
76 6in drain holes through foot strip
77 Stemhead fitting with double rollers
78 Accommodation ladder
79 Ensign staff, 5ft 6in ash
80 Foremast of pitch pine or silver spruce, 5in dia, 22ft 6in to the underside of the truck, with two yards
81 After mast of pitch pine or silver spruce 4in dia, 14ft 3in to the underside of the truck
82 Jackstaff
83 Deck foot strips
84 Foot stop
85 Flag locker
86 Depth charge
87 10ft dinghy
88 A/S crane
89 18in bollard
90 24in bollard
91 Fairlead
92 Lift off hatch
93 Conning stool
94 Compass
95 Brass plate
96 Naptha tank
97 Main switchboard

98 Shaft bearing
99 Wood ladder
100 Strum box
101 Sliding hatch
102 3-pounder gun
103 Windlass
104 Main hatch
105 .025in brass deadwood supports
106 Funnel supplied to shipbuilders to be riveted to base plate and secured to deck by .375in dia bolts
107 Space between centre fore and aft was zinc-lined to stow perishable stores
108 All windows fixed
109 Chart table
110 Line of depth charge release gear (under deck)
111 Metal plate at base of funnel
112 Brass louvre to trunk to galley
113 Double diagonal caulked decking
114 Lighting set (later MLs)
115 Upper deck locker with nest of drawers on port side
116 Floor level about 10in below the level of engine bearers
117 Door 24in × 24in, two hinges, four clips and catch (with rubber insert)

*Note*: The position of depth charges was fixed on each boat to the satisfaction of the overseer. D/C loading: one crane and two sockets. No lower rails were fitted in the way of DCs.

Wheelhouse and upper deck detail, as
designed

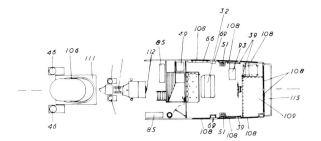

Deck plan, as designed

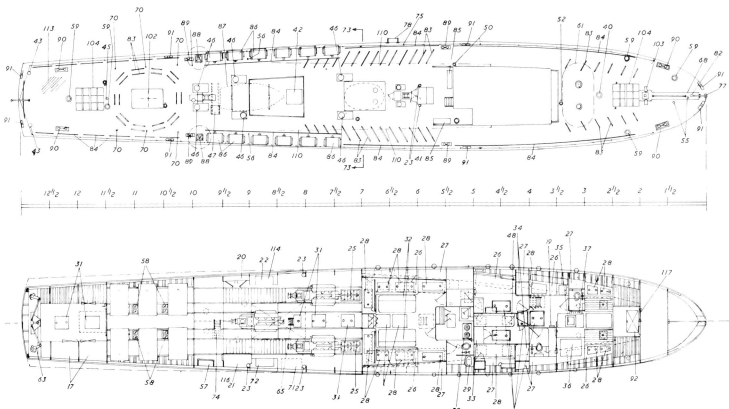

Plan below deck, as designed

*ML 100 again in late 1941. Note the four smoke
floats stowed amidships.*
Imperial War Museum

ML 106 in late 1942 as a minelayer, armed with one 3-pounder Mark I, twin .303in
Lewis guns, twin .5in machine guns on Mark IV mounting and six ground mines.

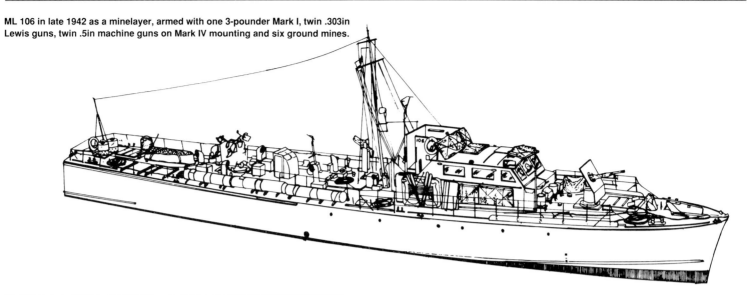

ML 107 in June 1942 as modified for special service with the Naval Intelligence
Division, transporting agents; a single 20mm Oerlikon has been added aft.

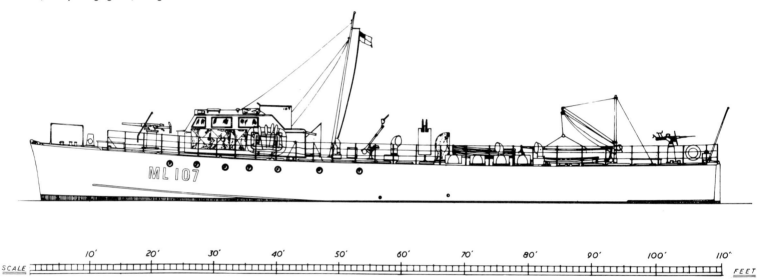

SCALE  10'  20'  30'  40'  50'  60'  70'  80'  90'  100'  110'  FEET

*A third view of ML 100 as a minelayer in late 1941.*
*Note that she retained her Holman projector.*
Imperial War Museum

# The Fairmile B type motor launch

The second type to come from the Fairmile organisation was from an Admiralty design completed just before the war by Sydney Graham and tested in the experimental tank at Haslar, Gosport. The hull form was known to be favourable, as regards both resistance and sea-keeping ability. The general arrangement outline was also drawn to meet the known requirements for a wooden motor launch. The Admiralty gave its approval for rapid production of the new design, the B type ML, by the newly formed Fairmile organisation.

The lines and general arrangement drawings were turned over to Fairmile, and the company arranged the scheme of framing to suit their system of prefabricated construction.

The original design for a round bilge ML had provided for three Hall-Scott Defender engines, but reluctantly it was decided to fit just two engines and accept the loss of speed that this would entail. This decision was prompted by the limited supply of the Hall-Scott engines from America. It was, however, quickly pointed out that, with only two engines per boat, half as many boats again could be built from the same supply.

To ensure that mass-production was implemented, the Admiralty instructed Fairmile to name an adequate number of yacht-building firms willing to become involved in the production process. The Admiralty stated that it would refrain from placing orders for other naval craft with those particular firms.

The general particulars of the new type were:

Length: 112ft
Beam: 18ft 3in
Draught: 4ft 10in forward; 5ft 1/2in aft
Engines: two Hall-Scott Defenders, each of 600bhp max
Fuel storage below deck: 2305 gallons
Maximum speed: 20 knots
Maximum continuous speed: 17.5 knots
Endurance at maximum speed: 600 nautical miles
Endurance at 12 knots: 1500 nautical miles
Displacement: 67 tons in early boats; 85 tons in later boats with increased armament

Accommodation was provided for two officers, two petty officers and twelve to fourteen ratings. As originally placed into service for coastal escort duties, the B type carried a 3-pounder gun of 1880 vintage aft, two .303in Lewis guns and twelve depth charges. Asdic was fitted as standard.

The first B type order, for thirteen units, was placed on 22 September 1939 (along with the repeat A type order); this was followed

*MLs 113 and 120 on exercise off Great Yarmouth, 1941.* Author's collection

*ML 145 in January 1942, armed with a 3-pounder,
Holman projector, 20mm Oerlikon, twin .303in
Vickers MGs on the bridge wings and four depth
charges. A fairmile A type can be seen in the
background.* Imperial War Museum

by a further order for 120 on 8 January 1940, another sixty-five on 21 May, thirty-two in August, plus four more, then eighteen, and so the orders continued, with about 650 of the class eventually built worldwide. A number, under construction at Hong Kong, Singapore and Rangoon, were lost before completion when the Japanese invaded. Eighty were built in Canada, in thirteen different boatyards (see below). Others were constructed from kits sent out to Karachi, Alexandria, Cario, Auckland, Jamaica, Bermuda, Calcutta, Capetown and other places.

Very early in the war it was proposed to use the B type with the option of variations in armament. To this end, steel deck strips were fitted, with tapped holes to suit the base securing bolts of different types of equipment. Thus depth charge chutes, torpedo tube supports, changes in gun mountings, mine rails and mine chutes, and many other items could be fitted as required. It was possible to change the role of the B at 48 hours' notice. A shoreside crane was required, but it was necessary only to remove the bolts that secured the existing weapons fit, lift the weapons off, and replace them with the required weapons system secured to another set of tapped deck strips. Thus, the Fairmile B became a veritable maid of all work and, being constructed in kit form in boatyards all over the world, was soon adapted for a variety of local conditions.

The lines of the B were attractive, and in general they were excellent sea boats. Two types of conditions required careful handling, however. First, in a short sea, as in the North Sea, the B had difficulty handling a strong breeze, above Force 7. This was especially noticeable if the sea was astern or quartering, when the flat transom stern was frequently thrown up and blown about, and the boat stood a good chance of broaching. Second, in a long open sea, such as was frequent on the West Coast, though the boat could take far more punishment than the crew (as was discovered in heavy weather trials) steering down-wind in a Force 8 was dangerous. In very heavy weather, such as a Force 10, the old trawler dodge of steaming two or three points off the wind at just steerage-way speed was used. If the boat steered further off, four or five points, there was a danger that she would go broadside on, and full power was frequently necessary on the lee main engine to push her back. Trim, too, had a considerable effect on steering. Trimming the

bow down beyond Fairmile's recommendation caused serious problems, even at slow speed with moderate seas astern. Trimming by the stern was bad for speed, but good for heavy weather, and on occasions the steering gear compartment was ballasted with extra weight, such as depth charges, to trim aft as a precaution against bad weather.

The main engines were provided under Lend-Lease from America, as fitted in the As, and details are given in that section.

To increase range, particularly en route to foreign stations, deck fuel tanks were fitted as a temporary measure, with the resultant problem of top weight. Those units fitted out for foreign service were copper sheathed.

The B type made up numbers where there were shortages of motor launches, and as a result was given whatever weapons could be found at the time. Two flotillas were fitted with two ex-American 21in torpedo tubes, removed from the fifty Lend-Lease Town class ex-World War I destroyers. When so equipped, in spite of a speed of only about 20 knots, they were intended to act as torpedo boats in the event of the invasion of England. The following units were so equipped: nos 112, 113, 114, 116, 117, 119, 120, 178 and 206 of the 2nd ML Flotilla.

In general, the tubes were removed when the invasion threat passed, but they were retained in the 9th ML Flotilla at Gibraltar for anti-submarine work. The idea was that two Bs should work as a team patrolling the entrance to the Straits, one with a full depth charge complement and no torpedoes, the other with only two depthcharges and full tubes. The plan was that the U-boat was to be detected and brought to the surface by depth charge attack, and was then torpedoed by the other unit before its gun armament could be brought into use. After a period, with negative results, the tubes were removed and the flotilla was sent on to Malta for refitting as inshore minesweepers with Oropesa sweep gear.

ML 173 had been fitted with tubes, and during an earlier refit at Gibraltar the 3-pounder gun had been replaced by a single 20mm Oerlikon. Later, when the boat was modified for minesweeping, a 40mm Bofors Mark III was mounted on the focs'l. The 9th Flotilla was then used for minesweeping on the western coast of Greece, including the Gulf of Patras, and then on the Adriatic coast following the 8th Army's advance to Ancona.

Other variations were introduced. Twelve MLs were fitted with A frames for sweeping acoustic mines in shallow waters. The sound box operated with a 12in square diaphragm driven by a Kango hammer, and actuated mines at a similar distance to the 19in hammer box on the fleet sweepers. Other MLs were fitted with an additional generator and batteries for magnetic minesweeping with a Mark VIII LL sweep, with the power cables stowed on the upper deck and with an acoustic SA towed box sweep streamed from a gantry over the bows, sweeping for both magnetic and acoustic mines.

The Bs came into their own as minesweepers at Malta. The Mark V Oropesa sweep was originally produced for use in battleship picket boats or similar small craft, and was therefore designed with the requirement of light weight, in order to permit handling by two men in a limited working space. This sweep came into prominence in 1942 at Malta, where fleet minesweepers were reduced to a state of complete ineffectiveness by Axis air cover from Italy and Sicily. A flotilla of Bs was hurriedly equipped with the Mark V sweep in order that an incoming convoy could be swept in. The success achieved was remarkable, for the MLs swept over 100 moored mines. The Admiralty gave instructions that trials be carried out to determine the potential of this equipment in all B type MLs.

It was found that at 8 knots the sweep was very temperamental and required favourable weather conditions. The wire reels were found to be quite unsuitable, but no alternative was available; the

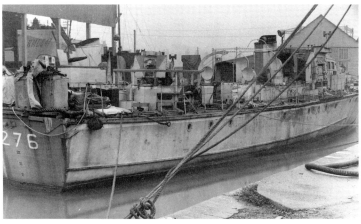

*ML 359 in the eastern Mediterranean in late 1944.
She carries a 40mm Bofors forward, two single 20mm
Oerlikons and two single 'poached' Italian Bredas
aft. Built by Anglo American, Cairo, she was ceded
to the Italian Navy in 1946.* Imperial War Museum

*Below: Early Bs during training, taken from an A
type; these boats are from the second division of the
1st ML Flotilla out of Great Yarmouth in May
1941.* Author's collection

*ML 276 refitting at Vosper's yard in 1944. The mast
has been removed, and towing plates and two CSAs
fitted.* Vosper Thornycroft (UK) Ltd

sweep gear therefore had to be towed from the after bollards, as the reels and deck fittings could not take the strain of towing. The Mark V* was used as a precursor sweep in advance of the fleet minesweepers in any large operation whenever shallow-laid moored mines were suspected. With the invasion of Sicily and Italy, in due course, much Italian minesweeping equipment was obtained and put into use.

Oropesa equipped MLs were used during the Normandy landings on 6 June 1944, with twenty in the British sector and sixteen units in the US sector using the Mark V* sweep. The Mark VII Oropesa had much improved equipment and could sweep at over 10 knots without overloading the engines, but it was not developed in time to be of service in the invasion; it was gradually phased into service from late 1944.

Other Bs were fitted for minelaying, both of moored contact type mines or influence ground mines, and this equipment can be seen in the armament section.

In 1944, with the European invasion being planned, a number of Bs were modified as navigational leaders, to lead landing craft to their selected beaches. Topweight was reduced by removing the funnel exhaust (like the A type) and fitting dumbflow exhausts. A lattice mast was fitted abaft the bridge to support the weight of a lantern protecting an Air Ministry Type QH2 radar (RN Type 970). Additional navigational aids were fitted – an echo sounder and asdic recorders, a pitometer or Chernikeef log recorder, and a direction finding loop control, as well as the standard compass and a 9- or 20-mile wire measuring set to aid accurate navigation.

Other flotillas were modified in the UK for service as gunboats in the Far East. The Bs were selected due to their lower maintenance requirement and longer range, compared with the existing Vosper MTBs, which were on station and suffering from local conditions. (In May 1942 three flotillas of 72ft Vosper MTBs, under construction in the USA, were to be delivered to India as deck cargo; in the event, two were lost during delivery, and it was decided to operate the remainder as two eleven-boat flotillas, the 16th and 17th MTB Flotillas.)

In May 1942 six Bs were already under construction in Calcutta and Bombay, under English (mostly Cornish) shipwrights. Their hulls were of Burma teak, and kits of both electrical and mechanical equipment were supplied from the UK. They were to form the 55th ML Flotilla, with MLs 474 and 476 to be launched later. HDMLs were to join from both Indian and UK shipyards. These gunboats were sent to reinforce the MLs on station against the Japanese established in the islands and coastlines of Burma (see

*ML 338 as a minesweeper in 1945. She is fitted with
a 40mm Bofors Mark III forward, two single 20mm
Oerlikons, Oropesa sweep gear and six depth charges.*
Courtesy F Kennedy

*From Trombay to Changi . . . the Story of Arakan Coastal Forces*, by
O A Goulden, for more detail).

A number of MLs had earlier been upgunned to assist with
coastal convoy protection, using the ex-destroyer 2-pounder Mark
II mounting, with its 200 rounds per minute firepower. This was in
turn replaced by the greater punch, but slower operation, of the
manually operated elderly 6-pounder for use in the Far East, which
in its turn was to have been replaced by a heavier gun still.

In those ML gunboats sent to Burma, the depth charge equipment was removed (the waters were too shallow to operate submarines), and the 6-pounder gun was fitted after some local hull
strenghthening. A twin 20mm Oerlikon Mark IX mounting was
fitted amidships, with a manual 2-pounder Mark VII mounting aft.
Radar and hydrophones were also added and funnels were removed. Those units sent from the UK made their way out via
South Africa and were used in support of the Arakan landings in
1945. (See the drawing of ML 303.)

Thirteen units were converted as ambulance launches for the
War Office and manned by the RASC (Royal Army Service Corps).
The story starts in November 1944, when 467 Company, RASC
(Motor Boat) took over MLs 166 and 167 from the RN. These two
units were standard Bs, and the army crews spent a few days seeing
just how the RN made them work.

The following spring, two specially converted MLs came south
to the Isle of Wight. For a long time it had been common gossip
that motor launches were being converted for use as ambulance
launches, but the first had come off a slipway in Barking Creek in
the previous April. She retained the same hull and bridge, but had
gained a large deckhouse abaft the funnel. This addition was a
sickbay for ten stretcher cases, and the previous wardroom flat had
been converted into a lower sickbay to take an additional four
stretcher cases and six bed cases, making a total of twenty patients
in all. Officers were accommodated forward, and the radio room
was squeezed into the wheelhouse.

*Boulters* was the first conversion, and when *Abingdon* joined her,
MLs 166 and 167 also went into the shipyards for conversion, to
become *Hambledon* and *Iffley* (all the launches were named after
locks on the Thames) in January 1945. While the two new boats
were being commissioned, 935 Company, RASC (Ambulance
Launch) came into being.

The Company establishment provided for fifteen ambulance
launches and a headquarters ship, in which the usual sickbays were
fitted out as a company office. The new Army unit was designed to
be entirely water-borne and independent of a shore base. Each
launch was to have a crew of two officers (captain and subaltern),

coxswain and second cox, four deckhands, three engineers and an
electrician. There was also accommodation for RAMC (Corpsmen)
personnel. The launches were accepted by the Admiralty, checked
and passed over to the Army. In war theatres it was planned that
the Navy would fuel them, and C/F bases would provide for any
repairs over and above normal maintenance.

For the new Company it was to be a rather hectic summer.
Officers, engineers and deck crews had to be found and trained.
The new craft had to be ferried from builders' yards all round the
coast, and they arrived in groups. The officer commanding, with
his No 2, had to cope with organising the mobilisation as well as all
the other problems, when the new Company was split into small
groups and was picking up new boats from all directions.

*ML 337 converted for wire minesweeping in 1945,
with a 40mm forward, a single 20mm Oerlikon and
Oropesa sweep gear. Note the 291 radar at the
masthead.* Courtesy Ralph Eastwood

To aid with sea training, and at the same time save the running
hours on the new engines for the long passage to the Far East (for
that was their planned destination), the hard worked and now elderly ML 171 (completed in October 1940), was borrowed from
the RN. Her captain, coxswain and chief mechanic were retained.
Each week she was crewed with trainee officers and other ranks,
cruising up and down the Channel on both day and night passages,
tackling all types of navigation and putting into every available type
of harbour. In two months, ML 171 steamed 2500 sea miles.

As they completed their training periods, the new Army crews
moved aboard their ships, and the flotilla started to form. *Benson,
Clifton, Boveney, Abingdon* and *Bray* joined to the first division.
The second consisted of *Goring, Cleeve, Boulters, Cookham* and
*Culham*.

By the third week of August those units, with *Chertsey* as HQ
ship, were nearly ready to depart. They had all worked up in the
Channel, and in some cases had combined training with useful
operations. *Abingdon* had visited Antwerp with replacements for a
Motor Boat Company, and *Boulters* had ferried men and equipment to the Channel Islands. Ambulance launches had been proved
to work, and had lost none of the B type's sea-keeping qualities in
the conversion.

The third division, which was to follow separately, was beginning to form, but, as mobilisation date approached, the war against
Japan ended with the dropping of the two Atomic bombs; VJ Day
was just ten days before the start of the division's voyage, which
was duly cancelled.

Over forty Bs were fitted out as Rescue MLs (see the lists). They
carried a power-operated 2-pounder forward, or in some cases a
twin .5in Mark V power-operated mounting. The main visual dif-

RML 529 in May 1944 in Portsmouth Harbour, with HM King George aboard, reviewing some of the assembled invasion forces. She carries a power-operated 2-pounder forward, twin .303in Vickers GO MGs and a single 20mm aft. She has an RAF-type aircraft direction finder sighted above her wheelhouse, and a small sickbay-cabin aft.
Imperial War Museum

An RML (possibly 538) under tow, on 5 December 1944. Imperial War Museum

RML 531 at sea. Imperial War Museum

A group of Bs alongside. All carry 3-pounder Hotchkiss Mark V mountings. The location is not known, but is probably abroad. Imperial War Museum

Q 179 at Copenhagen in May 1945. The other boats to starboard are both navigational leaders and are fitted with masthead ASV radar. One of these boats can be identified as ML 159. Courtesy J Davis

ference, apart from reduced offensive armament, was the large deckhouse abaft the funnel, which was used to accommodate any recovered aircrews. To aid the recovery and search for survivors, the vessels were fitted with a prominent aircraft type direction finder above the wheelhouse.

From the late summer of 1940, the B type joined the fleet worldwide in increasing numbers. They were used for close anti-submarine escorts in coastal waters, or as smoke layers to protect convoys from air attack or long-range guns off Dover. They formed the bulk of the naval taskforce in the St Nazaire raid in March 1943, suffering many losses. The use of high octane petrol was a source of constant danger in all British Coastal Forces, and a number of B types were lost as the result of fires or the explosion of petrol vapour.

In night actions against minelaying E-boats off the East Coast, the B type boats were frequently referred to as 'British destroyers' by the Germans, because they had funnels.

## Some special units

After completing in September 1942, ML 570 was returned to undergo new engine trials. Her Hall-Scott engines were removed and two experimental Perkins T12 high speed diesels were fitted (see the photographs). Following acceptance trials off Southend, she was attached to the Captain ML base at the Hamble river, where she joined a small band of other experimental Coastal Forces units. She then carried out an extended series of sea trials to prove

*ML 172 off Gibraltar on anti-submarine patrol (taken from ML 173).* Author's collection

*A B type ML looking aft, leading a section of landing craft in September 1943. Note the fresh Oerlikon magazine on the ready use locker.* Imperial War Museum

*MLs 276 and 345 under refit at Vosper's yard in
1944. RML 547 is under cover, and two 71ft 6in
British Power Boats are moored astern.*
Vosper Thornycroft (UK) Ltd

*ML 173's bridge, taken at Gibraltar. The bridge is
relatively spartan, with a magnetic compass, voice
pipes and a semi-permanent signal lamp.*
Author's collection

the diesel engines. Apparently only three of the engines were built,
from a design for the Air Ministry intended to compete with the
pre-war German Junkers Jumo diesel aircraft engine. Owing to
problems in aero engine production, however, they were passed
over to the Admiralty for further development.

ML 570 eventually became operational, attached to the 2nd ML
Flotilla. Her funnel had been removed and her armament consisted

*ML 181 and sisters at HMS* Hornet *in 1945.*
Courtesy J Davies

of a 3-pounder forward, two single 20mm Oerlikons, depth charges
and a Y gun. However, her story does not finish here. In 1945 her
forward messdeck was strengthened and she undertook sea trials
with the new 4.5in 8cwt gun on the prototype Mark II manual
mounting, a low-velocity howitzer designed to sink non-armoured
targets such as junks, sampans and other soft-skinned targets in the
Far East. (The war ended before this weapons system was put into
production with its new sighting system, although it later saw limited service aboard some Fast Patrol Boats in the late 1950s – see
the weapons system details, page 213ff.)

ML 472 was an experimental anti-submarine trials vessel based
at Fairlie in Scotland, at the Underwater Weapons Research
Establishment. Between times she served at Tobermory, under the
overall command of the redoubtable 'Puggy' (or 'Monkey')
Stephenson, Vice-Admiral (retired), serving as Commodore Western Isles, at the initial working-up base for all types of escort and
A/S vessels.

When he joined, the new CO of ML 472 found the ship in poor
repair and the crew's morale low. She had not had a refit, or her
crew leave, for some time. A half-pattern Hedgehog A/S mortar
had previously been fitted on the focs'l, with inadequate stiffening.
Trials of that weapon were being carried out with the original fixed
asdic, and each time the weapon was fired the deckhead opened up;
the messdeck was very wet indeed. A report was written to Commodore Stephenson detailing her defects, and with the support of
the NOIC at Fairlie (whom the new CO had known at Cambridge),
another report was submitted suggesting that trials be postponed
until she had been refitted and rearmed. Within a short time, ML
472 was sent to Robertson's yard at Sandbanks (Holy Loch) for a
long refit, rearming and new asdic gear. New RDF (radar) was also
specified. The CO recommended that it should not be fitted unless
the funnel and other topweight were removed, and dumb-flow side
exhausts fitted. The constructors turned down that proposal, but
because the inclining trials that followed raised concern about her
stability, the fitting of RDF was quietly forgotten. Like the fixed
A/S gear, the RDF equipment was anyway very indifferent, except
in the still and sheltered waters of *Seahawk*.

However, the new training asdic and aircraft-type gyro compass,
together with the split Hedgehog, was 'splendid equipment'. On
their return to Fairlie, ML 472 and her crew had much success
hunting 'Mickey Mouse' midget submarines, in weather up to
Force 6–7. Later, returning to Tobermory, she found herself acting

as a target for radar callibration trials for big ships.

A story of those days:

> By chance no one had thought of the effect on an ML of attacking a shallow target, only 20–30ft deep, with hedgehog bombs – which explode on contact. A technique had been worked out, by eye and stopwatch, without using asdic.
>
> Commodore Stephenson, who had seen the report, leapt at the error and told Fairlie that he intended to find out, and that he would organise it. The charts were examined to find a flat rock area at a depth of 20ft or so, the nearest being south of Canna Island.
>
> On a hot summer's day, 472 set off with Q 453 as safety vessel and observer. On arrival, several lines of armed lead soundings were made to confirm the data on the chart. The bottom was rock and kept clear by sluicing tidal streams, and a dan buoy was laid in position to simulate the spot where the target was to be. This buoy attracted a small gaggle of ducks on the glassy water. As the boat, travelling at close on 20 knots, roared up, the ducks were still swimming around, but as the hedgehog fired and the projectiles soared upwards, the now terrified ducks flew off as the cascading V of bombs came down . . . all except one duck, which dived. There was a hell of a bang as the bombs hit the bottom, half a cable ahead. The lower deck had been cleared earlier, but everyone was shaken up severely. Then . . . up in the air, turning over and over, went the poor old duck. The ML had passed the test and a boat was dropped to recover the dan, and the duck. It was discovered that, apart from a tuft of feathers round the Parson's Nose, the bird was completely bald and very seriously dead.

The Fairmile B also made a major contribution to Commonwealth and other navies. Over 160 Bs were destined to serve under Allied flags, or to be sold off at the conclusion of hostilities to form the basis of navies for the newly independent nations.

Seven were allocated to Norwegian crews shortly after their completion in late 1940 and early 1941, and manned by these crews until the summer of 1941, when their ships' companies transferred to new Fairmile D motor gunboats. Subsequently these Bs reverted to the RN. The Free French Navy, too, was well represented among users of Bs, manning the type from the summer of 1941 to the summer of the following year. Twelve units were provided, with four of these being lost at St Nazaire on 28 March 1942, alongside RN units. Three more were allocated to France in August 1944.

*ML 122 in 1941, showing a rather basic weapons fit.*
Wright & Logan

*ML 120, fitted with two 21in tubes, in June 1942.*
Wright & Logan

*ML 181 off Flensburgh in 1945. She still retains a twin .5in Mark IV mounting, but has been modified for limited ice navigation.* Courtesy J Davies

*The launch of the first Fairmile built in New Zealand, 12 September 1943. ML 403 was later leader of the 80th ML Flotilla.* Courtesy Ken Cassells

*Early days; a B type at sea. No gun shield was fitted at this stage.* Imperial War Museum

The Royal Canadian Navy, besides manning those units constructed in Canada for the RCN, manned four further units in the autumn of 1942. The Royal Indian Navy was provided with ever-increasing numbers, the majority constructed in Indian boatyards with engines and equipment shipped out. By the end of the conflict the RIN total had reached twenty-seven.

The Royal New Zealand Navy built all twelve RNZN-crewed MLs in local yards, and most of those vessels were sold out of service in 1947. However, ML 409 was re-purchased in 1953, re-engined with new commercial diesels, and served for another ten years. Australia, too, provided thirty-five Bs, built in her own shipyards (ML 828 was cancelled), and these joined the Far East Fleet from the summer of 1943. All were retained until 1949, with the exception of ML 827, which sank while under tow after grounding off New Guinea in November 1944.

As the war in Europe came to an end, there was less need for the hard-worked MLs in such numbers. The Italian Navy saw the promise of these useful craft and purchased twenty in late 1945 and early 1946. The Royal Netherlands Navy had preceded them by a few months, borrowing or purchasing seven, some to be retained (sold outright) in 1947.

A number of the units that had earlier been provided for the Free French were given to the Burmese RNVR in 1945, with later additions taking the Burmese total to seven.

The South African Navy was lent two (nos 119 and 135) in 1945, while the Greek Navy borrowed or purchased fourteen between 1945 and 1947, most of which were to remain in Greek

*A selection of Wright & Logan photographs, from Jack Kennedy and taken at Newhaven, showing ML 116, in June 1942 and fitted as a torpedo boat with ex-US Navy 21in tubes.* Wright & Logan

service until the early 1960s. Eight were purchased by Turkey on 2 July 1946, and one single unit, ML 310, which had been lost off Tjebia Island in February 1942, was recovered by the Japanese to become their *Suikei 12*.

It is of interest to note that ten B types were lost by fire or explosion unconnected with enemy action during the war, as follows: ML 133 was lost by fire off the West Scottish coast in May 1943; in February 1942, 169 was lost by fire at Gibraltar; ML 242 became a constructive total loss by fire off West Africa in November the same year; in August, ML 301 was lost by fire and explosion at Freetown, and in July 1944 two boats – 265 and 287 – were lost by fire at the same location; in June 1944, ML 385 was lost by fire and explosion off Alexandria, while in March, 387 was lost by internal explosion at Beirut; during May, at Maddalena, 444 became another constructive total loss due to an engine room explosion, to be disposed of by October that year; the last such loss was ML 449, which was listed 'for disposal' in September 1945, after fire damage in the Mediterranean. This list shows why commanding officers were always apprehensive when starting up main engines.

## Fairmile B class data

**Pennant numbers**   112–311, 336–500, 511–600, 801–933 (050–129 all RCN)
**Designed for the Admiralty by W J Holt**
**Built by 43 boatyards in the UK and 38 abroad**
**Construction**   Round bilge type, prefabricated, double diagonal mahogany plywood frames. Hull subdivided into 12 compartments. Twin underslung rudders.
**Dimensions**   Length overall 112ft 0in, beam 18ft 3in, draught 3ft 8in forward, 4ft 9in aft, freeboard amidships 7ft 0in
**Displacement**   65 tons (first 12 units); 73–85 tons remainder, depending on armament.
**Machinery**   Two Hall-Scott Defender petrol engines, each 600hp; auxiliary engine Stuart 24-volt lighting set.
**Speed**   20 knots at 2200rpm maximum, 16.7 knots at 1800rpm continuous.
**Range**   1500 miles at 12 knots.
**Fuel capacity**   2305 gallons; additional upper deck stowage for 345 gallons.
**Heating and cooking**   Coal ranges in galley.
**Wheelhouse and Steering**   The original boats had armoured wheelhouses and internal hydraulic steering; later, dual steering of the Reid or Mathway Positive type was fitted.
**Communications**   W/T, asdic and echo sounding sets; radar was fitted later (see drawings); CSA smoke apparatus.
**Armament**   As an escort, one 3-pounder Mk I aft, two .303in Lewis guns, twelve depth charges; as increased for anti-submarine duties, one 3-pounder forward, one single 20mm Oerlikon amidships, one twin 20mm Oerlikon aft, twin .303in GO MGs on bridge wings, fourteen depth charges in chutes, one Y gun with four reloads, one Holman projector.
For minelaying the Y gun and depth charges were landed and nine moored or eight ground mines were carried.
During 1941 fifty units were fitted with two ex-US 21in torpedo tubes for anti-invasion duties.
By 1944 a 2in Rocket Flare launcher had replaced the Holman projector.
Other units were fitted for minesweeping duties (see drawings).

*ML 187, in July 1942, coming alongside at Newhaven.* Wright & Logan

*ML 150 in February 1942, with a 3-pounder forward, two 21in tubes and a 2-pounder Rolls-Royce gun aft.* Wright & Logan

*ML 189 in July 1942; she is similar to 187 in that both retain a Holman projector and both have the same funnel markings.* Wright & Logan

**ML 345 in January 1944 – general arrangement**

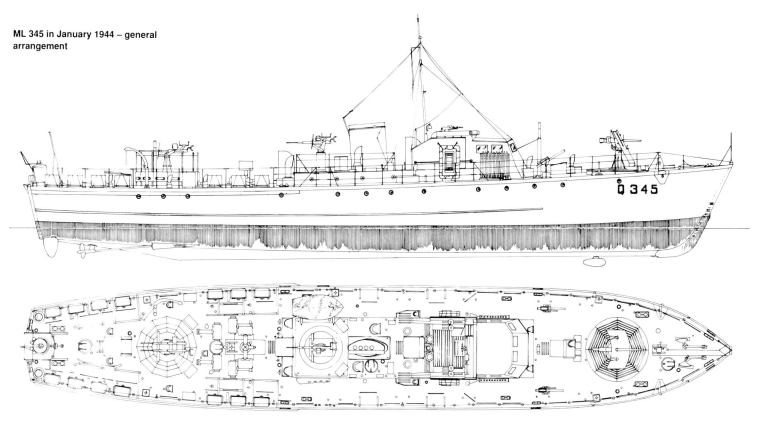

*ML 190, from the same flotilla as 187 and 189 (see p38), at the same date and location.*
Wright & Logan

*ML 214 in June 1942, showing typical armament of the period – a 3-pounder, Holman projector, twin .303in Vickers GO machine guns, and a single 20mm Oerlikon aft, with four depth charges.*
Wright & Logan

**ML 345 in January 1945, internal profile**

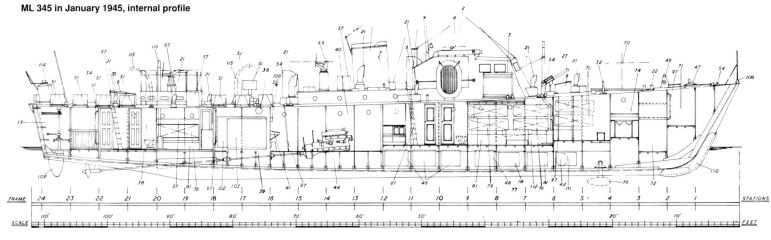

**ML 345 deck plan**

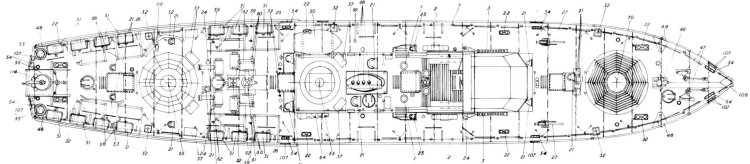

1   .303in ready use locker
2   Carley float life raft
3   2in rocket flare launcher ready use stowage
4   Twin .303in machine guns
5   Steaming light
6   Hatch
7   Mast step
8   Bridge
9   Compass
10   Wheelhouse
11   Chart table
12   Settee berth
13   Instrument panel
14   Loudspeaker
15   Hinged seat
16   Anti-submarine sounder
17   Anti-submarine recorder
18   Throttle controls
19   Engineroom telegraph
20   Log and clock panel
21   Cowl ventilator
22   Bollard
23   W/T starter box
24   Hand bilge pump deckplate
25   Waterproof ventilator
26   Sink
27   2in rocket flare launcher
28   Petty Officer's cabin
29   Petty Officers' WC
30   Awning stanchion deck plates
31   3-pounder ready use lockers
32   King post for crane
33   Steering gear
34   Bosun's store
35   Magazine
36   Fuel tank for auxiliary machinery
37   Wardroom
38   Officers WC

39   Fuel tank compartment
40   Engineroom
41   Log desk
42   Paraffin tank
43   Wardrobe
44   Hall-Scott Defender petrol engine
45   Lubricating oil tank
46   Fresh water tanks (140 and 110gal)
47   CQR anchor
48   Towing eyeplate
49   Windlass
50   10ft sailing dinghy
51   Depth charge
52   Depth charge crane stowage
53   Emergency tiller
54   Roller fairlead
55   Seat for type B CSA
56   Base plate
57   20mm Oerlikon ready use locker
58   Moored mine seat
59   Swan neck vent
60   Fuel tank sounding pipe
61   Y type depth charge gun
62   Depth charge with stalk (reload)
63   Stowage for A/S batteries
64   Accommodation ladder (stowed)
65   Twin 20mm Oerlikon on Mark IX mounting
66   20mm Oerlikon on Mark VII mounting
67   Funnel (not fitted on all B class boats
68   Engine exhaust
69   Lubricating oil filler
70   3-pounder on Mark V HA/LA mounting
71   Forepeak store
72   Chain locker
73   Shelf

**ML 345 bridge and wheelhouse detail**

74   Crew's washplace
75   Crew's WC
76   Asdic gear
77   Table
78   Seat
79   Folding cot
80   Watertight door
81   Lock seat
82   Blanket stowage
83   Radio room
84   Signal key
85   Transmitter
86   Galley
87   Dresser
88   Cooking range
89   Heating stove
90   Lobby
91   Domestic water tank (over)
92   Work bench
93   Engine spares
94   Raised floor plate over batteries
95   Generator (A/S)

96   Lighting set
97   Ladder
98   Officers' pantry
99   Plate rack
100   Provision store
101   Key rack
102   Fuel tank (542gal)
103   Fuel tank (407gal)
104   Mirror
105   Locker for engineer's spares
106   Fuel gauge panel
107   Chaffing strip
108   Bullring stemhead
109   Twin rudders
110   Steel buttress shoe
111   Coal bin
112   Crew space
113   Radio receiver
114   Chemical smoke apparatus
115   A/S or D/C crane
116   Stove chimney

**Fairmile B lines**

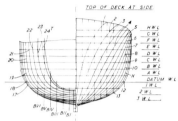

*The repair of one of the Bs after the Dieppe raid.* Imperial War Museum

**ML 345 accommodation deck plan**

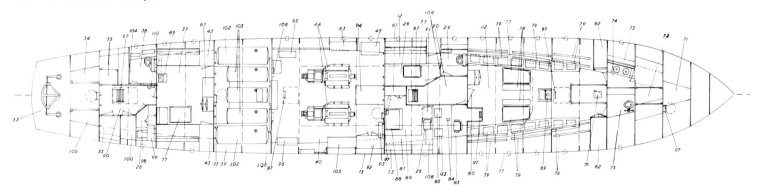

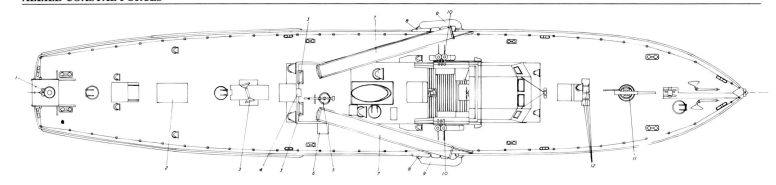

**Fairmile B torpedo boat armament layout**

1. Type B CSA (chemical smoke-making apparatus)
2. Gun deck pad
3. Torpedo loading chock
4. Torpedo cartridge ready use locker
5. Holman projector
6. Holman ready use locker
7. 21in ex-US Navy torpedo tubes
8. Sponson
9. Coir fender
10. Twin .303 GO Vickers machine guns
11. 3-pounder on Mark I mounting
12. 3-pounder ready use lockers

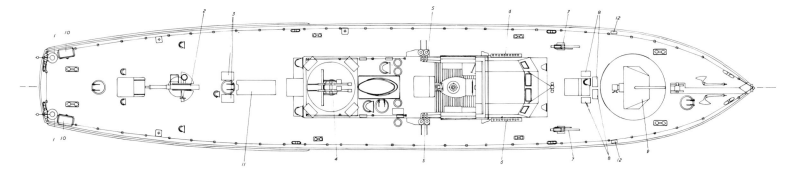

**Fairmile B gunboat armament layout**

1. Type B CSA
2. 2-pounder Vickers 40mm on Mark II mounting
3. 2-pounder ready use locker
4. Twin 20mm Oerlikon on Mark IX mounting
5. Twin .303 in GO Vickers machine guns
6. Ready use 2in rocket flares
7. 2in rocket flare launcher
8. 6-pounder ready use lockers
9. 6-pounder Mark VI HA/LA mounting
10. Two depth charges
11. Y gun deck pad (Y gun deleted)
12. Pad for hydrophone gear

**Right and below right: Fairmile B typical constructional sections**

1. Deck inner skin ⁵⁄₁₈ mahogany, outer skin teak
2. Shelf (pitch pine 7in × 3in)
3. Clamp (pitch pine 3½ × 3in)
4. King plank (pitch pine 8in × 1½in)
5. Face piece (teak 2in × ⁵⁄₁₈in
6. No 10 stringer
7. No 9 stringer
8. No 8 stringer
9. No 7 stringer
10. No 6 stringer
11. No 5 stringer
12. No 4 stringer
13. No 3 stringer
14. No 2 stringer
15. No 1 stringer
16. Hog (oak 14in × 3½in)
17. Keel (pitch pine 8in sided)
18. Frames (bonded plywood 1in birch or 1¼in col pine)
19. Deck beam (BC pine 3in × 1½in)
20. Engine bearer
21. Side coamings (1in plywood)
22. 7in dia opening lights
23. 7in dia fixed lights
24. Planking (mahogany inner skin, ⁵⁄₁₈in thick; outer skin, ¾in thick; skins laid diagonally in opposite directions at 45 degrees
25. Belting (pitch pine or elm 4in × 1¼in)

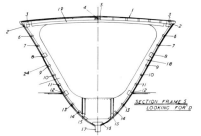

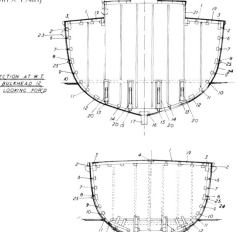

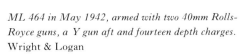

*ML 464 in May 1942, armed with two 40mm Rolls-Royce guns, a Y gun aft and fourteen depth charges.*
Wright & Logan

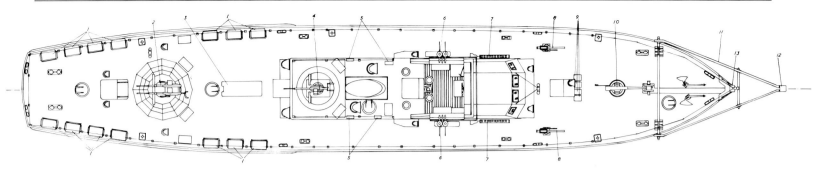

**Fairmile B minesweeper with A frame and accoustic sweep**

1   Fourteen depth charges
2   Twin 20mm Oerlikon on Mark IX

mounting
3   Y gun deckpad (Y gun deleted)
4   Single 20mm Oerlikon on Mark VII
   mounting
5   Hand grenade locker

6   Twin .303in GO Vickers machine
   guns
7   2in rocket flare stowage
8   2in rocket flare launcher
9   3-pounder ready use locker

10   3-pounder HA/LA mounting
11   A frame in stowed position
12   Mathematical box
13   Gallows for securing A frame

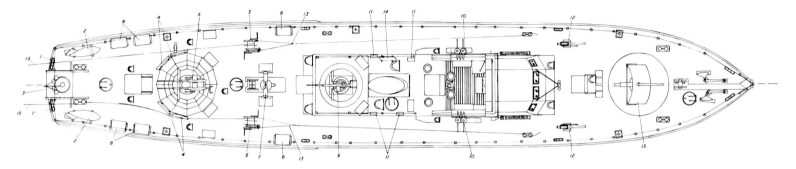

**Fairmile B minesweeper with Oropesa Mark V for moored mines**

1   Type F minesweeping fairlead
2   Float sweep
3   Chemical smoke apparatus

4   Stowage for spare kite otters
5   Non purchase reel
6   Twin 20mm Oerlikon on Mark IX
   mounting
7   Y gun with no reloads
8   Six depth charges

9   Single 20mm Oerlikon on Mark VII
   mounting
10   Twin .303 GO Vickers machine guns
11   Hand grenade locker
12   2in rocket flare launcher
13   Bridle and stay

14   Stowage for additional kite otters
15   3-pounder on HA/LA mounting
16   Sweep wire ¾in BMMW, 1¼BMMW
   with arming cutters

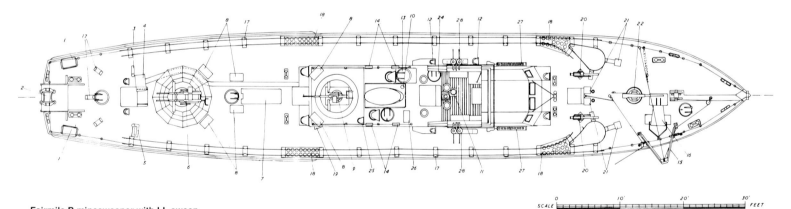

**Fairmile B minesweeper with LL sweep and SA towed box for ground mines**

1   Two depth charges
2   LL fairlead cable roller
3   Hinged cable holder
4   Terminal box
5   Portable cable holder
6   Twin 20mm Oerlikon on Mark IX
   mounting
7   Y gun deck pad (Y gun deleted)

8   20mm Oerlikon ready use locker
9   Single 20mm Oerlikon on Mark VII
   mounting
10   Nautral exhaust from pulse generator
11   Forced exhaust from battery room
12   Natural supply to battery room
13   Hatch to generator room
14   Hand grenade locker

15   Gallows
16   SA box
17   Cable holders
18   Bridge over fairlead
19   'Clam cable' extractor
20   2in rocket flare launcher
21   3-pounder ready use locker
22   3-pounder on HA/LA mounting

23   Forced supply to generator
24   Additional hatch to battery room
25   Forced supply to generator
26   Fireworks tank
27   2in rocket flare stowage
28   Twin .303in GO Vickers machine
   guns

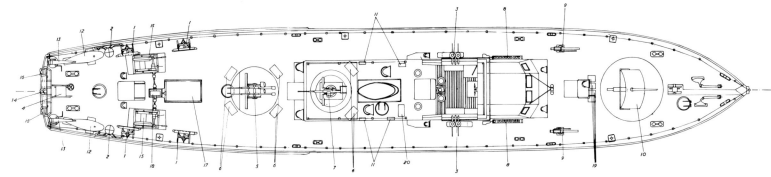

**Fairmile B minesweeper with Oropesa Mark VII for moored mines**

1  Monoplane Otter (port or starboard)
2  Kite depressor
3  Twin .303 GO Vickers machine guns
4  Type J dual hand-operated geared winch
5  Twin 20mm Oerlikon on Mark IX mounting
6  20mm Oerlikon ready use locker
7  Single 20mm Oerlikon on Mark VII mounting
8  2in rocket flare stowage
9  2in rocket flare launcher
10  3-pounder HA/LA mounting
11  Hand grenade locker
12  Float
13  M/S davit
14  Kite fairlead
15  Power winch
16  Roller fairlead
17  Winch motor housing
18  Winch gear box
19  3-pounder ready use locker
20  Fireworks tank

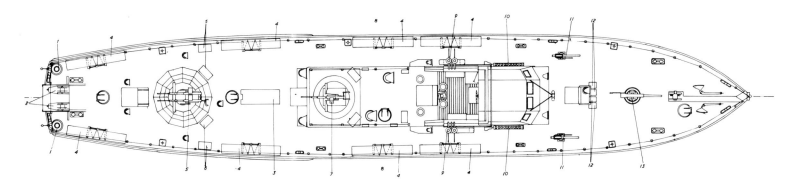

**Fairmile B minelayer with Mark IX ground mines**

1  Type B chemical smoke apparatus
2  Taut wire measuring gear
3  Y gun deck pad (Y gun deleted)
4  Ground mines (Mark IX or M Mark III or M Mark V, etc)
5  Twin 20mm Oerlikon on Mark IX mounting
6  20mm Oerlikon ready use locker
7  Single 20mm Oerlikon on Mark VII mounting
8  Hand grenade locker
9  Twin .303in GO Vickers machine guns
10  2in rocket flare stowage
11  2in rocket flare launcher
12  3-pounder ready use locker
13  3-pounder on HA/LA mounting

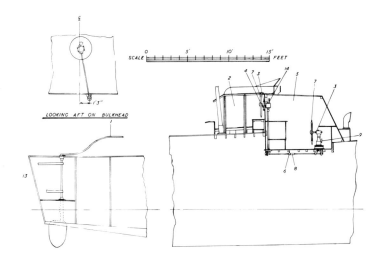

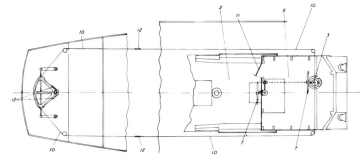

**Arrangement of hand steering gear with wire rope emergency control**

1  Hand tiller
2  Bridge
3  Helm indicator
4  Clutch for bridge steering
5  Wheelhouse
6  Steady bracket
7  Ship's wheel (3ft dia)
8  Expansion coupling
9  Clutch for wheelhouse steering
10  Wire rope
11  Wheelhouse door
12  Stretching screw
13  Dummy post carrying quadrant and tiller
14  Helm indicator for wheelhouse steering wheel, always in gear

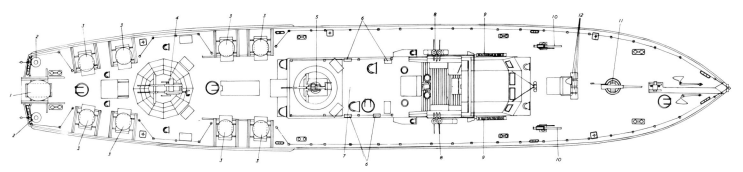

**Fairmile B minelayer with Mark XV or Mark XIX moored mines**

1   Moored mine Mark XV or Mark XIX, or taut wire measuring gear
2   Type B chemical smoke apparatus
3   Mine Mark XV or Mark XIX (eight or nine carried, as shown)
4   Twin 20m Oerlikon on Mark IX mounting
5   Single 20mm Oerlikon on Mark VII mounting
6   Hand grenade locker
7   Funnel exhaust deleted
8   Twin .303in Vickers GO machine guns
9   2in rocket flare stowage
10  2in rocket flare launcher
11  3-pounder on Mark I mounting
12  3-pounder ready use locker

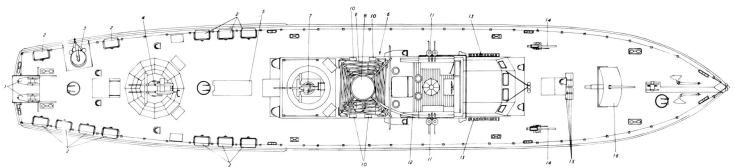

**Fairmile B navigational leader (1944)**

1   Taut wire measuring gear
2   Twelve depth charges
3   No 1 type chemical smoke apparatus
4   Twin 20mm Oerlikon on Mark IX mounting
5   Bed for Y gun (Y gun deleted)
6   Funnel exhaust deleted
7   Single 20mm Oerlikon on Mark VII mounting
8   Radar type 971
9   Trellis mast
10  Hand grenade locker
11  Twin .303in Vickers GO machine guns
12  Radar power lead
13  2in rocket flare stowage
14  2in rocket flare launcher
15  3-pounder ready use locker
16  3-pounder on HA/LA mounting

*ML 861 converted for minesweeping in the Mediterranean in 1945.* Author's collection

*'Mind the posties's bike' – ML 113 coming alongside in 1941.* Author's collection

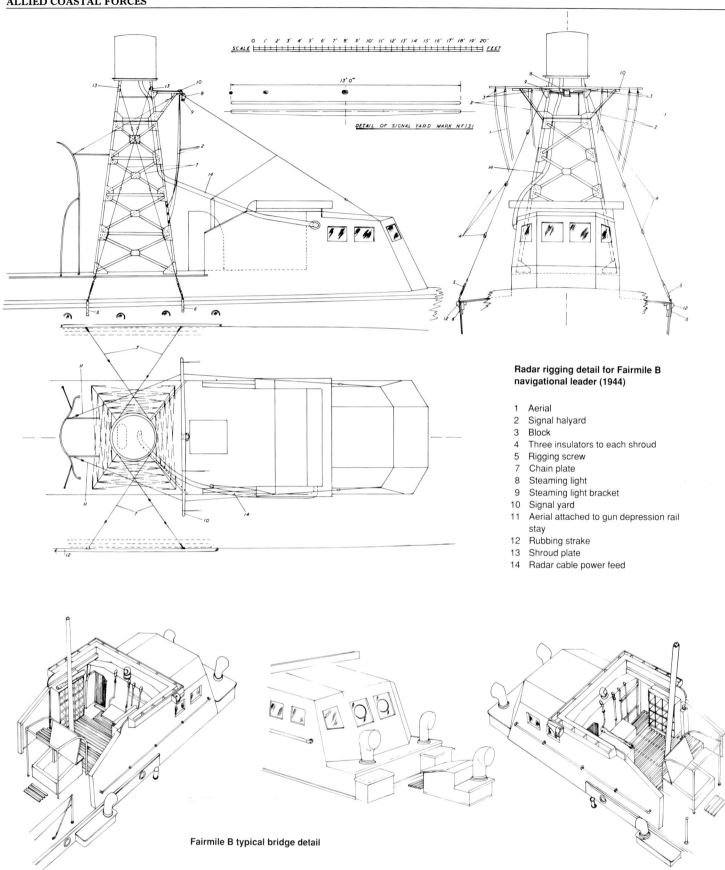

SCALE |0' 1' 2' 3' 4' 5' 6' 7' 8' 9' 10' 11' 12' 13' 14' 15' 16' 17' 18' 19' 20'| FEET

13' 0"

DETAIL OF SIGNAL YARD MARK NF131

**Radar rigging detail for Fairmile B navigational leader (1944)**

1   Aerial
2   Signal halyard
3   Block
4   Three insulators to each shroud
5   Rigging screw
7   Chain plate
8   Steaming light
9   Steaming light bracket
10  Signal yard
11  Aerial attached to gun depression rail stay
12  Rubbing strake
13  Shroud plate
14  Radar cable power feed

Fairmile B typical bridge detail

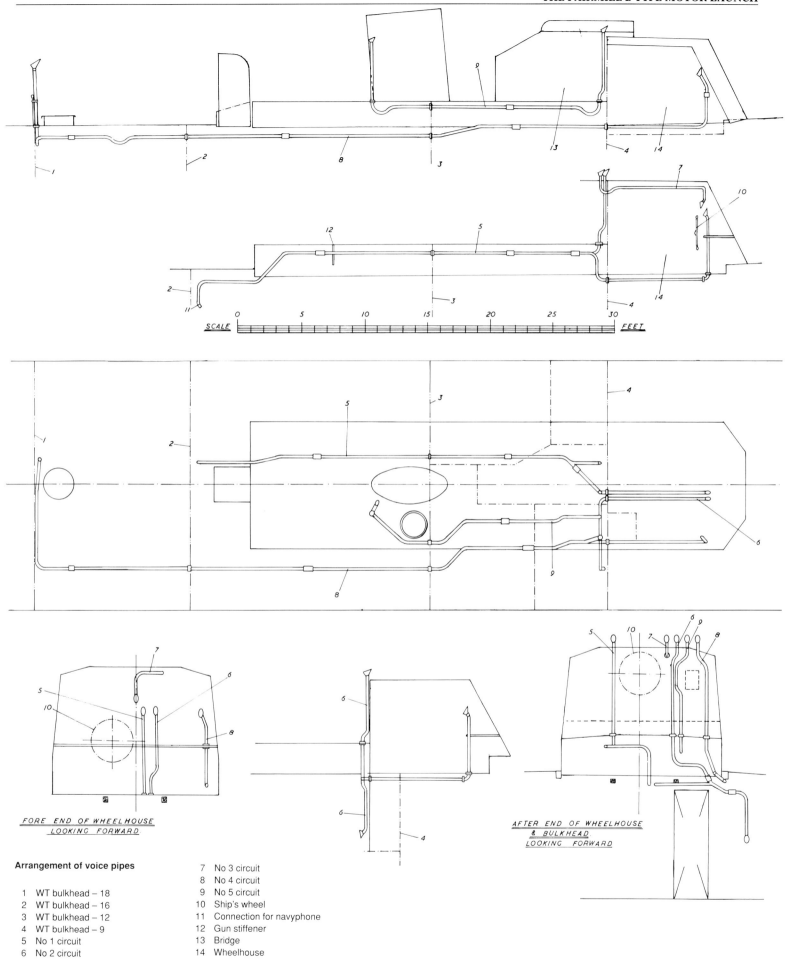

SCALE 0 5 10 15 20 25 30 FEET

FORE END OF WHEELHOUSE
LOOKING FORWARD

AFTER END OF WHEELHOUSE
& BULKHEAD
LOOKING FORWARD

**Arrangement of voice pipes**

| | |
|---|---|
| 1 WT bulkhead – 18 | 7 No 3 circuit |
| 2 WT bulkhead – 16 | 8 No 4 circuit |
| 3 WT bulkhead – 12 | 9 No 5 circuit |
| 4 WT bulkhead – 9 | 10 Ship's wheel |
| 5 No 1 circuit | 11 Connection for navyphone |
| 6 No 2 circuit | 12 Gun stiffener |
| | 13 Bridge |
| | 14 Wheelhouse |

Stanchion detail – athwart strut at
transom (left) and stanchion at
gangway with narrow spread (right)

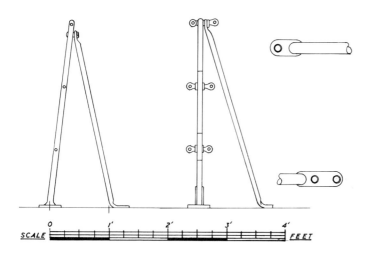

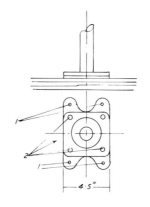

**Tapped base plate for portable
stanchions**

1  Four CSK holes, ⅜in dia.
2  Four holes tapped for ⅝in set bolts

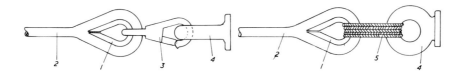

**Guard rail assembly at gangway**

1  Thimble
2  Guardrail wire
3  Spring hook
4  Eyenut on stanchion
5  Lashing

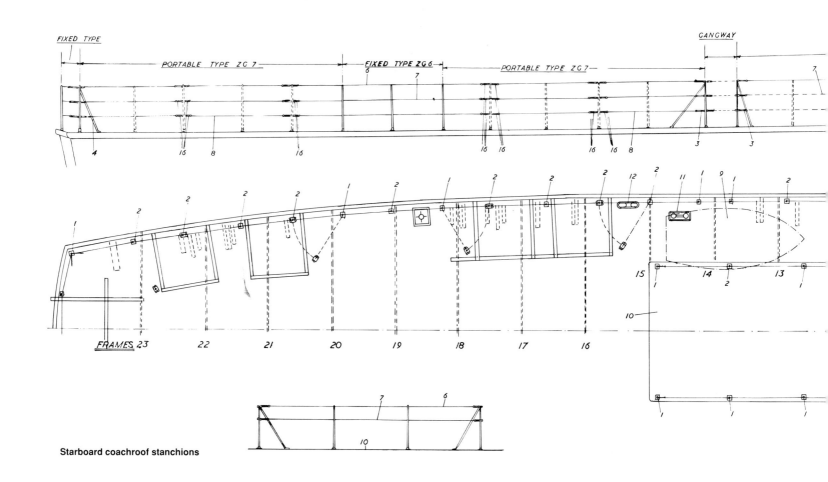

**Starboard coachroof stanchions**

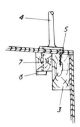
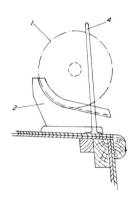

## Guard rails and stanchions

1 Fixed stanchion
2 Portable stanchion
3 Thimble and lashing
4 Straining strut
5 Wire rove
6 Top wire, 1⅛in circ 6/9 GFS wire
7 Centre wire, 1in circ 6/9 GFS wire
8 Lower wire, 1in circ 6/9 GFS wire
9 Dinghy stowage
10 Coachroof
11 Bollard
12 Fairlead
13 Open gangway
14 End of bridge bulwark
15 Wire mesh
16 Lashing

## Depth charge arrangement

1 Depth charge
2 Chute
3 Shelf
4 Stanchion
5 4in screw
6 Clamp
7 6in bolt

Note that when depth charges were carried the centre and lower wires in way of these were unshipped.

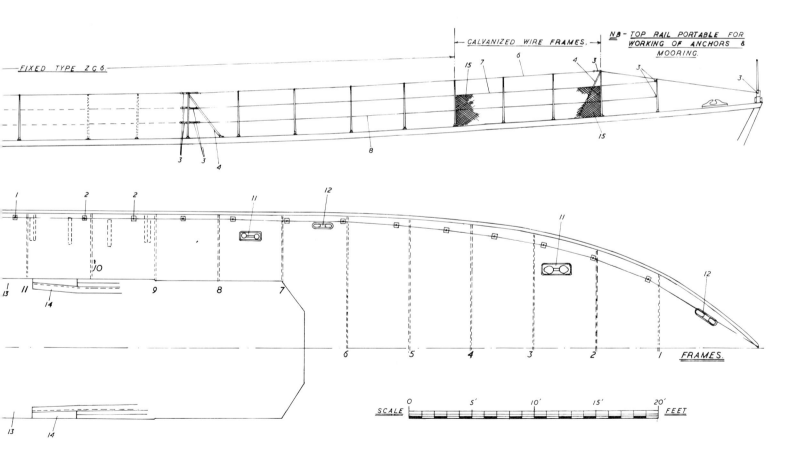

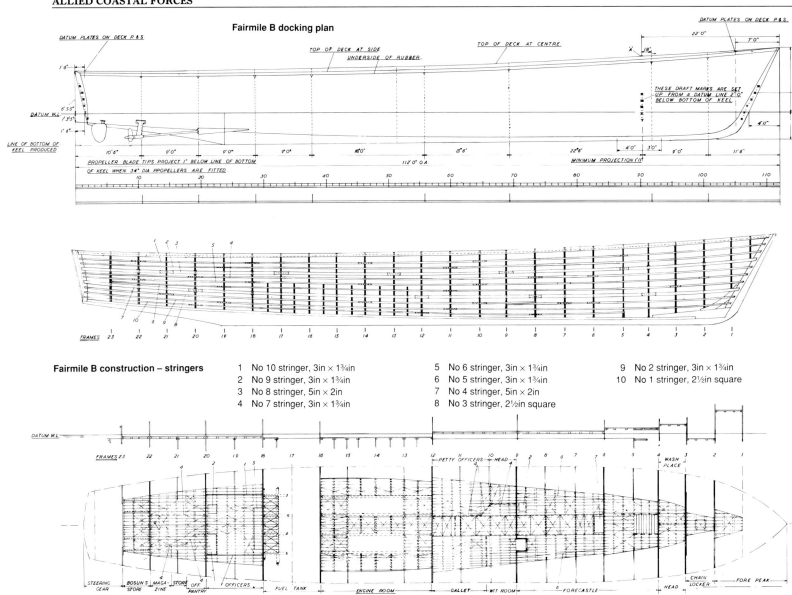

**Fairmile B docking plan**

**Fairmile B construction – stringers**

| | | | | | |
|---|---|---|---|---|---|
| 1 | No 10 stringer, 3in × 1¾in | 5 | No 6 stringer, 3in × 1¾in | 9 | No 2 stringer, 3in × 1¾in |
| 2 | No 9 stringer, 3in × 1¾in | 6 | No 5 stringer, 3in × 1¾in | 10 | No 1 stringer, 2½in square |
| 3 | No 8 stringer, 5in × 2in | 7 | No 4 stringer, 5in × 2in | | |
| 4 | No 7 stringer, 3in × 1¾in | 8 | No 3 stringer, 2½in square | | |

**Fairmile B cabin sole and framing**

| | | | | | |
|---|---|---|---|---|---|
| 1 | Front of settee | 3 | Seat and locker | 5 | Sideboard and dressing table | 7 | Mess traps |
| 2 | Stove | 4 | Bulkhead | 6 | Locker front | | |

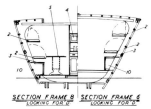
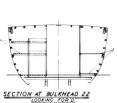
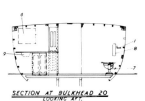
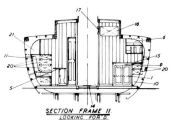

**Fairmile B simplified hull sections**

| | | | | | |
|---|---|---|---|---|---|
| 1 | Shelf | 8 | Hinged wash basin | 17 | Sliding window |
| 2 | Berth | 9 | Sink | 18 | Mirror |
| 3 | Locker seat | 10 | Locker | 19 | Dressing table |
| 4 | Mess traps | 11 | Hinge-up berth | 20 | Drawer |
| 5 | Table | 12 | Settee | 21 | Cupboard |
| 6 | Plate rack | 13 | Wardrobe | | |
| 7 | WC | 14 | Hatch | | |
| | | 15 | Dresser | | |
| | | 16 | Fresh water tank | | |

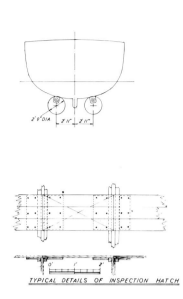

DISPLACEMENT SCALE

TYPICAL DETAILS OF INSPECTION HATCH

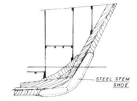

STEEL STEM SHOE

**Detail of bulkheads and trimmers**

1 Cabin sole
2 Portable hatch
3 Straps 5¼in × ¾in
4 Bulkhead cant
5 Trimmer

**Detail of deckhouse**

1 Engineroom telegraphs
2 Signalling key
3 WT recess in bulkhead 9
4 WT starter switch
5 Settee berth
6 Folding seat
7 Sliding window
8 Wheel
9 Compass

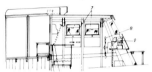

*The after end of ML 570, showing her two single
20mm mountings, Y gun and depth charges.*
Courtesy Harold Hawkins BEM

*Below right: RML 511 in June 1942, armed with
twin .5in MGs in the power-operated Mark V
mounting forward and twin .303in MGs. This boat
later became* River Lady, *then* Western Diver.
Wright & Logan

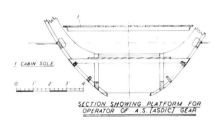

1 CABIN SOLE.

SECTION SHOWING PLATFORM FOR
OPERATOR OF A.S. (ASDIC) GEAR

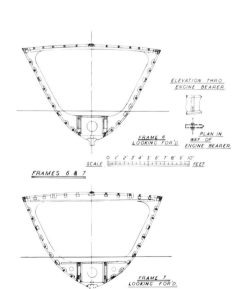

FRAMES 6 & 7

FRAME 7
LOOKING FOR'D.

ELEVATION THRO
ENGINE BEARER

PLAN IN
WAY OF
ENGINE BEARER

FRAME 8
LOOKING FOR'D

SCALE          FEET

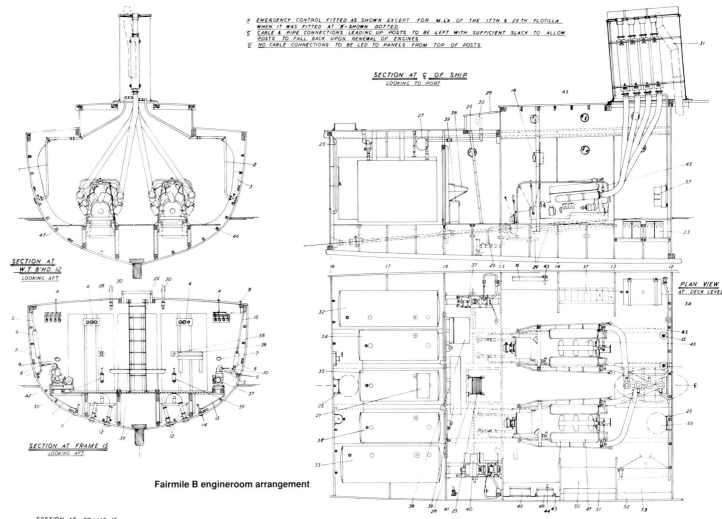

'A' EMERGENCY CONTROL FITTED AS SHOWN EXCEPT FOR M.L's OF THE 17TH & 26TH FLOTILLA
WHEN IT WAS FITTED AT 'B'-SHOWN DOTTED.
'C' CABLE & PIPE CONNECTIONS LEADING UP POSTS TO BE LEFT WITH SUFFICIENT SLACK TO ALLOW
POSTS TO FALL BACK UPON RENEWAL OF ENGINES
'D' NO CABLE CONNECTIONS TO BE LED TO PANELS FROM TOP OF POSTS.

_SECTION AT ℄ OF SHIP_
LOOKING TO PORT

_PLAN VIEW_
AT DECK LEVEL

_SECTION AT_
_W.T. B'HD. 12_
LOOKING AFT.

_SECTION AT FRAME 15_
LOOKING AFT.

**Fairmile B engineroom arrangement**

_SECTION AT FRAME 15_
LOOKING FOR'D

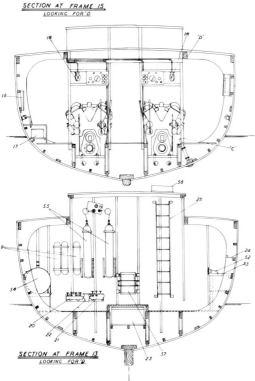

_SECTION AT FRAME 13_
LOOKING FOR'D

| | | | |
|---|---|---|---|
| 1 | Cooling water discharge overboard from starboard engine | 29 | Engine drip trays |
| 2 | Cooling water discharge overboard from port engine | 30 | Gooseneck vent |
| 3 | Lockheed gear panel | 31 | Galley uptake (fitted to home service boats only) |
| 4 | Petrol gauges | 32 | 542gal port outer fuel tank |
| 5 | 1in bore pipe | 33 | 542gal starboard outer fuel tank |
| 6 | Silencer | 34 | 407gal port inner fuel tank |
| 7 | Junction box | 35 | 407gal centre fuel tank |
| 8 | 1¼in bore pipe | 36 | 407gal starboard inner fuel tank |
| 9 | Drain plug | 37 | 75kw Stuart Turner asdic generator |
| 10 | ⅜in OD water outlet | 38 | Watchkeeper's log desk |
| 11 | Seacock for 15kW generating set cooling water | 39 | Engineer's form (seat) |
| 12 | Seacocks for main engine cooling water | 40 | Bilge pump |
| | | 41 | Auxiliary engien bilge discharge |
| 13 | ⅜ OD circulating water suction | 42 | 15kw Stuart turner lighting set |
| 14 | Seacock for A/S generating set cooling water | 43 | Port engine bilge discharge |
| | | 44 | Starboard engine bilge discharge |
| 15 | ¾in bore pipe | 45 | Handrail |
| 16 | Lockheed steering gear panel | 46 | Port Hall-Scott Defender main engine |
| 17 | A/S batteries | 47 | Starboard Hall-Scott Defender main engine |
| 18 | Engineroom telegraphs | |
| 19 | Fire extinguishers | 48 | Main electrical switchboard |
| 20 | Bilge suction valve chest | 49 | Auxiliary electrical switchboard |
| 21 | Bilge pump suction valve chest | 50 | Locker for engine spares |
| 22 | Mud box | 51 | Engine gasket locker |
| 23 | Main battery | 52 | Engineer's vice |
| 24 | Shelf | 53 | Work bench cupboard (under) |
| 25 | Ladder | 54 | Lubricating oil tank |
| 26 | By-pass to thermostat | 55 | Air bottles for Holman projector (if fitted) |
| 27 | Daily service fuel tanks for auxiliary engines | 56 | 20in escape hatch |
| | | 57 | Main switch |
| 28 | Engineroom hatch | 58 | Stern tube thermometer |
| | | 59 | Lubricator |

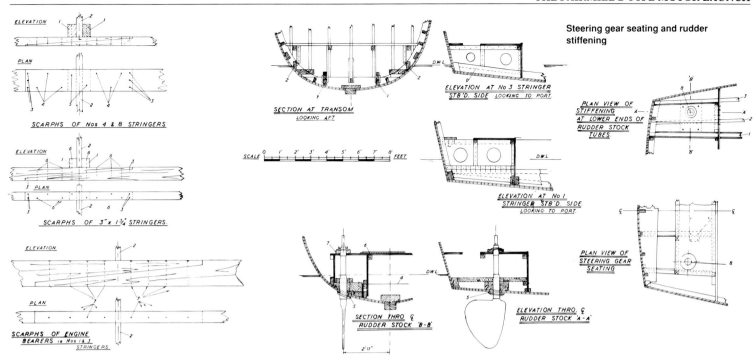

ELEVATION

PLAN

**SCARPHS OF Nos 4 & 8 STRINGERS**

ELEVATION

PLAN

**SCARPHS OF 3" x 1¾ STRINGERS.**

ELEVATION

PLAN

**SCARPHS OF ENGINE BEARERS ie Nos 1 & 3 STRINGERS**

SCALE 0 1 2 FEET

**SECTION AT TRANSOM**
LOOKING AFT

SCALE 0 1 2 3 4 5 6 7 8 FEET

**ELEVATION AT No 3 STRINGER**
STB'D. SIDE LOOKING TO PORT

**ELEVATION AT No 1 STRINGER STB'D SIDE**
LOOKING TO PORT.

**SECTION THRO ℄ RUDDER STOCK 'B-B'**

2' 11"

**ELEVATION THRO ℄ RUDDER STOCK 'A-A'**

**Steering gear seating and rudder stiffening**

**PLAN VIEW OF STIFFENING AT LOWER ENDS OF RUDDER STOCK TUBES**

**PLAN VIEW OF STEERING GEAR SEATING**

**Detail of scarphs**

1  Pad
2  Frame
3  Copper jack nail 1¾ × 8g
4  Copper nails 2½in × 6g
5  Galvanised iron nail 5½ × 3.8in
6  Copper nails 3½in × 6g
7  Copper nails 5½in × 4g

1  No 1 stringer
2  No 2 stringer
3  No 3 stringer
4  Top of engine bearers
5  Hardwood pad shaped to fit hull and flange of bottom bearing
6  1in thick teak pad under steering gear
7  Teak chocks
8  Centre of rudder stock
9  Plywood lapped 2½in No 3 stringer

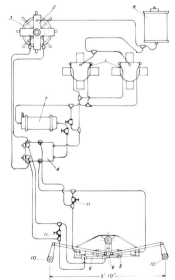

**Lockheed steering gear**

1  Four-cylinder pump driven by main engine
2  Steering transmitter
3  Handwheel
4  Control valve
5  Tiller operating cylinder
6  Auxiliary cylinder
7  Purolator valve
8  Fluid supply tank at highest point in system
9  Steering slave cylinder
10  Rudder head
11  By-pass (to be opened to permit emergency operation by hand tiller)

*The bows of ML 173 in the Mediterranean in 1945.*
*She was fitted with a 40mm Bofors Mark III at*
*Malta and converted for minesweeping.*
Author's collection

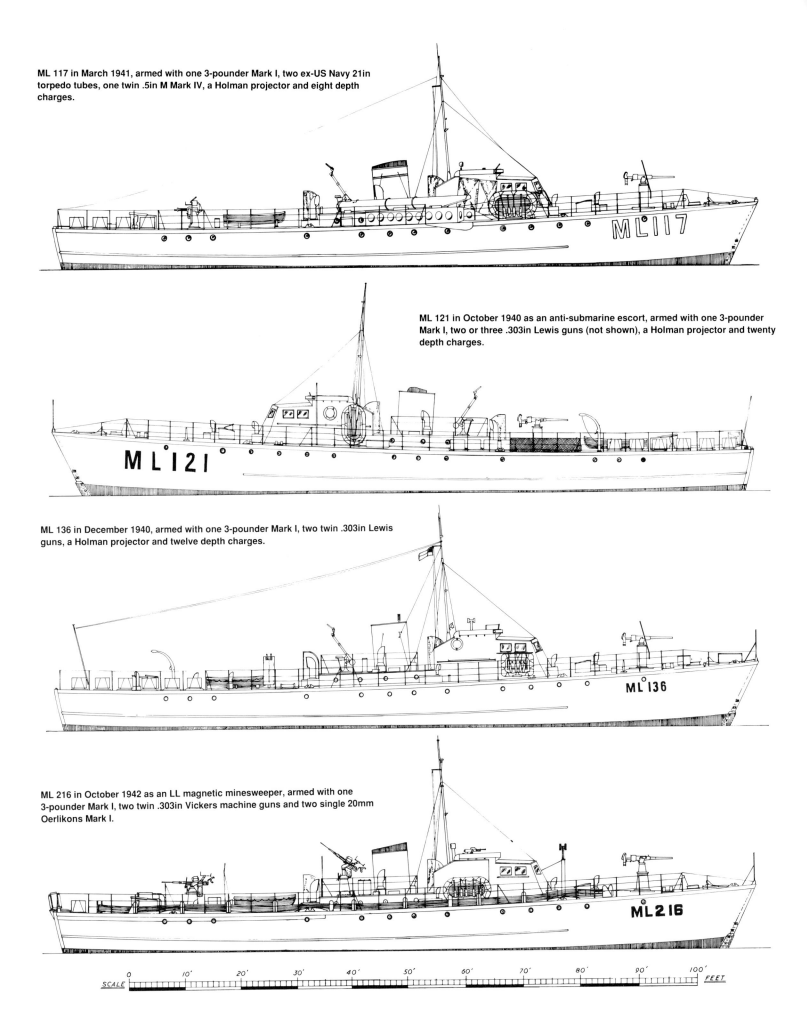

ML 117 in March 1941, armed with one 3-pounder Mark I, two ex-US Navy 21in torpedo tubes, one twin .5in M Mark IV, a Holman projector and eight depth charges.

ML 121 in October 1940 as an anti-submarine escort, armed with one 3-pounder Mark I, two or three .303in Lewis guns (not shown), a Holman projector and twenty depth charges.

ML 136 in December 1940, armed with one 3-pounder Mark I, two twin .303in Lewis guns, a Holman projector and twelve depth charges.

ML 216 in October 1942 as an LL magnetic minesweeper, armed with one 3-pounder Mark I, two twin .303in Vickers machine guns and two single 20mm Oerlikons Mark I.

SCALE    0    10'    20'    30'    40'    50'    60'    70'    80'    90'    100'    FEET

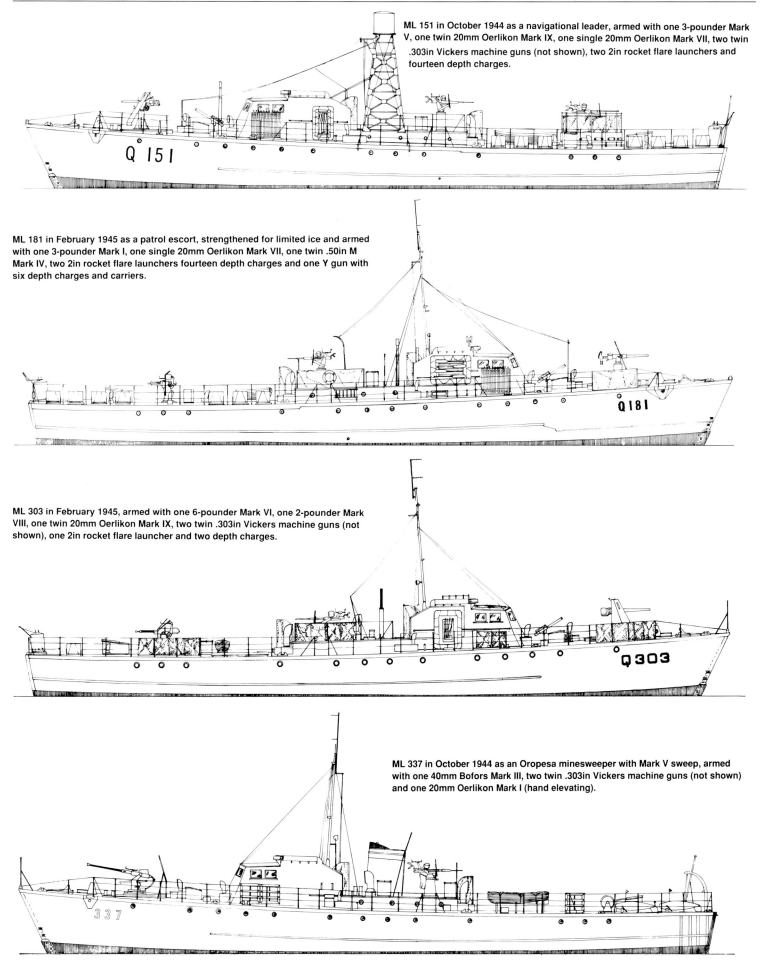

ML 151 in October 1944 as a navigational leader, armed with one 3-pounder Mark V, one twin 20mm Oerlikon Mark IX, one single 20mm Oerlikon Mark VII, two twin .303in Vickers machine guns (not shown), two 2in rocket flare launchers and fourteen depth charges.

ML 181 in February 1945 as a patrol escort, strengthened for limited ice and armed with one 3-pounder Mark I, one single 20mm Oerlikon Mark VII, one twin .50in M Mark IV, two 2in rocket flare launchers fourteen depth charges and one Y gun with six depth charges and carriers.

ML 303 in February 1945, armed with one 6-pounder Mark VI, one 2-pounder Mark VIII, one twin 20mm Oerlikon Mark IX, two twin .303in Vickers machine guns (not shown), one 2in rocket flare launcher and two depth charges.

ML 337 in October 1944 as an Oropesa minesweeper with Mark V sweep, armed with one 40mm Bofors Mark III, two twin .303in Vickers machine guns (not shown) and one 20mm Oerlikon Mark I (hand elevating).

ML 145 in January 1942, armed with one 3-pounder 50° conversion, one single 20mm Oerlikon Mark 1, one Holman projector and four depth charges; note the deck mountings for torpedo tubes, mines, etc.

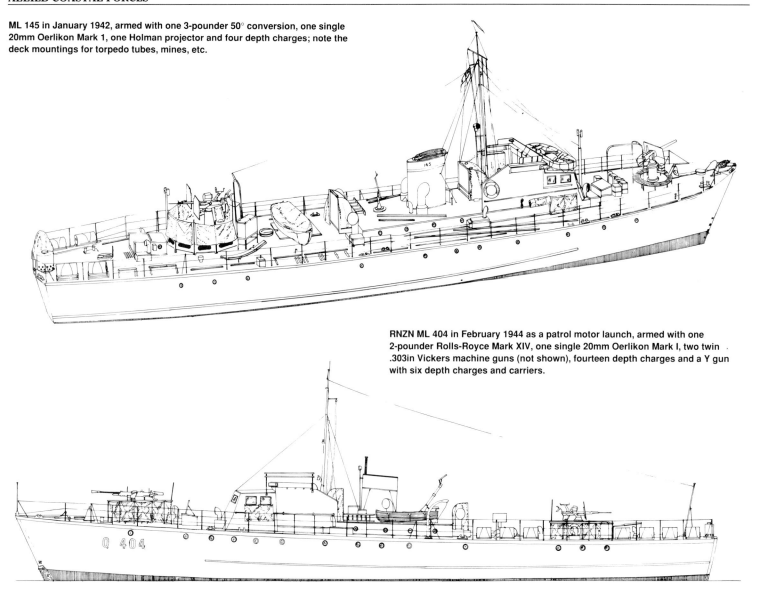

RNZN ML 404 in February 1944 as a patrol motor launch, armed with one 2-pounder Rolls-Royce Mark XIV, one single 20mm Oerlikon Mark I, two twin .303in Vickers machine guns (not shown), fourteen depth charges and a Y gun with six depth charges and carriers.

ML 570 in March 1945, armed with one 4.5in 8cwt gun on a Mark II (manual) mounting, two single 20mm Oerlikons Mark I, two twin .303in Vickers machine guns, fourteen depth charges and a Y gun with six depth charges and carriers.

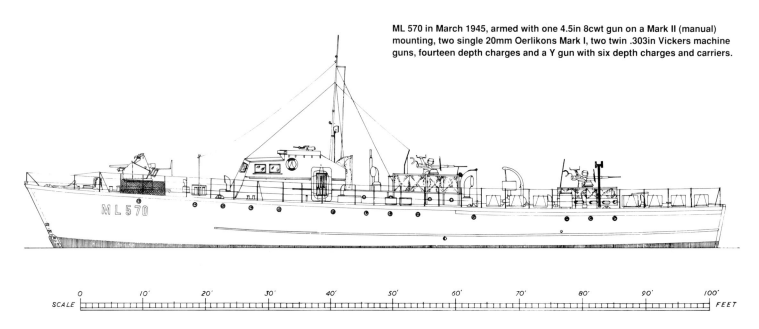

SCALE | 0 | 10' | 20' | 30' | 40' | 50' | 60' | 70' | 80' | 90' | 100' FEET

ML 338 in January 1945 as an Oropesa minesweeper with Mark VII sweep, armed with one 40mm Bofors Mark III, two twin .303in Vickers machine guns (not shown), one 20mm Oerlikon Mark I (hand elevating), one twin 20mm Oerlikon Mark IX and six depth charges.

US SC 1472 (ex ML 398) in October 1943 as a Fairmile B type wooden submarine chaser, armed with one 3in/50 Mark 22, two single 20mm Oerlikons on USN mountings, two Mark 20 Mousetraps, twelve depth charges and a Y gun with six depth charges and carriers.

RML 529 in May 1944 as a rescue motor launch, armed with one 2-pounder Mark VIII on a Mark XVI (power) mounting, one single 20mm Oerlikon Mark I (hand elevating), two twin .303in Vickers machine guns (not shown) and six depth charges.

Fairmile B ambulance launch RASC *Boulters* in January 1945; no armament was carried.

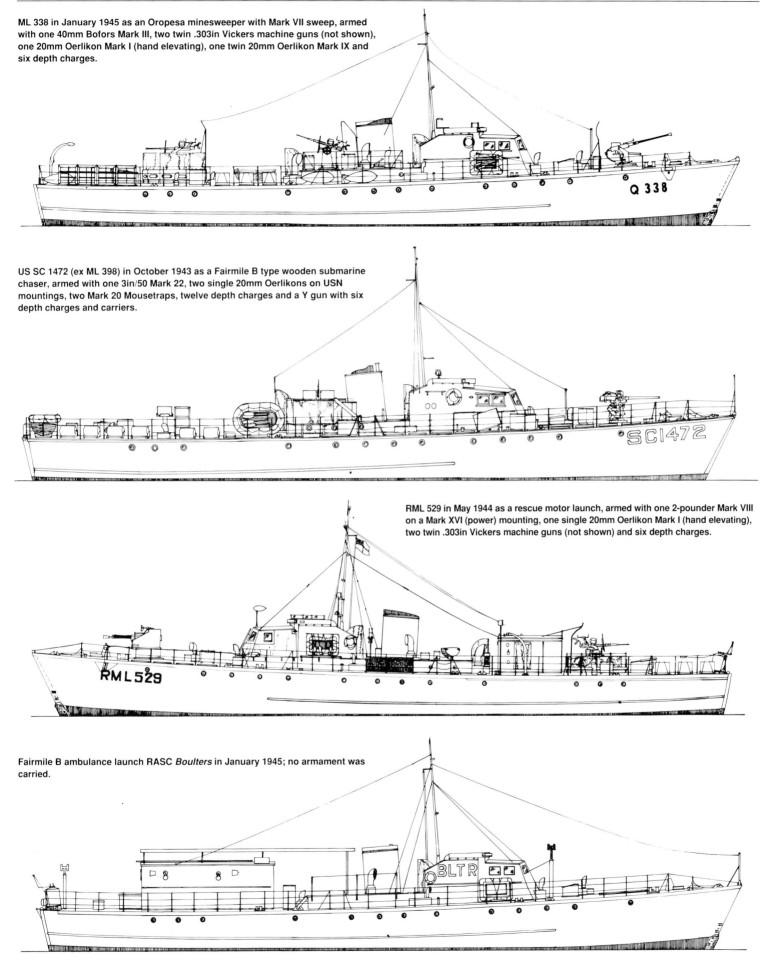

# Construction list

| ML | Builder | Completed | Fate |
|----|---------|-----------|------|
| 112 | 71 | 22. 9.40 | Sold 27.2.46 |
| 113 | 64 | 12. 8.40 | Sold 3.46 = *Pendennis* |
| 114 | 13 | 24. 8.40 | For disposal 1946 |
| 115 | 54 | 18. 9.40 | Sold 10.46 |
| 116 | 22 | 14. 9.40 | For disposal 4.46 |
| 117 | 37 | 26.10.40 | Sold 1946 = yacht *Savourna* by 1959 |
| 118 | 57 | 7.10.40 | Sold 1946 = *Marandis* |
| 119 | 47 | 12. 9.40 | Lent SAN 1945; for disposal 1945 |
| 120 | 2 | 8.10.40 | Sold 1946 = *Onetwenty* 1947 |
| 121 | 52 | 12. 9.40 | Sold in Egypt circa 1947 |
| 122 | 22 | 16.10.40 | Lent RNN 13.12.40 to 23.8.41; for disposal 10.45 |
| 123 | 21L | 5.41 | FF *St Ronan* 5.41 to 7.42; sold 1946 |
| 124 | 22 | 13.11.40 | To STT 1946; for disposal 10.47 |

**120 ordered 8.1.40**

| ML | Builder | Completed | Fate |
|----|---------|-----------|------|
| 125 | 24 | 9.11.40 | Lent RNN 23.12.40 to 23.8.41; for disposal 10.45 |
| 126 | 41 | 19. 9.40 | Lost 27.11.43 after being torpedoed by U-boat |
| 127 | 13 | 7.11.40 | Mined 22.11.40 in the Thames Estuary |
| 128 | 30 | 10.40 | RNN 13.12.40 to 23.8.41; for disposal 1.46 |
| 129 | 40 | 14.10.40 | Bombed 22.3.42 off Algeria |
| 130 | 21L | 9.10.40 | Sunk off Malta 7.5.42 by gunfire from E-boats |
| 131 | 21L | 27.11.40 | Sold 3.47 |
| 132 | 33 | 9.11.40 | CTL by bombing 21.3.42 and interned at Bone on 22nd |
| 133 | 37 | 12.12.40 | Lost 11.5.43 by fire off west Scottish coast |
| 134 | 54 | 29.10.40 | For disposal 10.46; became Egyptian *Hamza* |
| 135 | 25 | 10.10.40 | Lent SAN 1945; sold at Malta 11.46 |
| 136 | 47 | 26.11.40 | Sold Holland 3.47 = Y861 |
| 137 | 11 | 26.11.40 | For disposal 10.45 |
| 138 | 2 | 19.11.40 | Lent R Neth N 10.11.45 to 1953, then sold |
| 139 | 21L | 17.12.40 | For disposal 10.45 |
| 140 | 21L | 31. 1.41 | For disposal 10.45 |
| 141 | 40 | 23.12.40 | For disposal 10.45 |
| 142 | 13 | 26.11.40 | Sold 1946 = *Tregarth* |
| 143 | 21L | 13. 2.41 | R Neth N 10.11.45 to 10.4.46; sold .46 = *Gay Tulip* |
| 144 | 25 | 12.11.40 | Mined 22.9.41 in the Channel |
| 145 | 21L | 25. 3.41 | ML(A).1 from 7.45; sold 1946 |
| 146 | 21L | 1. 3.41 | For disposal 10.45 |
| 147 | 13 | 12.40 | CTL 3.11.44 off Portsmouth; for disposal 4.45 |
| 148 | 57 | 10.12.40 | ML(A).2 from 7.45; sold 1946 |
| 149 | 67 | 20. 2.41 | ML(A).3 from 7.45; sold 1946 |
| 150 | 50 | 6. 3.41 | Sold 3.48 |
| 151 | 50 | 25. 2.41 | For disposal 10.45 |
| 152 | 30 | 18.12.40 | ML(A).4 from 7.45; for disposal 6.46 |
| 153 | 44 | 19. 1.41 | For disposal 7.46; = yacht *Ginasal* |
| 154 | 52 | 5.11.40 | = ML2154 = *Squirrel* 1956; BU 6.58 |
| 155 | 71 | 11.12.40 | = ML2155; sold 1961 |
| 156 | 68 | 18.12.40 | Scuttled at St Nazaire 28.3.42; salved = ML2156; sold 51 |
| 157 | 63 | 9.10.40 | Sold 2.46 |
| 158 | 63 | 5. 5.41 | Sold 27.2.46 |
| 159 | 41 | 23.11.40 | Sold 2.46 |
| 160 | 47 | 27.12.40 | Bombed 6.5.42 at Brixham |
| 161 | 21L | 10. 4.41 | R Neth N 4.1.45 to 27.8.46; sold 1946 |
| 162 | 22 | 3.12.40 | R Neth N 4.1.45 to 10.4.46; sold 9.46 |
| 163 | 48L | 12. 2.41 | Sold 1947 = *Armanda* |
| 164 | 11 | 18.12.40 | R Neth N 4.1.45 to 10.4.46; sold 9.46 |
| 165 | 36 | 10.12.40 | For disposal 10.45 |
| 166 | 65 | 1. 1.41 | WD *Hambledon* 1.45; for disposal 5.47 |
| 167 | 65 | 1.41 | WD *Iffley* 1.45; for disposal 5.47 |
| 168 | 69 | 23.11.40 | For disposal 5.46 |
| 169 | 35 | 27.11.40 | Lost by fire 15.2.42 at Gibraltar |

**Codes for builders**

| | |
|----|---|
| 1 | Alcock Ashdown, Karachi |
| 2 | Aldous Successors, Brightlingsea |
| 3 | Alexandria (no further details known) |
| 4 | Anglo-American Nile Tourist Company, Cairo |
| 5 | Associated Boat Builders, Auckland, New Zealand |
| 6 | Austins, East Ham, London |
| 7 | Bailey, Auckland, New Zealand |
| 8 | Bay Yacht, Wallasea |
| 9 | Beheral Company, El Gamel, Egypt |
| 10 | Belmont Dock, Kingston, Jamaica |
| 11 | Boat Construction Company, Falmouth |
| 12 | Bombay Dockyard |
| 13 | Brook Marine, Oulton Broad, Lowestoft |
| 14 | C L Burland, Bermuda |
| 15 | Burn & Company, Calcutta |
| 16 | Camper & Nicholson, Gosport |
| 17 | Cape Province, South Africa |
| 18 | Cardnel L, Maylandsea |
| 19 | Collins, Lowestoft |
| 20 | Thomas Cook, Cairo |
| 21L | Curtis, Looe |
| 21P | Curtis, Par |
| 22 | Dickie, Bangor and Tarbert |
| 23 | Diesel Constructors, Isleworth |
| 24 | Doig, Grimsby |
| 25 | Dorset Yacht, Hamworthy |
| 26 | Egyptian Motors and Marine |
| 27 | Garden Reach, Calcutta |
| 28 | Green Point Boatyard, Sydney, Australia |
| 29 | Halvorsen, Sydney, Australia |
| 30 | Harris, Appledore |
| 31 | India General Navigation, Calcutta |
| 32 | Irrawadi Flotilla Company, Rangoon |
| 33 | Itchenor Shipyard |
| 34 | Johnson & Jago, Leigh on Sea, Essex |
| 35 | King, Burnham on Crouch |
| 36 | Kris Cruisers, Isleworth |
| 37 | Lady Bee, Isleworth |
| 38 | Le Blanc Shipbuilding, Weymouth, Nova Scotia |
| 39 | Louw & Halvorsen, Capetown, South Africa |
| 40 | Mashford Brothers, Cremyll |
| 41 | Jas Miller, St Monance |
| 42 | H Mohatta, Karachi |
| 43 | William Osborne, Littlehampton |
| 44 | H J Percival, Horning, Norfolk |
| 45 | Rangoon Dockyard (contracts were transferred to Calcutta) |
| 46 | Risdon Beazley, Northam Bridge |
| 47 | Alexander Robertson, Sandbank |
| 48L | Leo Robinson, Oulton Broad, Lowestoft |
| 48T | Leo Robinson, Tewkesbury |
| 49 | John Sadd, Maldon, Essex |
| 50 | Sheerness Dockyard |
| 51 | Shipbuilders Limited, Auckland, New Zealand |
| 52 | Jas Silver, Rosneath and Dumbarton |
| 53 | Singapore Harbour Board |

| ML | Builder | Completed | Fate |
|----|---------|-----------|------|
| 170 | 2 | 1.41 | For disposal 5.46 |
| 171 | 64 | 21.10.40 | WD *Richmond* 6.45; for disposal 5.47 |
| 172 | 21L | 16. 3.41 | For disposal 5.46 |
| 173 | 21L | 17. 1.41 | For disposal 5.46 |
| 174 | 43 | 12.40 | For disposal 5.46 |
| 175 | 52 | 20. 1.41 | For disposal 5.46 |
| 176 | 54 | 12.40 | For disposal 5.46 |
| 177 | 68 | 12.40 | Lost at St Nazaire 28.3.42 |
| 178 | 48 | 24. 6.41 | Sold 1946 |
| 179 | 65 | 16. 2.41 | Sold 2.46 |
| 180 | 19 | 18. 2.41 | Sold 1948 = *Matapan* |
| 181 | 49 | 24. 1.41 | Lent R Neth N 1945; sold R Neth N 3.47 |
| 182 | 48T | 2. 8.41 | FF 1.4.42 to 12.8.42; sold 2.46 |
| 183 | 22 | 10. 2.41 | Lost 11.2.45 in collision with East Pier, Dieppe |
| 184 | 30 | 10. 2.41 | Sold 3.46 |
| 185 | 60 | 20. 5.41 | Sold 3.46 |
| 186 | 13 | 28. 1.41 | Sold 3.46 |
| 187 | 11 | 11. 2.41 | Sold 11.6.47 at Singapore |
| 188 | 22 | 25. 3.41 | For disposal 11.45 at Freetown |
| 189 | 25 | 4. 2.41 | Sold 11.6.47 at Singapore |
| 190 | 54 | 19. 3.41 | For disposal 10.45 |
| 191 | 33 | 15. 5.41 | Burma RNVR 11.45; for disposal 6.46 |
| 192 | 56 | 1. 8.41 | FF 1942; lost at St Nazaire 28.3.42 |
| 193 | 44 | 27. 3.41 | Sold 11.6.47 at Singapore |
| 194 | 34 | 29. 1.41 | Sold 11.6.47 at Singapore |
| 195 | 63 | 21. 1.41 | Sold 3.47 |
| 196 | 41 | 1. 2.41 | = ML2196; to Norwich Sea Cadets 1958 = *Lord Nelson* |
| 197 | 47 | 24. 2.41 | Sold 1946 = *Cory 3* |
| 198 | 71 | 18. 3.41 | Sold 1946 = *Cory 4* |
| 199 | 64 | 19.12.40 | Sold 8.46 |
| 200 | 52 | 22. 2.41 | For disposal 1.46 at Trincomalee |
| 201 | 52 | 27. 3.41 | Sold 11.6.47 at Singapore |
| 202 | 37 | 15. 3.41 | Sold 2.46 at Trincomalee |
| 203 | 41 | 24. 6.41 | For disposal 10.45 |
| 204 | 46 | 27. 2.41 | To Burma RNVR 1.11.45; for disposal 1946 |
| 205 | 60 | 28. 6.41 | FF *Ouessant* 5.42 to 8.42; for disposal 1946 |
| 206 | 2 | 5. 3.41 | Sold Hampton Sea Scouts 10.46 |
| 207 | 34 | 11. 3.41 | Sold 3.46 |
| 208 | 46 | 12. 3.41 | RNN 12.3.41 to 10.42; for disposal 10.45 |
| 209 | 60 | 25. 8.41 | For disposal 11.45 at Freetown |

| | |
|----|----|
| 54 | Solent Shipyard, Sarisbury Green |
| 55 | South African Railways, East London, South Africa |
| 56 | Southampton Steam Joinery, Southampton |
| 57 | Sussex Shipbuilders, Shoreham |
| 58 | Taikoo Dockyard, Hong Kong |
| 59 | Task Railway and Port Service, Dar-es-Salaam |
| 60 | Jas Taylor, Chertsey |
| 61 | Thesen, Knysna, South Africa |
| 62 | Thomson and Balfour, Bo'ness |
| 63H | Thornycroft, Hampton |
| 63S | Thornycroft, Singapore |
| 64 | Tough Brothers, Teddington |
| 65 | J W & A Upham, Brixham |
| 66 | Voss Limited, Auckland, New Zealand |
| 67 | Vosper, Portsmouth |
| 68 | Wallasea Bay Yacht Yard, Rochford |
| 69 | William Weatherhead, Cockenzie |
| 70 | Williams, East London, South Africa |
| 71 | Woodnutt, Bembridge, Isle of Wight |
| 72 | Woods, Potter Heigham |
| 73 | Norman Wright, Brisbane, Australia |

More detailed addresses are shown for the UK-built Fairmiles in the British Fairmile lists.

*ML 570 alongside a fleet destroyer on VE Day, 1945. The short 4.5in Mark I manual mounting can just be seen.* Courtesy Harold Hawkins BEM

| ML | Builder | Completed | Fate |
|---|---|---|---|
| 210 | 43 | 7. 4.41 | RNN 5.4.41; mined 15.2.44 off Dieppe |
| 211 | 13 | 3. 3.41 | Sold 1947 |
| 212 | 22 | 5. 3.41 | Sold 1946 = yacht *Yvonne II* |
| 213 | 40 | 11. 4.41 | For disposal 11.45 |
| 214 | 36 | 10. 3.41 | Sold 11.6.47 at Singapore |
| 215 | 18 | 7. 5.41 | Sold 1947 |
| 216 | 37 | 28. 5.41 | Mined 19.9.44, foundered on 28th, North Sea |
| 217 | 22 | 5.41 | = ML2217 = Nigerian *Sapele* 20.7.59 |
| 218 | 69 | 17. 3.41 | For disposal 9.45 |
| 219 | 43 | 17. 5.41 | Grounded near Stornoway 21.11.41, CTL |
| 220 | 64 | 2.41 | = ML2220; RNVR 12.47; sold 20.8.56 |
| 221 | 35 | 24. 2.41 | = ML2221; to Connahs Quay SCC 1958 |
| 222 | 24 | 20. 4.41 | = ML2222; for disposal 1956 |
| 223 | 47 | 5.41 | = ML6002; = ML2223 = Nigerian *Calabar* 7.59 |
| 224 | 8 | 13. 3.41 | For disposal 3.46 |
| 225 | 2 | 25. 4.41 | WD *Maple Durham* 6.45, conversion not completed; for disposal 10.45 |
| 226 | 11 | 8. 4.41 | For disposal 11.45 at Freetown |
| 227 | 6 | 21. 5.41 | Sold 1947 = *Syrinx* |
| 228 | 64 | 15. 4.41 | For disposal 11.45 at Freetown |
| 229 | 25 | 7. 4.41 | For disposal 11.45 |
| 230 | 13 | 28. 3.41 | Lost in collision 17.8.45 Indian waters |
| 231 | 57 | 19. 5.41 | For disposal 11.45 at Freetown |
| 232 | 52 | 4.41 | Greek *Domakos* 7.45 on loan; BU 1947 |
| 233 | 30 | 31. 3.41 | Lent RNN 31.3.41 – 23.8.41; for disposal 10.45 |
| 234 | 22 | 15. 9.41 | WD *Marlow* 6.45, conversion not completed; disposal 10.45 |
| 235 | 22 | 27. 5.41 | Sold 1946 = yacht *Pauline* |
| 236 | 65 | 9. 6.41 | For disposal 2.46 |
| 237 | 65 | 22. 5.41 | = ML2237; sunk 8.10.52 as gunfire target |
| 238 | 47 | 14.11.41 | For Italian Navy 7.1.46 |
| 239 | 54 | 22. 5.41 | WD *Marsh* 6.45, conversion not completed; disposal 10.45 |
| 240 | 62 | 9. 4.41 | For Italian Navy 7.1.46 |
| 241 | 21L | 19. 5.41 | For disposal 10.45 |
| 242 | 21L | 28. 5.41 | CTL by fire 29.11.42, West Africa |
| 243 | 69 | 26. 5.41 | For disposal 1.46 |
| 244 | 44 | 3. 7.41 | To France 16.8.44 = V101 |

**65 ordered 21.5.40**

| ML | Builder | Completed | Fate |
|---|---|---|---|
| 245 | 50 | 14. 7.41 | FF *St Guenole* 7.41 – 7.42; sold 11.6.47 at Singapore |
| 246 | 50 | 21. 7.41 | FF *St Ives* 7.41 – 7.42; Burma RNVR 11.45; disposal 1.46 |
| 247 | 65 | 19. 7.41 | FF *St Alain* 7.41 – 7.42; Burma RNVR 11.45; disposal 1.46 |
| 248 | 13 | 4.41 | = ML2248; sold 3.7.54 |
| 249 | 68 | 27. 4.41 | WD *Molesey* (i) 6.45; conversion not completed; disposal 10.45 |
| 250 | 21 | 11. 7.41 | = ML2250; sold 1962 |
| 251 | 21 | 7.41 | Lost 6.3.43 in collision in the Atlantic |
| 252 | 56 | 17. 2.41 | Sold 1946 = yacht *Cheriton* |
| 253 | 49 | 5. 5.41 | For disposal 10.45 |
| 254 | 65 | 8. 5.41 | For disposal 10.45 |
| 255 | 40 | 18. 7.41 | For disposal 12.45 |
| 256 | 21L | 25. 6.41 | For disposal 4.47 |
| 257 | 21L | 8.41 | For disposal 10.45 |
| 258 | 25 | 28. 5.41 | Mined 15/16.9.44 off Rimini; for disposal 1.45 |
| 259 | 48L | 3. 7.41 | Sold 7.46 |
| 260 | 63 | 22. 5.41 | R Neth N 4.1.45 – 9.46; for disposal 9.46 |
| 261 | 11 | 11. 6.41 | For disposal 11.45 at Freetown |
| 262 | 19 | 18. 6.41 | FF 1941; lost 28.3.42 at St Nazaire |
| 263 | 30 | 10. 6.41 | For disposal 11.45 at Freetown |
| 264 | 34 | 20. 5.41 | Sold 11.46 |
| 265 | 46 | 30. 5.41 | Lost 1.7.44 by fire at Freetown |
| 266 | 35 | 19. 5.41 | To France 16.8.44 = V103 1946 |
| 267 | 54 | 25. 7.41 | FF 1941; lost 28.3.42 at St Nazaire |
| 268 | 25 | 17. 7.41 | FF 1941; lost 18.3.42 at St Nazaire |
| 269 | 69 | 28. 7.41 | FF *Béniquet* 4.42 – 8.42; Burma RNVR 10.45; disposal 12.45 |
| 270 | 13 | 26. 6.41 | Scuttled 28.3.42 at St Nazaire |

*ML 173 fitted for minesweeping, with twin .303in Vickers MGs on the bridge and a single 20mm aft of the funnel. Note the spare minesweeping floats and otters stowed on the upper deck.* Author's collection

| ML | Builder | Completed | Fate |
|---|---|---|---|
| 271 | 11 | 14. 7.41 | To France 16.8.44 = V102 |
| 272 | 8 | 29. 5.41 | For disposal 11.45 at Freetown |
| 273 | 43 | 17. 9.41 | For Italian Navy 24.1.46 |
| 274 | 34 | 16. 6.41 | For disposal 11.45 at Freetown |
| 275 | 62 | 26. 6.41 | For disposal 10.45 |
| 276 | 21P | 12. 9.41 | For disposal 10.45 |
| 277 | 65 | 13. 7.41 | For disposal 11.45 at Freetown |
| 278 | 2 | 7.10.41 | For disposal 11.45 at Freetown |
| 279 | 30 | 7.41 | For disposal 11.45 at Freetown |
| 280 | 21L | 9.41 | For Italian Navy 7.1.46 |
| 281 | 13 | 19. 7.41 | For disposal 11.45 at Freetown |
| 282 | 33 | 2.10.41 | Sold 3.46 |
| 283 | 44 | 25. 9.41 | To Italian Navy 10.12.45 |
| 284 | 52 | 4. 9.41 | PO 4.8.45 |
| 285 | 54 | 18. 9.41 | For disposal 11.45 at Freetown |
| 286 | 24 | 29. 8.41 | For disposal 10.45 |
| 287 | 6 | 23. 8.41 | Lost 1.7.44 by fire at Freetown |
| 288 | 18 | 19. 8.41 | Foundered 11.10.41 off Hartlepool |
| 289 | 8 | 15. 8.41 | For disposal 11.45 at Freetown |
| 290 | 13 | 18. 9.41 | Sold at Freetown 12.45 |
| 291 | 43 | 30. 9.41 | For disposal 10.45 |
| 292 | 40 | 30.10.41 | CTL by mine 19.6.44; PO 3.7.45 |
| 293 | 25 | 10. 9.41 | PO 8.45 |
| 294 | 49 | 25. 8.45 | For disposal 10.45 |
| 295 | 21L | 21.10.41 | Greek *Doliana* 1946 – 52, = ML2295; sold 25.1.56 |
| 296 | 25 | 8.10.41 | For disposal 11.45 at Freetown |
| 297 | 65 | 10. 9.41 | For disposal 1.46 |
| 298 | 25 | 21.11.41 | Lost 28.3.42 at St Nazaire |
| 299 | 37 | 4.12.41 | Laid up 9.46 |
| 300 | 69 | 30. 9.41 | For disposal 10.45 |
| 301 | 2 | 2.12.41 | Lost 9.8.42 by explosion at Freetown |
| 302 | 35 | 6. 9.41 | To France 16.8.44 = V104 |
| 303 | 41 | 14.10.41 | FF 4.42 – 8.42; sold 2.46 at Trincomalee |
| 304 | 30 | 8.10.41 | For disposal 10.45 |
| 305 | 34 | 9.41 | Sold 1.46 at Freetown |
| 306 | 54 | 18.12.41 | Lost 28.3.42 at St Nazaire; = German RA9 |
| 307 | 21L | 7.11.41 | Greek *Doxaton* on loan 21.6.45 – .61; sold 7.4.61 |

*Two views of the bow and stem of ML 261 under repair on the slip at Freetown.* Author's collection

| ML | Builder | Completed | Fate |
|----|---------|-----------|------|
| 308 | 21L | 30.11.41 | Sold 1948 at Malta |
| 309 | 65 | 16.11.41 | Sold 1946 = *River Lady* |

**2 accepted 28.6.40 as gift from Singapore Harbour Board**

| ML | Builder | Completed | Fate |
|----|---------|-----------|------|
| 310 | 53 | 29.11.41 | Lost 15.2.42 Tjebia Is; = Japanese *Suikei 12* |
| 311 | 53 | 29.11.41 | Lost 14.2.42 by Japanese gunfire in Banka Strait |

**24 ordered 28.7.40**

312 to 335 completed as Motor Gunboats

**32 ordered 21.8.40**

| ML | Builder | Completed | Fate |
|----|---------|-----------|------|
| 336 | 11 | 12. 9.41 | To Italian Navy 3.12.45 |
| 337 | 22 | 18.11.41 | = ML2337; sold 25.9.56 |
| 338 | 46 | 28. 9.41 | = ML2338; sold 17.12.55 |
| 339 | 8 | 16.10.41 | Torpedoed 7.10.42 by E-boats off Cromer |
| 340 | 48T | 19. 1.42 | Sold 4.47 at Malta |
| 341 | 19 | 27.10.41 | Greek *Drama* on loan 26.7.45 – 1960; sold 7.4.61, BU |
| 342 | 34 | 10.10.41 | = ML2342; sold 26.11.62 to BU |
| 343 | 63 | 10.41 | For disposal 10.45 |
| 344 | 13 | 22.10.41 | Sold 1946 = *Glen Tor* |
| 345 | 23 | 30. 3.42 | Sold 1946 = *Warrior Geraint* yacht |
| 346 | 41 | 11.41 | Sold 1946 = *Merrie Golden Hind* |
| 347 | 46 | 17.10.41 | Sold 1.47 = yacht *Venturer* |
| 348 | 20 | 26. 5.42 | Sold 1.47 |
| 349 | 20 | 2. 6.42 | For Italian Navy 7.1.46 |
| 350 | 20 | 15. 8.42 | Sold 1.47 |
| 351 | 20 | 9.42 | For Italian Navy 14.1.46 |
| 352 | 4 | 9. 6.42 | Bombed 14.9.42 at Tobruk |
| 353 | 4 | 26. 5.42 | Bombed 14.9.42 at Tobruk |
| 354 | 4 | 19. 5.42 | For Italian Navy 24.1.46 |
| 355 | 4 | 18. 4.42 | For Italian Navy 10.12.45 |
| 356 | 4 | 10. 7.42 | For Italian Navy 14.1.46 |
| 357 | 4 | 1. 8.42 | = ML2357; to Bermondsey SCC 1958; sold 1961 |
| 358 | 4 | 9.42 | Lost 12.11.43 off Leros |
| 359 | 4 | 31.10.42 | To Italian Navy 18.12.46 |
| 360 | 4 | 12.42 | = ML2360; sold 18.3.59 |
| 361 | 4 | 1.43 | Greek *Karpathos* 1945 |
| 362 | 53 | — | Launched 16.8.41, lost incomplete at Singapore |
| 363 | 53 | — | Launched 19.8.41, lost incomplete at Singapore |
| 364 | 53 | — | Launched ?, lost incomplete at Singapore* |
| 365 | 53 | — | Launched ?, lost incomplete at Singapore* |
| 366 | 59 | 4.43 | Sold 11.6.47 at Singapore |
| 367 | 59 | 4.43 | Sold 11.6.47 at Singapore |

* One of these was launched by the Japanese at their Patrol boat No 111 in 5.43

**4 ordered 27.8.40**

| ML | Builder | Completed | Fate |
|----|---------|-----------|------|
| 368 | 14 | 3.12.42 | To RCN 12.42; sold 1946 in Bermuda |
| 369 | 14 | 31.12.42 | To RCN 12.42; sold 1946 in Bermuda |
| 370 | 10 | 7. 9.42 | Sold 1946 in Bermuda |
| 371 | 10 | 16. 9.42 | Sold 1946 in Bermuda |

**18 ordered 21.8.40**

| ML | Builder | Completed | Fate |
|----|---------|-----------|------|
| 372 | 53 | — | Lost 1.42 on stocks at Singapore |
| 373 | 53 | — | Lost 1.42 on stocks at Singapore |
| 374 | 53 | — | Lost 1.42 on stocks at Singapore |
| 375 | 53 | — | Lost 1.42 on stocks at Singapore |
| 376 | 58 | — | Lost 12.41 on stocks at Hong Kong |
| 377 | 58 | — | Lost 12.41 on stocks at Hong Kong |
| 378 | 10 | 3.11.42 | To RCN 11.42; sold 1945 in Trinidad |
| 379 | 10 | 31.10.42 | To RCN 11.42; sold 1945 in Trinidad |
| 380 | 39 | 9.42 | To RIN; sold 1947 |
| 381 | 39 | 10.42 | Sold 10.45 at Bombay to BU |
| 382 | 39 | 11.42 | Sold 10.45 at Bombay to BU |
| 383 | 39 | 28.11.42 | Sold 10.45 at Bombay to BU |
| 384 | 20 | 12.42 | To Italian Navy 18.12.45 |
| 385 | 20 | 1.43 | Unfit 6.44 and PO 16.6.44 at Alexandria |
| 386 | 4 | 27. 4.43 | To Turkey 2.7.46 = AB1 |
| 387 | 4 | 1. 6.43 | Lost 5.3.44 by internal explosion at Beirut |

*A set of three pictures of an unknown B in the Greek Islands, camouflaged during daylight hours.* Author's collection

*The same unit, fitted for dropping agents among the Islands.* Author's collection

*A clearer view of the same unit's equipment. She carries a Rolls-Royce gun forward, twin MGs, a single 20mm Oerlikon and a folding boat in addition to her own dinghy.* Author's collection

| ML | Builder | Completed | Fate |
|---|---|---|---|
| 388 | 53 | — | Lost 1.42 on stocks at Singapore |
| 389 | 53 | — | Lost 1.42 on stocks at Singapore |

**2 ordered 27.8.40 at Singapore, re-ordered 22.2.42**

| ML | Builder | Completed | Fate |
|---|---|---|---|
| 390 | 12 | 16. 5.44 | RIN; sold 1947 |
| 391 | 12 | 11.44 | RIN; sold 1947 |

**8 ordered 12.8.41**

| ML | Builder | Completed | Fate |
|---|---|---|---|
| 392 | 38 | 26. 9.42 | To USN 12.42 = SC1466; for disposal 30.1.48 |
| 393 | 38 | 26. 6.42 | RCN 6.42; USN 12.42 = SC1467; sold 1949 |
| 394 | 38 | 1.10.42 | To USN 12.42 = SC1468; for disposal 20.1.48 |
| 395 | 38 | 26. 9.42 | To USN 12.42 = SC1469; for disposal 30.1.48 |
| 396 | 38 | 23.10.42 | To USN 12.42 = SC1470; sold 13.2.47 |
| 397 | 38 | 23.10.42 | To USN 12.42 = SC1471; for disposal 30.1.48 |
| 398 | 38 | 5.12.42 | To USN 12.42 = SC1472; for disposal 4.3.48 |
| 399 | 38 | 5.12.42 | To USN 12.42 = SC1473; for disposal 21.4.48 |

**20 ordered 4.9.41**

| ML | Builder | Completed | Fate |
|---|---|---|---|
| 400 | 7 | 18.11.42 | RNZN = *Kahu* 1.4.44; sold 1947 = *Dolphin* |
| 401 | 7 | 1. 4.43 | RNZN; sold 1947 = yacht *Mahurangi* |
| 402 | 7 | 11.43 | RNZN; sold 1947 = yacht *Ngaroma* |
| 403 | 5 | 21.10.42 | RNZN; sold 1947 = *Tiare* |
| 404 | 5 | 1. 2.43 | RNZN; sold 1947 = *Wailana* |
| 405 | 5 | 5.43 | RNZN; sold 1947 = *Marlyn* |
| 406 | 5 | 7.43 | RNZN; sold 1947 = *Rodney Farry* |
| 407 | 51 | 8. 3.43 | RNZN; sold 1947 = yacht *Deborah Bay* |
| 408 | 51 | 8. 8.43 | RNZN; sold 1947 = yacht *Karamana* |
| 409 | 51 | 8.43 | RNZN; sold 1947 = *Iris Moana*. Repurchased 1953 = *Iris Moana* (ML3570) = *Maori* 1961; sold 1963 |
| 410 | 66 | 1.43 | RNZN; sold 1947 = yacht *La Reta* |
| 411 | 66 | 20.12.43 | RNZL; = ML3571 = *Kahu* (ii) 1953 = *Philomel* 1961; sold 1965 ferry |
| 412 | 27 | 30.11.43 | RIN; sold 1947 |
| 413 | 27 | 29.11.43 | RIN; sold 1947 |
| 414 | 27 | 1. 3.44 | RIN; sold 1947 in Burma |
| 415 | 27 | 8. 3.44 | RIN; sold 1947 in Burma |
| 416 | 31 | 20.11.43 | RIN; sold 1947 |
| 417 | 31 | 20.11.43 | RIN; sold 1947 |
| 418 | 27 | 15. 3.44 | RIN; sold 1947 in Burma |
| 419 | 15 | 4. 1.44 | RIN; sold 1947 at Bombay |

**2 ordered Singapore 4.9.41 and re-ordered 12.1.42**

| ML | Builder | Completed | Fate |
|---|---|---|---|
| 420 | 12 | 17. 3.44 | RIN; = ML6420; sold 1947 |
| 421 | 12 | 31. 1.45 | RIN; sold 1947 |

**2 ordered Singapore 4.9.41 and re-ordered 28.11.41**

| ML | Builder | Completed | Fate |
|---|---|---|---|
| 422 | 10 | 21. 4.43 | Sold 1946 in Trinidad |
| 423 | 10 | 24. 4.43 | Sold 1946 in Trinidad |

**8 ordered Singapore 21.8.40 and re-ordered 1.42**

| ML | Builder | Completed | Fate |
|---|---|---|---|
| 424 | 28 | 28. 1.43 | RAN; for disposal 3.47 |
| 425 | 28 | 6. 2.43 | RAN; for disposal 3.47 |
| 426 | 28 | 5. 3.43 | RAN; for disposal 3.47 |
| 427 | 28 | 15. 3.43 | RAN; for disposal 3.47 |
| 428 | 28 | 31. 3.43 | RAN; for disposal 3.47 |
| 429 | 28 | 15. 4.43 | RAN; for disposal 3.47 |
| 430 | 28 | 6. 5.43 | RAN; sunk 14.8.44 by S/M gunfire off New Guinea |
| 431 | 28 | 14. 5.43 | RAN; for disposal 3.47 |

**4 ordered 26.7.40**

| ML | Builder | Completed | Fate |
|---|---|---|---|
| 432 | 53 | 21. 1.42 | Lost 1.42 by bombing at Singapore |
| 433 | 53 | 21. 1.42 | Lost 15.2.42 by gunfire in Banka Straits |
| 434 | 58 | — | Lost incomplete 12.41 at Hong Kong |
| 435 | 58 | — | Lost incomplete 12.41 at Hong Kong |

**2 ordered 26.7.40 at builder 45, re-ordered 14.1.41**

| ML | Builder | Completed | Fate |
|---|---|---|---|
| 436 | 31 | 29. 4.43 | For disposal 1947 |
| 437 | 31 | 9. 5.43 | To Burma Government 1948 = *Mermaid* |

**4 ordered 26.7.40 (last 3 originally builder 31)**

| ML | Builder | Completed | Fate |
|---|---|---|---|
| 438 | 31 | 30. 4.42 | RIN 1944; sold 1947 |
| 439 | 27 | 12.42 | RIN 1944; sold 1947 |

*MLs 574 and 305 refitting at Freetown.*
Author's collection

| ML | Builder | Completed | Fate |
|---|---|---|---|
| 440 | 27 | 14. 4.42 | RIN 1944; sold 1947 |
| 441 | 15 | 8.42 | RIN 1944; sold 1947 |

**36 ordered 29.4.41 (MLs 462–465 originally intended for Singapore)**

| ML | Builder | Completed | Fate |
|---|---|---|---|
| 442 | 60 | 13. 1.42 | For disposal 10.45 |
| 443 | 13 | 30.11.41 | Mined 12.7.44 off west coast of Italy |
| 444 | 62 | 26. 9.41 | CTL 22.5.44 by engine room explosion; disposal 10.44 |
| 445 | 65 | 12.12.41 | For disposal 10.45 |
| 446 | 11 | 21.11.41 | Scuttled 28.3.42 at St Nazaire |
| 447 | 44 | 8. 1.42 | Lost 28.3.42 at St Nazaire |
| 448 | 64 | 11.41 | For disposal 10.45 |
| 449 | 56 | 14. 4.42 | For disposal 9.45 after fire damage in the Mediterranean |
| 450 | 6 | 17.11.41 | Sold 3.48 |
| 451 | 30 | 17.11.41 | Sold 1946 |
| 452 | 40 | 8. 1.42 | For disposal 10.45 |
| 453 | 60 | 14. 4.42 | Sold 1947 = yacht *Nepeta* |
| 454 | 47 | 16. 1.42 | Sold 5.46 |
| 455 | 69 | 11.41 | Sold 4.3.46 |
| 456 | 49 | 5. 1.42 | Sold 1946 |
| 457 | 34 | 21.11.41 | Lost 28.3.42 at St Nazaire |
| 458 | 21L | 1. 1.42 | To Italian Navy 10.12.45 |
| 459 | 54 | 24. 2.42 | To Italian Navy 22.5.46 |
| 460 | 22 | 21. 1.42 | CTL by grounding 5.1.45 Mediterranean; disposal 4.45 |
| 461 | 18 | 20.11.41 | = ML2461; sold 20.7.56 |
| 462 | 25 | 15.12.41 | = ML2462; sold 18.3.59 |
| 463 | 2 | 25. 1.42 | To Italian Navy 3.12.46 |
| 464 | 24 | 12.41 | To STT 1947; sold 1949 |
| 465 | 21L | 18. 2.42 | Sold 1946 = yacht *Dorasta* |
| 466 | 33 | 31. 3.42 | Mined 25.3.45 off Walcheren |
| 467 | 46 | 6.12.41 | For disposal 10.45 |
| 468 | 46 | 29. 1.42 | For disposal 9.45 |
| 469 | 34 | 15. 1.42 | To Italian Navy 3.12.46 |
| 470 | 44 | 17. 3.42 | Sold 1946 in Trinidad |
| 471 | 11 | 1. 4.42 | To Italian Navy 24.1.46 |
| 472 | 54 | 17. 4.42 | For disposal 10.45 |
| 473 | 69 | 3. 2.42 | For disposal 10.45 |
| 474 | 31 | 22. 4.43 | RIN; sold 1947 |
| 475 | 31 | 10. 5.43 | RIN; sold 1947 |
| 476 | 27 | 14. 4.42 | RIN; sold 1947 |
| 477 | 27 | 12.42 | RIN; sold 1947 |

**23 ordered 27.8.41**

| ML | Builder | Completed | Fate |
|---|---|---|---|
| 478 | 62 | 1.42 | Greek *Kalini* = *Eleptheron* on loan 7.46; sold 7.4.61 |
| 479 | 19 | 1. 4.42 | Sold 1946 in Trinidad |
| 480 | 21L | 6. 2.42 | For disposal 4.46 at Malta |
| 481 | 21L | 9. 4.42 | Sold 1946 in Trinidad |
| 482 | 6 | 26. 2.42 | Sold 1946 in Trinidad |
| 483 | 41 | 2.42 | Lent Greek Navy 1946; for disposal 1964 |
| 484 | 54 | 5. 5.42 | Sold 1945 in Trinidad |
| 485 | 18 | 30. 3.42 | Sold 1945 in Trinidad |
| 486 | 34 | 10. 3.42 | Sold 1945 in Trinidad |
| 487 | 34 | 13. 4.42 | Sold 1945 in Trinidad |
| 488 | 37 | 28. 3.42 | To Hounslow SCC 6.46 |
| 489 | 41 | 1. 3.42 | = ML2489; sold 1961 |
| 490 | 21L | 17. 3.42 | For disposal 10.45 |
| 491 | 11 | 5.42 | = ML2491; sold 7.4.61 |
| 492 | 2 | 13. 5.42 | Sold 1946 = *Pride of Paignton* |
| 493 | 21L | 5.42 | = ML2493; sold 1956 |
| 494 | 62 | 19. 3.42 | For disposal 9.45 |
| 495 | 69 | 5.42 | Chelsea SCC *Loyalty* by 1957 |
| 496 | 37 | 2. 7.42 | Sold 20.1.59 |
| 497 | 56 | 7.42 | Sold 1947 |
| 498 | 46 | 15. 4.42 | *Sea Eagle* 1955; Derry SCC 11.57; sold 20.9.63 |
| 499 | 46 | 5.42 | Sold 4.3.46 |
| 500 | 22 | 7.42 | Sold 20.4.46 |

*HMS* Hornet *in 1945, showing a 71ft 6in British Power Boat, ML 570 with her 'gun' and a Fairmile D. Note the background – 'Suicide Bridge' was known to all Coastal Forces and submariners.*
Courtesy Harold Hawkins BEM

| ML | Builder | Completed | Fate |
|----|---------|-----------|------|
| **1 ordered 27.1.40** | | | |
| 501 | 16 | — | Lost 3.41 by bombing while building; replaced by 501(ii) building for Turkey and completed as MGB |
| **17 ordered 27.8.41 (RMLs)** | | | |
| 511 | 65 | 6.42 | Sold 1947 |
| 512 | 24 | 6.42 | Sold 18.9.58 |
| 513 | 21L | 20. 6.42 | Sold 4.3.46 |
| 514 | 6 | 5. 5.42 | For disposal 12.45 |
| 515 | 19 | 6.42 | Sold 18.9.58 = *Dear Pal* |
| 516 | 69 | 6.42 | Sold 3.46 = yacht *Padua* |
| 517 | 49 | 20. 5.42 | Sold 1946 |
| 518 | 41 | 1. 6.42 | Sold 1946 = yacht *Commodore* |
| 519 | 2 | 7.42 | Sold 1946 |
| 520 | 6 | 5.11.42 | Sold 1946 |
| 521 | 21L | 6.42 | Sold 1946 = yacht *Aramel* |
| 522 | 34 | 25. 6.42 | Sold 1946 |
| 523 | 44 | 2. 7.42 | For disposal 12.45 |
| 524 | 33 | 3. 9.42 | Sold 1946 = yacht *Maraya* |
| 525 | 21L | 24. 7.42 | Sold 3.46 = *Lenrodian* |
| 526 | 54 | 27. 8.42 | Sold 3.46 |
| 527 | 13 | 9. 9.42 | For disposal 11.45 |
| **73 ordered 28.11.41 and 18.5.42 (528 to 553 were RMLs)** | | | |
| 528 | 48L | 11.10.42 | For disposal 11.45; sold = *Escapade* |
| 529 | 41 | 14. 7.42 | Thames SCC *Darling* 1957; sold 7.63 |
| 530 | 21L | 24. 8.42 | Sold 3.46 |
| 531 | 44 | 22. 9.42 | For disposal 11.45 |
| 532 | 34 | 13. 7.42 | For disposal 11.45 |
| 533 | 21L | 2. 9.42 | Sold 1946 |
| 534 | 18 | 9. 7.42 | Sold 3.46 |
| 535 | 69 | 8.42 | Sold = *Western Lady* 1947 |
| 536 | 54 | 9.10.42 | For disposal 12.45 |
| 537 | 22 | 22.10.42 | For disposal 12.45 |
| 538 | 49 | 9.10.42 | For disposal 12.45 |
| 539 | 21L | 25. 9.42 | Sold 1947 |
| 540 | 65 | 1.12.42 | For disposal 1.46; sold = *The Dansant* |
| 541 | 19 | 16. 9.42 | For disposal 11.45; sold = *Mastiff* |
| 542 | 6 | 22. 7.42 | For disposal 11.45; sold = *Western Lady II* 1947 |
| 543 | 34 | 20. 8.42 | For disposal 12.45 |
| 544 | 21L | 10.42 | For disposal 12.45; sold = yacht *Xrona* |
| 545 | 69 | 9.42 | For disposal 1.46 |
| 546 | 41 | 15. 9.42 | For disposal 1.46 |
| 547 | 24 | 10.42 | For disposal 1.46 |
| 548 | 34 | 25. 9.42 | For disposal 11.45 |
| 549 | 6 | 23. 9.42 | For disposal 11.45 |
| 550 | 44 | 16.12.42 | Sold 1946 = *Starlena* |
| 551 | 62 | 17.11.42 | For disposal 11.45 |
| 552 | 41 | 14.10.42 | For disposal 11.45 |
| 553 | 56 | 28.12.42 | For disposal 11.45 |
| 554 | 21L | 10.42 | Greek *Kassos* 1945 – 52; = ML2554; sold 25.9.56 |
| 555 | 54 | 21.12.42 | WD *Sonning* 13.3.46; for disposal 3.48 |
| 556 | 21L | 12.42 | Sold 8.10.47 at Alexandria |
| 557 | 21L | 12.42 | Lent WD 13.3.46, permanently transferred 12.47 |
| 558 | 33 | 12. 2.43 | Mined 5.5.45 in the Adriatic |
| 559 | 2 | 29. 1.43 | Sold 1948 at Malta |
| 560 | 18 | 20.10.42 | For disposal 10.47 at Alexandria |
| 561 | 69 | 11.42 | Greek *Karpathos* on loan 1946 = ML2561; BU 1.55 |
| 562 | 13 | 16. 2.43 | Damaged 6.10.44 and for disposal 11.44 |
| 563 | 54 | 3. 3.43 | Mined 16.8.44 in the Mediterranean |
| 564 | 34 | 14.11.42 | = ML2564; sold 22.11.56 |
| 565 | 22 | 5. 3.43 | Greek *Kos* on loan 1946 – 52, = ML2565; BU 1.55 |
| 566 | 21L | 1.43 | For disposal 10.47 at Alexandria |
| 567 | 44 | 12. 4.43 | = ML2567; sold 18.3.59 |
| 568 | 21L | 2.43 | = ML2568; sold 25.9.56 |

| ML | Builder | Completed | Fate |
|----|---------|-----------|------|
| 569 | 19 | 15. 1.43 | = ML2569; sold 25.1.56 |
| 570 | 6 | 25. 9.42 | Sold 1949 |
| 571 | 60 | 19. 2.43 | = ML2571; sold 1963 |
| 572 | 34 | 20.12.42 | Sold 1957 |
| 573 | 41 | 21. 1.43 | Lent RNN 25.1.43 – 18.12.45; for disposal 12.45 |
| 574 | 41 | 15. 1.43 | Sold 1.46 at Freetown |
| 575 | 34 | 2. 2.43 | = ML2575; sold 7.56 |
| 576 | 60 | 13. 7.43 | = ML2576; sold 27.1.56 |
| 577 | 34 | 5. 3.43 | WD *Sunbury* 1945 – 28.4.50; ML2577; sold 20.7.56 |
| 578 | 41 | 14. 4.43 | Greek *Khalki* on loan 31.7.45 – 60; sold 7.4.61 |
| 579 | 41 | 3. 6.43 | Bombed 26.10.43 at Leros |
| 580 | 34 | 20. 4.43 | Sold 2.47 at Alexandria |
| 581 | 34 | 5.43 | = ML2581; sold 19.2.59 |
| 582 | | 24. 9.43 | = ML2582; lost 5.6.52 off Holland by crashed aircraft |
| 583 | | 12.10.43 | = ML2583; sold 1962 |
| 584 | 34 | 7.43 | To Turkey 2.7.46 = AB2 |
| 585 | 41 | 19. 7.43 | = ML2585; sold 1961 at Malta |
| 586 | 41 | 31. 8.43 | = ML2586; sold 18.3.59, BU |
| 587 | 34 | 8.43 | Sold 1946 = yacht *La Contenta* |
| 588 | 60 | 12. 1.44 | Sold 3.46 = *Mary Lou* |
| 589 | 21L | 12.43 | Sold 3.46 |
| 590 | 34 | 17. 9.43 | For disposal 1.46 |
| 591 | 21L | 18. 4.44 | Foundered 9.5.45 in tidal wave in Sitang River, Burma |
| 592 | 41 | 15.11.43 | = ML2592; sold 1961 |
| 593 | 34 | 19.10.43 | = ML2593; *Sea Eagle* 1956; sold 30.12.58 |
| 594 | 33 | 5. 4.44 | Sold 2.46 at Trincomalee |
| 595 | 21L | 16. 6.44 | = ML6004 = ML2595; for disposal 1953 |
| 596 | 69 | 18. 1.44 | Sold 3.46 |
| 597 | 34 | 24.11.43 | Sold 1947 |
| 598 | 41 | 29.11.43 | Sold 8.46 |
| 599 | 69 | 16. 4.44 | Sold 2.46 at Trincomalee |
| 600 | 21L | 20. 9.44 | Sold 1946 = yacht *Lady Penelope* 1947 |

**MLs 601–798 ordered 15.3.40 (12 boats), 27.4.41 (28 boats) and 28.11.41 were completed as MGB/MTBs**

**8 ordered 28.11.41 (originally intended for Singapore)**

| | | | |
|----|---------|-----------|------|
| 801 | 28 | 29. 5.43 | RAN. Sold 1949 |
| 802 | 28 | 15. 6.43 | RAN. Sold 1949 |
| 803 | 28 | 8. 7.43 | RAN. Sold 1949 |
| 804 | 28 | 15. 7.43 | RAN. Sold 1949 |
| 805 | 28 | 3. 8.43 | RAN. Sold 1949 |
| 806 | 28 | 8. 9.43 | RAN. Sold 1949 |
| 807 | 28 | 13. 9.43 | RAN. Sold 1949 |
| 808 | 28 | 23. 9.43 | RAN. Sold 1949 |

**4 ordered 27.5.42 (first two builder 29, second two builder 73)**

| | | | |
|----|---------|-----------|------|
| 809 | 28 | 7.10.43 | RAN. Sold 1949 |
| 810 | 28 | 25.10.43 | RAN. Sold 1949 |
| 811 | 28 | 5.11.43 | RAN. Sold 1949 |
| 812 | 28 | 4.12.43 | RAN. Sold 1949 |

**16 ordered 19.5.42**

| | | | |
|----|---------|-----------|------|
| 813 | 29 | 16.11.42 | RAN. Sold 1949 |
| 814 | 29 | 16.11.42 | RAN. Sold 1949 |
| 815 | 73 | 11. 1.43 | RAN. Sold 1949 |
| 816 | 73 | 1. 6.43 | RAN. Sold 1949 |
| 817 | 29 | 16. 2.43 | RAN. Sold 1949 |
| 818 | 29 | 29. 3.43 | RAN. Sold 1949 |
| 819 | 29 | 10. 5.43 | RAN. Sold 1950 |
| 820 | 29 | 21. 6.43 | RAN. Sold 1949 |
| 821 | 29 | 29. 7.43 | RAN. Sold 1949 |
| 822 | 29 | 30. 8.43 | RAN. Sold 1949 |
| 823 | 29 | 30. 9.43 | RAN. Sold 1949 |
| 824 | 29 | 18.11.43 | RAN. Sold 1949 |
| 825 | 29 | 1. 2.44 | RAN. Sold 1949 |
| 826 | 73 | 1. 1.44 | RAN. Sold 1949 |

*The funnel exhaust of ML 869, seen in August 1945.*
Author's collection

| ML | Builder | Completed | Fate |
|---|---|---|---|
| 827 | 73 | 19. 4.44 | RAN. Grounded 17.11.44 Jacquinot Bay, New Guinea; sank on 20th in tow of *Cambrian Salvor* |
| 828 | — | Cancelled? | |

**6 ordered 28.11.41**

| ML | Builder | Completed | Fate |
|---|---|---|---|
| 829 | 39 | 14. 1.43 | RIN 4.45; sold 1946 |
| 830 | 39 | 27. 2.43 | Stranded E Indies 16.10.44; sold 2.46 |
| 831 | 61 | 18. 8.43 | RIN 4.45; for disposal 7.46 |
| 832 | 61 | 18. 8.43 | RIN 4.45; for disposal 7.46 |
| 833 | 59 | 31. 5.44 | Sold 11.6.47 at Singapore |
| 834 | 59 | 12.44 | Sold 2.46 |

**8 ordered 18.5.42**

| ML | Builder | Completed | Fate |
|---|---|---|---|
| 835 | 4 | 8. 8.43 | Bombed 12.10.43 at Leros |
| 836 | 4 | 29. 7.43 | To Turkey 2.7.46 = AB3 |
| 837 | 4 | 31. 3.44 | To Turkey 2.7.46 = AB4 |
| 838 | 4 | 1. 1.44 | To Turkey 2.7.46 = AB5 |
| 839 | 4 | 25. 5.44 | To Italy 28.12.45 |
| 840 | 4 | 15. 6.44 | = ML2840 = *Watchful* 7.55; for disposal 1962 |
| 841 | 4 | 8.10.43 | For disposal 5.46 |
| 842 | 4 | 26.11.43 | To Turkey 2.7.46 = AB6 |

**3 ordered   . .42**

| ML | Builder | Completed | Fate |
|---|---|---|---|
| 843 | 42 | 28. 8.44 | RIN; sold 1947 |
| 844 | 42 | 28.10.44 | RIN; sold 1947 |
| 845 | 42 | — | RIN; cancelled 2.45 |

**12 ordered 30.8.42**

| ML | Builder | Completed | Fate |
|---|---|---|---|
| 846 | 39 | 24. 7.43 | RIN 1945; BU 1946 |
| 847 | 39 | 7.11.43 | For disposal 2.46 |
| 848 | 39 | 25. 2.44 | For disposal 2.46 |
| 849 | 55 | 25. 2.44 | For disposal 2.46 |
| 850 | 70 | 19. 9.44 | Sold 11.6.47 at Singapore |
| 851 | 70 | 19. 9.44 | Sold 11.6.47 at Singapore |
| 852 | 61 | 20. 2.44 | For disposal 2.46 |
| 853 | 61 | 20. 2.44 | For disposal 2.46 |
| 854 | 39 | 7.11.43 | For disposal 2.46 |
| 855 | 39 | 22. 1.44 | For disposal 2.46 |
| 856 | 55 | 6. 4.44 | For disposal 2.46 |
| 857 | 55 | 6. 4.44 | For disposal 2.46 |

**2 ordered 3.10.42**

| ML | Builder | Completed | Fate |
|---|---|---|---|
| 858 | 10 | 5.44 | Sold 1945 in Trinidad |
| 859 | 10 | 19. 8.44 | Sold 1945 in Trinidad |

**40 ordered 22.12.42 (plus ML872 ordered 31.12.42)**

| ML | Builder | Completed | Fate |
|---|---|---|---|
| 860 | 20 | 20. 5.44 | To Italy 28.12.45 |
| 861 | 20 | 10. 5.44 | Greek *Tsaltaltza*. On loan 12.11.45 – 61; sold 27.4.62 |
| 862 | 20 | 25. 2.44 | To Turkey 2.7.46 = AB7 |
| 863 | 20 | 11. 3.44 | To Turkey 2.7.46 = AB8 |
| 864 | 4 | 22. 4.44 | Greek *Nissiros* on loan 9.5.47 – 64; sold 15.11.65 |
| 865 | 4 | 6. 5.44 | To Italy 28.12.45 |
| 866 | 20 | 27. 6.44 | = ML2866; BU 1.55 |
| 867 | 20 | 12. 7.44 | Greek *Karpentisi* on loan 12.11.45 – 60; sold 1962 |
| 868 | 9 | 4.45 | For disposal 2.46 |
| 869 | 9 | 4.45 | = ML6005 = ML2869; sold circa 1951 in Ceylon |
| 870 | 4 | 2. 8.44 | Mined 15.10.44 off Piraeus |
| 871 | 4 | 4.45 | For disposal 2.46 |
| 872 | 1 | 8. 5.45 | RIN; sold 1947 |
| 873 | 4 | 4.45 | Sold 1946 |
| 874 | 4 | 4.45 | For disposal 2.46 |
| 875 | 20 | 4.45 | For disposal 2.46 |
| 876 | 20 | 16. 3.45 | For disposal 2.46 |
| 877 | 4 | 3. 4.45 | For disposal 2.46 |
| 878 | 4 | 23. 3.45 | For disposal 2.46 |
| 879 | 20 | 3. 4.45 | For disposal 2.46 |
| 880 | 20 | 3. 4.45 | For disposal 2.46 |
| 881 | 4 | 19. 4.45 | For disposal 2.46 |
| 882 | 4 | 30. 3.45 | WD *Marsh* 1946 – 49; = ML2882; sold 16.11.56 |

*Upper deck detail of ML 348 in the Mediterranean in 1945.* Courtesy Alf Pavitt

| ML | Builder | Completed | Fate |
|----|---------|-----------|------|
| 883 | 26 | 12. 4.45 | WD 7.46 – 28.4.50; for disposal 1951 |
| 884 | 26 | 23. 4.45 | WD 7.46 – 50; for disposal 1951 |
| 885 | 4 | 20. 7.45 | For disposal 1.46 |
| 886 | 4 | 9. 8.45 | WD *Molesey* (ii) 7.46 – 22.9.49 = ML2886; sold 21.11.56 |
| 887 | 3 | — | Cancelled circa 6.45 |
| 888 | 3 | — | Cancelled circa 6.45 |
| 889 | 20 | 14. 4.45 | WD *Shepperton* 7.46 – 49 = ML2889; sold 21.11.56 |
| 890 | 20 | 3.45 | WD *Shiplake* 1946 – 49; for disposal 1950 |
| 891 | 17 | 28. 3.44 | Mined 21.1.45 off Ramree Island, Burma |
| 892 | 17 | 28. 3.44 | For disposal 2.46 |
| 893 | 17 | 1. 6.44 | For disposal 2.46 |
| 894 | 61 | 1. 6.44 | For disposal 2.46 |
| 895 | 61 | 25. 5.44 | For disposal 2.46 |
| 896 | 61 | 25. 5.44 | For disposal 2.46 |
| 897 | 17 | 7. 3.45 | Sold 11.6.47 at Singapore |
| 898 | 17 | 7. 3.45 | Sold 11.6.47 at Singapore |
| 899 | 17 | 7. 3.45 | Sold 11.6.47 at Singapore |
| 900 | 17 | 7. 3.45 | Sold 11.6.47 at Singapore |

**33 ordered 30.8.42**

| ML | Builder | Completed | Fate |
|----|---------|-----------|------|
| 901 | 34 | 31.12.43 | = ML6006 = ML2901; RNVR 1951; sold 20.8.56 |
| 902 | 41 | 27. 2.44 | Sold 1947 = yacht *Dame de Coeur* |
| 903 | 34 | 11. 2.44 | For disposal 1946 |
| 904 | 41 | 28. 4.44 | Burma RNVR 11.45; for disposal 1.46 |
| 905 | 60 | 10. 5.44 | Lost 9.5.45 in a tidal wave in the Sitang River, Burma |
| 906 | 60 | 28. 7.44 | = ML2906; sold 10.50 |
| 907 | 34 | 7. 4.44 | Scuttled off Singapore 1947 as unserviceable |
| 908 | 60 | 18. 5.45 | WD *Benson* 1.45; for disposal 9.46 |
| 909 | 34 | 4.44 | For disposal 2.46 |
| 910 | 41 | 29. 6.44 | For disposal 10.45 |
| 911 | 34 | 8 6.44 | For disposal 1.46 |
| 912 | 69 | 22. 7.44 | = ML6007 = ML2912; sold 15.9.58 |
| 913 | 33 | 11.44 | Sold 7.3.46 = yacht *Lulworth Castle* |
| 914 | 41 | 5.44 | For disposal 1.46 |
| 915 | 34 | 11. 7.44 | For disposal 1.46; sold = yacht *Ififa* |
| 916 | 69 | 16. 9.44 | Mined 8.11.44 off Dutch coast |
| 917 | 44 | 3. 8.45 | WD *Caversham* 1.45; sold 1946 = yacht *Sea Kayem* |
| 918 | 34 | 27. 8.44 | Sold 2.12.49 = yacht *Lavender Lady* |
| 919 | 41 | 9.10.44 | = ML2919; for disposal 1.53 |
| 920 | 72 | 7.45 | WD *Cleeve* 1.45; for disposal 11.45 |
| 921 | 69 | 22.11.44 | = ML2921; sold 4.2.57 |
| 922 | 60 | 7.45 | WD *Chertsey* 1.45; for disposal 11.45 |
| 923 | 34 | 7.12.44 | Sold 14.7.47 at Singapore |
| 924 | 41 | 16.12.44 | Sold 4.3.46 |
| 925 | 6 | 20. 4.45 | WD *Boulters* 1.45; for disposal 11.45 |
| 926 | 19 | 17. 7.45 | WD *Culham* 1.45; for disposal 11.45 |
| 927 | 34 | 18. 5.45 | WD *Abingdon* 1.45; sold 1946 |
| 928 | 41 | 5.45 | WD *Boveney* 1.45; for disposal 11.45 |
| 929 | 43 | 27. 6.45 | WD *Goring* 1.45; for disposal 11.45 |
| 930 | 18 | 7.45 | WD *Clifton* 1.45; for disposal 10.46 |
| 931 | 71 | 7.45 | WD *Cookham* 1.45; for disposal 1.46 |
| 932 | 34 | 7.45 | WD *Bray* 1.45; for disposal 11.45 |
| 933 | 6 | 8.45 | WD *Hurley* 1.45; for disposal 10.46 |

**4 ordered 30.6.44**

| ML | Builder | Completed | Fate |
|----|---------|-----------|------|
| 4001 | 61 | 9. 3.45 | Sold 11.6.47 |
| 4002 | 61 | 9. 3.45 | Sold 11.6.47 at Singapore |
| 4003 | 61 | 15. 4.45 | = ML6008 = ML2156; sold 1951 in Ceylon |
| 4004 | 61 | 15. 4.45 | For disposal 2.46 |

*A 20mm Oerlikon mounting aboard an unknown B in the Mediterranean. Note the substantial gun safety rails.* Author's collection

# The Canadian Fairmile B type

Canada, too, was woefully short of warships at the outbreak of the war, and, when offered the chance to build Fairmiles, eventually built eighty. Fifty-nine of these were built in boatyards on the Great Lakes, fourteen on the west coast and the remainder at Weymouth, Nova Scotia.

The first twenty-four were ordered in January or April 1941, and began to enter service in the autumn of that year. Twelve more were ordered in July, followed by eighteen in February 1942, with the final twenty-six in October.

The first thirty-six boats were originally designated CML 01–36 (Coastal Motor Launch), with the numbers 001–036 painted up; these and later units were listed and painted up as Q 050–Q 129 later.

The first sixty-two displaced 79 tons with a beam of 17ft 10in, but they were otherwise very similar to their British counterparts. The Hall-Scott engines came from the same source, giving them an endurance of 1455 miles at 7 1/2 knots. The remaining boats had the same displacement, but a beam of just 17ft. These were powered by the more powerful Sterling engines of 1400 bhp, giving

*Q-070 newly commissioned in March 1942.*
Author's collection

22 knots maximum speed for a short period and an endurance of 1925 miles at 7 1/2 knots.

The Canadian B types played a vital role as escort vessels in the St Lawrence River and the Gulf of St Lawrence, and as close escorts to convoys between Newfoundland, the offshore islands and the mainland. They carried out anti-submarine patrols, and port defence and rescue duties, thus releasing the few larger escort craft for duties elsewhere.

In 1942 the decision was made to send two flotillas for the winter period to the Caribbean, where U-boats were enjoying a high success rate due to the shortage of US escorts and their operational inexperience. The 72nd and 73rd Flotillas (each of six boats) left Halifax in mid-December for Trinidad via Boston and other ports south. Stress of inclement weather on the way forced the 72nd Flotilla to return after reaching Savannah, Georgia, but the remaining units operated until the spring out of Miami and Key West under the orders of the local US commander.

Early in June 1943, ML 053 recovered two mines, intact, from a field laid by U 119 in the approaches to Halifax. Others were engaged in anti-espionage efforts, intercepting spies landed from a U-boat, and working towards the boat's eventual destruction. MLs 052, 062 and 063 were transferred to the Free French forces in

Feburary 1943, and stationed at St Pierre and Miquelon under operational control of the Flag Officer, Newfoundland. Most were sold at the end of hostilities, but six were retained in service as training ships on the Great Lakes until the 1960s.

I am grateful to the Canadian Archives for their assistance, and have redrawn a selection of their data. While obviously influenced by the US armament industry, the armament fit in early Canadian Bs comprised one 3-pounder forward and twin .5in water-cooled Colt machine-guns aft, backed up by .303in Lewis or .300 Savage guns. Later the armament was virtually standardised at three single 20mm Oerlikons. An interesting local construction change was the introduction of circular wheelhouse windows in many units. Trials were also carried out by the fitting of the American Mousetrap mounting, an ahead-throwing anti-submarine weapon for small ships. Photographs of this can be seen in the weapons section.

### Fairmile Bs in the United States Navy

It is a little-known fact that Lend-Lease also worked in reverse during World War II. A number of British products were urgently required to aid the US war effort shortly after the declaration of war by the US government. By the spring of 1942, when the United States was reeling from the onslaught of German U-boats on merchant shipping off the east coast (called the 'happy hunting ground' by U-boat COs), serious defects in the US coastal defence had become obvious. The difficulties had begun during the winter.

At a German conference on December 12 1941, it was resolved on Hitler's order to carry the U-boat war into American coastal waters. Initially only six of the larger 740-ton U-boats were despatched. They left the Biscay ports between 18 and 30 December, with orders to penetrate the northern end of the coastal route

*The Canadian MLs 072, 058 and 073 nearing completion, in late 1941.* Author's collection

between Newfoundland and New York, near the assembly ports of the convoys bound for the UK. Their success was immediate. By the end of January thirty-one ships, totalling nearly 200,000 tons, had been sunk off the United States and Canadian coasts. This German success soon spread southward off Hampton Roads and Cape Hatteras, and then on to the coast of Florida. Many merchant ships were completely unprotected, and many coastal towns were not even blacked out to hinder the U-boats' navigation. Along this undefended coastline the precious tanker fleet moved in procession, to and from the oil ports of Venezuela and the Gulf of Mexico. The Caribbean Sea, too, offered a wealth of targets, and the U-boats concentrated chiefly on the tankers; neutral ships as well as those of the Allies were sunk. Week by week the losses increased. In February losses in the Atlantic rose to seventy-one ships, totalling 384,000 tons, all but two of which were sunk in the American zone. This was the highest rate of loss to date, but it was soon surpassed. This havoc was caused by no more than twelve to fifteen U-boats.

The protection afforded by the United States Navy was for several months hopelessly inadequate. The USN had provided fifty old destroyers and ten Revenue cutters to the Royal Navy earlier in the war, but those vessels were now sorely missed by the United States. Coastal Air Defence had not been developed, and no plans had been made for coastal convoys, nor for the small craft necessary for their protection.

On 10 February Churchill, unasked, offered twenty-four of the Royal Navy's best-equipped anti-submarine trawlers and ten Flower class corvettes with their trained crews, to help fill the gap. They were welcomed, and the first arrived in New York early in

March, with twenty-three arriving by the 12th of that month. At the same time, Churchill promised that bombing attacks in force would be made by the RAF on ports where U-boats were known to be re-fitting or building, with improved day and night air patrols over the Bay of Biscay in order to destroy as many U-boats as possible en route.

By 1 April, through frantic efforts, it became possible for the US Navy to institute at least a partial convoy system. At first this consisted of no more than a process of daylight hops of about 120 miles between protected anchorages by groups of ships under escort, with all shipping brought to a standstill at night. On any one day during that period, there were upwards of 120 ships of varying sizes requiring protection between Florida and New York. The delays involved in this partial convoy system could not be avoided, and it was not until 14 May that the first fully organised convoy sailed from Hampton Roads for Key West. Nevertheless, by the end of the month the chain along the east coast from Key West northward was at last complete. Relief was immediate, and although the U-boats continued attacking the Allied shipping, losses were much reduced.

What other British efforts could be spared to assist the American struggle against the U-boats? Fifteen Flower class corvettes under construction in Canadian shipyards for the Royal Navy were made available, but the US only took eight and the remainder were returned to the RN. In general the Flower class corvette, a small steel steam-powered vessel of less than 1000 tons and 205ft overall, designed in emergency conditions in 1939, was intended for use as a coastal escort vessel. In the Royal Navy, under force of circumstances, the Flowers were mainly used as ocean escorts, but in US hands they reverted to their designed function, and were generally more heavily armed than their British counterparts.

Eight Fairmile B type motor launches ordered for the RN on 12 August 1941 and under construction in the Canadian Le Blanc yard at Weymouth, Nova Scotia (RN nos 392–399), were also offered. They were all delivered by the autumn of 1942, with the authorised American armament of a 3in/23 gun forward, two 20mm Oerlikons, two K-guns with six charges, twelve depth charges, and two Mark 20 Mousetraps forward. SC (Submarine Chasers) 1466–73, as they were numbered, were quickly used on coastal convoy protection.

### Canadian Fairmile B class data

The first thirty-six boats were originally designated CML 01–36 (with nos 001–036 painted up); these and the later boats were listed as Q050–Q129 later.

**First 62 boats**  79 tons. 112ft 0in overall, 17ft 10in beam, 4ft 9in draught. Two Hall-Scott petrol engines, 1260bhp. 20 knots (max), 16.5 knots sea speed. Endurance 1455 miles at 7.5 knots.

**Following boats**  79 tons. 112ft 0in overall, 17ft 0in beam, 4ft 9in draught. Two Sterling petrol engies, 1400bhp. 22 knots (max). Endurance 1925 miles at 7.5 knots.

**Armament**  Originally one 3-pounder, two 5in machine guns; by 1945 four units had one 3-pounder and three machine guns, the rest had three single 20mm Oerlikons.

**Builders**

Benson, Vancouver (8 units)
Greavette, Gravenhurst, Ontario (9)
Grew, Pentetanguishene, Ontario (8)
Hunter, Orillia, Ontario (6)
Le Blanc, Weymouth, Nova Scotia (7)
Mac Craft, Sarnia, Ontario (8)
Midland Boat Works, Ontario (8)
Minette Shields, (Port Carling) Bracebridge, Ontario (10)
Star (Mercers), New Westminster (5)
Taylor, Toronto (9)
Vancouver Shipyard (5)

More heavily armed than the RN and Canadian Bs, they carried a crew of twenty-eight on a displacement of 73 tons. All survived the war, with SCs 1466, 1469 and 1471 being transferred to Mexico, rearmed with a 40mm Bofors, and renumbered SC 11, 12 and 13. The Fairmiles were generally dismissed in US circles as a British adaptation of the earlier US-built submarine chaser supplied to the RN in World War I, and regarded merely as a stopgap until the 110ft wooden US-built submarine chasers could be produced in large numbers.

*ML 124 as a UNTD cadet training ship in 1947.*
Author's collection

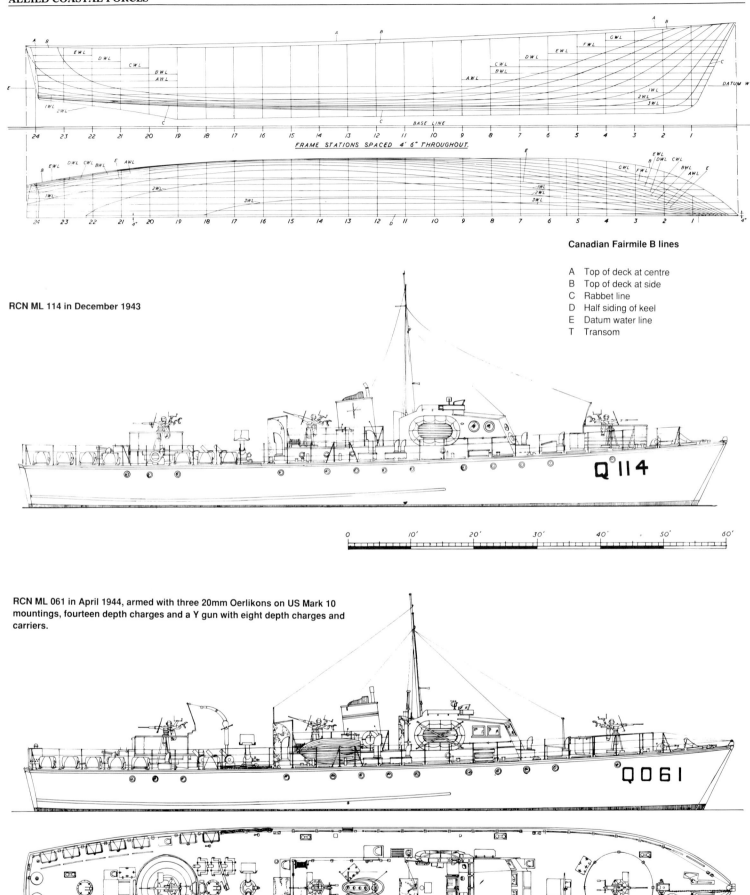

FRAME STATIONS SPACED 4' 6" THROUGHOUT.

**Canadian Fairmile B lines**

A   Top of deck at centre
B   Top of deck at side
C   Rabbet line
D   Half siding of keel
E   Datum water line
T   Transom

RCN ML 114 in December 1943

RCN ML 061 in April 1944, armed with three 20mm Oerlikons on US Mark 10 mountings, fourteen depth charges and a Y gun with eight depth charges and carriers.

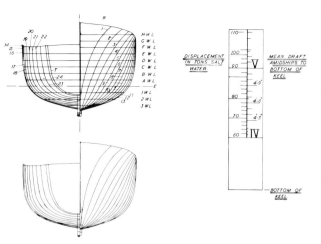

*ML 098 and others (probably 099 and 100) fitting out at Grew, Pentetanguishene, Ontario, in late 1942.* Author's collection

**RCN ML 070 in April 1942**

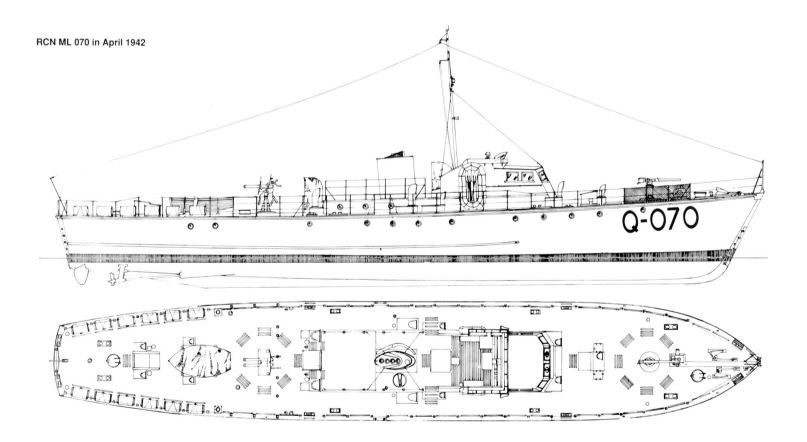

**RCN ML 070 internal profile**

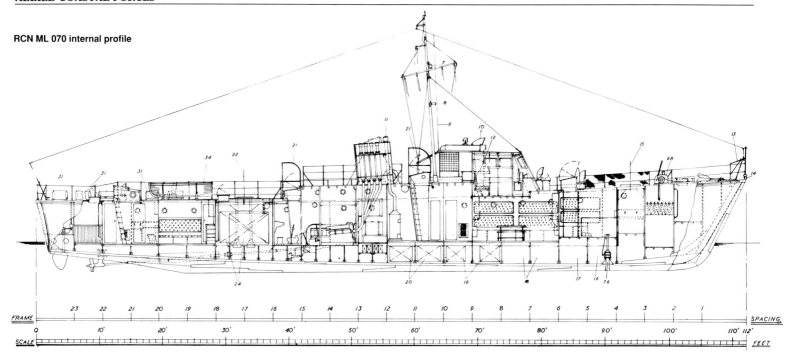

**RCN ML 070 upper deck plan**

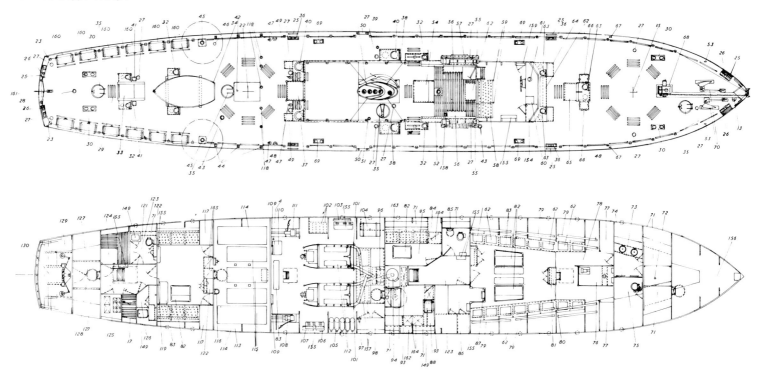

**RCN ML 070 cabin sole plan**

**Canadian Fairmile B typical internal profile**

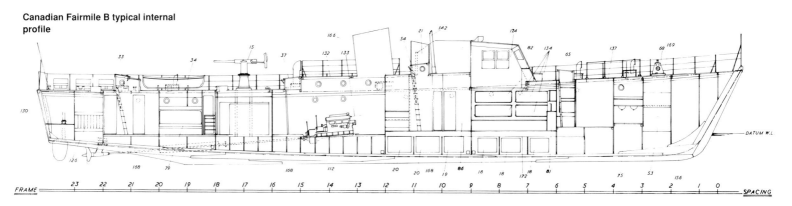

**Canadian Fairmile B typical upper deck plan**

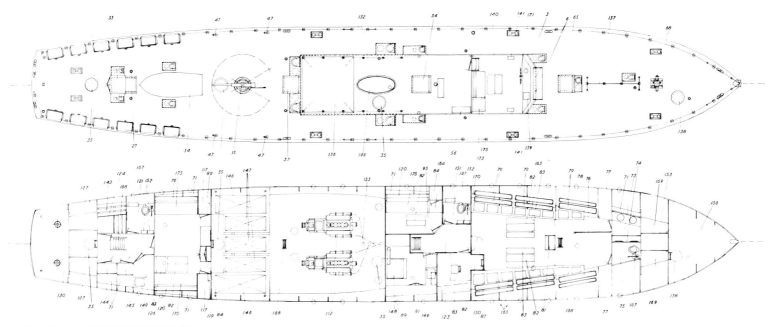

**Canadian Fairmile B typical cabin sole plan**

| | | | |
|---|---|---|---|
| 1 Armour plate top and back | 46 3in hand bilge pump socket | 91 Galley | 137 Hand rail |
| 2 Steadying bar (grab rail) | 47 2in swan neck vent | 92 Fresh water tank above | 138 Hatch to peak |
| 3 Compass | 48 Steel tread strips | 93 Water heater expansion tank | 139 Recorder |
| 4 Voice pipe | 49 Ready use lockers for .5in | 94 Hot water heater | 140 Chart room |
| 5 Searchlight | ammunition (eight box capacity) | 95 Petty Officers' compartment | 141 D/C recorder |
| 6 Clearview screen | 50 Side ladder deck sockets | 96 Main switch cabinet | 142 Mast |
| 7 Masthead light | 51 Wash deck hose connection | 97 Vice | 143 Sparred shelves |
| 8 Horn | 52 Wash deck hose rack | 98 Work bench | 144 Gunner's stores |
| 9 W/T lead | 53 Forward datum plate | 99 Galley stove | 145 Paymaster's stores |
| 10 Glass windscreen | 54 Coachroof hatch | 100 Main batteries | 146 Fuel tank, 545gal |
| 11 Liverpool head spark arrester | 55 Life raft | 101 Instrument panels | 147 Fuel tank, 410gal |
| 12 Folding chart table | 56 Flag locker | 102 A/S batteries | 148 Coal cooking range |
| 13 Anchor davit | 57 Step well | 103 Steering gear panel | 149 Sink |
| 14 Roller stemhead fitting | 58 Seat (portable hatch under) | 104 Lubricating oil tank | 150 Wireless room |
| 15 3-pounder Mark VII | 59 Stanchion | 105 $CO_2$ fire equipment | 151 Petty Officers' WC |
| 16 A/S asdic compartment | 60 A/S recorder | 106 Main switchboard | 152 Toilet locker |
| 17 Store | 61 Binnacle | 107 Auxiliary switchboard | 153 Chain locker |
| 18 Coal bin, 7cwt. | 62 Locker | 108 Lighting set | 154 Fuse cabinet |
| 19 Fresh water tank, 110gal | 63 8in cowl vent | 109 Fuel gauges | 155 Radiator |
| 20 Fresh water tank, 140gal | 64 Meat safe | 110 Desk | 156 Forepeak |
| 21 Canvas canopy | 65 Focs'l hatch | 111 A/S generator | 157 main batteries |
| 22 Twin .5in Colt machine guns | 66 3-pounder ready use ammunition | 112 Hall-Scott gasoline engine | 158 W/T lead |
| 23 After datum plate | 67 A/S datum plate | 113 Fuel tank space | 159 Switch cabinet |
| 24 Fuel tanks | 68 Windlass | 114 Fuel tank, 542gal | 160 Standard depth charge |
| 25 Chaffing strip | 69 18in bollard | 115 Fuel tank, 407gal | 161 Flag staff |
| 26 21in roller fairlead | 70 COR anchor | 116 Paraffin tank | 162 Cooker |
| 27 3in mushroom vent | 71 Shelf | 117 Wardrobe | 163 Lockers under |
| 28 Emergency hand tiller | 72 Chain pipe | 118 Fuel tank sounding pipe | 164 Drawers |
| 29 Tread strips | 73 Focs'l wash place | 119 Keyboard | 165 Dressing table |
| 30 24in bollard | 74 Towel racks and mirrors | 120 Hinged berth | 166 Funnel |
| 31 Depth charges | 75 Focs'l WC | 121 Officers' WC | 167 WC |
| 32 6in cowl vent | 76 A/S equipment | 122 Cabinet | 168 Ladder |
| 33 Officers' companion | 77 Hanging space | 123 Lobby | 169 Stowage space |
| 34 10ft dinghy | 78 Focs'l | 124 Provisions | 170 Hand pump |
| 35 20in WT scuttle | 79 Folding cot | 125 Magazine | 171 Ship's wheel |
| 36 18in fairlead | 80 Radiator under | 126 Officers' pantry | 172 Top of engine bearers |
| 37 Engineroom hatch | 81 Mess traps | 127 Bin | 173 Hatch to radio room |
| 38 Life preserver | 82 Table | 128 Bosun's store | 174 Wheelhouse |
| 39 Lubricating oil filler cap | 83 Seat | 129 Lockheed steering gear | 175 Settee bed |
| 40 12in cowl vent | 84 Cupboard | 130 Steering compartment | |
| 41 Detonator locker for depth charges | 85 Folding wash basin | 131 Navigation light | |
| 42 Fuel tank filling pipe | 86 W/T office | 132 Coachroof | |
| 43 4in hand bilge pump socket | 87 Ladder to wheelhouse | 133 Exhaust led up funnel | *Note*: These lists are taken from the |
| 44 Stanchions to hinge down port and | 88 Plate rack | 134 Cot | original drawings and the nomenclature |
| starboard | 89 Dresser | 135 Chain locker | shown is that used by the RCN – slightly |
| 45 Depth charge crane socket | 90 Hood over stove | 136 Portable hatch | different from RN practice. |

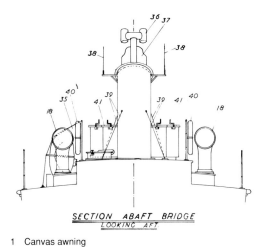

SECTION ABAFT BRIDGE
LOOKING AFT

1 Canvas awning
2 Pipe rails
3 Siren
4 Ship's bell
5 Flare launcher
6 Ship's wheel – bridge
7 Ship's wheel – wheelhouse
8 Log book stowage
9 Magnetic compass
10 8in signal lamp
11 Windscreen
12 Wind deflector
13 Sparred grating
14 Wheel box
15 Chart table
16 Sleeping berth (under)
17 Wooden ladder
18 Cowl vent
19 Aerial entry box
20 Captain's chair on top of flag locker
21 Cleats for signal halyards
22 Clear view screen
23 Forestay fitting
24 Foot strips
25 Plot cover
26 Navigation light
27 Binocular box
28 Glass port
29 Voice pipe
30 Door
31 Electric switch panel
32 Plot recorder
33 Engineroom telegraph
34 Deck and fire bucket stowage
35 10ft dinghy
36 Galley funnel
37 Funnel exhaust wind deflector

**Bridge and wheelhouse detail**

38 Aerials to signal yards
39 Funnel guys
40 Life buoy
41 Ready use ammunition locker
42 Flare stowage
43 Patent log recorder
44 Signal book locker
45 Aerial to main yard

46 Flag locker
47 Engine exhaust pipes
48 Tool box
49 W/T hatch
50 Mushroom ventilator
51 Toe rails
52 Grab rail

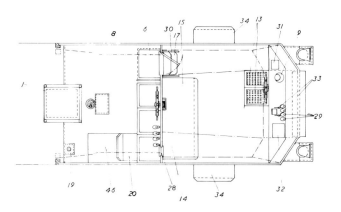

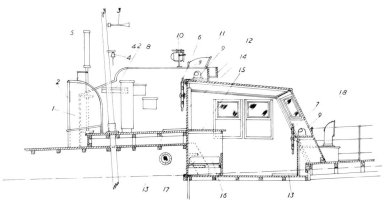

# Construction list

| ML | Builder | Completed | Fate |
|---|---|---|---|
| **24 ordered 3.1.41 or 7.4.41** | | | |
| 050 | 8 | 18.11.41 | For disposal 8.7.45 |
| 051 | 8 | 24.11.41 | For disposal 23.6.45 |
| 052 | 11 | 31.10.41 | FF *Galantry* on loan 14.1.43; for disposal 25.7.45 |
| 053 | 11 | 17.11.41 | For disposal 10.6.45 |
| 054 | 3 | 17.10.41 | For disposal 8.7.45 |
| 055 | 3 | 6.11.41 | For disposal 10.6.45 |
| 056 | 3 | 24.11.41 | For disposal 10.6.45 |
| 057 | 9 | 28.10.41 | For disposal 8.7.45 |
| 058 | 9 | 24.11.41 | For disposal 14.7.45 |
| 059 | 9 | 25. 5.42 | For disposal 27.5.46 |
| 060 | 5 | 1.11.41 | For disposal 17.6.45 |
| 061 | 5 | 11.11.41 | For disposal 7.5.46 |
| 062 | 7 | 18. 4.42 | FF *Langlade* on loan 1943–45; = PTC762 1949 = *Wolf* listed to 1959 |
| 063 | 7 | 18. 4.42 | FF *Colombier* 1943–45; for disposal 25.7.45 |
| 064 | 6 | 15. 5.42 | For disposal 17.6.45 |
| 065 | 6 | 15. 5.42 | For disposal 14.7.45 |
| 066 | 12 | 6. 3.42 | For disposal 12.10.45 |
| 067 | 12 | 27. 3.42 | Sold 1946 = *Stranger II* |
| 068 | 2 | 7. 3.42 | For disposal 12.10.45; sold = *Salvor* 1948 |
| 069 | 2 | 28. 3.42 | For disposal 6.10.45 |
| 070 | 10 | 14. 3.42 | For disposal 12.10.45; sold = *Machigonne* |
| 071 | 10 | 15. 4.42 | For disposal 7.11.45; sold = *Gulf Wing* |
| 072 | 4 | 24.11.41 | For disposal 17.7.45 |
| 073 | 4 | 24.11.41 | For disposal 17.7.45 |
| **12 ordered 22.7.41** | | | |
| 074 | 9 | 26. 5.42 | For disposal 23.6.45 |
| 075 | 9 | 22. 6.42 | For disposal 17.7.45 |
| 076 | 9 | 22. 6.42 | For disposal 17.7.45 |
| 077 | 3 | 2. 6.42 | For disposal 17.7.45 |
| 078 | 3 | 2. 6.42 | For disposal 17.7.45 |
| 079 | 11 | 27. 5.42 | = PTC779 1949 = *Raccoon* listed to 1959 |
| 080 | 11 | 17. 6.42 | For disposal 13.6.45 |
| 081 | 8 | 27. 5.42 | For disposal 15.6.45 |

**Codes for builders**

1. Armstrong, Victoria
2. Benson, Vancouver
3. Greavette, Gravenhurst, Ontario
4. Grew, Pentetanguishene, Ontario
5. Hunter, Orillia, Ontario
6. Le Blanc, Weymouth, Nova Scotia
7. Mac Craft, Sarnia, Ontario
8. Midland Boat Works, Ontario
9. Minette-Shields, (Port Carling), Bracebridge, Ontario
10. Star (Mercers) New Westminster, British Columbia
11. Taylor, Toronto
12. Vancouver Shipyard
13. Victoria Machinery

*ML 075 fully fitted and ready for sea.*
Author's collection

| ML | Builder | Completed | Fate |
|---|---|---|---|
| 082 | 8 | 27. 5.42 | Damaged and for disposal 1.45 |
| 083 | 6 | 25. 5.42 | For disposal 13.6.45 |
| 084 | 6 | 18. 6.42 | For disposal 15.6.45 |
| 085 | 5 | 13. 6.42 | For disposal 13.6.45 |

**18 ordered 16.2.42**

| | | | |
|---|---|---|---|
| 086 | 11 | 26.10.42 | For disposal 30.6.45 |
| 087 | 11 | 9.11.42 | For disposal 29.6.45 |
| 088 | 11 | 10. 5.43 | For disposal 22.6.45 |
| 089 | 3 | 15.10.42 | For disposal 29.6.45 |
| 090 | 3 | 19.11.42 | For disposal 9.7.45 |
| 091 | 3 | 17. 5.43 | For disposal 14.7.45 |
| 092 | 5 | 2.11.42 | For disposal 22.6.45 |
| 093 | 5 | 2.11.42 | For disposal 1.7.45 |
| 094 | 8 | 19.11.42 | For disposal 23.6.45 |
| 095 | 8 | 12. 5.43 | For disposal 1.7.45 |
| 096 | 9 | 9.11.42 | For disposal 30.6.45 |
| 097 | 9 | 16.11.42 | For disposal 19.6.45 |
| 098 | 4 | 7.11.42 | For disposal 7.7.45; sold = yacht *Le St Barnabe* |
| 099 | 4 | 7.11.42 | For disposal 22.6.45; sold = *Dipedon* |
| 100 | 4 | 7.11.42 | For disposal 7.7.45 |
| 101 | 7 | 7.11.42 | For disposal 9.7.45; sold = yacht *Edmar* |
| 102 | 7 | 14.11.42 | For disposal 22.6.45 |
| 103 | 7 | 18.11.42 | For disposal 7.7.45 |

**26 ordered 10.42**

| | | | |
|---|---|---|---|
| 104 | 7 | 4. 8.43 | = PTC704 1949 = *Cougar*; listed to 1959 |
| 105 | 7 | 5. 9.43 | For disposal 15.9.45 |
| 106 | 4 | 28. 8.43 | = PTC706 1949 = *Beaver*; listed to 1959 |
| 107 | 4 | 11. 9.43 | For disposal 15.9.45 |
| 108 | 8 | 13. 8.43 | For disposal 14.7.45 |
| 109 | 5 | 23. 8.43 | For disposal 14.7.45 |
| 110 | 9 | 7. 8.43 | For disposal 9.7.45 |
| 111 | 6 | 9. 9.43 | = PTC711 1949 = *Moose*; listed to 1956 |
| 112 | 11 | 25.10.43 | To RCMP 1945 = *Fort Walsh* |
| 113 | 11 | 20.11.43 | For disposal 21.7.45 |
| 114 | 3 | 23.11.43 | To RCMP 1945 = *Fort Selkirk* |
| 115 | 7 | 16.11.43 | For disposal 21.7.45 |
| 116 | 5 | 12. 7.44 | = PTC716 1949 = *Reindeer*; listed to 1957 |
| 117 | 4 | 16.11.43 | To RCMP 1945 = *Fort Steel* |
| 118 | 8 | 6.11.43 | For disposal 23.7.45 |
| 119 | 9 | 16.11.43 | To RCMP 1945 = *Fort Pitt* |
| 120 | 6 | 27. 1.44 | For disposal 23.7.45; sold = yacht *Osceola* |
| 121 | 6 | 17. 4.44 | = PTC721 1949; listed to 1953 |
| 122 | 12 | 17. 5.44 | For disposal 3.10.45; sold = yacht *Malibu Tyee* |
| 123 | 12 | 10. 6.44 | For disposal 3.10.45; sold = yacht *Malibu Marlin* |
| 124 | 12 | 30. 6.44 | = PTC724 1949 = *Elk*; listed to 1958 |
| 125 | 10 | 22. 7.44 | For disposal 3.10.45; sold = yacht *Malibu Tilikum* |
| 126 | 10 | 7. 8.44 | For disposal 3.10.45; sold = *Princess Malibu* |
| 127 | 10 | 27. 9.44 | For disposal 3.10.45; sold = *Chief Malibu* |
| 128 | 2 | 29. 7.44 | For disposal 3.10.45; sold = *Princess Louisa Inlet* |
| 129 | 2 | 16.10.44 | For disposal 3.10.45; sold  yacht *Malibu Inez* |

*ML 121 escorting the surrendered U-889 into harbour in May 1945.* Author's collection

# The Fairmile C type motor gunboat

As noted above, the Norman Hart designed prototype Fairmile became the A type while under construction and proved the viability of the Fairmile mass construction method, being followed by a further eleven units. While it is fair to say that the design did have the inherent problems of short range and poor manoeuvrability, all twelve boats were in service by the summer of 1940, at a time when escorts were in very short supply and Britain was expecting invasion at any time.

The navy required additional gunboats as soon as possible, and an improved design was still at the planning stage. (This was to be the D type with four engines of increased power, but the prototype was not to be laid down until 1 June 1941.) However, the building jigs for the A type were still available, so it was decided to make use of them as an interim measure. The A type design had at least proved sound and seaworthy, and could be modified and improved.

The decision was made to construct a number of improved A type Fairmiles, exactly similar as regards construction and accommodation, but fitted with three supercharged Hall-Scott Defender engines, each rated at 900hp. The opportunity was also taken to remedy some of the earlier design defects. The bridge was redesigned in line with motor torpedo boat practice and to take up less deck area, fuel capacity was increased from the original 1200 to 1800 gallons, and the armament fit was much improved. While the hull lines remained identical, in fact the width of the focs'l was slightly reduced (see drawing).

*Q 328 and 330; Fairmile C Motor Gunboats, early in 1942. Comparison of these with the A type reveals the same hull lines but improved MTB type upperworks, with heavier armament.*
Imperial War Museum

Twenty-four such motor launches, to be kown as the type C, were ordered on 27 August 1940 and the first keel was laid down on 1 December. The designed displacement was 66½ tons and would give a maximum speed of 27 knots, some 2 knots more than the original A. However, armament and other equipment inevitably increased the actual displacement, which became 72 tons, thus reducing the speed by half a knot and giving a maximum continuous speed of 22 knots. The improved fuel capacity gave a range of 305 miles.

The first of these new motor launches joined the Coastal Forces early the following summer. The C type suffered from similar manoeuvring problems to those encountered in the A type because of the large deadwood aft, but the two underslung rudders placed right aft on the transom were given a greater surface area by the addition of extra plating to improve the turning circle. This modification was probably undertaken after the first of the class sea trials. Little has been published abut the C class boats, which were used mainly as close-escort vessels for East Coast convoys.

MGB 325 joined the 16th MGB Flotilla for just such duties, and was based, as were most of the class, at Great Yarmouth (HMS *Midge*). She was ordered to Portland to carry out sea trials on the new 2-pounder Rolls-Royce gun, and later, while she was having the mounting removed, her CO was asked if he would undertake an operation to pick up a British agent, as a sister gunboat was unserviceable due to a machinery breakdown. The CO of the original vessel undertook to navigate, and that evening MGB 325 sailed for the Points de Bihit, an outcrop of rock in Lannion Bay near Trebeurden. No signal was received from the shore, however, so the attempt was abandoned and the unit returned to Portland undetected.

In October 325 was again withdrawn from her usual patrol duties

and ordered to carry out another ferry trip, this time from Felixstowe to the Dutch coast. On that flat featureless coast, however, the pickup point was difficult to identify, and when it was at last located, fog set in and the mission had to be abandoned. A month later another trip was made to land two British agents. They were to be dropped by the gunboat's first lieutenant, but during the approach the small dinghy overturned and the three occupants had to swim ashore. All three were captured the next day by German soldiers. The two agents were shot and the first lieutenant became a POW.

Another of the class, also used on occasion for clandestine purposes, was MGB 314. However, she was also lent to the Combined Operations command as part of the covering force for the raid on St Nazaire, in which the ex-American destroyer HMS *Campbeltown* was to be rammed into the lock gates while commandos carried over in motor launches (Fairmile Bs and Cs) were to land and destroy the port installations. Commander Robert Ryder RN, Commanding Officer Naval Forces, and his staff were aboard MGB 314. The operation was in the main successful, but many

*Fairmile Cs at Dover, in late spring 1942. MGB 324 is nearest, with 328 outboard, 322 astern and 330 outboard of her. Note the differences in detail, gun safety rails, etc.* Imperial War Museum

lives were lost. MGB 314 was severely damaged and during the return voyage, in worsening weather, she had to be sunk by other British units. Her place was subsequently taken by MGB 318.

Although British gunboats were heavily armed for their size at that stage of the war, when they were used on agent dropping operations in occupied Europe their commanding officers had strict orders not to open fire except in extreme circumstances of self defence.

Apart from air operations undertaken on behalf of SOE, the 15th MGB Flotilla became the principal means of maintaining communications across the Channel with occupied France. Other units attached to the 15th Flotilla were MA/SB 36, MGB 2003, MGB 2009, MTB 718, MGB 503, MGB 507 and possibly ML 107.

Clear photographs of the class later in the war are unobtainable, but the records make it clear that they were upgunned. MGB 332 carried a French 75mm gun aft in place of her Rolls-Royce 2-pounder, but it was found that this heavier weapon was too long to fire broadside, as the gun crew had virtually to hang over the side to reload. It was soon removed and replaced by a power-operated 2-pounder, although conflicting reports state that power-operated mountings were not fitted aft as there were no hydraulic pressure lines from the engines. Although classed as gunboats, the Cs were rather lively and not steady gun platforms.

Apparently 318 had single 20mm Oerlikons in place of the twin .5in Mark V power-operated turrets, but she retained her Holman projector. In general, this rather inferior equipment was removed and replaced by a single 20mm Oerlikon as the supply of those guns improved. By late 1943 to early 1944, the Rolls-Royce gun was removed and replaced by the 2-pounder gun on the manual Mark VIII mounting.

In general the C types were very similar in appearance, with little to distinguish one from another. While 317 was under construction prior to trials, her CO asked for the mast to be raked at a greater angle than on the plans, to give a more yacht-like appearance. This was done (though no photographs are available to prove it), but a special one-off bracket had to be made to fit the masthead radar aerial. The IFF receivers were fitted in various places on Cs, either on the mast or on a short pole mast on the side of the bridge, as on the Ds.

The Cs were generally well regarded and very soundly constructed, as is proved by the photograph of MGB 321 after being rammed by her sister 315 on 11 April 1943 (see page 89). The rubbing strake was apparently altered – raised or lowered – to reduce spray coming inboard at speed, but this was a local modification and something also tried on the later Camper & Nicholson boats. All twenty-four units of the C type served in home waters, with five lost to enemy action.

## Fairmile C class data

**Pennant numbers** MGB 312–335, twenty-four units.

**Designed by** Norman Hart (as the A type).

**Built by a total of thirteen firms.**

**Construction** Hard chine prefabricated double diagonal mahogany hull. Plywood frames, hull subdivided into nine watertight compartments. Two underslung rudders.

**Dimensions** Length overall 110ft 0in, beam 17ft 5in, draught 5ft 0in forward, 6ft 3in aft, freeboard 6ft 0in.

**Displacement** As designed, 72 tons.

**Machinery** Three Hall-Scott supercharged petrol engines, 900hp each. Sided exhaust. Auxiliary engine Stuart 24-volt lighting set.

**Speed** 26.6 knots at 2100rpm maximum, 23.6 knots at 1700rpm continuous.

**Endurance** 500 nautical miles at 12 knots.

**Fuel capacity** 1800 gallons; flexible tanks were later fitted, for 2600 gallons.

**Heating and cooking** Paraffin cooking and heating, later changed to coal heating.

**Wheelhouse and steering** Originally inside hydraulic steering, later changed to dual with upper bridge steering in the armoured upper bridge.

**Communications** W/T radar (type 286), echo sounding sets, CSA smoke apparatus.

**Complement** Two officers, fourteen men.

**Armament** As designed, one 2-pounder QF Mark IIC gun on Mark XV (power) mounting or one 40mm gun on H/A Mark II (manual) mounting forward, two twin .5in Vickers machine guns in Mark V (power) mountings amidships, Holman projector (if fitted), Rolls-Royce 2-pounder aft, Two twin .303in Vickers GO machine guns on the bridge. As rearmed, two 2-pounder power mountings, forward and aft, single or twin 20mm Oerlikons in place of the twin .5in, single or twin 20mm in place of the Holman projector. Four depth charges were retained throughout.

*A Senior Officer's Boat – MGB 330 at Lowestoft in May 1942.* Wright & Logan

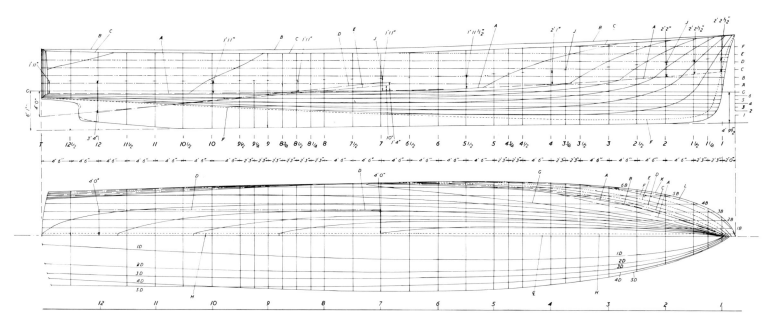

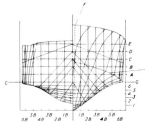

*HALF TRANSOM*

**Fairmile C lines**

A  Chine line
B  Top of deck at centre
C  Top of deck at side
D  Wing engine propeller shaft line
E  Centre engine propeller shaft line
F  Rabbet line
G  Designed water line
H  Half siding of keel at rabbet line
J  Lower edge of spray break and rubber
    on skin of ship (measurements taken
    vertically above chine)
K  Top of deck at side for A class
L  Top of deck at side for C class

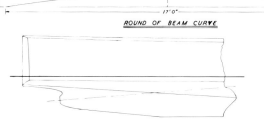

*ROUND OF BEAM CURVE*

*MODIFIED SHAPING OF FAIRING OF DEADWOOD FOR BOATS
FOLLOWING M.G.B. 312.*

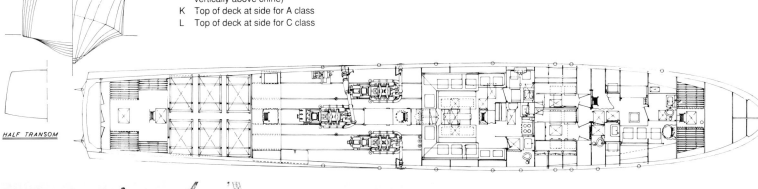

**Fairmile C typical cabin sole plan**

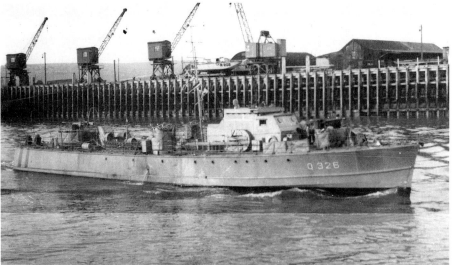

*MGB 326 at Lowestoft in 1942.* Wright & Logan

*Opposite: ML 312 off Cowes in June 1941. The CO,
Lt A R H Nye, is on the bridge. This picture was
taken during acceptance trials and before the
2-pounder gun was fitted.* Imperial War Museum

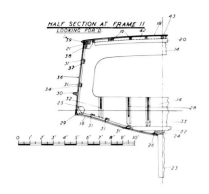
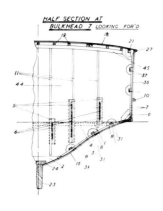
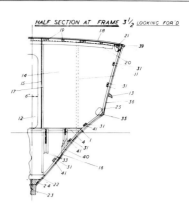

**Fairmile C typical constructional sections**

1   Cabin sole, ¾in pine
2   8in × 2in English oak double floors
3   1½in × 1⅜in Canadian rock elm double face pieces
4   2in × 1½in pitch pine bearers
5   Stiffener forms
6   Fillet on aft side
7   Canadian rock elm fillets 3in × 1½in (double on fore side, single on aft side)
8   10in × 5in × 1½in English oak pads
9   1½in English oak chine pad
10  Chine rubber 3in × 3in Canadian rock elm
11  3in × 1¾in pitch pine stiffeners
12  3ft 0in × 6ft 0in opening
13  Chine rubber, 4in × 4in Canadian rock elm

14  1in plywood frame
15  ⅝in T & G bulkhead
16  Outer bottom planking (¾in mahogany), inner ⅝in mahogany, with unbleached oiled calico between
17  3in × 1¾in pitch pine corner post
18  Outer deck planking ⁹⁄₁₆ teak, inner ½in mahogany
19  Deck stringer
20  3in × 1½ face piece
21  Clamp (2⅞in × 3⅜in pitch pine)
22  4in × 2in English oak floor
23  9in–8in pitch pine keel
24  15in × 3½in Canadian rock elm hog
25  1½in English oak pad
26  Watercourse

27  Deck rubber 3½in × 2½in Canadian rock elm
28  Engine bearers (2¾in plywood)
29  Chine apron filling and bone (Canadian rock elm)
30  4in × 3in Canadian rock elm chine rubber
31  Wedge
32  Plywood bearer notched over frame
33  1½in × 1⅜in Canadian rock elm face pieces
34  Slot for stringer
35  Chine bone (Canadian rock elm)
36  Outer side planking ¾in mahogany, inner ½in mahogany
37  3in × 1¾in Canadian rock elm stringer

38  Shelf (6⅞in × 2⅞in pitch pine)
39  Deck rubber (2½in × 3½in Canadian rock elm)
40  Frame face pieces (1½in × 1¾in Canadian rock elm each side)
41  Stringers (3in × 1¾in Canadian rock elm)
42  2in × 1½in Canadian rock elm face piece
43  2½in × 2½in pitch pine
44  WT bulkhead planking 2⅝in mahogany
45  3in × 1½in Canadian rock elm face pieces (double)

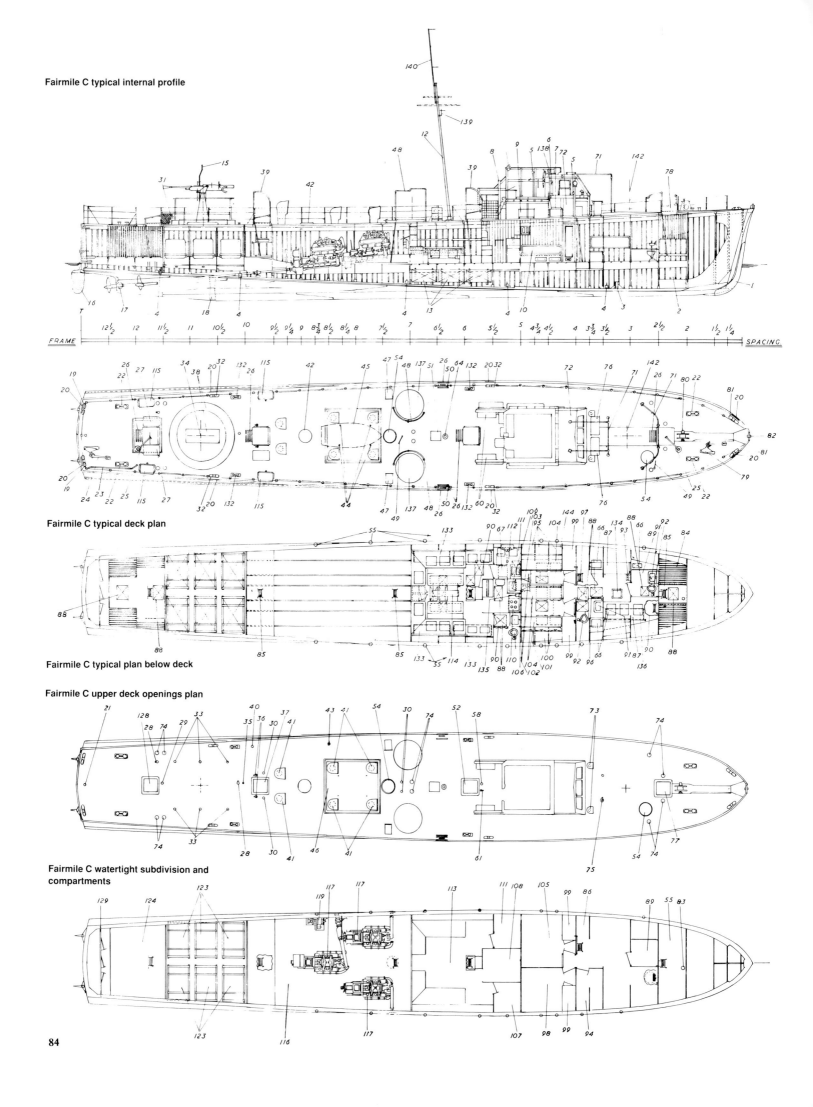

Fairmile C typical internal profile

Fairmile C typical deck plan

Fairmile C typical plan below deck

Fairmile C upper deck openings plan

Fairmile C watertight subdivision and
compartments

84

1 Stem shoe
2 Chain locker
3 Asdic gland
4 Strum box
5 Voice pipe from W/T room
6 Folding chart table
7 Upholstered seat
8 Aerial lead in
9 Fresh water tank, 215gal
10 HInged upholstered back
11 Centre engine bearer
12 Mast; 21ft 3in from deck to truck, 5in dia at base
13 Fresh water tank, 100gal
14 Battery space
15 Aerial staff; 6ft 9in above top of gun, 1in dia pipe
16 Extension plates fitted to rudders
17 Shroud plate, flush with hull
18 ⅜in naval brass plates
19 21in fairlead
20 Chaffing strip
21 Hand steering gear housing
22 24in bollard
23 Hard tiller in stowed position
24 84lb COR anchor
25 Ammunition hoist
26 Footstrips
27 Ammunition locker for 2-pounder Rolls-Royce gun
28 3in dia hand pump
29 Petrol filling cap
30 3in dia mushroom vent
31 Wire mesh
32 18in fairlead
33 Petrol sounding pipe
34 Rolls-Royce 2-pounder gun
35 Fuel shut-off
36 Swan neck vent
37 Hatch to engine room
38 Gun platform
39 Canopy frame
40 Lubricating oil filler
41 10in dia Revon vent
42 Pad for Holman projector
43 Deck wash hose connection
44 Lifting eye bolts
45 10ft dinghy
46 Semi-portable hatch
47 Ammunition locker for .5in MGs
48 Gun stops for twin .5ins
49 Hook for escape hatch
50 Accommodation ladder fitting
51 Meat safe
52 Hatch to crew's quarters
53 Vegetable locker
54 20in circular scuttle
55 5in dia mushroom vent
56 Navigation light
57 Handrail
58 Fresh water filer
59 Step
60 Lewis gun stowed on top of locker
61 Fresh water air vent
62 Ladder to bridge
63 Flag locker
64 Mast bracket
65 Accommodation ladder in stowed position
66 Locker
67 Hinged seat
68 Carley float
69 Hose rack
70 Bridge deck with batten floor
71 Gun stops for 2-pounder gun
72 Wheelhouse
73 6in dia Revon Vent
74 5in dia mushroom vent

75 4in hand pump
76 Ready use ammunition locker
77 Hatch to forward magazine
78 Windlass handle (to be stowed on side of hatch)
79 140lb CQR anchor
80 Davey windlass
81 21in roller fairlead
82 Stemhead fitting
83 Hole for chain
84 Stowage for ammunition boxes
85 Ladder to deck
86 Space for oilskins
87 Two folding cots
88 Floor hatch
89 Petty Officers' WC
90 Blackout curtains
91 Wash basin
92 WC
93 Rifle rack
94 Officers' WC
95 Shelf above
96 Radiator
97 Ladder to wheelhosue
98 Officers' cabin
99 Fitted wardrobe
100 Cupboard
101 Corner cupboard above
102 Dressing table
103 Serving hatch
104 Settee berth
105 Petty Officer's cabin
106 Asbestos sheet
107 Crew's toilet
108 Galley
109 Sink
110 Paraffin stove
111 W/T room
112 Instrument table
113 Crew space
114 Table
115 Space for oilskins
116 Engineroom
117 Supercharged Hall-Scott Defender petrol engine
118 Battery covers
119 105kw lighting set
120 Workbench
121 Tool locker under
122 Bilge pump
123 Fuel tank, each 300gal
124 Stowage space for ammunition
125 Spare gear cupboard
126 Lubricating oil tank
127 WT door
128 Hatch to after magazine and tank room
129 Battened space to protect steering gear
130 Kent clear view screen
131 Box for manoeuvring balls and cones
132 18in bollard
133 Folding cot
134 Asdic cover
135 Halliday electric boiler
136 Seat
137 Twin .5in MGs on Mark V power mounting
138 Magnetic compass
139 IFF aerial (Type 240 or 241)
140 Type 286 PU aerial
141 Ship's wheel
142 2-pounder power mounting
143 Main engine throttles
144 Drawers under

**Right: engineroom detail**

**Bridge detail**

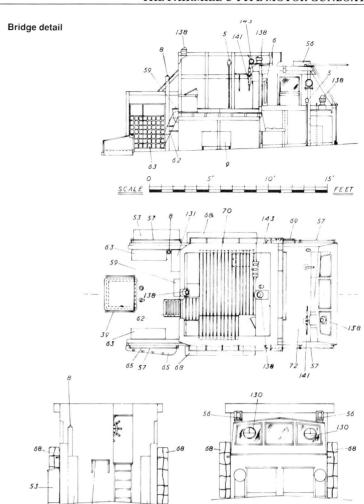

SCALE 0 5' 10' 15' FEET

VIEW FROM AFT

VIEW FROM FOR'D

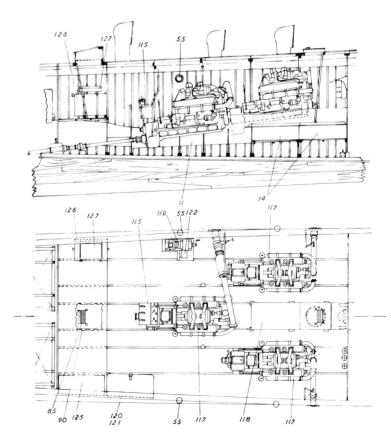

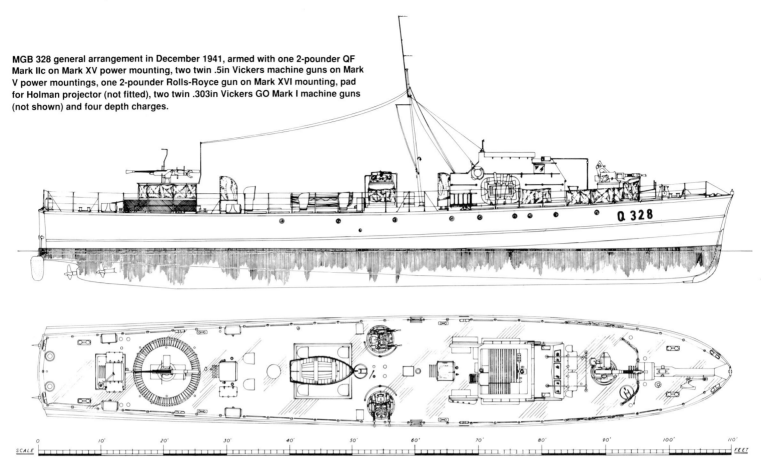

MGB 328 general arrangement in December 1941, armed with one 2-pounder QF Mark IIc on Mark XV power mounting, two twin .5in Vickers machine guns on Mark V power mountings, one 2-pounder Rolls-Royce gun on Mark XVI mounting, pad for Holman projector (not fitted), two twin .303in Vickers GO Mark I machine guns (not shown) and four depth charges.

*MGB 321 off Great Yarmouth in spring 1943.* Author's collection

*MGB 321 again; the censor could not delete the weather in this view!* Author's collection

MGB 328 internal profile

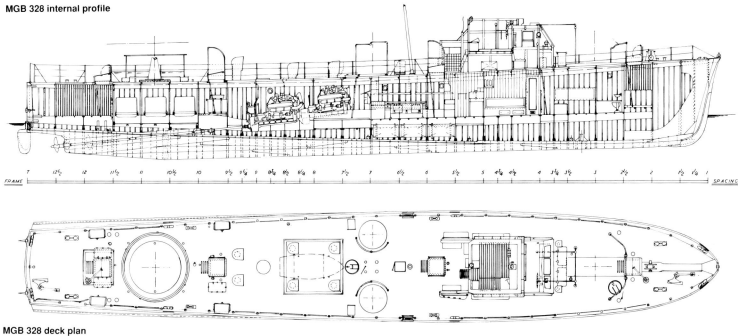

MGB 328 deck plan

MGB 317 in March 1942, armed with one 40mm Vickers Mark II gun on Mark II mounting, two twin .303in Vickers machine guns (not shown), two twin .5in Vickers machine guns on Mark V power mounting, Holman projector, one 2-pounder Rolls-Royce gun on Mark XIV manual mounting, smoke floats and four depth charges.

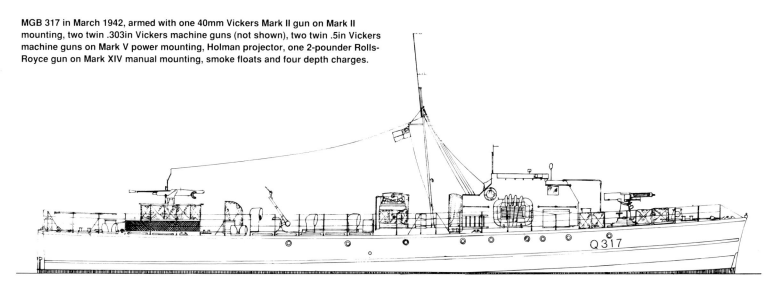

MGB 317 in October 1944, armed with one 2-pounder QF Mark VIII gun on Mark XVI power mounting, two twin .303in Vickers GO machine guns (not shown), two twin .5in Vickers machine guns on Mark V power mountings, one single 20mm Oerlikon Mark IIA, one 2-pounder QF Mark VIII* gun on Mark VIII manual mounting, CSA, smoke floats and four depth charges.

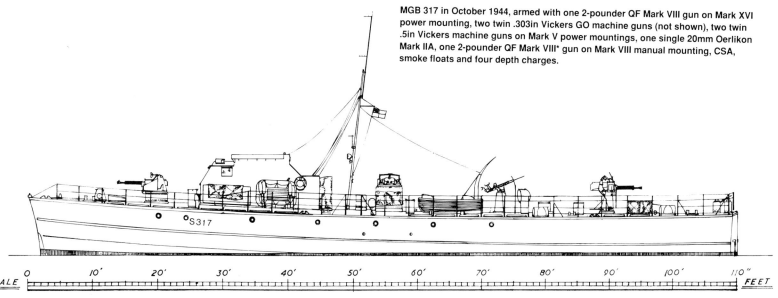

SCALE

0   10'   20'   30'   40'   50'   60'   70'   80'   90'   100'   110" FEET

MGB 332 in December 1945, armed with one 2-pounder Mark IIc gun on Mark XV power mounting, one 2-pounder Mark VIII gun on Mark VIII manual mounting, two twin .303in Vickers machine guns (not shown), two single 20mm Oerlikons on Mark IIa mountings, one twin 20mm Oerlikon on Mark IX manual mounting, CSA, smoke floats and four depth charges.

*MGB 321 off Great Yarmouth early in 1942. The censor has deleted her pennant number.*
Author's collection

# Construction list

| MGB | Builder | Completed | Fate |
|---|---|---|---|
| **24 Motor Launches ordered 27.8.40 and rated Motor Gun Boats 1.8.41** | | | |
| 312 | 13 | 16. 6.41 | For disposal 10.45 |
| 313 | 7 | 12. 6.41 | Lost by mine or torpedo 16.8.44 off Normandy |
| 314 | 4 | 26. 6.41 | Scuttled 28.3.42 after damage at St Nazaire |
| 315 | 10 | 10. 7.41 | For disposal 10.45 |
| 316 | 12 | 19. 5.41 | For disposal 10.45 |
| 317 | 10 | 3. 9.41 | For disposal 10.45 |
| 318 | 1 | 6. 7.41 | For disposal 10.45 |
| 319 | 2 | 4. 9.41 | For disposal 1.46 |
| 320 | 10 | 23. 8.41 | For disposal 10.45 |
| 321 | 11 | 9. 7.41 | For disposal 10.45 |
| 322 | 4 | 27. 9.41 | For disposal 10.45 |
| 323 | 5 | 11. 7.41 | To ship target trials 2.46 |
| 324 | 13 | 4. 9.41 | For disposal 10.45 |
| 325 | 3 | 9. 9.41 | For disposal 3.46 |
| 326 | 11 | 18. 8.41 | Sunk by mine off Normandy 28.6.44 |
| 327 | 9 | 22. 8.41 | For disposal 10.45 |
| 328 | 6 | 13.10.41 | Sunk by gunfire of German surface craft in the Dover Straits 21.7.42 |
| 329 | 1 | 25. 9.41 | For disposal 10.45 |
| 330 | 12 | 25. 7.41 | To ship target trials 1946 and destroyed by 10.48 |
| 331 | 12 | 13. 8.41 | For disposal 10.45 |
| 332 | 11 | 8.10.41 | For disposal 10.45 |
| 333 | 13 | 16.10.41 | For disposal 10.45 |
| 334 | 4 | 9.10.41 | For disposal 10.45 |
| 335 | 4 | 10.10.41 | Sunk by gunfire from German surface craft in the North Sea 10.9.42 |

## Codes for builders

1   Aldous Successors Ltd, The Shipyard, Brightlingsea
2   Brooke Marine Ltd, Oulton Broad, nr Lowestoft
3   Frank Curtis Ltd, Looe, Cornwall
4   A M Dickie & Sons, Bangor, North Wales
5   Kris Cruisers (1934) Ltd, Riverside Yard, Ferryll Road, Isleworth
6   Lady Bee Ltd, Shoreham-by-Sea, Sussex
7   James N Miller & Sons Ltd, East Shore, St Monance
8   William Osbourne Ltd, Littlehampton, Sussex
9   Risdon Beazley Ltd, Clausentum Yard, Northam Bridge, Southampton
10   Alex Robertson (Yachtbuilders) & Sons Ltd, Sandbank, Argyllshire
11   James A Silver Ltd, Rosneath, Dumbartonshire
12   Tough Bros Ltd, Teddington Wharf, Manor Road, Teddington
13   Woodnutt & Co Ltd, St Helens, Isle of Wight

*Proof, if it is needed, of the soundness of the Fairmile construction method: MGB 321 after being rammed by her sister, MGB 315, on 11 April 1943.*
Author's collection

# The Fairmile D type MTB/MGB

The type D was produced to combat the known advantages of the German S-boat (from *Schnellboot*, but always called E-boats by the Allies). Their low silhouette and excellent sea-keeping qualities were much sought after, and they were more heavily armed than the British 'short boats'. Their powerful Mercedes-Benz light-weight diesel engines of over 2000hp had the advantage of less volatile fuel than that used by the British petrol engines, and the E-boat type as a whole constituted a very effective and relatively cheap weapons system from the start of the war, without any real Allied counterpart. Of round-bilge form, suitable for very high speed, they were designed to attack with torpedoes or to lay mines in the coastal waters around Britain. Their gun armament was primarily defensive; the E-boat made its attack and then made off at very high speed, its steel hull giving a maximum ability to maintain high speed in rough conditions.

British short-hulled, hard-chine MTBs were not capable of challenging E-boats effectively, since they could not maintain their maximum speed in adverse sea conditions. Their armament of .303in and .5in weapons was largely ineffective, and their 21in torpedoes were of no help against targets of such high speed and shallow draught.

The Fairmile A was too slow at 25 knots to catch E-boats, as was the later and improved C type gunboat, so a new design was required. This, then, was the genesis of the staff requirement for a 'long' boat design, capable of a heavier fit of automatic weapons and of higher speed with better sea-keeping, and able to meet the E-boat on more level terms; this was later expanded to provide an offensive torpedo armament, making the Ds the most potent and heaviest armed coastal forces type of any navy.

The lines of the D were developed at the Admiralty by William John Holt, then head of the boat section of the Royal Corps of Naval Constructors. The distinctive hull form was developed, figuratively speaking, by splicing a destroyer type bow on to a fast motor boat stern. The hull form was tested in the Admiralty Experimental Tank at Haslar towards the end of 1939, though with the testing of variations it was not to take its final shape until March 1941. It was then linked with the powerful American Packard petrol engine, again provided under Lend-Lease, with four engines, and four propeller shafts fitted into the wide after-hull.

Fairmile construction techniques had proved themselves, and the D type was built in some thirty small shipyards in the UK, being supplied in kit form, as for the previous designs. Building proceeded alongside construction of the B type, with some yards constructing both types at the same time. The D was designed for a displacement of about 80 tons, with a top speed of about 31 knots, but as in the case of all British Coastal Forces designs, the additional weight of heavier armament increased the displacement, thereby reducing the maximum speed.

The prototype D, MGB 601, was constructed by Tough Brothers at Teddington on the Thames, and not far from Cobham. She was laid down on 1 June 1941, launched on 4 October, and, after trials, handed over on 20 February 1942. Tough Bros had already had experience of Fairmile construction methods, as they had been contracted to build the second B, ML 113, and had completed it before ML 112. At that time the company was employing only about sixteen men, and 14-hour days were worked, but the work-

*MGB 658 at Manfredonia in March 1945. She has*
*two 6-pounders on power-operated Mark VII*
*mountings, sided 20mms and a 2in rocket flare*
*projector on her forward mounting. Ready use rockets*
*are stowed about her wheelhouse. She has also*
*acquired a US Navy SO radar and mainmast.*
Courtesy Len (Rover) Reynolds

*MGB 601 on acceptance trials in March 1942.*
*No torpedoes or torpedo scallops were provided,*
*but there was a 2-pounder, two twin .5in on*
*power-operated Mark V mountings, a Holman*
*projector on the coachroof and a twin 20mm on a*
*power-operated Mark V mounting aft. Depth charges*
*and Type 291 radar were also fitted.*
Courtesy Fairmile (Marine Consultants) Ltd

*MGB 605 with a Senior Officer's stripe on her bow,*
*in company with MGB 610 off the Dorset coast in*
*summer 1942. Note the Type 241 (IFF interrogator)*
*on the wheelhouse roof.* Central Press Photos Ltd

force was soon expanded, with new buildings and expansion of the ground area, to fulfil the agreed contracts.

Like the B type, the D was constantly improved as a result of operational war experience and improved production from the armament industry. The first twelve units were ordered as MGBs on 15 March 1941, with another four ordered the following month. These (601 to 616), the first orders, can easily be distinguished in photographs by the fact that they did not have torpedo scallops cut into the hull forward of the bridge, although many were later modified to carry either two 18in tubes mounted on high beds aft, or, in the case of 617 to 632, were completed with two 21in tubes, both with additional height on the torpedo tube beds to clear the hull when firing. Nos 633 to 696 were constructed with scallops, but again not all were rated as motor torpedo boats. As was usual with all Fairmile types, armament could be changed for operational reasons at relatively short notice. Nos 697 to 800 were classified as combined MTB/MGBs, most of them having four 18in torpedo tubes, others only two 21in tubes.

The last fifty-eight units, ordered on 26 March 1943, including 5001 to 5020 (the ultimate wartime Ds), reverted to the heavier punch of two 21in tubes, which, with the heavier warhead, was retained for postwar Fairmile Ds and, in general, for postwar Coastal Forces designs.

It must be remembered that, with the large number of Ds built (229), there were many slight appearance and armament variations. The other 'long' Fairmile types – the As and Cs – only served in home waters, but the Bs served worldwide, and the Ds performed sterling service both in home waters and in every area of the Mediterranean. There was a constant increase in weapons and equipment, with the increased displacement further reducing maximum speed. The earlier Ds made 30 knots at 91 tons displacement, which was later increased to 32½ knots at 98 tons when reduction gearboxes were fitted to the main engines. From 1944, increased

*Job No 602 at Tough Brothers' yard, showing the
keel and transom. The D type on the right is probably
the prototype, ML 601, in a much more advanced
state of construction.*
Courtesy Fairmile (Marine Consultants) Ltd

*The framing of ML (later MGB) 601, showing the
typical Fairmile construction methods.*
Courtesy Fairmile (Marine Consultants) Ltd

armament in the shape of two power operated 6-pounder Mark IIA
guns in Mark VII mountings, one forward and one aft, plus four
18in tubes, and twin power operated 20mm Oerlikons in Mark V
mountings, with radar, rocket flare launchers, and other equipment
brought the displacement up to 120 tons, and a corresponding
reduction in speed to 29 knots. The resultant overloading of the
main engines also decreased their reliability.

The effects of weather both on boats and crew comfort were
severe. Wetness was influenced by the hull form, and with her
sharp bow, good flare and knuckle, and more rounded hull form
aft, the D was drier than most. However, the boats were built of
wood, and wooden hulls 'worked'; it was found that when pounding at speed into a head sea, particularly a short sharp sea, the hull
began to strain. When I visited a houseboat, ex MTB 618, at
Shoreham in 1984, I was shown the area under the forward messdeck where large angle irons had been worked into the framing to
give added strength (she had been a Norwegian-manned boat and
frequently visited Norwegian waters on operations). With operations further afield, other problems were met. Steep and violent
seas were encountered in the Mediterranean. Units driven at high
speed into short head seas to take up tactical positions off the
Cape Bon Peninsula from bases such as Bone, were prone to breaking their plywood frames forward. In addition, the keel scarfs were
liable to ease and work, and the scarfs of the gunwales and the deck
stringers in the way of the engineroom were liable to crepitation or
cracking. It therefore became necessary to double the number of
of frames to act as tension strips to prevent fracture. Steel fish-
plates, some 10ft long, were fitted over keel scarfs found subject to
lates, some 10ft long, were fitted over keel scarfs found subject to
movement, acting as strength members. Margin plates, too, were
fitted adjacent to the engine case coaming to strengthen the deck,
thereby compensating for a local hull weakness caused by the large

*A view not normally seen: the propeller shafts, A
brackets and rudders of MGB 601.*
Courtesy Fairmile (Marine Consultants) Ltd

*MGB 601 taking shape. Note the prefabricated*
*frames and scrap wood distance pieces.*
Courtesy Fairmile (Marine Consultants) Ltd

*MGB 601 just prior to planking.*
Courtesy Fairmile (Marine Consultants) Ltd

area of open deck. Additional strength and deck stiffening were built in when heavier armament was fitted, particularly under the foredeck in the messdeck area.

As noted above, local changes could be made for operational reasons, such as the removal of torpedo tubes for operational minelaying sorties. Many MGBs in the Mediterranean were modified locally, with their twin .5in Mark V gun tubs landed and single, or in some cases twin, 20mm Oerlikon mountings fitted in their place.

In all, 229 Ds were ordered, with one (5027) cancelled. Of these, nineteen were completed as long-range rescue craft for the Royal Air Force, being fitted with a purely defensive 20mm Oerlikon armament. In addition, a further twenty-one were transferred to the RAF towards the end of 1944.

At the end of the war in 1945, although a number of Ds had been earmarked to operate in the Far East against the Japanese, numbers were reduced sharply; by the end of 1946 only about two dozen Ds remained in service with the Royal Navy.

A general summary of the D type is as follows: of the first ninety-six units, half were completed as MGBs, with the other half modified or built as MTBs. After MGB 696, all boats were defined as MTBs, and carried a combined torpedo and gun armament with a consequent reduction in speed. All MTBs completed as such – up to 723 – carried two 21in torpedo tubes, but those numbered between 724 and 800 were built with deck strips for four 18in tubes. The final group, 5001 to 5029, reverted to the two heavier 21in fit, as did postwar boats. Of the forty-eight units completed as MGBs, two flotillas (sixteen boats) went to the Mediterranean under their own power in the summer of 1943 (see *Gunboat 658*, by Len Reynolds). They, or those that survived, remained as gunboats throughout their service. The four flotillas of D type MGBs in home waters were redesignated MTBs in the autumn of 1943, and when actually refitted for that role, received only 18in tubes, which is a useful recognition feature.

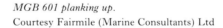

*MGB 601 planking up.*
Courtesy Fairmile (Marine Consultants) Ltd

*MGB 601's bridge – a relatively simple layout
compared with later units, with compass, voice pipes,
bell pushes and engineroom telegraphs.*
Courtesy Fairmile (Marine Consultants) Ltd

*Bridge and coachroof under construction.*
Courtesy Fairmile (Marine Consultants) Ltd

*601 starting to come together at Teddington. Note the
gun mounting pad, welded hatches, mushroom
ventilators, etc. A B type can be seen fitting out
alongside.*
Courtesy Fairmile (Marine Consultants) Ltd

D type MGBs served in the 17th to 22nd MGB flotillas, and the early MTBs in the 30th to 35th MTB flotillas. During the summer of 1943 those flotillas were renumbered to become the 50th to 61st, although not respectively. The Ds continued this progression of flotilla numbers, which by 1945 extended to the 73rd MTB Flotilla, and, as far as I know, the only exception to boats serving in those flotillas was MTB 718, which served in the 15th MGB Flotilla (later the 71st). In addition to the two flotillas of MGBs sent to the Mediterranean, two flotillas of MTBs were dispatched at the same time, but as a result of the substantial losses suffered on operations, from both gunfire and mines, an additional flotilla of MTBs (the 59th) was sent out at the end of October 1944. Apart from those noted, all the other 'Dog' boats, as they were popularly known, served in home waters.

In addition to serving as MTBs, MGBs, or in the combined dual-purpose role, the 64th Flotilla boats were fitted for the role of minelaying (see the armament section on Coastal Forces minelaying fittings), while the 66th operated in the anti-submarine role, carrying thirty-two depth charges in place of their torpedo tubes, and being fitted with type 143E asdic. Towards the end of 1944 the 55th Flotilla boats landed their torpedo tubes and main gun armament, and were equipped with depth charges for Operation Shellfish, the destruction of the new German Oyster (pressure-operated) mines laid off the invasion beaches. The Oyster mine had been predicted, and very restrictive speed scales issued to the fleet in an effort to combat them. The seriousness of the threat posed to the Allied build-up called for every effort to be made to combat this unsweepable mine, a number of which were soon recovered intact. Some of the D class, aided by the entire flotilla of steam gunboats, were particularly useful in this role, as they were large enough to carry the heavy minesweeping equipment at higher speeds. The first experimental sweep used three Ds towing a sound source, an SA sweep, in fact the pipe noisemaker or Foxer towed anti-acoustic

*MGB 664 in spring 1943. She is armed with a
2-pounder forward, a twin .5in, a twin 20mm on a
power mounting (in place of the Holman) and a
6-pounder on a Mark VI mounting aft. She has
torpedo scallops, but was not fitted with tubes. She
was modified in late 1944 to a LRRC for the RAF.*
Imperial War Museum

torpedo device as used by convoy escort vessels. With a combination of depth charges, their wakes at high speed and magnetic or
acoustic sweep gear, they were able to overcome the oyster mines.

Unlike the more numerous B type, few experiments were carried
out in the D. MGB 675 was fitted with davits aft for the transportation of two Chariots (manned torpedoes), to attack targets in Norway, while MGB 613 mounted a single 2-pounder Mark VIII gun
on the Mark VIII mounting on her focs'l, a weapon usually found
on Flower class corvettes or fleet minesweepers of the Bangor class.

The D type suffered from the usual armament procurement
problems when they were first built – they were given what was
available. The early units were provided with a 2-pounder pom-
pom forward, at first the Mark XV mounting (the first power-
operated turret), then the improved Mark XVI mounting. The
twin Vickers .5in machine guns in the power-operated Mark V
were mounted each side of the bridge. To provide extra splinter
protection, splinter mattresses were frequently secured around the
gun tub and on the wheelhouse roof as protection against enemy air
attack by machine gun or cannon. Two twin .303in Vickers gas-
operated guns on handheld mounts were fitted in the bridge wings;
these were ineffective against aircraft, but useful in close fighting
alongside, as was the box of hand grenades which most Coastal
Forces craft acquired.

A Holman projector was fitted to the coachroof, and a twin
20mm Oerlikon was fitted, on a power-operated Mark V mounting,
just coming off the production lines. A number of the earlier units
completed with a single 20mm Oerlikon aft, due to shortfalls in the
production of the twin Mark V. In later MGBs this mounting was
re-sited on the coachroof, the Holman deleted, and an old manual

*MGB S 613 in Haslar creek late in 1942. A unit of
the 18th MGB flotilla, she was based at Portsmouth.
Note the manual 2-pounder Mk VIII mounting
forward, the Holman projector and the single 20mm
Oerlikon on a hand raised mounting aft; this is a
non-standard weapons fit.* MoD (Navy)

*MTB 650 in early 1943, with two 21in torpedo
tubes. She retains her searchlight and Holman
projector, but has a 2-pounder on a Mark XVI
power-operated mounting forward.* MoD (Navy)

*MGB 642, followed by MGB 647, leaving Algiers
on 2 April 1943. Both belonged to the 19th Flotilla.*
Imperial War Museum

6-pounder Hotchkiss gun, usually of nineteenth-century vintage, was fitted aft. By the middle months of 1944 boats were completing with the new semi-automatic 6-pounder Mark VII mounting, which was fitted forward and aft, and, to reduce topweight, a manual twin 20mm Oerlikon Mark IX mounting on a wooden sparred gun platform, where it gave an excellent arc of fire.

Postwar, the Ds were fitted with improved weapons, as shown in the GA drawings.

## Allied and Commonwealth-manned Fairmile Ds

While the vast majority of D types were manned by the Royal Navy, albeit with many, many officers and ratings from overseas, the Royal Norwegian Navy crewed over twenty units of the Free Norwegian Navy. Originally they had manned Fairmile Bs, but as Ds were completed from the spring and summer of 1942, the Norwegians took these over, undertook trials, and operated them from Scottish ports against Axis forces in Norway, suffering a number of losses. MGB 631 was stranded while on operations off Norway in March 1943 and captured by the Germans, while 626 was lost by an explosion at her base in Lerwick the following November. Another, 712, became a constructive total loss after grounding in Scottish waters in January 1945 and was disposed of within six months. MTB 715 was another casualty, lost by explosion at Fosnavaag in Norway on 19 May 1945.

Those units operated by the Free Norwegian Navy included 618, 619, 620, 623, 625, 627, 631, 653, 688, 704, 709, 711, 712, 713, 715, 716, 717, 719, 720, 722, and 723, with eight surviving boats sold to Norway in 1946 (713, 716, 717, 719, 720, 721, 722 and 723).

*Two views of MTB 655 off Cowes in January 1943,
after her completion at Littlehampton. She carries
the usual armament fit for that period, but no
Holman.* MoD (Navy)

*MGB 660 and MTB 633 at Bastia in early 1944.*
*The gunboat has had her twin .5in MGs replaced by*
*single 20mms, but retains the punch of her 6-pounder*
*aft. Note that towing plates were now standard, but*
*both have low-power stern lights of a different*
*pattern, possibly a local modification.*
Imperial War Museum

The Royal Canadian Navy crewed two flotillas of Coastal Forces types. A proposal had been made in 1942 that the RCN should form a British-based flotilla of motor craft, but this was not acted upon as Canada at that time had no such craft. A year later the Admiralty offered to supply and maintain such boats if the RCN would man them. Accordingly two flotillas were formed in early 1944; the 29th, equipped with 71ft 6in British Power Boats, and the 65th, with Fairmile Ds (MTBs 726, 727, 735, 736, 743, 744, 745, 746, 748 and 797). Both flotillas took part in a variety of pre-invasion operations off the coast of France, and in protecting the flanks of the invasion forces. After D-Day they assisted in preventing German E-boats and larger craft from attacking the cross-Channel reinforcements to the beach heads. All the Canadian Ds survived the war to be sold in the early 1950s.

## Fairmile D class data

**Designed by the Admiralty.**
**Built at a total of thirty British yards.**
**Dimensions**  Length overall 115ft 0in, length on waterline 110ft 0in, beam 20ft 10in, draught 4ft 9in.
**Displacement**  As designed, 85 tons; actual, 105 tons (and above).
**Machinery**  Four Packard 12-cylinder 1250bhp supercharged 4M 2500 petrol engines. Dumbflow exhaust. Specimen revolutions: 1000rpm = 12 knots, 1500rpm = 17 knots, 1800rpm = 21 knots, 2000rpm = 25 knots, 2400rpm = 30 knots (short periods only).
**Speed**  34.5 knots design maximum (at 85 tons), 29.5 knots design continuous; 32.0 knots actual maximum (at 105 tons, with reduction gear; early units 30.0 knots at 105 tons, with direct drive), 27.0 knots actual continuous (at 105 tons, with reduction gear; early units 25.0 knots at 105 tons, with direct drive). These are average trial figures for new craft.
**Range at maximum continuous speed**  506 nautical miles.
**Fuel capacity**  5200 gallons.
**Steering**  Mathway manual gear (other types also fitted).
**Radar and electronics aerials fitted**  Type 286 (from late 1941), Type 242 IFF Interrogator, Type 253 IFF Transponder, Type 291U (from 1943), Type 241 IFF Interrogater, US Navy SO Type (from 1944), Type 286U (from early 1945).
**Underwater detection apparatus**  Hydrophone Type 715A.
**For armament variations see drawings.**

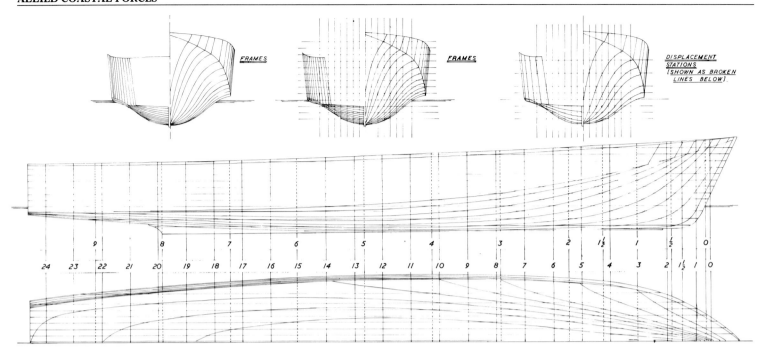

**Fairmile D lines**

*N.B:- TORPEDO HULL SCALLOPS ARE NOT SHOWN.*

**Fairmile D constructional sections**

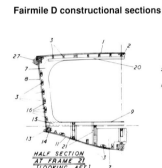

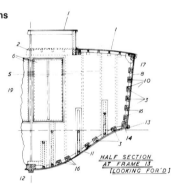

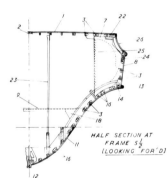

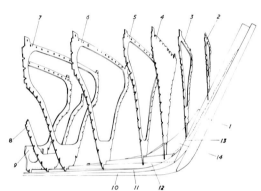

**Fairmile D forward bulkheads and frames**

1  Deck planking two thicknesses ¹⁵⁄₃₂in teak
2  King plank, 3in × 1½in teak
3  Spurce stringers, 3in × 1¾in
4  Pitch pine keel, 12in × 7in
5  Spruce bulkhead stiffeners, 3in × 1¾ in
6  Plywood wit door, 1in
7  Plywood frame, 1in
8  Mahogany planking – outer ⅝in, inner ½in
9  Pine cabin sole, ¾in

10  Oak stringer face pieces – 1½in × 1⅜ in
11  Mahogany planking – outer ¾in, inner ⅝in
12  Canadian rock elm false keel, 6in × 2in
13  Mahogany rubber, 3⅜in × 2½in
14  Chine rail, 6in × 4in
15  Spruce bearer, 3in × 1¾in
16  Mild steel lugs, 14 gauge
17  mild steel knee, 12 gauge
18  Mild steel flanged bracket, ³⁄₁₆in

19  Mahogany WT bulkhead, 3½in thicknesses
20  2lb mild steel angle – 2ft ½in × 1½in
21  Pitch pine vertical posts
22  Silver spruce deck former
23  Steel pillar, 2in dia
24  Silver spruce side former
25  Mild steel wing bulkhead, ³⁄₁₆in
26  Scallop planking – two thicknesses of ⅜in silver spruce doubled with 3½in teak fore and aft over skin
27  English elm in wake of mien shutes, 9½in × 5in

1  Stem
2  Frame 0
3  Frame 1
4  Watertight bulkhead 1½
5  Frame 2
6  Frame 3
7  Frame 4
8  Frame 5
9  Frame 6
10  False keel
11  Keel
12  Deadwood
13  Apron
14  Stem knee

**Detail of letters, numerals and Mark figures**

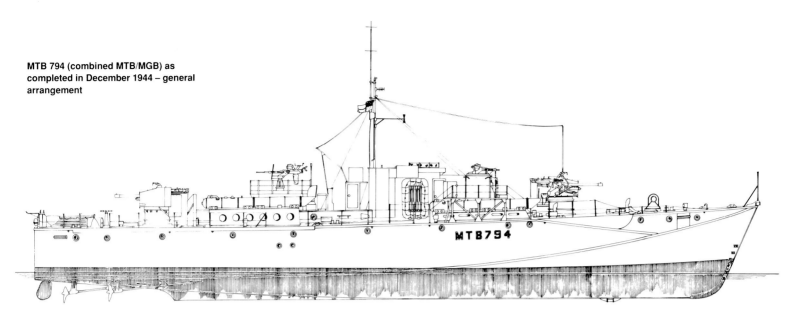

MTB 794 (combined MTB/MGB) as
completed in December 1944 – general
arrangement

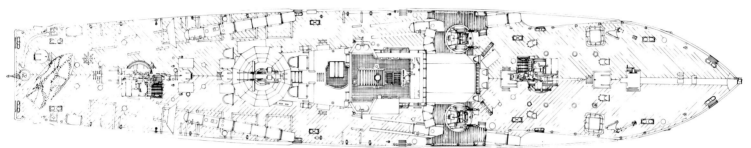

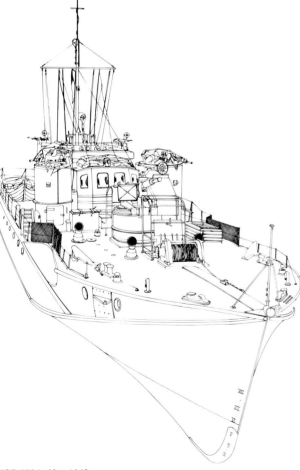

MGB 673 in May 1943

*An upper deck view off Algiers on 2 April 1943 of a
D type (633-640), showing an early Mark V power-
operated mounting. The unit on her port quarter is
MTB 636, and both units are of the 32nd MTB
Flotilla. (636 was lost the following October).*
Imperial War Museum

**MTB 794 internal profile**

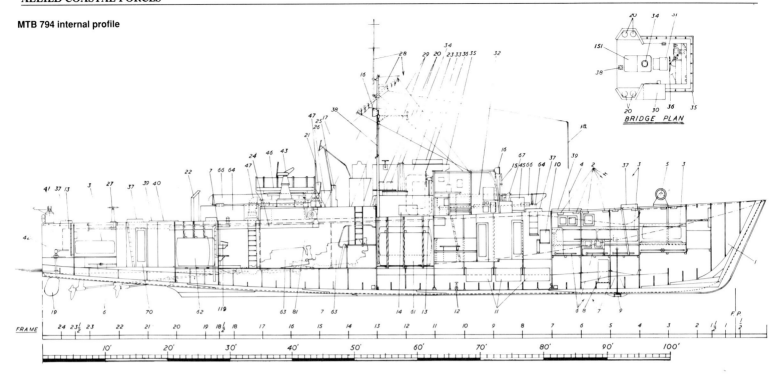

**MTB 794 deck plan**

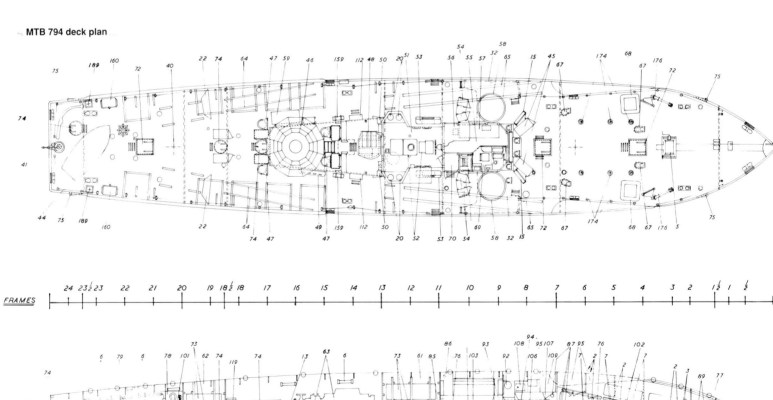

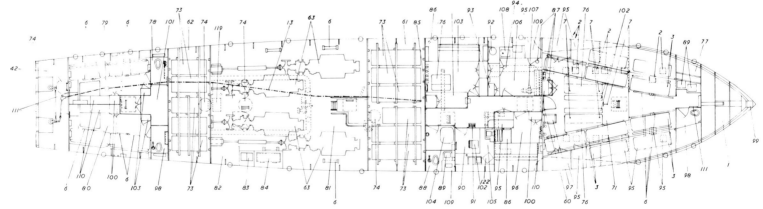

**MTB 794 plan below deck**

*MTB 724 in September 1943. Her armament is four*
*18in tubes, a 2-pounder forward, a 6-pounder aft,*
*two twin .5in mountings, one twin 20mm and two*
*depth charges.* MoD (Navy)

1 Forepeak
2 Respirator racks
3 Pipe cot
4 6-pounder on Mark VII or 2-pounder Mark XVI mounting
5 Anchor windlass (various makes)
6 Electric heater
7 2in dia steel pillar
8 Fresh water tank (45gal)
9 Hydrophone oscillator
10 Hand-up ammunition platform
11 Fresh water tank (110gal)
12 Pitometer log
13 Steering gear lead
14 Fresh water tank (35gal)
15 2in rocket flare stowage (if fitted)
16 Loudhailer (fitted in various positions)
17 TW12 aerial
18 Mast on Mark VII mounting (if fitted)
19 Twin rudders
20 .303in ready use ammunition bin
21 Mast crutch (normally stowed)
22 Torpedo blast screen
23 Pattern 23 life raft (other types carried)
24 Ventilator trunking
25 Flag locker
26 20mm Oerlikon ready use ammunition locker
27 Mathway steering pedestal and wheel (emergency position)
28 Type 291 U radar aerial (differing sets fitted)
29 TCS aerial

30 Chart table under cover
31 Stool
32 Wooden catwalk over torpedo tube
33 Windscreen
34 Standard compass
35 Wind deflector
36 Ship's wheel
37 Hatch
38 Mast
39 Gun bed
40 After 6-pounder on Mark VII or Mark VI mounting
41 Chemical smoke apparatus (plus smoke floats)
42 Steering gear compartment
43 Twin 20mm Oerlikon on Mark IX mounting
44 10ft dinghy
45 6-pounder ready use ammunition locker
46 Wooden stepped Oerlikon gun platform
47 18in cowl vent
48 Compass and searchlight platform
49 Accommodation ladder (stowed)
50 Hand grenade ready use locker
51 Bridge deck
52 Wood platform
53 Wood platform
54 .5in machine gun ready use ammunition locker
55 Chart house
56 Plotting table
57 Settee berth (locker under)
58 Twin .5in Vickers machine guns on

Mark V power operated mounting
59 Locker for deck gear (portable)
60 Watertight door
61 Forward fuel tank space
62 After fuel tank space
63 Packard marine engine model 4M 2500
64 18in torpedo tube deck seat
65 21in torpedo tube deck seat
66 18in torpedo tube LC Mark II
67 6in waterbox vent
68 Denton life float
69 Radar office
70 Lobby
71 Forward messdeck
72 WT hatch
73 Copper fuel tanks
74 WT scuttle
75 Towing bracket
76 Hinged flap table
77 Crew's washplace
78 Petty officers' washplace
79 Petty officers' cabin (four men)
80 Crew's mess (aft – four men)
81 Engineroom
82 Workbench
83 Waste bin
84 Spares locker
85 Small cupboard
86 Chest of drawers
87 Fire extinguisher
88 Officers' WC
89 Washbasin
90 W/T office
91 Rifle rack
92 Water heater
93 Food locker
94 Plate rack
95 Shelves (over)
96 CO's cabin
97 Oilskin locker

98 Crew's WC
99 Stem
100 Wardrobe
101 Magazine
102 Seat
103 Wardroom
104 Shower
105 Bench
106 Galley
107 Fan
108 Sink
109 Lockers
110 Dresser
111 Mirror
112 Step-up
113 Floor hatch
114 Towel bar
115 Blackout curtain
116 Stowage space
117 Zinc lined lockers
118 Mattress as seat back
119 Engineroom watchkeeper's desk
120 Pistol box
121 Generators under floor
122 Radio
123 Provision locker
124 2-pounder ammunition tank
125 Voice pipe
126 Battery seating
127 Steel ladder
128 Hand bilge pump
129 Shaft cover
130 Battery (under)
131 Generator
132 Stowage for sixteen boxes of 20m ammunition
133 2-pounder gun spares box
134 6-pounder gun spares box
135 6-pounder Hotchkiss on Mark VI mounting (manual)

*Key continued on p103*

**Fairmile D MGB typical internal profile**

**Fairmile D MGB typical deck plan**

**Fairmile D MGB plan below deck**

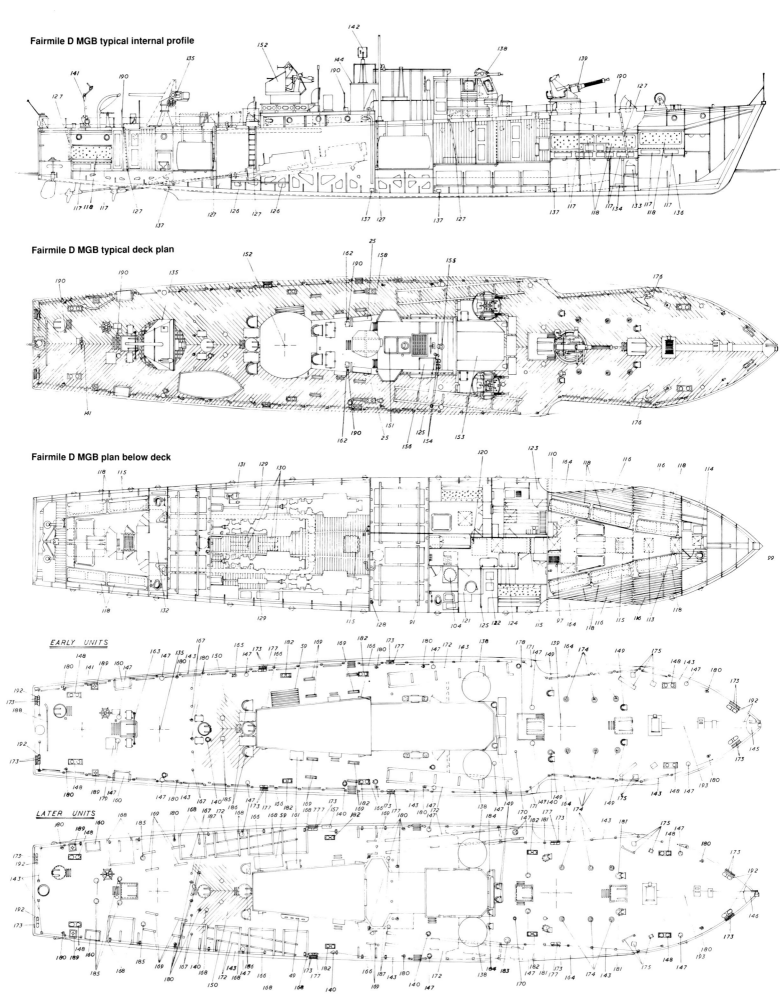

*EARLY UNITS*

*LATER UNITS*

102

*Key continued from p101*

136 Bosun's store
137 Strum box
138 Twin .5in on Mark V (power) mounting
139 2-pounder on Mark XV or XVI (power) mounting
140 Hand bilge pump deck plate
141 Holman projector
142 20in searchlight projector
143 Guard rail
144 Searchlight platform
145 Guide pulley fitted to stem head fitting

146 Metal bullring with deck plate
147 5in dia mushroom vent
148 24in bollard
149 6in dia cowl vent
150 Diagonal teak deck planking
151 Lift-up hatch to space under bridge deck
152 Twin 20mm Oerlikon on Mark V mounting
153 Charthouse roof
154 Main engine throttles
155 Pelorus
156 Locker for stowage of electrical gear (under)
157 Deck pad for hydrophone gear

158 Entrance to engineroom (under)
159 Torpedo impulse charge box
160 Depth charge
161 Firework tank
162 Grenade ready use locker
163 Gun depression rail
164 Hull torpedo scallops
165 Hose wash deck connection
166 Exhaust on coachroof side
167 Sounding deck plate
168 Seat for moored mines
169 Torpedo loading chock tapping strip
170 Fresh water filling deck plate
171 Brass datum plate for torpedo tubes
172 Torpedo girder tapping strip

173 Chafing strip
174 Decklight
175 CQR anchor chocks
176 CQR anchor
177 18in fairlead
178 Portable deck plate
179 Holman RU locker
180 2in dia swan neck vent
188 Emergency tiller
189 Seat for depth charge davit
190 Grab stanchion
191 Deck foot strips
192 21in roller fairlead
193 Wood chafing strip

**MTB 794 hull subdivisions and access**

1 WT bulkhead 1½
2 WT bulkhead 7
3 WT bulkhead 11
4 WT bulkhead 13
5 WT bulkhead 18½
6 WT bulkhead 20
7 WT bulkhead 23½
8 Forepeak
9 Crew's WC
10 Crew's washplace
11 Forward messdeck
12 WT door
13 CO's cabin
14 WT office
15 Officers' WC
16 Lobby
17 Galley
18 Wardroom
19 Forward fuel tank compartment
20 Engineroom
21 After fuel tank compartment
22 Magazine
23 Petty officers' cabin
24 Seamen's mess
25 Petty officers' WC
26 Crew's WC
27 Steering gear compartment
28 Transom

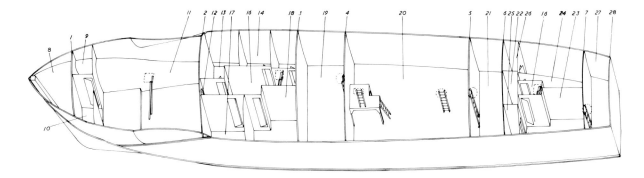

*MGB 658 at Manfredonia in March 1945. She has
two 6-pounders on power-operated Mark VII
mountings, sided 20mms and a 2in rocket flare
projector on her forward mounting. Ready use rockets
are stowed about her wheelhouse. She has also
acquired a US Navy SO radar and mainmast.*
Courtesy Len (Rover) Reynolds

**Opposite: Fairmile D MGB deck
openings and fittings plans**

*MGB 658 on the floating pontoon dock in Msida
Creek, Malta, taken in December 1943 (on one of the
few photographic films then on the island).*
Courtesy Len (Rover) Reynolds

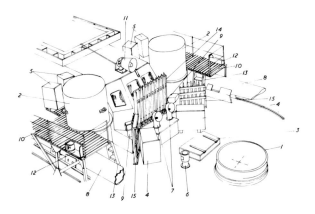

1   Deck support for 6-pounder QF Mark VII mounting
2   .5in twin on Mark V (power) mounting
3   WT hatch to forward messdeck
4   6-pounder ready use ammunition locker
5   .5in ready use ammunition locker
6   5in dia vent
7   6in dia cowl vent
8   18in torpedo tubes
9   6in dia Revon vent
10  Wooden catwalk over tubes
11  Loudhailer
12  Navigation light
13  Wooden ladder
14  Ready use stowage for ten 2in rockets
15  Ready use stowage for five 2in rockets

**Details of windlass**

**MTB armament fittings**

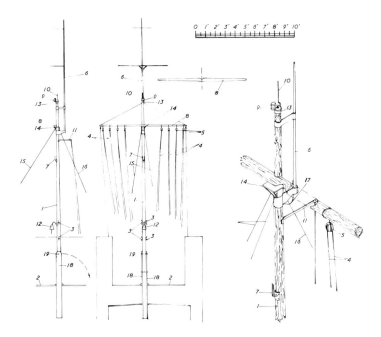

1   Wood mast
2   Bridge deck
3   Cleats
4   Signal halyard
5   Halyard block
6   RDF aerial mast
7   Steaming light bracket
8   Signal yard
9   Masthead signal lamp
10  Vertical conductor
11  Ensign strut
12  Ship's bell
13  Masthead cap
14  Mast spider band
15  Forestay
16  Backstay
17  RDF power cable
18  Mast support
19  Pivot for lowering mast (early Type 286 radar shown)

**Details of masts**

LATER UNITS WERE FITTED WITH FIGHTING LIGHTS & LOUDSPEAKERS AS SHOWN BELOW

**Below: Fairmile D displacement scale**

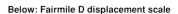

*MGB 778 showing her forefoot, May 1945.*
Courtesy Ford Jenkins

**Guardrail detail**

1 Stanchion
2 Upper deck
3 Shelf
4 Clamp
5 Bolt
6 Screw
7 Deck socket
8 Eyebolt

**CQR anchor detail**

**Magnetic compass binnacle (later units)**

*3 BALL FIXED STANCHION*   *2 BALL HINGED STANCHION*   *1 BALL HINGED STANCHION*

*MTB 710 in late 1943; she was lost to a mine in the Adriatic in April 1945.* MoD (Navy)

*A bow view of MTB 634 in May 1945, with US S0 radar – a local, unofficial fitting.* Author's collection

*The old and the new at Felixstowe in 1944 – an unidentified D being passed by a loaded sailing barge.* Author's collection

**Layout of main fuel tanks, piping, etc**

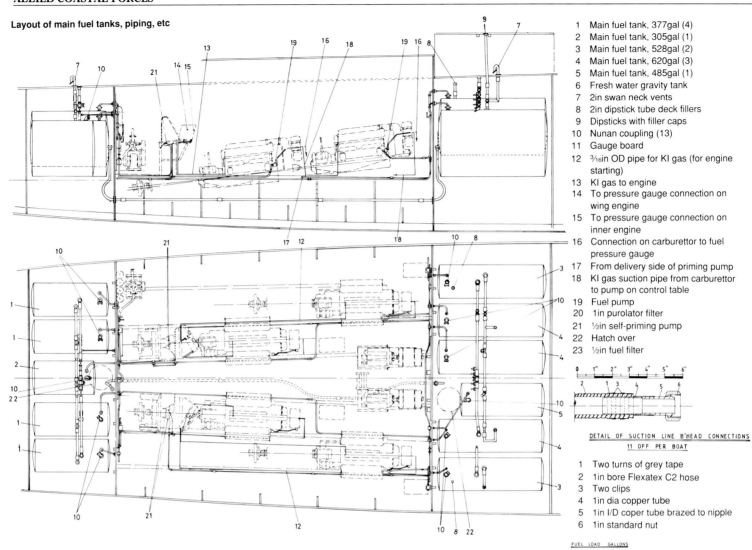

1  Main fuel tank, 377gal (4)
2  Main fuel tank, 305gal (1)
3  Main fuel tank, 528gal (2)
4  Main fuel tank, 620gal (3)
5  Main fuel tank, 485gal (1)
6  Fresh water gravity tank
7  2in swan neck vents
8  2in dipstick tube deck fillers
9  Dipsticks with filler caps
10  Nunan coupling (13)
11  Gauge board
12  ³⁄₁₆in OD pipe for KI gas (for engine
    starting)
13  KI gas to engine
14  To pressure gauge connection on
    wing engine
15  To pressure gauge connection on
    inner engine
16  Connection on carburettor to fuel
    pressure gauge
17  From delivery side of priming pump
18  KI gas suction pipe from carburettor
    to pump on control table
19  Fuel pump
20  1in purolator filter
21  ½in self-priming pump
22  Hatch over
23  ½in fuel filter

**DETAIL OF SUCTION LINE B'HEAD CONNECTIONS**
**11 OFF PER BOAT**

1  Two turns of grey tape
2  1in bore Flexatex C2 hose
3  Two clips
4  1in dia copper tube
5  1in I/D coper tube brazed to nipple
6  1in standard nut

**Right: Fairmile D MGB speed, range
and fuel load data**

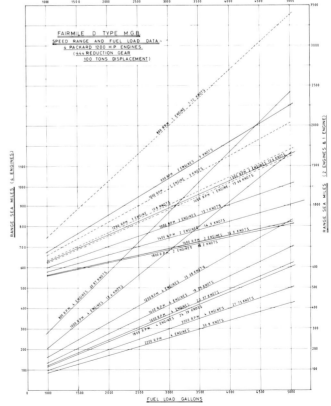

*Out looking for trouble – MGB 778 and sisters, after
the tide had turned, early in 1945.* Author's
collection

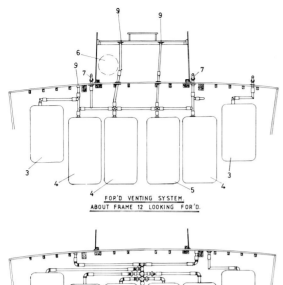

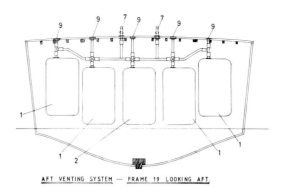

AFT VENTING SYSTEM — FRAME 19 LOOKING AFT

FOR'D VENTING SYSTEM.
ABOUT FRAME 12 LOOKING FOR'D.

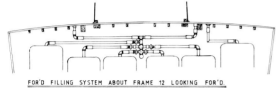

FOR'D FILLING SYSTEM ABOUT FRAME 12 LOOKING FOR'D.

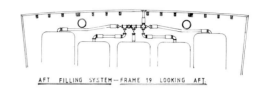

AFT FILLING SYSTEM — FRAME 19 LOOKING AFT.

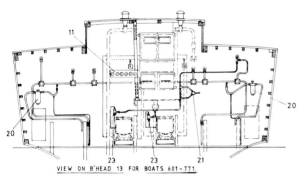

VIEW ON B'HEAD 13 FOR BOATS 601~771.

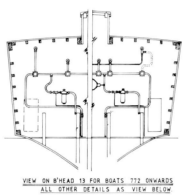

VIEW ON B'HEAD 13 FOR BOATS 772 ONWARDS
ALL OTHER DETAILS AS VIEW BELOW.

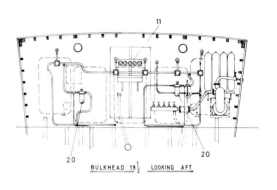

BULKHEAD 18½ LOOKING AFT

*MTB 774 in late 1945, with four torpedo tubes, two 6-pounders on Mark VII mountings, two twin .5in mountings, one twin 20mm on a Mark IX mounting. She is seen after a refit, where type 268 radar was added.* MoD (Navy)

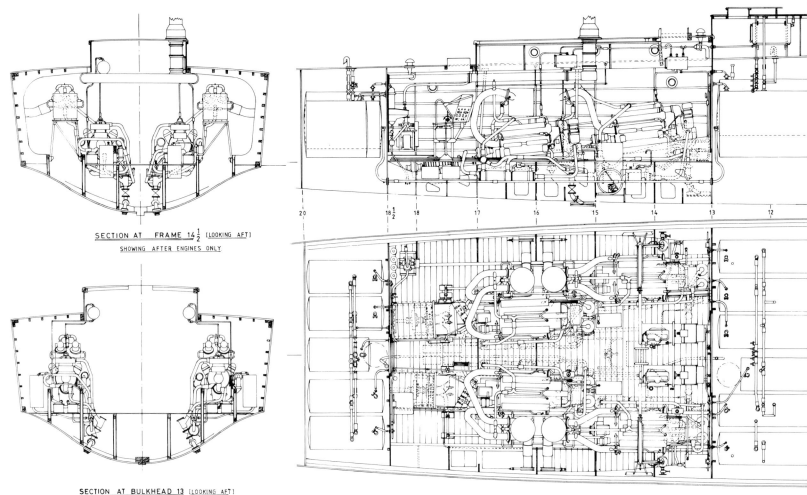

SECTION AT FRAME 14½ [LOOKING AFT]
SHOWING AFTER ENGINES ONLY

SECTION AT BULKHEAD 13 [LOOKING AFT]
SHOWING FOR'D ENGINES ONLY.

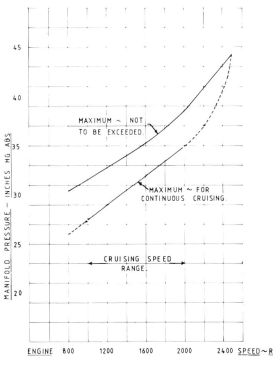

*Above left: The Royal Air Force's Navy – LRRC 003 in Mounts Bay, showing an all-defensive armament of 20mm Oerlikons. She was ex MTB 5004.* Courtesy John Pritchard

*Left: LRRC 007, ex MTB 5014; she too retains the D type appearance. Note the long-range deck tanks on the upper deck.* Imperial War Museum

Fairmile D engineroom general arrangement (boats 673, 772–800, 5001–5029, less 5027)

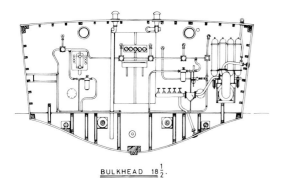

BULKHEAD 18½.

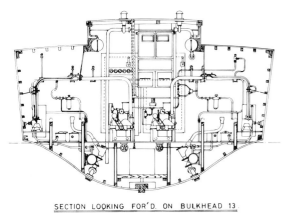

SECTION LOOKING FOR'D. ON BULKHEAD 13

**Opposite: Fairmile D manifold pressures (100 Octane fuel)**

*Right: MTB 5003 in July 1945 – the ultimate wartime boat, with 21in tubes. Compare her weapon fit with that of MGB 601.* Imperial War Museum

*LRRC 003 in Newlyn Harbour, early in 1946.* Courtesy John Pritchard

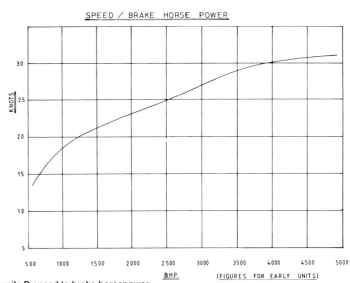

SPEED / BRAKE HORSE POWER

Fairmile D speed to brake horsepower table (early units)

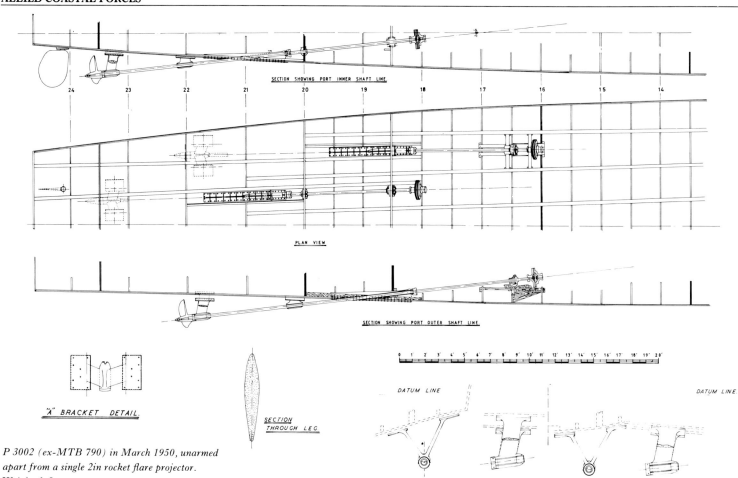

SECTION SHOWING PORT INNER SHAFT LINE

24  23  22  21  20  19  18  17  16  15  14

PLAN VIEW

SECTION SHOWING PORT OUTER SHAFT LINE

"A" BRACKET DETAIL.

SECTION THROUGH LEG.

0  1'  2'  3'  4'  5'  6'  7'  8'  9'  10'  11'  12'  13'  14'  15'  16'  17'  18'  19'  20'

DATUM LINE                    DATUM LINE.

STARBOARD WING BRACKET          STARBOARD INNER BRACKET

*P 3002 (ex-MTB 790) in March 1950, unarmed apart from a single 2in rocket flare projector.*
Wright & Logan

**Below and opposite: Fairmile D propeller shaft detail**

SECTION ON
FRAME 19
LOOKING FOR'D

SECTION ON
FRAME 21
LOOKING FOR'D

SECTION 12' 0" FOR'D OF TRANSOM
LOOKING FOR'D.

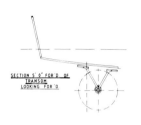

SECTION 5' 0" FOR'D OF
TRANSOM
LOOKING FOR'D.

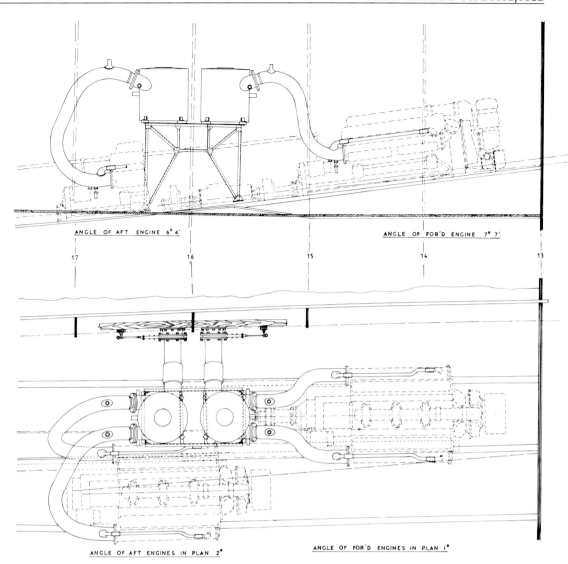

ANGLE OF AFT ENGINE 6° 4'          ANGLE OF FOR'D ENGINE 7° 7'

ANGLE OF AFT ENGINES IN PLAN 2°          ANGLE OF FOR'D ENGINES IN PLAN 1°

**Below and right: Layout of dumbflow exhaust system (boats 673 and 772 onwards)**

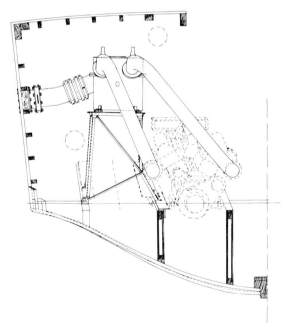

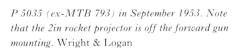

*P 5035 (ex-MTB 793) in September 1953. Note that the 2in rocket projector is off the forward gun mounting.* Wright & Logan

MGB 601 in March 1942, armed with one 2-pounder Mark XV gun, two twin .5in machine guns on Mark V (power) mountings, two twin .303in Vickers machine guns (not shown), one twin 20mm Oerlikon Mark V, a Holman projector and two depth charges.

MGB 613 in October 1942, armed with one 2-pounder Mark VIII gun, two twin .5in machine guns on Mark V (power) mountings, two twin .303in Vickers machine guns (not shown), a single 20mm Oerlikon Mark I, a Holman projector and two depth charges.

MTB 655 in January 1943, armed with one 2-pounder Mark XVI gun, two twin .5in machine guns on Mark V (power) mountings, two twin .303in Vickers machine guns (not shown), one twin 20mm Oerlikon Mark V, two 21in torpedo tubes and two depth charges.

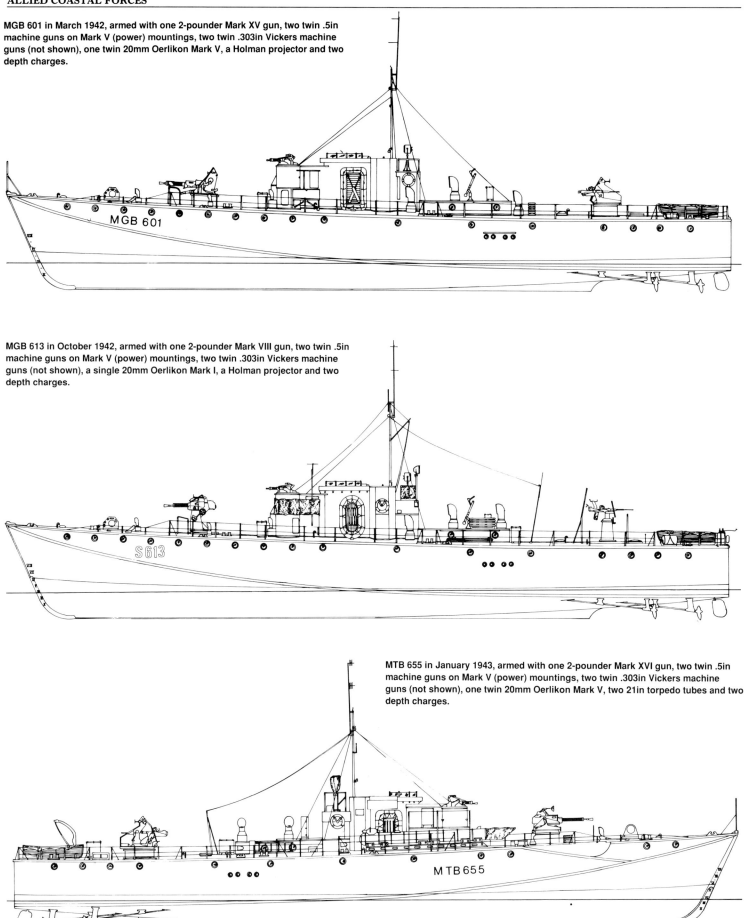

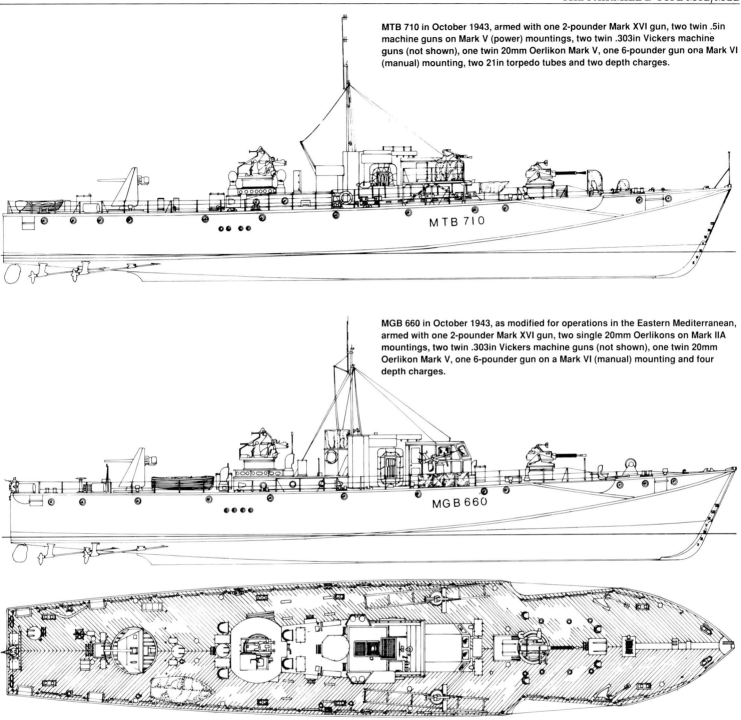

**MTB 710 in October 1943, armed with one 2-pounder Mark XVI gun, two twin .5in machine guns on Mark V (power) mountings, two twin .303in Vickers machine guns (not shown), one twin 20mm Oerlikon Mark V, one 6-pounder gun on a Mark VI (manual) mounting, two 21in torpedo tubes and two depth charges.**

**MGB 660 in October 1943, as modified for operations in the Eastern Mediterranean, armed with one 2-pounder Mark XVI gun, two single 20mm Oerlikons on Mark IIA mountings, two twin .303in Vickers machine guns (not shown), one twin 20mm Oerlikon Mark V, one 6-pounder gun on a Mark VI (manual) mounting and four depth charges.**

*P 5015 (ex-MTB 5015) in November 1951, and armed with weapons systems that appeared as hostilities ended: two 4:5in Mark I (power-operated) mountings and the twin 20mm Mark 12A mounting.* Wright & Logan

MTB 629 in May 1944, armed with one 2-pounder Mark XVI, two twin .5in machine guns on Mark V (power) mountings, two twin .303in Vickers machine guns (not shown), one twin 20mm Oerlikon on a Mark V (power) mounting, a Holman projector, two 21in torpedo tubes and two depth charges.

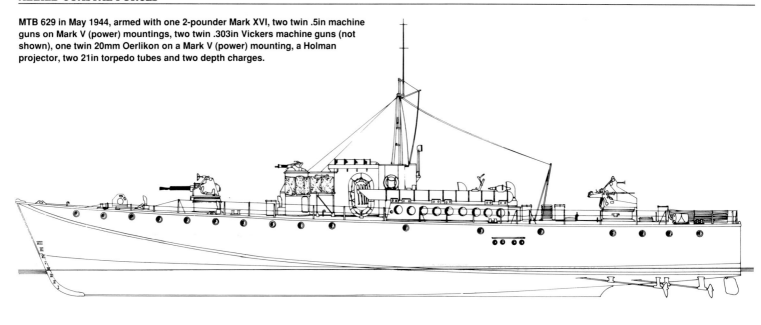

MTB 624 in June 1944, armed with one 6-pounder gun on a Mark VII mounting, two twin .5in machine guns on Mark V (power) mountings, two twin .303in Vickers machine guns (not shown), one twin 20mm Oerlikon on a Mark V (power) mounting, a Holman projector, two 21in torpedo tubes and two 2in rocket flare launchers.

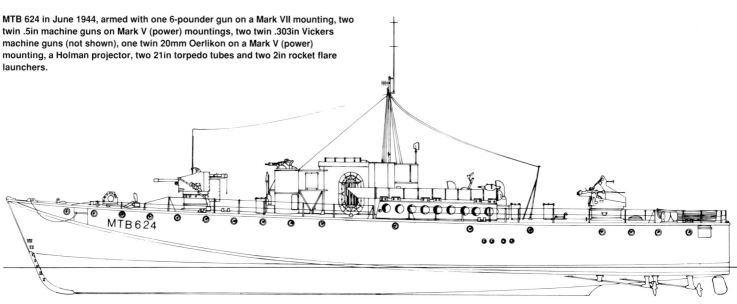

MTB 605 in November 1944, armed with one 6-pounder gun on a Mark VII mounting, two twin .5in machine guns on Mark V (power) mountings, two twin .303in Vickers machine guns (not shown), one twin 20mm Oerlikon on a Mark IX mounting, one 6-pounder gun on a Mark VI mounting, two 18in torpedo tubes, two depth charges, a single 2in rocket flare launcher and provision for mines.

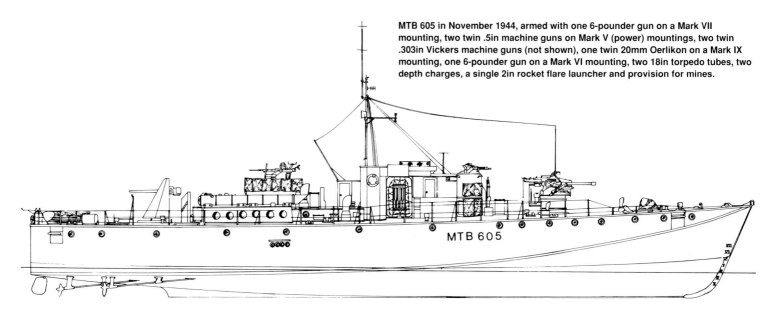

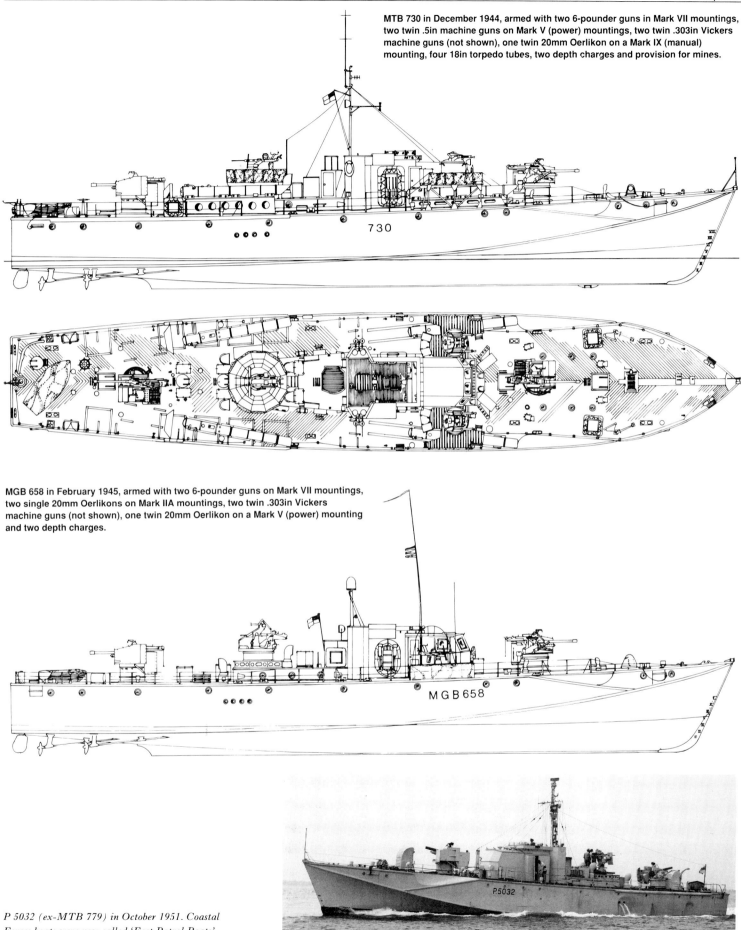

MTB 730 in December 1944, armed with two 6-pounder guns in Mark VII mountings, two twin .5in machine guns on Mark V (power) mountings, two twin .303in Vickers machine guns (not shown), one twin 20mm Oerlikon on a Mark IX (manual) mounting, four 18in torpedo tubes, two depth charges and provision for mines.

730

MGB 658 in February 1945, armed with two 6-pounder guns on Mark VII mountings, two single 20mm Oerlikons on Mark IIA mountings, two twin .303in Vickers machine guns (not shown), one twin 20mm Oerlikon on a Mark V (power) mounting and two depth charges.

MGB658

*P 5032 (ex-MTB 779) in October 1951. Coastal Forces boats were now called 'Fast Patrol Boats'.*
Wright & Logan

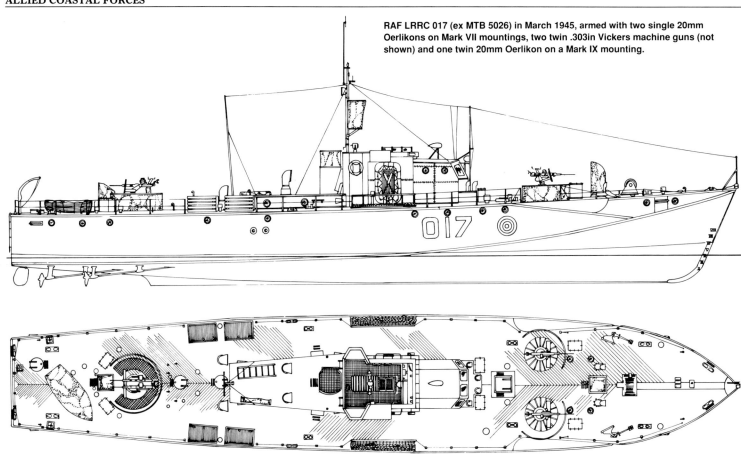

RAF LRRC 017 (ex MTB 5026) in March 1945, armed with two single 20mm Oerlikons on Mark VII mountings, two twin .303in Vickers machine guns (not shown) and one twin 20mm Oerlikon on a Mark IX mounting.

MTB 5003 in July 1945, armed with two 6-pounder guns on Mark VII mountings, two twin .5in machine guns on Mark V (power) mountings, two twin .303in Vickers machine guns (not shown), one twin 20mm Oerlikon on a Mark IX mounting, two 21in torpedo tubes, two depth charges, a single 2in rocket flare launcher and provision for mines.

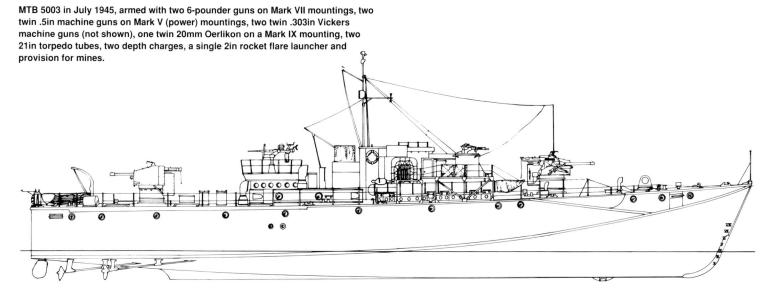

*P 5031 (ex-MTB 758) in February 1953, armed with two 4:5in Mark I mountings, one twin 20mm Oerlikon on a Mark 12A mounting and two 21in torpedo tubes.* Wright & Logan

MASB (Motor Anti Submarine Boat) 5013 in July 1948, armed with a single 40mm
Bofors gun on a Mark VII mounting, a split Hedgehog mounting, two 2in rocket
flare launchers and provision for four depth charges.

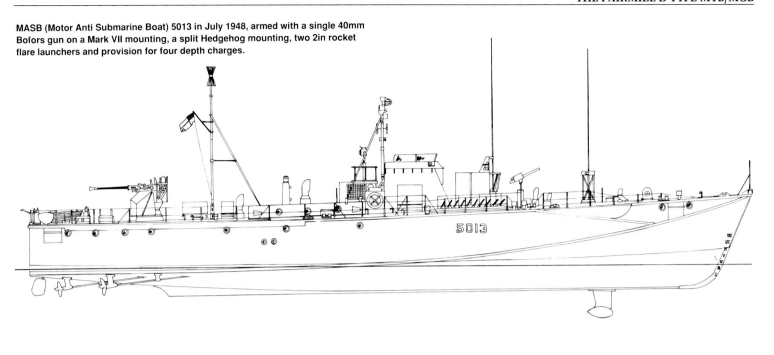

FPB 5001 (ex MTB 780) in June 1954, armed with two 4.5in guns on Mark
I mountings, one twin 20mm Oerlikon on a Mark XII mounting, one 2in rocket
flare launcher and provision for mines and depth charges.

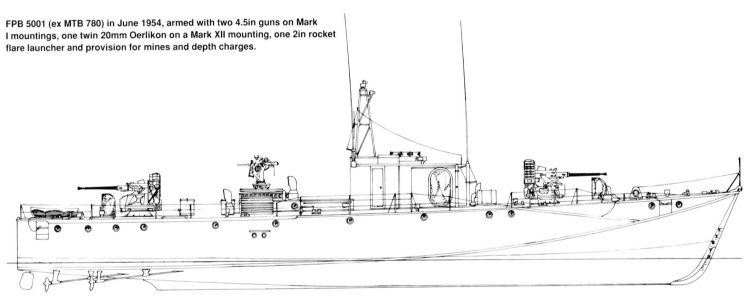

FPB 5031 (ex MTB 758) in February 1953, armed with two single 40mm Bofors guns on
Mark XII mountings, one twin 20mm Oerlikon on a Mark XII mounting, one 2in rocket
flare launcher (on the 40mm mounting) and provision for mines and depth charges.

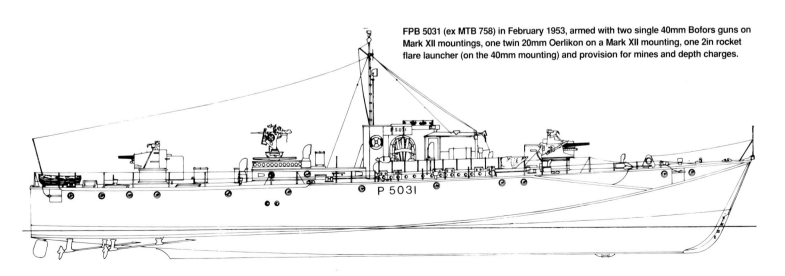

**FPB 5035 (ex MTB 793) in September 1955, armed with two 4.5in guns on Mark I mountings, one twin 20mm Oerlikon on a Mark XII mounting, two 2in rocket flare launchers and provision for mines and depth charges.**

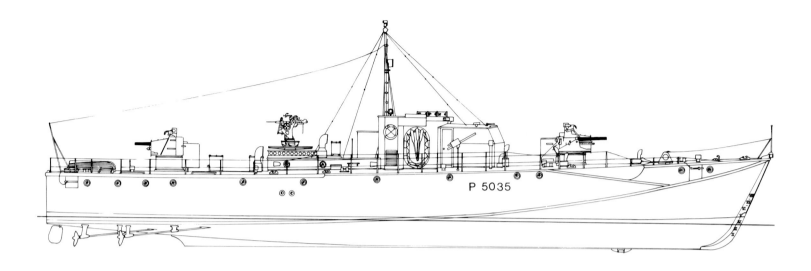

P 5035

*Ds with teeth; a unit of the 5th MGB Flotilla in 1944.* Imperial War Museum

*LRRC 003 at sea, with her twin 20mm Oerlikon on a Mark IX mounting manned. Note the 'spanner' life raft stowed on the guard rail.*
Courtesy John Pritchard

# Construction list

| No | Builder | Completed | Fate |
|---|---|---|---|
| **12 MGBs ordered 15.3.41 (all became MTBs in 9.43.*)** | | | |
| 601 | 25 | 9. 3.42 | Sunk 24.7.42 in action in the Dover Straits |
| 602 | 13 | 8.42 | To SCC 10.45; sold 21.2.56 |
| 603 | 25 | 25. 7.42 | For disposal 10.45 |
| 604 | 7B | 24. 7.42 | For disposal 10.45 |
| 605 | 15 | 16. 6.42 | Lost 17.2.45 in collision with wreck off Ostend |
| 606 | 27 | 7. 7.42 | Sunk 3/4.11.43 in action off the Dutch coast |
| 607 | 21 | 6.42 | For disposal 10.45 |
| 608 | 21 | 8.42 | For disposal 1.46 |
| 609 | 12 | 9. 6.42 | To SCC 10.45; sold circa 1952 |
| 610 | 28 | 30. 6.42 | To SCC Falmouth 4.46 and Weymouth 8.50; disposal 1.64 |
| 611 | 4 | 15. 9.42 | Sold .46 |
| 612 | 10 | 10. 7.42 | To SCC 12.45; for disposal 7.48 |
| **4 MGBs ordered 27.4.41 (all became MTBs in 9.43*)** | | | |
| 613 | 10 | 9. 9.42 | For disposal 10.46 |
| 614 | 28 | 6. 8.42 | For disposal 11.45 |
| 615 | 7T | 9.42 | For disposal 10.45 |
| 616 | 15 | 19. 8.42 | To SCC Exeter .47; for disposal .55 |
| **24 ordered 27.4.41 as MLs = MGBs, and became MTBs** | | | |
| 617 | 15 | 8.10.42 | Lent to Sea Scouts 1946; sold 7.7.53 |
| 618 | 11 | 27. 6.42 | RNN 6.42–.44; for disposal 1.45 |
| 619 | 9 | 23. 8.42 | RNN 8.42–7.44; for disposal 10.45 |
| 620 | 7B | 6. 9.42 | RNN 11.42–8.43; for disposal 3.46 |
| 621 | 21 | 10.42 | To SCC 4.46; sold 10.2.55 |
| 622 | 4 | 10.11.42 | Sunk 10.3.43 by German destroyers off Terschelling |
| 623 | 27 | 27. 8.42 | RNN .42–.44; for disposal 5.47 |
| 624 | 9 | 19.10.42 | To SCC Aberystwyth 12.45; for disposal 5.64 |
| 625 | 18 | 4. 9.42 | RNN .42; lost 1944 in Scottish waters |
| 626 | 25 | 24. 7.42 | RNN 6.42; lost 22.11.43 by explosion at Lerwick |
| 627 | 11 | 7.10.42 | RNN 9.42–.44; for disposal 4.45 |
| 628 | 26 | 11.42 | For disposal 10.45 |
| 629 | 7T | 1.12.42 | For disposal 10.45 |
| 630 | 18 | 5.11.42 | To SCC .45; sold by 1949 |
| 631 | 12 | 8.42 | RNN 1942; stranded 14.3.43 on coast of Norway and captured by Germans |
| 632 | 13 | 12.42 | For disposal 10.45 |
| 633 | 9 | 23.11.42 | Lost 30.1.46 on passage Malta–Alexandria |
| 634 | 15 | 27.11.42 | Lost 30.1.46 on passage Malta–Alexandria |
| 635 | 3 | 11.42 | Damaged 1944 and reported 7.45 as sunk as a target off Malta |
| 636 | 21 | 1.43 | Sunk in error by MGB 658 in action off Elba |
| 637 | 18 | 1.43 | Lost 30.1.46 on passage Malta–Alexandria |
| 638 | 7B | 14.12.42 | Lost 30.1.46 on passage Malta–Alexandria |
| 639 | 4 | 9. 3.43 | Sunk 28.4.43 by Italian tb *Sagittario* off Pantellaria |
| 640 | 27 | 1.11.42 | Mines 26/27.6.44 off Vada, Italy |
| **16 MGBs ordered 18.11.41 (641–648, 657–663 & 674)** | | | |
| 641 | 24 | 29.12.42 | Sunk 14/15.7.43 by shore batteries, Messina Straits |
| 642 | 11 | 7. 3.43 | Lost 30.1.46 on passage Malta–Alexandria |
| 643 | 28 | 22.12.42 | Lost 30.1.46 on passage Malta–Alexandria |
| 644 | 25 | 12.42 | Mined 26.6.43 off Sicily and scuttled |
| 645 | 10 | 12.42 | For disposal 8.45 |
| 646 | 17 | 19.11.42 | For disposal 8.45 |
| 647 | 7B | 24. 2.43 | Scuttled 9.46 off Malta |
| 648 | 9 | 10. 1.43 | Bombed 14.6.43 in central Mediterranean |
| MGBs continued at no 657 | | | |
| **44 ordered 28.11.41. as MLs = MGBs, and converted to MTBs (649–656, 664–673 and 675–700)** | | | |
| 649 | 17 | 7. 1.43 | For disposal 9.45; Mediterranean |
| 650 | 3 | 1.43 | To RAF .45 = LRRC020 |
| 651 | 25 | 1.43 | For disposal 9.45; Mediterranean |
| 652 | 10 | 25. 1.43 | For disposal 10.45; Mediterranean |

**Codes for builders**

1 Aldous Successors Ltd, Brightlingsea
2 Austins of East Ham Ltd, London E6
3 Boat Construction Co Ltd, Falmouth
4 Brooke Marine Ltd, Oulton Broad, nr Lowestoft
5 Cardnell Brothers, Maylandsea, Althorne, nr Chelmsford
6 Collins Pleasurecraft Co Ltd, Oulton Broad, nr Lowestoft
7B A M Dickie & Sons, Bangor, North Wales
7T A M Dickie & Sons, Tarbert, Argyllshire
8 J S Doig (Grimsby) Ltd, Grimsby Docks
9 Dorset Yacht Co Ltd, Lake Road, Hamworthy, Poole
10 S B Hall, Galmpton, Brixham, Devon
11 P K Harris & Sons Ltd, New Quay Dry Docks, Appledore
12 William King (Burnham-on-Crouch) Ltd
13 Kris Cruisers (1934) Ltd, Riverside Yard, Ferryll Road, Isleworth
14 Lady Bee Ltd, Shoreham-by-Sea, Sussex
15 William Osbourne Ltd, Littlehampton, Sussex
16 H T Percival, Yacht Station, Horning, Suffolk
17 Risdon Beazley Ltd, Clausentum Yard, Northam Bridge, Southampton
18 Alex Robertson (Yachtbuilders) & Sons Ltd, Sandbank, Argyllshire
19 Leo A Robinson, Oulton Broad, nr Lowestoft
20 John Sadd & Sons Ltd, Maldon, Essex
21 James A Silver Ltd, Rosneath, Dumbartonshire
22 Solent Shipyards Ltd, Bursledon Bridge, Sarisbury Green, Hants
23 Sussex Shipbuilding Co Ltd, Shoreham-by-Sea
24 Thomson & Balfour, Victoria Saw Mills, Bo'ness
25 Tough Brothers Ltd, Teddington Wharf, Teddington
26 J W & A Upham, Brixham, Devon
27 Wallasea Bay Yacht Station Ltd, Wallasea Bay, nr Rochford
28 Woodnutt & Co Ltd, St Helens, Isle of Wight
29 Herbert Woods, Broads Haven, Potter Heigham, Great Yarmouth

*MGBs 602–616 (also MTBs 664, 673 and 675–680) were to have become MTBs 499–521 respectively

| No | Builder | Completed | Fate |
|---|---|---|---|
| 653 | 18 | 3.43 | RNN 1943–44; for disposal 12.45 |
| 654 | 14 | 19. 2.43 | Damaged 1944 and for disposal 1.45 |
| 655 | 15 | 1.43 | Mined 22.3.45 in the Adriatic |
| 656 | 27 | 24.12.42 | For disposal 9.45; Mediterranean |

MTB continued at no 664

**MGBs continued**

| No | Builder | Completed | Fate |
|---|---|---|---|
| 657 | 28 | 9. 2.43 | CTL by mine 11/12.9.44 Mediterranean; 'to BU' 12.44 |
| 658 | 26 | 4.43 | Lost 30.1.46 on passage Malta-Alexandria |
| 659 | 3 | 5.43 | Lost 30.1.46 on passage Malta–Alexandria |
| 660 | 4 | 21. 4.43 | For disposal 2.46 |
| 661 | 18 | 5.43 | For disposal 6.46 |
| 662 | 9 | 8. 4.43 | For disposal 2.46 |
| 663 | 15 | 8. 3.43 | Mined 10.10.44 in the Adriatic |

MGBs continued at no 674

**MTBs continued**

| No | Builder | Completed | Fate |
|---|---|---|---|
| 664 | 7T | 1. 4.43 | To RAF 1.44 = LRRC021 1945 |
| 665 | 11 | 5. 5.43 | Sunk 15.8.43 by shore batteries at Messina |
| 666 | 9 | 10. 6.43 | Sunk 4/5.7.44 in action off IJmuiden |
| 667 | 12 | 28.12.42 | For disposal 9.45 to 7.46 in the Mediterranean |
| 668 | 24 | 26. 3.43 | To SCC 12.45 |
| 669 | 14 | 29. 4.43 | Sunk 26.10.43 in action off Norway |
| 670 | 27 | 7. 3.43 | Lost 30.1.46 on passage Malta-Alexandria |
| 671 | 7B | 16. 5.43 | Sunk 24.4.44 in action off Cape Barfleur |
| 672 | 21 | 4.43 | For disposal 10.45 |
| 673 | 25 | 6.43 | To RAF 1945 = LRRC022 |

MTBs continued at no 675

**MGBs continued**

| No | Builder | Completed | Fate |
|---|---|---|---|
| 674 | 25 | 6. 5.43 | For disposal 6.46 |

**MTBs continued**

| No | Builder | Completed | Fate |
|---|---|---|---|
| 675 | 18 | 7.43 | To RAF 5.45 = LRRC023 |
| 676 | 17 | 13. 5.43 | To RAF 6.45 = LRRC024 |
| 677 | 10 | 5.43 | To RAF 6.45 = LRRC025 |
| 678 | 3 | 7.43 | To RAF 6.45 = LRRC026 |
| 679 | 7B | 7.43 | To RAF 6.45 = LRRC027 |
| 680 | 17 | 4.43 | To RAF 6.45 = LRRC028 |
| 681 | 4 | 20. 7.43 | Sunk 10.6.44 in action off the Dutch coast. |
| 682 | 27 | 5.43 | To RAF .45 = LRRC029 |
| 683 | 21 | 7.43 | To RAF 5.45 = LRRC030 |
| 684 | 28 | 28. 4.43 | To RAF .45 = LRRC031 |
| 685 | 9 | 7.43 | For disposal 4.49 |
| 686 | 15 | 9. 6.43 | Lost 22.11.43 by fire at Lerwick |
| 687 | 11 | 31. 7.43 | Paid off 24.10.44 for transfer to RAF = LRRC032 |

*LRRCs 001 and 003 alongside at Newlyn, early in 1946.* Courtesy John Pritchard

| No | Builder | Completed | Fate |
|---|---|---|---|
| 688 | 7T | 7.43 | RNN 8.43–1944; to RAF 1945 = LRRC = LRRC034 |
| 689 | 10 | 7.43 | To RAF 6.45 = LRRC033 |
| 690 | 3 | 15. 9.43 | Lost 18.1.45 in collision with wreck, North Sea |
| 691 | 18 | 8.43 | To RAF 5.45 = LRRC035 |
| 692 | 14 | 7.43 | To RAF 1945 = LRRC036 |
| 693 | 12 | 5.43 | To RAF 5.45 = LRRC037 |
| 694 | 24 | 26. 7.43 | To RAF 5.45 = LRRC038 |
| 695 | 4 | 30.10.43 | To RAF 1945 = LRRC039 |
| 696 | 13 | 15. 4.44 | For disposal 10.45 |
| 697 | 28 | 7.43 | Mined 17.4.45 in the Adriatic |
| 698 | 27 | 7.43 | Lost 30.1.46 on passage Malta–Alexandria |
| 699 | 9 | 10.43 | For disposal 10.45 to 7.46, Mediterranean |
| 700 | 15 | 7.43 | Lost 30.1.46 on passage Malta–Alexandria |

**23 ordered 7.4.42**

| No | Builder | Completed | Fate |
|---|---|---|---|
| 701 | 26 | 10.43 | To SCC Bideford 1946 |
| 702 | 11 | 31.10.43 | To STT 1946 |
| 703 | 25 | 8.10.43 | For disposal 9.45 to 7.46, Mediterranean |
| 704 | 15 | 11.43 | RNN 12.44; for disposal 1946 |
| 705 | 17 | 7. 8.43 | Mined 23.3.45 in the Adriatic |
| 706 | 17 | 10.43 | For disposal 9.45 to 7.46, Mediterranean |
| 707 | 3 | 11.43 | Lost 18.4.44 in collision with L'Escarmouche north of Ireland |
| 708 | 10 | 11.43 | Scuttled 5.5.44 after bombing in error by Allied aircraft in the Channel |
| 709 | 7T | 2.44 | RNN 1944–45; for disposal 1.47 |
| 710 | 15 | 18. 9.43 | Mined 10.4.45 in the Adriatic |
| 711 | 4 | 2. 4.44 | RNN Hauk 1944–46; for disposal 1947 |
| 712 | 27 | 10. 2.44 | RNN 1944–7.45; CTL 25.1.45 by grounding in Scottish waters; for disposal 7.45 |
| 713 | 9 | 10.12.43 | RNN 1944; sold Norway 1946 |
| 714 | 7B | 10.43 | To SCC 4.46; sold 18.11.55 |
| 715 | 28 | 9.12.43 | RNN 1944; lost 19.5.45 by explosion at Fosnavaag, Norway |
| 716 | 21 | 4.44 | RNN 1944; sold to Norway 1946 |
| 717 | 7B | 1. 2.44 | RNN .44; sold Norway 1946 |
| 718 | 18 | 3.44 | To SCC Tyne 1946 |
| 719 | 14 | 2.44 | RNN 1944; sold Norway 1946 |
| 720 | 12 | 11.43 | RNN 1944; sold Norway 1946 |
| 721 | 5 | 15.10.43 | RNN 1944; sold Norway 1946 |
| 722 | 24 | 3.44 | RNN 1944; sold Norway 1946 |
| 723 | 11 | 27. 4.44 | RNN 1944; sold Norway 1946 |

**48 ordered 30.8.42**

| No | Builder | Completed | Fate |
|---|---|---|---|
| 724 | 27 | 7. 9.43 | To SCC Norwich 12.45; sold 24.7.54 |
| 725 | 3 | 3.44 | To SCC Pwllheli 10.45; sold 12.9.51 |
| 726 | 7B | 2. 3.44 | RCN 3.44–5.45; SCC Wisbech 7.46; sold by 1950 |
| 727 | 10 | 27. 2.44 | RCN 2.44–6.45; SCC Twickenham 1946; sold 20.12.51 |
| 728 | 15 | 21.12.43 | To SCC Cardigan 1946; sold 1948 |
| 729 | 4 | 7.44 | Sold 21.9.47 |
| 730 | 28 | 28. 4.44 | To SCC 4.46; sold 27.5.58 |
| 731 | 18 | 7.44 | = MTB3001 1949 = MASB3001 1953; SCC Birkenhead 10.57 |
| 732 | 9 | 17. 4.44 | Sunk in error 28.5.44 by La Combattante in action in the Channel |
| 733 | 14 | 8. 6.44 | To SCC Plymouth 3/46 |
| 734 | 24 | 30. 5.44 | Bombed in error 26.6.44 by Allied aircraft off Normandy and scuttled |
| 735 | 25 | 26. 2.44 | RCN 2.44–5.45; SCC Ellesmere 1.46; sold 14.6.56 |
| 736 | 25 | 4.44 | RCN 4.44–5.45; SCC Fraserburgh 7.46 |
| 737 | 8 | 5.44 | Lent Brighton Nautical Training College 1945 |
| 738 | 17 | 15.12.43 | To SCC Ipswich 1.46; sold 25.4.58 |
| 739 | 29 | 27. 4.44 | = MTB3039 1949; for disposal 4.52 |
| 740 | 6 | 8. 8.44 | To SCC Norwich 1946 |
| 741 | 7T | 7.44 | To SCC Goole 1946; sold 26.11.57 |
| 742 | 20 | 4.44 | To SCC Parkeston 2.46 |
| 743 | 1 | 13. 4.44 | RCN 3.44–5.45; lent Sea Scouts 1946; sold 23.1.57 |
| 744 | 17 | 3.44 | RCN 3.44–5.44; to RAF 1945 = LRRC040 |
| 745 | 2 | 29. 1.44 | RCN 1.44–5.45; to STT 1946; for disposal 1946 |

*FPB 5001 (ex-MTB 780) in June 1954, fitted as a control ship for Coastal Forces. Her armament consists of two 40mm Bofors Mark VII mountings and a twin 20mm Mark 12A mounting.*
Wright & Logan

| No | Builder | Completed | Fate |
|---|---|---|---|
| 746 | 21 | 19. 5.44 | RCN 5.44–5.45; SCC Gloucester 12.45; sold 20.5.55 |
| 747 | 23 | 6.44 | To SCC 3.46; sold 19.2.58 |
| 748 | 15 | 19. 2.44 | RCN 2.44–5.45; SCC Barnes 3.46; sold 1953 |
| 749 | 15 | 4. 4.44 | To STT 1946 |
| 750 | 7B | 5.44 | = MTB3002 1949 = MASB3002 1953; to SCC 1956; sold 1967 |
| 751 | 27 | 25. 5.44 | To SCC Poplar 10.45; sold 23.1.57 |
| 752 | 9 | 6.44 | To SCC 10.45 |
| 753 | 3 | 7.44 | To SCC Bermondsey 11.45; sold 22.10.56 |
| 754 | 22 | 12.44 | To SCC Connahs Quay 5.46; sold 17.9.54 |
| 755 | 26 | 9.44 | To SCC Scarborough; sold 13.10.55 |
| 756 | 29 | 31. 7.44 | To SCC Hull 1.46; sold 8.11.54 |
| 757 | 11 | 29. 6.44 | To SCC Worcester 1.46; sold 25.1.52 |
| 758 | 18 | 10.44 | = MTB5031 1949; sold 14.6.56 |
| 759 | 28 | 7.44 | To SCC Barnstaple 4.46; sold 25.11.54 |
| 760 | 10 | 6.44 | To SCC Bristol 4.46; sold 18.9.58 |
| 761 | 1 | 9. 8.44 | To SCC Chelmsford 1.46; sold 25.3.63 |
| 762 | 4 | 6.10.44 | For disposal 10.45 |
| 763 | 5 | 6.44 | To SCC Stockton 1.46; sold 17.5.56 |
| 764 | 21 | 9.44 | For disposal 5.46 |
| 765 | 16 | 30.10.44 | To SCC Sunbury 12.45; sold 22.2.55 |
| 766 | 27 | 10. 8.44 | To SCC Clydebank .46; sold 10.2.55 |
| 767 | 3 | 19.12.44 | For disposal 1.47 |
| 768 | 24 | 26. 8.44 | To SCC Newark 12.45; sold 30.11.55 |
| 769 | 12 | 6.44 | To SCC Fareham 1946; sold 24.4.56 |
| 770 | 19 | 11.12.44 | To SCC Cleethorpes 4.46; sold 26.11.57 |
| 771 | 7B | 5. 8.44 | To SCC Southend 1946; sold 25.11.54 |

**58 ordered 26.3.43**

| No | Builder | Completed | Fate |
|---|---|---|---|
| 772 | 17 | 12. 7.44 | To SCC Chelsea 1.46; sold 29.4.55 |
| 773 | 2 | 29. 6.44 | To STT 1946; for disposal 10.47 |
| 774 | 23 | 11.44 | Sold 1948 |
| 775 | 10 | 8.44 | To SCC 12.45; sold 17.9.54 |
| 776 | 14 | 8.44 | Lost 14.2.45 by fire and explosion in Ostend harbour |
| 777 | 7B | 21.10.44 | To SCC Peterborough 1946; sold 15.11.51 |
| 778 | 9 | 11.44 | To SCC Purfleet 1946; sold 25.7.55 |
| 779 | 28 | 16.10.44 | = MTB 5032 1949; sold 16.1.55 |
| 780 | 13 | 11. 1.45 | = MTB 5001 1949; sold 23.10.57 |
| 781 | 8 | 11.44 | To SCC Penarth 4.46; sold 22.7.52 |
| 782 | 27 | 25.10.44 | Mined 29.12.44 off the Schelde |
| 783 | 5 | 7.45 | Sold 1947 |
| 784 | 25 | 29. 9.44 | Sold 7.1.48 |
| 785 | 4 | 12. 3.45 | = MTB 5033 1949; sold 17.10.55 |
| 786 | 22 | 12. 7.45 | Sold 1949 |
| 787 | 15 | 6.44 | = MTB 5034 1949; sold 17.6.49 |
| 788 | 11 | 127. 2.45 | Lent Sea Scouts 1946; sold 18.6.55 |
| 789 | 17 | 17.10.44 | Lost 14.2.45 by fire and explosion at Ostend |
| 790 | 3 | 7.45 | = MTB 5003(ii) 1949; sold 25.11.53 |
| 791 | 24 | 4.11.44 | Lost 14.2.45 by fire and explostion at Ostend |
| 792 | 25 | 1. 3.45 | Sold 7.1.48 |
| 793 | 18 | 5. 3.45 | = MTB 5035 1949; sold 25.4.58 |
| 794 | 29 | 22.12.44 | = MTB 5036 1949; sold 24.4.58 |
| 795 | 15 | 8.44 | = MTB 5037 1949; for disposal 1952 |
| 796 | 20 | 31.10.44 | Lent Sea Scouts 1946; sold 7.54 |
| 797 | 7T | 1.45 | RCN 12.44–5.45; for disposal 1947 |
| 798 | 2 | 16.10.44 | Lost 14.2.45 by fire and explosion at Ostend |
| 799 | 16 | 6.45 | To RAF 7.45 = LRRC001 |
| 800 | 9 | 7.45 | To RAF 7.45 = LRRC002 |
| 5001 | 28 | 18.12.44 | Sunk 6/7.4.45 in action, North Sea |
| 5002 | 27 | 12.44 | Sold 1957 |
| 5003 | 21 | 7.45 | Sold 8.3.48 |
| 5004 | 21 | 9.45 | To RAF 9.45 = LRRC003, SCC Sittingbourne 1949; sold 6.56 |
| 5005 | 15 | 7.11.44 | Sold 28.2.52 |
| 5006 | 3 | 8.45 | To RAF 8.45 = LRRC004 |
| 5007 | 10 | 3.45 | Sold 17.11.50 |

*LRRC 001 leaving Newlyn for the last time on her way to be sold.* Courtesy John Pritchard

| No | Builder | Completed | Fate |
|---|---|---|---|
| 5008 | 12 | 6.45 | Sold 20.7.56 |
| 5009 | 14 | 5. 4.45 | Sold 17.3.56 |
| 5010 | 7B | 1.45 | = MTB 3050 1949 = MASB 3050 1953; sold 20.7.55 |
| 5011 | 24 | 28. 3.45 | = LRRC005 3.45 |
| 5012 | 2 | 3.45 | = LRRC006 3.45 |
| 5013 | 17 | 3.45 | = MTB 3053 1949 = MASB 3053 1953; to SCC 1957; sold 3.69 |
| 5014 | 28 | 3.45 | To RAF 3.45 = LRRC007 |
| 5015 | 5 | 3.45 | Sold 23.10.57 |
| 5016 | 27 | 3.45 | To RAF 3.45 = LRRC008 |
| 5017 | 7T | 7.45 | To RAF 7.45 = LRRC009 |
| 5018 | 18 | 7.45 | To RAF 7.45 = LRRC010 |
| 5019 | 17 | 13. 4.45 | To RAF 4.45 = LRRC011 |
| 5020 | 15 | 12.44 | For disposal 12.56; sold 18.9.58 |
| 5021 | 11 | 9. 7.45 | To RAF 7.45 = LRRC012 |
| 5022 | 25 | 19. 4.45 | To RAF 4.45 = LRRC013 |
| 5023 | 10 | 14. 7.45 | To RAF 7.45 = LRRC014, to SCC 1948; sold 18.9.58 |
| 5024 | 7B | 5. 5.45 | To RAF 5.45 = LRRC015 |
| 5025 | 27 | 8.45 | To RAF 8.45 = LRRC016 |
| 5026 | 15 | 17. 3.45 | To RAF 3.45 = IRRC017 |
| 5027 | 17 | — | Cancelled 12.44 |
| 5028 | 28 | 5.45 | To RAF 5.45 = LRRC018 |
| 5029 | 24 | 12. 7.45 | To RAF 7.45 = LRRC019 |

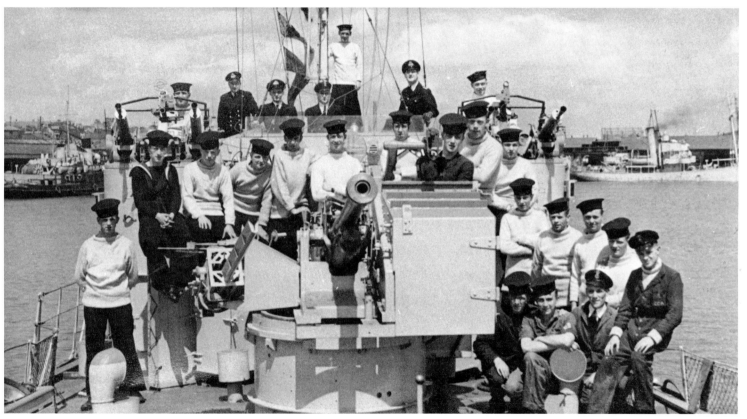

*This is their home; the ship's company of MGB 768 gathered round the forward 6-pounder in the autumn of 1944.* Courtesy Malcolm Boast (this was his father's boat)

# The Fairmile F type MGB 2001

By late 1941, in the light of operational experience gained with the Fairmile D, it was obvious that the maximum speed of about 31 knots would be decreased as more and more weight was added in the shape of weapons and operational equipment, and therefore that more powerful main engines were required.

The 12-cylinder Packard 4M 2500 supplied under Lend-Lease from America was rated at 1200hp at 2400rpm, and it was felt that the design was not capable of much greater power without re-design. The radical alternative proposal was made that a current radial aircraft engine should be used. These engines were much more powerful, and though they were air cooled, they were light and compact and the problems of engine cooling did not seem insurmountable.

After discussion, it was decided to test the 18-cylinder Bristol Centaurus, which was then under development for the next generation of heavy fighter for the Royal Air Force. The Centaurus had first run in July 1935 and had been type-tested in 1939 at 2000hp. It had been overlooked by the Air Ministry until 1943, despite the fact that the Centaurus 4S prototype reached a speed of 421mph in a Hawker Tornado in October 1941. By late 1942 the two-speed supercharged development was type tested at 2375hp and cleared for production as the Mark V, with the Mark XI at 2520hp.

Fairmile decided that an engineering test bed vessel, based on the hull of the D type, was sufficient for a trial, and design went ahead. The Air Ministry, however, was not happy that the navy should make first use of the new power unit, since few of the Centaurus engines were then obtainable. It was therefore decided, as an interim measure, to use the 1350hp Hercules radial engine from the same Bristol stable. The Hercules had fourteen cylinders with a cubic capacity of 2360cu in (as opposed to the larger 3270cu in of the Centaurus) and had first run in January 1936. The prototype produced 1290hp and its development had continued. On 87 octane fuel the Hercules produced 1425hp, and on 100 octane, 1590hp (the RN used 100 octane fuel aboard MTBs).

The Hercules was in full production, and in squadron service, being fitted to the twin-engined Beaufighter, the Short Stirling (the RAF's first four engined bomber), and the then mainstay of Bomber Command, the Halifax. It was also used in the Short Sunderland flying boat. For Fairmile's purposes, the engine was sound and proven.

MGB 2001, as the prototype was numbered, was ordered on 7 April 1942 from Kris Cruisers (1934) Ltd at Isleworth, near Cobham; the company had already constructed Fairmile B, C and D types, so was fully conversant with Fairmile methods. Her keel was laid on 6 June. The engineroom layout was a new venture, with air cooling required in volume, but it was felt that all problems could be resolved by the time the larger engine became available.

MGB 2001 completed on 26 April 1944, a building time of 98 weeks, and the engineroom arrangements proved successful, despite large upper deck air intakes and exhausts trunked to provide the huge volume of cooling air. The cooling fan required over 400hp alone. The noise of all fifty-six cylinders at full throttle is difficult to imagine, as is the solution of the silencing problems.

No drawings of MGB 2001 are known to exist, and photographs are very rare. One photograph taken with a pocket camera, contrary to wartime instructions, is reproduced here, but details of the boat are very indistinct. The drawings of the Fairmile collection at Woolwich Arsenal, part of the National Maritime Museum collection, contain no details of MGB 2001 at all.

The records indicate that MGB 2001 was designed to be 80 tons displacement, but completed overweight at 99 tons. Her length overall was 115ft, and her beam 21ft 3in, as for the D type. Armed as a gunboat, she mounted one 6-pounder forward, a 2-pounder pom-pom in a power mounting aft, two single 20mm Oerlikons and two .5in twins in Mark V power-operated mountings. Two twin .303in Vickers gas-operated machine guns were sided on the bridge wings.

Her four Bristol Hercules radial engines of 6600 hp (an increase of 1800hp over the D type) gave a top speed of 30 knots, but no doubt problems with the installation remained to be solved. MGB 2001 was never operational and was palced on the disposal list in June 1945. What the potential of four Centaurus Mark VI supercharged engines of 2520hp each, giving a total of 10,080hp, could have been is not known, but a likely speed would have been in the region of 34–36 knots.

The developed engine was used in the RAF's Tempest Mark II, as well as in the Fleet Air Arm's Hawker Sea Fury, which saw service in Korea, and also in the Firebrand torpedo bomber.

The disposal of MGB 2001 was not the end of the attempt to use air-cooled aero engines in fast warship types. In 1947 a smaller but similar vessel was completed for the Bristol Aeroplane Company. Unarmed and designed as an air sea rescue launch named *Celerity*, she too was powered by four Bristol Hercules 1630bhp radial engines. Designed by Fred Cooper, she was also built by Kris Cruisers. *Celerity* was 105ft long, with a beam of 22ft, and displaced 80 tons. Her hard-chine hull was constructed of double-diagonal mahogany with an outer skin of hiduminium – a light alloy of aluminium, magnesium and manganese – which was also used in her superstructure for lightness. She had a maximum speed of 40 knots, and a cruising range of 4200 miles was expected from her trials. Despite its potential, however, this private-venture design failed to arouse sufficient Admiralty interest to result in an order.

*The only photograph I can find of MGB 2001 – the Fairmile F – taken in 1944 from a 2½ × 1½ snapshot. She is the centre boat in the background.* Author's collection

# The Fairmile H type LCI (S) and LCS (L) (2)

In 1942, when the whole of Western Europe was occupied by Axis forces, it was felt that comparatively large-scale Commando type raids from a base in Britain would be a useful means of probing enemy defences and tying down additional troops. Various ideas were therefore put forward for a 'giant raiding craft', as the ideal transport for such raids was then envisaged.

Inevitably at that period of the war, no additional shipbuilding capacity was available, so that construction of the raiding craft could not be undertaken when the proposal was first mooted.

In April 1942, however, a firm requirement was produced for a craft to carry 200 fully equipped troops, compared with the thirty-five men carried in the current LCA (Landing Craft Attack). The new design was to have a speed of 17 knots (as against the LCA's 8 knots) and beaching draughts not much greater than those of the present craft.

The Thornycroft Company had earlier made investigations into wooden landing craft, but it was agreed that steel hulls would be required in order to combine the requirements of load and shallow draught. The use of steel, however, would have come into conflict with the construction of destroyers, both planned and building.

American help was therefore sought, and before the end of the year a design for the new type LCI(L) – Landing Craft Infantry (Large) – had been produced in the United States. This design was based on the original drawings prepared in the UK to the original requirements, and the craft proved ideal for the future operational use, both in European and Far Eastern waters.

At the same time, British staff requirements were reduced to suit British construction capacity, in order that an alternative, smaller design should be available which nevertheless still fulfilled the basic requirements of the original proposal. To this end, the assistance of the Fairmile Company was sought, and Fairmile produced the H type from their offices. Typical Fairmile construction techniques were used, with all items, as usual, prefabricated. The scantlings were in some cases reduced from those then fitted in coastal forces craft, but it was felt that the new vessel, being much more sedate in performance, would not be subjected to the pounding and stress so typical in MTBs and MGBs. The deck and sides were planked in sheets of plywood, laid double diagonal. In spite of the comparative lightness of the hull, the vessel was built to carry a very heavy load of personnel, as well as a considerable weight of protection in the shape of ¼in DIHT steel sheeting fitted as scales.

In a few cases the scantlings were found wanting, but in general the craft did all that was required of them. They were not designed to beach themselves, but did so on occasion with no ill effects. The

## Fairmile H type data

### LCI (S)

**Description**  Medium-sized British infantry carrier designed for raiding operations. Wooden hull and general design were the same as LCS (L), with troops disembarking over four bow ramps or gangways. Stowage for eighteen bicycles on deck.

**Numbers**  501–540

**Dimensions**  Length overall 105ft 1in, beam 21ft 4in; draught 2ft 10in forward, 3ft 8in aft (loaded).

**Displacement**  63 tons (light), 100 tons (loaded).

**Machinery**  Two 1120hp or 1500hp supercharged Hall-Scott petrol engines. Silencers fitted. Twin screws.

**Speed**  15 knots maximum at 2000rpm, 13.25 knots continuous at 1600rpm.

**Range**  550 nautical miles at 15 knots, 700 at 12.5 knots.

**Fuel capacity**  4000 gallons

**Crew**  Two officers and fifteen men, with accommodation.

**Capacity**  Six officers and ninety-six men, fully equipped, below deck.

**Armament**  Two 20mm Oerlikons (or more), two .303 Lewis guns.

**Armour**  10lb DIHT plating to deck sides, gun positions, generator house and forward bulkhead, ¼in plate to bridge.

**Losses**  511, 512, 517, 524, 531, 532, 537 and 540.

### LCS (L) (2)

**Description**  Support craft designed to accompany landing craft in long-range operations. Hull and many details were the same as LCI (S); the craft was, however, not intended to beach.

**Numbers**  251–260.

**Dimensions**  Length overall 105ft 1in, beam 21ft 5in; draught 2ft 3in forward, 3ft 0in aft (light), 3ft 8in forward, 3ft 4in aft (loaded).

**Displacement**  84 tons (light), 116 tons (loaded).

**Machinery**  Two Hall-Scott petrol engines (some supercharged). 31in screws.

**Speed**  14.75 knots.

**Range**  700 nautical miles at 12.5 knots.

**Fuel capacity**  4000 gallons.

**Crew**  Two officers and twenty-three men, with accommodation.

**Armament**  One 6-pounder in a tank turret, two 20mm Oerlikons, one twin .5in PO Vickers machine gun, two .303in Lewis guns, one 4in smoke mortar.

**Armour**  10lb DIHT plating to deck, hull sides and gun positions; ¼in plating to bridge.

**Losses**  252, 256 and 258.

hull sides, bridge and gun positions were protected, and the troop spaces were completely enclosed rather than open to the elements as in previous landing craft. Disembarkation was made easier and more rapid by four brows or gangways which were easily rolled over the bow. Eighteen pedal cycles were stowed on the upper deck to allow troops some mobility ashore. Two 20mm Oerlikons amidships provided some covering fire against aircraft and light vehicles

*LCI(S) 501 – the Fairmile H type. Capacity was*
*six officers and ninety-six fully equipped troops,*
*disembarking over four bow ramps.*
Imperial War Museum

on shore, later units had two additional 20mm Oerlikons mounted further aft, and the troops embarked carried their own personal weapons.

Ten units were converted while under construction to Landing Craft, Support (Large) (Mark 2). The earlier LCS(L) 1 had been provided with a 2-pounder gun in a tank turret, and this weapon had been found to lack the required firepower. In order to provide some fire support at close range, particularly when enemy tanks were feared before our Allied tanks could be landed, the new LCS(L) 2 was armed with the more potent 6-pounder in a tank turret, as well as two single 20mm Oerlikons behind armoured bulwarks and twin power-operated .5in Vickers machine guns aft, with a 4in smoke mortar sited well forward.

No records are available of building dates for these minor craft, but the first order was placed in May 1942 and the first boat was delivered by February the next year. As was usual with Fairmile designs, they were constructed from kits, assembled in smaller British boatyards.

Although they were designed as infantry assault vessels or gun support craft, the Fairmile Hs were also used in a number of other roles, such as supply-carrying and casualty evacuation, and others were equipped with CSA to lay smoke screens.

Of the first group, one was lost in home waters, five at Normandy, one at Walcheren and another in a location not stated. Of the ten conversions, one was lost in home waters and three at Walcheren.

*The LCS(L) (2), converted to carry gun armament to support landing craft in long-range operations, but not intended to beach.* Imperial War Museum

## Construction list

| Builder | Number |
|---|---|
| Austins of East Ham Ltd, London (Yard: Twinn Wharf, Abbey Road, Barking) | 507, 251, 257 and 260 (4) |
| Brook Marine Ltd, Oulton Broad, Lowestoft, Norfolk | 512, 513, 514, 515, 255, 538, 539 and 534 (8) |
| Cadnell Brothers, Riverside Estate, Maylandsea, Althorne, near Chelmsford | 502 and 523 (2) |
| Collins Pleasurecraft Company Ltd, Oulton Broad, nr Lowestoft, Norfolk | 520 and 532 (2) |
| Frank Curtis Ltd, Looe, Cornwall | 503, 508, 516, 519, 521, 527, 528 and 529 (8) |
| A M Dickie & Sons, Bangor, North Wales | 254 (1) |
| J S Doig (Grimsby) Ltd, Grimsby Docks | 510 and 531 (2) |
| Itchenor Shipyard Ltd, Itchenor, near Chichester | 526 (1) |
| Leo A Robinson, Broadside Launch Works, Oulton Broad, nr Lowestoft, Norfolk | 511 and 533 (2) |
| John Sadd & Sons Ltd, Maldon, Essex | 505 and 256 (2) |
| Solent Shipyards Ltd, Bursledon Bridge, Sarisbury Green, Hants | 506, 252, 258 and 536 (4) |
| Southampton Steam Joinery Company Ltd, Southampton | 518 (1) |
| Thomson and Balfour, Victoria Saw Mills, Bo'ness | 509 and 524 (2) |
| H T Percival, Yacht Station, Horning, Norfolk | 253, 259 and 537 (3) |
| W Weatherhead and Sons, West Harbour, Cockenzie | 504, 517, 522, 530, 535 and 540 (6) |

**Opposite: Fairmile H type LCI (S) general arrangement, internal profile and plan below decks**

| | |
|---|---|
| 1 | Steering gear compartment |
| 2 | Generator room |
| 3 | WC |
| 4 | Engineroom |
| 5 | Fuel tank compartment |
| 6 | Hall-Scott petrol engine |
| 7 | Generator set |
| 8 | Fuel tanks, 500gal each |
| 9 | 20mm ready use ammunition lockers |
| 10 | Wardroom (eight to ten officers) |
| 11 | Galley |
| 12 | Radio room |
| 13 | Stowage for twelve cycles |
| 14 | Cork floatnets |
| 15 | Sickbay and troops |
| 16 | Messdeck (forty troops) |
| 17 | Messdeck (twenty-nine troops) |
| 18 | Bridge |
| 19 | Compass |
| 20 | Ship's wheel |
| 21 | 20mm Oerlikon mounting |
| 22 | 18in vent |
| 23 | 9in vent |
| 24 | Fresh water tanks, 100 gal each |
| 25 | Engineroom and NCOs' mess |
| 26 | Disembarkation hatch |
| 27 | Landing gangway, 30ft × 2ft |
| 28 | Armoured bulkhead |
| 29 | Bosun's store |
| 30 | Forepeak |
| 31 | Washdeck locker |
| 32 | Spare gear locker |
| 33 | Warping winch |
| 34 | Chemical smoke aparatus |
| 35 | Provision room |
| 36 | Twin rudders |
| 37 | Dumbflow silencer |
| 38 | Watchkeeper's desk |
| 39 | Bollards |
| 40 | Conning tower (later reduced) |
| 41 | Pole mast |

**Opposite: Fairmile H type LCS (L) (2) sheer elevation**

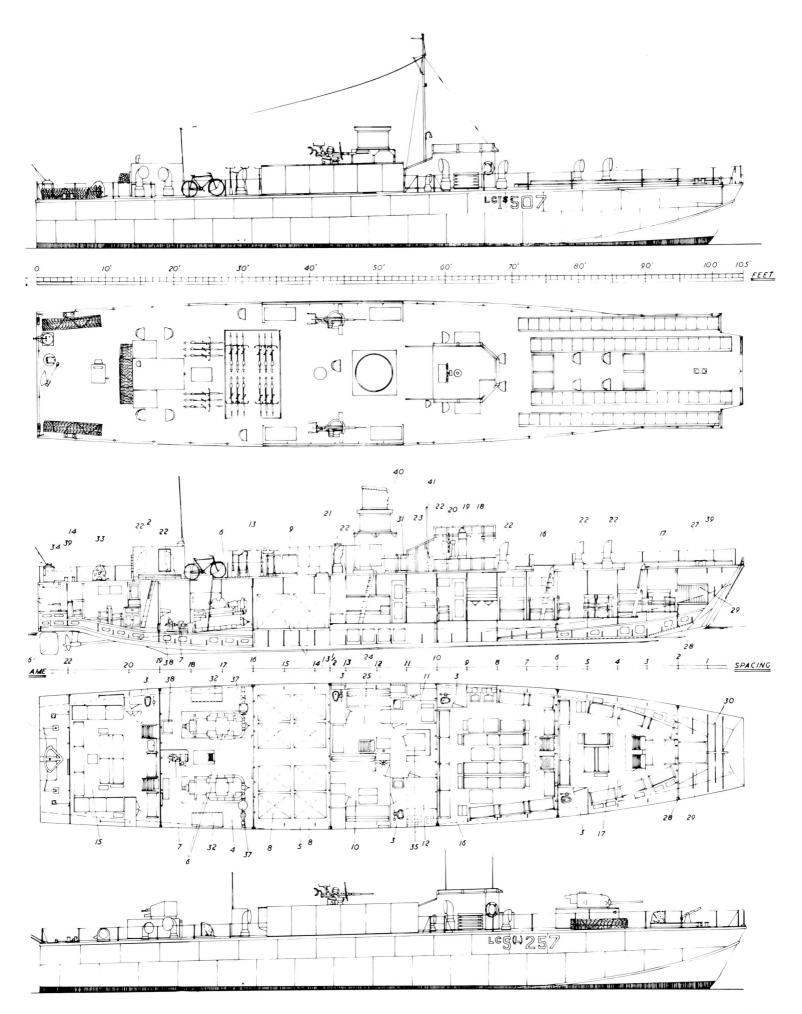

LCI$507

0    10'    20'    30'    40'    50'    60'    70'    80'    90'    100'  105'    _FEET_

40  41

14  22 2  22    6   13   9   21  22  31 23 22 20 19 18  22  16  22  22  17  27 39

34 39  33

29

28

6  22   20  19 38 7 18  17  16  15  14 13½ 13  24 12  11  10  9  8  7  6  5  4  3  2  1   SPACING

AME

3 38  32 37    2 25  11  3    30

15    7  32 4 37  8  5 8   10   3  35 12  16    3  17    28  29
6

LCS(4)257

127

# The 72ft harbour defence motor launch

The 72ft HDML has been included here even though it was conceived before the Fairmile organisation was properly in being, because it nevertheless was an important naval motor launch type. The HDML was constructed using normal shipbuilding practice, rather than from prefabricated kits in the manner of the other Fairmile ML types

In late 1939 the Admiralty prepared the design of a small wooden motor launch which, armed with depth charges, asdic (sonar) and a small gun, would be used to protect estuaries and harbours against infiltration by enemy submarines.

The Admiralty requirements were for a craft not exceeding 72ft in length, and thus capable of being shipped abroad as deck cargo for operations wherever such vessels were required, particularly in less hostile holding operations.

The design was of round bilge form with the hull subdivided into eight watertight compartments, with the short hull having two underslung rudders for maximum manoeuvrability against an underwater target in a confined area.

The HDMLs were to be driven by two diesel engines, and a number of different makes were used: Buda Lanova, Gleniffer, Hercules, Gray, Gardner, or – as shown in these drawings – Thornycroft designs. The horsepower was from 130 to 150 each, depending upon make, which gave a maximum speed of 11 to 12 knots on a displacement of some 46 to 54 tons.

Hull construction was of double diagonal planking with formed transverse timbers, outside longitudinal stringers and reinforcing timbers at intervals inside the stringers. This system of framing proved to be both strong and very resilient, verified by the fact that a small number of HDMLs are still in existence as yachts.

Early boats were planked with mahogany, but when this became scarce it was necessary to use larch for planking, which in some cases led to leaky boats (and was specially subject to dry rot). The use of larch was discontinued as soon as the supply of mahogany improved.

Asdic was to be standard equipment, and in general the class was armed with a single 3-pounder Mark I mounting or the 2-pounder sub-calibre gun, carried forward of the bridge. Later, when supply became easier for the RN, and with both home-built and US Lend-Lease guns available, a single 20mm Oerlikon mounting was also carried aft. Early units had whatever could be found for close-range defence, usually one or two .303in Lewis guns or a stripped Lewis on a pedestal mount, or .303in Hotchkiss guns. Later, again as supply improved, two twin .303in Vickers gas-operated mountings were also carried in the bridge wings. Later again the armament was further improved by the retrofitting of a second 20mm forward. Other boats carried a 2-pounder Mark IIC mounting, a weapon dating from between the wars.

The normal offensive punch was eight depth charges, which were dropped over the sides from the standard depth charge chute. A box of grenades was usually carried on the upper deck for close defence, to prevent boarders.

The main fuel tanks held 1250 gallons in four tanks situated forward of the engineroom, combined with 300 gallons in the en-

*ML 1031 in September 1940, armed with a 3-pounder Mark I forward, a .303in Hotchkiss gun aft and eight depth charges. Note the reduced open bridge of the early units.* Imperial War Museum

*HDML 1221 in August 1943, with a 2-pounder forward and a 20mm Oerlikon aft. She was one of eight units rigged for sailing to increase range.*
Imperial War Museum

gineroom tanks, giving an endurance of about 2000 miles at 10 knots, and deck tanks could be fitted to extend ferry range.

Accommodation was provided for two officers, two petty officers and eight ratings. The wheelhouse in early units was fitted with protective plating, but later units had their bridge armoured instead of the wheelhouse.

Orders for these yacht-type craft were placed only with boatyards that were well equipped, as with the exception of such fittings as shaft brackets, steering gear, rudders and naval equipment such as asdic, radio and weapons, the builder was required to produce the whole ship.

The HDMLs proved to be excellent sea boats, and the large numbers produced were in use in every war theatre, in general for similar duties to those of the larger Fairmile B class motor launches. Designed by J W 'Bill' Holt, they were a very successful and pleasing craft. In his postwar reading of the papers on Coastal Force Design at the spring meeting of the eighty-eighth session of the Institution of Naval Architects, held on 27 March 1947, Bill Holt was full of praise for the success of the design, which was obviously one of his favourites, and of which he was justifiably proud.

In a seaway the HDMLs seemed to possess an unusual harmony of weight, form, bouyancy and hull shape in relation to pitching and speed, which enabled them to move in rhythm with the sea, and to make the very best of prevailing conditions.

Some 486 units were ordered during the war, and in general there were few visual differences. The bridge was lengthened after early boats were completed, and obviously, with some fifty-seven different builders undertaking their construction in all the Allied nations, there were small local variations in material and some equipment.

Early units were shipped abroad to their new operational areas, but with the loss of shipping from torpedo attack by U-boats, and the lack of suitable deckspace, arrangements were soon put in hand for them to proceed on their own keels, normally in groups or flotillas. Those destined for service in the Mediterranean or tropical stations were copper bottomed during building, while those that were to serve in Iceland were provided with additional insulation and heating. They made these journeys under their own steam.

Eight HDMLs were required for service in the West Indies, and, to ensure that they could make the long haul from the Cape Verde Islands to the USA, they were provided with an outfit of sails. Two tabernacle masts were fitted. The foremast carried a standing lug and jib, with the mizzen mast a standing lug. A large square sail

was also provided for running before the wind. This long passage was never made, however, as those particular boats joined the forces engaged in the North African landings after their arrival at Gibraltar.

Later, as D-Day for the Allied landings on the French mainland approached, there was an urgent need for inshore minesweepers to operate off the invasion beaches, and many HDMLs were fitted to tow one leg of an Oropesa wire sweep, to make safe passage for larger craft in more sheltered waters.

Others were fitted as navigational leaders to assist groups of landing craft to locate their correct beach or landing area, and were fitted with radar and other navigational equipment towards this end. ML 1407 was one so equipped. She was originally completed at McLean's yard at Renfrew in December 1943. In March 1944 she was converted to a navigational leader by Power Boats at Poole, to be ready for D-Day.

Alterations included the installation of radar (type 291U), type 253 IFF transponder, radar cabin, QH2 (tree) extra W/T, more advanced asdic with a repeater on the bridge, Chernikeeff log, echo sounder, fighting lights and plenty of splinter mats. A wooden high chair was built on the bridge for the senior officer. The wheelhouse and all doors were fitted with blackout curtains. As built, ML 1407 had a 2-pounder gun forward, but this was changed for a single 20mm Oerlikon. Small depth charges were carried, and were later used to attack the small Biber one-man submarines used against the invasion forces. She captured one, which can now be seen at the Imperial War Museum in London. This submarine was captured by lassooing the periscope, and towed back to harbour.

ML 1407 was navigational leader for Force J, in charge of one of the minefree swept channels on D-Day, then engaged in shepherding boats off the beach-head, escorting cross-Channel convoys, and buoy laying and location with Trinity House. Later she was used in the defence of the mouth of the Scheld and for patrols off Ostend and Flushing.

During Operation Neptune (the naval portion of Operation Overlord, the D-Day landing), the 150th and 151st HDML

*ML 1070 in May 1941, another early unit. She was armed with a 2-pounder on a Mark IX mounting, with two single .303in gas-operated Vickers MGs on the bridge wings. The bridge area is now enlarged. The covered weapon on the pedestal mounting aft is probably a .303in Lewis gun.*
Imperial War Museum

Flotillas carried out two major diversionary operations and a protective operation, codenamed Taxable, Glimmer and Big Drum.

Taxable and Glimmer involved radar spoofing, balloons, radio spoofing and noise-making equipment to mislead the enemy into believing that assaults were to be made in the Pas de Calais area. Big Drum was entirely a radar jamming operation off the Cherbourg peninsula, to prevent German radars from detecting the US assault convoys in the western assault areas. These three vital operations, close in on the enemy shore, were probably the most important offensive operations performed by HDMLs throughout the war.

The first of the small HDMLs were ordered on 17 January 1940, with thirty-three units (Nos 1001 – 1033) ordered from seventeen builders at small shipyards in the United Kingdom. These ranged from Lymington (6 units) to Harland & Wolff, Belfast (2), Isleworth (1), Shoreham (3), East Molesey (2), Littlehampton (2), Whitstable (2), Hamworthy (2), Bideford (2), Wroxham, Norfolk (2), Lowestoft (2), the Clyde (2), Clynder (2) and Poole, Dorset (1).

Six more were ordered on 14 February, then one more, then another twenty-one on 29 June, followed by further units in groups of four, five, nine and so on, with most yards taking on the construction of one, two or three boats at a time. A total of 108 was built in 1940, and 100 during 1941. Twenty were built for the Royal Indian Navy in 1942, plus seventy-six in the UK, nine for the Royal Australian Navy, with twenty-four ordered under Lend-Lease from Dodge, Newport News, Ellsworth, Maine, Rye NY, Washington, New Jersey, California, Michigan and other yards in the USA. Other Commonwealth nations contributed their share to the vast programme, and HDMLs were constructed at Mombasa, Karachi, Bombay, Calcutta, Rangoon, Tasmania, Adelaide, Durban, Alexandria, Singapore, Colombo, and other places. With the fall of Singapore, a number under construction were captured on the stocks by the Japanese, and others already ordered were never laid down.

HDMLs served in the Royal New Zealand, Royal Australian, Royal Indian and South African navies, with many also being crewed by Free French and other nations in exile. Over forty units were lost by enemy action during the war, with others lost to natural hazards or on passage or as freight.

*HDML 1024 in June 1941. One of the first group ordered on 17 January 1940, she became Air Safety Launch 3 and is seen here apparently on her builder's trials. The only armament shown is paired .303in Vickers GO guns. Imperial War Museum*

These mass-produced small motor launches made a great reputation for themselves during the war. They were very sea-kindly, with reliable engines, and as they were diesel-powered there was less of a fire risk than was the case with their larger sisters. Their actual service far exceeded the duties visualised when their original Staff Requirements were outlined; they proved to be maids of all work. HDMLs rendered great service during the evacuation of Crete; they played their part in the Allied landings in North Africa, Sicily, Normandy and the South of France, and in operations against the Japanese in the Arakan. They were also used for convoy escort duties off the north and west coasts of Africa.

Like the larger B type Motor Launch, the 72ft HDML was crewed by many exiled navies, and the type was much sought after by foreign navies for postwar patrol work.

Two were captured by Axis forces at Tobruk (1039 and 1069) on 20 June 1942, and a number were captured while under construction at Hong Kong and Singapore, when these cities were occupied by the Japanese. One early Singapore-built HDML was saved by the Japanese after being lost in early 1942 in Malayan waters, and became the Japanese *Suikei* 11.

The Free French Navy was well represented, with eleven HDMLs in 1943, a further ten during 1944, two in 1945, ten more in 1946, plus one for service in French Indo-China and one other sold to France in January 1948.

The Royal Indian Navy was allocated its first HDML in 1942, three in 1943 and six more the following year, most of which served until 1946. The Turkish Navy, at the time an uneasy neutral, was to have nine. The first of these (ML 1153), however, was lost on passage out in September 1942, but the eight others were transferred during 1943.

ML 1074 was commissioned in the Royal Australian Navy in October 1942, and joined by 1129 the following month and 1161 in early 1943. Of thirty units ordered on 30 June 1942 in the USA,

Nos 1338–47 and 1352–59 were for the RAN, with 1348–51 for the RNZN and the remainder, 1360–67, for the RN on Lend-Lease. The three UK-built boats were followed by both locally-built units and US-built boats during 1944–45. During the war these HDMLs served as far afield as New Guinea, Borneo, Timor and the Philippines. By 1948 nineteen boats had been paid-off and sold, and four transferred to the RN in 1950 (and later to the Philippines Navy). One was wrecked in August 1952 and another sold in 1958. Three units (MLs 1321,1324 and 1325) were reclassified as Seaward Defence Boats and underwent modernisation refits, being lengthened by approximately 8ft (amidships), and having new diesel engines. The first was sold in August 1971, the second dismantled in 1982 and the last, 1325, unarmed, was still in service as a general-purpose tender in 1984.

The Royal New Zealand Navy acquired a total of sixteen units: the four noted above, four built in Burnham-on-Crouch in the UK and eight constructed in two boatyards in Cairo. One other, ML 1090, was allocated in June 1942, but was lost the following month while being transported out. Postwar, those that were retained were re-engined and the upperworks modified, and used for inshore survey work until the late 1970s.

Eight units (1197–1204), ordered on 15 November 1941 in South African boatyards for the RN, were transferred to the South African Navy before completion, to be joined by a further three boats in 1944 (1330–1332).

The Royal Netherlands Navy gathered together a number as the war in Europe drew to a close. Of sixteen ordered from American yards under Lend-Lease, six were supplied on completion, followed by another seven from both British and US sources, two more in 1946 and three more the following year.

The Greek Navy borrowed or purchased seven 72ft MLs, six in 1945 and an additional unit in 1947. Burma found them ideal craft for their new peacetime navy. First the Burmese RNVR was provided with four in 1945, then these boats were presented to the Government as gifts and followed by a total of thirteen more purchased the following year. Nearer home, Italy purchased eight in 1946, Portugal bought two for Macao in April 1947, and eight were purchased by China the same year. Malaya found them very useful for her long coastline, purchasing nine between 1947 and 1958.

Other nations purchased the HDMLs in small numbers during 1946; the Palestine Government two, the Palestine Police two, Is-

*HDML 1234 in October 1942, with the typical armament fit of the period.* Imperial War Museum

*HDML 1240 in July 1943, crewed by the Free French. Note the sprinkle of RN ratings on the upper deck. An off-loaded Liberty ship can be seen in the background.* Imperial War Museum

rael one, the Singapore Customs two, and a single unit was obtained for the Penang Pilot Service. In 1947 the Pakistan Navy purchased four and in 1958 the Philippine Navy bought five. Nigeria bought a single unit in 1959 and Iran purchased three, one during 1948, another the following year and the last in 1956.

## Harbour Defence Motor Launch data

**Numbers** ML 1001–1600.

**Dimensions** Length 72ft (oa), 70ft (pp), beam 15ft; draught 4ft 6in to 5ft 6in.

**Displacement** 46 tons, 54 tons deep load.

**Machinery** Twin diesel engines with six different manufacturers used; 300bhp Gardner, 320bhp Gleniffer, 330bhp Gray, 480bhp Hercules, 300bhp Buda Lanova or 260bhp Thornycroft. A Stuart 24-volt lighting set was fitted.

**Speed** 11–12½ knots maximum, 11.4 knots continuous (according to make).

**Range** 1000 nautical miles at 12 knots, 2000 at 10 knots.

**Fuel capacity** 1500 gallons, with provision for additional long-range deck tanks of 200 gallons.

**Heating and cooking** Paraffin cooking range; coal stoves for mess-deck heating. A paraffin-burning refrigerator was fitted for overseas postings.

**Communications** W/T and asdic; Type 291 radar and Type 253 IFF fitted later.

**Complement** Two officers, two petty officers, eight to ten ratings.

**Armament** One 3-pounder Mark I mounting or one 2-pounder Mark IX mounting, two .303in Lewis or stripped Lewis guns, eight depth charges. A single 20mm Oerlikon was added by 1943, with two 20mm mountings later. By 1945 the majority had two 20mm or one 2-pounder and one 20mm, four .303in Vickers GO Mark I (two twins), plus four to eight depth charges.
Other armament variations included: (84 boats) one 3-pounder, one 20mm, four MGs, eight depth charges; (46 boats) two 20mm (singles), four MGs, eight depth charges; (50 boats) two .5in MGs (two singles), one 20mm, eight depth charges; (22 boats) one 3-pounder, one 2-pounder, one 20mm, four MGs, eight depth charges; (13 boats) one 40mm (Bofors), one 20mm, four MGs, eight depth charges.

# Construction list

| ML | Builder | Engines | Completed | Fate |
|---|---|---|---|---|
| **33 ordered 17.1.40** | | | | |
| 1001 | 30 | Th | 2. 6.41 | = SML1 1945; for disposal 1949 |
| 1002 | 51 | Th | 1. 8.41 | = ASL17; sold 1946, = yacht *Le Cheval Noir* |
| 1003 | 56 | Th | 3. 1.41 | Lost 20.4.41 in transport on passage to Malta |
| 1004 | 56 | Th | 1. 2.41 | To Italy 26.3.46 |
| 1005 | 23 | Th | 17. 2.41 | Sold 10.46 at Malta |
| 1006 | 23 | Th | 4. 4.41 | For disposal 1.46 at Freetown |
| 1007 | 51 | Th | 14. 2.41 | For disposal 9.46; sold, = yacht *Naar* |
| 1008 | 51 | Th | 12. 6.41 | = ASL1; for disposal 8.46 |
| 1009 | 4 | Th | 29. 3.41 | WD TC1009 9.45; sold 1946, = *Cynthia Dawn* |
| 1010 | 4 | Th | 18. 5.41 | = FDB59; sold 14.6.48 |
| 1011 | 39 | Ga | 16.11.40 | Bombed 10.5.41 on passage Suda to Crete |
| 1012 | 39 | Ga | 10. 2.41 | To Italy 26.3.46 |
| 1013 | 6 | Ga | 5. 4.41 | WD TC1013 9.45; for disposal 11.46 |
| 1014 | 6 | Ga | 22. 5.41 | For disposal 1.46 at Freetown |
| 1015 | 7 | Ga | 24. 2.41 | Lost 10.43 in a gale, eastern Mediterranean |
| 1016 | 7 | Ga | 4. 4.41 | For disposal 1.46 at Freetown |
| 1017 | 21 | Gl | 6. 2.41 | To Italy 26.3.46 |
| 1018 | 21 | Gl | 6. 3.41 | For disposal 1.46 at Freetown |
| 1019 | 11 | | 30. 3.41 | For disposal 6.45 |
| 1020 | 11 | | 19. 6.41 | = ASL2; for disposal 8.46 |
| 1021 | 47L | Th | 9. 5.41 | = FDB57; sold to France 12.7.46, = VP25 |
| 1022 | 47L | Th | 3. 9.41 | = FDB60; sold 17.12.47, later = French VP26 |
| 1023 | 49 | Th | 1. 2.41 | To Italy 26.3.46 |
| 1024 | 49 | Th | 22. 3.41 | = ASL3; sold 1946, = yacht *Miarka* |
| 1025 | 6 | Ga | 18. 6.41 | = FDB69; sold 1947 |
| 1026 | 6 | Ga | 16. 6.41 | = FDB33; sold 1947, = yacht *Wings of Morn* |
| 1027 | 12 | Gl | 9. 5.41 | = FDB46; for disposal 1.46 |
| 1028 | 12 | Gl | 5. 8.41 | To Italy 26.3.46 |
| 1029 | 33 | Gl | 9.40 | For disposal 7.46 |
| 1030 | 33 | Gl | 11.11.40 | Lost 28.5.41 on passage Suda to Crete |
| 1031 | 6 | Ga | 9.40 | = ASL4; for disposal 8.46 |
| 1032 | 6 | Ga | 11.40 | To Greece on loan 1947–62; sold 1962 |
| 1033 | 8 | Ga | 9. 4.41 | = FDB47; for China 1.46, transferred 1947* |
| **6 ordered 14.2.40** | | | | |
| 1034 | 21 | Gl | 29. 3.41 | = FDB48; sold 7.47 |
| 1035 | 21 | Gl | 4.41 | = FDB49; sold 7.47 |
| 1036 | 11 | Gl | 20. 8.41 | = FDB50; for disposal 1.48 |
| 1037 | 6 | Ga | 3. 1.41 | Lost 20.4.41 in a transport vessel torpedoed in Atlantic |
| 1038 | 6 | Ga | 24. 1.41 | To WD 2.7.46 |
| 1039 | 38 | Ga | 26.11.40 | Captured by Axis forces at Tobruk 20.6.42 |
| **1 ordered 22.5.40** | | | | |
| 1040 | 39 | Th | 10. 6.41 | = ASL18; for disposal 8.46 |
| **21 ordered 29.6.40** | | | | |
| 1041 | 39 | Ga | 29. 5.41 | For disposal 1.46 at Freetown |
| 1042 | 39 | Ga | 7. 5.41 | For disposal 1.46 at Freetown |
| 1043 | 39 | Ga | 8. 6.41 | WD TC1043 9.45, for disposal 5.47 |
| 1044 | 39 | Ga | 19. 8.41 | For disposal 11.45 in West Africa |
| 1045 | 8 | | 6. 6.41 | WD TC1045 9.45, for disposal 1946 |
| 1046 | 6 | Ga | 9. 7.41 | For disposal 4.46 |
| 1047 | 6 | Ga | 22. 8.41 | = FDB51; to China 1947 |
| 1048 | 33 | Gl | 10. 2.41 | To WD 2.7.46 |
| 1049 | 33 | Gl | 11. 4.41 | = ASL5; for disposal 8.46 |
| 1050 | 33 | | 21. 7.41 | For disposal 6.46 |
| 1051 | 38 | Ga | 10. 2.41 | Lent to Greece 4.9.45; sold in Greece 1961 |
| 1052 | 38 | Ga | 8. 5.41 | For disposal 1.46 at Freetown |
| 1053 | 38 | Ga | 12. 7.41 | = SML2 1945, = SML322 1949; sold 20.4.59 |
| 1054 | 11 | Ga | 6.11.41 | CTL 11.10.43 by stranding near Heugh Light, Tees |

**Codes for engines**

BL = Buda Lanova
Gl = Gleniffer
H  = Hercules
Ga = Gardner
Gr = Gray
Th = Thornycroft

**Key to usage codes**

| | |
|---|---|
| ASL | Air Safety Launch |
| CTL | Constructive Total Loss |
| FDB | Fast Despatch Boat |
| ML(A) | Motor Launch (Air Service) |
| MSU | Mediterranean Survey Unit |
| SML | Survey Motor Launch |
| WD | War Department (Royal Army Service Corps) |

\* She and MLs 1047, 1058, 1059, 1068 and 1390 were transferred to China in place of Chinese Government vessels seized in 1940 and lost.

| | | | | |
|---|---|---|---|---|
| 1055 | 11 | Ga | 14. 3.42 | For disposal 7.46; sold, = yacht *Gerenik* |
| 1056 | 23 | | 18. 8.41 | = ASL6; for disposal 8.46 |
| 1057 | 23 | | 30. 9.41 | Lost by accident 13.10.44 off Kilindini, Kenya |
| 1058 | 57 | Ga | 8. 9.41 | = FDB52; to China 1947 |
| 1059 | 57 | Ga | 27. 9.41 | = FDB53; to China 1947 |
| 1060 | 57 | Ga | 12. 1.42 | CTL by ammunition explosion 6.8.44 in the Poole area |
| 1061 | 57 | Ga | 23. 4.42 | To Royal Indian Navy 5.43; for disposal 6.46 |

**5 ordered 26.7.40**

| | | | | |
|---|---|---|---|---|
| 1062 | 52S | Th | 1.42 | Lost 16.2.42 by Japanese gunfire, Banka Strait |
| 1063 | 52S | Th | 1.42 | Lost 1.3.42 at Tanjong Priok* |
| 1064 | 8 | Ga | 3. 7.41 | = FDB61; sold 1947 |
| 1065 | 7 | Ga | 16. 7.41 | For disposal 11.45 in West Africa |
| 1066 | 7 | Ga | 20. 8.41 | For disposal 11.45 in West Africa |

* Either 1062 or 1063 was salvaged by the Japanese and became *Suikei* 11

**4 ordered 31.7.40**

| | | | | |
|---|---|---|---|---|
| 1067 | 37 | | 8. 5.41 | = FDB34; sold France 1.48, = VP24 |
| 1068 | 37 | | 25. 6.41 | = FDB54; to China 1947 |
| 1069 | 56 | | 28. 5.41 | Captured by enemy forces at Tobruk 20.6.42 |
| 1070 | 56 | | 28. 5.41 | = FDB55; sold 1948 |

**3 ordered 13.8.40 and 2 ordered 14.9.40**

| | | | | |
|---|---|---|---|---|
| 1071 | 49 | Ga | 21. 8.41 | = FDB56; sold 11.47 |
| 1072 | 49 | Ga | 13.10.41 | To Free French Navy 30.8.43, = French VP21 1945 |
| 1073 | 47T | Ga | 18. 5.41 | To Royal Indian Navy 1943; for disposal 1946 |
| 1074 | 47T | Ga | .42 | Commissioned in Royal Australian Navy 7.10.42; sold 24.1.48 |
| 1075 | 47L | Th | 11.12.41 | = ASL19; for disposal 8.46, = *Ancelia* |

**9 ordered 2.9.40**

| | | | | |
|---|---|---|---|---|
| 1073 | 34 | | 1. 8.41 | Sold 22.12.45 at Freetown |
| 1077 | 34 | | 12. 8.41 | For disposal 12.45 at Freetown |
| 1078 | 34 | Gl | 17.11.41 | For disposal 12.45 at Freetown |
| 1079 | 34 | Gl | 6. 4.42 | Royal Indian Navy 1943–46; sold 1947 |
| 1080 | 15 | Ga | 8.10.41 | = ML3501, = Malay *Sri Kedah* 22.6.51 |
| 1081 | 8 | Ga | 19. 9.41 | = SML3 1945, SML323 1949; to Iran |
| 1082 | 8 | Ga | 1.12.41 | Sold 22.7.47 |
| 1083 | 7 | Ga | 23.10.41 | Lost 20.2.44 by grounding in the Aegean Sea |
| 1084 | 7 | Ga | 19. 1.42 | Royal Indian Navy 2.4.42 to 1946; sold 1947 |

**5 ordered 14.10.40 and 2 (1088 and 1089) 18.10.40**

| | | | | |
|---|---|---|---|---|
| 1085 | 51 | Ga | 16. 9.41 | = SML4 1945, = SML324 1949; sold 9.6.59 |
| 1086 | 51 | Ga | 4.11.41 | For disposal 10.46 |
| 1087 | 51 | Ga | 3. 1.42 | Royal Indian Navy 2.4.42 to 1944; sold 1947 |
| 1088 | 33 | Gl | 24.11.41 | Sold 1946 at Kilindini |
| 1089 | 33 | Gl | 29. 5.42 | Sold 1.46 at Freetown |
| 1090 | 45 | Ga | 22. 1.42 | To Royal NZ Navy 6.42; lost 11.7.42 in transport out |
| 1091 | 45 | Ga | 16. 7.42 | = SML5 1945, = SML325 1949; sold 22.7.58 |

**4 ordered 23.10.40**

| | | | | |
|---|---|---|---|---|
| 1092 | 21 | Gl | — | Destroyed on stocks by bombing 4/5.5.41 |
| 1093 | 21 | Gl | — | Destroyed on stocks by bombing 4/5.5.41 |
| 1094 | 21 | Gl | — | Destroyed on stocks by bombing 4/5.5.41 |
| 1095 | 21 | Gl | — | Destroyed on stocks by bombing 4/5.5.41 |

**4 ordered 27.12.40**

| | | | | |
|---|---|---|---|---|
| 1096 | 52S | | — | Lost at fall of Singapore (launched 1.6.41) |
| 1097 | 52S | | — | Lost at fall of Singapore (launched 10.6.41) |
| 1098 | 40 | Ga | 2.42 | For disposal 1.47 at Hong Kong |
| 1099 | 40 | Ga | .42 | For disposal 1.46 at Trincomalee |

**5 ordered 15.5.40 (to Burma account)**

| | | | | |
|---|---|---|---|---|
| 1100 | 28 | | 7.41 | Royal Indian Navy 1944; sold 1947 |
| 1101 | 28 | | 7.41 | Royal Indian Navy 1944; sold 1947 |
| 1102 | 28 | | 10.41 | Royal Indian Navy 1944; for disposal 3.47 |
| 1103 | 28 | | 10.41 | Royal Indian Navy 1944; sold 1947 |
| 1104 | 46 | | 30. 6.41 | Royal Indian Navy 1944; sold 1947 |

**Codes for builders**

| | |
|---|---|
| 1 | Ackerman, Azusa, California, USA |
| 2 | Africa Mirine, Mombasa |
| 3 | Alcock Ashdown, Karachi |
| 4 | Anderson Rigden & Perkins, Whitstable |
| 5 | Armedi Shipyard, Bombay |
| 6 | Berthon Boat, Lymington, Dorset |
| 7 | Blackmore, Bideford, Devon |
| 8 | Bolson, Poole, Dorset |
| 9 | Bombay Dockyard |
| 10 | Bombay Steam Navigation |
| 11 | Bunn, Wroxham, Norfolk |
| 12 | Bute Slip, Clyde, Scotland |
| 13 | Dodge, Newport News, USA |
| 14 | Edgar, Rye, New York, USA |
| 15 | Elkins, Christchurch, Dorset |
| 16 | Elscot, City Island, New York, USA |
| 17 | Everett, Washington, USA |
| 18 | Freeport Shipyard, Long Island, USA |
| 19 | Garden Reach, Calcutta |
| 20 | Grays Harbor, Aberdeen, Washington, USA |
| 21 | Harland & Wolff, Belfast, Northern Ireland |
| 22 | Harris & Parsons, Greenwich, Rhode Island, USA |
| 23 | Hillyard, Littlehampton, West Sussex |
| 24 | Hiltebrant, Kingston, USA |
| 25 | Hooghly Dock and Engineering, Calcutta |
| 26 | Huskins Yacht Corporation, USA |
| 27 | India General Navigation, Calcutta |
| 28 | Irrawadi Flotilla Company, Rangoon |
| 29 | Jack, Launceston, Tasmania |
| 30 | Lady Bee, Isleworth |
| 31 | Leek, New Jersey, USA |
| 32 | MacFarland, Adelaide, Australia |
| 33 | McGruer, Clynder, Scotland |
| 34 | McLean, Renfrew, Scotland |
| 35 | Madden & Lewis, Sausalito, California, USA |
| 36 | Mohatta, Karachi |
| 37 | Moody, Swanwick Shore, Southampton |
| 38 | Morgan Giles, Teignmouth, Devon |
| 39 | Newman, Hamworthy, Dorset |
| 40 | Nichol, Durban, South Africa |
| 41 | Pehara, Alexandria, Egypt |
| 42 | Perkins & Vaughan, Wickford, Rhode Island, USA |
| 43 | Purdon & Featherstone, Hobart, Tasmania |
| 44 | Quincy Adams, USA |
| 45 | Ranalah Yacht Yard, Wooton, Isle of Wight |
| 46 | Rangoon Dockyard, Rangoon |
| 47L | Robinson, Lowestoft, Norfolk |
| 47T | Robinson, Tewkesbury, Gloucestershire |
| 48 | Scindia, Bombay |
| 49 | Sittingbourne Shipbuilding Company, Kent |
| 50 | Spadbrow, Durban, South Africa |
| 51 | Sussex Ship Building Company, Shoreham, Sussex |
| 52 | Thornycroft, Hampton |
| 53 | Thornycroft, Singapore |
| 54 | Thorsen, Ellsworth, Maine, USA |

| ML | Builder | Engines | Completed | Fate |
|---|---|---|---|---|
| **4 ordered 27.11.40** | | | | |
| 1105 | 2 | Ga | 3. 3.43 | = ML3502, = Malay *Sri Trengganu* 1949 |
| 1106 | 2 | Ga | 3. 8.43 | Sold to Portugal 20.4.47 for Macao |
| 1107 | 2 | Ga | 30.11.43 | Sold 4.48 |
| 1108 | 2 | Ga | 6. 6.44 | Sold to Portugal 20.4.47 for Macao |
| **12 ordered 8.1.42 for the Royal Indian Navy** | | | | |
| 1109 | 36 | Gl | 15. 5.44 | Sold 1947 |
| 1110 | 36 | Gl | 1. 5.44 | = ML3110 8.51 |
| 1111 | 36 | Gl | 6.44 | Sold 1947 |
| 1112 | 25 | Gl | 6.12.44 | = ML3112 8.51 |
| 1113 | 25 | Gl | 24.12.44 | Sold 1947 |
| 1114 | 10 | Gl | 21. 1.44 | For disposal 11.46 |
| 1115 | 19 | Gl | 10. 6.43 | For disposal 11.46 |
| 1116 | 9 | Gl | 4.44 | For disposal 11.46 |
| 1117 | 9 | Gl | 23. 3.44 | = ML3117 8.51 |
| 1118 | 27 | Gl | 11.11.44 | = ML3118 8.51 |
| 1119 | 27 | Gl | 27. 7.44 | Lost 7.10.44 in Indian waters |
| 1120 | 19 | Gl | 22. 7.43 | Sold 1947 |
| **46 ordered 30.5.41** | | | | |
| 1121 | 51 | Th | 10. 7.42 | Lost – foundered off Pantellaria 31.12.43 |
| 1122 | 51 | Th | 29. 5.42 | Sold 1946 |
| 1123 | 51 | Th | 2. 8.42 | Sold 10.46 |
| 1124 | 51 | Th | 2.10.42 | To Turkey 1943, = LM1 |
| 1125 | 6 | Ga | 28. 4.42 | Royal Australian Navy 1943; Royal Indian Navy 1944; sold 1947 |
| 1126 | 6 | Ga | 21. 5.42 | Sold Palestine Police 27.6.46 |
| 1127 | 6 | Ga | 9. 6.42 | Free French 16.11.43, = French VP9 1944 |
| 1128 | 6 | Ga | 30. 6.42 | French VP6 1944 |
| 1129 | 52H | Th | 23. 4.42 | Royal Australian Navy 7.11.42; sold 10.12.47 |
| 1130 | 52H | Th | 30. 4.42 | Sold 1946 |
| 1131 | 52H | Th | 12. 5.42 | Sold 1946 |
| 1132 | 52H | Th | 13. 6.42 | Free French 20.9.43, = French VP8 1944 |
| 1133 | 52H | Th | 27. 6.42 | Free French 1.9.43, = French VP7 1944 |
| 1134 | 52H | Th | 13. 8.42 | For disposal 7.46 at Gibraltar |
| 1135 | 52H | Th | 18. 9.42 | To Turkey 3.43, = LM2 |
| 1136 | 52H | Th | 22.10.42 | French VP14 1944 |
| 1137 | 47L | Th | 10. 9.42 | Sold 18.12.45 at Freetown |
| 1138 | 47L | Th | 17.11.42 | Free French 5.43, = French VP2 1944 |
| 1139 | 47T | Ga | 3. 7.42 | = French VP16 1944 |
| 1140 | 8 | Ga | 19. 6.42 | = Air Safety Launch 7, = *Gannet* 1946; sold 1.3.57 |
| 1141 | 8 | Ga | 12.10.42 | Free French 30.8.43, = French VP22 1944 |
| 1142 | 57 | Ga | 4. 7.42 | French VP13 14.1.44 |
| 1143 | 57 | Ga | 20. 8.42 | French *Palmyre* 1944, = VP31 |
| 1144 | 57 | Ga | 10.11.42 | French VP15 26.2.44 |
| 1145 | 57 | Ga | 26.11.42 | To Palestine Police 5.1.46 |
| 1146 | 4 | Th | 6. 6.42 | Sold 1946 |
| 1147 | 4 | Th | 22. 5.42 | For disposal 6.45 |
| 1148 | 37 | Ga | 23. 4.42 | Royal Indian Navy 1943; sold 1947 |
| 1149 | 37 | Ga | 29. 5.42 | Greek *Klissoura* 4.9.45; for disposal 1962 |
| 1150 | 7 | Ga | 10. 5.42 | Sold 22.7.47 |
| 1151 | 7 | Ga | 6.42 | Royal Indian Navy 1944; sold 1947 |
| 1152 | 7 | Ga | 2. 7.42 | French VP11 1944 |
| 1153 | 7 | Ga | 18. 8.42 | To Turkey 1942, lost 9.42 on passage out |
| 1154 | 11 | Th | 30. 1.43 | Mined 14.5.43 at Bizerta |
| 1155 | 11 | Th | 2. 4.43 | To Italy 26.3.46 |
| 1156 | 12 | Gl | 10.11.42 | Sold 1946 |
| 1157 | 12 | Gl | 30.12.42 | Lost 4.43 in transport |
| 1158 | 23 | Th | 11. 5.42 | To Palestine Government 2.46 |
| 1159 | 23 | Th | 8. 6.42 | For disposal 7.46 at Alexandria |
| 1160 | 49 | Th | 4. 6.42 | Sold 22.12.45 at Freetown |
| 1161 | 49 | Th | 8.42 | Royal Australian Navy 9.1.43; sold 10.12.47, = *Los Negros* |
| 1162 | 15 | Ga | 14. 5.42 | Sold 1946 |

| 55 | Truscott, St Joseph, Michigan, USA |
|---|---|
| 56 | Walker, Colombo, Ceylon (now Sri Lanka) |
| 57 | Woods, Potter Heigham, Norfolk |

*HDML 1245 in April 1943, prior to her transfer to Turkey in October.* Imperial War Museum

*The wheelhouse and armoured window covers of HDML 1246. They were clipped shut, particularly during the hours of darkness, to prevent light escaping from the wheelhouse. They also gave protection to the helmsman.* Courtesy Roy Tyldesley

| 1163 | 15 | Ga | 31.12.42 | Torpedoed 5.1.45 in the Adriatic |
|------|-----|------|----------|----------------------------------|
| 1164 | 56 | Th | 18. 9.42 | French *Baalbek* 1944, = VP32 |
| 1165 | 56 | Th | 16.10.42 | Sold 1946 |
| 1166 | 56 | Th | 2. 2.43 | French VP5 1945, = *La Belle Brise* 1952 |

**2 ordered 17.6.41 and 2 ordered 26.6.41**

| 1167 | 52S | | — | Lost on stocks at the fall of Singapore |
|------|-----|------|----------|----------------------------------|
| 1168 | 52S | | — | Lost on stocks at the fall of Singapore |
| 1169 | 52S | | — | Lost on stocks at the fall of Singapore |
| 1170 | 52S | | — | Lost on stocks at the fall of Singapore |

**24 ordered 21.2.42 on Lend-Lease agreement**

| 1171 | 13 | Gr | 11.12.42 | Returned United States Navy 3.47 at Bombay |
|------|-----|------|----------|----------------------------------|
| 1172 | 13 | Gr | 16.12.42 | Returned United States Navy 3.47 at Bombay |
| 1173 | 13 | Gr | 7. 1.43 | Returned United States Navy 3.47 at Bombay |
| 1174 | 13 | Gr | 16. 1.43 | Returned United States Navy 3.47 at Bombay |
| 1175 | 13 | Gr | 12. 2.43 | Returned United States Navy 3.47 at Bombay |
| 1176 | 13 | Gr | 12. 2.43 | Returned United States Navy 3.47 at Bombay |
| 1177 | 13 | Gr | 12. 2.43 | Returned United States Navy 3.47 at Bombay |
| 1178 | 13 | Gr | 4. 3.43 | Returned United States Navy 3.47 at Bombay |
| 1179 | 13 | Gr | 4. 3.43 | Lost 21.8.44 in a hurricane off Jamaica |
| 1180 | 13 | Gr | 4. 3.43 | Returned United States Navy 3.47 at Bombay |
| 1181 | 13 | Gr | 23. 3.43 | Returned United States Navy 3.47 at Bombay |
| 1182 | 13 | Gr | 23. 3.43 | Returned United States Navy 3.47 at Bombay |
| 1183 | 35 | Gr | 3.43 | Royal New Zealand Navy, = P3551 1950, = *Mako* 1956 |
| 1184 | 35 | Gr | 3.43 | Royal New Zealand Navy, = P3552 1950, = *Paea* 1956 |
| 1185 | 35 | Gr | 4.43 | Royal New Zealand Navy, = Army *Bombardier* 1948, = *Manga*, = *Olphert* |
| 1186 | 35 | Gr. | 5.43 | Royal New Zealand Navy; sold 5.47 |
| 1187 | 17 | Gr | 5.43 | Royal New Zealand Navy, = 35556B, = *Tarapunga* |
| 1188 | 17 | Gr | 5.43 | Royal New Zealand Navy, = 3556A, = *Takupu* 1955 |
| 1189 | 17 | Gr | 5.43 | Sold 1946 |
| 1190 | 17 | Gr | 6.43 | Royal New Zealand Navy, = 3562, = *Olphert* 1956, = *Parore* 1967 |
| 1191 | 20 | Gr | 8.43 | Royal New Zealand Navy, = 3553, = *Tamaki* 1961, = *Kahawai* 4.66 |
| 1192 | 20 | Gr | 8.43 | Royal New Zealand Navy, = 3554, = *Irirangi* 1961, = *Maroro*, sold 1972 |
| 1193 | 20 | Gr | 8.43 | Royal New Zealand Navy, = 3555, = *Viti* 1955, = *Ngapona* 1959, = *Tamure* 1967; sold 1973 |
| 1194 | 20 | Gr | 8.43 | Royal New Zealand Navy, = *Ngapona* 1948, = 3561 1950; stranded 8.11.57 and broken up |

**2 ordered 4.6.41**

| 1195 | 2 | Ga | 12.44 | For disposal 1945 |
|------|-----|------|----------|----------------------------------|
| 1196 | 2 | Ga | — | Cancelled 1945 (launched 9.45) |

**8 ordered 25.11.41 for Royal Navy and transferred to South African Navy before completion**

| 1197 | 40 | Ga | 24. 7.43 | Listed to 1961 |
|------|-----|------|----------|----------------------------------|
| 1198 | 40 | Ga | 26. 7.43 | Listed to 1951 |
| 1199 | 40 | Ga | 20. 7.43 | Listed to 1951 |
| 1200 | 40 | Ga | 4. 8.43 | Listed to 1961 |
| 1201 | 40 | Ga | 6. 8.43 | Listed to 1951 |
| 1202 | 40 | Ga | 3. 8.43 | Listed to 1961 |
| 1203 | 50 | Ga | 22. 7.43 | Listed to 1961 |
| 1204 | 50 | Ga | 10.12.43 | Listed to 1961 |

**4 ordered 17.7.41**

| 1205 | 55 | Gl | 29.12.44 | Lent to Burma 1946; listed to 1949 |
|------|-----|------|----------|----------------------------------|
| 1206 | 55 | Gl | 28. 6.45 | Lent to Burma 4.46; sold to Burma 1949 |
| 1207 | 55 | Gl | — | Cancelled 29.12.44 |
| 1208 | 55 | Gl | — | Cancelled 1944 |

**2 ordered 30.6.41 and 2 ordered 1.7.41**

| 1209 | 39 | Ga | 11. 5.42 | Sold 18.12.45 at Freetown |
|------|-----|------|----------|----------------------------------|
| 1210 | 39 | Ga | 25. 6.42 | Sold 1946, = yacht *Perchance* |
| 1211 | 52H | Th | 24.11.42 | For disposal 6.46 at Alexandria |
| 1212 | 52H | Th | 11.12.42 | Lost in transport from the UK 4.43 |

| ML | Builder | Engines | Completed | Fate |
|---|---|---|---|---|
| **8 ordered 15.11.41*** | | | | |
| 1213 | 52S | | — | Lost on stocks at fall of Singapore, 2.42 |
| 1214 | 52S | | — | Lost on stocks at fall of Singapore, 2.42 |
| 1215 | 52S | | — | Lost on stocks at fall of Singapore, 2.42 |
| 1216 | 52S | | — | Lost on stocks at fall of Singapore, 2.42 |
| 1217 | 52S | | — | Lost on stocks at fall of Singapore, 2.42 |
| 1218 | 52S | | — | Lost on stocks at fall of Singapore, 2.42 |
| 1219 | 52S | | — | Lost on stocks at fall of Singapore, 2.42 |
| 1220 | 52S | | — | Lost on stocks at fall of Singapore, 2.42 |
| **16 ordered 17.12.41** | | | | |
| 1221 | 37 | Ga | 6. 8.42 | Greek *Bizani*, on loan 22.8.45; for disposal 1962 |
| 1222 | 37 | Ga | 9. 3.43 | Sold 1946 |
| 1223 | 51 | Th | 9. 3.43 | French VP3 1945 |
| 1224 | 51 | Th | 6.43 | Sold 1947, = yacht *Santa Clara* |
| 1225 | 39 | Ga | 6. 8.42 | French VP12 1944 |
| 1226 | 39 | Ga | 12.10.42 | Mined off Alexandropolis 4.10.45 (Eastern Mediterranean) |
| 1227 | 49 | Th | 24.11.42 | Sunk by gunfire of German surface craft off Piraeus 5.10.44 |
| 1228 | 49 | Th | 23. 1.43 | French VP6 1944 |
| 1229 | 33 | Th | 19.10.42 | Sold 1946, = French VP749 |
| 1230 | 33 | Th | 3.12.42 | Scuttled off Malta, 9.46 |
| 1231 | 7 | Ga | 7.10.42 | Free French 30.8.43, = VP23, = French VP758 |
| 1232 | 7 | Ga | 23.11.42 | Sold 1946 |
| 1233 | 4 | Th | 2.10.42 | Free French 1.6.43, = VP3 |
| 1234 | 4 | Th | 19.10.42 | For disposal 1.46 at Gibraltar |
| 1235 | 23 | Th | 4. 9.42 | For disposal 1.46 at Gibraltar |
| 1236 | 23 | Th | 21.10.42 | Sold 1947, = yacht *Neba* |
| **8 ordered 18.12.41** | | | | |
| 1237 | 6 | Th | 30. 7.42 | Scuttled off Malta 9.46 |
| 1238 | 6 | Th | 17. 9.42 | Sold 11.46 |
| 1239 | 6 | Th | 14.10.42 | To Italy 26.3.46 |
| 1240 | 6 | Th | 14.11.42 | Free French 1.6.43, = VP4 |
| 1241 | 34 | Th | 5. 2.43 | Scuttled off Malta 9.46 |
| 1242 | 34 | Th | 31. 4.43 | For disposal 9.46 |
| 1243 | 34 | Th | 29. 5.43 | To Turkey 18.11.43, = LM8 |
| 1244 | 34 | Th | 20. 8.43 | Lost in transit from the UK 25.11.43 |
| **16 ordered 21.2.42** | | | | |
| 1245 | 47T | Ga | 3. 4.43 | To Turkey 26.10.43, = LM7 |
| 1246 | 47T | Ga | 14. 4.43 | To the Palestine Police 5.1.46 |
| 1247 | 47T | Th | 22. 4.43 | Sold 3.47 |
| 1248 | 47L | Th | 2. 6.43 | To Singapore Customs 4.7.46, = *Panah* |
| 1249 | 39 | Ga | 11.11.42 | Free French 16.4.43, = VP1 |
| 1250 | 39 | Ga | 1.12.42 | Free French 16.12.43, = VP10 |
| 1251 | 39 | Ga | 25. 1.43 | To Italy 26.2.46 |
| 1252 | 39 | Ga | 19. 2.43 | Greek *Farsala* on loan 9.11.45; sold 1962 |
| 1253 | 39 | Ga | 5. 4.43 | Sold 11.46 |
| 1254 | 39 | Ga | 15. 4.43 | Mediterranean Survey Unit 1 1946; sold 9.47 |
| 1255 | 6 | Th | 11.12.42 | Sold 1.46 at Freetown |
| 1256 | 6 | Th | 18. 1.43 | To Turkey 7.8.43, = LM3 |
| 1257 | 6 | Th | 18. 2.43 | Sold 5.46, = yacht *Marica* 1948 |
| 1258 | 6 | Ga | 1. 4.43 | Sold 3.47 |
| 1259 | 6 | Ga | 28. 4.43 | Hull damage 10.44, paid off 31.10.44 to be broken up |
| 1260 | 6 | Ga | 28. 6.43 | Sold to Holland 1946 |
| **8 ordered 29.3.42 for the Royal Indian Navy** | | | | |
| 1261 | 9 | Th | 18.11.45 | Royal Pakistan Navy 1947, = ML3517 1951 |
| 1262 | 9 | Th | 11.45 | Royal Pakistan Navy 1947, = ML3518 1951 |
| 1263 | 9 | Th | 16. 1.45 | Royal Pakistan Navy 1947, = ML3519 1951 |
| 1264 | 9 | Th | — | Cancelled 1945 |
| 1265 | 36 | Th | 28. 9.44 | Sold 1947 |
| 1266 | 36 | Th | 7.11.44 | Royal Pakistan Navy 1947, = ML3520 1951 |
| 1267 | 36 | Th | 11. 3.44 | Sold 1947 |

* It is doubtful if any of these eight were in fact laid down

*HDML in June 1945 at Marseille; by this time she had become the Free French VP 1. Note the detail of the 2-pounder gun.* Imperial War Museum

*HDML 1294 in July 1943. She was built by the Sussex Ship Building Company at Shoreham.* Imperial War Museum

| | | | | |
|---|---|---|---|---|
| 1268 | 48 | Th | 29. 1.45 | Sold 1947 |

**42 ordered 24.4.42**

| | | | | |
|---|---|---|---|---|
| 1269 | 23 | Ga | 7. 1.43 | Sold 8.46 |
| 1270 | 23 | Ga | 1. 4.43 | Sold 1946 |
| 1271 | 23 | Ga | 22. 4.43 | Sold 5.46, = *Madonna Ta Pompei* |
| 1272 | 23 | Ga | 5. 7.43 | Lent to Burma 8.45, sold to Burma 1.48 |
| 1273 | 4 | Th | 6. 3.43 | French VP82 1946 |
| 1274 | 4 | Th | 23. 1.43 | = FDB62; sold 14.6.48 |
| 1275 | 4 | Th | 21. 6.43 | For disposal 1947 at Singapore |
| 1276 | 37 | Ga | 21. 1.43 | = FDB63; sold 7.47 |
| 1277 | 37 | Ga | 20. 3.43 | To Israel 1946 |
| 1278 | 37 | Ga | 20. 5.43 | For disposal 1946; sold, = yacht *Lady Walrus* |
| 1279 | 12 | Gl | 24.11.43 | = FDB70, = ML3511; sold 1948, = *Islandu* |
| 1280 | 12 | Gl | 25. 4.44 | = ML3503; sold 1958, = *Lady Ellen* |
| 1281 | 49 | Th | 19. 5.43 | Sold 13.10.49 |
| 1282 | 49 | Th | 26. 7.43 | To Turkey 26.10.43, = LM6 |
| 1283 | 52H | Th | 25. 3.43 | To WD 1946; sold, = *Amanda Mary* 1948 |
| 1284 | 52H | Th | 3. 4.43 | Sold 11.46, = yacht *Nejm* |
| 1285 | 52H | Th | 27. 4.43 | To Singapore Government 16.7.46 |
| 1286 | 52H | Th | 22. 4.43 | To Burma 2.4.46 |
| 1287 | 52H | Th | 25. 6.43 | To Singapore Customs 6.7.46 |
| 1288 | 52H | Th | 26. 5.43 | To Panang pilots 1946 |
| 1289 | 52H | Th | 2. 7.43 | Lost 25.11.43 on passage abroad |
| 1290 | 52H | Th | 23. 7.43 | Sold 1946 |
| 1291 | 52H | Th | 28. 8.43 | Sold 1946 |
| 1292 | 51 | Ga | 8. 6.43 | Greek *Distraton* on loan 4.9.45; sold 1962 |
| 1293 | 51 | Ga | 1. 6.43 | Sold to France 1.7.46 for Indo China |
| 1294 | 51 | Ga | 20. 7.43 | To Turkey 26.10.43, = LM5 |
| 1295 | 51 | Ga | 12.11.43 | = FDB74, = ML3512; sold 17.11.58 |
| 1296 | 33 | Gl | 29. 1.43 | To Turkey 7.8.43, = LM4 |
| 1297 | 33 | Gl | 10. 4.43 | Sold 1946 |
| 1298 | 33 | Gl | 17. 6.43 | Sold to Burma Government 2.4.46 |
| 1299 | 33 | Gl | 5. 8.43 | Burma RNVR 8.45; sold to Burma 1946 |
| 1300 | 7 | Ga | 20. 1.43 | = FDB64; sold 6.48 |
| 1301 | 7 | Ga | 6. 4.43 | = Mediterranean Survey Unit 2 1946, = SML352 (*Meda*); sold 25.6.66 |
| 1302 | 7 | Ga | 19. 4.43 | Sold 11.46, = *Santa Katerina* |
| 1303 | 7 | Ga | 15. 6.43 | Cannibalised 5.46 in India |
| 1304 | 57 | Ga | 20. 4.43 | Burma RNVR 8.45; gift to Burma 1.48 |
| 1305 | 57 | Ga | 5.43 | Sold 1947, = yacht *Lewina* |
| 1306 | 57 | Ga | 13. 8.43 | Burma RNVR 8.45; gift to Burma 1.48 |
| 1307 | 57 | Ga | 20. 9.43 | Greek *Karia* on loan 11.45; for disposal 1961 |
| 1308 | 11 | Gl | 4. 9.43 | Sold 5.46 at Gibraltar |
| 1309 | 11 | Gl | 4. 2.44 | = FDB 75; sold 14.4.48 |
| 1310 | 11 | Gl | 5. 5.44 | = FDB 79; sold 1947, = yacht *The Bee* |

**6 ordered 31.8.42**

| | | | | |
|---|---|---|---|---|
| 1315* | 41 | Gr | 15. 5.45 | = FDB40; for disposal 1946 |
| 1316 | 41 | Gr | 30. 5.45 | = FDB41; for disposal 1946 |
| 1317 | 41 | Gr | 19. 6.45 | = FDB42; for disposal 1946 |
| 1318 | 41 | Gr | 30. 6.45 | = FDB43; lent WD 1945; for disposal 1946 |
| 1319 | 41 | Gr | 8.45 | = FDB44; for disposal 1946 |
| 1320 | 41 | Gr | 31. 7.45 | = FDB45; for disposal 1946 |

**6 ordered 27.6.42 for Royal Australian Navy**

| | | | | |
|---|---|---|---|---|
| 1321 | 43 | B | 11.11.43 | (Commissioned) sold 7.71 |
| 1322 | 43 | B | 17. 1.44 | (Commissioned) to Philippines Navy 1958 |
| 1323 | 32 | B | 21. 1.44 | (Commissioned) to Iran 21.6.56 |
| 1324 | 32 | B | 12. 6.44 | (Commissioned) listed to 1964 |
| 1325 | 29 | B | 4.11.43 | (Commissioned) listed 1964 |
| 1326 | 29 | B | 19. 1.44 | (Commissioned) to Philippines Navy 1958 |

**3 ordered 24.5.43 for Royal Australian Navy**

| | | | | |
|---|---|---|---|---|
| 1327 | 32 | B | 29. 5.44 | (Commissioned) to Philippines Navy 1958 |
| 1328 | 32 | B | 16. 1.45 | (Commissioned) to Philippines Navy 1958 |
| 1329 | 32 | B | 14. 6.44 | (Commissioned) to Philippines Navy 1958 |

*4 (MLs 1311–1314) projected or ordered 1942 in Ceylon; cancelled

| ML | Builder | Engines | Completed | Fate |
|----|---------|---------|-----------|------|
| **8 ordered 20.10.43** | | | | |
| 1330 | 40 | Ga | 23. 6.44 | To South African Navy 1944; laid up 30.7.45 |
| 1331 | 40 | Ga | 28. 6.44 | To South African Navy 1944; laid up 8.3.46 |
| 1332 | 40 | Ga | 25. 6.44 | To South African Navy 1944; laid up 28.7.45 |
| 1333 | 40 | Ga | 15. 9.44 | = ML3505; Malayan *Sri Pahang* 17.5.58 |
| 1334 | 40 | | 16.10.44 | = ML3506; Malayan *Sri Negri Sembilan* 9.50 |
| 1335 | 40 | | 2. 1.45 | = ML3507; Malayan *Sri Perak* 4.3.54 |
| 1336 | 40 | | 30. 9.44 | To Malaya 7.47 |
| 1337 | 40 | | 11.12.44 | Lent to Holland 1946–49; for disposal 1962 |
| **30 ordered 30.6.42 in the USA\*** | | | | |
| 1338 | 31 | H | 31. 5.44 | (Commissioned) sold 1949 |
| 1339 | 31 | H | 15. 6.44 | (Commissioned) sold 1949 |
| 1340 | 53 | H | 12. 5.44 | (Commissioned) sold 1949 |
| 1341 | 53 | H | 1. 12.44 | (Commissioned) sold 1949 |
| 1342 | 53 | H | 24. 7.44 | (Commissioned) sold 1949 |
| 1343 | 53 | H | 3.10.44 | (Commissioned) sold 1949 |
| 1344 | 54 | H | 9.45 | Sold 1949 |
| 1345 | 54 | H | 5.45 | Sold 1949 |
| 1346 | 54 | H | 6. 1.45 | (Commissioned) sold 1949 |
| 1347 | 54 | H | 31.12.44 | (Commissioned) sold 1949 |
| 1348 | 1 | H | 3.44 | (Commissioned) = 2563, = *Pegasus* 1956, = *Kuparu* 1967, = *Toroa* 1968 |
| 1349 | 1 | H | 3.44 | (Commissioned) = 3565, = *Wakefield* 1956, = *Haku* 1.64 |
| 1350 | 1 | H | 3.44 | (Commissioned) = 3564, = *Toroa* 1956, = *Koura* 1967 |
| 1351 | 1 | H | 3.44 | (Commissioned) sold 1947, = *Aotearoa* by 1951 |
| 1352 | 18 | H | 12. 5.44 | (Commissioned) sold 1949 |
| 1353 | 18 | H | 18.10.44 | (Commissioned) sold 1949 |
| 1354 | 18 | H | 11.12.44 | (Commissioned) sold 1949 |
| 1355 | 18 | H | 11.12.44 | (Commissioned) sold 1949 |
| 1356 | 16 | H | 20.12.44 | (Commissioned) sold 1949 |
| 1357 | 16 | H | 4.11.44 | (Commissioned) sold 1949 |
| 1358 | 16 | H | 21.10.44 | (Commissioned) sold 1949 |
| 1359 | 16 | H | 22. 9.44 | (Commissioned) sold 1949 |
| 1360 | 14 | | 25.10.43 | = FDB28; returned US Navy at Bombay 3.47 |
| 1361 | 14 | | 22.12.43 | = FDB29; returned US Navy at Bombay 3.47 |
| 1362 | 14 | | 21.11.43 | = FDB30; returned US Navy at Bombay 3.47 |
| 1363 | 14 | | 15. 2.44 | = FDB31; returned US Navy at Bombay 3.47 |
| 1364 | 13 | H | 20. 7.43 | Returned US Navy at Bombay 3.47 |
| 1365 | 13 | H | 9.10.43 | Returned US Navy at Bombay 3.47 |
| 1366 | 13 | H | 27.10.43 | Returned US Navy at Bombay 3.47 |
| 1367 | 13 | H | 27.10.43 | Returned US Navy at Bombay 3.47 |
| **8 ordered 11.9.42** | | | | |
| 1368 | 39 | Ga | 9. 6.43 | To Burma Navy 2.4.46 |
| 1369 | 39 | Ga | 25. 6.43 | Burma RNVR 8.45; gift to Burma 1.48 |
| 1370 | 56 | Gl | 6. 4.45 | To France 1.7.46, = VP72 |
| 1371 | 56 | Gl | — | Cancelled 1944 |
| 1372 | 6 | Th | 28. 7.43 | To France 1946 |
| 1373 | 6 | Th | 24. 8.43 | For disposal 1946 |
| 1374 | 37 | Ga | 31. 7.43 | To Burma Government 2.4.46 |
| 1375 | 37 | Ga | 2.10.43 | Greek *Kastraki* on loan 13.11.45; for disposal 1961 |
| **22 ordered (date not established)** | | | | |
| 1376 | 7 | Ga | 5. 7.43 | Sold to Malay Government 7.47 |
| 1377 | 7 | Ga | 4. 9.43 | To France 1.7.46, = VP71 |
| 1378 | 7 | Ga | 11.10.43 | = FDB80, = *Isis*, = ML3513; sold 11.58 at Hong Kong |
| 1379 | 7 | Ga | 17.11.43 | = FDB81; sold 1947 |
| 1380 | 33 | | 16. 9.43 | Lost 1.5.44 in the Agean – cause unreported |
| 1381 | 33 | | 11.43 | Captured 26.8.44 at Sirini by five Axis craft |
| 1382 | 4 | Th | 3. 9.43 | = ASL8; for disposal 8.46 |
| 1383 | 4 | Th | 30.12.43 | = FDB86; sold 10.46 |

\*1338–1347 and 1352–1359 for Royal Australian Navy (1338–1139 and 1352–1355 originally intended for the Royal New Zealand Navy); 1360–1367 for the Royal Navy on Lend-Lease

*HDML 1282 in July 1943. Note that no Carley floats were carried, but that she had two spanner rafts instead. She was sold to Turkey the following October.* Imperial War Museum

*HDML 1368 in June 1943, in home waters. She was sold to the Burmese Navy in 1946. Her smart appearance shows why the 72ft ML was much sought after as a private yacht post war.* Imperial War Museum

| 1384 | 39 | Ga | 11.43 | For disposal at Malta 8.46 |
|---|---|---|---|---|
| 1385 | 39 | Ga | 8.43 | = 3508, = Malay *Sri Kelantan* 23.12.50 |
| 1386 | 39 | Ga | 9.43 | = 3509; to Malay Government 1949 |
| 1387 | 39 | Ga | 29.12.43 | = FDB76, = *Thames* 1949, = ML3516, = *Medusa* 1960 |
| 1388 | 49 | Th | 25.11.43 | CTL by grounding near Hartlepool 24.12.43 |
| 1389 | 49 | Th | 12. 2.44 | = FDB58; to Iran 1.49 (listed in Iran Navy 1951 but reported as CTL by grounding near Fort William and sold 1.50) |
| 1390 | 6 | Ga | 9.43 | = FDB85; to China 1947 |
| 1391 | 6 | Ga | 11.43 | = FDB72, = ML3515; to Nigeria 11.3.59 |
| 1392 | 6 | Ga | 20.12.43 | = FDB73; sold 10.47 |
| 1393 | 6 | Ga | 10. 2.44 | = Survey ML6 1945; Survey ML326 1949; sold 20.4.59 |
| 1394 | 34 | Gl | 8.43 | Sunk at Trincomalee 1946 |
| 1395 | 34 | Gl | 10.43 | Sold 11.46, = yacht *Dorina* |
| 1396 | 47L | Th | 27. 3.44 | = FDB82; sold 1947, = *Pride of the Dart* |
| 1397 | 47L | Th | 7. 7.44 | FDB65; sold to Iran 8.10.48 |

**26 ordered 19.3.43**

| 1398 | 15 | Ga | 6.43 | Sold to Malay Government 7.47 |
|---|---|---|---|---|
| 1399 | 15 | Ga | 3.44 | Sold 2.46 |
| 1400 | 15 | Ga | 24. 1.45 | = FDB35; to Royal Netherlands Navy 15.5.46 |
| 1401 | 23 | Ga | 5.44 | Sold 1946, = yacht *Keredon* |
| 1402 | 23 | Ga | 16. 7.44 | = FDB66, = ML3514; sold 1958 |
| 1403 | 4 | Th | 8.44 | Sold 2.46 |
| 1404 | 4 | Th | 25. 5.44 | = ASL9; for disposal 8.46 |
| 1405 | 39 | Ga | 3.44 | = FDB83; to China 1947 |
| 1406 | 39 | Ga | 5.44 | = FDB84; to China 1947 |
| 1407 | 34 | Gl | 12.43 | To Royal Netherlands Navy 31.10.45 |
| 1408 | 34 | Gl | 29. 2.44 | = FDB78; sold 25.5.48 |
| 1409 | 7 | Ga | 12.43 | To Royal Netherlands Navy 31.10.45 |
| 1410 | 7 | Ga | 22. 2.44 | = ASL10; for disposal 8.46 |
| 1411 | 7 | Ga | 2. 5.44 | = Survey ML7 1945, = Survey ML327 1949; expended 6.53 as part of Coronation celebrations in Plymouth Sound |
| 1412 | 7 | Ga | 30. 5.44 | = ASL11; for disposal 8.46 |
| 1413 | 6 | Ga | 3.44 | Sold 1946 |
| 1414 | 6 | Ga | 4.44 | Sold 1946, = yacht *Aisha* |
| 1415 | 33 | Gl | 30.12.43 | = ASL12; for disposal 8.46 |
| 1416 | 33 | Gl | 1. 2.44 | = ASL13; for disposal 8.46 |
| 1417 | 33 | Gl | 28. 3.44 | Mined off Flushing 15.2.45 and lost in tow |
| 1418 | 33 | Gl | 4.44 | Sold 1946 |
| 1419 | 57 | Ga | 6. 3.44 | = ASL14, = *Peregrine* 1946; sold 20.8.58 |
| 1420 | 57 | Ga | 28. 4.44 | = ML3510; sold at Hong Kong 5.59 |
| 1421 | 37 | Ga | 23.12.43 | = FDB77; sold 1947 |
| 1422 | 37 | Ga | 3. 3.44 | = ASL15; for disposal 8.46 |
| 1423 | 37 | Ga | 4.44 | To France 1946, = VP747 |

**16 ordered 1.5.43**

| 1424 | 36 | Th | 22. 5.45 | To Burma 4.4.46 |
|---|---|---|---|---|
| 1425 | 36 | Th | 10. 7.45 | To France 3.46, = VP41 |
| 1426 | 36 | Th | — | Cancelled 1.46 |
| 1427 | 36 | Th | — | Cancelled 1.46 |
| 1428 | 3 | Th | — | Cancelled |
| 1429 | 3 | Th | — | Cancelled |
| 1430 | 48 | Gl | 5.10.45 | For disposal in India 7.46 |
| 1431 | 48 | Gl | — | Cancelled 1945 |
| 1432 | 10 | Gl | 11.12.45 | To France 1.7.46, = VP81 |
| 1433 | 5 | Gl | — | Cancelled 6.45 |

**16 ordered 25.3.44 (Lend-Lease)**

| 1440* | 24 | | 29. 3.45 | = FDB15; to Royal Netherlands Navy by US Navy 1945 |
|---|---|---|---|---|
| 1441 | 24 | | 20. 4.45 | = FDB16; returned to US Navy 10.45 |
| 1442 | 24 | | 20. 4.45 | = FDB17; returned to US Navy 10.45 |
| 1443 | 24 | | 6.45 | = FDB18; returned to US Navy 10.45 |
| 1444 | 18 | | 26. 4.45 | = FDB19; returned to US Navy 10.45 |

\* Nos 1434–1439 were ordered in India and cancelled

| ML | Builder | Engines | Completed | Fate |
|---|---|---|---|---|
| 1445 | 18 | | 6. 4.45 | = FDB20; returned to US Navy 10.45 |
| 1446 | 18 | | .45 | = FDB21; returned to US Navy 15.8.45 |
| 1447 | 44 | H | 16.12.44 | Returned to US Navy at New York 1.46 |
| 1448 | 44 | H | 1. 1.45 | Returned to US Navy at New York 1.46 |
| 1449 | 44 | H | 17. 3.45 | = FDB32; to Royal Netherlands Navy by US Navy 1945 |
| 1450 | 22 | | 4. 1.45 | = FDB11; to Royal Netherlands Navy by US Navy 1945 |
| 1451 | 22 | | 26. 3.45 | = FDB22; to Royal Netherlands Navy by US Navy 1945 |
| 1452 | 22 | | 19. 4.45 | = FDB23; returned US Navy 10.45 |
| 1453 | 42 | | 24. 1.45 | = FDB12; to Royal Netherlands Navy by US Navy 1945 |
| 1454 | 42 | | 13. 3.45 | = FDB24; to Royal Netherlands Navy by US Navy 1945 |
| 1455 | 42 | | 2. 4.45 | = FDB25; returned US Navy 10.45 |

**16 ordered 7.8.43**

| ML | Builder | Engines | Completed | Fate |
|---|---|---|---|---|
| 1456 | 7 | Ga | 25. 7.44 | Lent to Burma 8.45; gift to Burma 1.48 |
| 1457 | 7 | Ga | 21. 9.44 | To France 1.7.46, = VP42 |
| 1458 | 23 | Ga | 27.11.44 | Sold 1947 |
| 1459 | 23 | Ga | 6. 3.45 | = FDB36; for disposal 9.46 at Calcutta |
| 1460 | 23 | Ga | — | Cancelled 1944 |
| 1461 | 33 | Gl | 7. 6.44 | = ASL16; for disposal 8.46 |
| 1462 | 33 | Gl | 27. 7.44 | Lent to Burma 8.45; gift to Burma 1.48 |
| 1463 | 33 | Gl | 18. 9.44 | Lent to Burma 8.45; gift to Burma 1.48 |
| 1464 | 33 | | — | Cancelled 1944 |
| 1465 | 6 | Ga | 26. 5.44 | Sold 1945 |
| 1466 | 6 | Ga | 25. 7.44 | = FDB67; sold 1947 |
| 1467 | 6 | Ga | 28. 9.44 | Lent to Burma 8.45; gift to Burma 1.48 |
| 1468 | 6 | Ga | 11.12.44 | Sold 1947 |
| 1469 | 49 | Th | 4. 7.44 | = FDB68; sold 9.9.47 |
| 1470 | 49 | Th | 3.10.44 | To Royal Netherlands Navy 1947 |
| 1471 | 49 | Th | 9. 1.45 | = FDB71; sold 4.3.48 |

**4 ordered 25.3.44 (Lend-Lease)**

| ML | Builder | Engines | Completed | Fate |
|---|---|---|---|---|
| 1472 | 26 | | 13. 3.45 | = FDB13; to Royal Netherlands Navy by US Navy 1945 |
| 1473 | 26 | | 17. 1.45 | = FDB14; to Royal Netherlands Navy by US Navy 1945 |
| 1474 | 26 | | 17. 3.45 | = FDB26; to Royal Netherlands Navy by US Navy 1945 |
| 1475 | 26 | | 17. 3.45 | = FDB27; to Royal Netherlands Navy by US Navy 1945 |

**3 ordered 10.1.44**

| ML | Builder | Engines | Completed | Fate |
|---|---|---|---|---|
| 1476 | 34 | Gl | 11. 8.44 | Sold 11.47 |
| 1477 | 34 | Gl | 12. 9.44 | Lent to Burma 8.45; gift to Burma 1.48 |
| 1478 | 34 | Gl | 19.11.44 | Lent to Burma 8.45; gift to Burma 1.48 |

**16 ordered 29.11.44**

| ML | Builder | Engines | Completed | Fate |
|---|---|---|---|---|
| 1479 | 4 | Th | 12.10.44 | To Royal Netherlands Navy 1947 |
| 1480 | 4 | Th | 17. 2.45 | For disposal 7.46 at Bombay |
| 1481 | 47L | | — | Cancelled 1945; completed as a yacht |
| 1482 | 47L | | — | Cancelled 1945 |
| 1483 | 6 | | 20. 2.45 | = FDB37; for disposal 1946 |
| 1484 | 6 | | — | Cancelled 1944 |
| 1485 | 6 | | — | Cancelled 1944 |
| 1486 | 7 | Ga | 22.11.44 | Lent to Burma 8.45; gift to Burma 1.48 |
| 1487 | 7 | | — | Cancelled 1944 |
| 1488 | 37 | Ga | 11.11.44 | Lent to Burma 8.45; gift to Burma 1.48 |
| 1489 | 37 | Ga | 27. 1.45 | = FDB38; to Royal Netherlands Navy 1945 |
| 1490 | 33 | | — | Cancelled 1944 |
| 1491 | 33 | | — | Cancelled 1944 |
| 1492 | 33 | | — | Cancelled 1944 |
| 1493 | 39 | Ga | 6. 2.45 | = FDB39; to Royal Netherlands Navy 1945 |
| 1494 | 39 | | — | Cancelled 1944 |

**Harbour defence motor launch typical sheer elevation, internal profile, deck plan and plan below deck (MLs 1129–1136)**

1 Deck fitting to emergency tiller
2 Hatch to after peak
3 10ft sailing dinghy
4 Holman projector chock
5 Companion
6 Fuel tank filler
7 Lubricating oil filler
8 Gravity tank fuel filler
9 Deck light
10 Bilge pump deck fitting
11 Deck filer to paraffin tank
12 M/S socket for davit
13 CQR anchor
14 MV with fan under
15 Stove pipe
16 Windlass
17 Davit
18 Mushroom vent
19 Ready use locker
20 Vegetable safe
21 Warp crate
22 3in dia vent
23 8in dia vent
24 Machine gun mounting
25 Ladder
26 4in dia vent
27 Mast
28 After peak
29 Wardroom
30 Keyboard
31 Shelves
32 W/T room
33 POs' cabin
34 150gal fuel tank
35 Lister auxiliary engine
36 Batteries
37 Stool
38 Engineroom
39 Workbench
40 Vice
41 20gal oil tank
42 50gal gravity tank
43 Portable decking
44 Sea inlet
45 Fuel tank, 345gal
46 Fuel tank, 315gal
47 Passage
48 Galley
49 Hinge-up table
50 Sink
51 Cupboard
52 Asdic gear
53 Refrigerator
54 Coal locker
55 Alternator
56 Crew's WC
57 Wash basin
58 Forepeak
59 Settee berths with foam cushions
60 Hinged cot frames
61 Portable water tank under table
62 Loudspeakers
63 Fan
64 Wheelhouse
65 Throttles
66 Voice pipes
67 Chart table
68 A/S recorder
69 Rifle rack
70 Pistol rack
71 First aid chest
72 Blackout curtain
73 Compass

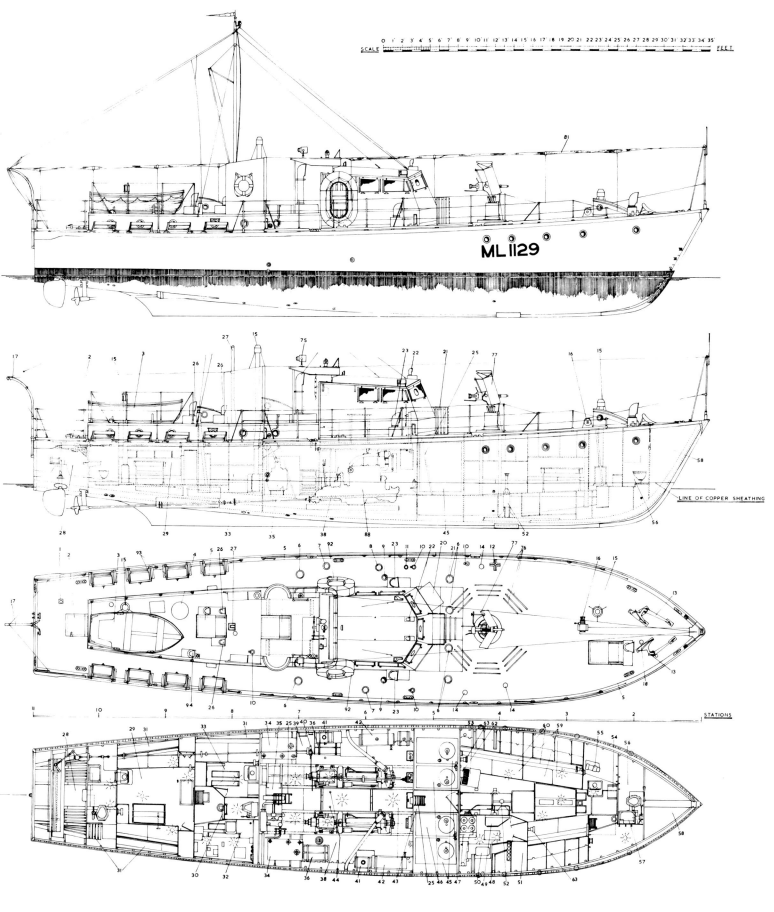

| | | | |
|---|---|---|---|
| 74 | Flag locker | 79 | Masterhead light |
| 75 | 10in signal lamp | 80 | Navigation light |
| 76 | Foot strips | 81 | Awning |
| 77 | 2-pounder gun | 82 | Carley float |
| 78 | 20mm Oerlikon | 83 | Depth charge rack |

| | |
|---|---|
| 84 | 6in dia vent |
| 85 | Stanchion |
| 86 | Safety rail |
| 87 | Mark VII depth charge |
| 88 | Thornycroft 260bhp diesel engine |

| | |
|---|---|
| 92 | Carley float |
| 93 | Depth charge rack |
| 94 | 6in dia vent |

Harbour defence motor launch typical
sheer elevation, internal profile, deck
plan and plan below deck (MLs 1283–
1291); (right and opposite:) bridge plan
and sections

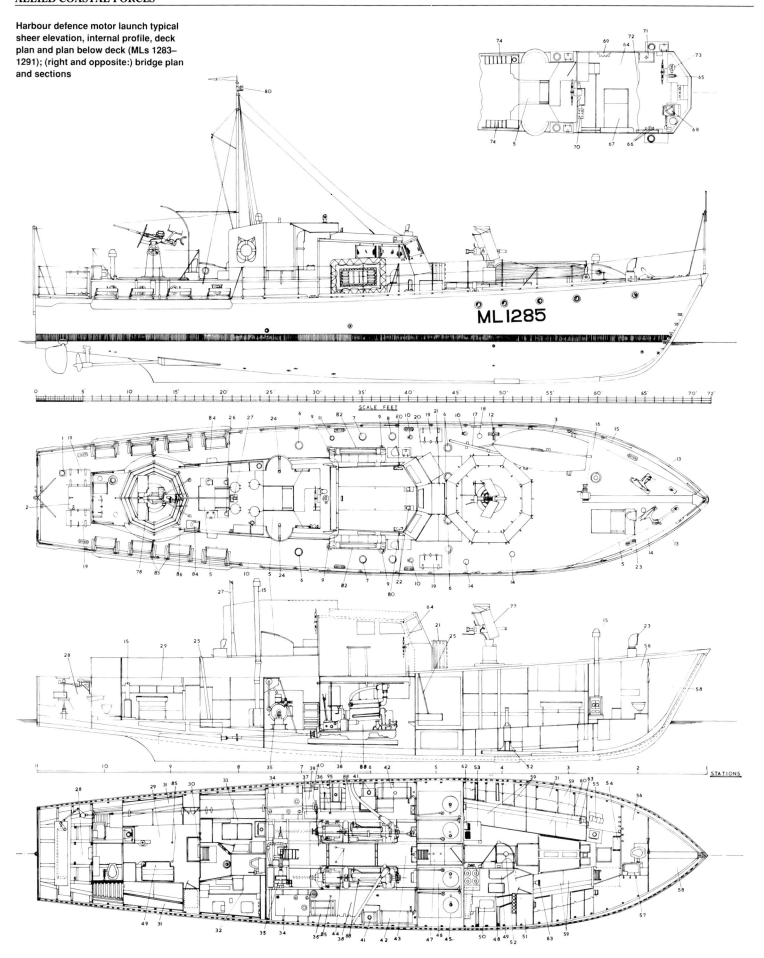

SCALE FEET

STATIONS

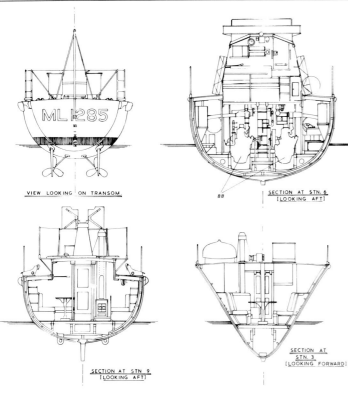

VIEW LOOKING ON TRANSOM

SECTION AT STN. 6
[LOOKING AFT]

SECTION AT STN 9
[LOOKING AFT]

SECTION AT
STN. 3
[LOOKING FORWARD]

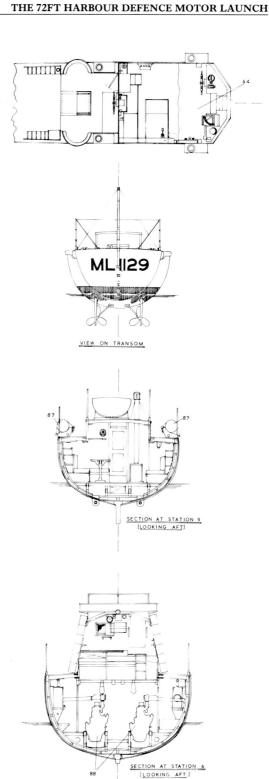

VIEW ON TRANSOM

SECTION AT STATION 9
[LOOKING AFT]

SECTION AT STATION 6
[LOOKING AFT]

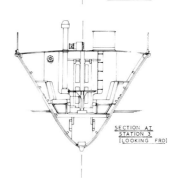

SECTION AT
STATION 3
[LOOKING FRD]

| | |
|---|---|
| 1 Deck fitting to emergency tiller | 47 Passage |
| 2 Hatch to after peak | 48 Galley |
| 3 10ft sailing dinghy | 49 Hinge-up table |
| 4 Holman projector chock | 50 Sink |
| 5 Companion | 51 Cupboard |
| 6 Fuel tank filler | 52 Asdic gear |
| 7 Lubricating oil filler | 53 Refrigerator |
| 8 Gravity tank fuel filler | 54 Coal locker |
| 9 Deck light | 55 Alternator |
| 10 Bilge pump deck fitting | 56 Crew's WC |
| 11 Deck filer to paraffin tank | 57 Wash basin |
| 12 M/S socket for davit | 58 Forepeak |
| 13 CQR anchor | 59 Settee berths with foam cushions |
| 14 MV with fan under | 60 Hinged cot frames |
| 15 Stove pipe | 61 Portable water tank under table |
| 16 Windlass | 62 Loudspeakers |
| 17 Davit | 63 Fan |
| 18 Mushroom vent | 64 Wheelhouse |
| 19 Ready use locker | 65 Throttles |
| 20 Vegetable safe | 66 Voice pipes |
| 21 Warp crate | 67 Chart table |
| 22 3in dia vent | 68 A/S recorder |
| 23 8in dia vent | 69 Rifle rack |
| 24 Machine gun mounting | 70 Pistol rack |
| 25 Ladder | 71 First aid chest |
| 26 4in dia vent | 72 Blackout curtain |
| 27 Mast | 73 Compass |
| 28 After peak | 74 Flag locker |
| 29 Wardroom | 75 10in signal lamp |
| 30 Keyboard | 76 Foot strips |
| 31 Shelves | 77 2-pounder gun |
| 32 W/T room | 78 20mm Oerlikon |
| 33 POs' cabin | 79 Masterhead light |
| 34 150gal fuel tank | 80 Navigation light |
| 35 Lister auxiliary engine | 81 Awning |
| 36 Batteries | 82 Carley float |
| 37 Stool | 83 Depth charge rack |
| 38 Engineroom | 84 6in dia vent |
| 39 Workbench | 85 Stanchion |
| 40 Vice | 86 Safety rail |
| 41 20gal oil tank | 87 Mark VII depth charge |
| 42 50gal gravity tank | 88 Thornycroft 260bhp diesel engine |
| 43 Portable decking | 92 Carley float |
| 44 Sea inlet | 93 Depth charge rack |
| 45 Fuel tank, 345gal | 94 6in dia vent |
| 46 Fuel tank, 315gal | |

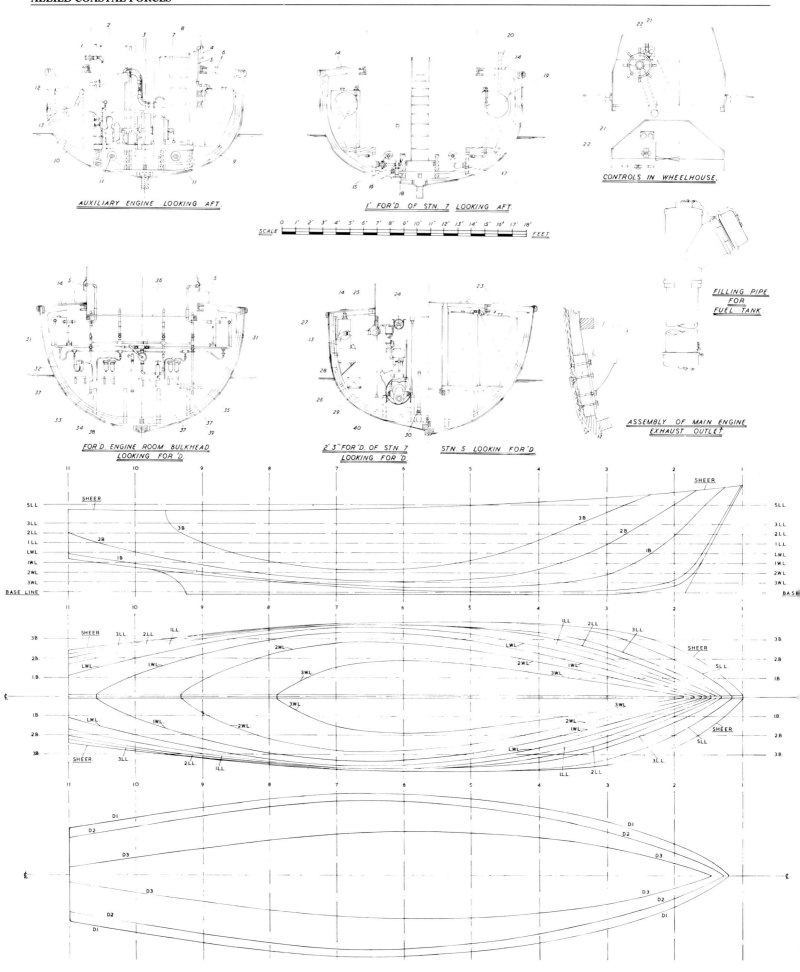

AUXILIARY ENGINE LOOKING AFT.

1' FOR'D. OF STN. 7 LOOKING AFT.

CONTROLS IN WHEELHOUSE.

SCALE — FEET

FILLING PIPE
FOR
FUEL TANK.

FOR'D. ENGINE ROOM BULKHEAD
LOOKING FOR'D

2' 3" FOR'D. OF STN. 7
LOOKING FOR'D

STN. 5 LOOKIN FOR'D.

ASSEMBLY OF MAIN ENGINE
EXHAUST OUTLET.

**Opposite: 72ft HDML typical
engineroom sections and details**

| | | | |
|---|---|---|---|
| 1 | Connection for deck washing, etc | 19 | Supply pipe from tank |
| 2 | Silencer (with slight fall towards outlet to be self draining) | 20 | Filling pipe in position |
| | | 21 | Instrument board carrying tachometers |
| 3 | Exhaust pipe between engine and silencer (lagged) | 22 | MRC fuel pump controls |
| 4 | Cover over vent | 23 | 8in screwed deck plate over filler |
| 5 | Vent pipe | 24 | Engineroom telegraph |
| 6 | Resistances | 25 | Support for exhaust pipe |
| 7 | Switchboard | 26 | Asdic batteries |
| 8 | Change-over switch | 27 | 20gal tank (port and starboard) |
| 9 | Gardner auxiliary unit | 28 | Tray under oil tank |
| 10 | Bench (semi-portable) | 29 | Instrument board on each engine |
| 11 | Watertight bulkhead gland | 30 | Port engine sea inlet |
| 12 | Stern tube water pressure gauge | 31 | Tank sight glass |
| 13 | Short length of rubber pipe | 32 | Auxiliary engine fuel filter |
| 14 | 6in screwed deck plate over filler | 33 | To after main tank |
| 15 | 2in OD copper pipe to auxiliary engine service pump | 34 | Port engine fuel filter |
| 16 | Sea inlet for service and circulating pumps on auxiliary engine | 35 | Starboard engine fuel filter |
| | | 36 | Semi-rotary hand pump |
| 17 | Water pump for stern tube bearings | 37 | Drip tray |
| 18 | Connection for auxiliary engine circulating pump | 38 | Filler pipe clipped to bulkhead |
| | | 39 | Auto Klean strainer |
| | | 40 | Thornycroft diesel engine |

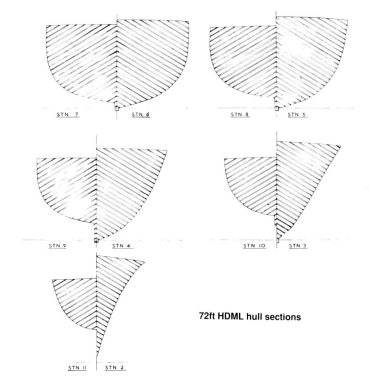

**72ft HDML hull sections**

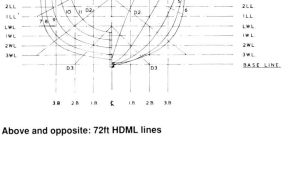

**Above and opposite: 72ft HDML lines**

**72ft HDML typical deck plan when fitted
with an Oropesa sweep**

| | | | |
|---|---|---|---|
| 1 | Roller fairlead | 27 | Vickers gas operated .303in machine gun |
| 2 | Towing bollard | | |
| 3 | Fairlead | 28 | Deck light |
| 4 | Bollard | 29 | 8in water box vent |
| 5 | Hatch to after peak | 30 | Open bridge |
| 6 | Mushroom vent | 31 | Kite otter multiplane |
| 7 | Stove pipe funnel | 32 | 8in water vent to engineroom |
| 8 | Non-purchase reel | 33 | Wheelhouse |
| 9 | Depth charge chute | 34 | Bowlight |
| 10 | 20mm Oerlikon on Mark IIA or Mark VII mounting | 35 | Oil fuel filling cap |
| | | 36 | 2-pounder ready use locker |
| 11 | Oerlikon ready use locker | 37 | Wash deck locker |
| 12 | 6in water box vent (wardroom) | 38 | Davit |
| 13 | 4in water box vent (petty officers' mess | 39 | Meat safe |
| | | 40 | Deck socket for A/S davit |
| 14 | Companion to wardroom, etc | 41 | 10ft sailing dinghy on chocks |
| 15 | Grenade box | 42 | 2-pounder Mark IIC mounting |
| 16 | Step | 43 | 4in waterbox vent |
| 17 | Ready use .303in magazine container | 44 | 9in cowl vent |
| 18 | W/T lead in | 45 | Stanchion socket |
| 19 | Mast tabernacle | 46 | Hand windlass |
| 20 | Deck pump | 47 | Companion to forward mess |
| 21 | Flag locker | 48 | 60lb CQR anchor |
| 22 | Fireworks tank | 49 | 80lb CQR anchor |
| 23 | Deck locker | 50 | 3½in cowl vent |
| 24 | Lifebuoy | 51 | Bullring |
| 25 | Float sweep | 52 | Jackstaff |
| 26 | Engineroom companion | | |

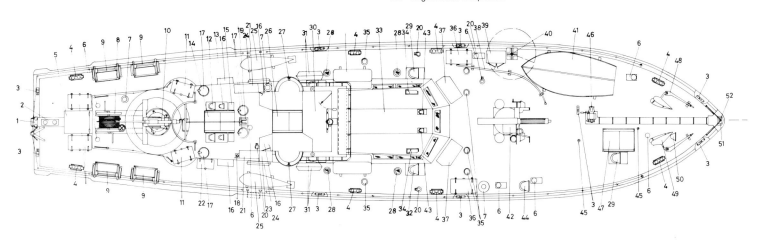

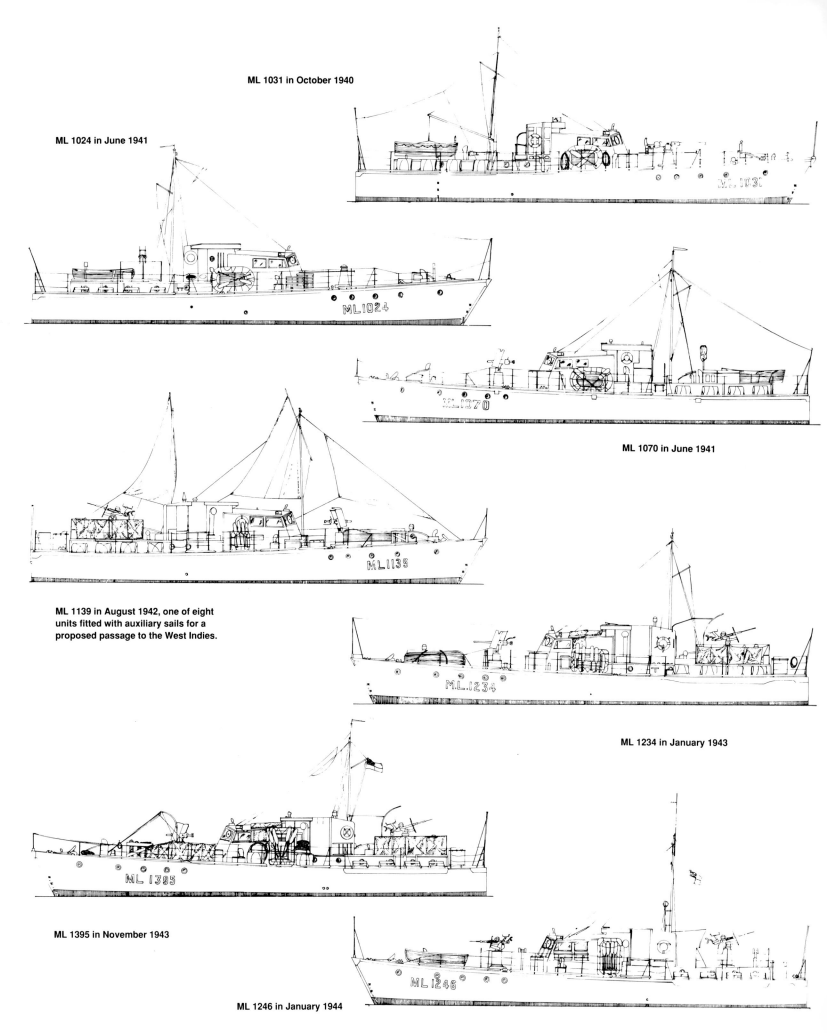

ML 1031 in October 1940

ML 1024 in June 1941

ML 1070 in June 1941

ML 1139 in August 1942, one of eight
units fitted with auxiliary sails for a
proposed passage to the West Indies.

ML 1234 in January 1943

ML 1395 in November 1943

ML 1246 in January 1944

# The US Navy SC 497 class 110ft subchaser

The ancestry of the SC 497 class 110ft subchaser of World War II can be traced to a similar design conceived in 1917. Realising that US involvement in World War I was imminent, the US Navy concluded that a large number of coastal patrol and anti-submarine craft would be required. To achieve the numbers needed, and to minimise the need to use strategic materials (namely steel) and skilled labour, these craft would have to be of wooden construction and capable of being built by small commercial boatyards.

Initially the Navy considered buying a number of 80ft Elco motor launches, 550 of which had been built for the Royal Navy in 1915–16. Designed for anti-submarine warfare, the 80ft Elcos were well liked by the Royal Navy, but they were too small and too primitively armed to be truly effective. Consequently, the Bureau of Construction and Repair Preliminary Design Division began a series of studies that would eventually result in the first 110ft SC design.

Outwardly similar to the World War II SCs, the original design had a slender wooden hull powered by three 220bhp Standard Motor Company petrol engines and was capable of about 17 knots. Trunk cabins were built above the main deck to provide sufficient headroom in the shallow hull. A small, simple pilothouse with wing extensions was mounted atop the forward trunk cabin. Armament varied somewhat; generally, either a 6-pounder or 3in/23 was mounted forward and a single Y gun aft.

These first SCs were built by both private and government yards. As the type had been designed for mass production, SC construction proceeded rapidly. On 19 August 1917 the US Navy commissioned SC 6, the first of its 110ft boats; two years later, on 26 August 1919, it commissioned SC 444, the last of 440 SCs eventually built for the USN and France.

During their fifteen months of combat service the SCs conducted patrol and anti-submarine operations along the Altantic Seaboard of the US and in European waters. However, like most war-expedient designs, they had short lives. By 1921 most of those in US Navy service had been decommissioned and sold. Of the survivors, only two, SC 412 and 437, were still in commission at the end of World War II.

Like their World War I counterparts, the SC 497 class subchasers were developed in response to the impending US involvement in another war. The design considerations were remarkably similar to those for the earlier craft: large numbers were required quickly, strategic materials and skilled labour were to be conserved, and contracts were to be let to many small boatyards.

In 1938 a patrol craft design competition was held. From the proposals received, two SC designs were selected and, in 1940, two prototypes (initially designated PC 449 and PC 450) were built.

PC 449 was designed by Elco, but built by Luders Marine Construction Company, while PC 450 was a modernised World War I design built by the American Car and Foundry. Outwardly, both designs differed little in appearance, dimensions, armament, and performance from their World War I counterparts. Both mounted a 3in/23 forward, and PC 450 was fitted with two depth charge tracks at the stern. Interestingly, neither mounted a Y gun. Each,

*Photographed on 19 May 1944, 25 years after her initial commissioning, SC 412 still retains most of her original WWI appearance. While superficially similar to her WWII sisters, she was nearly 2ft narrower, displaced about 20 tons less, and was much slower. US Navy*

### US 110ft subchaser data

Dimensional variation among the SCs built during World War II was extensive. The illustrative particulars shown below were taken from the Booklet of General Plans for SC 676 and SC 1474.

| | SC 676 | SC 1474 |
|---|---|---|
| **Builder** | W A Robinson | Quincy Adams Yacht Yard |
| **Length overall** | 111ft 6¾in | 110ft 0in |
| **Length on waterline** | 107ft 6in | 106ft 8¼in |
| **Beam** | 18ft 8½in | 18ft 7¾in |
| **Draught** | 5ft 9in | 5ft 1in |
| **Displacement** | 95 tons | 98 tons |
| **Armament** | one 3in/50 | one 40mm Mark 3 |
| | two 20mm Mark 4 | three 20mm Mark 10 |
| | two Mark 6 K guns | two Mark 6 K guns |
| | two stern depth charge tracks | ten Type C depth charge racks |
| | two Mark 20 mousetraps | two Mark 20 mousetraps |
| **Machinery** | two GM 'Pancake' diesels, each 1200shp | |
| | or | |
| | two GM 8-268A diesels, each 500shp | |

*SC 661 on the day of her commissioning, 6 October 1942. She displays the original SC armament of one 3in/23 forward and two single .50in machine guns amidships. No radar is fitted, but a crow's nest is mounted midway up the mast. US Navy*

however, was diesel-powered and twin screwed, which was a major departure from the earlier petrol-powered, triple-screw design.

Neither design proved successful, as performance and firepower were well below that needed to deal with modern submarines. On the verge of cancellation, the SC programme was saved primarily by the introduction of the so-called 'pancake' diesel developed by General Motors and a revised hull design. Developing twice the horsepower of the original GM 8-268A diesels (2400 against 1200shp), the new engines raised top speed from 17 knots to about 22 knots, although the range remained the same (about 1500 miles at 12 knots).

The new design commenced with SC 497, built by the Westergard Boat Works. As is often the case, however, the class leader was not the first to be completed. This honour went to SC 507, built by the Mathis Yacht Yard and completed on 19 January 1942, nearly three months earlier than SC 497.

Of all-wood construction, the SC's graceful hull incorporated longitudinal yellow pine or Douglas fir planking over 109 frames. A layer of ¾in white oak sheathing was applied the full length of the hull. On early boats this sheathing ran parallel to, and approximately 1ft above and below, the waterline. Beginning with SC 1474, the upper course of sheathing approximated the sheer line and met the stem at about the 8ft draught mark. Interestingly, the sheathing planks were spaced ⅛in apart. An external keel with extended skeg aft protected the lower part of the hull.

Watertight integrity was enhanced by seven watertight bulkheads, which divided the hull into the following compartments:

Forepeak
Forward crew's quarters
Magazine
Officers' quarters/radio and sound room
Engineroom
Fuel/freshwater tank space
After crew's quarters/galley
Lazarette

Additional fuel and freshwater tanks were located below the forward crew's quarters and officers' quarters

Two trunk cabins about 1ft high were incorporated to provide additional headroom in the relatively shallow hull. The forward trunk cabin extended from frame 37 (aft bulkhead of the magazine) to frame 71 (aft engineroom bulkhead). Access to the engineroom was through a companionway on the aft end of this trunk.

*Another view of 661 on her commissioning day. The K guns have not yet been fitted, although the mounting points can be seen to either side of the crewmember standing aft. The two racks on either side of the mizzen mast are for depth charge arbors. US Navy*

The aft trunk cabin was very small, extending only over part of the galley and the aft crew's head. On early SCs mounting only two 20mm, a companionway, vegetable locker, several vents, and a wherry were mounted on the roof. Later boats had a bandstand built over the after trunk for a third 20mm.

An austere pilothouse of ¾in plywood was mounted on the forward trunk cabin. Access to the pilothouse from the main deck was through a door to port on the aft bulkhead. Three hatches were fitted to the pilothouse floor for access from the engineroom, officers' quarters, and the radio and sound room. A large vent was installed to starboard on the aft bulkhead of the pilothouse.

As first designed, none of the SCs carried radar. In 1942 a number of SCs (including SC 712 and SC 738) were experimentally fitted with the Canadian SW-1C radar. As it became available in sufficient numbers, the standard SG surface search radar was mounted atop the mast.

The standard sonar type used was QC.

Eight SCs (644, 757, 1035, 1053, 1056, 1071, 1072 and 1366) were converted to motor gunboats (PGM 1–8) in November 1943. This conversion involved major alterations, including the removal of the pilothouse and all ASW gear. A simple open bridge replaced the original enclosed pilothouse. Single 40mm Mark 3 mounts were fitted fore and aft within semi-circular splinter shields. Two pairs of Mark 17 twin .5in turrets were installed on either side amidships. What appears to be SG radar was mounted atop a PT-style bipod radar mast aft of the open bridge.

These craft were originally intended to accompany PT boats on 'barge busting' operations, but proved too slow to keep up with their speedy companions. As a result, a number of older PTs were converted to the PGM role. Interestingly, three 77ft Elco PTs (PT 59, 60, and 61) had been converted to the PGM role in October 1943 and carried the same firepower on a hull 33ft shorter than, and with half the displacement of, the SC! These PT gunboats will be described in detail in a future volume.

Between 1943 and 1945 seventy-eight SCs were transferred to the Soviet Navy. These included: SC 500, 537–38, 634, 643, 646–47, 657, 660–61, 663, 673–75, 685, 687, 713, 719–721, 752, 754, 756, 774, 986, 997, 1007, 1011, 1021, 1031, 1060, 1073–76, 1283–87, 1295, 1324, 1364–65, 1475–93, 1496–99, 1502–08, 1510–12, and 1517. According to Meister (1977), 1477, 1485, 1507, and 685 were lost in action, the remainder being returned to the USN, scrapped, or scuttled by 1956. Efforts to obtain official information from Soviet sources were unsuccessful at the time of publication. Should additional official material become available, it will be included in a future volume.

*SC 756 on 17 June 1943, graphically displaying the cramped space aft on later boats. The two stern depth charge tracks have been landed and replaced by ten single Type C racks. Gone, too, are the mast and boom for handling depth charges. The K guns are now serviced by roller racks. US Navy*

*SC 696 at Daytona Beach, Florida, on 23 November 1942. While she mounts the original 3in/23 forward, the .50in MGs have been replaced by two 20mm Mark 4 mounts. Note that the pilothouse wing is only half as large as that fitted to SC 667. She was lost during a Luftwaffe raid on Palermo on 23 August 1943, when a 550lb bomb hit her pilothouse, causing fires which ultimately detonated her magazine. US Navy*

*SC 738 on 11 November 1942, sporting a Canadian SW-1C radar antenna. The mast and boom aft were for lifting depth charges to the K guns. US Navy*

**Summary of 110ft SC transfers to foreign navies during World War II**

| SC number | New name or number | Date transferred |
|---|---|---|
| **Brazil** | | |
| 763 | *Javari* | 7.12.42 |
| 762 | *Jutai* | 31.12.42 |
| 766 | *Jurvena* | 31.12.42 |
| 765 | *Jaguaro* | 16. 2.43 |
| 767 | *Jaguaribe* | 16. 2.43 |
| 1289 | *Jundiai* | 26. 4.43 |
| 1288 | *Jacui* | 19. 5.43 |
| 764 | *Jurua* | 31.12.44 |
| | | |
| **France** | | |
| 1335 | CH 52 | 12.11.43 |
| 1344 | CH 62 | 19.11.43 |
| 1336 | CH 51 | 24.11.43 |
| 1345 | CH 61 | 23.12.43 |
| 1337 | CH 71 | 29.12.43 |
| 1346 | CH 72 | 18. 1.44 |
| 517 | CH 82 | 16. 3.44 |
| 508 | CH 95 | 18. 3.44 |
| 498 | CH 142 | 18. 3.44 |
| 497 | CH 96 | 18. 3.44 |
| 516 | CH 81 | 19. 3.44 |
| 519 | CH 83 | 27. 3.44 |
| 507 | CH 85 | 29. 3.44 |
| 529 | CH 84 | 31. 3.44 |
| 1331 | CH 6 | 11. 4.44 |
| 977 | CH 94 | 18. 5.44 |
| 639 | CH 93 | 22. 5.44 |
| 697 | CH 92 | 22. 5.44 |
| 1359 | CH 5 | 26. 8.44 |
| 526 | CH 114 | 25. 9.44 |
| 693 | CH 107 | 27. 9.44 |
| 666 | CH 134 | 27. 9.44 |
| 638 | CH 116 | 27. 9.44 |
| 522 | CH 111 | 27. 9.44 |
| 506 | CH 113 | 27. 9.44 |
| 691 | CH 133 | 29. 9.44 |
| 1030 | CH 136 | 2.10.44 |
| 533 | CH 104 | 2.10.44 |
| 524 | CH 101 | 7.10.44 |
| 770 | CH 141 | 8.10.44 |
| 525 | CH 102 | 8.10.44 |
| 676 | CH 105 | 9.10.44 |
| 515 | CH 121 | 10.10.44 |
| 1043 | CH 125 | 10.10.44 |
| 655 | CH 144 | 23.10.44 |
| 690 | CH 106 | 24.10.44 |
| 978 | CH 145 | 26.10.44 |
| 979 | CH 146 | 27.10.44 |
| 534 | CH 122 | 28.10.44 |
| 1029 | CH 123 | 30.10.44 |
| 503 | CH 112 | 4.11.44 |
| 532 | | 16.11.44 |
| 651 | CH 135 | 16.11.44 |
| 535 | CH 143 | 16.11.44 |
| 695 | | 16.11.44 |
| 692 | CH 131 | 17.11.44 |
| 530 | CH 115 | 17.11.44 |
| 771 | CH 124 | 17.11.44 |

*A shortage of 3in/23s led to the introduction of the 3in/50 on the SCs. This 1 January 1943 view of SC 734 shows her in what appears to be Ocean Gray overall. Note the masthead platform for the soon-to-be-installed SG radar. The rectangular object midway up the mast is a lookout position. US Navy*

*SC 717 on 2 July 1944. Note that she carries a 40mm forward and three 20mm Mark 10s. SG radar has also been fitted, and the heavy Mark 4 20mm mounts have been landed to make room for the lighter Mark 10s. US Navy*

*SC 667 on 19 September 1942, the day before her commissioning. Note that she carries the original PC designator, changed just days later to SC. US Navy*

| SC number | New name or number | Date transferred |
|-----------|--------------------|------------------|
| **USSR** | | |
| 1283 | | 13. 7.43 |
| 1284 | | 23. 7.43 |
| 1285 | | 23. 7.43 |
| 1073 | | 13. 8.43 |
| 1286 | | 13. 8.43 |
| 1074 | | 13. 8.43 |
| 719 | | 14. 8.43 |
| 720 | | 24. 9.43 |
| 1075 | | 24. 9.43 |
| 1287 | | 27. 9.43 |
| 721 | | 27. 9.43 |
| 1484 | | 9. 5.44 |
| 1480 | | 17. 5.44 |
| 1488 | | 19. 5.44 |
| 1496 | | 20. 5.44 |
| 1489 | | 25. 5.44 |
| 1492 | | 7. 6.44 |
| 1490 | | 15. 6.44 |
| 1498 | | 24. 6.44 |
| 1481 | | 27. 6.44 |
| 1475 | | 1. 7.44 |
| 1476 | | 1. 7.44 |
| 1507 | | 4. 7.44 |
| 1517 | | 6. 7.44 |
| 1510 | | 7. 7.44 |
| 1485 | | 8. 7.44 |
| 1504 | | 11. 7.44 |
| 1502 | | 18. 7.44 |
| 1477 | | 19. 7.44 |
| 1493 | | 28. 7.44 |
| 1482 | | 8. 8.44 |
| 1511 | | 15. 8.44 |
| 1505 | | 20. 8.44 |
| 1486 | | 22. 8.44 |
| 1497 | | 23. 8.44 |
| 1491 | | 30. 8.44 |
| 1478 | | 2. 9.44 |
| 1508 | | 6. 9.44 |
| 1483 | | 9. 9.44 |
| 1506 | | 21. 9.44 |
| 1499 | | 22. 9.44 |
| 1503 | | 30. 9.44 |
| 1479 | | 3.10.44 |
| 1487 | | 12.10.44 |
| 1512 | | 21.10.44 |
| 713 | | 5. 5.45 |
| 537 | | 26. 5.45 |
| 646 | | 26. 5.45 |
| 647 | | 26. 5.45 |
| 661 | | 26. 5.45 |
| 674 | | 26. 5.45 |
| 687 | | 26. 5.45 |
| 657 | | 5. 6.45 |
| 660 | | 5. 6.45 |
| 663 | | 5. 6.45 |
| 673 | | 5. 6.45 |
| 986 | | 5. 6.45 |
| 1021 | | 5. 6.45 |
| 1060 | | 5. 6.45 |
| 500 | | 9. 6.45 |

| SC number | New name or number | Date transferred |
|-----------|--------------------|------------------|
| 634 | | 10. 6.45 |
| 675 | | 10. 6.45 |
| 1295 | | 10. 6.45 |
| 1324 | | 10. 6.45 |
| 685 | | 19. 7.45 |
| 643 | | 17. 8.45 |
| 752 | | 17. 8.45 |
| 754 | | 17. 8.45 |
| 997 | | 17. 8.45 |
| 1007 | | 17. 8.45 |
| 1011 | | 17. 8.45 |
| 774 | | 17. 8.45 |
| 1031 | | 17. 8.45 |
| 1364 | | 17. 8.45 |
| 1365 | | 17. 8.45 |
| 538 | | 18. 8.45 |
| 756 | | 2. 9.45 |

## Summary of SC losses during World War II

| SC | Date | Cause |
|------|----------|-------------------|
| 709 | 21. 1.43 | Grounding |
| 1024 | 2. 3.43 | Collision |
| 740 | 17. 6.43 | Grounding |
| 751 | 22. 6.43 | Grounding |
| 694 | 23. 8.43 | Air raid, Salerno |
| 696 | 23. 8.43 | Air raid, Salerno |
| 1067 | 19.11.43 | Foundered |
| 700 | 10. 3.44 | Accident |
| 984 | 9. 4.44 | Grounding |
| PGM7 | 18. 7.44 | Collision |
| 744 | 27.11.44 | |
| 521 | 10. 7.45 | Foundered |
| 636 | 9.10.45 | |

## Summary of PGM conversions

| PGM | SC | Date |
|-----|------|----------|
| 1 | 644 | 10.12.43 |
| 2 | 757 | 10.12.43 |
| 3 | 1035 | 10.12.43 |
| 4 | 1053 | 10.12.43 |
| 5 | 1056 | 10.12.43 |
| 6 | 1071 | 10.12.43 |
| 7 | 1072 | 10.12.43 |
| 8 | 1366 | 10.12.43 |

# Construction list

| SC | Builder | Keel laid | Launched | Completed |
|---|---|---|---|---|
| 497 | 42 | 7. 3.41 | 4. 7.41 | 15. 4.42 |
| 498 | 42 | 12. 3.41 | 21. 7.41 | 29. 4.42 |
| 499 | 13 | 24. 4.41 | 24.10.41 | 13. 3.42 |
| 500 | 13 | 27. 2.41 | 11.10.41 | 31. 3.42 |
| 501 | 33 | 29. 4.41 | 24. 1.42 | 30. 4.42 |
| 502 | 33 | 6. 5.41 | 31. 1.42 | 3. 6.42 |
| 503 | 31 | 30. 1.41 | 14. 3.42 | 13. 4.42 |
| 504 | 31 | 30. 1.41 | 21. 3.42 | 23. 4.42 |
| 505 | 25 | 24. 2.41 | 23. 2.42 | 10. 4.42 |
| 506 | 25 | 24. 3.41 | 30. 1.42 | 27. 4.42 |
| 507 | 26 | 6. 2.41 | 30. 6.41 | 19. 1.42 |
| 508 | 26 | 10. 2.41 | 25. 7.41 | 27. 3.42 |
| | | | | |
| 511 | 1 | 1. 8.41 | 1. 4.42 | 27. 6.42 |
| 512 | 1 | 12. 8.41 | 26. 3.42 | 10. 7.42 |
| 513 | 30 | 16. 5.41 | 20. 1.42 | 28. 3.42 |
| 514 | 30 | 14. 6.41 | 7. 3.42 | 12. 4.42 |
| 515 | 11 | 24. 4.41 | 20. 9.41 | 16. 4.42 |
| 516 | 11 | 7. 5.41 | 11.10.41 | 5. 5.42 |
| 517 | 11 | 22. 5.41 | 11.10.41 | 4. 5.42 |
| 518 | 11 | 2. 6.41 | 12.11.41 | 11. 5.42 |
| 519 | 39 | 2. 6.41 | 14. 3.42 | 21. 4.42 |
| 520 | 39 | 15. 7.41 | 18. 4.42 | 25. 5.42 |
| 521 | 2 | 5. 5.41 | 1. 2.42 | 15. 4.42 |
| 522 | 2 | 14. 5.41 | 18. 2.42 | 1. 5.42 |
| | | | | |
| 524 | 26 | 29. 4.41 | 19. 9.41 | 13. 4.42 |
| 525 | 26 | 3. 7.41 | 21.11.41 | 30. 4.42 |
| 526 | 26 | 29. 7.41 | 30.12.41 | 11. 5.42 |
| 527 | 26 | 4. 9.41 | 21. 1.42 | 28. 5.42 |
| 528 | 26 | 24.10.41 | 17. 2.42 | 13. 6.42 |
| 529 | 26 | 24.11.41 | 16. 3.42 | 26. 6.42 |
| 530 | 42 | 27. 3.41 | 16. 8.41 | 12. 5.42 |
| 531 | 42 | 27. 3.41 | 4. 9.41 | 27. 5.42 |
| 532 | 25 | 19. 4.41 | 7. 4.42 | 15. 5.42 |
| 533 | 25 | 5. 5.41 | 13. 4.42 | 5. 6.42 |
| 534 | 25 | 23. 5.41 | 27. 4.42 | 10. 7.42 |
| 535 | 25 | 18. 6.41 | 9. 7.42 | 21. 7.42 |
| 536 | 22 | 29. 4.41 | 3. 5.42 | 1. 4.42 |
| 537 | 22 | 29. 4.41 | 21. 3.42 | 27. 4.42 |
| 538 | 22 | 17. 5.41 | 1. 4.42 | 9. 5.42 |
| 539 | 22 | 17. 5.41 | 7. 4.42 | 28. 5.42 |
| 540 | 32 | 28. 7.41 | 6. 4.42 | 22. 4.42 |
| 541 | 32 | 1. 8.41 | 11. 4.42 | 5. 5.42 |
| | | | | |
| 628 | 30 | 25. 8.41 | 15. 4.42 | 29. 4.42 |
| 629 | 30 | 3. 9.41 | 27. 4.42 | 15. 5.42 |
| 630 | 26 | 22.12.41 | 18. 4.42 | 5. 8.42 |
| 631 | 26 | 27. 1.42 | 19. 6.42 | 19. 8.42 |
| 632 | 26 | 23. 2.42 | 25. 6.42 | 2. 9.42 |
| 633 | 26 | 20. 3.42 | 3. 7.42 | 9. 9.42 |
| 634 | 26 | 27. 4.42 | 10. 7.42 | 26. 9.42 |
| 635 | 26 | 6. 6.42 | 14.10.42 | 23.10.42 |
| 636 | 39 | 29. 8.41 | 14. 5.42 | 11. 7.42 |
| 637 | 39 | 24.12.41 | 10. 6.42 | 31. 7.42 |
| 638 | 11 | 11. 8.41 | 20.12.41 | 27. 6.42 |
| 639 | 11 | 16. 8.41 | 31.12.41 | 21. 6.42 |
| 640 | 11 | 30. 8.41 | 17. 1.42 | 11. 7.42 |
| 641 | 11 | 7.11.41 | 12. 2.42 | 10. 7.42 |

## Codes for builders

| | | | |
|---|---|---|---|
| 1 | American Cruiser | 23 | Larson Boat Shop |
| 2 | Annapolis Yacht Yard | 24 | Liberty Drydock |
| 3 | Burger Boat | 25 | Luders Marine Construction |
| 4 | Calderwood Yacht Yard | 26 | Mathis Yacht Building |
| 5 | Dachel-Carter Shipbuilding | 27 | Perkins & Vaughan |
| 6 | Daytona Beach Boat Works | 28 | Peterson Boat Works |
| 7 | Delaware Bay Shipbuilding | 29 | Peyton |
| 8 | Dingle Boat Works | 30 | Quincy Adams Yacht Yard |
| 9 | Donovan Contracting | 31 | Rice Brothers |
| 10 | Dooley's Basin and Drydock | 32 | Robinson Marine Construction |
| 11 | Elizabeth City Shipyard | 33 | Seabrook Yacht |
| 12 | Fellows & Stewart | 34 | Simms |
| 13 | Fisher Boat Works | 35 | Snow Shipyards |
| 14 | George W Kneass | 36 | Thomas Knutson Shipbuilding |
| 15 | Gulf Marine Ways | 37 | Ventnor Boat Works |
| 16 | Harbor Boat Building | 38 | Victory Shipbuilding |
| 17 | Harris & Parsons | 39 | Vinyard Boat Building |
| 18 | Hiltebrant Dry Dock | 40 | W A Robinson |
| 19 | Inland Waterways | 41 | Weaver Shipyards |
| 20 | Island Dock | 42 | Westergard Boat Works |
| 21 | John E Matton | 43 | Wilmington Boat Works |
| 22 | Julius Petersen | | |

*SC 1049 on the ways at Ventnor Boat Works on 1 May 1943. Note the large diesel exhaust amidships.* US Navy

*SC 736 on 24 February 1943. The mast has not yet been modified to carry the SG antenna. She mounts a 3in/50 forward.* US Navy

| SC | Builder | Keel laid | Launched | Completed |
|---|---|---|---|---|
| 642 | 22 | 28.10.41 | 30. 5.42 | 4. 8.42 |
| 643 | 22 | 21.11.41 | 10. 6.42 | 5. 8.42 |
| 644 | 22 | 29.11.41 | 27. 6.42 | 2.10.42 |
| 645 | 22 | 1. 2.42 | 26. 7.42 | 2. 9.42 |
| 646 | 32 | 23. 9.41 | 21. 5.42 | 1. 7.42 |
| 647 | 32 | 23. 9.41 | 27. 6.42 | 3. 8.42 |
| 648 | 7 | 10.10.41 | 18. 4.42 | 11. 7.42 |
| 649 | 7 | 16.10.41 | 18. 4.42 | 31. 7.42 |
| 650 | 42 | 21.10.41 | 30. 4.42 | 20. 7.42 |
| 651 | 42 | 4.11.41 | 14. 5.42 | 8. 8.42 |
| 652 | 22 | 5.12.41 | 18. 4.42 | 16. 6.42 |
| 653 | 22 | 15.12.41 | 18. 4.42 | 6. 7.42 |
| 654 | 42 | 18. 9.41 | 4. 5.42 | 18. 7.42 |
| 655 | 42 | 11.10.41 | 12. 5.42 | 8. 8.42 |
| 656 | 35 | 6.12.41 | 2. 5.42 | 6. 8.42 |
| 657 | 35 | 20.12.41 | 22. 6.42 | 31. 8.42 |
| 658 | 1 | 8.12.41 | 6. 6.42 | 12. 8.42 |
| 659 | 1 | 16.12.41 | 29. 6.42 | 1.10.42 |
| 660 | 3 | 24.12.41 | 20. 6.42 | 18. 9.42 |
| 661 | 3 | 30.12.41 | 26. 6.42 | 6.10.42 |
| 662 | 13 | 4.11.41 | 11. 4.42 | 29. 5.42 |
| 663 | 13 | 4.11.41 | 22. 4.42 | 1. 7.42 |
| 664 | 5 | 19.11.41 | 21. 5.42 | 8. 8.42 |
| 665 | 5 | 25.11.41 | 12. 5.42 | 10. 8.42 |
| 666 | 41 | 16.10.41 | 17. 3.42 | 2. 9.42 |
| 667 | 41 | 16.10.41 | 4. 4.42 | 20. 9.42 |
| 668 | 6 | 5.11.41 | 12. 3.42 | 2. 7.42 |
| 669 | 6 | 17.11.41 | 21. 3.42 | 17. 7.42 |
| 670 | 19 | 17.11.41 | 6. 7.42 | 21. 8.42 |
| 671 | 19 | 17.11.41 | 8. 8.42 | 7.10.42 |
| 672 | 36 | 29.10.41 | 2. 5.42 | 15. 6.42 |
| 673 | 36 | 7.11.41 | 16. 5.42 | 6. 7.42 |
| 674 | 18 | 31.10.41 | 13. 3.42 | 12. 8.42 |
| 675 | 18 | 13.11.41 | 19. 3.42 | 10. 9.42 |
| 676 | 40 | 31. 1.42 | 23. 6.42 | 27. 7.42 |
| 677 | 40 | 27. 2.42 | 27. 7.42 | 19. 8.42 |
| 678 | 36 | 10. 3.42 | 17. 8.42 | 6.11.42 |
| 679 | 36 | 4. 3.42 | 29. 8.42 | 18.12.42 |
| 680 | 36 | 17. 3.42 | 7. 9.42 | 30. 1.43 |

| SC | Builder | Keel laid | Launched | Completed |
|---|---|---|---|---|
| 681 | 36 | 24. 3.42 | 20. 9.42 | 6. 3.43 |
| 682 | 1 | 8. 4.42 | 18. 9.42 | 1.11.42 |
| 683 | 1 | 9. 4.42 | 14.10.42 | 21.11.42 |
| 684 | 1 | 6. 7.42 | 21.11.42 | 11.12.42 |
| 685 | 1 | 9. 7.42 | 25. 3.42 | 12. 5.42 |
| 686 | 1 | 30.11.42 | 15. 4.43 | 26. 6.43 |
| 687 | 1 | 21. 1.43 | 5. 6.43 | 18. 8.43 |
| 688 | 2 | 25. 4.42 | 22. 8.42 | 28.11.42 |
| 689 | 2 | 27. 4.42 | 15. 8.42 | 2.11.42 |
| 690 | 2 | 22. 5.42 | 7. 9.42 | 16.12.42 |
| 691 | 2 | 31. 5.42 | 19. 9.42 | 30.12.42 |
| 692 | 4 | 26. 3.42 | 25. 9.42 | 25.11.42 |
| 693 | 4 | 15. 5.42 | 24.10.42 | 12. 1.43 |
| 694 | 6 | 21. 3.42 | 25. 5.42 | 6. 9.42 |
| 695 | 6 | 21. 3.42 | 4. 7.42 | 19.10.42 |
| 696 | 6 | 26. 3.42 | 6. 8.42 | 25.11.42 |
| 697 | 6 | 31. 3.42 | 15. 8.42 | 24.12.42 |
| 698 | 7 | 1. 3.42 | 7. 8.42 | 28. 9.42 |
| 699 | 7 | 8. 3.42 | 7. 9.42 | 14.10.42 |
| 700 | 7 | 25. 3.42 | 7. 9.42 | 2.11.42 |
| 701 | 7 | 18. 4.42 | 17. 9.42 | 9.12.42 |
| 702 | 7 | 2. 5.42 | 10.10.42 | 18.12.42 |
| 703 | 7 | 19. 5.42 | 28.11.42 | 5. 1.43 |
| 704 | 11 | 7. 3.42 | 6. 4.42 | 24. 9.42 |
| 705 | 11 | 7. 3.42 | 24. 4.42 | 29. 9.42 |
| 706 | 11 | 14. 3.42 | 26. 6.42 | 7.10.42 |
| 707 | 11 | 11. 4.42 | 10. 6.42 | 14.10.42 |
| 708 | 11 | 3. 5.42 | 26. 6.42 | 23.10.42 |
| 709 | 11 | 10. 6.42 | 15. 7.42 | 6.11.42 |
| 710 | 10 | 11. 3.42 | 7. 9.42 | 12.11.42 |
| 711 | 10 | 8. 4.42 | 17.10.42 | 26.12.42 |
| 712 | 13 | 16. 3.42 | 25. 7.42 | 10. 9.42 |
| 713 | 13 | 18. 4.42 | 25. 7.42 | 22.10.42 |
| 714 | 13 | 24. 4.42 | 17. 9.42 | 12.11.42 |
| 715 | 13 | 14. 5.42 | 23.10.42 | 26.11.42 |
| 716 | 13 | 18. 5.42 | 20.11.42 | 11.12.42 |
| 717 | 13 | 30. 7.42 | 14.12.42 | 6. 5.43 |
| 718 | 13 | 22. 9.42 | 31. 3.43 | 19. 5.43 |
| 719 | 13 | 22. 9.42 | 3. 4.43 | 10. 7.43 |
| 720 | 13 | 16.11.42 | 10. 4.43 | 27. 7.43 |

*A large number of SCs were transferred to the Soviet Union during WWII, including SC 1075, seen here on 9 August 1943 before her transfer.* US Navy

*Another view of SC 736.* US Navy

| SC | Builder | Keel laid | Launched | Completed |
|---|---|---|---|---|
| 721 | 13 | 16.11.42 | 17. 4.43 | 7. 8.43 |
| 722 | 16 | 5. 3.42 | 15. 5.42 | 14.11.42 |
| 723 | 16 | 6. 3.42 | 10. 6.42 | 7.12.42 |
| 724 | 16 | 6. 4.42 | 2. 7.42 | 23.12.42 |
| 725 | 16 | 7. 4.42 | 23. 7.42 | 31.12.42 |
| 726 | 16 | 8. 4.42 | 12. 8.42 | 18. 1.43 |
| 727 | 16 | 7. 5.42 | 7. 9.42 | 9. 2.43 |
| 728 | 16 | 8. 5.42 | 16.12.42 | 8. 3.43 |
| 729 | 16 | 9. 5.42 | 25. 1.43 | 19. 4.43 |
| 730 | 18 | 23. 3.42 | 5. 6.42 | 16.11.42 |
| 731 | 18 | 23. 3.42 | 17. 6.42 | 30.11.42 |
| 732 | 18 | 11. 4.42 | 27. 6.42 | 18.12.42 |
| 733 | 18 | 6. 6.42 | 10. 8.42 | 8. 1.43 |
| 734 | 23 | 15. 4.42 | 18. 7.42 | 28.12.42 |
| 735 | 23 | 20. 4.42 | 29. 8.42 | 12. 3.43 |
| 736 | 24 | 11. 4.42 | 29.10.42 | 25. 2.43 |
| 737 | 24 | 18. 4.42 | 15.12.42 | 20. 5.43 |
| 738 | 22 | 7. 3.42 | 27. 6.42 | 19.10.42 |
| 739 | 22 | 20. 3.42 | 4. 7.42 | 27. 6.42 |
| 740 | 22 | 24. 3.42 | 14. 7.42 | 13.11.42 |
| 741 | 22 | 1. 4.42 | 3. 8.42 | 14.12.42 |
| 742 | 22 | 22. 4.42 | 17. 8.42 | 5. 1.43 |
| 743 | 22 | 24. 4.42 | 26. 8.42 | 25. 2.43 |
| 744 | 30 | 18. 2.42 | 23. 5.42 | 10. 7.42 |
| 745 | 30 | 7. 3.42 | 15. 6.42 | 6. 8.42 |
| 746 | 30 | 1. 4.42 | 8. 7.42 | 16. 8.42 |
| 747 | 30 | 9. 4.42 | 28. 7.42 | 11. 9.42 |
| 748 | 30 | 27. 4.42 | 21. 8.42 | 28. 9.42 |
| 749 | 30 | 25. 5.42 | 7. 9.42 | 26.10.42 |
| 750 | 30 | 15. 6.42 | 26. 9.42 | 12.11.42 |
| 751 | 30 | 8. 7.42 | 15.10.42 | 27.11.42 |
| 752 | 32 | 8. 5.42 | 7.12.42 | 9. 1.43 |
| 753 | 32 | 8. 5.42 | 4. 1.43 | 25. 3.43 |
| 754 | 32 | 6. 6.42 | 23. 2.43 | 25. 4.43 |
| 755 | 32 | 20. 6.42 | 3. 4.43 | 16. 5.43 |
| 756 | 32 | 9. 7.42 | 15. 5.43 | 19. 6.43 |
| 757 | 32 | 16. 7.42 | 17. 6.43 | 24. 7.43 |
| 758 | 32 | 6. 8.42 | 28. 7.43 | 28. 8.43 |
| 759 | 32 | 20. 8.42 | 26. 8.43 | 25. 9.43 |
| 760 | 40 | 14. 3.42 | 11. 8.42 | 10. 9.42 |
| 761 | 40 | 14. 3.42 | 24. 8.42 | 24. 9.42 |
| 762 | 40 | 23. 3.42 | 14. 9.42 | 7.10.42 |
| 763 | 40 | 23. 3.42 | 25. 9.42 | 20.10.42 |
| 764 | 40 | 3. 4.42 | 12.10.42 | 30.10.42 |
| 765 | 40 | 8. 4.42 | 12.11.42 | 3.12.42 |

| SC | Builder | Keel laid | Launched | Completed |
|---|---|---|---|---|
| 766 | 40 | 9. 4.42 | 27.10.42 | 14.11.42 |
| 767 | 40 | 18. 4.42 | 7.12.42 | 2. 1.43 |
| 768 | 33 | 8. 4.42 | 8. 8.42 | 9.11.42 |
| 769 | 33 | 8. 4.42 | 23. 8.42 | 4.12.42 |
| 770 | 33 | 15. 7.42 | 18.10.42 | 31.12.42 |
| 771 | 33 | 18. 8.42 | 5.11.42 | 25. 1.43 |
| 772 | 29 | 23. 5.42 | 7. 9.42 | 15. 4.43 |
| 773 | 29 | 23. 5.42 | 17.10.42 | 12. 5.43 |
| 774 | 29 | 11. 6.42 | 27.10.42 | 28. 6.43 |
| 775 | 29 | 12. 6.42 | 28.11.42 | 22. 7.43 |
| 977 | 34 | 26. 4.42 | 10.10.42 | 19.11.42 |
| 978 | 34 | 9. 5.42 | 10.10.42 | 8.12.42 |
| 979 | 34 | 23. 5.42 | 9.12.42 | 9. 1.43 |
| 980 | 34 | 18. 6.42 | 9.12.42 | 5. 2.43 |
| 981 | 39 | 14. 3.42 | 14. 8.42 | 2.10.42 |
| 982 | 39 | 18. 4.42 | 7. 9.42 | 31.10.42 |
| 983 | 39 | 14. 5.42 | 5.11.42 | 16. 1.43 |
| 984 | 39 | 10. 6.42 | 19.12.42 | 25. 6.43 |
| 985 | 21 | 3. 4.42 | 18. 9.42 | 17.12.42 |
| 986 | 21 | 18. 4.42 | 13.11.42 | 26. 4.43 |
| 987 | 21 | 15. 6.42 | 10. 4.43 | 4. 6.43 |
| 988 | 21 | 7.11.42 | 1. 6.43 | 12. 7.43 |
| 989 | 21 | 9.12.42 | 25. 6.43 | 30. 7.43 |
| 990 | 14 | 20. 8.42 | 7.12.42 | 10. 3.43 |
| 991 | 14 | 20. 8.42 | 20. 1.43 | 30. 4.43 |
| 992 | 14 | 20. 8.42 | 31. 3.43 | 5. 6.43 |
| 993 | 14 | 16.11.42 | 1. 5.43 | 30. 6.43 |
| 994 | 14 | 16.11.42 | 24. 5.43 | 22. 7.43 |
| 995 | 14 | 16.11.42 | 5. 6.43 | 14. 8.43 |
| 996 | 20 | 30. 3.42 | 7. 9.42 | 5.11.42 |
| 997 | 20 | 2. 4.42 | 21.10.42 | 23.12.42 |
| 998 | 20 | 17. 4.42 | 13.11.42 | 30. 4.43 |
| 999 | 20 | 29. 4.42 | 9.12.42 | 17. 5.43 |
| 1000 | 8 | 21. 4.42 | 22.10.42 | 14. 2.43 |
| 1001 | 8 | 1. 5.42 | 5.11.42 | 2. 3.43 |

*SC 1506 on 15 July 1944, showing the ultimate*
*configuration. Note that the 12ft wherry now sits*
*transversely aft on a low cradle; earlier boats carried*
*their wherries longitudinally on a high tubular cradle.*
*SC 1506 served with the Soviet Navy until 1955,*
*when she was scuttled in the Barents Sea along with*
*twenty-nine other SCs.* US Navy

| | | | | |
|---|---|---|---|---|
| 1002 | 8 | 15. 7.42 | 4. 3.43 | 13. 5.43 |
| 1003 | 12 | 8. 4.42 | 25. 7.42 | 24.12.42 |
| 1004 | 12 | 8. 4.42 | 1. 8.42 | 21. 1.43 |
| 1005 | 12 | 13. 4.42 | 15. 8.42 | 24. 2.43 |
| 1006 | 12 | 13. 4.42 | 7. 9.42 | 3. 5.43 |
| 1007 | 12 | 4. 5.42 | 14.11.42 | 3. 5.43 |
| 1008 | 12 | 8. 5.42 | 19.11.42 | 15. 6.43 |
| 1009 | 12 | 18. 7.42 | 25.11.42 | 25. 6.43 |
| 1010 | 12 | 30. 7.42 | 12.12.42 | 15. 7.43 |

| SC | Builder | Keel laid | Launched | Completed |
|---|---|---|---|---|
| 1011 | 12 | 17. 8.42 | 16.12.42 | 29. 7.43 |
| 1012 | 12 | 7. 9.42 | 28.12.42 | 18. 8.43 |
| 1013 | 25 | 23. 3.42 | 22. 7.42 | 19. 9.42 |
| 1014 | 25 | 21. 2.42 | 26. 7.42 | 28. 8.42 |
| 1015 | 25 | 4. 5.42 | 30. 8.42 | 19.10.42 |
| 1016 | 25 | 3. 6.42 | 4. 9.42 | 14.12.42 |
| 1017 | 25 | 8. 6.42 | 28.10.42 | 28.12.42 |
| 1018 | 25 | 14. 4.42 | 21.11.42 | 19. 1.43 |
| 1019 | 25 | 13. 4.42 | 1.12.42 | 12. 2.43 |
| 1020 | 25 | 7. 8.42 | 23.12.42 | 18. 5.43 |
| 1021 | 25 | 14. 8.42 | 1. 2.43 | 28. 4.43 |
| 1022 | 25 | 18. 9.42 | 23. 3.43 | 8. 6.43 |
| 1023 | 26 | 15. 6.42 | 16.11.42 | 18.11.42 |
| 1024 | 26 | 29. 6.42 | 28.11.42 | 3.12.42 |
| 1025 | 26 | 27. 8.42 | 17.12.42 | 22.12.42 |
| 1026 | 26 | 7. 9.42 | 8. 1.43 | 13. 1.43 |
| 1027 | 26 | 7. 9.42 | 26. 1.43 | 2. 2.43 |
| 1028 | 26 | 21.10.42 | 21. 2.43 | 27. 3.43 |
| 1029 | 9 | 27. 4.42 | 31. 8.42 | 13.11.42 |
| 1030 | 9 | 4. 5.42 | 31. 8.42 | 13.11.42 |
| 1031 | 28 | 28. 4.42 | 3.10.42 | 8. 1.43 |
| 1032 | 28 | 19. 5.42 | 17.10.42 | 25. 1.43 |
| 1033 | 28 | 17. 6.42 | 12.11.42 | 26. 3.43 |
| 1034 | 28 | 4. 8.42 | 2. 1.43 | 2. 4.43 |
| 1035 | 28 | 9. 7.42 | 12. 4.43 | 6. 5.43 |
| 1036 | 28 | 7. 9.42 | 10. 5.43 | 27. 5.43 |
| 1037 | 28 | 31.10.42 | 29. 5.43 | 24. 6.43 |
| 1038 | 28 | 28.11.42 | 12. 6.43 | 16. 7.43 |
| 1039 | 31 | 14. 4.42 | 28. 7.42 | 15.10.42 |
| 1040 | 31 | 14. 4.42 | 1. 8.42 | 27.10.42 |
| 1041 | 31 | 14. 5.42 | 13. 8.42 | 9.11.42 |

*SC 1499 under way on 24 July 1944. The extended sheathing is visible just forward of the bow wave.*
US Navy

*SC 1335 on Long Island Sound, New York, on 11 August 1943, with a 40mm Mark 3 carried forward. Note the height of the wherry cradle and the lack of a pilothouse wing.* US Navy

| SC | Builder | Keel laid | Launched | Completed |
|---|---|---|---|---|
| 1042 | 31 | 11. 5.42 | 15. 8.42 | 28.11.42 |
| 1043 | 31 | 3. 8.42 | 15.10.42 | 31.12.42 |
| 1044 | 31 | 4. 8.42 | 17.10.42 | 25. 1.43 |
| 1045 | 31 | 19. 8.42 | 19.11.42 | 18. 2.43 |
| 1046 | 31 | 18. 8.42 | 21.11.42 | 27. 3.43 |
| 1047 | 37 | 24. 4.42 | 15.11.42 | 30. 1.43 |
| 1048 | 37 | 28. 4.42 | 12.12.42 | 8. 4.43 |
| 1049 | 37 | 2. 5.42 | 2. 5.43 | 9. 6.43 |
| 1050 | 37 | 4. 5.42 | 9. 5.43 | 4. 8.43 |
| 1051 | 37 | 8. 5.42 | 19. 6.43 | 29. 7.43 |
| 1052 | 37 | 14. 5.42 | 26. 6.43 | 6. 9.43 |
| 1053 | 43 | 11. 4.42 | 7. 9.42 | 17. 3.43 |
| 1054 | 43 | 11. 4.42 | 19. 9.42 | 6. 4.43 |
| 1055 | 43 | 2. 5.42 | 10.10.42 | 10. 5.43 |
| 1056 | 43 | 14. 5.42 | 2.11.42 | 15. 6.43 |
| 1057 | 15 | 7. 5.42 | 11.11.42 | 18. 5.43 |
| 1058 | 15 | 7. 5.42 | 1.12.42 | 17. 6.43 |
| 1059 | 19 | 20. 5.42 | 28.11.42 | 25. 2.43 |
| 1060 | 19 | 8. 7.42 | 1.12.42 | 13. 4.43 |
| 1061 | 17 | 23. 5.42 | 26. 9.42 | 5. 1.43 |
| 1062 | 17 | 3. 6.42 | 23.12.42 | 27. 2.43 |
| 1063 | 38 | 22. 6.42 | 28.11.42 | 8. 1.43 |
| 1064 | 38 | 9. 7.42 | 16. 1.43 | 17. 4.43 |
| 1065 | 27 | 27. 5.42 | 17.10.42 | 30.12.42 |
| 1066 | 27 | 2. 6.42 | 14.11.42 | 27. 2.43 |
| 1067 | 26 | 19.11.42 | 9. 3.43 | 3. 4.43 |
| 1068 | 26 | 10.12.42 | 26. 3.43 | 13. 4.43 |
| 1069 | 26 | 30.12.42 | 17. 4.43 | 26. 4.43 |
| 1070 | 26 | 21. 1.43 | 3. 5.43 | 24. 5.43 |
| 1071 | 26 | 6. 2.43 | 20. 5.43 | 8. 6.43 |
| 1072 | 26 | 10. 3.43 | 17. 6.43 | 28. 6.43 |
| 1073 | 26 | 31. 3.43 | 30. 6.43 | 19. 7.43 |
| 1074 | 26 | 20. 4.43 | 12. 7.43 | 28. 7.43 |
| 1075 | 26 | 11. 5.43 | 27. 7.43 | 11. 8.43 |
| 1076 | 26 | 29. 5.43 | 12. 8.43 | 23. 8.43 |
| 1266 | 30 | 28. 7.42 | 9.11.42 | 12. 2.43 |
| 1267 | 30 | 20. 8.42 | 12.12.42 | 27. 2.43 |
| 1268 | 30 | 7. 9.42 | 29.12.42 | 13. 3.43 |
| 1269 | 30 | 26. 9.42 | 24. 2.43 | 10. 4.43 |

| SC | Builder | Keel laid | Launched | Completed |
|---|---|---|---|---|
| 1270 | 30 | 15.10.42 | 24. 2.43 | 26. 4.43 |
| 1271 | 30 | 9.11.42 | 31. 3.43 | 15. 5.43 |
| 1272 | 30 | 1.12.42 | 19. 4.43 | 4. 6.43 |
| 1273 | 30 | 28.12.42 | 8. 5.43 | 30. 6.43 |
| 1274 | 30 | 4. 1.43 | 22. 5.43 | 24. 7.43 |
| 1275 | 30 | 15. 1.43 | 5. 6.43 | 17. 8.43 |
| 1276 | 11 | 7. 9.42 | 27.10.42 | 4. 3.43 |
| 1277 | 11 | 7. 9.42 | 27.10.42 | 11. 3.43 |
| 1278 | 11 | 7. 9.42 | 7.12.42 | 16. 3.43 |
| 1279 | 11 | 7. 9.42 | 27.10.42 | 25. 3.43 |
| 1280 | 11 | 27.10.42 | 6. 2.43 | 22. 4.43 |
| 1281 | 11 | 27.10.42 | 5. 2.43 | 30. 4.43 |
| 1282 | 11 | 7.12.42 | 6. 2.43 | 13. 5.43 |
| 1283 | 11 | 31.12.42 | 20. 2.43 | 6. 6.43 |
| 1284 | 11 | 5. 2.43 | 26. 3.43 | 18. 6.43 |
| 1285 | 11 | 9. 2.43 | 17. 4.43 | 4. 7.43 |
| 1286 | 11 | 22. 2.43 | 15. 5.43 | 20. 7.43 |
| 1287 | 11 | 19. 4.43 | 5. 6.43 | 29. 7.43 |
| 1288 | 40 | 27. 7.42 | 24.12.42 | 12. 2.43 |
| 1289 | 40 | 19. 8.42 | 8. 2.43 | 12. 3.43 |
| 1290 | 40 | 28. 8.42 | 16. 3.43 | 15. 4.43 |
| 1291 | 40 | 22. 9.42 | 30. 3.43 | 3. 5.43 |
| 1292 | 40 | 5.10.42 | 17. 4.43 | 19. 5.43 |
| 1293 | 40 | 20.10.42 | 24. 4.43 | 4. 6.43 |
| 1294 | 40 | 28.12.42 | 4. 6.43 | 7. 7.43 |
| 1295 | 40 | 21. 1.43 | 23. 7.43 | 12. 8.43 |
| 1296 | 40 | 11. 2.43 | 20. 8.43 | 16. 9.43 |
| 1297 | 40 | 19. 3.43 | 2. 9.43 | 8.10.43 |
| 1298 | 27 | 7. 9.42 | 19. 3.43 | 30. 4.43 |
| 1299 | 27 | 7. 9.42 | 10. 4.43 | 1. 6.43 |
| 1300 | 27 | 7. 9.42 | 8. 5.43 | 3. 7.43 |
| 1301 | 27 | 7. 9.42 | 15. 5.43 | 3. 8.43 |
| 1302 | 6 | 15. 8.42 | 31.10.42 | 27. 3.43 |
| 1303 | 6 | 4. 9.42 | 28.11.42 | 1. 5.43 |
| 1304 | 6 | 12. 9.42 | 16. 1.43 | 14. 6.43 |
| 1305 | 6 | 19. 9.42 | 15. 2.43 | 11. 8.43 |
| 1306 | 6 | 6.10.42 | 25. 3.43 | 1. 9.43 |
| 1307 | 6 | 20.10.42 | 15. 4.43 | 29. 9.43 |
| 1308 | 6 | 28.11.42 | 15. 5.43 | 1.11.43 |
| 1309 | 2 | 7. 9.42 | 26. 2.43 | 3. 5.43 |
| 1310 | 2 | 7. 9.42 | 28. 2.43 | 22. 5.43 |
| 1311 | 2 | 28. 9.42 | 10. 4.43 | 12. 6.43 |
| 1312 | 2 | 9.10.42 | 26. 4.43 | 1. 7.43 |
| 1313 | 2 | 2.10.42 | 3. 5.43 | 19. 7.43 |

*SC 727 in difficulties at Okinawa in the Autumn of 1945, following a typhoon. The large hull numbers are unusual. US Navy*

*Photographed on 14 May 1943, SC 712 has a pair of Mousetraps forward of her 3in/23 and a Canadian SW-1C radar on the masthead. Note that her ready service lockers for the 7.2in ASW rockets are mounted transversely forward of the pilothouse; most SCs carried these lockers facing forward. US Navy*

| SC | Builder | Keel laid | Launched | Completed |
|---|---|---|---|---|
| 1314 | 2 | 3. 3.43 | 12. 6.43 | 16. 8.43 |
| 1315 | 22 | 11. 8.42 | 3. 3.43 | 12. 6.43 |
| 1316 | 22 | 18. 8.42 | 11. 3.43 | 18. 6.43 |
| 1317 | 22 | 2. 9.42 | 20. 3.43 | 5. 7.43 |
| 1318 | 22 | 8. 9.42 | 2. 4.43 | 9. 8.43 |
| 1319 | 22 | 24. 9.42 | 12. 4.43 | 26. 8.43 |
| 1320 | 22 | 10.10.42 | 17. 4.43 | 22. 8.43 |
| 1321 | 17 | 7. 9.42 | 6. 2.43 | 5. 4.43 |
| 1322 | 17 | 26. 9.42 | 8. 4.43 | 2. 6.43 |
| 1323 | 17 | 24.12.42 | 15. 5.43 | 5. 8.43 |
| 1324 | 17 | 4. 2.43 | 22. 7.43 | 24. 9.43 |
| 1325 | 7 | 7. 9.42 | 11. 2.43 | 19. 4.43 |
| 1326 | 7 | 7. 9.42 | 24. 2.43 | 3. 5.43 |
| 1327 | 7 | 7.10.42 | 24. 3.43 | 4. 6.43 |
| 1328 | 7 | 9.10.42 | 21. 4.43 | 30. 6.43 |
| 1329 | 34 | 10.10.42 | 19. 4.43 | 8. 5.43 |
| 1330 | 34 | 30.10.42 | 19. 4.43 | 29. 5.43 |
| 1331 | 34 | 16.12.42 | 2. 6.43 | 7. 2.43 |
| 1332 | 34 | 16.12.42 | 17. 7.43 | 6. 8.43 |
| 1333 | 36 | 21. 8.42 | 24. 4.43 | 23. 6.43 |
| 1334 | 36 | 22. 8.42 | 8. 5.43 | 16. 7.43 |
| 1335 | 36 | 15. 9.42 | 5. 6.43 | 11. 8.43 |
| 1336 | 36 | 17. 9.42 | 22. 5.43 | 26. 8.43 |
| 1337 | 36 | 28. 9.42 | 19. 7.43 | 15. 9.43 |
| 1338 | 36 | 19.10.42 | 7. 8.43 | 29. 9.43 |
| 1339 | 36 | 24.10.42 | 21. 8.43 | 6.11.43 |
| 1340 | 36 | 7.11.42 | 18. 9.43 | 3.12.43 |
| 1341 | 31 | 21.10.42 | 14. 1.43 | 25. 5.43 |
| 1342 | 31 | 21.10.42 | 16. 1.43 | 14. 6.43 |
| 1343 | 31 | 23.11.42 | 20. 2.43 | 9. 8.43 |
| 1344 | 31 | 24.11.42 | 27. 3.43 | 16. 8.43 |
| 1345 | 31 | 21. 1.43 | 10. 4.43 | 12. 9.43 |
| 1346 | 31 | 22. 1.43 | 29. 4.43 | 24.10.43 |
| 1347 | 13 | 15. 2.43 | 15. 7.43 | 27. 8.43 |
| 1348 | 13 | 17. 2.43 | 12. 8.43 | 25. 9.43 |
| 1349 | 13 | 27. 4.43 | 11. 9.43 | 16.10.43 |

| SC | Builder | Keel laid | Launched | Completed |
|---|---|---|---|---|
| 1350 | 13 | 27. 4.43 | 6.10.43 | 6.11.43 |
| 1351 | 39 | 7. 9.42 | 11. 3.43 | 30. 4.43 |
| 1352 | 39 | 14. 9.42 | 21. 4.43 | 18. 6.43 |
| 1353 | 39 | 5.11.42 | 3. 6.43 | 4. 8.43 |
| 1354 | 39 | 19.12.42 | 10. 8.43 | 29. 9.43 |
| 1355 | 25 | 14.11.42 | 12. 4.43 | 9. 7.43 |
| 1356 | 25 | 5. 1.43 | 7. 6.43 | 16. 8.43 |
| 1357 | 25 | 13. 2.43 | 21. 6.43 | 30. 8.43 |
| 1358 | 4 | 1.10.42 | 22. 2.43 | 20. 4.43 |
| 1359 | 4 | 2.11.42 | 3. 4.43 | 3. 6.43 |
| 1360 | 4 | 22. 2.43 | 22. 6.43 | 20. 8.43 |
| 1361 | 4 | 3. 4.43 | 24. 7.43 | 13.10.43 |
| 1362 | 29 | 7.11.42 | 24. 4.43 | 6. 9.43 |
| 1363 | 29 | 14.11.42 | 29. 5.43 | 29. 9.43 |
| 1364 | 29 | 28.11.42 | 10. 7.43 | 2.11.43 |
| 1365 | 29 | 24. 4.43 | 29. 9.43 | 2. 1.44 |
| 1366 | 43 | 2.11.42 | 1. 5.43 | 1. 5.43 |
| 1367 | 43 | 25.11.42 | 27. 5.43 | 10. 9.43 |
| 1368 | 43 | 28.11.42 | 21. 6.43 | 9.10.43 |
| 1369 | 43 | 9.12.42 | 19. 7.43 | 12.11.43 |
| 1370 | 12 | 7.12.42 | 20. 5.43 | 6. 9.43 |
| 1371 | 12 | 10.12.42 | 22. 5.43 | 30. 9.43 |
| 1372 | 12 | 19.12.42 | 8. 6.43 | 1.11.43 |
| 1373 | 12 | 23.12.42 | 19. 6.43 | 1.11.43 |
| 1374 | 12 | 26.12.42 | 5. 7.43 | 14.11.43 |
| 1375 | 12 | 29.12.42 | 31. 7.43 | 24.11.43 |
| 1474 | 30 | 3. 6.43 | 11. 1.44 | 8. 4.44 |
| 1475 | 30 | 3. 6.43 | 8. 2.44 | 29. 4.44 |
| 1476 | 30 | 15. 6.43 | 8. 3.44 | 17. 5.44 |

*A view aft on SC 729; the 20mm guns have not yet been fitted, although the mountings are in place. Note the placement of the wherry on the early boats.*
US Navy

| SC | Builder | Keel laid | Launched | Completed |
|---|---|---|---|---|
| 1477 | 30 | 7. 7.43 | 22. 3.44 | 9. 6.44 |
| 1478 | 30 | 21. 7.43 | 24. 4.44 | 13. 7.44 |
| 1479 | 30 | 17. 8.43 | 5. 6.44 | 24. 8.44 |
| 1480 | 31 | 19. 4.43 | 1.10.43 | 9. 4.44 |
| 1481 | 31 | 15. 4.43 | 16.10.43 | 16. 5.44 |
| 1482 | 31 | 18. 5.43 | 14.12.43 | 27. 6.44 |
| 1483 | 31 | 21. 5.43 | 16.12.43 | 23. 7.44 |
| 1484 | 6 | 10. 7.43 | 27.10.43 | 10. 4.44 |
| 1485 | 6 | 24. 7.43 | 30.11.43 | 29. 5.44 |
| 1486 | 6 | 5. 8.43 | 15. 1.44 | 21. 7.44 |
| 1487 | 6 | 23. 9.43 | 11. 3.44 | 30. 9.44 |
| 1488 | 11 | 10. 7.43 | 24. 8.43 | 5. 4.44 |
| 1489 | 11 | 8. 4.43 | 25. 9 43 | 11. 4.44 |
| 1490 | 11 | 14. 8.43 | 16.10.43 | 6. 5.44 |
| 1491 | 11 | 25. 8.43 | 30.10.43 | 14. 7.44 |
| 1492 | 34 | 23. 6.43 | 8.12.43 | 22. 4.44 |
| 1493 | 34 | 28. 6.43 | 22. 2.44 | 12. 6.44 |
| 1496 | 39 | 5. 6.43 | 1.12.43 | 7. 4.44 |
| 1497 | 39 | 23. 8.43 | 4. 5.44 | 10. 7.44 |
| 1498 | 36 | 14. 8.43 | 21. 3.44 | 15. 5.44 |
| 1499 | 36 | 4. 9.43 | 27. 4.44 | 2. 8.44 |
| 1502 | 4 | 14. 7.43 | 27.11.43 | 1. 6.44 |
| 1503 | 4 | 14. 8.43 | 22. 5.43 | 22. 8.44 |
| 1504 | 9 | 29. 7.43 | 16. 4.44 | 24. 5.44 |
| 1505 | 9 | 30. 7.43 | 30. 4.44 | 18. 6.44 |
| 1506 | 9 | 7. 8.43 | 14. 5.44 | 17. 7.44 |
| 1507 | 17 | 15. 7.43 | 26. 1.44 | 15. 5.44 |
| 1508 | 17 | 12. 8.43 | 8. 5.44 | 22. 7.44 |
| 1509 | 17 | 12. 8.43 | 8. 5.44 | 22. 7.44 |
| 1510 | 27 | 3. 7.43 | 9.12.43 | 18. 5.44 |
| 1511 | 27 | 12. 7.43 | 3. 4.44 | 3. 7.44 |
| 1512 | 27 | 27. 7.43 | 15. 6.44 | 26. 9.44 |
| 1517 | 22 | 14. 8.43 | 12. 4.44 | 20. 5.44 |

*Note*: The gaps in hull number sequences are a result of the USN practice of numbering patrol craft consecutively, regardless of type. The numbering sequence included the 110ft SC, the 136ft PCS, the 173ft PC, and the 180ft PCE.

*A view aft on SC 639 on 20 June 1942.* US Navy

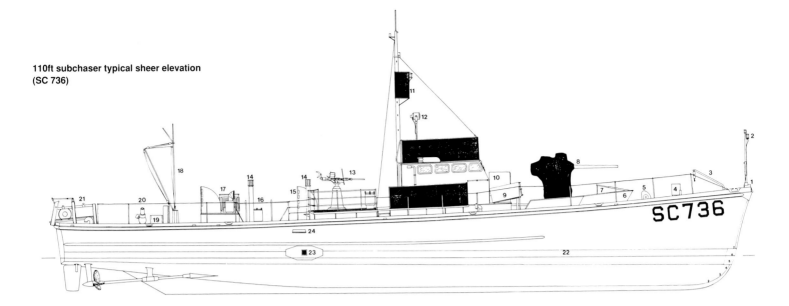

**110ft subchaser typical sheer elevation
(SC 736)**

| | | | |
|---|---|---|---|
| 1 | Bullnose | 13 | 20mm Mark 4 |
| 2 | Bow light | 14 | Smoke pipe |
| 3 | Anchor davit | 15 | Companionway |
| 4 | Vent | 16 | Liferaft support |
| 5 | Windlass | 17 | Vegetable locker |
| 6 | Breakwater | 18 | Depth charge topping lift |
| 7 | Booby hatch | 19 | Depth charge rack |
| 8 | 3in 50 Mark 22 | 20 | Mark 6 K gun |
| 9 | 7.2in ASW projectile ready service locker | 21 | Depth charge track |
| 10 | 3in/50 ready service locker | 22 | Hull sheathing |
| 11 | Crow's nest | 23 | Diesel exhaust |
| 12 | Searchlight | 24 | Grab rail |

These drawings are representative of the early configuration of the SC 497 class subchaser. Craft with the 3in/23 did not have the raised platform within the breakwater. The original design mounted single, water-cooled .50 calibre machine guns on Mark 3 mounts in the positions occupied by the 20mm Mark 4. The initial design used a more normal strut arrangement, with the aft strut forward of the propeller.

*An excellent closeup of the foredeck of SC 729. Note the two styles of anchors and the Mark 20 Mousetraps. The two cylindrical objects between the launchers are vents. US Navy*

*This bow view of SC 1049 shows to good advantage the hull sheathing between the 3ft and 7ft draught marks. On SC 1474 and later boats, this sheathing extended upwards several feet more. US Navy*

*SC 729 being fitted out at Harbor Boat in early 1943. Her Mousetraps have been fitted and she carries a 3in/50 Mark 22 forward. On the 3in/50 boats, a platform was built up inside the spray shield to the level of the trunk cabin. The framing for this platform can be seen on the incomplete SC at the top of the picture. Two licence-built 72ft Vosper MTBs can just be seen beyond the incomplete SC. US Navy*

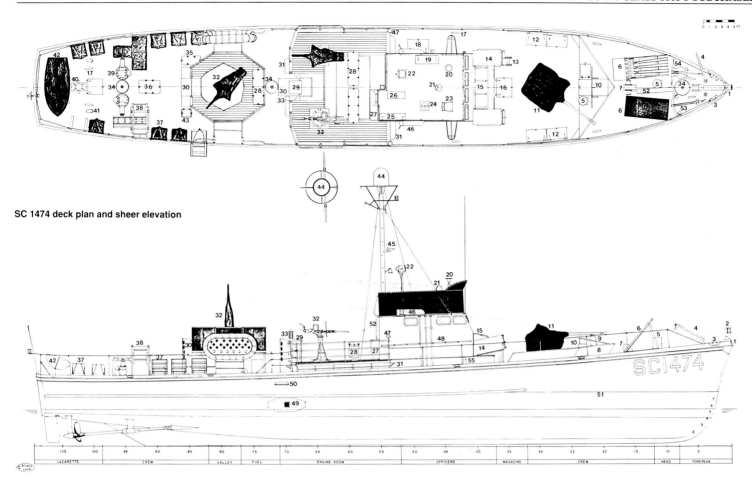

**SC 1474 deck plan and sheer elevation**

| | | | |
|---|---|---|---|
| 1 | Bullnose | 16 | Hatch to magazine |
| 2 | Bow light | 17 | Cleat |
| 3 | Fairlead | 18 | 7.2in ASW projectile fuse locker |
| 4 | Anchor davit | 19 | Explosive signal locker |
| 5 | Vent | 20 | Gyro repeater |
| 6 | Mousetrap | 21 | Binnacle |
| 7 | Windlass | 22 | Searchlight |
| 8 | Breakwater | 23 | Chair |
| 9 | Depression rail | 24 | RDF loop |
| 10 | Booby hatch | 25 | Recognition light locker |
| 11 | 40mm Mark 3 | 26 | Vent |
| 12 | 40mm ready service locker | 27 | Signal flag locker |
| 13 | Reel | 28 | 20mm ready service locker |
| 14 | 7.2in ASW projectile ready service locker | 29 | Log desk |
| 15 | 40mm ready service locker | 30 | Companionway |
| | | 31 | Step |

| | | | |
|---|---|---|---|
| 32 | 20mm Mark 10 | 47 | Pelorus |
| 33 | Smoke pipe from galley | 48 | Grab rail |
| 34 | Manhole cover | 49 | Diesel exhaust |
| 35 | Depth charge marker ready service locker | 50 | Grab rail |
| 36 | Smoke pot locker | 51 | Hull sheathing above and below waterline |
| 37 | Type C depth charge roll-off rack | 52 | Scuff plate for anchor chain |
| 38 | K gun ready service rack | 53 | Stock anchor |
| 39 | K gun | 54 | Danforth anchor |
| 40 | Towing bitt | 55 | Fuel oil vent |
| 41 | Gooseneck vent | | |
| 42 | 9ft wherry | | |
| 43 | K gun impulse charge locker | | |
| 44 | SG radar dome | | |
| 45 | Horn | | |
| 46 | Side light | | |

These general arrangement drawings show the ultimate configuration of the SC 497 class subchaser. The bandstand for the aft 20mm was built over the aft trunk cabin.

*A number of SCs were converted to gunboats (PGM) to counter barge traffic in the Pacific. PGM 7 (ex-SC 1072), seen here on 7 January 1944 at Newport Beach, California, mounts a 3in/23 forward, four twin .50in Mark 17 turrets amidships, and a 40mm Mark 3 aft. Note the radically modified bridge structure. US Navy*

**SC 1474 internal profile**

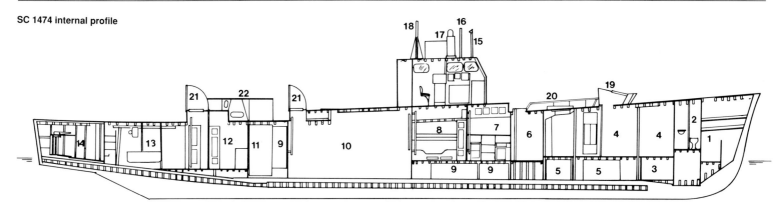

| | | | |
|---|---|---|---|
| 1 | Forepeak | 7 | Radio/sound room |
| 2 | Crew's WC | 8 | Officers' quarters |
| 3 | Chain locker | 9 | Fuel oil tanks |
| 4 | Forward crew's quarters | 10 | Engineroom |
| 5 | Fresh water tank | 11 | Fresh water tank |
| 6 | Magazine | 12 | Galley |

| | | | |
|---|---|---|---|
| 13 | Aft crew's quarters | 19 | Booby hatch |
| 14 | Lazarette | 20 | Breakwater |
| 15 | Voice tube | 21 | Companionway |
| 16 | Gyro compass stand | 22 | Bandstand for 20mm |
| 17 | Binnacle | | |
| 18 | Searchlight stand | | |

**SC 1474 details of pilothouse**

1  Antenna spreader
2  Sidelight
3  Grab rail
4  40mm ready service locker
5  Whip antenna
6  Fire hose rack
7  Blinker light
8  SG radar dome
9  Vertical ladder
10  Vent
11  Signal flag locker
12  7.2in ASW projectile fuse locker
13  Companionway
14  Canvas dodger
15  Trunk cabin (shown without platform
    for 20mm)

The pilothouse on earlier SCs generally
had four windows per side and did not
have the extension on the starboard side
aft. Pilothouse wings of different lengths
were also installed port and starboard on
earlier craft.

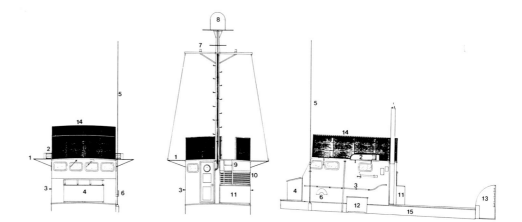

*Another view of SC 729 being fitted out. Note how
bare the open bridge is. The vertical lockers are ready
service for the 3in/50. US Navy*

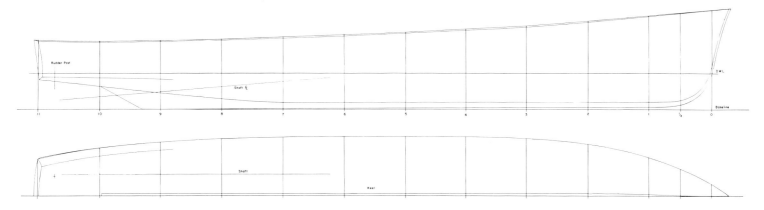

**110ft subchaser lines and stern profile**

**110ft subchaser construction and fastening detail**

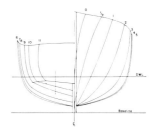

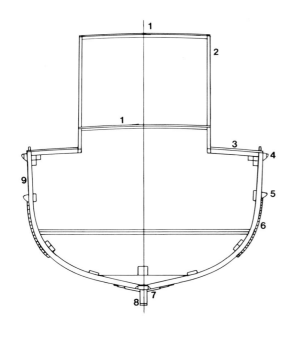

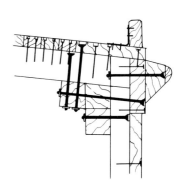

1  Pilothouse roof and deck, ¾in, 5-ply Douglas fir covered with 8oz cotton duck
2  Pilothouse sides, ¾in, 5-ply Douglas fir covered with 8oz cotton duck or mahogany veneer
3  Deck, 1¾in × 2¾in Douglas fir planking
4  Upper guardrail, 3in × 6in yellow pine (inner), 1⅛in × 3in white oak
5  Lower guardrail, 3in × 6in yellow pine (inner), 1⅛in × 3in white oak
6  Hull sheathing, ¾ × 4in white oak with ⅛in spacing
7  Garboard strake, 2¼in × 11in yellow pine
8  Keel, 7in × 12in white oak
9  Hull planking, yellow pine or Douglas fir

**SC 1474 deck plan and sheer elevation**

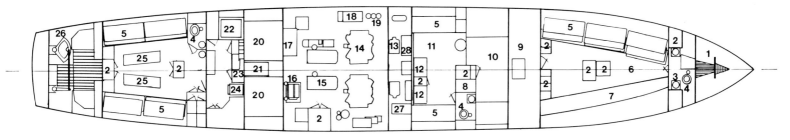

| | | | |
|---|---|---|---|
| 1  Forepeak | 8  Shower | 15  Generator | 22  Refrigerator |
| 2  Locker | 9  Magazine | 16  Hot water boiler | 23  Sink |
| 3  Wash basin | 10  Radio/sound room | 17  Work bench | 24  Range |
| 4  WC | 11  Officers' quarters | 18  Starting batteries | 25  Table |
| 5  Berth (double or triple) | 12  Desk | 19  $CO_2$ bottles | 26  Steering quadrant |
| 6  Forward crew's quarters | 13  Heat exchanger | 20  Fuel oil tank | 27  Switch board |
| 7  Settee | 14  Diesel | 21  Freshwater tank | 28  Lubrication oil tank |

**Aft bunk cabin on subchasers without the 20mm bandstand**

1  Hand hold
2  Companionway
3  Vegetable locker
4  Vent
5  Cowl vent
6  Trunk cabin
7  Raised cowl vent box
8  Plug over alternative cowl vent location

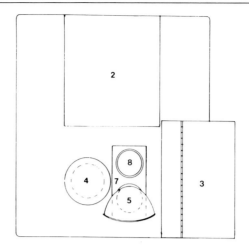

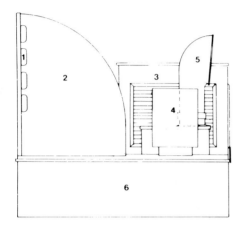

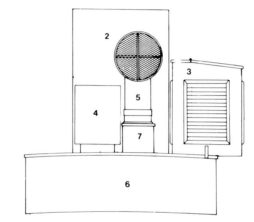

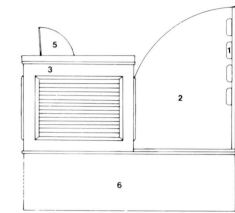

# Depth charges and anti-submarine equipment

The records of U-boat losses during World War II reveal none attributed to attacks by Coastal Forces or motor launches in particular, although these units spent a great deal of time on convoy protection duties. There is proof that CFs were particularly useful in the role of defending the Allied invasion beaches against the many small one-man units sent in to destroy ships unloading off the beachhead, where they had some small success, although many were sunk, damaged or driven off. One Biber type (No 105) is now on display at the Imperial War Museum, having been captured by a motor launch.

The standard depth charge was the main armament of the anti-submarine armed craft, especially the early A and B type Fairmiles, as well as the 72ft ML, and up to four was a standard armament fit for both short and long MTB and MGB types.

Early in the war MA/SBs had single or twin racks for three or six depth charges, fitted aft for dropping over the stern. This was improved by a single chute fitted along the deck edge, where the charge was simply released and rolled over the side. Some units had hydraulic release gear operated from the bridge, but in most cases it was necessary to release the securing strop by hand, to drop the charges in single or double sets as required. The drawings show both the charges and various racks and chutes employed during the war.

During the Great War, 96,403 depth charges were manufactured for the use by the Royal Navy and Allies. Some 186 U-boats failed to return to their bases. Destroyers and patrol craft were credited with sinking thirty-five by depth charge; ten were caught in nets and destroyed; five were sunk by the use of towed explosive sweeps; and twenty by gunfire and ramming.

The history of the depth charge began immediately after the outbreak of that war. In October 1914 Admiral Jellicoe requested the immediate development of a 'mine' to be fired by hydrostatic

*After deck view of an A type, probably ML 110, in May 1941. Note the detail of the depth charges, early type smoke floats, twin .303in Lewis guns and the 3-pounder aft. Part of the Holman projector ammunition box can be seen behind the rivets of the funnel casing.* The Motor Boat

pressure for the destruction of enemy submarines, the mine to be triced up astern and let go when over the estimated position of the submarine. In the meantime, a civilian, H J Taylor, had on his own account designed a hydrostatically operated pistol for such a purpose. He had one made and arranged for it to be tested at the Battersea Polytechnic, where he was then an instructor. He proved as resourceful in finding a means of testing his pistol as he was in designing it. When it was discovered that a pressure head of 80ft required for operating it was not immediately available, he utilised some pipes intended for building operations that were lying around; by erecting them vertically end to end, he provided himself with the test tank of the required depth, in which the pistol could be made to operate by lowering it from the top. Trials were successful, and he forwarded the details to the Admiralty.

The net result was that, in June 1915, Mr Taylor was invited to join HMS *Vernon* to work on the project, thus becoming the first civilian member of what was later known as the Admiralty Mining Establishment (from which he retired in December 1945).

In August drawings of the new mine were circulated and Chatham Dockyard received orders to make twenty-five sets of dropping gear. The L class destroyers were to be fitted with 'Egerton depth charges' as they came in to refit, as were the M class of the 10th Flotilla. The depth charge offered a means of combatting the U-boat menace, particularly with the introduction of the type D* charge with 120lb of TNT and the type D with 300lb. However, production was slow, and during the early months of 1917 the allowance per destroyer was only two of each type. By mid-July weekly production was about 140 and by the end of the year 800.

The depth charge remained substantially unaltered in form from its inception. It was essentially a cylinder of ⅛in steel plate, 18in in diameter and 26in long, containing some 300lb of explosive. A central tube was fitted to hold the firing mechanism, which consisted of a pistol and primer. The pistol operated when a head of 50ft had been built up in the primer tube; the rate of water entry could be controlled by bringing into play one of a series of orifices, by rotating an external handle, the effect being to increase the time, and therefore the depth, at which the 50ft head was reached. The primer was coupled to a device termed the 'primer placer', which permitted a 3in axial movement of the primer while retaining complete watertightness of the tube.

During the next war a great deal of operational research was carried out to establish why the explosion of the depth charge was not causing the destruction of the U-boat. All manner of problems were examined, including the working of the ship, which could cause the charge to hold for a fraction of time. It was essential to keep the chutes and dropping gear free, particularly when the gear was exposed to the corrosive action of sea air and sea water, such as aboard Coastal Forces vessels. There were no facilities to run steam heating coils, as in the case of larger A/S vessels, but it was still necessary to guard against the non-operation of traps or the American Y gun, if fitted, due to accumulations of ice and snow.

At the same time it was difficult to reload racks or throwers at sea, when new depth charges (if carried at all) would have to be brought up from below deck; this is why the reloading crane or derrick was normally stowed away. The depth charge was regarded as a single-use weapon, and there were generally no replacements, apart from those for the Y gun, if fitted.

Early in the war the surviving D and D* charges were supplied,

*Cleaning fish after dropping a depth charge aboard
HMNZML 401 on 29 July 1943 in the Hauraki
Gulf, New Zealand. Part of the Y gun is shown.*
Courtesy Ken Cassells

until stocks were finished. The standard depth charge was the Mark VII, little different from the original. It weighed 410lb, the charge being 396lb of explosive. The depth charge could be fused to explode at 50ft increments from 50 to 300ft, the then supposed maximum diving depth of submarines. The sinking rate was 10ft per second.

While the Fairmiles lacked throwers to bracket the target, they could only drop charges over the side. However, in an effort to increase the sinking rate of the charge, a cast iron weight was secured to one end, which increased the rate to 16½ft per second. At the same time the pistol was modified, so that the standard Mark VII depth charge now had depth settings available of 50, 100, 150, 250, 350 and 500ft. However, this heavier charge was not issued to Coastal Forces. During the war years the explosive filling was improved with the introduction of Minol and Torpex, which increased the explosive power roughly in the proportion of 1:1.5:2. By 1944 the smaller Mark XII depth charge, with a 55lb Minol charge, was issued in limited numbers to Coastal Forces for use against midget submarines and similar devices. A flotilla of Ds was converted to combat the considerable numbers of these vessels which tried to penetrate and attack the off-loading major units anchored off the beachheads.

The depth charge was normally in three states of readiness: (1) as supplied or transported on arrival on board, where the charge was complete with pistol and detonator, but the primer was not inserted; (2) primed (immediately after leaving harbour), but with the primer inserted in the 'safe' position and a rubber cover on the pistol; and (3) ready for dropping, with the primer in the ready position and the depth set, and the depth-setting key and the rubber cover removed. In the event of an attack on a U-boat or other target, the engineroom would first be informed when circumstances permitted.

It was quite common to see a 40-gallon drum stowed on the upper deck. This was secured to a depth charge, apparently to slow its rate of sinking in order that the charge could be dropped in the path of an enemy ship – in particular an E-boat, which found the volume of water thrown up by a shallow set charge quite disturbing, especially in night actions.

The equipment fitted to locate underwater targets has a long and complicated history. In December 1916 the Anti-Submarine Division commenced its duties by collecting operational intelligence, and deploying the leading scientists of the day; the Royal Navy hydrophone research and training establishment was firmly

established at Hawkcraig Point, near the village of Aberdour in Fifeshire. A number of small units were allocated for research purposes. In August 1917 a new listening school and experimental station was located at Weymouth: HMS *Sarepta*, which was transferred to new buildings in Portland in April 1918. Other Royal Navy shore bases were set up elsewhere, both at home and abroad, for underwater sound research.

From those early efforts an impressive fund of knowledge was built up. The World War I hydrophone had many drawbacks (mainly because it was an entirely passive device), and a small British team started to investigate an active detection device in 1917. The first use of the word 'asdic' occurred in the 'Weekly report of experimental work at Parkeston Quay' (Harwich) dated 6 July 1918, where 'Asdics' replaced the section heading of 'supersonics', dealing with these experiments. This new terminology appeared in records very frequently from then on. In the inter-war years this subject was considered to be so secret that no public reference, even to quartz, was permitted – the code word in that case was 'asdivite'.

The word 'sonar' was coined in 1942, by the American underwater acoustics specialist and director of the wartime Harvard Underwater Sound Laboratory, FV (Ted) Hunt. He recalled that he simply intended it as a phonetic analogue to 'radar'. The American name was finally adopted by the Royal Navy in the early 1950s.

A number of different asdic sets were gradually developed between the wars, for both submarines and surface vessels. Asdic domes were slowly improved and the basic sets were modified accordingly. Each set normally consisted of an electrical set, including control instruments for transmission, reception and recording, and also a mechanical component, comprising the dome, housing arrangements, etc, which is now called the 'asdic hull outfit'. The various items were frequently modified and updated or improved during production. Set No 111 was introduced in late 1918, and was an experimental set used in the trials ship P 59. It was later standardised as the Type 112 from late 1919 and fitted to P boats; this was the precursor of the destroyer set, with a retracting cylindrical canvas dome. It was fitted to the 1st Anti-Submarine Flotilla from 1920 to 1921. The 113 was fitted to submarines and the 114 to destroyers from 1922, with the dome and directing gear from the Type 112 and electronics derived from Type 113. HMS *Heather* (of the Flower class) had the first standardised set in 1923, and this was then fitted to the 1st Anti-submarine Flotilla at Portland and the 6th Destroyer Flotilla.

Development continued through the Type 115 for destroyers 1923–25; Type 116 for submarines, 1926; Type 117 for destroyers, about 1927; Type 118 for submarines, 1928; and Type 119 for destroyers 1929–30 (the standard inter-war destroyer set, specially designed for the Mediterranean). The Type 120 was introduced in 1930 for submarines, and was an updated Type 118, fitted to the River and early S class boats. The Type 121 of 1931, for destroyers, was the first with a retracting streamlined dome, and was fitted in the D, E, F and G classes. Type 122 was the first set developed for trawlers and drifters with no electricity supply, an idea under development since 1927 and in use from 1927 to 1933, and was installed in drifters in 1940. The Type 123 of 1934 was basically similar, but improved on the 112 and was intended for trawlers, though during the war it was fitted to whalers, armed yachts, small minesweepers and other auxiliary vessels. Type 124, introduced 1934–7, was an updated Type 121 for destroyers and later for coastal sloops. Type 125 of 1936 was for survey ships. Type 126 was fitted to the two Australian sloops *Yarra* and *Swann*, to be superseded by the Type 127S. The Type 127 of 1937 was specially designed for coastal escort sloops and, with the Type 128, was the most extensively modified set of the coming war. The Type 127

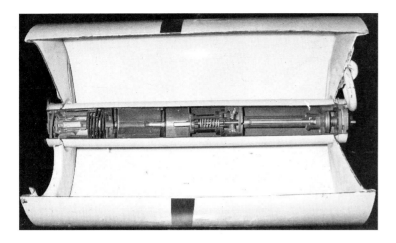

*The internal workings of a depth charge, showing the detonator, etc. The explosive has been removed. This is an exhibit at the RN Armament Museum at Priddy's Hard, Gosport.* Courtesy Jim Goss of NAVPIC

a tadpole-shaped dome, fixed transducer, and electronics derived from the Type 127, but it never proceeded beyond the design stage.

The Type 134, of 1939, was employed for Coastal Forces. It had a hand-operated retractable tadpole-shaped dome, which could not be housed. It carried two fixed transducers; one faced forward, and the other, which was double-faced, faced athwartships. The electrical gear was the same as the previous Type 127. The frequency range was 14–22kHz. Later a listening set, Type 142, was sometimes added for detecting U-boats by hydrophone effect. Some six variants were produced during the war. Type 134A was developed in 1941 for motor launches, and had a portable transducer unit. The Type 134B of 1942 had a single trainable transducer and an AVC receiver. The Type 134E of 1944 had a compass-stabilised training system, for improved accuracy, and these later sets were fitted before the Normandy landings for use against midget submarines. The Type 134S of 1945 had a reflecting plate in a dome for echo sounding, and was probably used for wreck detection.

In general, those craft employed on convoy escort duties operated in shallow waters, where pin-point navigation was required. Close inshore there was little risk of U-boats, but the set could also be used for depth sounding, to aid in bottom reading from the chart. Asdic operators were trained in considerable numbers for MLs and they performed a thankless task, searching and listening in uncomfortable conditions below deck.

Another aid in the fight against the U-boats, before the introduction of surface radar, was the use of 'Snowflake' illumination. This involved the use of star shells to light up and silhouette surfaced U-boats. Brief details of the projector for this system, and the 2in rocket launcher into which it was later developed in Coastal Forces, are given on pages 193–4 below.

was very widely fitted to escort sloops and other escort vessels such as old destroyers and the new frigates, when they were introduced. The Type 128 was the last pre-war destroyer set with the directing gear and dome as in the Type 121 and electronics as in the Type 127. The dome type depended on the ship speed, being fitted to the A, L and Hunt class destroyers as well as other wartime vessels with no space for the Type 144, as well as minelayers and minesweepers.

The Type 129 of 1937 was the first keel set for submarines. Type 130, of 1938, was designed for small craft and motor boats, and had

**Details of depth charge fittings**

1 After tank space hatch
2 Engineroom hatch
3 Mushroom vent
4 A/S davit – working radius 3ft 3in
5 D/C chute (Admiralty supply)
6 Multiple outer covering board
7 Deck stringer
8 Deck girder
9 Carling
10 Depth charge
11 Strut on frame 77
12 Six 1in × ⅜in dia hex-headed MS bolts
13 Fabricated davit tabernacle
14 Six 1¼in × ⅜in dia CSK MS bolts
15 Eight 5in × ⅜in dia snap-headed MS bolts
16 Pine levelling chock
17 Six 2½ × ⅜in dia hexheaded MS coachscrews
18 Six ½in No 10 brass CSK MS bolts
19 Two 1¼ × No 10 brass CSK wood screws
20 Spruce plug, 3½ in dia

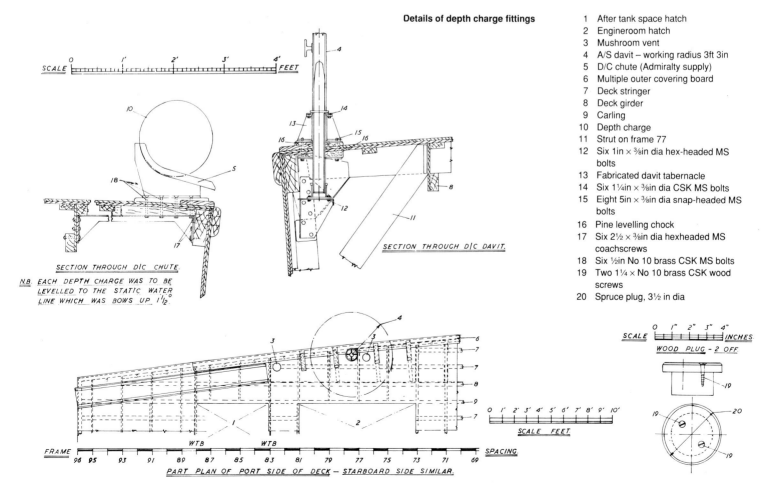

SCALE ⊢⊢⊢⊢⊢⊢ FEET

SECTION THROUGH D/C CHUTE.

N.B. EACH DEPTH CHARGE WAS TO BE LEVELLED TO THE STATIC WATER LINE WHICH WAS BOWS UP 1'½".

SECTION THROUGH D/C DAVIT.

SCALE FEET

SPACING

PART PLAN OF PORT SIDE OF DECK – STARBOARD SIDE SIMILAR.

SCALE ⊢⊢⊢⊢⊢ INCHES
WOOD PLUG – 2 OFF

**Depth charge in rack (c1940)**

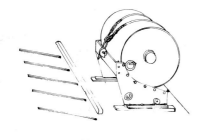

**BPB 70ft MASB single depth charge chute**

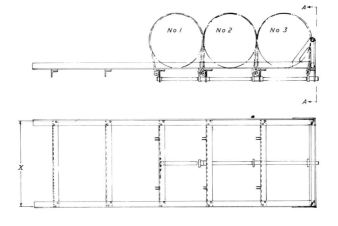

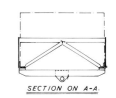

*SECTION ON A-A.*

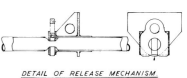

*DETAIL OF RELEASE MECHANISM.*

*N.B. 28·0" BETWEEN RAILS = X*

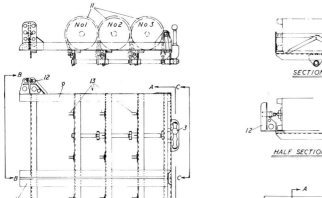

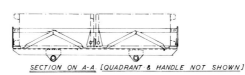

*SECTION ON A-A. [QUADRANT & HANDLE NOT SHOWN].*

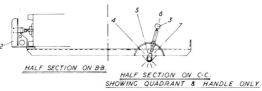

*HALF SECTION ON B-B.* *HALF SECTION ON C-C.*
*SHOWING QUADRANT & HANDLE ONLY.*

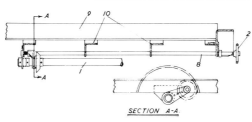

*SECTION A-A.*

**BPB 70ft MASB double depth charge chute**

1 Rotating release shaft
2 Selector handwheel
3 Firing gear assembly
4 Locked position
5 Release No 1
6 Release No 2
7 Release No 3
8 Control shafting
9 Framework
10 Athwartship member
11 Anchor wire
12 Bracket for detonating head striker
13 Wire anchors (adjustable)

**Y gun twin depth charge thrower (RN Mark III, ex US Navy)**

1 Hatch
2 Depth charge thrower MK III
3 Grab stanchion
4 Reload depth charge with arbor
5 Wooden depth charge pad
6 Wooden deck pad
7 Depth charge reload crane

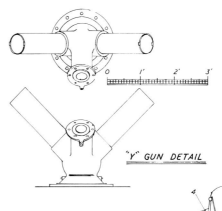

*"Y" GUN DETAIL*

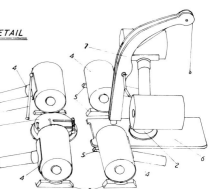

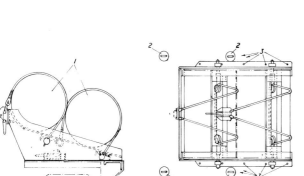

**Canadian Power Boat Co double depth charge chute**

1 Depth charge
2 ½in eye plates to take lashing as required
3 Ten ½in dia securing bolts

**Mark VII depth charge**

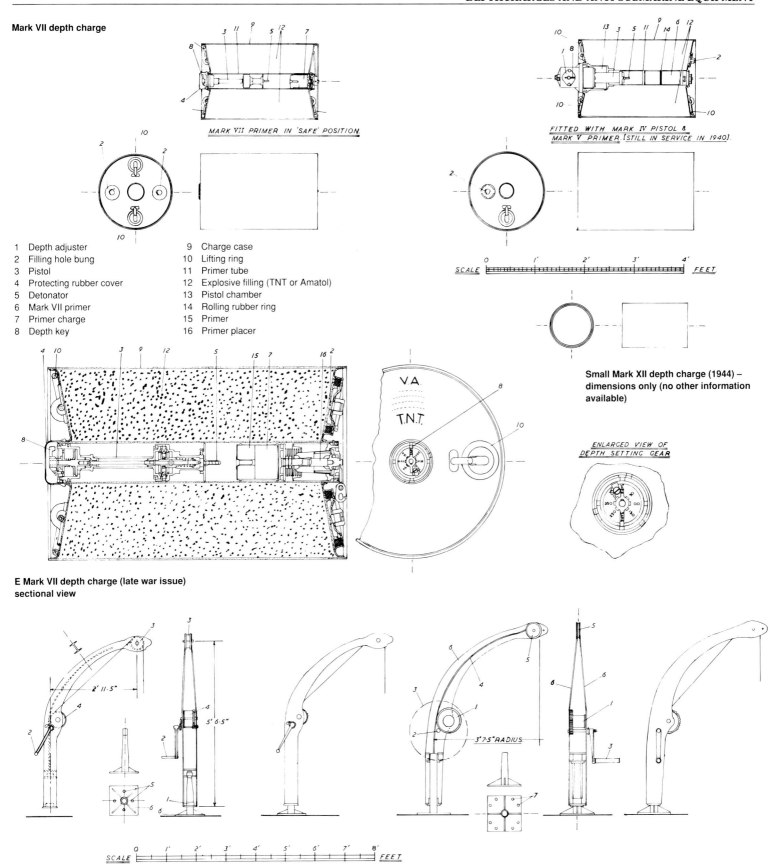

MARK VII PRIMER IN 'SAFE' POSITION.

FITTED WITH MARK IV PISTOL & MARK V PRIMER [STILL IN SERVICE IN 1940].

SCALE | FEET.

1  Depth adjuster
2  Filling hole bung
3  Pistol
4  Protecting rubber cover
5  Detonator
6  Mark VII primer
7  Primer charge
8  Depth key
9  Charge case
10  Lifting ring
11  Primer tube
12  Explosive filling (TNT or Amatol)
13  Pistol chamber
14  Rolling rubber ring
15  Primer
16  Primer placer

**Small Mark XII depth charge (1944) – dimensions only (no other information available)**

ENLARGED VIEW OF DEPTH SETTING GEAR

V.A.
T.N.T.

**E Mark VII depth charge (late war issue) sectional view**

SCALE | FEET

**4cwt depth charge crane**

1  Socket bearing
2  Winding handle (12in radius)
3  6½in dia pulley
4  6½ dia drum
5  ½in dia bolt holes
6  Base plate

**A/S crane and king pin**

1  Winding drum
2  Machine cut spur (six pinion gears)
3  Winding handle (12in radius)
4  25in mild steel rib
5  Mild steel lead sheave to suspension rope
6  25in mild steel side plates
7  ½in dia bolt holes

167

# British Coastal Forces radar

Naval radar in general should be seen in the context of overall naval preparation for war in the late 1930s. Britain was in many respects unprepared for war in 1939, whereas Germany had been allocating money and technical resources to weapons research for over five years. The difference in the quality of equipment of many kinds between the two nations was glaringly obvious during the first two years of the war. Though Britain had invented RDF (Radio Direction Finding), as it was first called, and was actually able to use it to great effect during the Battle of Britain, it was simply not availabe for many warships, and in particular not for Coastal Forces units. The RN did have simple gunnery control sets, but they were of limited use, and did not compare with the much more efficient German big ship gunnery control radar; Britain was unable to match the performance of the German gunnery control radar until late in the war.

Priority for Coastal Forces radar sets was low, partly because naval radar resources were at full stretch, and few resources were available to design and produce sets which would be small and light enough to be fitted in small craft. RN staff prejudice against the RNVR in general, and Coastal Forces in particular, also played some part. From these limited resources and a small number of dedicated men, however, CF radar was developed into a useful asset.

By 1942 there were about forty Coastal Forces boats based at HMS *Hornet* at Portsmouth, a typical base, and of those only the short MTBs (Vosper and White types) and the Fairmile C type MGBs had radar, almost all 286U sets. These were, according to those who operated them, of very limited value, and very unreliable. The aerial array was fixed to the masthead, pointing forward and the arrangement of the three dipole groups was such that the aerial transmission/reception signals occurred in three lobes, the strongest one being the centre lobe, with the two right and left wing lobes (angled out about 15 degrees) about two-thirds of the strength. So if the radar operator saw an echo on his CRT (cathode ray tube), the CO could only get a bearing on it by altering course both ways, until the operator could feel certain that his tube was showing the maximum height echo of the three possible traces (the centre lobe was not a narrow beam like that of a searchlight). On a flat calm sea, and when the CO had no other boats in close company, he could afford to comply, and results could be achieved, but, given the rarity of those conditions during operations in the North Sea or the Channel, it is small wonder that the young COs were not overly impressed with the performance of the radar; there was little indication of range and direction.

Added to these problems were the effects of conditions at sea, notably the rapid violent movements and the wet salt atmosphere. At sea the 'gremlins', prevalent from the beginning in RAF radar, were multiplied. In those early days, pulse transmitter output from the type 286U was from a pair of valves connected up as a flip-flop circuit, which gave only moderate power. To make the most of this, losses in the power feed up to the aerial array had to be minimised. A technical conflict arose in that the aerial array had to be as high as possible, in order to give a reasonable range, but long lengths of the flexible co-axial cables then available gave unacceptable loss of signal strength at the high transmission frequency used. The scientists therefore decided to use the shortest practicable lengths of flexible co-axial cable. One length was fitted from the transmitter to a junction box at the mast tabernacle, and another from the top of the mast and another junction box to the aerial array on its lightweight permalloy topmast. The two junction boxes were then connected by the main length of feed cable up the mast; this cable was of rigid pyrotenax and consisted of a copper tube about 20mm in diameter, which was earthed. At its centre was a solid pure copper conductor wire, about 4mm in diameter to carry the radar signals. The space between the two was filled with compressed magnesium oxide powder. This, when dry, was an excellent insulator and permitted very low loss of H/F radiation from the centre core. Unfortunately magnesium oxide is very, very hygroscopic – it readily absorbs moisture from the air. Therefore, it was essential to see that the outer tube of pyrotenax was properly sweated into each junction box, the latter then being filled to overflowing by pouring in hot pitch, before screwing back the lid. When this was done, preferably in hot dry weather, a megger test taken between core and outer sheath would indicate about 10 megohms. This reading seldom lasted very long; after a few weeks of sea time the CO would report that 'his b----- radar couldn't even pick up an echo from the Nab Tower at 2 miles'. The first test was always with the megger, and a reading of about 2 megohms, or less, was regularly found. If that was so, an opportunity to get the boat berthed under the quayside crane had to be organised; if the boat was operational, then its radar was out of action.

When the boat was eventually under the crane, the lower junction box had to be emptied, the cable parted and the mast lifted out on to trestles on the quay. There, radar mechanics would work along the pyrotenax with a giant 5-pint blowlamp (an ordinary 1-pint lamp was not enough to drive out the moisture). After the compulsory megger test had established that the insulation was again 10 megohms, the sweating-in and junction box refilling job had to be redone, and the mast had to be repainted in pusser's 'crabfat' grey, as the existing paint had been burnt off during the operation.

This operation was necessary whenever a boat was hauled up the slip for hull repairs in the boatshed, or if it had to go up Haslar Creek into Gunboat Yard for the engineers to do an engine change or similar job. If an urgent radar defect required a pyrotenax and junction box reconnection when the weather was inclement, then a tarpaulin was rigged to provide cover.

This tedious repair was the major problem, but not the only one. The low feeder insulation accounted for 80–90 per cent of the problems, but there were other, more technical difficulties with CF radar sets. The majority of radio valves were VR91s, pentodes (five pins), and their glass envelopes were completely shrouded by a cylindrical can, painted red, which was earthed so that stray radiations could not interfere with their function. In the early days most VR91s did not take kindly to violent physical shocks, such as those regularly produced by a hard-chine short boat trying 15 knots into a head sea in the Channel, when it was blowing a Force 5 or more. The valves tended regularly to fail, burn out, loosen one of the base pins, or even get shaken from their sockets. Dry-soldered joints in the circuit wiring, particularly those to the valve pin sockets, could also cause valve failure following a rough passage, and problems with joints were difficult to trace *in situ*. The only sure way was to remove the faulty set from the boat, take it to the workshop test bench and test through the circuit using an oscilloscope, with the aid of the circuit diagram.

If the problem was found to be a faulty valve, then it was simply replaced, but on occasion boats ran out of replacement VR91s faster than they were able to indent for new ones. When that hapened, a valve had to be 'won' from a boat under some sort of long refit, for temporary exchange.

By 1943 the supply of valves had much improved, with American VR91s available in quantity. It seems that there were few failures of the display CRTs, in spite of the number of functions that could be adjusted, and the high anode voltage applied to them. Many connections were made to their base pins, so that functions like brightness, vertical and horizontal shifts, focus, etc, could all be adjustable. The 286U tube had a left-to-right horizontal line scan, so the electronic controls of the tube's electron beam were crude and simple: one pair of capacitor plates vertically, and another pair horizontally; this was a great aid to reliability.

Yet another problem was with the connecting cables between the different units of the set. The cables were relatively short and flexible multicore, sheathed over their outer insulation with tinned copper braid to provide an earthed screen. The connecting plugs at each end were round and carried a cylindrical shroud milled on the outside and with a rather fine screw thread on the inside; thus, when the plug had been pushed home into its socket on the set unit, the outer shroud cover could be screwed home on the male screw thread of the set unit socket, completing the earthing screen connection to the set's unit chassis. Unfortunately, the outer shrouds were constructed of a kind of base cast alloy, which was prone to corrosion in the screw threads due to the salt air environment. After a period, as this built up, its presence upset the earthing connection, with various interference effects becoming evident, such as low and fuzzy echoes on the CRT scan, with lots of 'noise' all along the scan. On occasion a pair of grips was required to loosen the screw shroud, with the build-up of corrosion, and not infrequently the force required was enough to crack the shroud. In any event, the cleaning job on the connectors was a tedious process which took both care and time for the radio mechanics.

In the summer of 1942 new boats began to be fitted with 286PU sets. These were similar to the 286U apart from the aerial array. At the bottom of its permalloy topmast were two simple bearings and a lightweight pulley, the latter being connected to a similar pulley in the boat's radar office by a thin pair of wires running up the aftside of the mast. This simple modification now meant that the radar operator could rotate the aerial array from dead ahead through almost 180 degrees to either beam, and report any echoes seen with a bearing relative to the ship's heading. This avoided the need for the CO to alter course with the boat in order to get a more accurate bearing. The new layout of the dipole groups also did away with the two side-lobe transmissions which the 286U aerial had needed, so the operator had only a single echo from a given target, thus making his task easier. Stops were fitted to prevent the wires wrapping themselves around the mast.

When the new 286PU array became available in greater numbers, the older boats were retro-fitted with improved system. Then, in 1943, 286 sets began to be replaced by 291Us; these were basically the same as 286s, but with a number of internal electronic modifications, better transmission and modulator valves, and improved CRT controls. No progress was made, however, with the problem of the pyrotenax, and the 'down mast/up mast' routines still provided a major part of the workload, now added to by the complication of the lines which controlled aerial rotation.

1943 also saw a gradual expansion of *Hornet*'s involvement in the war, as more and more boats arrived and the workload increased. This expansion brought in additional staff, which included another PO radiomechanic to assist the Chief, a PO and a killick radar operator, so that training courses could be introduced for the individual MTB and MGB operators, as well as additional radiomechanics, including (towards the end of the year) a few WREN radiomechanics plus an assistant radar officer.

By mid-year responsibilities included maintenance of, and operator instruction in, the boats' radar sets, IFF sets, QH navigational sets and, for some strange reason, loud-hailers. Boats' W/T and R/T equipment, however, came under the control of the signals officer, who had his own PO telegraphist and radiomechanic staff.

By the autumn, the gradual expansion had taken on more of the look of an explosion, as flotilla after flotilla of boats berthed at *Hornet* – all kinds, Vosper and Samuel White short boats, 71ft 6in British Power Boats, MTBs and MGBs, Fairmile B, C and D types, HDMLs, and, early in 1944, a squadron of US Navy PT boats. These last had the US Navy SO radar, but though these sets were a great improvement on the RN equipment, the US Navy had their own radar technicians and a mobile workshop on the quayside. So many boats (over 140) were based at *Hornet* that berth space overflowed, and whole flotillas had to be berthed at nearby HMS *Dolphin* and at HMS *Vernon*, on the other side of the harbour.

Although the US SO set was not officially fitted to RN units, it was obtained by unofficial means, particularly in the Mediterranean. On some Fairmile D types, although in only limited numbers, friendly loans were organised.

Bob Fletcher, who operated the equipment, recalls its advantages over RN sets:

> I was most impressed with the SO, although I was not familiar with its innards. A couple of trips in a PT boat proved most informative. It had a much improved performance and a PPI (Plan Position Indicator) readout, nowadays a familiar item, but in those days an enormous step forward, compared to the linear scan as given by the 291U.

Interestingly enough, at about the same time some British boats were being fitted with a set working on the same principle, a continuously rotating paraboloid aerial inside a Perspex dome, and a PPI tube in the operator's office. This set, the type 970 (but known to the RAF as H2S – it was Air Ministry designed and produced), had been in use for some time before the RN received it, in Coastal Command Sunderland flying-boats and Liberators. It was not fitted to MTBs, but was fitted to those B types modified as navigational leaders, so that it is shown listed as either type.

The set itself performed well (as reported by CFVA members), and there were no pyrotenax gremlins to fight; the transmitter valves were in the Perspex radome with the aerial and rotated with it, so the cables up the lattice mast did not need to be low-loss for UHF. Serious difficulties remained, however, largely due to the insurmountable problem of the hostile sea environment in which the sets were required to perform.

The greatest advance in British radar design came following the invention of the magnetron transmitter and its application to 5cm wavelength (X band) equipment. This resulted in the type 268U set, which was fitted to some Samuel White boats in 1944 and a few Fairmile Ds and BPBs soon afterwards. These too overcame the pyrotenax problems. The only cables up the mast were those carrying the supply to the magnetron 'cheese' unit, and the Selsyn motor to rotate it; the radar signal went up via a length of hollow rectangular section waveguide (not a cable). In simple terms, this did for the electronic signal something akin to what an organ pipe did for a sound signal of a frequency tuned to the pipe. When a boat with a type 268U had a down-mast/up-mast job, reconnection of the lower end of the waveguide needed some care, but the task was nothing compared with the pyrotenax junction box job. Apart from this, when the set was operating, a small fan heater pumped warm air up the interior of the waveguide to keep it dry. Indeed, the whole set had been designed with a view to the operating conditions imposed on C/F craft by sea, vibration, gunfire, etc; its performance

**RDF outfit ATS (Type 286 PU) general
arrangement and details**

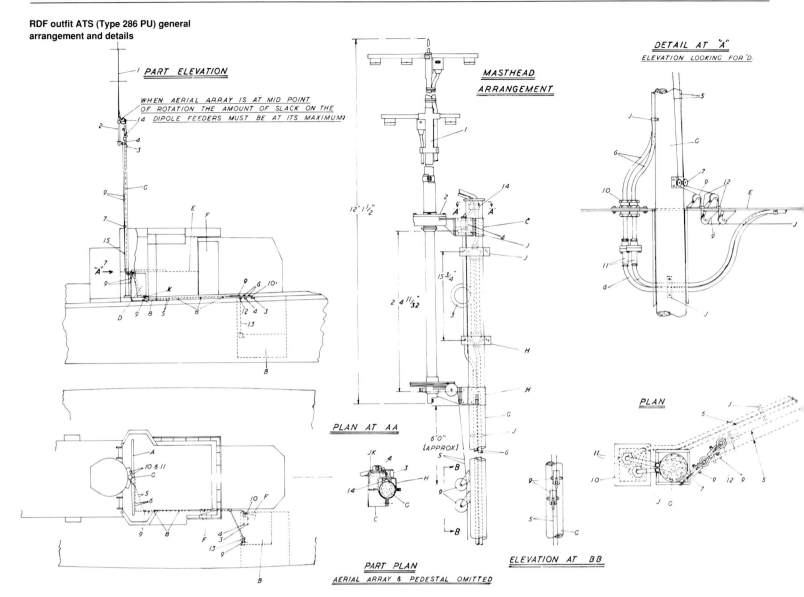

and general reliability were far superior to anything previously provided for small ships.

The other major aspect of Coastal Forces radar was IFF (Identification Friend or Foe). The idea behind IFF was that, if a friendly ship or aircraft were picked up by radar, the IFF set in the target responded to the incoming radar transmission by modulating and transmitting part of the signal in a regular pulse form, which made the target echo jump up and down on the searcher's radar scan (in the case of a set with a PPI, for instance a 970 or 268U, the target echo would brighten and dim in a rhythmical fashion). If the target echo did not pulse, but remained steady, it could be regarded as possibly (though not certainly) hostile. The sets themselves, and their service manuals, were classified Top Secret, and it was naturally regarded as essential that the enemy should not learn what radar frequencies they would respond to.

To prevent the enemy obtaining a set, each was fitted with an internal detonator, and standing orders required that if a boat (or RAF aircraft) became damaged in any way which meant that the unit might be captured by the enemy, a red button was to be pressed by the operator after an order from the CO, assuming that the latter had also taken the decision to destroy or sink the boat's confidential books. The design of the IFF set was such that firing the detonator effectively destroyed its valves and circuitry, without any of the debris coming out of the front of the case and thus

injuring the operator. Before a boat went out on an operation, and again whenever a set was refitted to a boat following any servicing in the workshop, the detonator circuit had to be checked. Testing it required a safety switch to be operated before (and during) the pressing of the red button; a red tell-tale lamp then lit up. At HMS *Hornet*, during the time one radar operator served there, there were four occasions on which the radiomechanic got the drill wrong, and blew up a perfectly good set. (On two of those occasions the same radiomechanic was responsible!). On another occasion he happened to be aboard the boat when the explosion occurred. Both he and the boat's CO scrambled down the companion to the radar office, to find it full of evil-smelling black smoke, and a white faced and frightened radiomechanic. At least this proved that the fragments of the set's interior had not been propelled out through its front panel.

Thus, although few sets were fitted in Coastal Forces craft, they were nevertheless steadily developed and improved, and those in service at the end of the war were vastly superior to the sets carried by the few enemy E-boats that had radar equipment (usually the senior officer's boat only).

Although the equipment was superbly constructed, the end product – the radar return – remained technically 2 – 3 years behind that of the RN large ship sets, and for that reason Coastal Forces radar was seldom used.

1 Mast 8ft 1in high complete with fittings (1 off)
2 Pedestal unit 19Q (1)
3 Transformer and matching unit for ATS (2)
4 2-way box junction (design C) for dipole feeders (2)
5 Steel wire rope, ESF galvanised, 6-strand, 19 wires per strand, ⅜in
6 Single core electric cable, pyrotenax mineral insulation, copper sheathed
7 1¼in pulleys with mast bracket (2 pairs)
8 1¼in pulleys with deck bracket (2 pairs)
9 2¼in pulley (deck mounted) (12)
10 Gland plate, 7½in × 6½in with two glands (2)
11 Coupling plug with special mineral insulation, ¾in diameter (2)
12 Gland for drive wire (4)
13 Training unit for ATS (1)

14 Clamp for ⅝in and 7⁄16in cables to mast (1)
15 2BA bottle screw (2)
16 Protecting cap for coupling socket (2)
17 Protecting cap for coupling plug (2)
A Aerial yard
B RDF office
C Upper pedestal securing board
D Locker
E Bridge deck
F Door
G Ship's mast
H Securing band
J Clip
K Bracket

*CLIP & BRACKET*

*PLAN*

*ELEVATION*

*DETAILS OF SECURING BANDS*

*UPPER PEDESTAL SECURING BAND*

NOTE – LOWER PEDESTAL SECURING BAND IS IDENTICAL IN ALL RESPECTS TO UPPER BAND EXCEPT FOR DIMENSION MARKED ✓ WHICH IS 3" FOR THE LOWER & 3·5" FOR THE UPPER.

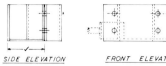
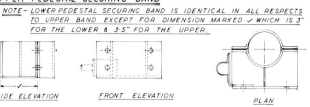

*SIDE ELEVATION*　　*FRONT ELEVATION*　　*PLAN*

0 1" 2" 3" 4" 5" 6" 7" 8" 9" 10" 11" 12"
*SCALE*　　　　*INCHES*

*SECURING BAND FOR TRANSFORMER & MATCHING UNIT*

*FRONT ELEVATION*　　*SIDE ELEVATION*　　*PLAN*

**Coastal Forces typical radar and IFF aerials**

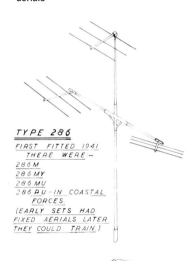

*TYPE 286*

FIRST FITTED 1941.
THERE WERE –
286 M
286 MY
286 MU
286 PU – IN COASTAL FORCES.
[EARLY SETS HAD FIXED AERIALS LATER THEY COULD TRAIN.]

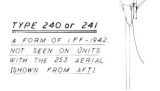

*TYPE 240 or 241*

A FORM OF IFF – 1942.
NOT SEEN ON UNITS WITH THE 253 AERIAL
[SHOWN FROM AFT.]

*TYPE 291 U*

FIRST FITTED 1943.

*TYPE 242*
[IFF INTERROGATOR].

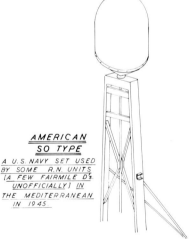

*AMERICAN SO TYPE*

A U.S. NAVY SET USED BY SOME R.N. UNITS [A FEW FAIRMILE D's UNOFFICIALLY] IN THE MEDITERRANEAN IN 1945

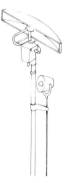

*TYPE 268 U & LOUD HAILER*

FIRST FITTED 1945

*TYPE 253*
[IFF TRANSPONDER].

**Radar rigging plan for Fairmile Bs modified as navigational leaders**

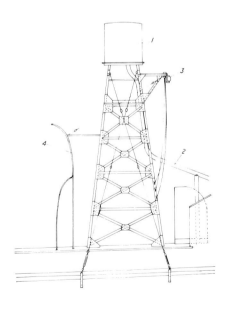

1 Type 971 lantern
2 Power feed
3 Steaming light
4 Gun safety rail

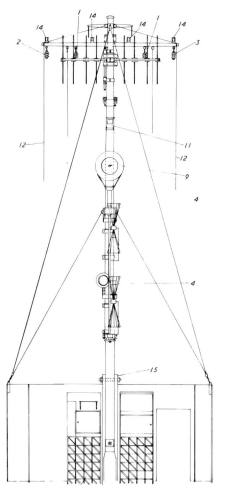

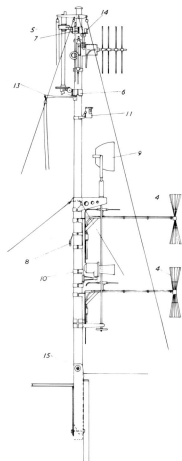

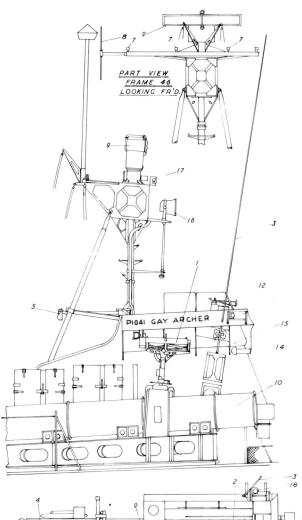

**Mast arrangement on Vosper MGB S10 (Boat 2186) in 1943**

1  Insulators port and starboard to take transmitting aerials (TW 12)
2  Insulator to take receiver second channel aerial
3  Insulator to take TCS aerial
4  ASH IFF transponder (Type 253)
5  RDF pedestal upper securing band
6  RDF pedestal lower securing band
7  Junction box securing clip and bracket
8  Guides for RDF training wire
9  Hailing apparatus APW 2041
10  Klaxon horn bracket
11  Masthead lamp
12  Signal yard shrouds
13  Ensign spur
14  Fighting lights (AP 3932; two red port, two green starboard)
15  Ply tabernacle
16  Flag lockers

**Typical postwar radar array (1953–4) on a short MTB/MGB**

1  Rocket projector
2  Azimuth repeater
3  Whip aerial
4  ATM compass
5  Shaded stern light
6  Pyrotechnic locker
7  Fighting lights
8  AJA Aerial
9  Decca marine radar Type 195
10  21in LC Mark 3 torpedo tube
11  Ready use rocket locker
12  Torpedo sight
13  Open bridge
14  Horn
15  Wind deflector
16  Loudhailer
17  Masthead light
18  Navigation light

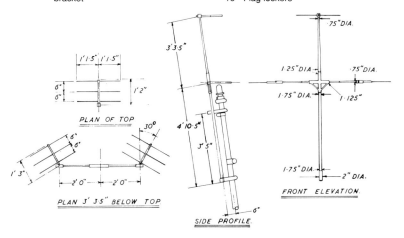

**RDF Type 286 aerial array, showing dimensions**

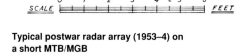

# British Coastal Forces camouflage

While a wide range of camouflage schemes were applied to RN and USN warships during World War II, those applied to Coastal Forces craft were relatively standardised and limited in number. The drawings which accompany this section illustrate the more commonly used schemes prepared for, but not limited to, the various Fairmile types. USN schemes and those for other RN types will be addressed in future volumes of this study.

of white and brown antifouling. On boats with coppered bottoms, the brown was to be omitted but the white was to be painted as shown. In practice, it appears that the white was seldom applied, the copper being left in its natural state. Even on uncoppered boats, the white does not appear to have been used very often, the entire underbody being painted with the darker antifouling up to the datum waterline.

**Camouflage drawing 1**

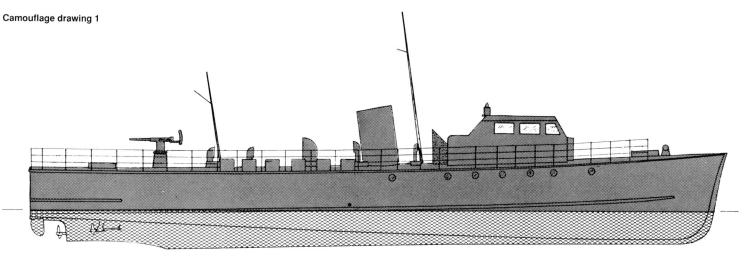

*Drawing 1*
This drawing depicts a Fairmile A in the then-standard (1941) Home Fleet scheme of overall dark grey (507A) with brown or black antifouling. Note that no countershading is in evidence, as this practice was not common until mid-1943. Later, this scheme was replaced by the standard light scheme of overall light grey (G.45) with dark blue-grey (B.15) decks and horizontal surfaces.

*Drawing 2*
Taken from a Fairmile drawing dated 24/8/43, this drawing depicts a modification of the standard light scheme applied to Fairmile Bs and HDMLs during this period. All horizontal surfaces were painted dark blue-grey (B.15), while all vertical surfaces were light grey (G.45). Countershading was in general use at this time and, in this instance, consisted of white enamel applied below all overhangs which might cast a shadow on a darker colour below. Rails, stanchions, and the interior of the bridge sides were also painted white, the deck in the bridge remaining dark blue-grey.
The area below the datum waterline was painted a combination

*ML 151 in 1941 with two ex-US Navy 21in torpedo tubes. She is camouflaged in the standard three-colour Western Approaches paint scheme.* Wright & Logan

**Camouflage drawing 2**

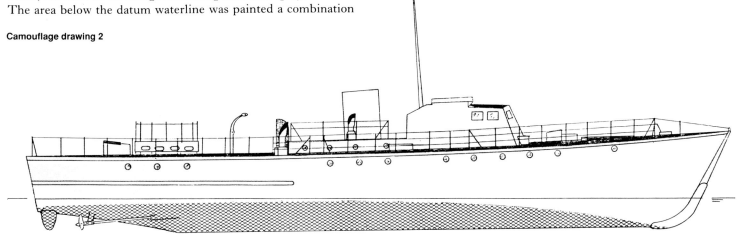

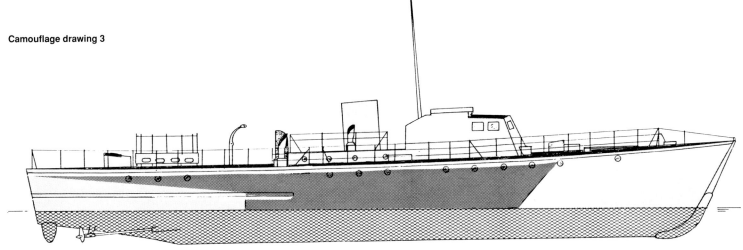

*Drawing 3*

This drawing depicts the dark modification of the standard light scheme, the only difference being a dark blue-grey (B.15) panel applied to the hull. Anti-fouling is standard black or brown.

*Drawing 4*

One of the more attractive camouflage schemes was the Peter Scott developed Western Approaches scheme. This example depicts an RCN Fairmile B during 1943. Eminently suited to the northern latitudes at which the RCN normally operated, this scheme consisted of an overall white with light blue (B.55) side panels and a darker deck, probably B.15. A variation on this scheme included the use of a light green along with the light blue, but green pigments were generally scarce and the blue predominated.

*ML 138 in August 1941 at Newhaven, painted in an Admiralty light disruptive paint scheme (white, greys and green – 507A, MS2, MS3 and 507C), suitable for use in overcast northern waters.* Wright & Logan

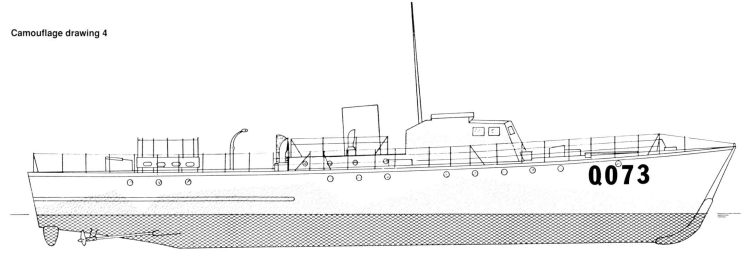

*A Norwegian-crewed unit (704–723) on operations from Lerwick, Scotland, to Norway. She has a Northern waters paint scheme and carries two 21in torpedo tubes, power-operated 6-pounder forward, manual 6-pounder aft, and a twin 20mm Oerlikon on the coachroof. She was probably a member of the 54th MTB Flotilla. It is just possible to pick out the different Norwegian caps in the original.* Imperial War Museum

**Camouflage drawing 5**

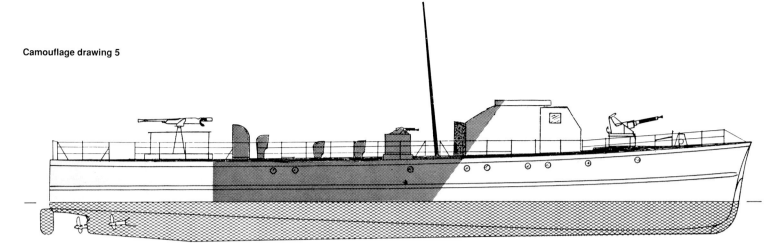

**Drawing 5**

This scheme appeared on several Fairmile Cs during 1944 (Q 328 in particular), and appears to have been a variation on the dark modification of the standard light scheme. The dark blue-grey (B.15) panel is carried on to the bridge and the Vickers Mark V turrets. Interestingly for this period, no countershading was evident in the photographs from which this drawing was prepared.

**Drawing 6**

This was the standard light scheme applied to the Fairmile D MTB/MGB. The large white area forward below the chine was a result of the very pronounced flare of the hull in this area. Variations on this scheme included the standard dark blue-grey panel amidships and, in some of the later boats, a triangular section of light grey which bisected the white section approximately between the torpedo cutout and the stem.

*MGB 322, a C type, in May 1942 at Lowestoft, painted in the Admiralty light disruptive scheme; she has the Senior Officer's broad mark at the bow, to distinguish her when on operations with her identical sisters.* Wright & Logan

**Camouflage drawing 6**

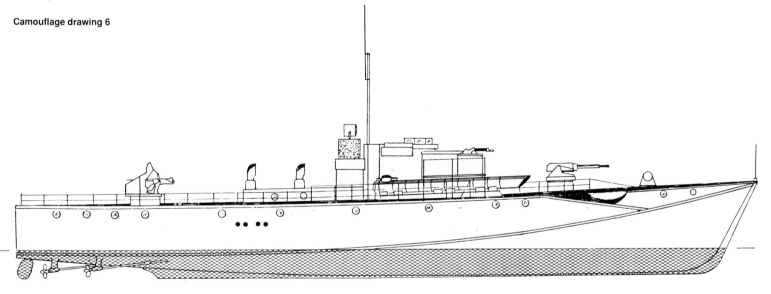

*ML 893 of the 37th ML Flotilla was built in Cape Province, South Africa, and appears to wear the Admiralty dark disruptive scheme devised for use in lighter, warmer climes.* Author's collection

Countershading was a common feature of Coastal Forces camouflage schemes, particularly since the boats usually operated at night and often engaged the enemy at close range, often under 100 yards. Countershading was applied to reduce the shadows in a boat's upperworks and to reduce the brightness of the highlights, thus making the boat less visible at close range. The dark shadows in a complicated structure such as a boat's bridge were often the first things to attract the eye, especially at night. The fundamental principle was simple: paint the highlights fairly dark and the areas of shadow as light as possible (that is, white).

To underscore the importance of countershading, the Admiralty issued very explicit directions for its application in Fleet Order 1575 Appendix. According to this instruction, the following areas were to be painted with white enamel:

the undersides of platforms and of all horizontal projections not normally visible from outboard;
the insides of ventilators and of enclosing surfaces not normally visible from outboard, except in the bridge;
the deck under under the guns, dinghy, depth charges, anchors, gratings, ammunition lockers, and any fitting raised more than 2in off the deck;
any horizontal surfaces which might throw light up into dense shadows;
that part of the hull either below the chine or normally in shadow due to flare;
the insides of the gun shields, winch, etc;
the masts, posts, guardrail stanchions;
the underside of the dinghy, the lower third of gun barrels, torpedo tubes, searchlights, throats of ventilators;
the average shadow areas on vertical or approximately vertical surfaces due to adjacent projections of any kind or to the areas in question being recessed.

Similarly, the following areas were to be painted dark blue-grey (B.15):

the deck and all horizontal surfaces visible from outboard;
the upper third of gun barrels, torpedo tubes, searchlights, and any other rounded or sloping surfaces which created highlights, such as the tops of ventilators, etc;
all surfaces inside the bridge [a direct contradiction to the instructions on the Fairmile plans mentioned earlier!]

Two other points of interest appear in this CAFO. First, it required that the camouflage paint be carried down to the waterline over the boot topping. Earlier CAFOs did not recommend painting *over* the boot topping; instead, they recommended not applying the boot topping but carrying the normal camouflage to the datum waterline. Second, it recommended painting the transom and all vertical surfaces in the superstructure running athwartships light grey (G.45).

Until early 1943, the Admiralty prescribed the use of matt paints for camouflage, primarily because matt paints were least likely to 'flash' when struck by either sun or moon light. Operational experience, however, soon showed that matt paints were very susceptible to wear and chalking, which quickly reduced their effectiveness.

*Units of the 50th MTB Flotilla, showing an interesting attempt at counter-shading on some boats. The picture shows MTBs 677 (SO), 676 and 679.*
Courtesy Leslie Sprigg.

### Paint formulae for A.1 type paints

| | | |
|---|---|---|
| G.5 | White lead oil paste | 72lb |
| | Black paste | 12lb |
| | Raw linseed oil | 16pt |
| | White spirit | 3pt |
| | Liquid dryers | 4pt |
| G.10 | White lead oil paste | 56lb |
| | Zinc oxide white | 21lb |
| | Raw linseed oil | 8pt |
| | White spirit | 14pt |
| | Liquid dryers | 3pt |
| | Blue black paste | 7lb |
| G.20 | White lead oil paste | 50lb |
| | Zinc oxide white | 28lb |
| | Green paste | ½lb |
| | Black paste | 1lb |
| | Raw linseed oil | 16pt |
| | White spirit | 8pt |
| | Liquid dryers | 3pt |
| | Paste ochre | 1½lb |
| G.45 | White lead oil paste | 50lb |
| | Blue black paste | 7lb |
| | Zinc oxide white | 28lb |
| | Raw linseed oil | 11pt |
| | White spirit | 10pt |
| | Liquid dryers | 3pt |
| B.15 | White lead oil paste | 61lb |
| | Blue black paste | 14lb |
| | Blue paste | 11½lb |
| | Green paste | 1lb |
| | Black paste | ½lb |
| | Raw linseed oil | 11pt |
| | White spirit | 10pt |
| | Liquid dryers | 3pt |
| B.30 | White lead oil paste | 58lb |
| | Blue black paste | 20lb |
| | Zinc oxide white | 9lb |
| | Blue paste | ½lb |
| | Green paste | ½lb |
| | Raw linseed oil | 11pt |
| | White spirit | 10pt |
| | Liquid dryers | 3pt |
| B.55 | White lead oil paste | 40lb |
| | Zinc oxide white | 47lb |
| | Blue black paste | 2lb |
| | Green paste | 2oz |
| | Raw linseed oil | 9pt |
| | White spirit | 11pt |
| | Liquid dryers | 3pt |

To counter this durability problem, the Admiralty approved the use of a semi-gloss paint, identified as A.1, in early 1943. At the same time, experiments were undertaken to determine the suitability of an even higher-gloss paint, type A.2. Interestingly, this latter type had the same gloss factor as the prewar 507 paints. Apparently the A.2 paint did not prove sufficiently more durable than the A.1 and it was not put into general use. A Fleet Order dated 28 June 1945 noted that a new resin-based paint was under development but, for the present, type A.1 would remain the standard camouflage paint.

Prior to 1943, camouflage paints were designated by either a 507 or MS prefix. The standard prewar mixes were:

507A – dark grey
507B – medium grey
507C – light grey

507A was applied to ships in home waters, while 507C was applied to ships on foreign station. This was reversed when the war began, with most Mediterranean Fairmile Ds, for instance, being painted overall dark blue-grey.

The 507 series was followed by the MS series, which incorporated blue and green tinting materials. These new shades included:

MS1  – a very dark, almost black, grey
MS2  – a dark grey
B5   – a dark blue-grey
MS3  – a dark green-grey
B6   – a medium grey
MS4  – a medium blue-grey
MS4a – a light grey

By 1943, however, the Admiralty wanted to simplify its paint designations and make their formulae more consistent. According to CAFO 2106 of 13 May 1943,

The shades of paints for use externally in HM ships will be referred to by a letter denoting the colour (B=Blue-

*MTB 5003 in July 1945, the ultimate wartime boat for the war in the Far East. She was camouflaged in Admiralty dark disruptive colours, but did not serve in Eastern waters as hostilities ended just as she was about to leave. Note the weapons fit: two 21in tubes, two 6-pounder Mark VIIs, twin 20mms and British Type 268U radar. Imperial War Museum*

grey, G=Grey) followed by a number denoting the reflection factor or tone of the paint; the higher the number, the lighter the tone.

These new shades and the shades they replaced were:

G.5   – MS1
G.10 – MS2 and 507A
G.20 – MS3
G.45 – 507C
B.15 – B5
B.30 – B6 and MS4
B.55 – MS4a and Western Approaches Blue

As a rule, RN coastal forces craft used only B.15, G.45, and white, especially during the latter stages of the war. The RCN, of course, used B.55 extensively.

*Artist's licence, not an all-American requisite – units of the 55th MTB Flotilla (ex-31st MTB Flotilla) at HMS Hornet in June 1944. Not all boats had the shark's teeth painted up, due to boat replacements. The nearest unit is MTB 628, with 629 and 621 astern and out of view. Imperial War Museum*

# Engines and engineering

The only genuine marine engine of British manufacture available just before World War II was the Thornycroft RY.12 petrol engine, developing only 650hp. This had gradually been developed and improved by Thornycroft from the similar engine used in Coastal Motor Boats during the Great War. It was supplied in the boats sold to the Philippines and China prior to the outbreak of hostilities in 1939. A more powerful engine was clearly needed.

The only other marine engine available was the 1000hp Isotta-Fraschini petrol marine engine, which had been sponsored by the Italian Government and was purchased from them by Vosper for use in their new designs. With an eye to the future, a finance group offered to set up a company to build Isottas in the United Kingdom, where a factory in Scotland was envisaged; the Admiralty, however, could not guarantee orders of sufficient numbers to justify the capital outlay, so the project was dropped.

Commander (E) Peter du Cane of Vosper repeatedly urged production. Two Isottas were purchased for the Vosper private-venture improved design (MTB 102), which developed 1150hp, and when the 1938 building programme was planned the Admiralty ordered thirty-nine such engines from Italy (thirty-six working engines and just three spares). About one third of the engines ordered were delivered before Italy entered the war. Fortunately, Vosper had taken delivery of a number of engines for boats being built by them for Romania, and requisitioning resulted in fifteen boats with these powerful Italian engines for the Royal Navy. The Isotta-Fraschini engine will be covered in a future volume.

Hubert Scott-Paine, who founded the British Power Boat Company and had constructed the first 60ft boats for the RN, had also foreseen the problems of supplying power units in the event of war.

*Not the best of conditions – working on the port Hall-Scott engine aboard ML 181.* Courtesy J Davies

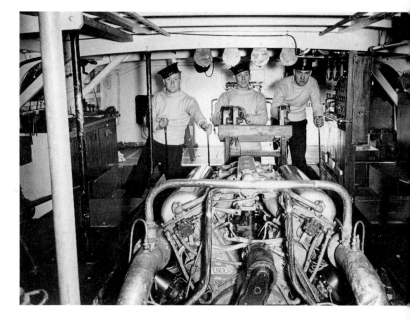

*Engineroom of a Fairmile A, showing the unsupercharged Hall-Scott Defender centre engine. Note the switchboard to port, with a workbench opposite.* The Motor Boat

The Napier Lion had been adapted for marine use, but was not sufficiently powerful, so for new ideas and improved boats he decided to adapt to marine use the new Rolls-Royce Merlin, and gained the contract for the conversion. However, Lord Beaverbrook, Minister of Aviation, quickly stopped this source of supply by insisting that every Merlin was required by the RAF for fighters; only a few British Power Boat craft, mainly for export (and requisitioning), were eventually equipped with Merlins (these will be covered in a future volume).

The Admiralty was therefore forced to turn to America for power units for the projected Motor Torpedo Boats. The first engines to arrive were unsupercharged 650hp Hall-Scott Defenders, ordered by Fairmile. These were obviously not capable of producing enough power for the short MTBs then building, since those vessels had been designed for 1150hp engines. Hall-Scott then delivered supercharged versions of the same engine, giving 900hp. These were fitted to the Fairmile C MGBs, and, in desperation, were also fitted in seven of the Vosper units; in consequence, the performance of the Vosper boats was painfully inadequate. Two MTB flotillas which included those units were based at Dover when the *Gneisenau* and *Scharnhorst* passed through on their 'Channel Dash', and the MTBs were unable to press home their attack.

Fortunately, the outstanding American Packard 4m–2500 petrol engine was then under development. Scott-Paine, who was in Canada and had realised that neither Isotta-Fraschini nor Rolls-Royce petrol engines were likely to be available to the Admiralty, assisted with the redesign of the Packard and sought to get it into production. Other sources were also investigated by the British Purchasing Commission, and the Admiralty was subsequently offered both the Packard and the Sterling Admiral. An order for 500 Packards was secured, later increased to 1000 with a reserve supply of Sterling Admirals. The vast resources of American industry soon ensured that a flood of engines, together with quantities of spares, began to be shipped to the UK. The powerplant problem was thus resolved, with both Allies using common power sources. (The Packard engine will be covered in a future volume.)

The advantages of the petrol engine can be summed up as speed of start and getaway, reduced engineroom complement and simplicity of engineering layout. The disadvantages were the inherent problems of the high-octane fuel carried and the constant risk of fire both from enemy action and fuel vapour leaks. To combat this ever-present risk, strict routines were laid down. The fuel supply to the engine carburettors was to be shut off at all times when the engine was not operating, and the battery circuits broken. Engine drip trays, savealls, etc, were to be kept clear of accumulations of oil and petrol. The bilge of the engine compartment was to be examined at frequent intervals and kept entirely free from fuel. No naked lights were to be used and no smoking was permitted in the engineroom or in the neighbourhood of the fuel tanks. A fire extinguisher was always to be kept in the engineroom available for instant use, with a second one in the immediate vicinity of the exit from that compartment.

When embarking fuel, smoking or naked lights were not allowed in the vicinity of the filling or venting positions and sentries were posted to ensure strict compliance. All fires in galleys or living quarters were to be extinguished if their chimneys were within 15ft of a filling or venting pipe. All side scuttles in or near the petrol lighter or other carrier were to be closed and secured until the lighter had left the boat. No radio transmission was to be carried out while embarking petrol, and no petrol tank was to be filled in excess of 95 per cent of its capacity. Cases of fire had occurred due to a spark caused by the discharge of the high potential electricity generated by friction in the hose filling during the embarkation of fuel, and earthing of the hose was therefore also paramount. Some COs remained very uneasy whenever engines were started, as a result of previous explosions caused by leakage or spills in the engineroom bilges.

When it was necessary to trail one (or more) shafts while running at slow speeds, difficulties due to overheating of the clutches were sometimes experienced. On passage, when instant readiness for full speed was not required, the sailing clutch and engine clutch of each trailing engine were disengaged so that the reduction gear and engine clutch discs were not rotating and there was therefore no pos-

*ML 476 of the Indian flotilla, undergoing an engine change at Ramree Island. Note the 40mm Bofors and CSA aft.* Author's collection.

sibility of overheating. The trailing shaft had to be stopped (by bringing the boat to rest) before sailing clutches could be engaged and all engines and full power became available.

On occasions when full speed might be required instantly, the sailing clutches of the trailing shafts were kept engaged and the engine clutches of those shafts were put into neutral, and the engines stopped but kept warm. As the engine clutch discs were then rotating with no positive oil supply, it was necessary to change over main engines at hourly intervals to prevent overheating clutches (AFO 4503/40).

Whenever an order was received which, if executed, would, in the opinion of the engineer officer (motor mechanic), tend to injure the machinery or cause a needless expenditure of fuel, he was to make a representation to this effect to the commanding officer, but unless the order was countermanded after his representation, he was to execute it. In any such occurrence the CO was to cause the order received and the representation made to be noted in the Engine Log Book. On all occasions before getting under way the engineering officer (senior motor mechanic), was to satisfy himself, by personal inspection and by actually working the steering gear and telegraphs, that those fittings were correct, free from obstruction and in good working order. A report to that effect was to be made to the CO at the same time that the main engines were reported ready, in conformity with the custom of the Service.

## The Hall-Scott Defender marine engine

The Hall-Scott Defender twelve-cylinder marine engine was supplied for Lend-Lease BAD-1009, contract number 11933 (Lot I, engines 34575–35000 inclusive and engines 62001–62301 inclusive, and Lot II, engines 62302–62321 inclusive), a total of 744 main engines. This was increased later in the war. They were made by the Hall-Scott Motor Car Company, a division of the American Car and Foundry Motors Company, of 2850 Seventh Street, Berkely, California. The Defender was designed and built for salt water service. Models 2286 and 3368 turned right-hand propellers; models 2287 and 3369 turned left-hand propellers. Maximum revolutions per minute were 2100; maximum horsepower of the standard engine, 630; octane rating of fuel, 87; number of cylinders, 12 (bore 5¾in, stroke 7in, cubic capacity 2.181cu in); direct drive or reduction gear drive was fitted, with 100 percent rpm in reverse. The approximate net weight of the standard engine with reduction gear (models 2286 and 2287) was 4600lb, of the supercharged engine with direct drive (models 3368 and 3369), 4125lb, and of the supercharged engine with reduction gear, 5400lb.

*Cylinder blocks* These were of the removable type, cast *en bloc* of chrome-nickel-molybdenum iron. Large removable plates on each block made the water jackets readily accessible for cleaning. The cylinder head hold-down studs passed through the block to the upper crankcase.

*Cylinder heads* These were cast from chrome-nickel-molybdenum iron. The complete valve actuating mechanism, including camshafts, valves, inserts for the exhaust valve seats, springs, rocker arms, rocker arm shafts and camshaft driving sprocket, was buried in the heads. The entire assembly could be removed and the valves ground on the bench. Large water jackets ensured proper valve and sparkplug cooling. An oil-tight rocker arm cover enclosed the entire valve mechanism.

*Upper crankcase* Also cast from chrome-nickel-molybdenum iron, the crankcase was suitably ribbed and webbed to ensure ample strength and rigidity. Seven main bearings were fitted, with forged steel bearing caps. The bearing material was a lead-bronze alloy.

*Lower crankcase* Cast (for lightness) from heat-treated aluminium alloy, the lower crankcase was highly resistant to salt water.

*Crankshaft* A chrome-nickel-molybdenum steel forging, the crankshaft turned on seven main bearings of 3¼in diameter with heavy web sections; it was drilled for pressure feed lubrication and fully counterbalanced.

*Connecting rods* Also chrome nickel steel forgings, the connecting rods were of I beam section, with heat-treated alloy connecting rod bolts and nuts. Lead-bronze bearing shells were fitted without shims and were dowelled into the forked rod. The outside of the shell was the bearing for the hardened and ground bore of the plain rod. The gudgeon pin end of the rod was fitted with a bronze bush taking 1⅜in diameter gudgeon pins.

*Pistons* These were of aluminium alloy, with a solid skirt. Aluminium gudgeon pin end caps were fitted, and the gudgeon pins themselves were of case-hardened steel, and of the full floating type. High-compression pistons were fitted.

*Reverse gear* Designed to give 100 percent rpm in reverse, the reverse gear was equipped with ball bearings and large thrust bearings.

*Reduction gear* This was 2-to-1 ratio. Equipped with trailing clutches, the reduction gears were of the double-helical type, fitted with ball bearings on the pinion shaft and Timken roller thrust bearings on the gear wheel shaft.

*Auxiliaries* Duplicate generators and oil pumps were mounted on each side of the engine, and the steering pump and bilge pump were driven by two triple-strand roller chains, themselves driven by sprockets geared to the crankshaft. Adjustable sprockets were provided for chain tension adjustment.

*Oil pumps* Two oil pumps were mounted on the rear face of the sprocket housing, one on each side of the engine. Each pump contained two sets of gears – one set for scavenging and one set for high-pressure lubrication.

*Oil lubrication system* The scavenging half of each pump took oil from the rear sump and pumped it back to the main sump; the pressure half of each pump took oil from the main sump and forced it through the oil filters and oil coolers into the main oil line in the upper crankcase, whence it was distributed to all moving parts in the cylinder head, the sprocket housing, the reverse and reduction gears and the seven main bearings. The connecting-rod bearings were pressure lubricated through drilled passages in the crank webs from the main bearings. An oil-pressure regulating valve was mounted on the forward end of the upper crankcase between the cylinder banks.

*Water pump* Two gear type self-priming pumps were fitted, one on each side of the engine, bolted directly to the upper crankcase. Grease cups provided lubrication of the pump spindles.

*Water circulation* From the intake scoop and strainer, the water passed through the water pump into the oil coolers. From the oil coolers some of the water went into the cylinder blocks, then into the cylinder heads. Some of the water went from the coolers into

*Engine replacement aboard ML 181 at Flensburgh* (HMS Gadfly) *in 1945.* Courtesy J Davies

the exhaust manifold, then into the cylinder heads. From the cylinder heads the water passed into the water jackets of the intake manifold, then to the exhaust pipe jacket and overboard. A thermostat was installed at the outlet from the engine to bypass warm water back to the water pump suctions until the engine reached a normal running temperature.

*Generators* Two generators were fitted, one on each side of the engine, though a single large generator was fitted instead to the later engines (after engine serial No 29149). They were voltage and current regulated, each having a capacity of 260 watts (or 650 watts in the case of the single large generator). Two twelve-point distributors were fitted. Ignition was so arranged that each distributor fired one set of sparkplugs in each bank of cylinders.

*Starter* One 24-volt starter was used, designed with reduction gear drive to increase starting torque.

*Oil filters* Oil filters were mounted on each side of the engine. Filtering elements were metal edge type, cleaned by rotating a T handle.

*Oil coolers* The oil cooler units were fitted on each side of the engine. They were of ample size to maintain proper oil temperature.

*Exhaust manifolds* These were cast iron, water jacketed, and had two expansion joints in the jacket.

*Intake manifolds* These were cast iron, water jacketed and carried three marine type non-flooding updraft Zenith carburettors. Carburettors were mounted in the V between the cylinder blocks. The supercharged engines had four carburettors attached to the upper side of the supercharger.

*Fuel system* Two camshaft-driven pumps, one on the forward end of each cylinder head, provided the fuel. Regulating valves in the pumps maintained fuel pressure between 2 and 3lb per square inch.

To clarify reference to engines as right or left hand or forward or after end, the following definitions are used:

*A supercharged Hall-Scott petrol engine fitted in Vosper's MTB 36. Three supercharged engines produced only 25 knots maximum.* Vosper Thornycroft (UK) Ltd

*Right-hand engine* – one that turns the propeller in a clockwise or right-hand rotation when viewed from the driving or propeller shaft end, regardless of the engine rotation.

*Left-hand engine* – one that turns the propeller in an anticlockwise or left-hand rotation when viewed from the driving or propeller shaft end, regardless of the engine rotation.

*Forward end of the engine* – the flywheel end or end opposite the driving or reverse gear end.

The engine electrical system was specially shielded to suppress electromagnetic disturbance. Disturbance or interference from the engine electrical system w.. usually of sufficient amplitude to distort the W/T (radio) signals to a point where clear and effective reception was impossible.

The Hall-Scott engine was reliable, well liked and capable of very long running between overhauls, provided that routine maintenance was carried out. These engines indeed served worldwide with few problems, even where few spares were available.

The above description covers the main engine details of the Fairmile A, B and C types, but the story of the 72ft motor launches was somewhat different. Here again, there was no development before the war and little money to encourage research in the more economical diesel engine. The Germans had produced very powerful and generally reliable diesels, which were fitted to the E-boats, but there was no corresponding engine unit available in the UK. In 1938 the Turkish Government, through the British Admiralty, placed a contract with Camper & Nicholson Ltd of Gosport for the construction of eight large motor gunboats. This development was encouraged by the Admiralty, no doubt on the grounds that the design and construction work involved would ultimately be of benefit to Britain in her own MGB programme. The propulsion machinery specified was three Paxman sixteen-cylinder VRB diesel engines, each rated at 1000hp at 1650rpm. Unfortunately the first of the Paxman diesel 16 VRB engines was giving trouble on the test bed and the first motor launch, MTB 501, had therefore to be completed with 1250hp Packard petrol engines. A few days after

*A Perkins T.12 High Speed Diesel fitted to ML 570.*
*Only three were built.* Courtesy Harold Hawkins BEM

her acceptance in February 1942, this rather elegant vessel suffered a violent explosion and sank, fortunately without loss of life. By this time the Paxman diesel engine was becoming available, having been de-rated to 800hp at 1500 rpm, and seven units, MGBs 502–508, were completed in 1943. The value of the diesel engine, with its less volatile fuel which avoided the hazards of fire and explosion prevalent in the more powerful petrol engines of the period, was recognised.

With the introduction of the 72ft motor launch in ever-increasing numbers, the fitting of lower-power commercial diesel engines was authorised, but none was produced in sufficient quantities for complete standardisation throughout the class. A number of different makes were fitted: two Gardners each of 300bhp, two 320bhp Gleniffers, two 330bhp Grays, two 480bhp Hercules, two 300bhp Buda Lanovas or two 260bhp Thornycrofts. In spite of the small differences in power, it seems there was little to choose between these types, and all proved reliable in service throughout the world, although no doubt there were many problems with the issue and distribution of spares.

### The Stuart-Turner auxiliary dynamo engine

The auxiliary dynamo engine was in constant use, supplying electrical power and recharging batteries. Its speed was regulated automatically by a governor, the mixture being maintained at the correct strength by the cone and air sleeve, whatever the position of the throttle. However, owing to variation in the quality of petrol, slight adjustment was necessary, and this had to be done when the engine was warm. The cylinder of the water-cooled engine had to be felt, or the outflow inspected, to establish that the pump was cooling correctly. The seacock and weed trap needed regular attention, particularly in coastal waters and rivers. It was imperative that the plant was maintained regularly and the filters under the petrol cock and carburettor cleaned at regular intervals.

A choked jet was the most frequent cause of trouble, followed closely by the plug, which had to be clean and adjusted to .015in. Carbonisation in the exhaust system was another problem, causing a gradual build-up of back pressure, which reduced the revolutions, and thus the voltage, by gradually slowing the plant down. The dynamo ball bearings required attention every twelve months and the brushes had to be checked to make sure that they were not sticking. The normal charging rate was 22 amperes for a period up to 10 hours, or until the specific gravity was 1.280. The charge rate

could be increased during the early part of the charging, provided that the line voltage was kept below 26 volts. The maximum charging rate was 35 amperes, for a period of up to three hours. The average voltage was not to exceed 35 volts during the maximum charge. The temperature was not to exceed 100 °F, or 10 degrees above the air temperature in hot climates.

### Steering gear

The original Fairmile B types, as well as the As, had hydraulic steering, but this was later changed to dual steering (from the bridge or wheelhouse) of the Reid or Mathway Positive type, presumably because of problems due to hydraulic leaks, particularly in action.

A diagrammatic layout of the original arrangement is included here, redrawn from the Fairmile ML Engineering Handbook, dated February 1941. Its workings can best be understood from the drawing. The main units consist of two pumps (4 and 4A) driven by the main engines, one steering transmitter (2) with a handwheel, a control valve (5) and a tiller operating cylinder (6) complete with its auxiliary cylinder (3).

When the engines were running, the pumps delivered fluid through their outlets (A and A1) into the control valve (5), entering by inlet (B). When idling (that is, when the wheel was amidships), this fluid passed through the control valve, coming out at the outlet (C) and returning to the pumps through inlets (D) and (D1), thus completing the circuit. There was no resistance to the fluid flow other than slight pipe friction, and the pumps therefore ran easily.

Operation of the steering handwheel on the transmitter unit (2) in a clockwise direction delivered fluid out of connection (E) and into the auxiliary tiller operating cylinder (3) at connection (F), tending to force the piston rod in this auxiliary cylinder to the left, and thus to rotate the centre pivot shaft in a clockwise direction. The linkage used converted this into an anticlockwise direction at the rudder stocks.

The auxiliary slave cylinder could not move the rudder, and the

*A set of four variable-pitch propellers manufactured*
*by Rotol Airscrews Ltd of Gloucester and*
*experimentally fitted for trials to the D type MGB*
*602. These propellers were electrically operated.*
Courtesy Fairmile (Marine Consultants) Ltd.

*An insight into the problems of a new small ship engineroom layout: a wooden mock-up of the projected pipe layout, showing pipe runs for four Packard petrol engines for the prototype MGB 601.*
Courtesy Fairmile (Marine Consultants) Ltd

*This is the result – a view of 601's engineroom. Note the Dumbflow exhaust on the far bulkhead, throttles, control panel and workbench.*
Courtesy Fairmile (Marine Consultants) Ltd

result of the effort on the handwheel was to generate pressure in pipe (G), and this pressure passed into the control valve through connection (H) and operated an internal piston-type valve. This piston valve diverted the flow of fluid from the pump so that it came through outlet (J) instead of (C) and entered the main tiller-operating cylinder (6) through connection (K), passing into the cylinder via the hollow piston rod and moving the cylinder barrel towards the left, thereby turning the rudder in an anticlockwise direction.

The pump continued to feed the main tiller-operating cylinder in this manner as long as pressure was maintained in pipe (G) by continued rotation of the handwheel. The piston rod in the auxiliary cylinder was connected to the main cylinder and moved across at the same rate; three to four turns of the handwheel were necessary for the whole stroke.

Fluid ejected from the opposite end of the auxiliary cylinder during movement came out of connection (L) and re-entered the transmitter unit by connection (M). Fluid ejected from the opposite end of the main cylinder came out of connection (N), and entered the Control Valve at connection (P). It then left the Control Valve at connection (C) and returned to the pumps at (D) and (D1).

When the handwheel was either released or held stationary after the required movement of the rudder had been made, the main tiller operating cylinder tended to over-run the movement of the auxiliary cylinder, thus pulling it momentarily towards the left. This released the pressure in pipe (G) and returned the piston valve within the control valve (5), to a position allowing free passage for the fluid in at (B) and out at (C), thus giving the pumps a free circuit and permitting the system to idle freely. The fluid was locked in the main cylinder, and thus held the rudder over. Movement of the rudder in the opposite direction was of course obtained by an anti-clockwise rotation of the handwheel of the transmitter unit. This caused the control valve to divert the delivery of the fluid from the pump so that it came out of connection (P) and into the main operating cylinder at (N).

*MGB 658 fuelling at Bastia from the petrol barge Crete, in April 1944. It was necessary to filter all 100 octane fuel through a chamois leather stretched over a collar within half an old 40gal oil drum. This was a very tedious, slow process, involving washing the chamois in petrol frequently. No smoking was allowed, but fuelling was the cause of many serious fires. Note the fire extinguisher and liferaft.*
Courtesy Len (Rover) Reynolds

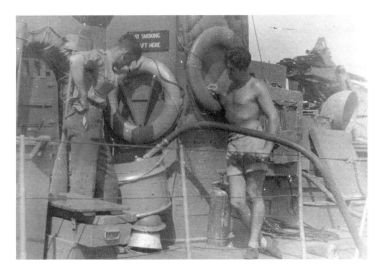

The maximum speed of operation depended upon the speed at which the pumps were driven, but the system was generally arranged to give about 3 seconds from midships to hard-over, under normal operating conditions. The power required varied from 1 to 2½hp.

If the pumps stopped – due to the stopping of the main engines, or the bypass valve (14) being opened – the system automatically changed over to give manual operation, but of course this increased the number of turns of the handwheel necessary for a given movement of the rudder. Under power operation approximately 3½ turns on the handwheel were necessary for the full angular movement of the rudder, hard-over to hard-over, for the standard types of gear. Under manual operation, the number of turns increased to approximately 19½. As a further emergency measure, a hand tiller could be attached to the centre pivot of the rudder gear, but screw-down globe valves Nos 12 and 13 had to be opened to permit a free circuit for the fluid in the system when such hand steering was in operation.

It was imperative that all traces of air should be excluded from the system, as its presence would cause a sudden loss of pressure and uneven wheel effort, giving a spongy feeling to the system. Bleeding of the system of pipes and operating gear was necessary after installation and when any part of the piping or equipment had been disconnected, or if the fluid header tank had inadvertently been allowed to empty itself. Only genuine Lockheed 'Orange fluid' was to be used, as the use of any other fluid would damage the rubber cups and seals, and cause ultimate failure. The fluid tank was never allowed to drop lower than half-full, and the tank was topped-up when required to within about 1in of the underside of the cover.

**Hall-Scott Defender marine petrol engine as supplied under Lend-Lease – general arrangement (as fitted to Fairmile A boats)**

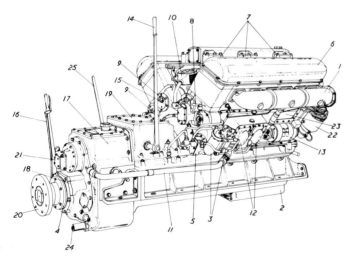

| | | | |
|---|---|---|---|
| 1 | Exhaust manifold | 14 | Clutch lever |
| 2 | Engine sump | 15 | Bilge pump |
| 3 | Oil filters | 16 | Sailing clutch lever |
| 4 | Packing gland | 17 | Reduction gear |
| 5 | Oil pumps | 18 | Thrust bearing |
| 6 | Chain driven camshafts | 19 | Clutch inspection cover |
| 7 | Three Zenith carburettors | 20 | Driving coupling |
| 8 | Bilge pump clutch | 21 | Reduction gear oil pump |
| 9 | Timing chain adjustment | 22 | Radio-shielded distributor |
| 10 | Backfire arrester | 23 | Cylinder block clean-out plates |
| 11 | Circulating pipe | 24 | Cooling water inlet |
| 12 | Oil coolers | 25 | Mechanical control clutch lever |
| 13 | Generator | | |

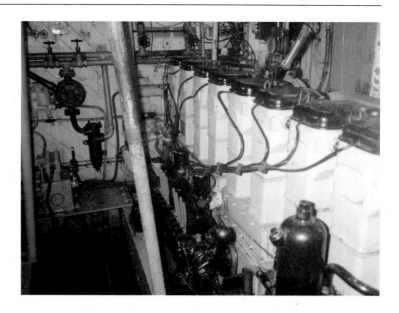

*The starboard main engine of* Medusa *(ex-HDML 1387) on 13 November 1988.* Author's collection

*A view of* Medusa's *engineroom on the same day.* Author's collection

*Whoops! – this crane on the quayside at Manfredonia toppled aboard a HDML while loading a new engine. A second crane was called to help. Note the amused onlookers.* Courtesy Len (Rover) Reynolds

**Hall-Scott Defender elevations and plan**

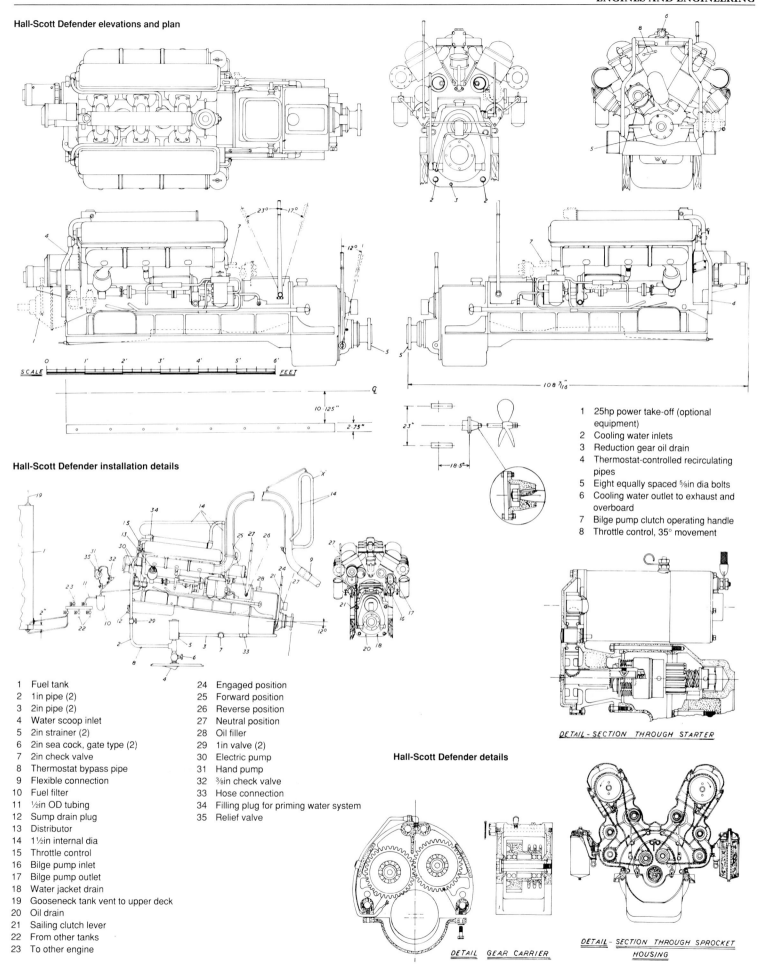

SCALE  0  1'  2'  3'  4'  5'  6'  FEET

10·125"

2·75"

108⁷⁄₁₆"

23°

18·5"

1  25hp power take-off (optional equipment)
2  Cooling water inlets
3  Reduction gear oil drain
4  Thermostat-controlled recirculating pipes
5  Eight equally spaced ⁵⁄₈in dia bolts
6  Cooling water outlet to exhaust and overboard
7  Bilge pump clutch operating handle
8  Throttle control, 35° movement

**Hall-Scott Defender installation details**

1  Fuel tank
2  1in pipe (2)
3  2in pipe (2)
4  Water scoop inlet
5  2in strainer (2)
6  2in sea cock, gate type (2)
7  2in check valve
8  Thermostat bypass pipe
9  Flexible connection
10  Fuel filter
11  ½in OD tubing
12  Sump drain plug
13  Distributor
14  1½in internal dia
15  Throttle control
16  Bilge pump inlet
17  Bilge pump outlet
18  Water jacket drain
19  Gooseneck tank vent to upper deck
20  Oil drain
21  Sailing clutch lever
22  From other tanks
23  To other engine
24  Engaged position
25  Forward position
26  Reverse position
27  Neutral position
28  Oil filler
29  1in valve (2)
30  Electric pump
31  Hand pump
32  ⅜in check valve
33  Hose connection
34  Filling plug for priming water system
35  Relief valve

DETAIL - SECTION THROUGH STARTER

**Hall-Scott Defender details**

DETAIL  GEAR CARRIER

DETAIL - SECTION THROUGH SPROCKET HOUSING

**Standard instruments**

A  Water thermometer
B  Fuel primer pump
C  Fuel pressure gauge
D  Oil thermometer
E  Tachometer
F  Oil pressure gauge
G  Reduction gear oil pressure gauge

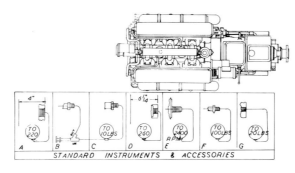

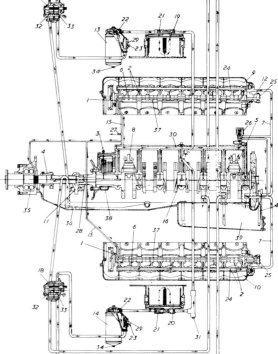

**Detail of water pump**

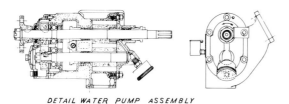

**Hall-Scott Defender supercharged 900hp marine petrol engine – general arrangement (as fitted to Fairmile C MGBs)**

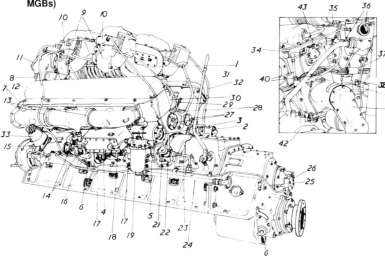

| | |
|---|---|
| 1  Supercharger | 23  Oil scavenge suction from reverse gear |
| 2  Bilge pump | |
| 3  Tachometer drive | 24  After water pump suction from reduction gear |
| 4  Oil cooler | |
| 5  Filter bypass | 25  Scavenge oil from sump to reduction gear pump |
| 6  Seawater inlet | |
| 7  Steam vent | 26  Reduction gear oil pump (AEW reversible Duplex) |
| 8  Oil return to sump | |
| 9  Carburettor (Zenith 1510 MV) | 27  Camshaft driving chain adjustment |
| 10  Carburettor anti-freeze muff | 28  Pressure oil to valve gear |
| 11  Skew gear blower drive | 29  Oil from main galley to filter |
| 12  Scavenge oil return to sump | 30  Filter for oil to blower bearings |
| 13  Expansion joint clamping straps | 31  Breather from sprocket casing |
| 14  Water inlets from forward pump and oil cooler to exhaust manifold and block | 32  Scavenge oil to anit-freeze muffs |
| | 33  Distributor |
| | 34  Fuel inlet |
| 15  Dipstick and hand scavenge pump | 35  Fuel line to starboard carburettor |
| 16  Cooled oil to main gallery | 36  Water outlets from induction manifold |
| 17  Forward and after seawater pump | 37  Pressure oil to power take-off |
| 18  Pressure oil to cooler | 38  Fuel relief valve |
| 19  Oil filter (Cuno Auto Klean) | 39  Oil pressure relief valve |
| 20  Oil scavenge suction from sump screen | 40  Oil return to sump |
| | 41  Starter (Leece-Neville 24v) |
| 21  Pressure oil to filter | 42  Generator (Delco-Remy 24v) |
| 22  Oil pump (pressure and scavenge) | 43  Fuel pump (Chandler Hill Titan) |

**Hall-Scott Defender oil circulation diagram**

1  Spray to sprocket chain and all accessory drive sprockets
2  Pressure to rocker arm bearings and camshaft
3  Gear carrier external line sprays on gear teeth at point of contact
4  Reverse gear shifter collar assembly
5  Spray to piston pin and cylinder walls
6  Exhaust rocker arm shoe spray line
7  Cylinder head drain pipe (external)
8  Pressure to connecting rod bearings
9  Left hand bank cylinder head
10  Right hand bank cylinder head
11  Reverse gear intermediate pinion
12  Pressure to fuel pump shaft
13  Left hand bank dual filter
14  Right hand bank dual filter
15  Cylinder head external line
16  Pressure to main bearings
17  Left hand bank pump
18  Right hand bank pump
19  Left hand bank cooler

20  Right hand bank cooler
21  Cooler bypass valve
22  Filter bypass valve
23  Return to sump (internal)
24  Hollow rocker arm shaft
25  Mechanical fuel pump
26  Pressure regulating valve
27  Pressure gauge connection
28  Drive flange bushing
29  Presssure relief valve
30  Main oil line
31  Temperature gauge connection (on inboard side only)
32  Scavenge side
33  Pressure side
34  Drain
35  Thrust bearing
36  Scavenge sump
37  Camshaft
38  Gear trough
39  Main sump
40  Oil level gauge and hand scavenge pump

**Fuel system diagram**

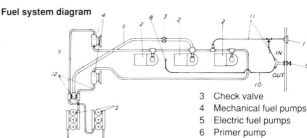

1  Pressure gauge (maintain 3lb/sq in at carburettor)
2  Carburettor

3  Check valve
4  Mechanical fuel pumps
5  Electric fuel pumps
6  Primer pump
7  Filter
8  Primer jet
9  ½in OD tubing
10  ⅛in OD tubing
11  ³⁄₁₆in OD tubing
12  ⅜in OD tubing
13  To fuel tanks

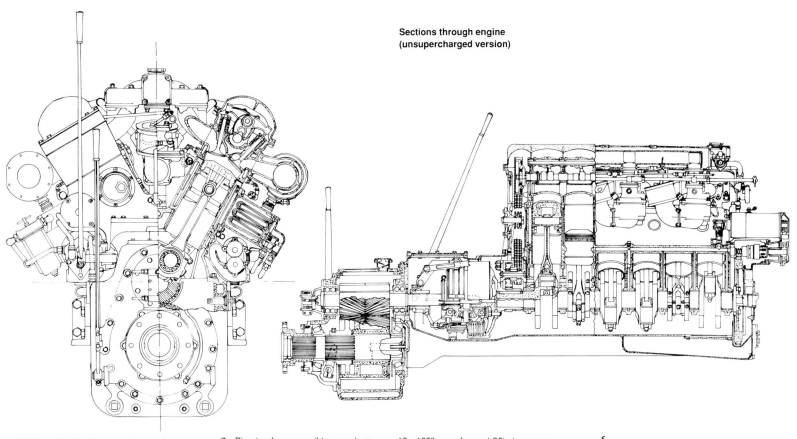

Sections through engine
(unsupercharged version)

**Hall-Scott Defender supercharged
900hp engine elevations and plan**

1  Forward
2  Netural
3  Reverse
4  Engaged
5  Water filler cap
6  Auxiliary water connection

7  Pipe tap for sump oil temperature
   connection
8  Plug oil drain
9  Reduction gear oil drain
10 Water drain both sides
11 Approx centre of gravity
12 Power take-off (optional) 25hp at
   1000rpm

13 160lb max force at 36in to engage
   hand lever
14 Bilge pump clutch operating handle
15 Cooling water inlets

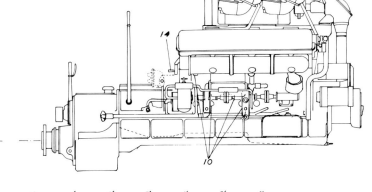

SCALE    0    1'    2'    3'    4'    5'    6'    FEET

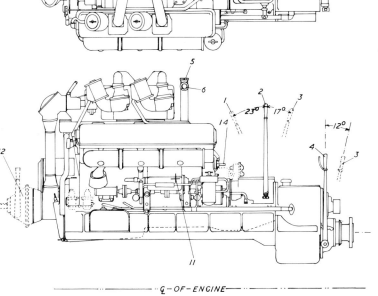

℄ – OF – ENGINE

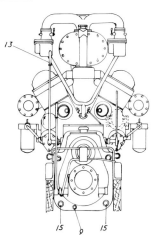

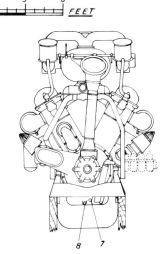

**Reverse gear detail**

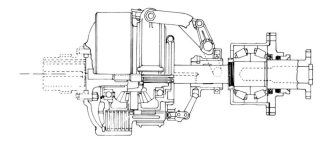
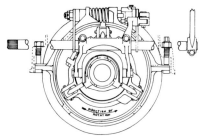
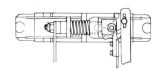

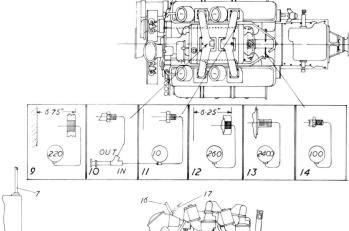

**Details of engine installation and instruments**

1  2in seacocks (4)
2  2in strainer (4)
3  Fuel filter
4  To other engines
5  From other tanks
6  Fuel tank
7  Tank vent to upper deck
8  Thermostat bypass pipe
9  Water thermometer (to 220°)
10  Fuel primer pump
11  Fuel pressure gauge (to 10lb)
12  Oil thermometer (to 260°)
13  Tachometer (to 2400rpm)
14  Oil pressure gauge (to 100lb)
15  Bearing capable of taking propeller thrust
16  Throttle control carburettor control lever (may be set at any angle), 4⅜in long and with a total travel of 70°
17  Throttle closed position

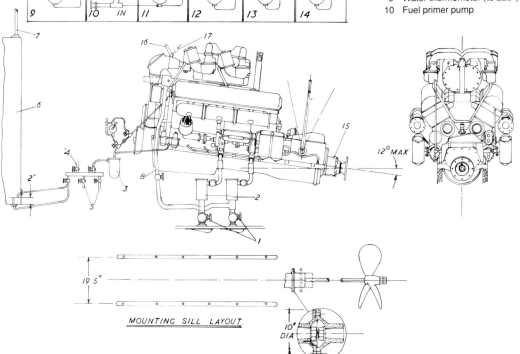

**Cylinder head and upper crankcase detail**

A  UNSUPERCHARGED.
B  SUPERCHARGED.

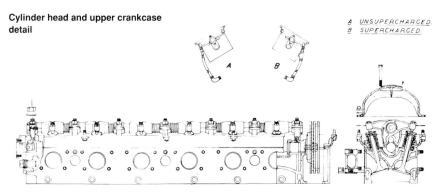
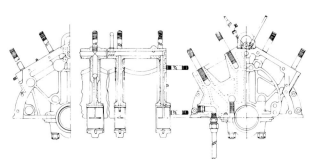

## Fuel system diagram (supercharged engine)

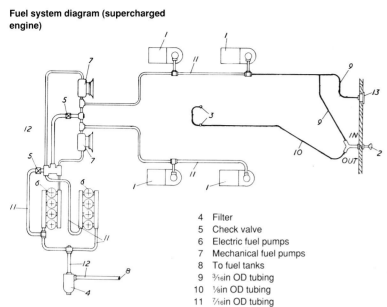

4  Filter
5  Check valve
6  Electric fuel pumps
7  Mechanical fuel pumps
8  To fuel tanks
9  ³⁄₁₆in OD tubing
10  ¹⁄₈in OD tubing
11  ⁷⁄₁₆in OD tubing
12  ⁵⁄₈in OD tubing
13  Pressure gauge to maintain 3lb pressure at the carburettor

1  Carburettor
2  Primer pump
3  Primer jets

## Fuel system diagram (unsupercharged engine)

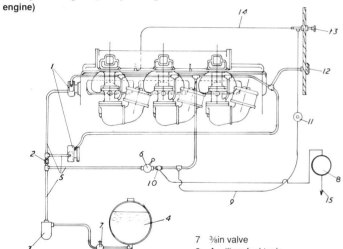

7  ³⁄₈in valve
8  Auxiliary fuel tank
9  ³⁄₁₆in OD pipe
10  Switch cock on port engine for filling auxiliary fuel tank
11  Fuel reservoir
12  Petrol pressure gauge
13  Primer pump
14  ¹⁄₈in OD pipe
15  To Stuart Turner engine

1  Dual fuel pumps
2  Check valve
3  Filter
4  Main fuel tanks
5  ³⁄₈in OD piping
6  Hand primer pump

## Lockheed steering gear and pipe layout diagram

Medusa's *Telefex bridge telegraph.*
Courtesy David Fricker

# Habitability

The effect of weather on any small warship and its crew is severe; conditions are uncomfortable at best, and usually the higher the speed at which the vessel is required to operate, the more uncomfortable conditions become. When they were free to adjust their speed to suit the weather or wave conditions, Coastal Forces vessels proved to be extremely seaworthy craft, with a very large reserve of buoyancy, a good range of stability and adequate hull strength. However, when forced to the limit in bad weather, particularly in head seas and at speed, the craft and their fittings frequently suffered damage. Early in the war much of this damage was attributed to the inexperience of the ship designers and the young crews, but repairs and local stiffening reduced such damage significantly as experience was gained, and thereafter commanding officers who broke frames, (except due to enemy action) became quite unpopular.

The effect of pitch, heave and roll on the crew was accentuated by the added problems of inadequate weatherproof clothing, and was not helped by the effects of noise and vibration and, frequently, seasickness.

The crews, who were in the main highly motivated volunteers, were generally young men, but those who were physically unable to stand the strain had to be transferred to other duties, such as general service ships.

This book is concerned in general with round-bilge hull forms common to the slower motor launches; these were better in head seas but rolled very heavily at slow speeds or in cross seas, since the motion was usually too severe for bilge keels to stay attached. Wetness was influenced considerably by the hull form, and with a sharp bow, good flare and knuckle, the Fairmile D, at least, was drier than many other designs. In the Cs, however, a spray rail was fitted; the placing of this was very critical and could determine whether the bridge and foredeck were very wet or dry.

Life became more tolerable for Coastal Forces crews when proper weatherproof clothing was issued later in the war, but prior to this waterproof gear had consisted of jerseys, duffle coats and a towel around the neck to keep out the water, all of which rapidly became soaked. The issue of hot kye was much better than tea or coffee and helped bridge and gun crews to stay awake and alert for long periods in wet and cold exposed positions as necessary. Goggles were tried, but were found to be worse than useless when exposed to spray, which swiftly caused them to mist up, so that eyes too became very tired.

Below decks, the tiring effects of violent motion were compounded by the noise and vibration of the main engines. Two or three main engines, with superchargers (if equipped) gulping air, plus the step-up gear train, engine reduction gear boxes, reciprocating hydraulic pumps for steering gear and power gun mountings, as well as auxiliary generators to charge batteries or provide power, caused considerable noise. Ear plugs were provided, but crews commonly plugged their ears with cotton wool.

The high noise levels had direct operational effects. In the event of a malfunction with the engine HT lead, interference from the engines was constant on the radio transmitter/receiver; the routine was to wear headphones on the temples and, when the boat's call sign was heard, to request the CO to reduce speed, or even to stop engines altogether until the radio transmission, both receiving and sending, was completed.

To crew members in the engineroom, the problem of nauseating petrol or lubricating oil fumes from the bilge or when taking temperature readings or changing tanks, was another hazard, always with the attendant risk of fire in the case of the enemy action, due to the huge volume of high-octane petrol carried.

The asdic operators in motor launches had to cope with a cramped office and the task of listening continuously on the asdic equipment, which for most of the war remained non-directional. The task of the radar operator, in those boats so equipped, was similarly demanding.

In home waters crews generally lived ashore, as operations were of short duration, but conditions in the mess were always cramped, with little room for the stowage of personal items. The wooden bulkheads sweated and the forward messdecks were usually heated by a coal stove, with a limited amount of fuel. Later, matters were improved, with electric heaters built in, but this required an increase in generating load. As more and more equipment and armament was added, additional crew had also to be carried. The galley was of limited use at sea, normally restricted to providing hot drinks and bully beef sandwiches; messing conditions can generally be described as 'cosy', that is, cramped.

Early in the war, the COs were usually from the Royal Navy, and they had their own routines. At least one, on putting to sea in a ML, insisted on having warm water poured into his sea boots; his theory was that, if his feet were to be wet, they might at least be warm.

In general, as Coastal Forces craft were built by yachtbuilders, the messdeck fittings, though basic, were well finished. All Tough Brothers boat fittings, for example, were apparently French polished, rather than being varnished.

While the A and C type Fairmiles all operated in home waters, the Ds served as far from their home bases as the Eastern Mediterranean, and the crews lived on board. The Bs served worldwide, as did the 72ft MLs; in the tropics the lack of special equipment was a particular hardship. Air-conditioning was not fitted, just awnings rigged to keep the upper deck out of the sun while the boat was in harbour. There was limited water, and, as no evaporators were fitted, water rationing was frequent. Food was picked up from local sources, and crews often spent weeks away from base, with no mail or other additional comforts. A shower could be rigged from the firemain, and washing facilities added to the cramped living conditions on board, but inadequate toilet facilities ashore and the problems of prickly heat and other local drawbacks like mosquitoes often meant that boats remained anchored offshore for long periods. In these conditions, diseases were easily transmitted; stomach problems were always prevalent and all drinking water had to be boiled.

However, in general crews remained fit and well, suffering the privations with wry humour, making the best of what was locally available and working as a close-knit team. Other publications have described life on board in greater detail, however, and further detail is not necessary here.

# The Holman projector

The Holman projector was a cheap stopgap weapon, a simple system, operated by compressed air or steam, for throwing a Mills bomb into the path of low-flying aircraft. The projector consisted of a barrel about 4ft 6in long, attached to a receiver and mounted so that it could be pointed or trained in any direction. It required a working deck area of 4ft 9in radius. There were four types of projector put into service:

The *Mark I* was triggered automatically when the Mills bomb in its tin reached the base of the barrel, in a similar manner to a mortar; no trigger or firing gear was used.
The *Mark IIA* was fired by a twist grip, similar to that on a motor cyle of the period; the firing gear operated valves in the receiver, and launched the bomb, which had been loaded and was already at the base of the barrel.
The *Mark IIS* was similar to the Mark IIA, but was operated by steam pressure from the ship's boiler.
The *Mark III* was fired by an explosive propellant.

In the first three types, pressure on the gauge should show 160lb, with a minimum pressure of 100lb. The Mark II allowed complete control of firing, after the bomb had been loaded. There was a simple sight at the muzzle end of the barrel, and, lower down, a pair of handles. When these were twisted, the right handle actuated the firing rod, which, if the projector was cocked, pressed down the trigger and opened the pilot valve below it. The lower end of the barrel was normally closed by a valve, which opened automatically when the pilot valve was lifted from its seat.

With the Mark IIA, two high-pressure air bottles were connected by a coupler to a regulating valve, which reduced the pressure to that suitable for operating the weapon. From the regulator, air passed through a flexible pipe to the projector receiver. The receiver was fitted with a stopcock on its inlet, a draincock for blowing down, and a pressure gauge with a plunger which protruded from its casing when the air was at a pressure for safe firing. The high-pressure air bottles were situated in the engineroom.

*The Holman projector aboard ML 110 of the 1st ML Flotilla, based at Great Yarmouth. Also visible are a twin .303in Lewis gun and a 3-pounder aft. Note the sub leader half band on the funnel. ML 206 (B type) is tied up astern.* The Motor Boat

The Mark IIS was connected to the ship's main system, the receiver being lagged, and having a draincock with a permanent weep. However, it was not usually fitted with a pressure gauge or stopcock. The only Coastal Forces type where the Mark IIS was fitted were the Steam Gunboats, but it was fitted to many trawlers and Bangor class Fleet Minesweepers early in the war.

The ammunition for all these types was the Mills bomb, supplied ready for use in open-ended tins, in sealed cases of twenty-four. The safety pins were in position and were withdrawn only when the tin was held at the muzzle lip of the projector during the loading operation. On firing, the tin fell away from the bomb when it had travelled about 100ft from the muzzle; this took about half a second. When the tin fell away, the side lever of the bomb fell out, releasing the spring plunger, and the fuse was started. The bomb then burst 3 seconds after the starting of the fuse.

The range of the weapon depended upon a number of variables, including the ship's speed and the wind direction and velocity, but it was usually in the region of about 600 to 650ft. The bombs, in their cans, could be loaded as fast as the weapon was able to fire them, each in its turn falling the whole way down the barrel, opening the automatic valve with its own weight and then being ejected. The sight comprised a straight bar, fixed at an angle of 20° below the bore of the gun. For the first round, the bar was pointed ahead of the approaching target and the aim was then corrected by observation of the flight of the bombs. The bombs or grenades were supposed to burst on, or ahead of, the target, as those falling astern would have no effect. The maximum elevation of the weapon was 85°, the minimum 5° and an adjustable depression stop was provided to prevent firing into the ship's structure.

The Holman projector was widely regarded as a disaster, and offered no improvement whatever to any boat's armament fit. It was still specified on Coastal Forces drawings up to 1943 (though not always fitted). By March 1941 some 1051 had been supplied to merchant ships as a form of defence. However, it rarely featured on a Coastal Forces action station watch bill, which indicates that it was rarely used.

On the other hand, it was a superb weapon for firing cans, large potatoes and the like, in the course of beery inter-flotilla battles. During a night bombing raid by German aircraft at Yarmouth, some Fairmile Bs fired their Holmans in anger and only succeeded in bringing down the Norfolk Electricity Grid cables, which crossed the river Yare on very high pylons, plunging the area into darkness.

Later in the war, more sophisticated ammunition was developed for this weapon system. A 10lb anti-submarine bomb round (shown in detail in the drawings) was produced (though never fully implemented in service) and a more efficient parachute flare, the Illuminating Projectile No 2 Mark I, which saw more general service.

Holman projectors were fitted to Fairmile As as built, some (but not all) Fairmile Bs, early Fairmile Ds, many British Power Boat MGBs, steam gunboats in 1942, the Vosper MGB 510 and a few 72ft HDMLs.

**Holman projector general arrangement**

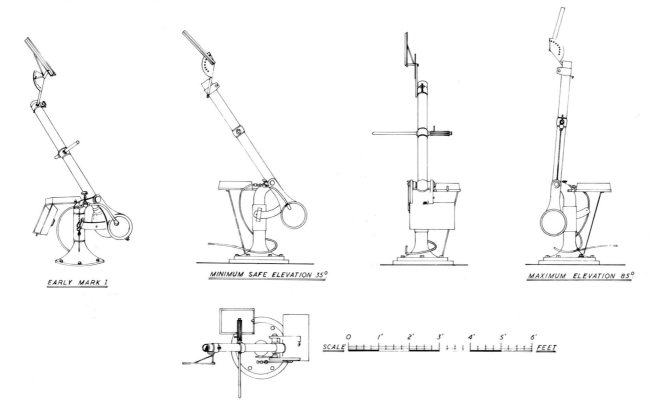

EARLY MARK I

MINIMUM SAFE ELEVATION 35°

MAXIMUM ELEVATION 85°

SCALE 0 1' 2' 3' 4' 5' 6' FEET

**Holman projector illuminating projectile No 2 Mark I**

1 Striker cover
2 Safety pin
3 Striker
4 Striker spring
5 410 cartridge
6 Nose cap
7 Safety fuse
8 Ignition and ejection charge
9 Flare unit
10 Body
11 Parachute case
12 Parachute
13 Millboard disc
14 Central tube
15 Fins
16 Tail bolt
17 Tulip spring
18 Gas check plate
19 Gas check
20 Firing cartridge

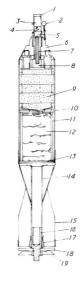

**Holman projector 10lb underwater bomb Mark I**

1 Plug
2 Sealing washer
3 Topping
4 CE exploders
5 TNT filling
6 Body
7 Composition RD 1006 or 1061
8 Tail tube
9 Fins
10 Tail bolt

# The PAC rocket

The parachute and cable rocket was a device for placing a strong wire vertically over the ship into the path of an attacking aircraft. There was a parachute at each end of the wire, and the effect on an aircraft striking the wire was to make it swerve violently, and possibly crash into the sea. Alternatively, the aircraft might swerve before it reached the wire, thus being put off its sighting run.

The projector consisted of a drawn-steel tube, supported on a baseplate. A hinged breech with a spring catch was fitted for insertion of the firing cartridges. The percussion firing mechanism consisted of a simple cocking handle, firing pin and trigger, which was operated by pulling a lanyard. The combined ramrod-cleaner was used for ejecting the cartridge, and a gunpowder rocket was used for projecting the cable. At the head of the rocket was a tin container which housed the upper parachute, ejection of which was effected by a small gunpowder charge. Attached to the bottom of the parachute container was a painted canvas cover which, when the rocket was in the projector, slipped over the outside of the muzzle and prevented water getting down into the barrel. Attached to the head of the rocket were two stirrups and a bridle, to which was fastened some 5ft of cable. The cable was covered with asbestos

at the rocket end and had a spliced eye at the other, where it was shackled to the main cable. A 60 grain cartridge was used to start the rocket on its path and ignite the propellant.

The main container was a galvanised metal box divided into two compartments. The larger contained a length of cable which was shackled to the short length attached to the rocket bridle. The smaller contained the lower parachute which was shackled to the lower end of the cable. This parachute was folded against a strong spring inside a small metal container. The lid of the container was kept in position by a spring clip retained by a wooden peg, to which was attached a 90ft tripping line. When the lower end of the main cable was 90ft clear of the ship, the tripping line became taut and pulled out the retaining peg, thus allowing the parachute to be ejected. The rocket reached its maximum height 4 or 5 seconds after discharge, and burst, leaving the wire suspended by the top parachute. The suspended wire then fell, and was thus in its correct position for a very short time only; accurate timing of the discharge was therefore essential.

Even less effective than the Holman projector, the PAC could not be aimed, but was usually fired when the enemy aircraft was 500 to 700 yards away, and approaching at a speed of between 200 and 250 knots. Fired about 5 seconds before the aircraft was estimated to be overhead (better a little too early than too late), it remained an inconvenience rather than a threat, and was a single-shot system, since it took far too long to reload for a second attempt.

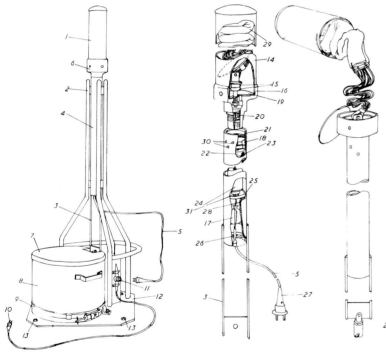

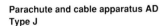

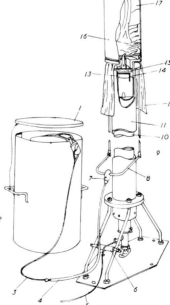

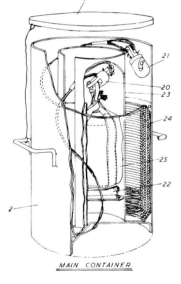

MAIN CONTAINER

**Parachute and cable apparatus AD Type J**

1 Head canister
2 Projector rails
3 R/G/D stirrup
4 Propelling tail
5 Firing lead
6 Socket
7 Removable lid
8 Main container
9 Clamping band
10 Remote plug
11 Projector socket
12 Bse plate
13 Securing bolts
14 Parachute head
15 Rubber shock absorbers
16 Ejector cup
17 Bag filled with silica gel
18 Shell ring springs
19 Piston plate
20 Ejector contents
21 Shell ring
22 Head obturator
23 Igniter
24 Cordite
25 Tail obturator
26 Closing disc
27 Flexible plug
28 Venturi
29 Parachute
30 Locking pins
31 Grid

**PAC apparatus details**

1 Removable lid
2 Main container
3 Flexible tail
4 Asbestos sleeve
5 Firing lanyard
6 Lanyard roller
7 Cone
8 Stirrup
9 Bridle
10 Rocket
11 Barrel
12 Canvas gaiter
13 Clay
14 Quickmatch
15 Burster
16 Parachute head
17 Parachute
18 Sealing band
19 Cap
20 Swivel at bottom of wire
21 Swivel at top of wire
22 Trail parachute
23 Centre tube
24 Coils of KBID wire
25 Lower parachute contained in canvas bag

# The 2in rocket flare

Snowflake illumination, the use of star shells to illuminate or silhouette targets, particularly surface U-boats, was an important technique in Coastal Forces from the beginning. The principle was developed further in the rocket flare, with the 2in rocket launched from a projector rail fitted usually on the forward gun mounting, or from single pedestal projectors located above the torpedo tubes. The rocket was made in three parts: the head, which contained a ballistic cap, the parachute and cable secured to the flare candle; the main body, which contained the cordite fuel (the cordite was ignited electrically by brass contact nuts in the base, the gasses passing through a venturi and powering the rocket); and the four tail fins, which were clipped in position.

The 2in rocket parachute flare was a development of the earlier high-explosive rocket (also shown in the drawings), in which the wind vane arming head was used to fire explosive shells at enemy aircraft. The shell head screwed into the propelling unit of the rocket. When fired electrically, the rocket was driven along the projector rail, which directed it while it was travelling comparatively slowly, though accelerating violently. The rocket accelerated for the first 600ft of its flight path and did not attain its maximum velocity until it reached about 2000ft; the direction of the rocket, and therefore its position when bursting, was much affected by wind direction, speed of the ship, and other variables. The flare slowly floated down on its parachute, illuminating the target on its way, so the rocket was normally aimed beyond the target.

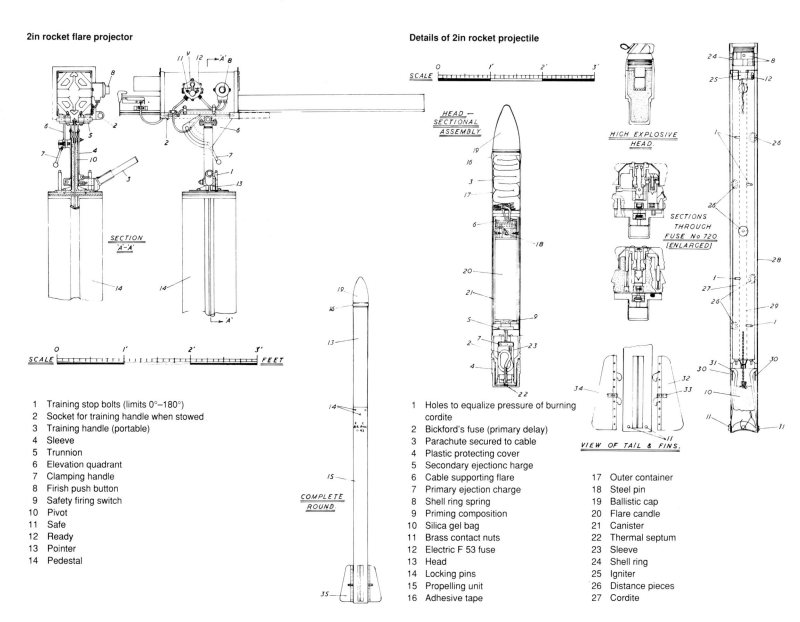

**2in rocket flare projector**

**Details of 2in rocket projectile**

1 Training stop bolts (limits 0°–180°)
2 Socket for training handle when stowed
3 Training handle (portable)
4 Sleeve
5 Trunnion
6 Elevation quadrant
7 Clamping handle
8 Firish push button
9 Safety firing switch
10 Pivot
11 Safe
12 Ready
13 Pointer
14 Pedestal

1 Holes to equalize pressure of burning cordite
2 Bickford's fuse (primary delay)
3 Parachute secured to cable
4 Plastic protecting cover
5 Secondary ejectionc harge
6 Cable supporting flare
7 Primary ejection charge
8 Shell ring spring
9 Priming composition
10 Silica gel bag
11 Brass contact nuts
12 Electric F 53 fuse
13 Head
14 Locking pins
15 Propelling unit
16 Adhesive tape
17 Outer container
18 Steel pin
19 Ballistic cap
20 Flare candle
21 Canister
22 Thermal septum
23 Sleeve
24 Shell ring
25 Igniter
26 Distance pieces
27 Cordite

# Smoke floats and smoke-making apparatus

Smoke floats were used primarily to assist units to evade an attacker, and could be used with effect either by day or night. They were not normally used onboard at night, however, as their ignition tended to give away the ship's position.

All smoke floats supplied were of the floating type and could be used from their usual stowage position aft, or dropped astern. They usually burnt for approximately ten minutes, giving off a thick, acrid white smoke.

They were never stowed below deck, due to the risk of fire and the danger that smoke confined below deck would make it impossible to locate and put out any such fire. The canisters were handled carefully to avoid damage to their casing, which would cause the contents to leak. If ignited onboard, they were to be secured to a steel deck or plate away from inflammable material, because of the intense heat they developed when in use. However, being stowed on the upper deck and open to the elements, they were liable to corrosion from the effects of rain or sea spray and they were checked frequently and maintained in good condition; the paint was touched up as necessary, with great care taken not to cover the identifying or distinguishing marks. Green was the distinctive colour paint used.

On occasion a weakened float would split when moved, and the contents were very corrosive. In one incident a crew member suffered extensive leg burns and months in hospital for skin grafts when the float split, splashing three seamen; the legs of their overalls burnt completely away, and his two colleagues saved themselves only by jumping overboard.

To make smoke, the brass cap of the igniter and the paper disc underneath were removed. The priming, with a tab of matchbox composition, was rubbed. This was found under the lighter cap. If the priming failed to ignite, the compound could be lit with a port fire or red hot poker (should one be available). It was necessary to wait until the igniter had started to burn properly if the float was to be pushed overboard. Floats were normally put overboard in pairs, as the smoke screen varied considerably according to the weather conditions. It was only on a damp overcast day, and in a wind of less than 10 knots, that one float was likely to produce an effective screen. A float could sink quite rapidly if its buoyancy chamber was damaged. During manufacture, two holes were provided in the buoyancy chamber, which were sealed by soldered discs. These discs, too, were susceptible to damage. Sinking holes were provided in the buoyancy chamber for stability and to sink the float after approximately an hour's immersion.

Information about CSA – Chlor-Sulphonic Acid smoke-producing apparatus – is scarce, apart from the fact that there were two types carried by Coastal Forces. The smaller, early type was a cylinder on its side, and the later type a larger cylinder with two smaller cylinders secured to it. Some had the smaller cylinders on the after side, while on others the smaller cylinders were attached to the forward or inboard side. The smoke produced, by chemical means, was white and very dense and was piped out astern low over the water surface. Its effect lasted up to 20 minutes.

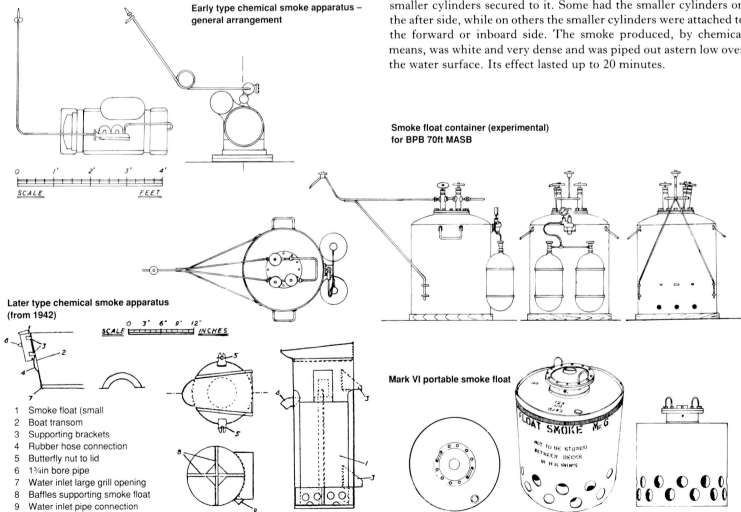

**Early type chemical smoke apparatus – general arrangement**

SCALE     FEET

**Smoke float container (experimental) for BPB 70ft MASB**

**Later type chemical smoke apparatus (from 1942)**

SCALE   INCHES

1   Smoke float (small
2   Boat transom
3   Supporting brackets
4   Rubber hose connection
5   Butterfly nut to lid
6   1¾in bore pipe
7   Water inlet large grill opening
8   Baffles supporting smoke float
9   Water inlet pipe connection

**Mark VI portable smoke float**

FLOAT SMOKE Mk G
NOT TO BE STOWED BETWEEN DECKS IN H M SHIPS

# The .303in Lewis machine gun

The Lewis gun was the first light automatic machine gun to be used in large numbers in time of war. It served in the Belgian Army in 1913, and, shortly afterwards, the British Army undertook to equip its infantry regiments with the weapon; BSA (Birmingham Small Arms Co Ltd) obtained the rights to manufacture the weapon under licence.

The Lewis was first used in 1914, during the retreat of the Belgian Army, and a small number were issued to British units. It was manufactured in very large numbers during the Great War: six guns could be produced for each .303in Vickers machine gun. Weighing only 26lb, it could easily be carried by one man, which enabled the weapon to keep pace with the movement of infantry. To reduce weight further, the cooling jacket could be removed, and the gun was extensively used in this form on aircraft of the RFC (Royal Flying Corps).

The gun was developed by one Samuel Maclean, from an original idea of Colonel Isaac Lewis of the USA, and, as originally patented, it was to have been a heavy or medium machine gun, cooled by air or water, and mounted upon a tripod. The first production weapons omitted the large cooling jacket, which was added when the gun was developed into a light machine gun. The expansion of the hot muzzle gasses induced a flow of air into the rear of the jacket, allowing a cooling flow of air to pass through the cooling fins of the aluminium radiator by a venturi action, the muzzle of the gun being to the rear of the front jacket opening.

Colonel Lewis had energetically promoted his new weapon in the USA, but only after the war in Europe had proved the worth of the weapon was the gun adopted there.

The Lewis gun continued in service with European and Asian armies until the late 1930s, when it was replaced by new weapons. In the British army its place was taken by the famed Bren, also mass-produced by BSA. After the retreat of the BEF from Dunkirk in 1940, and the loss of much of the army's modern equipment, and in view of the expected invasion of the South Coast by German forces, the Lewis gun was re-issued from reserve stocks stored from the last war.

Between the wars, the Royal Navy continued to be equipped with the Lewis as its standard close-range air defence weapon. It was the only suitable gun available, and was pressed into service on ships of every type. Large numbers of requisitioned trawlers were equipped with the weapon, and it was the gun armament of the motor torpedo boats of the early years, in the shape of the quadruple mounting, as shown in the accompanying photographs. In fact, as late as 1942 new corvettes were still going to sea with twin .303in Lewis guns on the bridge wings, while awaiting issue of the 20mm Oerlikon. The weapon was also issued in bulk to the DEMS (Defensively Equipped Merchant Ships).

The Lewis and Savage-Lewis were almost identical, both with a rate of fire of 500–600 rounds per minute. The Lewis fired .303in ammunition with a rimmed cartridge case, while the Savage-Lewis, of American pattern, supplied under the terms of Lend-Lease, used a .300in round with a rimless case. As a rapid means of identification, a 2in wide red band was painted round the body of the gun in front of the magazine post, and the rear half of the centre magazine disc was similarly painted.

Either a magazine holding 97 rounds or a smaller type holding 47 rounds was issued. Differing types of .303in ammunition were also issued; the normal magazine loading consisted of the following quantities of each: 50 percent tracer, 25 percent incendiary and 25 percent semi-armour-piercing, loaded in the memorable order

*Pre-war anti-aircraft defence: two quad .303in Lewis machine gun mountings aboard 60ft British Power Boat MTBs nos 14–18)* Imperial War Museum

TITS, TITS, TITS, etc (the tracer rounds were included to assist the aimer in following the line of sight).

Care and maintenance of the weapon was simple. The gun was unloaded and the bore and chamber were sponged out, the bolt was worked to ensure a smooth free movement, the whole action was lubricated and a fresh magazine was replaced. This was part of the daily routine.

A weekly routine consisted of lubricating the feed pawls, and an examination of the magazines to ensure that they were not bent or damaged, and that they were free from grit. After checking with the officer-of-the-watch, a short burst of some five rounds was fired on a safe bearing, with warning to other ships in company. If all was found to be in order, then the barrel was sponged out and the magazine refilled. In the case of DEMS the allowance was 200 rounds per gun, per year, and only ball ammunition (that is, solid shot) with a few tracer rounds was to be expended.

With close-range weapons such as the Lewis and .303in Vickers machine guns, fire was restricted to about 400 yards. If these weapons were fired at longer ranges, then the chances were that the magazine would require changing when the aircraft was at its nearest and most vulnerable point. The instructions were that, when the enemy aircraft's speed was up to 300mph, fire should commence some 2–300 yards ahead of the target, to allow for deflection.

The automatic action of the Lewis gun was similar to that of other machine guns. The cartridge, on being fired by the striker, travelled along the barrel, driven by the expanding pressure of the gasses. Just before it reached the muzzle, part of those gasses were trapped in the gas port, and passed down into the gas cylinder. In the gas cylinder was a gas piston, on the rear of which was the striker post and striker. The still-expanding gas forced the piston to the rear, which put tension upon the return spring, in the same manner as if the cocking handle had been pulled to the rear. At the same time the striker travelled along the groove in the bolt, unlocking the bolt from the breech end and carrying the bolt to the rear.

*A Fairmile A at sea. She is fitted with two twin
.303in Lewis guns, with limited splinter shields. Note
the body belt support (not the most comfortable
position when closed up).* Imperial War Museum

## The .303in Lewis Mark I gun data

| | |
|---|---|
| **Length** | 50in |
| **Weight (unloaded)** | 26lb |
| **Magazine capacity** | 47 or 97 rounds |
| **Rate of fire** | 550 rounds per minute (approximately) |
| **Muzzle velocity** | 2450ft per second |

heavily, the weapon could be fired by sight, allowing for deflection. This required considerable practice, but was often successful on occasions when the Lewis was the only weapon available, at least causing the pilot to lose his aim when bombing or straffing the ship.

The crew of the Lewis was normally two, the first to aim and fire the weapon, and the second to reload. For the aimer it was advisable to wear a scarf or towel around the neck, in order to prevent the hot ejected cartridge cases from falling down openings in clothing; on major warships, white anti-flash gear was normally worn when closed up at action stations.

Some 90 percent of stoppages in the Lewis gun were a result of lack of care, most of which could be remedied by the immediate action of the gunner. The cause of the fault could usually be found quickly by feeling for the position of the cocking lever when the weapon stopped firing.

The Lewis Mark I remained virtually unchanged throughout its long service.

On the front face of the bolt were spring extractors, which gripped the rim of the just-fired cartridge case. Additional movement to the rear of the piston, striker and bolt actuated an ejector, which threw the empty case aside, and out through an opening in the right-hand side of the gun. If the trigger was still squeezed, then the striker and bolt moved forward again, and the tension of the spring in the magazine provided a fresh live round, so that the cycle could continue.

The basic Mark I gun remained in use, or available for issue, from October 1915 until 1946. The method of fire in naval use, known simply as 'hosepiping', was to put up a curtain of fire through which an enemy aircraft had to fly. Unfortunately, the light round was not capable of stopping a contemporary aircraft, and would only cause its loss if the pilot were hit, or some vital part of the aircraft were damaged.

If tracer ammunition was not available, or the ship was rolling

*Fairmile As at HMS* Hornet *on 10 September 1942.
Crew members are shown working on a stripped
20mm Oerlikon and a pedestal-mounted twin Lewis.
Note the collection bag for cartridge cases.*
Imperial War Museum

*A twin Lewis mounted on an early Coastal Forces
vessel. This is a posed shot, as the foresight is down.*
Imperial War Museum

*Lewis gunners aboard a 70ft British Power Boat MASB (50–67 group) in February 1941. Note the substantial gun safety rails.* Imperial War Museum

.303in Lewis gun general arrangement and details

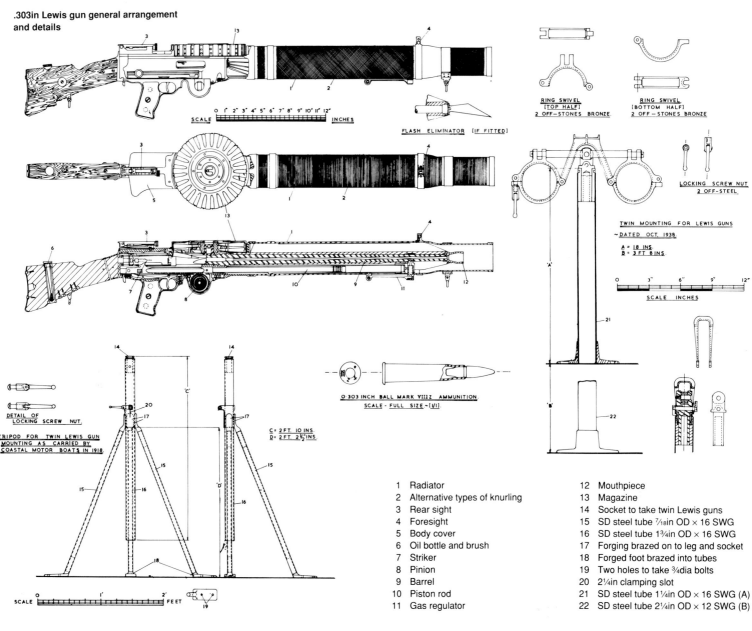

| | | | |
|---|---|---|---|
| 1 | Radiator | 12 | Mouthpiece |
| 2 | Alternative types of knurling | 13 | Magazine |
| 3 | Rear sight | 14 | Socket to take twin Lewis guns |
| 4 | Foresight | 15 | SD steel tube 7/8in OD × 16 SWG |
| 5 | Body cover | 16 | SD steel tube 1¾in OD × 16 SWG |
| 6 | Oil bottle and brush | 17 | Forging brazed on to leg and socket |
| 7 | Striker | 18 | Forged foot brazed into tubes |
| 8 | Pinion | 19 | Two holes to take ¾dia bolts |
| 9 | Barrel | 20 | 2¼in clamping slot |
| 10 | Piston rod | 21 | SD steel tube 1¼in OD × 16 SWG (A) |
| 11 | Gas regulator | 22 | SD steel tube 2¼in OD × 12 SWG (B) |

# The .303in Vickers gas-operated machine gun

The Vickers gas-operated gun was a development of earlier Vickers machine guns dating from the Great War. It was introduced in the Royal Navy in 1940, but had a previous history as an air weapon with the RAF.

It had a high rate of fire combined with a smooth action, and was fully automatic. The mechanism was simple, and had few working parts. It could be stripped for cleaning in less than 60 seconds, and the barrel could be readily removed and exchanged without stripping any other part of the gun. One special feature was that the gun had no external moving parts.

Ammunition was fed from a spring-loaded drum magazine, which was situated on the top of the gun. This, too, could be removed or exchanged without stripping any other part of the gun.

The action of the gun was simple; after the first round had been loaded and fired, motive power was obtained by deflecting a portion of the propelling gas through a hole in the barrel near the muzzle, on to a piston. The piston was driven to the rear, compressing the return springs and unlocking and drawing back the breech block. As it moved to the rear, this ejected the empty cartridge case from the chamber up against a deflector on the mounting.

The piston, and consequently the breech block, were held in the rear or 'cocked' position by a sear, until the firing control mechanism was operated. The operation of the mechanism released the sear, allowed the return springs to expand and drive forward the piston and breech block, which pushed a fresh round from the magazine into the chamber. When the breech block was locked, the piston continued to move forward and struck the floating firing pin situated in the breech block, which fired the next round.

As long as the firing mechanism was operated, the gun continued to fire automatically until the ammunition in the magazine was expended.

In the quadruple mounting, the four guns were fired by means of

## The .303in Vickers gas-operated Mark I No 5 gun (1940) data

| | |
|---|---|
| **Length of gun overall with flash eliminators** | 3ft 4in |
| **Length of barrel** | 1ft 8in |
| **Weight of gun (approximate)** | 20lb |
| **Weight of mounting for four guns** | 126lb |
| **Rifling** | |
|   **Type** | left-hand |
|   **Twist** | 1 in 10 |
|   **Number of grooves** | 5 |
| **Ammunition used** | all types of Mark VIII SAA |
|   **Capacity of magazine** | 100 rounds |
|   **Method of feed** | magazine |
|   **Rate of fire** | 950 rounds per minute (approximate) |

twin handgrips horizontally disposed on each side of the mounting. The guns, being air cooled, could in an emergency fire several hundred rounds almost continuously, but cooling, either by interrupted fire or by water, was advisable to prevent overheating and wear. Bursts of twenty rounds or so could be maintained for about 500 rounds.

The action of the magazine was as follows: the main spring, through the medium of the top plate, ensured that a fresh round was always in position in the lips of the magazine, and ready to be engaged by the feed piece. As the round was removed, the main spring rotated the top plate, which carried the ammunition with it until the next round was retained by the lips.

The quadruple mounting was designed for attachment to the standard pattern ring mounting, and consisted of the following major parts:

**.303in Vickers GO No 5 Mark I machine gun (1940) – elevation, plan and section**

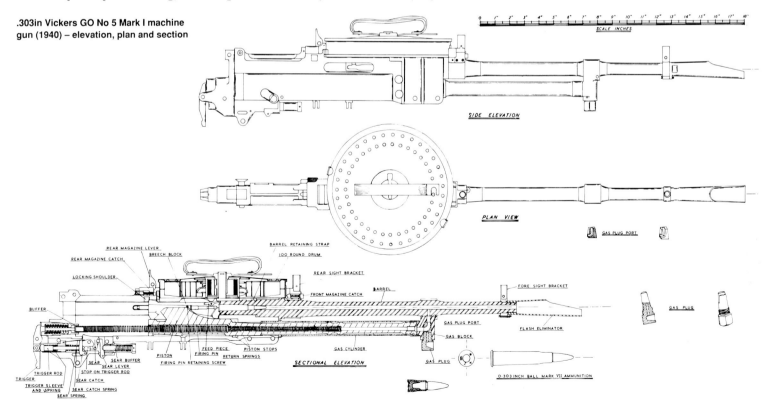

(1) the cradle, on which the guns were mounted;

(2) the shoulder rest, (with spray shield), which in conjunction with the firing grips on the cradle enabled the direction of the guns to be controlled;

(3) the firing gear, which enabled either two or four guns to be fired simultaneously; and

(4) the sights.

The gun was found in single, twin or quadruple mountings, the most familiar of which were the twin fittings carried by British Coastal Forces vessels, usually above the after end of the torpedo tubes. The gun was also carried by Air Sea Rescue launches operated by the RAF, and usually two single mountings were carried by British submarines.

**General arrangement for Coastal Forces single and twin mountings**

1 Body extension
2 Wooden hand grip
3 Trigger
4 Later 100-round magazine
5 Used cartridge case chute

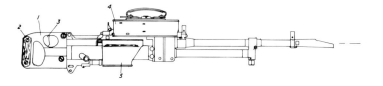

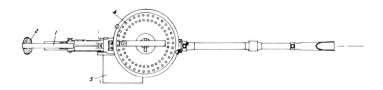

*Twin .303in Vickers gas-operated Mark I guns and 18in torpedo tubes.* Courtesy Al Ross II

**.303in Vickers machine gun on single pedestal mounting**

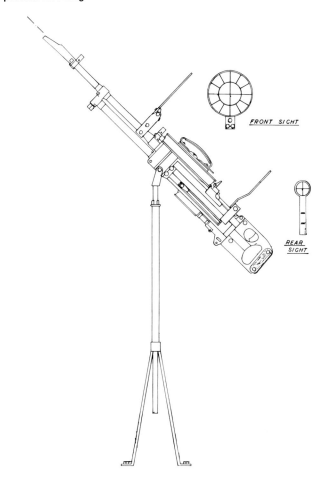

**Quadruple mounting with single pivot traverse – general arrangement and details**

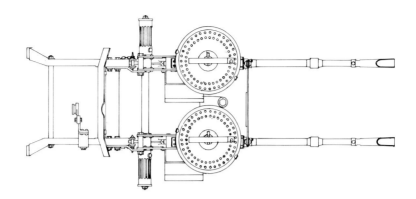

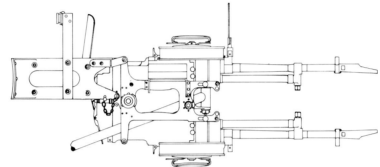

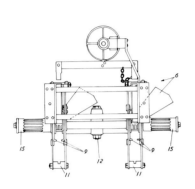

1  Spray shield
2  Shoulder rest hinge pin
3  Foresight
4  Backsight
5  Shoulder rest
6  Deflector
7  Elevating spindle
8  Cradle side plates
9  Bracket locating rear of gun body
10  Gun body securing bolt
11  Block retaining rear of gun body
12  Elevating and training bracket
13  Shoulder rest securing pin
14  Barrel strap retaining pin
15  Firing grip
16  Locating pin
17  Eye piece
18  Adjusting sleeve
19  Lock nut
20  Connecting rod
21  Pawl
22  Locking sleeve
23  Joint pin
24  Firing grip spindle
25  Firing grip bush
26  Safety catch
27  Firing lever

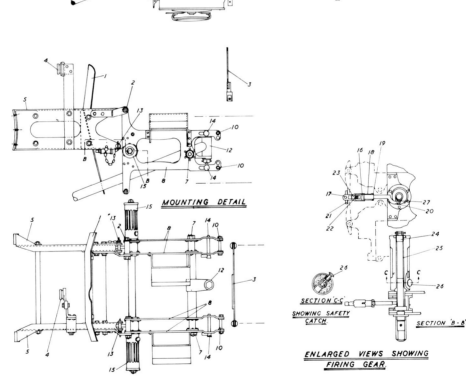

*MOUNTING DETAIL*

*SECTION 'C-C'*
*SHOWING SAFETY CATCH*

*SECTION 'B-B'*

*ENLARGED VIEWS SHOWING FIRING GEAR.*

# The 3-pounder Hotchkiss gun

Although the name Hotchkiss is usually associated with the large French armaments manufacturer, the company had British connections, and these were responsible for the light, quick-firing 3-pounder and 6-pounder guns used in large RN warships to counter torpedo boat attack.

Benjamin Berkely Hotchkiss was born in Watertown, Connecticut, USA, in 1825. He was apprenticed to Colt's Patent Fire Arms Company, where he helped to design some of that company's revolvers. His designs for barrel rifling improved the accuracy of Colt weapons, and a new percussion fuse of his invention was accepted by the United States government.

In 1867, finding little backing or encouragement in America and wishing to expand his horizons, he emigrated to France, where he produced a design for a metal cartridge case which was adopted by the French government and put into production at the St Etienne arsenal. Four years later he designed a five-barrelled 37mm revolving gun for rapid fire, for both the army and for the navy as a defence against torpedo boats. A hand crank controlled the loading, firing, extraction and barrel rotation operations of the weapon. Four versions were manufactured and the design was also enlarged to produce a 40mm version for fortress defence and 47mm and 57mm versions for naval use.

By 1884 Hotchkiss, now eminent in the armaments industry, amalgamated with the much acclaimed British inventor, engineer and gunmaker Sir William Armstrong, who founded the armament and engineering works at Elswick, just outside Newcastle. The 6-pounder 57mm and 3-pounder 47mm guns were produced at these works. The French parent company, after the death of Hotchkiss in 1885, continued the development of heavy machine guns and produced the Hotchkiss model 1914, which was to become the main French machine gun during the Great War and was still on that army's lists until 1944. It was also copied by the Japanese and produced with modifications for their army.

However, the 3-pounder 47mm (1.850in bore) weapon is the subject here, and was introduced in 1886 as a rapid-fire gun to keep off enemy torpedo boats. It was mounted high up, where the larger 6-pounder guns were considered too heavy, and carried in large numbers in major RN warships by the turn of the century, many being manufactured at the Elswick works. In use in a lesser role during the Great War, many were fitted to smaller craft such as minesweeping trawlers and drifters, where the simple and hardy design required little maintenance. After that war, many were used as subcalibre and saluting guns, or placed in storage. This meant that a reserve was held, and by World War II 550 Mark I and 91 Mark I* mountings survived from stock, with 31 high-angle Mark IV mountings. The gun was also put into use in new Mark V and a few Mark VI mountings, as well as conversions of the existing Mark I and I* to 50° capability for a limited dual-purpose role.

The object of this exercise was to make use of existing weapons in updated gun mountings to arm the new and requisitioned craft pressed into service on the outbreak of the war. These weapons, elderly in the extreme, were carried in a multitude of small craft, new constructions such as the Fairmile A and B types, the 72ft harbour defence motor launch, small requisitioned drifters and small trawler types used in inshore patrol and minesweeping duties.

Though the gun itself was obsolete, it was still capable of providing some form of defence against small units or surfaced U-boats. It was of robust construction and the sea environment did not

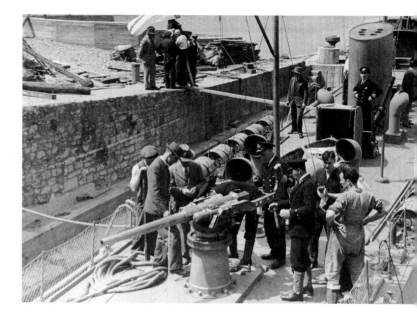

*A Fairmile A fitting out in dry dock, having just been fitted with a 3-pounder Mark I. She has twin .303in Lewis guns on a pedestal carried only on the starboard side, such was the shortage of weapons.* Author's collection

unduly affect its performance. There were no sophisticated aiming controls; the existing telescope sights, where fitted, proved adequate, and the larger 6-pounder, with its heavier punch, was fitted to many of the Fairmile D motor gunboats, as well as those Bs sent out to the Far East as gunboats.

The basic design of the 3-pounder was so effective that it was retained in the fleet as a saluting gun up until the 1970s, and is still to be found on some shore bases in this role today.

Of the total of 2950 guns on naval books, at least 1002 had been lost or stricken by 1939, and nearly all of those that survived were

*A 3-pounder aboard a B of the Indian Flotilla at the landing at Kankhaw, with twin .303in Bren guns. Note the swivel aerial fitting on the gun shield, and the Bs passing.* Courtesy George Hay

*A 3-pounder Hotchkiss on a Mark I mounting, and twin Lewis guns, shown on an A type of the 1st ML Flotilla out of Great Yarmouth in May 1941.*
Author's collection

Mark Is. High-explosive rounds were carried, with common shell also carried in the early part of the war. The unconverted Mark I and I* mountings allowed 25° maximum elevation, converted mountings 50°, the Mark V 70° and the Mark VI, which had rubber recoil buffers, 60°. The maximum range was about 6000 yards.

**3-pounder Hotchkiss gun on Mark I (naval) mounting**

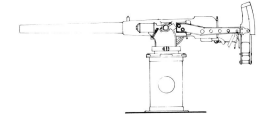

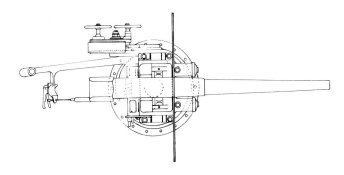

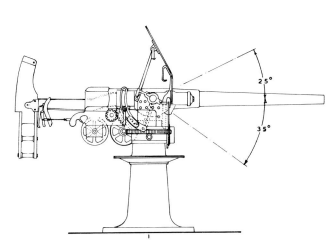

### The 3-pounder Hotchkiss gun data

**Bore**    1.350in (47mm)
**Weight including breech mechanism**    528lb
**Lenght overall**    80.635in
**Length of bore**    74.06in
**Weight of projectile**    3.30lb
**Propellant charge**    0.465lb
**Muzzle velocity**    1884ft per second
**Maximum range**    tables to 6500yd at 20° 41′

**Mark I mounting**
  Weight of mounting    7cwt 0qr 9lb
  Weight of mounting with gun    11cwt 2qr 19lb
**Mark I\* mounting**
  Weight of mounting    7cwt 3qr
  Weight of mounting with gun    12cwt 0qr 4lb
**50° Conversion mounting**
  Weight of mounting without shield    7cwt 3qr
  Weight of shield    3cwt 2qr
  Weight of mounting with shield and gun    15cwt 3qr 8lb
**Mark V mounting**
  Weight of mounting without shield or balance weight    14cwt 3qr 5lb
  Weight of shield and balance weight    13cwt 1qr 13lb
  Weight of mounting complete    32cwt 2qr 26lb
  Number of holding-down bolts    12 of ¾in diameter
  Pitch diameter of bolts    2ft 9in
**Mark VI mounting**
  Weight of mounting without shield and shield supports    16cwt 1qr 14lb
  Weight of shield and shield supports    7cwt 2qr 6lb
  Number of holding-down bolts    10 of ⅞in diameter
  Pitch diameter of bolts    2ft 3¼in
**Mark VI\* mounting**
  Weight of mounting without shield and shield supports    12cwt 0qr 18lb
  Weight of shield and shield supports    7cwt 2qr 6lb
  Weight of mounting complete    25cwt 1qr 4lb
(Other mountings as Mark VI)

The Mark I* mounting differed from the Mark I in that it was fitted with a telescopic sight on the left of the gun and an automatic brake on the right of the gun. For the Mark I mounting, the pedestal was conical in shape and was bolted to the deck by twelve ⅞in bolts. On the top of the pedestal was fitted the holding-down ring, secured by eighteen ⅞in bolts. The gun cradle was a single bronze casting which supported the gun in trunnion boxes. The 50° conversion mounting was a Mark I or I* converted for high angle/low angle firing, the limits being 47° and 8° respectively.

**3-pounder Hotchkiss gun on Mark I\* mounting**

SCALE FEET

**Details of the 3-pounder Hotchkiss
Mark I* mounting**

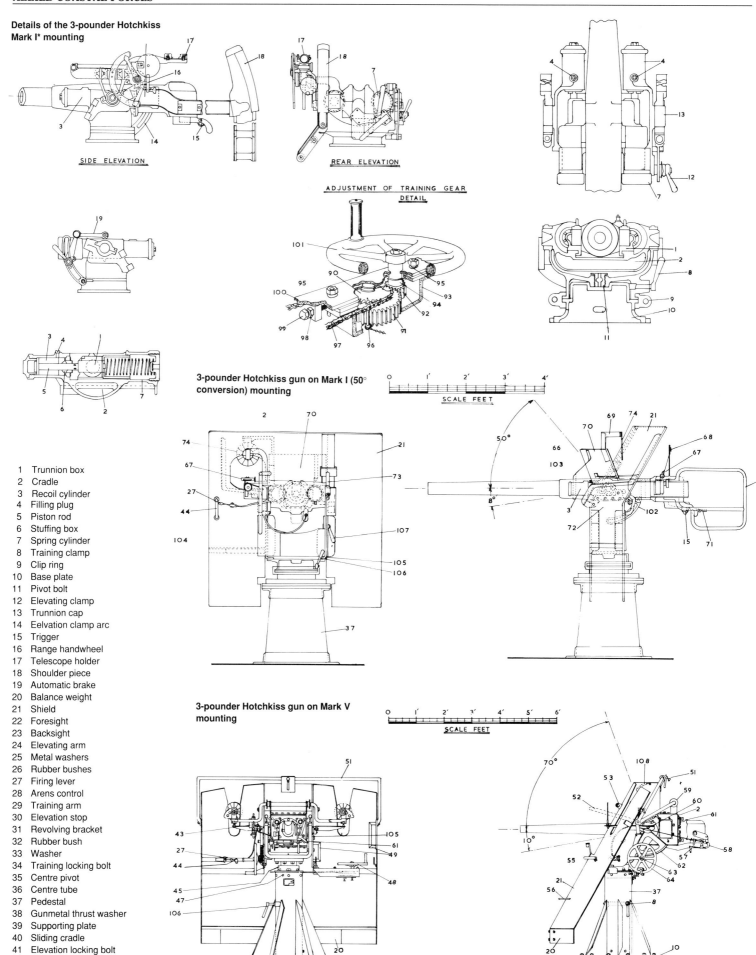

SIDE ELEVATION

REAR ELEVATION

ADJUSTMENT OF TRAINING GEAR
DETAIL

**3-pounder Hotchkiss gun on Mark I (50°
conversion) mounting**

SCALE FEET

**3-pounder Hotchkiss gun on Mark V
mounting**

SCALE FEET

1   Trunnion box
2   Cradle
3   Recoil cylinder
4   Filling plug
5   Piston rod
6   Stuffing box
7   Spring cylinder
8   Training clamp
9   Clip ring
10  Base plate
11  Pivot bolt
12  Elevating clamp
13  Trunnion cap
14  Eelvation clamp arc
15  Trigger
16  Range handwheel
17  Telescope holder
18  Shoulder piece
19  Automatic brake
20  Balance weight
21  Shield
22  Foresight
23  Backsight
24  Elevating arm
25  Metal washers
26  Rubber bushes
27  Firing lever
28  Arens control
29  Training arm
30  Elevation stop
31  Revolving bracket
32  Rubber bush
33  Washer
34  Training locking bolt
35  Centre pivot
36  Centre tube
37  Pedestal
38  Gunmetal thrust washer
39  Supporting plate
40  Sliding cradle
41  Elevation locking bolt

**Mark V mounting details of cradle**

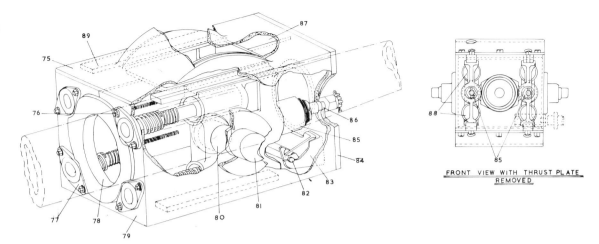

FRONT VIEW WITH THRUST PLATE REMOVED

**3-pounder Hotchkiss gun on Mark VI mounting**

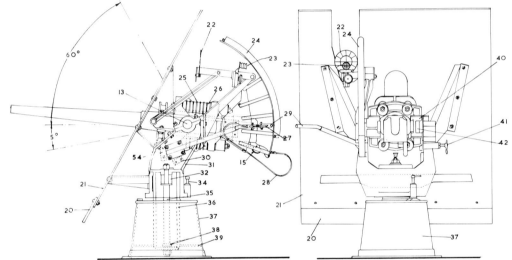

SCALE FEET

**3-pounder Hotchkiss gun on Mark VI* mounting**

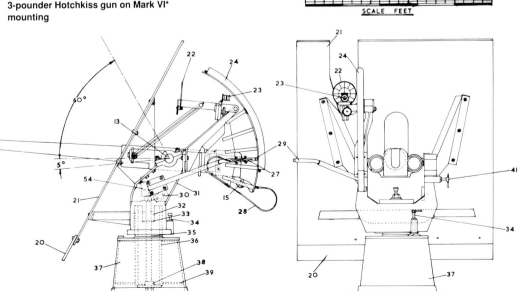

SCALE FEET

# The 2-pounder Mark XI and XII guns

The 2-pounder Mark XI and XII guns on the Mark IX mounting formed the main armament on the 72ft harbour defence motor launch and were also found on auxiliary vessels – drifters, etc. The gun was formerly the sub-calibre gun used in place of the 4.7in and 4in quick-fire guns, and was converted by fitting a percussion mechanism, which was fired by Bowden wire control from a pistol grip on the mounting.

The gun consisted of a steel barrel with a breech ring prepared for the reception of the breech mechanism screwed over the rear end and secured by a check screw. The exterior of the barrel was prepared with a screw thread on to which was screwed the inner sleeve on the cradle of the mounting.

The mounting was designed to enable the 2-pounder sub-calibre gun to be used as a high angle/low angle weapon in small auxiliary craft. The only differences in the mounting between the two types of gun were that the sleeves which screwed on to the guns differed in length, but fitted on to a common cradle, and that the torque plates, which prevented the gun turning when the shell was fired, differed in design.

The pedestal was a drum of welded steel construction, bolted to the deck by sixteen ⅝in bolts, and contained a fixed hollow steel tube. An inner tube formed a centre pivot 6in in diameter, around which the carriage was free to rotate.

The carriage was a gunmetal casing, fitting closely round the centre pivot and having a steel spindle attached to it, which projected through the steel tube. The steel spindle passed out through the bottom of the tube and was fitted with a nut, which resisted any tendency of the mounting to jump on firing. The lower end of the tube also passed through a rubber buffer and a ball race, to which by means of a steel collar it transmitted the weight of the carriage and the whole of the revolving structure. On firing, the downward thrust was partially cushioned by the rubber buffer, but was finally taken direct on the pivot.

The gun cradle was of a new type to the navy and was designed to absorb the gun recoil in two sets of rubber buffers, one above and the other below the gun. It consisted of an inner and outer gunmetal sleeve, held apart by the rubber buffers, the gun being screwed into the inner sleeve which then, on firing, recoiled within the outer sleeve. The inner sleeve was closed in front by a gunmetal fermature bush, secured by four ⅜in hexagon-headed screws. On the outer sleeve were formed the trunnion pins, by which the weight of the gun and cradle were supported in the trunnions of the carriage.

The gun was locked in the inner sleeve and prevented from rotating by gunmetal pads, screwed to a pressed steel housing in halves which enveloped the breech. The pressed steel housing extended to the rear, far enough to maintain contact with the breech during recoil.

On the left side of the outer sleeve was a facing for the attachment of the handle bar (four ⅜in screws), by which the gun was laid and trained. Note that the rear section of each buffer system (that is the wide rubber bush in the rear of the cradle diaphragm) did not take any part in absorbing the gun recoil, but helped to bring the gun to rest without a jar when it ran out. The normal length of recoil was about 2.75in for a 2lb shell. For scatter shot it was less.

A cartwheel foresight and bead backsight were provided, the sight bar moving parallel to the gun in elevation by reason of its attachment to the carriage on the one hand, and a steel bar projecting from the left hand side of the cradle on the other.

The maximum effective range of the weapon depended upon the type of ammunition used – high-explosive shell (range 1500 yards) or case shot (range 500 yards). It was ineffective to open fire at greater ranges than these.

Clear photographs of the 2-pounder Mark XI and XII guns, apart from general views of 72ft HDMLs, have proven impossible to obtain.

1   Foresight
2   Sightbar
3   Backsight
4   Sight rod
5   Sight arm
6   Rubber buffer
7   Fermeture bush
8   Outer sleeve
9   Elevating stop
10   Stauffer lubricator
11   Firing lever
12   Handle bar
13   Inner sleeve
14   Trunnion
15   Pressed steel housing in halves enveloping breech
16   Gunmetal pads screwed to housing
17   Adjustment
18   Bowden cable
19   Carriage
20   Training stop
21   Centre pivot
22   Pedestal
23   Hinged arm
24   Centre spindle
25   Rubber buffer
26   Thrust ball race
27   Barrel band

**2-pounder Mark XII gun on Mark IX mounting**

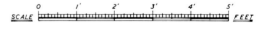

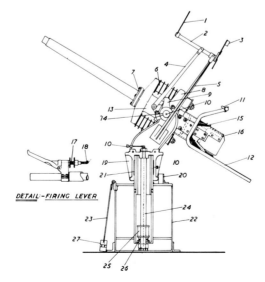

DETAIL:-FIRING LEVER

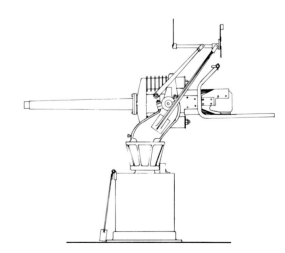

**2-pounder Mark XI gun on Mark IX mounting (without shield)**

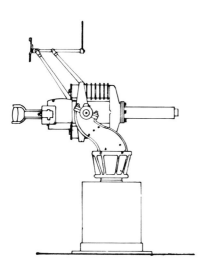

**The 2-pounder Mark XI and XII gun (1941) data**

**2-pounder sub-calibre gun Mark XI** (formerly sub-calibre gun of 4.7in and 4in QF guns)
    **Length of gun**   41.97in
    **Diameter of bore**   1.575in
    **Weight of one round**   2lb 10³⁄₁₆oz
**2-pounder sub-calibre gun Mark XII** (formerly sub-calibre gun of 4.7in and 4in BL guns)
    **Length of gun**   65.2in
    **Diameter of bore**   1.575in
    **Weight of one round**   2lb 15½oz

**Mark IX mounting**
    **Weight of mounting and gun without shield**   7¾cwt
    **Weight of shield**   2¼cwt
    **Number of holding-down bolts**   16
    **Diameter of holding-down bolts**   ⅝in
    **Pitch diameter of holding-down bolts**   20.75in
    **Crew**   Three (gunlayer, breechworker and loader)

**Ammunition (2-pounder QF Mark XI gun)**
    High explosive – (fuse No 240 or 241, the same as for the 2-pounder Mark VIII LV gun); Practice; Case shot; CP (common pointed)

The maximum effective range of this weapon depended on the type of ammunition being used.
    **HE shell**   range 1500 yards
    **Case shot**   range 500 yards

**2-pounder Mark XI gun on Mark IX mounting**

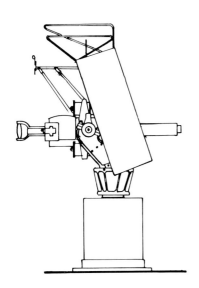
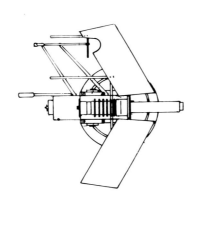
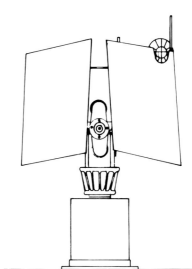

# The 2-pounder Vickers 40mm gun

The Royal Navy had adopted the Vickers pom-pom 2-pounder gun shortly before the Great War, and it was fitted to destroyers and other craft in large numbers during that conflict. The 2-pounder was, in effect, an oversized Maxim machine gun of 40mm calibre, which was belt fed and fired at about 60 rounds per minute. The Mark II gun was introduced in March 1915, with an automatic mechanism and a total weight with cooling water of 550lb; it had a 25-round fabric belt, giving a rate of fire of about 200rpm. The original Mark II gun suffered from mechanical problems, and the Mark II* was produced to improve the gun's functioning and reliability. Originally fitted to fleet destroyers, the older mountings were landed soon after the end of hostilities.

The mounting shown here, dating from 1929, was a somewhat improved version and was principally fitted to the older destroyers, 72ft HDMLs and other coastal craft such as the Fairmile C type motor gunboat, where the improved firepower was much sought after.

Photographs of this weapon on the 72ft HDML are scarce, but it was apparently issued in small numbers and proved to have more offensive potential than the 2-pounder Mark XII gun on the Mark IX mounting usually fitted, though at the cost of an additional weight penalty.

**2-pounder Vickers 40mm gun on HA Mark II mounting (1929) – general arrangement**

RIGHTHAND ELEVATION AT 80°.

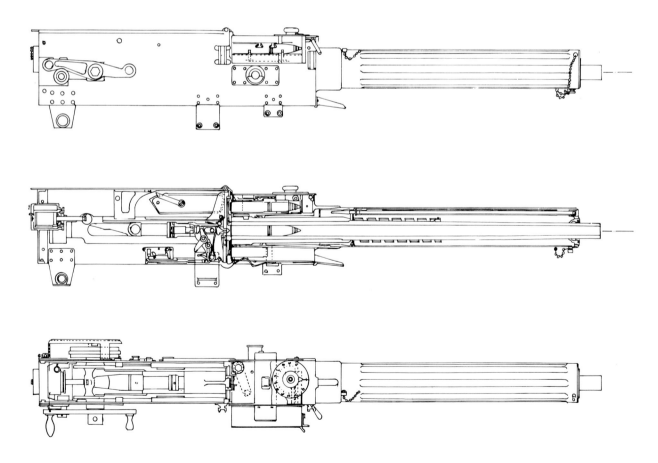

**2-pounder Vickers 40mm gun – profile, section and plan**

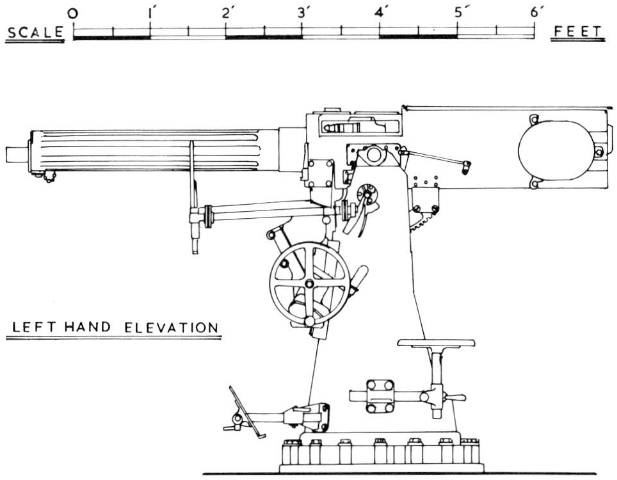

SCALE 0 1' 2' 3' 4' 5' 6' FEET

LEFT HAND ELEVATION

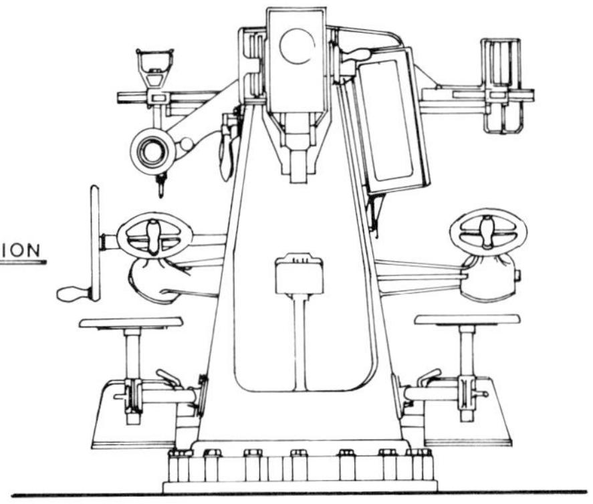

REAR ELELEVATION

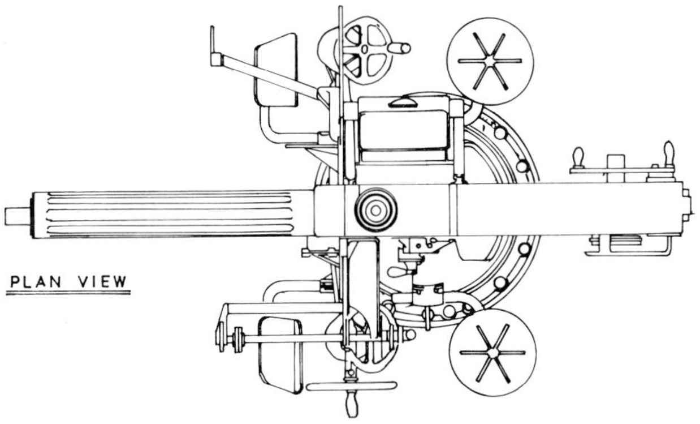

PLAN VIEW

## The 2-pounder Vickers 40mm gun (1929) data

**Calibre**   1.575in
**Muzzle velocity**   2000ft per second
**Pressure**   17 tons/sq in
**Muzzle energy**   55.5ft/tons
**Length of barrel**   39.37 calibres (62in)
**Length of rifling**   54.84in
**Twist in rifling**   1 turn in 30 calibres
**Number of grooves**   12
**Depth of grooves**   .0156in
**Width of grooves**   .322 to .311in
**Length of recoil**   3in (metal to metal)
**Maximum pull on trunnions**   2.1 tons
**Total length of gun**   95.65in
**Capacity of water jacket**   24 pints
**Rate of fire**   200 rounds per minute
**Maximum range**   7830 yards
**Height attained by projectiles at max. elevation**   14.515ft
**Total range at maximum elevation**   2400 yards
**Weight of gun complete with ammunition box and bracket**   584lb
**Weight of 25 rounds in belt**   75.5lb
**Weight of ammunition box**   17.5lb
**Weight of water in jacket**   32lb
**Weight of ammunition box bracket**   28lb

**The HA Mark II mounting**
  **Maximum elevation**   80°
  **Maximum depression**   6°
  **Upward lift**   3 tons
  **Downward blow**   3.5 tons
  **Speed of elevation**   7° per 1 revolution of handwheel
  **Speed of training**   7° per 1 revolution of handwheel

**Estimated weights**
**Gun**   4cwt 2qr 23lb
**Mounting**   6cwt 1qr 5lb
**Total**   14cwt 0qr 0lb

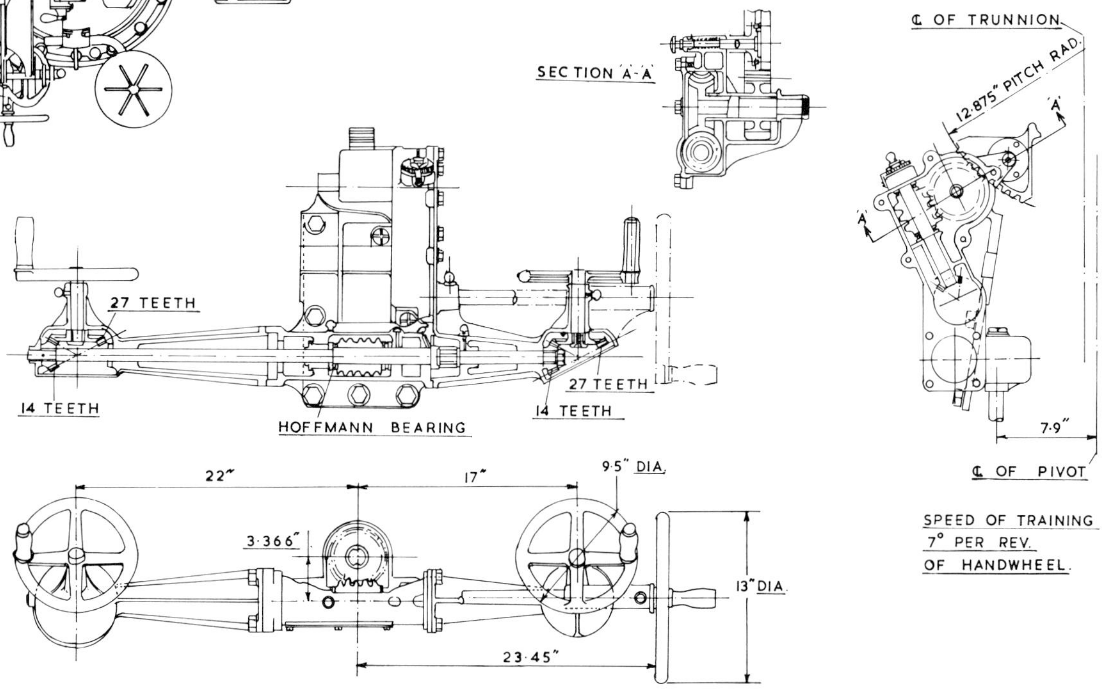

SECTION 'A-A'

₵ OF TRUNNION
12·875" PITCH RAD.
7·9"
₵ OF PIVOT

SPEED OF TRAINING
7° PER REV.
OF HANDWHEEL.

27 TEETH
14 TEETH
27 TEETH
14 TEETH
HOFFMANN BEARING

22"
17"
9·5" DIA.
3·366"
13" DIA.
23·45"

**Details of elevating and training gear**

# The 2-pounder Rolls-Royce 40mm SA gun

Rolls-Royce is well known for its wartime Merlin aero engine and its development, but little is known of the company's foray into the armament field. This part of its history was under the care of Dr Spirito Mario Viale, who was born in Turin in 1882. The son of a Staff-Major in the Italian Army, he moved to Paris after his graduation and spent the Great War working for the French and Italian governments, designing radial aero engines and developing synchronising gear for fighter aircraft. In 1919 he obtained a job as Chief Designer at Armstrong Siddeley and was involved with the design and development of the Jaguar, Lynx and Cheetah radial engines. During this time he became a naturalised British subject. In the early 1930s he returned to Northern Italy with his French-born wife and joined Isotta-Fraschini in Milan as their chief aero-engine designer. However, he soon found himself opposed to the Fascist regime in Italy and was encouraged to return to England. In 1938 he joined Rolls-Royce at Derby and, although engaged for aero engine work, he tended to float in a number of projects, eventually becoming chief designer for the new Armaments Division.

This was a new venture for Rolls-Royce and had been started with the idea of developing new guns specially adapted for aerial warfare, rather than building guns under licence from abroad or adapting them from land weapons. From the outset it was intended that the new department was to devote its energy to design and development, and that no large-scale production would be undertaken by the company. The new department had been set up following a meeting at the Air Ministry in November 1938, at which the question was asked how long it would take to produce a new machine cannon for aircraft. The reply given was five years, but the director of Rolls-Royce said that his company could do the job in eighteen months. Rolls-Royce got the contract.

The brief outline specification for the gun was issued on 23 November, but apart from fixing the calibre at 40mm and stating that the weapon was to be automatic, little further information was given. In fact, the final drawings and the specification of the ammunition to be used were only supplied in March 1939.

Dr Viale's 40mm gun had a hydraulic recoil mechanism and a completely original system of breech closure. The greatest innova-

*The 2-pounder Rolls-Royce gun aboard a Fairmile C MGB, with two sister boats following astern.*
Imperial War Museum

*The other side of the coin – the 2-pounder Rolls-Royce gun on a 15cwt truck for airfield defence. Note the barrage balloons high above.* Rolls-Royce Ltd

tion, however, was the use of aluminium alloy in the gun cradle and recoil mechanism.

The first gun was designed to have an automatic feed, holding nine rounds, the ammunition being supplied in clips of four. Design work started in March 1939, and the first gun, without a magazine and mounted on an old Victorian gun carriage (as shown in the photograph), was successfully proof fired at Woolwich Arsenal in December. Meanwhile, however, the Air Ministry had come to the conclusion that the war would be over before a gun of this calibre could be developed for use in aircraft, and the company was told that the project was no longer to be considered urgent.

At the same time, the Royal Navy began to take an interest in the new weapon. The RN urgently required a quick-firing, non-automatic 40mm weapon, as there was an extreme shortage of 2-pounder guns for Coastal Forces craft in general, and for the new Fairmile designs in particular, which were soon to be constructed in considerable numbers.

The navy's new Staff Requirement was provided in six weeks and the gun was tested at HMS *Excellent*, the Gunnery School, in

July 1940. These trials resulted in an order for the gun to be put into production. Dr Viale protested that the gun still required extensive development, and that the materials, maintenance procedures and operating conditions envisaged for an RAF weapon were unsuited to a gun intended for use at sea. He was, however, over-ruled, and an order was placed for 600 guns with the British United Shoe Machinery Company of Leicestershire.

The weapon was rapidly placed in service aboard motor gunboats and motor launches, and a further order for 600 was placed when the first contract was completed. Dr Viale's reservations quickly proved to be well-founded, however, and the gun's service was not as satisfactory as it might have been.

The gun could be ungainly, even when on target, if the loader was heavy-handed in putting in the next round, and in any seaway it was even more difficult. Nevertheless, if conditions were good it was a very accurate weapon and a good rate of fire could be maintained. The 2-pounder ammunition was self-destructing at 2500 yards or so, so it was possible to create a barrage around an incoming target, either aircraft or surface ship. A ready use ammunition tray was fitted to the right-hand side of the mounting, and the sights were of the cartwheel type, as on the 20mm Oerlikon.

In the same month as the weapon underwent its sea trials, the RAF had come forward with an urgent requirement for a version of the gun for airfield defence. The naval QF gun was fitted with an automatic hydraulic turret and mounted on a 15cwt Chevrolet truck.

Additional RAF work on the gun was also carried out, and some 300 guns were eventually bought by the Air Ministry from the Navy for use (after some modification) in Hurricanes. A small number of larger 57mm versions of the gun were fitted in the nose of Coastal Command de Havilland Mosquitoes to shoot up surfaced enemy U-boats or other ship targets.

In May 1943 the Armaments Department of Rolls-Royce closed down and the staff passed over to the more vital aero engine projects.

I am extremely grateful to Mr M H Evans of Rolls-Royce Employee Communications and Community Relations for the original general arrangement drawings and photographs of this interesting weapon, as well as copies of articles giving the information on the design and history of the weapon.

*Ready for proof firing, the prototype 2-pounder Rolls-Royce gun in the workshops.* Rolls-Royce Ltd

**2-pounder Rolls-Royce 40mm gun –
general arrangement and details**

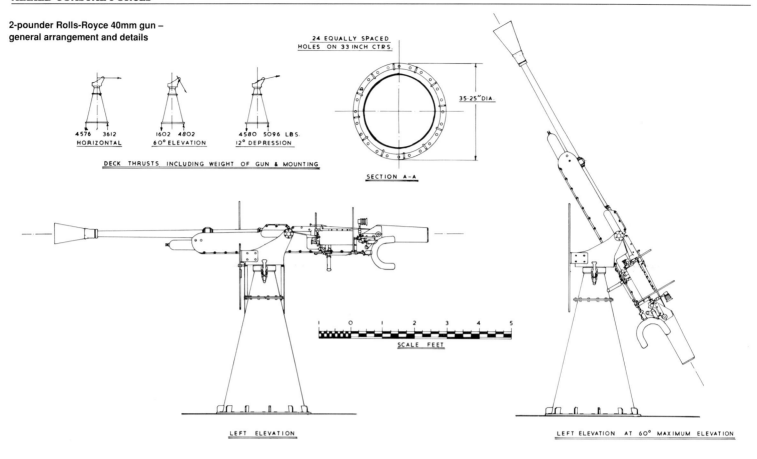

DECK THRUSTS INCLUDING WEIGHT OF GUN & MOUNTING

| 4576 | 3612 | 1602 | 4802 | 4580 | 5096 LBS. |
|---|---|---|---|---|---|
| HORIZONTAL | | 60° ELEVATION | | 12° DEPRESSION | |

24 EQUALLY SPACED
HOLES ON 33 INCH CTRS.

35·25" DIA.

SECTION A-A

SCALE FEET

LEFT ELEVATION

LEFT ELEVATION AT 60° MAXIMUM ELEVATION

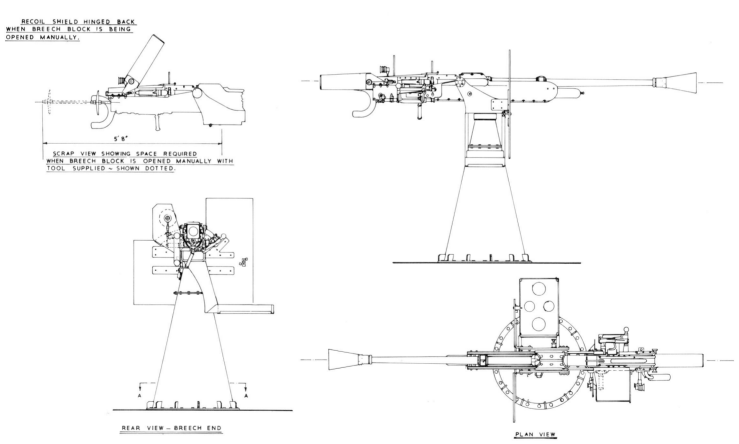

RECOIL SHIELD HINGED BACK
WHEN BREECH BLOCK IS BEING
OPENED MANUALLY.

5' 8"

SCRAP VIEW SHOWING SPACE REQUIRED
WHEN BREECH BLOCK IS OPENED MANUALLY WITH
TOOL SUPPLIED ~ SHOWN DOTTED.

REAR VIEW – BREECH END

PLAN VIEW

# The 4.5in 8cwt Mark I gun

By the spring of 1943 it had been found possible to fit the British Army's 6-pounder tank gun into the existing naval 2-pounder power-operated Mark XVI gun mounting, with a few necessary modifications, which significantly increased the the Coastal Forces firepower. This gun came into service from the autumn of 1943. Known as the naval 6-pounder Mark VII, it was issued to Fairmile Ds and other long gunboats, as well as to the British Power Boat 72ft 6in short boats, and will be covered in a future volume.

Even before its entry into service, it was recognised that the 6-pounder did not carry the necessary punch to sink armed trawlers, and that something like the US Navy's 4.5in gun would be required. In May 1944, a conference presided over by the Deputy First Sea Lord was convened to consider the application of the light 4.5in gun designed by DMD1, and the 95mm tank howitzer, for fitting in Coastal Forces craft, in particular for use in the Far East against Japanese forces. It was decided to place a pre-production order of eighteen of each weapon, with the necessary ammunition, and carry out comparative trials against a number of representative targets. Both types were designed for mounting in the power-operated Mark 2A 6-pounder 7cwt mounting.

The results of trials at Shoeburyness against box targets representing (a) a trawler; (b) a merchant ship; and (c) an R boat, were discussed at a meeting at the Admiralty on 26 June. The Director of Naval Ordnance considered that the Jefferis gun (the 4.5in) was undoubtedly superior to the 95mm against targets (a) and (b), and not significantly less effective against target (c). The 4.5in was therefore selected for production. Comparative specifications of the 4.5in and the 95mm guns are as follows:

|  | 4.5in | 95mm |
|---|---|---|
| Muzzle velocity | 1500ft per sec | 1050ft per sec |
| Weight of complete round | 22lb | 28lb |
| Weight of projectile | 15lb (5½lb HE) | 25lb (3lb HE) |
| Breech | Semi-automaic | Semi-automatic possible |
| Rate of fire | 10 to 15 rounds per minute | 10 to 15 rounds per minute |

Further trials were carried out in September 1945 against targets representing (a) an R boat; (b) a merchant ship; (c) a junk; (d) a sampan; and (e) an armoured fast barge. It was found that the shell was very effective against wooden hulled vessels and was also capable of causing considerable damage to merchant ships with mild steel hulls up to ⅝in thick. R and A trials were reasonably good, but jump was severe and was expected to be worse when the gun was mounted on a light craft. The captain of HMS *Excellent* (the Gunnery School) noted that the range should be set in increments of 400 yards so that any error due to uncorrected jump would be swamped by errors in range setting and estimation. Trials with a Sharklet anti-submarine diving projectile were also arranged.

In August 1944 it had been the intention to develop the Mark II hand-operated mounting to equip six flotillas of Fairmile B type gunboats earmarked for the Far East fleet, to replace their existing 6-pounders. This however, proved impossible due to delays with the development of both mountings. Trials were carried out aboard ML 570, as noted on page 35 above.

The weapons system has been redrawn for this book from information supplied by Priddy's Hard, and the GA drawings of the Mark II from photographs and post-war weapons fits. The Mark I mounting shown was a small power-operated mounting for the 4.5in low-velocity QF semi-automatic gun. The low velocity of the gun meant that the force of the recoil was not too great, and thus allowed a medium calibre weapon to be fitted in a small vessel without elaborate strengthening of the ship's structure.

*One of the few views of the Mark IV manual mounting aboard a B type. This weapon was also carried by trawlers.* Imperial War Museum

The inevitable disadvantages of this fitting were a low maximum range and slightly less accuracy than that of guns with a similar calibre and higher MV, but these had little significance when related to the purpose for which the equipment was intended, namely fairly heavy firepower at close ranges.

The whole mounting occupied a small space and was operated by a crew of four. Apart from the loading operation, complete control of the mounting was in the hands of one man, who laid, trained and fired the gun by the operation of a scooter control valve box.

Power was supplied by hydraulic pressure from a variable flow pump, which was designed to give a continuous supply of oil under pressure to a closed circuit.

Certain parts of the hydraulic system, including the variable flow pump, filter, header tank, relief valve, changeover cocks and drain valve, were on the fixed structure. The remaining parts of the system, comprising the rotating service joint, manual power unit (hand pump), changeover valve, scooter control, valve box, elevating cylinder, training motor and firing piston, were on the mounting.

The flow of liquid was uni-directional in the fixed structure and through the rotating service joint, the changeover valves and the master valve. In the elevating, training and firing units, the pressure and exhaust alternated in direction according to the position of their respective valves.

The mounting, power system and power units were of simple and robust construction, and maintenance was simplified by the fact that the power units were self-contained and self-lubricating, but the correct functioning of the working parts was only ensured by periodical examination of the power units and by constant attention to the lubricators at the accessible positions on the mounting.

The sight was somewhat new and unorthodox. It provided for adjustment in the ship's own speed, and automatically kept the correct deflection.

The steel gun comprised a short non-autofrettaged barrel and removable breech ring, screwed on over the rear end of the barrel and prevented from rotating by a conical ended securing screw, which fitted into a similarly shaped recess in the barrel.

The steel mounting support was cylindrical in shape, about 4ft in diameter and some 18in high, with a flange fitted at the top and bottom. The lower flange allowed the support to be bolted to the deck through a packing ring.

The upper flange carried the horizontal fixed roller path on which the whole weight of the moving structure bore. Outside the roller path, on a slightly higher level, was the fixed training rack – fitted with the teeth uppermost. Running around the outside of the training rack was the fixed ring, some 4in in depth and surmounted

*The trial 4.5in Mark II manual mounting aboard ML 570, 1945.* Courtesy Harold Hawkins BEM

by a dust plate. The inner surface of the fixed ring was machined to form a vertical roller path which prevented lateral play of the moving structure. Brackets secured to the upper flange carried the cam rail for safety firing gear, which prevented the gun from firing into its own superstructure. The lower half of the rotating service joint was fixed in the centre of the support, at about the deck level.

By January 1945 it was felt that the production of neither the Mark I nor the Mark II mounting was likely to commence before April 1945. At the same time, it was announced that MGB 538 (the last of the Vosper 1944 class, which by that time had been earmarked as a development vessel) would be equipped with the 4.5in Mark I.

In April it was stated that the 4.5in gun was further delayed and that the design of a development mounting was in hand. This new mounting was to incorporate either the new 4.5in gun or the existing 6-pounder Mark IIA gun. It was to have electrohydraulic drive and redesigned hydraulic components. This devleopment mounting was then designated for Vosper's MGB 538.

The first 4.5in 8cwt Mark I power-operated mounting was seen by April 1946, after the war's end, on MTBs 528 and 509 (both short boats – a Vosper 1944 class and a British Power Boats 1944 class respectively). These had replaced the 6-pounder Mark VII, which both boats had received on completion.

By the summer of 1946 the Fairmile D types 5007 and 5008 had the new weapons system fitted, again in place of the original

**4.5in gun on Mark I mounting — profiles and plan**

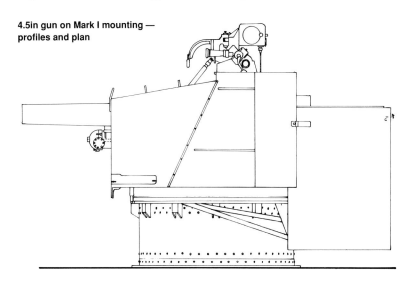

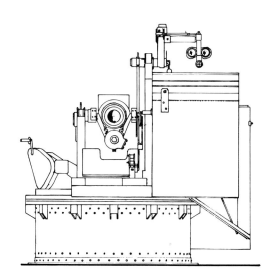

*A rear view of the short 4.5in Mark II mounting.*
Courtesy Harold Hawkins BEM

6-pounder, and at about the same time three Camper and Nicholson 1943 class boats – MTB 2016, 2017 and 2018 – had their forward 6-pounder replaced by a 4.5in mounting.

Coastal Forces were renumbered in mid-1949, after which both MTBs and MGBs were known as FPBs (Fast Patrol Boats). Prior to this date, the 71ft 6in British Power Boats 1944 class MTBs 509 and 520 and the 73ft Vosper 1944 class boats 528 and 530 are known to have been fitted with the 4.5in Mark I mounting. The Vosper experimental short boat 538, which was orginally intended to fit the first mounting, completed in August 1948 as MTB 538 and carried only a twin 20mm Oerlikon forward and four 18in torpedo tubes. During trials she landed this armament, and in early 1949, as an MGB, was fitted with a 4.5in Mark I mounting forward and the twin 20mm aft. Long boats included the three Camper and Nicholson boats mentioned above and the Fairmile D type MTBs 790, 5007, 5008 and 5009. Until 1949, the 4.5in gun merely replaced the 6-pounder forward (apart from 5008, where originally the after 6-pounder was retrofitted; later, she too had the heavier gun forward).

After mid-1949, the combined torpedo and gun armament was generally dropped and boats were fitted either as gunboats or torpedo boats. Short boats, with the 4.5in gun forward and a twin 20mm aft, included FPB 1027, 1030 and 1033. Long boats of the same period generally carried two 4.5in mountings and a twin 20mm amidships. The following Fairmile Ds were so fitted: FPB

## The 4.5in 8cwt QF Mark I gun (1949) data

| | |
|---|---|
| **Muzzle velocity** | 1500ft per second |
| **Maximum range** | 3000 yards |
| **Limits of elevation** | 12° to –10° |
| **Weight with breech mechanism** | 8cwt 0qr 0lb |
| **Weight without breech mechanism** | 7cwt 1qr 0lb |
| **Total length** | 89.06in |
| **Calibre** | 4.45in |
| **Length of bore** | 84in |
| **Capacity (total effective, including rifling grooves)** | 1167.75cu in |
| **Chamber** | |
|   **Capacity (total effective)** | 137.5cu in |
|   **Driving band design no** | NOD 6965/1 |
|   **Length to base of projectile** | 8.82in |
|   **Ramming** | 13.88in |
|   **Travel of projectile** | 75.18in |
| **Rifling system** | Polygroove plain section |
|   **Length** | 73.489in |
|   **Twist (uniform)** | 1 turn in 25 calibres, right-hand |
|   **Grooves (32)** | .036in depth; .291in width |
| **Position of centre of gravity from face of breech** | |
|   **Without breech mechanism, unloaded** | 33.87in |
|   **with breech mechanism, unloaded** | 30.85in |
| **Striker blow** | 25lb minimum |
| **Recoil** | |
|   **Metal to metal** | 31in |
|   **Working** | 29 to 30in |
|   **Capacity of recoil system** | 3 pints approx. |
| **Total weight of gun and cradle** | 11cwt |
| **The Mark I (power) mounting (1949)** | |
|   **Weight of turret without gun and cradle** | 1 ton 3cwt 3qr |
|   **Radial sweep of gun muzzle** | 5ft ⅝in |
|   **Radial sweep of loader's platform** | 5ft 2in |
|   **Speed of training** | 25° to 30° per second |
|   **Oil used in system** | DTD 44D (anti-freezing) |
|   **Quantity of oil in system** | 10 gallons |
|   **Working pressure** | 300lb per square inch |
|   **Stresses on firing limits in elevation and depression** | |
|     **Gun at 12° elevation** | 1.94 tons (downward blow) |
|     **Gun at 10° depression** | 1.14 tons (upward lift) |
| **Ammunition** | |
|   **Weight of assembled round** | 22lb |
|   **Length of assembled round** | 19in |

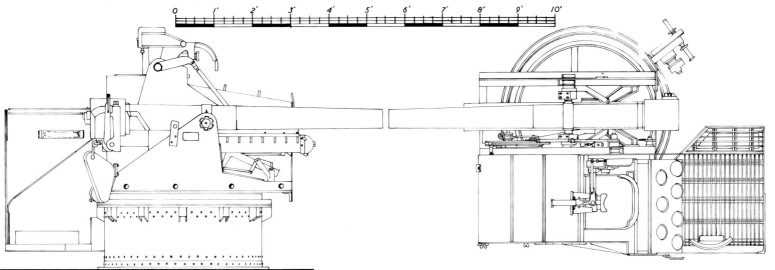

5001 (ex MTB 780), 5002, 5003 (ex MTB 790), 5007, 5008, 5009, 5015, 5020, 5031 (ex MTB 758), 5032 (ex MTB 779), 5033 (ex MTB 785), 5035 (ex MTB 793) and 5036 (ex MTB 794). A few others carried the 40mm Bofors Mark III when modified as control boats. Thus, by 1949 the heavier weapon had become the main gun of British Coastal Forces – no 6-pounders appear to have been carried after this date.

The 4.5 Mark I (power) mounting continued in service with the Gay class of 1953–4, and the subsequent Dark class of 1955–7, when these boats were fitted as gunboats, but the weapon faded from the service when the two operational squadrons of Dark boats paid off in 1957.

The only other craft known to have been fitted with the Mark II manual mounting were *Bold Pathfinder* and *Bold Pioneer*. These two experimental long boats carried two – one forward and one aft, with a single 40mm Bofors Mark VII mounting amidships. The last sighting of this gun seems to be the single Mark II mounting carried forward aboard *Bold Pathfinder* in 1961, when she was senior officer's boat of the Trials Squadron.

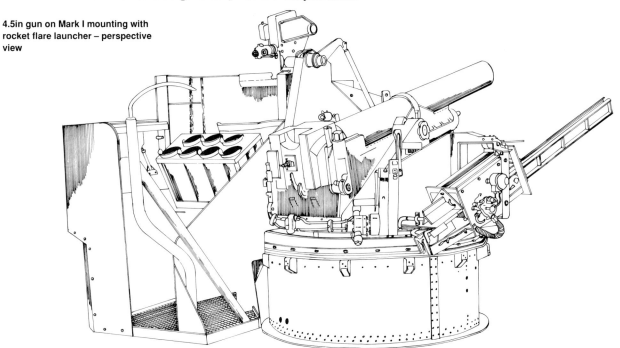

**4.5in gun on Mark I mounting with rocket flare launcher – perspective view**

**4.5in gun on Mark I mounting with rocket flare launcher – detail**

1  4.5in 8cwt Mark I gun
2  Lifting eye
3  Safety firing gear
4  Armoured shield
5  Sight link
6  Foresight
7  Sight binoculars
8  Deflection box
9  Speed setting knob
10  Range setting handle
11  Flexible drive from training rack
12  Control handles
13  Spray shield
14  Firing cylinder and piston
15  Gunlayer's seat
16  Ready use ammunition rack
17  Loader's backrest
18  Loader's folding seat
19  Elevating cylinder
20  Rotating service joint
21  Seat adjustment handle
22  Training motor
23  Training gear box
24  Safety cam rail
25  Training rack
26  Training rack pinion
27  Piston changeover valves
28  Base ring
29  Gun recoil mechanism
30  RSJ fixed support
31  2in flare projector
32  Manual drive unit
33  Oil pump
34  Gun trunnion
35  Sight trunnion
36  Loader's platform
37  Quick release belt
38  Spray shield hinge
39  Gunlayer's footrest
40  Gun firing cylinder and piston
41  Pressure relief valve
42  Flexible drive to deflection box

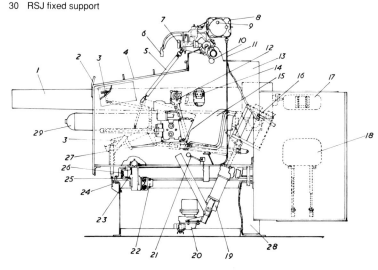

**Details of 2in rocket flare launcher**

**4.5in Mark I operating mechanism**

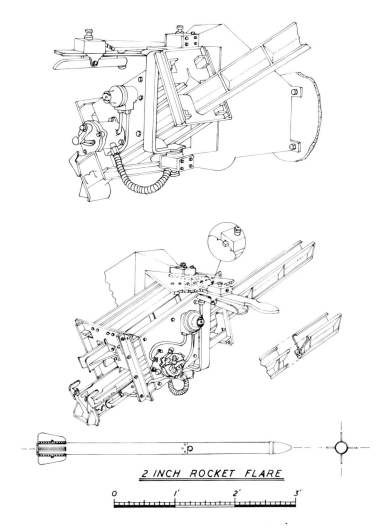

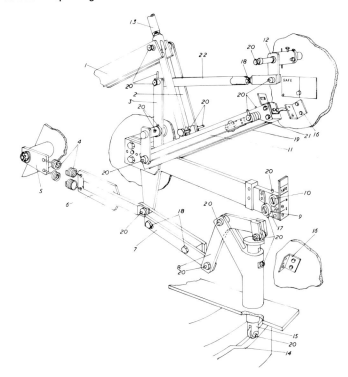

2 INCH ROCKET FLARE

| 1 | Sight drive lever | 12 | Control operating lever |
|---|---|---|---|
| 2 | Gun lever link | 13 | Sight operating link |
| 3 | Trip striker lever | 14 | Cam rail |
| 4 | Tension springs | 15 | Plunger |
| 5 | Rear spring plate | 16 | Index plate |
| 6 | Front spring plate | 17 | Cam lever |
| 7 | Adjustable plunger link | 18 | Adjustment |
| 8 | Plunger bell crank | 19 | Gun lever |
| 9 | Trip roller safe | 20 | Grease nipple |
| 10 | Trip roller fire | 21 | Trip striker |
| 11 | Trip striker link | 22 | Trip connecting link |

**4.5in Mark I gun – details**

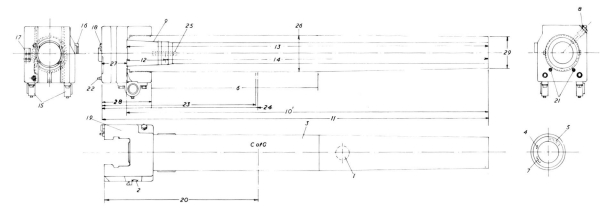

| 1 | 3in badge |
|---|---|
| 2 | Pin stop spring case |
| 3 | Barrel FL 12767 |
| 4 | No of forging |
| 5 | Mark of rifling |
| 6 | 35.97in parallel |
| 7 | Name of maker of steel |
| 8 | Screw, securing breech ring |
| 9 | Taper .03in per inch on diameter |
| 10 | Total length of barrel 84.0in |
| 11 | Total length of gun 89.06in |

| 12 | Length of chamber 8.82in |
|---|---|
| 13 | Length of bore 84.0in |
| 14 | Length of travel 75.18in |
| 15 | Actuating shaft bearing with bush tecalemit nipple and two securing bolts, each with locking plate |
| 16 | Breech mechanism lever stop plate with two securing screws |
| 17 | Firing lever retaining plate with four securing screws |
| 18 | Firing lever return plunger stop stud |

| | with check screw |
|---|---|
| 19 | Breech ring assembly FL 394A |
| 20 | Estimated centre of gravity without breech mechanism and unloaded, 33.87in |
| 21 | Plug extractor spring pocket |
| 22 | Firing lever axis stud with check screw |
| 23 | Estimated centre of gravity with breech mechanism and loaded, 30.5in |

| 24 | Estimated centre of gravity with breech mechanism but unloaded, 30.85in |
|---|---|
| 25 | Barrel key with two securing screws |
| 26 | 7.5in dia |
| 27 | 5.06in |
| 28 | 10.75in |
| 29 | 6.5in dia |

### 4.5in Mark I control mechanism

1. Control operating lever
2. Control pawl 'safe'
3. Control trip
4. Screw bolt for case
5. Control differential lever
6. Trigger return spring
7. Control pawl 'fire'
8. Control trip shaft
9. Control lever
10. Trigger cable
11. Grease nipple
12. Eccentric stop
13. Lower adjuster
14. Firing control valve
15. Upper adjuster
16. Pinjoint
17. Stop
18. Control spring

### 4.5in Mark I firing control valve

1. Constant exhaust
2. Safe side of gunfire piston
3. Constant pressure
4. Fire side of gunfire piston
5. To firing piston (alternate pressure and exhaust)

### 4.5in Mark I mounting – details of mechanism

1. Gun driving bracket
2. Elevating piston
3. Elevating cylinder
4. Elevating piston rod
5. Seal rings
6. Eye end
7. Pressure to depress
8. Exhaust from elevate
9. Pressure to elevate
10. Exhaust from depress
11. Ball valve
12. Annular recess
13. Control chamber
14. Dowel pin
15. Washer
16. Locknut
17. Top cap
18. Grease nipple
19. Seal gland
20. Locking wire
21. Seal washer
22. Locking ring

SAFETY FIRING GEAR.
[WITH SIGHT LEVER & SIGH OPERATING LINK ETC.]

GUN DRIVING BRACKET AND ELEVATING CYLINDER PIVOT.

FIRING GEAR.

OWN SPEED DEFLECTION SIGHT.

THE ELEVATING CYLINDER

SECTION X X

TRAINING MOTOR.

FIRING GEAR.

RIGHT HAND TRUNNION.

UNIVERSAL CONTROL VALVE BOX.

RECOIL CYLINDER & BREECH BLOCK.

CHANGE OVER VALVE UNIT.

## 4.5in Mark I details of sight

1 Binocular sight clamp
2 Clamp bracket
3 Locknut
4 Binocular clamp
5 Foresight
6 Clamping screw
7 Range selector body
8 Binoculars
9 Binocular spring
10 Backsight bead
11 Connection bar to cradle
12 Adjusting screw
13 Range setting handle
14 Sight trunnion
15 Sight bracket
16 Selector plate
17 Adjusting nut
18 Flexible drive from training gear box
19 Deflection box bracket
20 Deflection control rod extension
21 Slider guide
22 Deflection box
23 Deflection slider
24 Speed setting clamp
25 Needle roller
26 Speed setting scale
27 Bearing disc
28 Retaining ring
29 Horizontal adjustment locknut
30 Deflection lever
31 Enots lubricator
32 Tecalemit lubricator
33 Deflection pivot
34 Sight arm
35 Sight carrier
36 Pivot

37 Rubber eyepiece
38 Clamp ring
39 Tee bolt
40 Deflection lever pivot
41 Left hand thread
42 Spring
43 Trunnion
44 Right hand thread
45 Adjusting knob
46 Clip
47 Range setting selector plate
48 Range setting guide bracket
49 Vertical adjustment
50 Selector plate bolt
51 Setting index
52 Plunger
53 Plunger housing
54 Range cam
55 Cam housing
56 Movement of vessel
57 Training rack

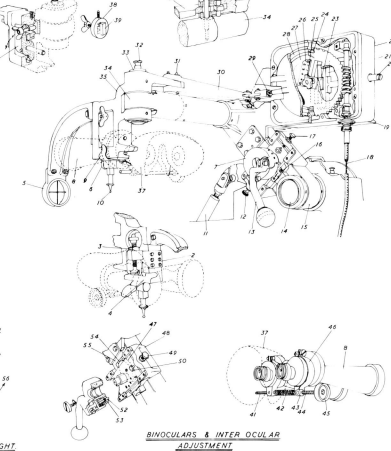

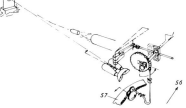

*DIAGRAM
SHOWING PRINCIPLE OF
OWN SPEED DEFLECTION SIGHT.*

*BINOCULARS & INTER OCULAR
ADJUSTMENT*

## 4.5in Mark I mounting pressure system diagram

1 Pressure
2 Exhaust
3 Firing control valve
4 Firing piston (to fire)
5 Firing push rod
6 Training gear box
7 Training motor
8 Training rack
9 Fixed structure
10 Relief valve
11 Elevating piston
12 Pressure and exhaust (alternating)
13 Trigger cable
14 Rotating service joint
15 Moving portion
16 Fixed portion
17 Gun bracket
18 Elevating control valve (to elevate)
19 Training control valve (to train left)
20 Change-over valves
21 Relief valve
22 Master valve (open)
23 Control column
24 Rotating arm
25 Bell crank lever
26 Firing control valve pressure and exhaust (constant)
27 Master valve lever
28 To manual power unit

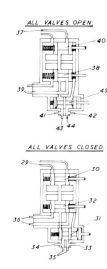

*ALL VALVES OPEN.*

*CLOSED* *OPEN*

*ALL VALVES CLOSED*

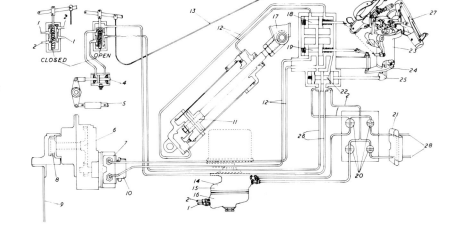

29 To elevating cylinder (liquid locked)
30 Elevation control valve neutral (valve closed)
31 Master valve closed
32 Training control valve neutral (valve closed)
33 Circulatory pressure to changeover valves

34 Circulatory pressure from changeover valves
35 Equalised circulatory pressure to firing valve
36 To training motor (liquid locked)
37 To elevating cylinder (pressure to depress)
38 Training control valve (to train right)

39 To training motor (pressure to train right)
40 Elevation control valve to depress
41 Pressure from changeover valves
42 Exhaust to changeover valves
43 Pressure to firing valve
44 Exhaust from firing valve
45 Master valve (open)

**4.5in Mark I recoil and runout mechanism**

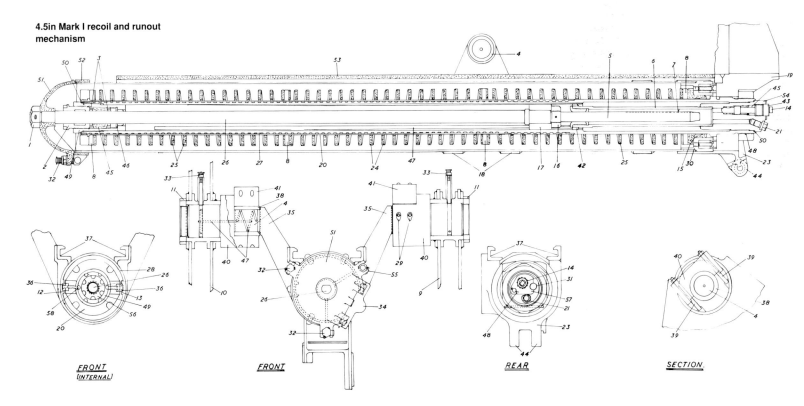

FRONT
[INTERNAL]

FRONT

REAR

SECTION.

| | | | |
|---|---|---|---|
| 1 | Piston rod nut | 16 | Recoil piston head locking nut |
| 2 | Stuffing box gland nut | 17 | Recoil piston head |
| 3 | Packing support collars | 18 | Trunion bands |
| 4 | Cradle trunnion | 19 | Gun slipper |
| 5 | Control rod | 20 | Run out spring compressor |
| 6 | Control chamber cylinder | 21 | Filling hole plug |
| 7 | Tapered flat | 22 | Gun securing nut |
| 8 | Separating disc | 23 | Transom bracket |
| 9 | Right hand trunion structure | 24 | Right hand spring |
| 10 | Left hand trunnion structure | 25 | Left hand spring |
| 11 | Trunion block locknut | 26 | Recoil piston rod |
| 12 | Right hand compressor guide | 27 | Recoil cylinder |
| 13 | Left hand compressor guide | 28 | Case |
| 14 | Run out adjusting valve | 29 | Stud(s) |
| 15 | Recoil cylinder bearing bush | 30 | Steel ring |
| 31 | Air plug | 46 | Leather |
| 32 | Hinge bolt | 47 | Groove |
| 33 | Lubricator | 48 | Keep pin |
| 34 | Inspection cover | 49 | Stuffing box |
| 35 | Trunnion arms | 50 | Copper washer |
| 36 | Guide key | 51 | Front cap |
| 37 | Slipper guides | 52 | Front band |
| 38 | Trunnion bush | 53 | Cradle |
| 39 | Stud(s) | 54 | Rear plug |
| 40 | Trunnion block | 55 | Securing lug |
| 41 | Trunnion cap | 56 | Stuffing box gland |
| 42 | Throttling bush | 57 | Valve locking plate |
| 43 | Gland nut | 58 | Stuffing box key |
| 44 | Lug(s) | | |
| 45 | Packing | | |

**4.5in gun on Mark II (manual) mounting – simplified layout**

**4.5in Mark II mounting – right hand elevation**

| | |
|---|---|
| 1 | Optical sight assembly right hand |
| 2 | Chain guard |
| 3 | Latch support frame |
| 4 | Support angle (top) |
| 5 | Support angle (bottom) |
| 6 | Rotation gear box |
| 7 | Braced foot stirrup |
| 8 | Rope catch net |
| 9 | Cable guard |

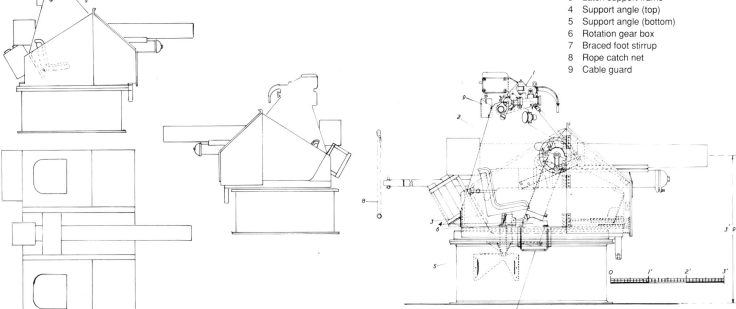

4.5in gun on Mark II (manual) mounting
– perspective views

# Minelaying equipment in Coastal Forces craft

As noted above, many MTBs, MGBs and MLs were capable of carrying and laying mines as an alternative armament. They were transported either in chutes for influence types or on short lengths of mine rail if of the contact type with a sinker. In both cases the mine was carried close to the ship's side and was released overboard.

To carry the additional weight involved, the hull had to be suitably stiffened. The chutes or rails were bolted to steel strips which rested on hardwood chocks, secured in place by bolts passing through the chocks, deck and stiffening. Two jigs and templates were used when drilling the holes in the chutes and rails respectively. This ensured that the rails were interchangeable with rails, and chutes with chutes, and that they could be fitted in any position on any ship. The steel strips were tapped to take ⅝in bolts. If the minelaying equipment was not required for an operation it could be landed, leaving the wooden blocks and steel strips bolted in place, and the rails and chutes could be stored. In preparation for a minesweeping sortie the chutes could be replaced in under 24 hours.

Mine chutes and rails were positioned relative to the hull rubbing strake, so that mines and fittings would not be damaged when coming alongside and to ensure that the mines would clear the ship's side when released and dropped.

The GA drawing of the D type shows alternative arrangements for both spherical mines and their sinkers and chutes for influence mines, while the deck layouts for the A and B type Fairmiles are shown in their relevant sections.

*Mark XVII moored mines aboard ML 493.*
Author's collection

The mine chutes were very similar to depth charge chutes, the mine being held in place by a wire and chain sling, secured by a tumbler hook. On release, the mine simply rolled out of the chute and over the ship's side. The chutes were supplied to Coastal Forces bases, and not allocated to any particular unit. The Mark II chute was designed to take mines up to 20½in diameter and, in the Mark II Mod 1, up to 24in diameter. Chain links were provided in the securing strops to enable smaller-diameter mines to be carried, depending upon the type of mine used on the minelaying operation.

The strops comprised a triangular link and two lengths of 1½in steel wire rope, with a heart-shaped thimble in each end. The wire legs were 3ft long and each was tailed with fourteen links of ⅝in chain, or nineteen links in the case of the Mark II Mod 1. The mine was secured in the chute by attaching the chain links under the securing bar, over the mine from outboard and securing the triangular link to the tumbler. The safety pin locking the tumbler release was removed and used as a handle for operating the tumbler to release the mine. The adjusting screws were fitted with locking nuts, and each sling was tested to one ton for safety.

Mine rails Mark I* were used for spherical mines with sinkers. They were bolted to the steel deck strips by ⅝in bolts. A hinged gap was fitted for use when loading the mines on to the rails. The mines were secured by stays, which were attached to two brackets situated one on each side of the rails and set up by bottlescrews. The rails were mounted as a unit complete with the mine trap Mark II, and the trap itself was simple to operate. A lever, moving in a horizontal plane, withdrew two trap toes and two spring-loaded check pawls, which protruded through the side plates of the rails. The toes prevented the mine from moving outboard until they were withdrawn, while the spring-loaded pawls prevented any inboard movement. The pawls could easily be depressed by the mine sinker as it moved inboard as, for example, when it was being loaded on to the rails by dockside crane.

The drawings show three influence mines and two moored contact types, as follows:

An A Mark I to IV, which was a ground influence mine laid either by RAF aircraft (by parachute) or by Coastal Forces. It had a magnetic induction, acoustic or magnetic-acoustic firing mechanism. It had a length of 13ft 8in overall, a diameter of 17.7in, and had a charge of 750lb Amatol or 775lb Minol.

A Mark XIX, which was a moored mine on a sinker. This was a contact switch horn mine of 31in diameter, which was laid by surface craft. It contained a 100lb charge of TNT, or, later, Amatol.

A larger Mark XX contact mine on a sinker, again contact switch horn armed and laid by surface craft, with a diameter of 40in and a length of 52in. This type contained a charge of 320lb or 500lb of TNT or Amatol. On occasion it was fitted with a lower antenna to give a greater radius of 'feel'.

An M Mark II, which was a ground influence mine laid by submarines, through the torpedo tubes (two per tube), or by surface craft. It had magnetic induction or acoustic firing, a length of 8ft and a diameter of 21in.

An A Mark III mine, which was another ground influence mine similar to the Mark I.

*Minelaying in the Mediterranean: ML 493's load of Mark XVII mines ready for dropping with their sinkers. Note the twin .303in Vickers GO guns in the foreground.* Author's collection

**Arrangement of mine and depth charge chutes on Vosper 70ft MTBs**

ARRANGEMENT OF MINE CHUTE     ARRANGEMENT OF D.C. CHUTE.     ARRANGEMENT OF PORTABLE MINE CHOCKS

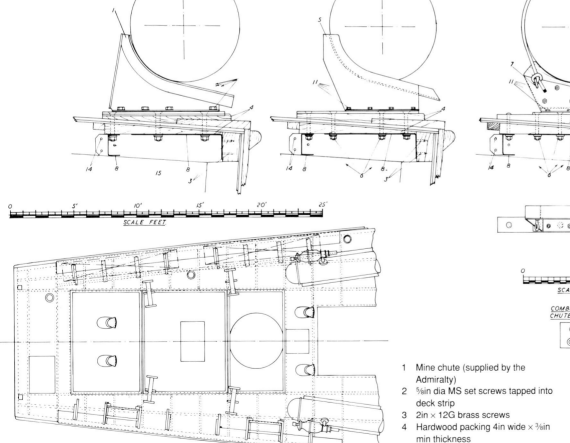

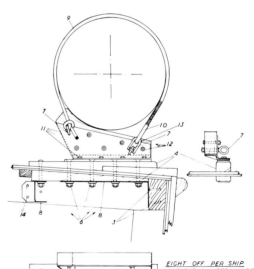

SCALE FEET.

EIGHT OFF PER SHIP
RIGHT & LEFT HANDED

SCALE INCHES

COMBINED DECK STRIP TO TAKE MINE & D.C.
CHUTE. 4 PAIRS OFF PER SHIP-HANDED-M.S

1 Mine chute (supplied by the Admiralty)
2 ⅝in dia MS set screws tapped into deck strip
3 2in × 12G brass screws
4 Hardwood packing 4in wide × ⅜in min thickness
5 Depth charge chute (supplied by the Admiralty)
6 ½in dia CSK MS bolts with nuts, washers and grommets
7 ½in dia eyebolt
8 ⅛in MS washer palte
9 1½in circular manila strop
10 Thimble
11 ⅜in dia MS set screws
12 ⅜in dia galvanised MS bolts
13 ⅜in dia shackle
14 ⁵⁄₁₆in dia bolts
15 ⅝in dia CSK MS bolts

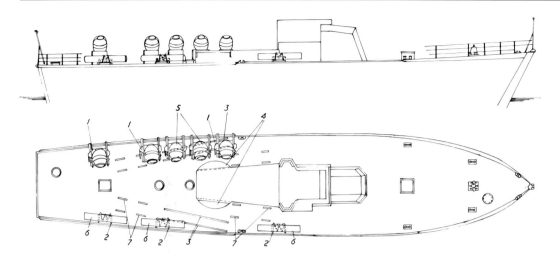

**Layout of Fairmile Ds fitted for minelaying**

1 Mine rail Mark I* with mine trap Mark II
2 Mine chute Mark II with hand release
3 18in torpedo tube tapping strips and deck pads
4 Gun platform hinged for 18in from outer edge to enable mines to be embarked
5 Moored mine unit
6 A mines
7 Torpedo loading chocks

**Mine chute Mark II**

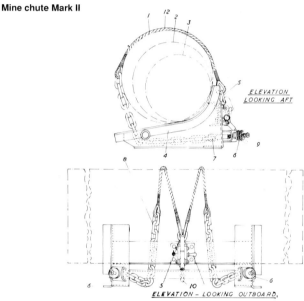

*A message chalked on a Mark XVII mine aboard ML 493.* Author's collection

1 20½in diameter mine
2 18in diameter mine
3 15¾in diameter mine
4 Chute frame
5 Triangular link
6 Adjusting screw and nuts

7 Chain links for adjusting pendant
8 'B' 14 links secured to thimble of pendant
9 'F' safety pin locking release
10 Safety pin 'F' used for released mine
11 Mark I mine chute release
12 Wire pendant with end links

**Mine rails Mark I***

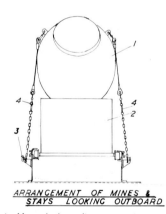 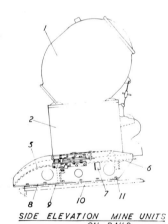

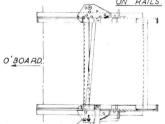

1 Moored mine unit
2 Sinker
3 Position of operating lever
4 Standard mine stay
5 Mine rail Mark I*
6 5° slope
7 Bracket for mine stay
8 Metal strip
9 Wood packing
10 Deck
11 ⅝in dia Whitworth bolts
12 Hinged gap in open position for loading rails
13 Mine trap Mark II

**Mine trap Mark II**

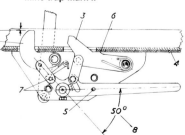

1 ³⁄₁₆in max
2 Trap toe
3 Check pawl
4 Side plate
5 Safety pin
6 Side plate to form stop for check pawl
7 Stop bolt eased to give toggle ⅛in past dead centre
8 50° movement of lever to release mine unit

**General arrangements of mines, rails
and chutes**

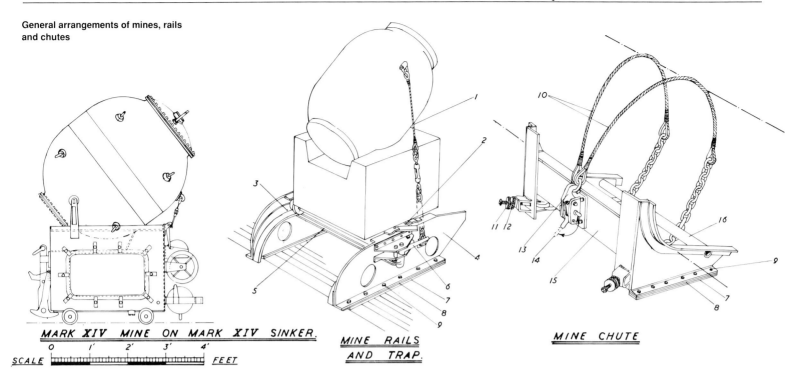

MARK XIV MINE ON MARK XIV SINKER.

SCALE | 0   1'   2'   3'   4' | FEET

MINE RAILS
AND TRAP.

MINE CHUTE

1  Standard mine stay
2  Gap opened for loading mine
3  Mine rail (Mark I)
4  Mine rail (Mark II)
5  Transfer rod
6  Release lever
7  Wood packing
8  Metal strip
9  ⅝in Whitworth bolts
10 Strops
11 Locking nut
12 Strop tensioning nut
13 Mine chute release
14 Safety pin used in this position to
   release mine
15 Mine chute (Mark II)
16 Securing bar

A - MINE "A" MARK I - IV.

**Mines laid by British Coastal Forces**

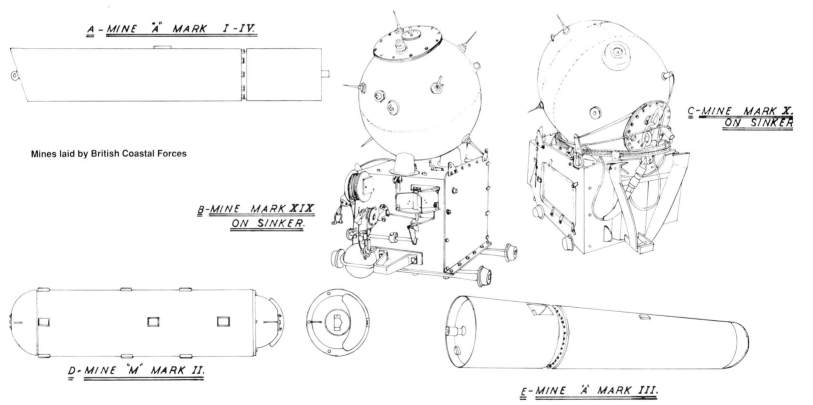

B - MINE MARK XIX
ON SINKER.

C - MINE MARK X.
ON SINKER

D - MINE "M" MARK II.

E - MINE "A" MARK III.

A  Ground influence mine laid by
   surface craft or aircraft by
   parachute – magnetic induction,
   acoustic or magnetic-acoustic
   firing; dia 17.7in, length 13ft 8in
   oa, charge 750lb amatol or 775lb
   minol

B  Moored contact switch horn mine,
   laid by surface craft; dia 31in,
   charge 100lb TNT or amatol

C  Moored contact switch horn mine,
   laid by surface craft; dia 40in,
   length 52in, charge 320lb or 500lb
   TNT or amatol

D  Ground influence mine laid by
   submarine or surface craft –
   magnetic induction or acoustic
   firing; dia 21in, length 8ft

E  Perspective view of A

# The US 3in/23 and 3in/50 guns

As designed, the SC 497 class boats mounted a 3in/23.5 Mark 14 forward and two single .5in Mark 3s on a platform aft of the pilot-house. When the 3in/23 proved unsatisfactory, it was replaced by a 3in/50 Mark 22. To accommodate this larger weapon, a platform, parallel to the waterline and rising almost to the level of the trunk cabin, was built inside the spray shield. Similarly, the .5s gave way to two 20mm Mark 4s, which, in turn, were replaced by three of the lighter 20mm Mark 10 mounts, two on the midships platform and a third on a raised platform over the galley.

Owing to a shortage of 3in/50s and a lack of satisfaction with its installation, the Navy decided to fit a 40mm Mark 3 to SC 508 in October 1942. Due to its light weight, tracer capability, and higher rate of fire, the 40mm became the standard main armament of the SC soon after.

The 3in/23.5 Mark 14 was a modification of the earlier Mark 13 'boat gun' and was commonly referred to as the Poole gun, after its manufacturer, the Poole Engineering and Machine Company. Fitted with a horizontal sliding wedge breech, the Mark 14 fired a 13lb shell at a muzzle velocity of 1650ft per second. Elevation limits were -15 degrees to +65 degrees.

The 3in/50 Mark 22 was the Navy's standard medium calibre dual-purpose weapon during World War II. The basic mount comprised a radially-expanded barrel attached by a bayonet mount to a housing containing a vertical sliding-wedge breech mechanism, which, in turn, was mounted on an open pedestal. Manually operated, the Mark 22 fired fixed-case ammunition, which was available in AA, APT, HE, HET, and illuminating rounds. Elevation limits were -10 degrees to +85 degrees.

## US 3in/23 and 3in/50 gun data

**3in/23.5 Mark 14 Mod 0**
**Type** Dual purpose, single mount
**Gun** Mark 14
**Max powder pressure** 13 long tons per square inch
**Muzzle velocity** 1650ft per second
**Barrel weight** 593lb
**Total weight** 1510lb
**Oscillating weight** 960lb
**Recoiling weight** 600lb
**Brake load** 14,710lb
**Trunnion pressure** 14,750lb (horizontal), 15,340lb (65° elevation)
**Elevation limits** +65° to −15°
**Max altitude** 16,000ft at 65°
**Max range** 10,100 yards at 45°
**Ammunition**
  **Projectiles** AA, 12.9lb; common, 13.0lb; illuminating, 13.0lb.
  **Cartridge** Case, 2.2lb; charge, 1.3lb nominal.

**3in/50 Mark 22**
**Type** Dual purpose, single mount
**Max powder pressure** 17 long tons per square inch
**Muzzle velocity** 2700ft per second
**Barrel weight** 1240lb
**Total weight** 6700 to 7510lb
**Oscillating weight** 3180 to 3780lb
**Recoiling weight** 1850lb
**Brake load** 27,500lb
**Elevation limits** +85° to −15°
**Max altitude** 29,800ft at 85°
**Max range** 14,600 yards at 45°
**Fixed ammunition**
  **AA** Projectile, Mark 27, 13.05lb; cartridge case Mark 3, 7.88lb; charge, 4lb; primer, Mark 14.
  **Illuminating** Projectile, Mark 25, 13.07lb; cartridge case, Mark 7, 7.0lb; charge, 4lb.
  **Armour piercing** Projectile, Mark 29, 13.07lb; cartridge case, Mark 9, 6.54lb; charge, 4lb.

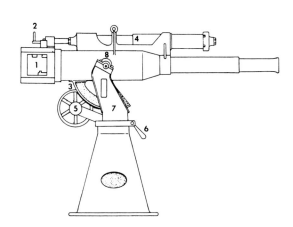

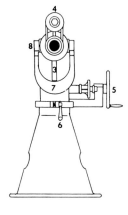

**US 3in/23.5 Mark 14 general arrangement**

1  Sliding breech
2  Breech operating mechanism
3  Elevating arc
4  Recoil cylinder
5  Elevating gear
6  Head lock
7  Stand
8  Trunnion

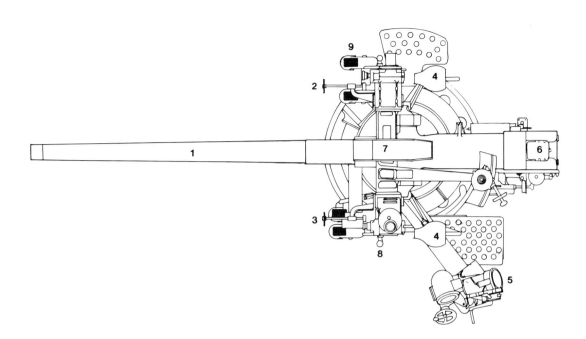

**3in/50 Mark 22 – plan view**

1  Barrel, Mark 21
2  Trainer's telescope
3  Layer's telescope
4  Seat
5  Fuse setting machine
6  Breech
7  Sight mechanism
8  Layer's handwheel
9  Firing pedal

**3in/50 Mark 22 – side elevation**

1  Barrel
2  Layer's sight
3  Recoil cylinder
4  Pointer's handwheel
5  Gear train
6  Fuse setting machine
7  Base ring
8  Breech
9  Stand, Mark 10

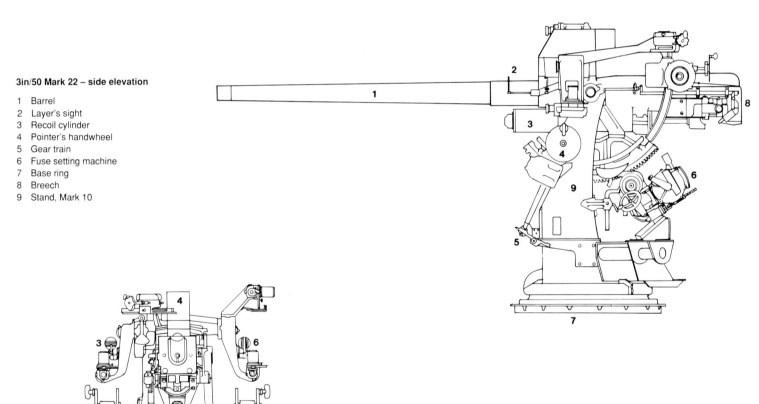

**3in/50 Mark 22 – rear view**

1  Fuse setting machine
2  Layer's handwheel
3  Layer's sight
4  Sight mechanism, Mark 16
5  Elevating arc
6  Trainer's sight
7  Trainer's handwheel
8  Firing pedals
9  Base ring
10  Stand

# The US 20mm Oerlikon

Two different marks of 20mm were fitted to the SCs: Mark 4 and Mark 10. The Mark 4 mount featured a cast pedestal and a variable height trunnion bracket. The pedestal was bolted to the deck, but the pedestal head, through which the column rose, rotated about the top of the pedestal and could be locked in any position by a clamping lever. The column could be raised about 15in by a hand-wheel mounted on the head. Mounted on top of the column were the trunnion bracket and pivot, which also provided support for the shield, cradle spiral spring, and cradle, to which the gun was bolted. The cradle spring, mounted around the left trunnion, had one end attached to the trunnion and the other to the spring case, thus acting as a counterbalance to the weight of the gun.

The Mark 10 was a much simpler and lighter mount than the Mark 4, which it replaced. In place of the cast column and variable height trunnion was a simple tripod welded to an open base ring. The trunnion bracket and pivot was mounted directly on top of the tripod. The remainder of the mount was identical to the Mark 4.

The gun was a 20mm 70 calibre weapon consisting of four main parts:

    barrel and breech casing
    breechblock
    recoil and counter-recoil system
    trigger mechanism and locking device

## US 20mm Oerlikon data

| | |
|---|---|
| **Type** | Single mount, manual |
| **Barrel weight** | 150lb |
| **Elevation limits** | +90° to −15° |
| **Cyclic** | 450rpm |
| **Muzzle velocity** | 2740ft per second |
| **Max altitude** | 10,000ft at 90° |
| **Max range** | 4800 yards at 35° |
| **Ammunition** | |
| **HE** | Projectile, .0271lb; case, .190lb; charge, 27.7 grams. |
| **APT** | Projectile, .0268lb; case, .180lb; charge, 27.7 grams. |

Designed for automatic firing only, the gun used some of the force developed by the explosion of the propellant to eject the empty cartridge, cock, reload, and fire the next round.

The 20mm fired fixed ammunition from a 60-round magazine at a cyclic rate of about 450rpm. In practice, an experienced crew could maintain a rate of about 300rpm. Usually, every other round or every third round in the spring-loaded magazine was a tracer.

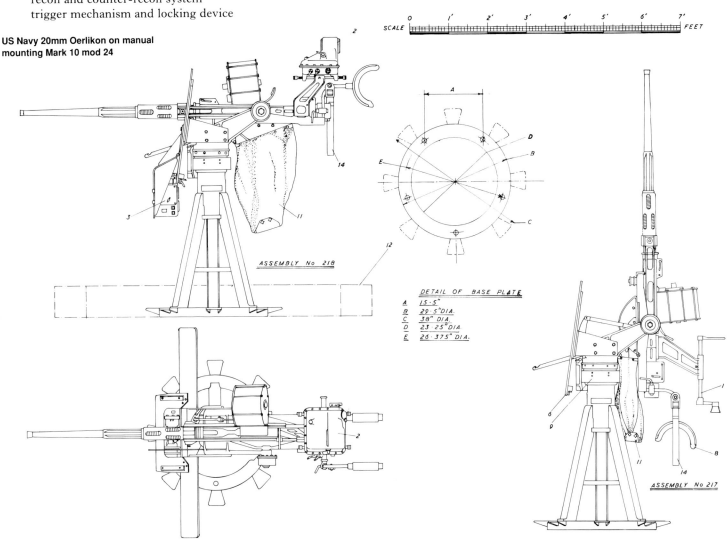

US Navy 20mm Oerlikon on manual mounting Mark 10 mod 24

ASSEMBLY No 218

DETAIL OF BASE PLATE

| | |
|---|---|
| A | 15.5" |
| B | 29.5" DIA. |
| C | 38" DIA. |
| D | 23.25" DIA. |
| E | 26.375" DIA. |

SCALE (0 to 7' FEET)

ASSEMBLY No 217

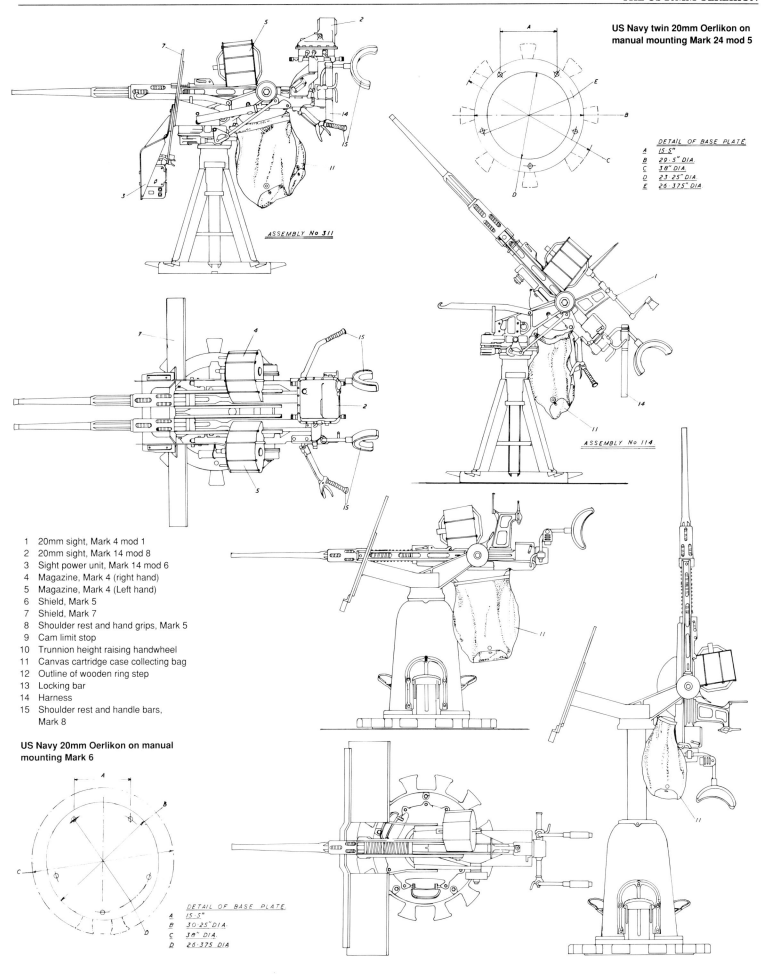

**US Navy twin 20mm Oerlikon on manual mounting Mark 24 mod 5**

ASSEMBLY No 311

ASSEMBLY No 114

DETAIL OF BASE PLATE
| | |
|---|---|
| A | 15·5" |
| B | 29·5" DIA. |
| C | 38" DIA. |
| D | 23·25" DIA. |
| E | 26·375 DIA. |

1  20mm sight, Mark 4 mod 1
2  20mm sight, Mark 14 mod 8
3  Sight power unit, Mark 14 mod 6
4  Magazine, Mark 4 (right hand)
5  Magazine, Mark 4 (Left hand)
6  Shield, Mark 5
7  Shield, Mark 7
8  Shoulder rest and hand grips, Mark 5
9  Cam limit stop
10  Trunnion height raising handwheel
11  Canvas cartridge case collecting bag
12  Outline of wooden ring step
13  Locking bar
14  Harness
15  Shoulder rest and handle bars,
    Mark 8

**US Navy 20mm Oerlikon on manual mounting Mark 6**

DETAIL OF BASE PLATE
| | |
|---|---|
| A | 15·5" |
| B | 30·25" DIA. |
| C | 38" DIA. |
| D | 26·375 DIA |

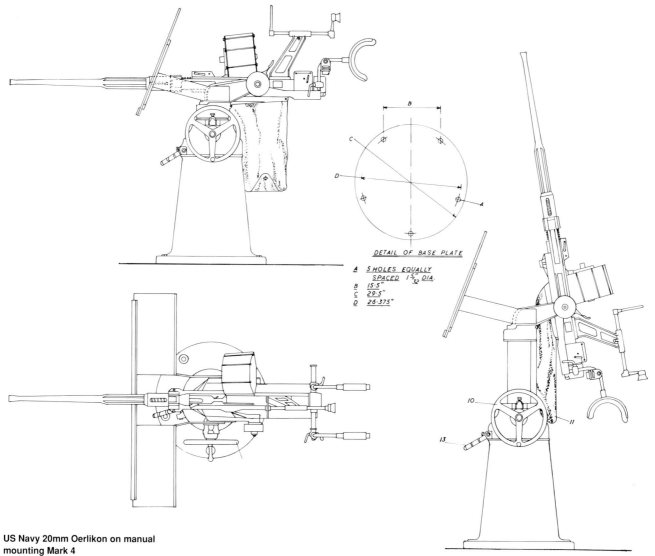

DETAIL OF BASE PLATE

A  5 HOLES EQUALLY
   SPACED 1 5/32" DIA.
B  15·5"
C  29·5"
D  26·375"

**US Navy 20mm Oerlikon on manual mounting Mark 4**

1  20mm sight, Mark 4 mod 1
2  20mm sight, Mark 14 mod 8
3  Sight power unit, Mark 14 mod 6
4  Magazine, Mark 4 (right hand)
5  Magazine, Mark 4 (Left hand)
6  Shield, Mark 5
7  Shield, Mark 7
8  Shoulder rest and hand grips, Mark 5
9  Cam limit stop
10  Trunnion height raising handwheel
11  Canvas cartridge case collecting bag
12  Outline of wooden ring step
13  Locking bar
14  Harness
15  Shoulder rest and handle bars,
    Mark 8

*A 40mm Bofors on a Mark III mounting aboard ML
173, fitted for minesweeping in the Mediterranean in
1945.* Author's collection

# The US 40mm Bofors Mark 3 gun

The 40mm Mark 3 was a naval version of the standard US Army M1 anti-aircraft weapon. The basic gun comprised the barrel, breech casing, and breech ring assemblies, breech operating mechanism, a portion of the firing mechanism, automatic loader assembly, automatic loading tray assembly, and recoil mechanism. The gun was supported by trunnions mounted on the sides of the breech casing, on the underside of which was mounted the elevating arc.

The mount comprised the top carriage, platform assembly, elevating mechanism, equilibrators, traversing mechanism, firing mechanism, and roller bearing, which bolted directly to the 3in/50 mounting points. Ring sights were provided for both the trainer and layer, who traversed and elevated the weapon manually.

The Mark 3 could be fired in either automatic or semi-automatic mode, the layer depressing a firing pedal with his right foot. Ammunition was available in HET and APT rounds, loaded in four-round clips.

**US 40mm Bofors Mark 3 data**

| | |
|---|---|
| **Type** | Single mount, manual |
| **Barrel weight** | 296lb |
| **Total weight** | 2440lb |
| **Oscillating weight** | 1042lb |
| **Recoiling weight** | 415lb |
| **Brake load** | 4800lb |
| **Elevation limits** | +90° to –6° |
| **Cyclic** | 160rpm |
| **Muzzle velocity** | 2890ft per second |
| **Max altitude** | 22,800ft at 90° |
| **Max range** | 11,000 yards at 42° |
| **Ammunition** | AA, AP, T – projectile, 1.98lb; case, 1.89lb; charge, 315 grams. |

1 Flash protector
2 Barrel
3 Recuperator spring cover
4 Recoil cylinder
5 Equilibriator
6 Foot rest
7 Firing pedal
8 Shell ejection chute
9 Elevater's sight
10 Side cover
11 Elevating gear
12 Carriage
13 Firing lever
14 Hand operating lever
15 Elevating arc
16 Safety lever
17 Shell guide
18 Rear chute
19 Ejected shell guide
20 Chute support
21 Training gear
22 Trainer's sight
23 Loader's platform
24 Base ring

**US Navy 40mm Bofors gun Mark 3**

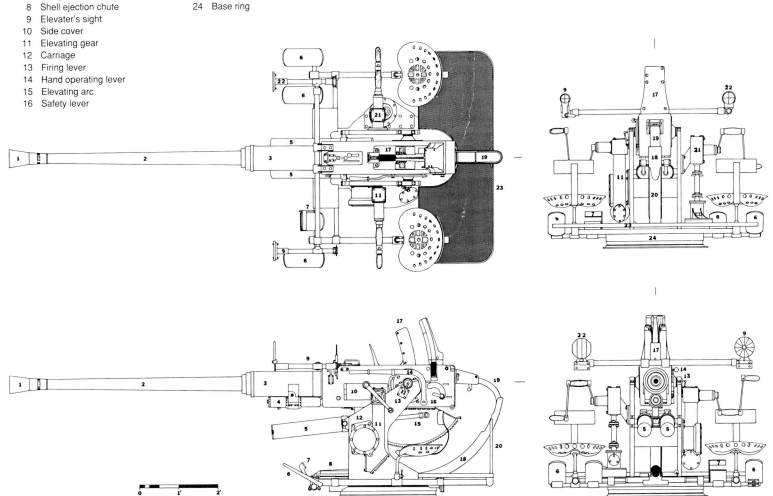

# US Navy anti-submarine equipment

The Mark 3 depth charge consisted of a sheet-steel cylinder approximately 28in long and 18in in diameter, a central tube containing a pistol, booster extender and booster, and 300lb of cast TNT. The pistol was adjustable and had indexed depth settings stamped on the face of the carrying flange. Sink rates varied between 6ft and 9ft per second and the effective range of relative damage varied between 30ft (fatal damage) and 90ft (moderate to slight damage).

The Mark 6 projector (K gun) consisted of a cast spherical expansion chamber with a 24in by 6in smooth bore tube set at a 45-degree angle. Set perpendicular to this tube was a casting housing the breech mechanism. The breech plug was an interrupted-screw type, housing a firing mechanism which provided for local percussion firing by lanyard. The entire unit was fixed, no provision being made for training or elevation. Variations in range were obtained by altering the weight of the impulse charge. Three standard weights of black powder charges were used to obtain ranges of 50, 75, and 120 yards.

In operation, an expendable arbor (a tube with a steel tray) was fitted into each projector tube and a depth charge was chained to the arbor. Once the range had been determined and the appropriate impulse charge inserted in the breech, firing was accomplished by percussion ignition of the impulse charge in the breech, the resulting gasses forcing the arbor out of the tube.

The Mark 20 Mousetrap projector was designed as a simple launcher for the 7.2in ASW projectile. The launcher consisted of a series of rails bolted together with a one or two degree spread and hinged to a box frame which was bolted to the deck. Electrical connections were provided at the aft end of the box frame and partially covered the rails when they were in the lowered position. When the rails were raised for firing, the blast plate was flipped aft to protect the deck from the blast of the four 7.2in projectiles.

The 7.2in projectile contained 30lb of TNT and a contact detonator within a cylindrical warhead, to which was attached a tail section consisting of a steel tube, fins and an impulse charge. Average range was about 200 yards. Firing to impact with the surface of the water took about 9 seconds, and the sink rate was about 4.5 seconds per 100ft.

*The first of three pictures of a Mousetrap trials installation aboard a Canadian B type ML, showing the launching frame and blast shield.* Courtesy Al Ross II

*A view from the bridge, with four Hedgehog bombs loaded in position.* Courtesy Al Ross II

**Type C depth charge rack**

1  Cable release
2  Cable
3  Cable tension adjustment
4  Track extension
5  Pulley for cable

This was the standard single depth charge roll-off rack fitted to small craft. The track extension appears to be unique to the SCs, and was needed to ensure that the depth charge cleared the side of the hull. The extension was normally secured to the rack in a vertical position, a line running between the end of the extension and a padeye on the rack. In action, the line was released and the extension lowered to follow the slope of the rack's rails.

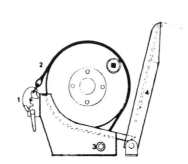

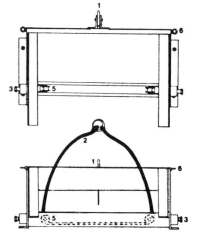

## US Mark 3 depth charge data

| | |
|---|---|
| **Length** | 27.626in |
| **Diameter** | 17.625in |
| **Weight** | 420lb |
| **Charge** | 300lb TNT |
| **Exploder** | Mark 6, 3.5 granular TNT |
| **Sink rate** | 6–9ft per second |
| **Effective radius of damage** | 30ft – fatal; 60ft – serious; 90ft – moderate to slight. |

### US Navy K gun – perspective view

1 Base
2 Expansion chamber
3 Tube
4 Breech mechanism
5 Percussion igniter
6 Arbor with tray

### Detail of depth charge arbor

1 Sleeve
2 Tray

### Mark 20 mousetrap

1 Projectile rail
2 Projectile stop
3 Hinged blast plate
4 Electrical connection for firing circuit
5 Hinged brace
6 Projectile brace
7 Base frame

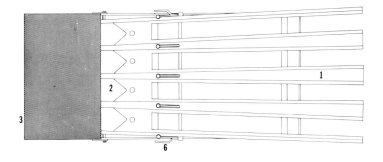

### 7.2in ASW projectile – exterior view

1 Impeller
2 Warhead
3 Tail tube
4 Fins

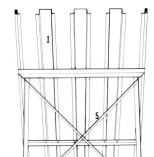

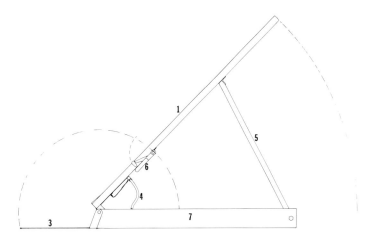

### 7.2in ASW projectile – internal view

1 Impeller cover
2 Impeller
3 Detonator
4 Charge
5 Propelling charge
6 Tail tube
7 Fins

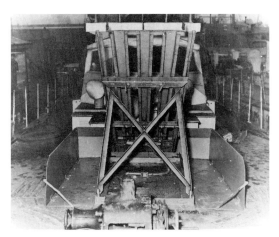

*Probably a different unit with the launching frame raised and a surrounding tray fitting.* Courtesy Al Ross II

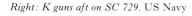

*Right: K guns aft on SC 729.* US Navy

233

# Disposition of motor launches 1939–45

Wooden motor launches were introduced during the first year of the war, and continued to be supplied in large numbers as the Fairmile company began mass production of the A and B types, followed by the Cs and Ds, as the war progressed. The 72ft Admiralty-designed motor launch joined the service in ever-increasing numbers from early 1941. These were re-classified as HDMLs (Harbour Defence Motor Launches) in early 1944. In 1948 those that survived in the RN were re-classified as SDMLs (Seaward Defence Motor Launches).

In 1945 seventy-six HDMLs became Fast Despatch Boats (FDBs) for operations in the Pacific, and nineteen became ASLs 1–19 (Air Safety Launches). They were just able to keep pace with the multitude of air operations in the Far Eastern theatre. They were used in this role until 1946, when they reverted to their former designation.

As noted above, twenty-six Fairmile Bs were also converted during building in 1945 to War Department Ambulance Launches and operated by the Royal Army Service Corps.

The most numerous types – the Fairmile B and the Admiralty designed HDML – both served worldwide, in every theatre of war. The larger A and C types were restricted to Home service. The multi-purpose D, however, as well as operating from the UK, also served with distinction in the Mediterranean and Aegean seas, and plans were developed to sail a flotilla out to the Far East for the war against Japan.

Flotillas were generally of eight boats, and by 1945 the 1st to the 59th flotillas and the 70th to the 82nd were of A and B type MLs. The 60th to 69th flotillas were RMLs (Rescue Motor Launches), with reduced armament. The 101st to the 156th flotillas were formed with 72ft HDMLs.

In June 1940 only three MLs were in commission, and these were used for training purposes. The position during the later war years was as shown in the table below.

**Number of flotillas (number of boats in brackets)**

| Area | January 1943 | January 1944 | May 1945 |
|---|---|---|---|
| Plymouth | 4½ (37) | 4 (39) | 4 (32) |
| Western Approaches | 8 (58) | 6 (28) | 3 (18) |
| Portsmouth | 8 (56) | 8 (54) | 9 (60) |
| Dover | 2 (9) | 3 (21) | 3 (16) |
| Nore | 8 (56) | 9 (49) | 17 (121)* |
| Rosyth | 2½ (8) | 1½ (12) | 1 (3) |
| Orkney & Shetland | 6 (41) | 4 (23) | 3 (18)** |
| Mediterranean | 13 (80) | 22 (171) | 23 (161) |
| Atlantic/Africa | 7 (50) | 9 (54) | 9 (57) |
| Eastern Fleet | 2 (13) | 12 (76) | 24 (149) |
| RAN & RNZN | 3 (15) | 4 (24) | 10 (54)† |
| Atlantic | 2 (12) | 1 (6) | 1 (7) |
| RCN – Atlantic | 7 (42) | 7 (42) | 9 (61) |
| RCN – Pacific | 1 (6) | 1 (6) | 1 (7) |

All areas also had a small number of MLs on special service or on operational or weapons trials.

\* Includes one flotilla attached ANCXF

\*\* Home Fleet Command at this date

† Plus thirty-four units in commission and not allocated to flotillas

By January 1947 only thirty-six MLs (all Bs or HDMLs) were in commission in Home waters and forty-two units abroad.

# Coastal Forced depot ships and shore bases 1939–45

Four ships were used as CF depot ships during the war, a trawler and three requisitioned passenger ships. The vast majority of craft were based at shore establishments, known as 'stone frigates' or parent ships, at various ports, from which the craft operated, and where ships' companies were messed, lived, and there were facilities for supply, pay etc. Some bases were specially allocated for the purpose, while others also had, as their main requirement, the duty of maintenance of patrol and minesweeping vessels, or anti-submarine vessels or other training roles.

**The Depot Ships**

HMS *Vulcan* (pennant T.51). A trawler, ex *Aston Villa*, built and engined by Smith's Dock Company in 1933 and purchased on 23 July 1936. She was of 623 tons, 398 tons gross, 155ft overall, with a beam of 26ft 6in and a draught of 10ft forward and 15ft aft. She was coal-fired, with triple expansion engines of 700ihp, which gave a maximum speed of 11½ knots. On her conversion to Service use she was unarmed, but in 1943 she acquired a single 20mm Oerlikon. Her conversion from a fishing vessel provided stowage for fifteen 18in torpedoes and fifty-eight depth charges for the flotillas under her care.

Her ten-year career in the Royal Navy was not uneventful. She commissioned at Portsmouth on 7 April 1937 for service with the Mediterranean Fleet. From June 1937 to December 1939 she was based at Malta. On 1 January 1940 she arrived at Portsmouth, and from February to the end of that year she was attached to the Nore Command and based at Felixstowe and Harwich, with a refit at

Wivenhoe from July to September to improve her facilities for the small craft. From February 1941 to 1946 she served with the Mediterranian Fleet, being based at Alexandria until mid-1943 then, following the land battles on the North African continent, at Benghazi, Brindisi, and back at Malta.

On 3 December 1943, while at Benghazi, she suffered some damage to her superstructure during an air raid when a nearby ship was blown up. She survived the war to return to the United Kingdom in late 1946, and until February 1947 she was based at Pembroke Dock under the Plymouth Command. On 5 February she was sold to Boston Deep Sea Fishing Ltd, renamed *Fotherby*, and resumed the career for which she had been designed and built.

HMS *Aberdonian* (pennant F.47). Considerably larger than the previous conversion, she was also much older. Built and engined by Henderson of Glasgow, she completed before the Great War, in May 1909. After civilian service she was requisitioned on 21 April 1940, and converted for her new duties by Harland & Wolff at North Woolwich. She was 2575 tons (deep), 1648 tons gross, 276ft 3in overall, with a beam of 36ft 3in and a draught of 14ft to 18ft. Still coal fired, she had a single triple expansion engine of 1530ihp, which gave a speed of about 11 knots. Her conversion had provided an armament of two single 12-pounder H/A guns and two quad .5in machine gun mountings for close-range anti-aircraft defence. She

*The Coastal Forces Depot Shop HMIS* Barracuda
*(ex-*Heinrich Jessen*) in India. Alongside are Bs and
Higgins LCPs.* Courtesy George Hay

## Coastal Forces shore establishments

| Name | Location | Commissioned | Paid off |
|---|---|---|---|
| HMS *Attack* | Portland | 15. 1.41 | 31.12.45 |
| HMS *Bee* | Weymouth | .42 | 10.43 |
| HMS *Bee* | Holyhead | 10.43 | 21. 7.45 |
| HMS *Beehive* | Felixstowe | 7.40 | 18.10.45 |
| HMS *Black Bat* | Plymouth | 2.44 | .45 |
| HMIS *Cheetah* (RIN) | Bombay | 8.42 | 31.12.45 |
| HMS *Flora II* | Invergordon | 4.42 | 11.43 |
| HMS *Grasshopper* | Weymouth | 15.10.43 | 28. 4.44 |
| HMS *Gregale* | Malta | 3.43 | 8.46 |
| HMS *Hornet* | Haslar, Gosport | 20.12.39 | 1950s |
| HMS *Mantis* (ex *Minos II*) | Lowestoft | 26. 7.42 | 6.45 |
| HMS *Minos II* | Lowestoft | .41 | 27. 7.42 (renamed) |
| HMS *Midge* | Great Yarmouth | 1.41 | 19. 7.45 |
| HMS *Mosquito* | Alexandria | 2.42 | 12.45 |
| HMS *Ragea* | Alexandria | 10.41 | 5.46 |
| HMS *Razorbill* | Algiers | 1.43 | 10.44 |
| HMS *St Christopher* | Fort William | 31.10.40 | 31.12.44 |
| HMS *Sandfly* | Peterhead | .41 | .45 |
| HMS *Seahawk* | Ardrishaig | 1. 1.41 | 12.44 |
| HMS *Tadpole* | Poole | 6.44 | 12.44 |
| HMS *Wasp* | Dover | .41 | 11.44 |

## Other shore establishments used by Coastal Forces

| Name | Location | Period used |
|---|---|---|
| HMS *Afrikander* | Simonstown | 1943–46 |
| HMS *Beaver* | Humber | 1942–44 |
| HMS *Benbow* | Trinidad | 1942–43 |
| HMS *Cicala* | Dartmouth | 1943– |
| HMS *Cormorant* | Gibraltar | 1942–44 |
| HMS *Edinburgh Castle* | Freetown | 1942–44 |
| HMS *Forte IV* | Falmouth | 1942– |
| HMS *Iron Duke* | Scapa Flow | 1942–43 |
| HMS *Melampus* | Bathurst, West Africa | 1943–45 |
| HMS *Mentor* | Stornoway | 1942– |
| HMS *Morgan* | Kingston, Jamaica | 1942– |
| HMS *Nile* | Alexandria | 1942–46 |
| HMS *St Angelo* | Malta | 1942–43 |
| HMS *Skirmisher II* | Milford Haven | 1942–44 |
| HMCS *Stadacona* | Halifax, Nova Scotia | 1942–44 |
| HMS *Stag* | Port Said | 1942–44 |
| HMS *Victory III* | Portsmouth | 1942– |
| HMS *Wildfire* | Sheerness | 1942– |

had stowage for twelve 21in torpedoes and up to twenty-four depth charges.

She commissioned in June 1940, and from that August until November 1941 she was based at Fort William under Western Approaches Command, attached to the CF shore base HMS *St Christopher*, which was training the crews of newly built MLs. From November to Januaary 1942 she was refitted at Pembroke Dock, and on completion of the refit was placed under Plymouth Command and based at Dartmouth until March 1945. From 4 March 1945 she was awaiting disarming and reconditioning, and was finally returned to her original owners on 4 December 1946.

HMS *Vienna* was some thirty years younger than the previous unit and was built and engined by John Brown on the Clyde, completing in July 1929. She was converted for naval duties by Green & Silley Weir at Blackwall from 17 July 1941 to 1 July 1942, in a major conversion and repair. Larger again than the previous two units, she was of 4218 tons gross, 365ft overall, with a beam of 50ft and a mean draught of 17ft 6in. With oil-fired boilers, she had two shaft turbines of 9600shp, giving her a designed speed of 21 knots. On her completion for war service she was fitted with a single 12-pounder on a HA mounting, two single 2-pounder Mark VIII mountings and eight single .303in Lewis guns. By 1943, after service on station, her armament had been increased by a further eight 20mm Oerlikons. During her conversion she was fitted for stowage of thirty-two 21in torpedoes and up to fifty depth charges.

On 13 July 1941, while on passage to Blackwall for the conversion, she was in collision with SS *Tamworth*. During her conversion, which lasted until July 1942, she was commissioned on 16 June 1942 and then underwent trials, and from 28 July to 24 August she underwent repairs on the Clyde. After further trials she underwent further alterations from 21 September to 21 October, and sailed in convoy to join the Mediterranean Fleet from November 1942. She was based at Algiers, following the Allied landings in North Africa, then Tunis and then Oran. She then moved north, and on 2 December 1943 was damaged by a bomb near miss at Bari. On 2 January 1944 she was again damaged by a near-miss bomb, and was towed to Brindisi, then to Taranto for repairs, which were undertaken there from 15 April until September. By this time her services were no longer required in that theatre, and on 31 October she was paid off and handed over to the Ministry of War Transport for disposal.

HMIS *Barracuda* (pennant F.140) was the ex-Danish *Heinrich Jessen*, built and engined by the Hong Kong & Whampoa Dock Company (though there is, in fact, some evidence that she was built in Japan, and towed to Hong Kong only to have her engines fitted) and completed in 1940. She escaped from Hong Kong, Singapore, Rangoon and Akyab as Japanese forces invaded, and was requisitioned for the Royal Indian Navy as a Coastal Forces Depot ship. Of 3335 tons (gross), she was 305ft overall, with a beam of 46ft 6in. Her maiden voyage was as the last ship to leave Hong Kong. At Singapore she managed to collect enough coal to be again the last ship to leave and reach Rangoon. Details of her armament are obscure, but no doubt she was equipped from a number of sources. From September 1942 to 1943 she was a depot ship for RIN motor launches (Fairmile Bs) based at Bombay, then Calcutta, where she stored and refuelled, then returned to mother the MLs at Kyaukpyu (for details see *From Trombay to Changi: the story of Arakan Coastal Forces*, published for the Arakan Coastal Forces Reunion Committee, and written by O A Goulden in 1987). In 1946 HMIS *Barracuda* was restored to her previous owners.

# The survivors

The Fairmile boats and the 72ft MLS were built to serve only a few years, and were regarded as expendable; nevertheless, a few still survive today.

The first to be brought to my attention was the 72ft ML *Medusa* (ex ML 1387). She is usually to be seen at Navy Days at Portsmouth. She is fitted with two 'handed' Gardner 8L3B diesel engines, the port engine of 1941 vintage and the starboard 1942. Both were refitted by the RN in 1965, prior to her disposal, and both have been refitted since by her present owners, The Medusa Trust. Each develops a nominal 152bhp, driving the ship at 10 knots. They are not fitted with hand starting gear, but have a rather elderly hand-cranked air compressor against the after engineroom bulkhead to charge the air start bottles. *Medusa* is in excellent condition and is slowly being restored to her original war appearance.

A Fairmile B type – ML 293 – is berthed at Princes Wharf at the Bristol Industrial Museum. She, too, is apparently little changed, although she has been re-engined with diesel engines. Her condition is excellent and she is the last B ML conforming to wartime standards; she is operated as a training ship. The Museum to Coastal Forces also owns a 55ft CMB (Coastal Motor Boat), a tug and the RAF's ML 2748.

For over forty years the Western Lady Ferry Service has operated a public ferry service during the summer months, weather permitting, between Brixham and Torquay. This service was inaugurated in 1946 by Mr Ron Edhouse, a Totnes baker, in partnership with his son. They purchased four Fairmile Bs, ex-rescue MLs, in 1946–47 and converted them. The petrol engines were removed and, after a number of suitability trials, replaced by Gardner 6 LX or LW twin diesel engines. The launches were named *Western Lady I* to *Western Lady IV* (ex-Rescue Motor Launches 535, 542, 497 and 526 respectively. *Western Lady II* was sold in 1955 for conversion to a luxury yacht based at Nice, while *Western Lady III* remained under the command of the same mas-

*RNZML* Kuparu *(P 3563), ex HDML 1348, at Gladstone Pier, Lyttleton, New Zealand, in March 1982.* Courtesy Ken Cassels

ter, Captain Don Jacobs, for over twenty years. *Western Lady IV* was purchased in 1947, having spent time in West Africa, where she had been partially converted below deck prior to her purchase. Another B, ex RML 511, was added to the fleet in the 1950s and named *River Lady*, later to be sold and re-christened *Western Diver* by her new owners. She worked in the Plymouth area until 1985 and apparently now has a new life in Holland.

In 1963 the Edhouse family sold the ferry service to M J and E D W Perrett, directors of the Torbay Boat Construction Company Limited, based at the Dolphin Shipyard, Galmpton, on the River Dart. In 1964 this company acquired another two boats, an ex-wooden BYMS Motor Minesweeper and a 72ft HDML. The latter, ex 1396, was converted and renamed *Pride of the Dart*, known affectionately as 'Pod'. *Western Lady III* and *IV* still provide the scheduled ferry service during the season, and *Western Lady I* is currently at the shipyard, where there are plans to refit her completely if finances permit. The two active units, plus *Pod*, have again passed their Board of Trade examination and were in use in the 1990 season.

Other privately owned yachts, generally Bs or HDMLs, still exist in various parts of the world. The Bs have invariably been re-engined with commercial diesel engines for economy and convenience. *Motonui* and *Iris Moana* are ex Bs in New Zealand, while another serves as a floating hotel on the Great Barrier Reef off Australia. It is possible that others still ply the Mediterranean and the Greek Islands. However, not all are abroad. The first 72ft ML – 1001 – still survives at Cardiff, now named MY *SM One*. Another *No LC2* is an ex HDML in the 1400 series, now based at Hamble. The yacht *Sarinda* is also an ex HDML, but no further details are available.

Other Fairmile types are common in British harbours, rivers and estuaries as static houseboats and are found in various states of repair. Their origins usually have to be established from their hull lines, as few retain their original bridge or upperworks. None that I have heard of are ex Bs or 72ft MLs (presumably these types were snapped up for conversions when they were of no further use); those to be seen are A, C or D types, though the majority belong to the Fairmile H class LCI or LCS, with steel plating holding them together.

The houseboat *Eidoron*, at Hayling Island, is apparently ex MGB 325, a C type. I am told that she still has her original bridge

*ML 293, almost as she was in the war, and still in good working condition, at the Bristol Industrial Museum, 1989.* Courtesy RG Morley

Medusa *in August 1988 at Vosper Pier, Gosport.* Courtesy David Fricker

*Former B type* Western Lady, *ex RML 535, laid up in August 1987.* Courtesy David Fricker

*The private launch* Motonui, *ex RNZML 406, was sold in 1947 and became a ferry in Auckland harbour until 1982, when she was sold and converted.* Courtesy Ken Cassells

*Ex ML 492, ex* Pride of Paignton, *as* Mars-Petra, *seen in January 1982 but alas now lost.* Courtesy David Fricker

*Ex MGB 324, H/B* Bellands, *at Shoreham in July 1986.* Courtesy David Fricker

*The bridge of* Western Lady III, *showing less equipment than in her war years. She is still going strong in 1990.* Courtesy David Fricker

*H/B* Eidoron, *ex MGB 325, is still original apart from a section abaft her bridge. She is claimed to be a C type, but seems more to resemble an A. She is seen here in August 1987.* Courtesy David Fricker

Western Lady III *departing Brixham in August 1987.* Courtesy David Fricker

*A collection of Old warriors: left to right, Fairmile Hs* Ciconia *and* Vanessa; *Little Susie (MTB 24);* Xoron *(MGB 321) and* Bosun *(ex LCA), at Bembridge in May 1986.* Courtesy David Fricker

*How the mighty are fallen – a derelict HB lying on the river Medway in April 1988. She was a D type, possibly ex LRRC 003, ex MTB 5004.*
Courtesy Philip Simons

and chartroom. The houseboat *Bellands*, at Shoreham, is her sister, ex MGB 324. I have no direct evidence, but photographs of these vessels tend to suggest, by the form of the upperworks, that both of these vessels may in fact be surviving As, and not Cs. The house-boat *Xoron*, at Bembridge on the Isle of Wight, is the ex C type MGB 321. The D type is represented by an un-named houseboat at berth 23 at Shoreham, the ex LRRC 029, ex MTB 682, and by a close sister at Chatham ex 030, ex MTB 683, which appears to be in better shape.

A B type named *Mars Petra*, ex *Pride of Paignton*, ex ML 492, survived until early 1982 near the John Foulkes boatyard on the River Hamble at Bursleden. She sank in March 1981 and was raised in April, but eventually was scrapped.

The remaining Fairmile types are the easily distinguished H class. One is at Crableck on the Hamble, one is the houseboat *Valeur* at Shoreham, another the houseboat *Ciconia* at Bembridge (with the remains of ML 284 alongside), another is at Quay Lane, Gosport, and a final survivor is a hulk on the River Medina.

*Medusa, ex HDML 1387, in April 1988 on the slip at Portland.* Courtesy David Fricker

*'POD' (Pride of the Dart) ex HDML 1396, laid up at Dartmouth in August 1987.*
Courtesy David Fricker

*MY SM One, ex HDML 1001, at Cardiff in December 1986.* Courtesy David Fricker

*Not landing – an end-on ex Fairmile H LCI (S) at Crableck on the river Hamble in April 1989.*

# Schedule of British builders of Fairmile Marine Company designs

A type, Nos 100–111
B type, Nos 112–309; 336–347; 442–473; 478–500; 511–600; 901–933
C type, Nos 312–335
D type, Nos 601–800; 5001–5029 (excluding 5027, cancelled)
F type, No 2001
H type, Nos LCI (S) 501–540; LCS (L) 251–260
36ft HLs 4428–4439; 441130–441164; 441532–441611
45ft MFVs 776–835

| Builders | Type | Boat numbers |
|---|---|---|
| Aldous Successors Ltd, The Shipyard, Brightlingsea | A | 110 |
| | B | 120, 138, 170, 206, 225, 278, 301, 463, 49, 519 & 559 |
| | C | 318,329 |
| | D | 743, 761 |
| Austins of East Ham Ltd, London E6 Yard: Twinn Wharf, Abbey Rd, Barking | B | 227, 287, 450, 482, 514, 542, 549, 520, 925, 933 |
| | D | 745, 773, 798, 5012 |
| | H | 507, 251, 257, 260 |
| Boat Construction Co Ltd, Office: 42 High Street Yard: Barracks Ope, Falmouth | B | 137, 164, 187, 226, 261, 271, 336, 446, 471, 491 |
| | D | 635, 650, 659, 678, 690, 707, 725, 753, 767, 790, 5006 |
| | HSL | 441164, 441534, 441535 |
| Brooke Marine Ltd, Oulton Broad, Nr Lowestoft, Norfolk | A | 103 |
| | B | 114, 127, 142, 147, 186, 211, 230, 248, 270, 281, 290, 344, 443, 527, 562 |
| | C | 319 |
| | D | 611, 622, 639, 660, 681, 695, 711, 729, 762, 785 |
| | H | 512, 413, 514, 515, 255, 538, 539, 534 |
| Cardnell Brothers, Riverside Estate, Maylandsea, Tilthorne, Nr Chelmsford | B | 215, 288, 461, 485, 534, 560, 930 |
| | D | 721, 736, 5015 |
| | H | 502, 523 |
| | MFV | 820, 821 |
| Collins Pleasurecraft Co Ltd, Oulton Broad Nr Lowestoft | B | 180, 262, 341, 479, 515, 541, 569, 926 |
| | D | 740, 783 |
| | H | 520, 532 |
| | MFV | 816, 817 |
| Frank Curtis Ltd, Looe, Cornwall | A | 105 |
| | B | 130, 131, 139, 140, 143, 145, 146, 161, 241, 242, 251, 256, 257, 280, 295, 307, 308, 458, 465, 480, 481, 490, 493, 513, 521, 525, 530, 533, 539, 544, 554, 557, 556, 566, 568, 582, 583, 589, 591, 595, 600 325 |
| | C | 503, 508, 516, 519, 521, 527, 528, 529 |
| | H | |
| Frank Curtis Ltd, Par, Cornwall | B | 123, 172, 173, 250, 276 |

| Builders | Type | Boat numbers |
|---|---|---|
| A M Dickie & Sons, Bangor, North Wales | A | 104 |
| | B | 122, 162, 103, 212, 235, 460, 500, 537, 565 |
| | C | 314, 322, 334, 335 |
| | D | 604, 620, 638, 647, 671, 679, 714, 717, 726, 750, 771, 777, 5010, 5024 |
| | H | 254 |
| | MFV | 792, 793 |
| A M Dickie & Sons, Tarbert, Argyllshire | B | 116, 124, 188, 217, 234, 337 |
| | D | 615, 629, 664, 688, 709, 741, 797, 5017 |
| | MFV | 799, 801 |
| Diesel Oil Vaporisers Ltd, 16 Town Wharf, Isleworth | MFV | 345 |
| J S Doig (Grimsby) Ltd Grimsby Docks | B | 125, 222, 286, 464, 512, 547 |
| | D | 737, 781 |
| | H | 510, 531 |
| Dorset Yacht Co Ltd, Lake Road, Hamworthy, Poole | B | 135, 144, 189, 229, 258, 268, 293, 296, 298, 462 |
| | D | 619, 624, 633, 648, 662, 666, 685, 699, 713, 732, 752, 778, 800 |
| S B Hall, Galmpton, Brixham, Devon | B | 179, 254, 277, 279 |
| | D | 612, 613, 645, 652, 677, 689, 708, 727, 760, 775, 5007, 5023 |
| | MFV | 782, 783, 798 |
| | HSL | 441140, 441141, 441146, 441147 |
| Hampton Launch Works Ltd | B | 157, 195, 260, 343 |
| P K Harris & Sons Ltd, New Quay Dry Docks, Appledore | B | 128, 152, 184, 233, 263, 279, 304, 451 |
| | D | 618, 627, 642, 665, 687, 702, 723, 757, 788, 5021 |
| | MFV | 794, 795 |
| Itchenor Shipyard Ltd, Itchenor, Nr Chichester | B | 132, 191, 282, 466, 524, 558, 594, 913 |
| | H | 526 |
| | HSL | 441148, 441149, 441156, 441157 |
| Johnson & Jago, Leigh Marshes, Leigh-on-Sea, Essex | B | 194, 207, 264, 274, 305, 342, 457, 469, 486, 487, 522, 532, 543, 548, 564, 572, 575, 577, 580, 581, 584, 590, 593, 597, 901, 903, 907, 909, 911, 915, 913, 923, 927, 932 |
| | MFV | 787, 788, 811, 812, 824 |
| | HSL | 441532, 441533 |
| William King (Burnham-on-Crouch) Ltd, High Street, Burnham-on-Crouch | B | 169, 221, 266, 302 |
| | D | 609, 631, 667, 693, 720, 769, 5008 |
| | MFV | 777, 786 |
| Leo A Robinson, Broadside Launch Works, Oulton Broad, Nr Lowestoft | B | 163, 259, 528 |
| | D | 770 |
| | H | 511, 533 |
| | HSL | 441154, 441155 |
| Leo A Robinson, Bathursts, St John's Bridge, Mythe Road, Tewkesbury | B | 178, 182, 340 |
| John Sadd & Sons Ltd, Maldon, Essex | B | 181, 253, 294, 456, 517, 538 |
| | D | 742, 796 |
| | H | 505, 256 |
| HM Dockyard, Sheerness, Kent | B | 150, 151, 245, 246 |

| Builders | Type | Boat numbers |
|---|---|---|
| James A Silver Ltd, Rosneath, Dumbartonshire | A | 101, 111 |
| | B | 121, 154, 175, 200, 201, 232, 284 |
| | C | 321, 326, 332 |
| | D | 607, 608, 621, 636, 672, 683, 704, 716, 764, 746, 5003, 5004 |
| | HSL | 4436, 4437, 4438, 4439, 441132, 441133, 441138, 441139 |
| Solent Shipyards Ltd, Bursledon Bridge, Sarisbury Green, Hampshire | B | 115, 134, 176, 190, 239, 267, 285, 306, 459, 472, 484, 526, 536, 555, 563 |
| | D | 754, 786 |
| | H | 506, 252, 258, 536 |
| Southampton Steam Joinery Co Ltd, 83 Whitworth Road, Southampton | B | 192, 252, 449, 497, 553 |
| | H | 518 |
| Sussex Shipbuilding Co Ltd, Shoreham-on-Sea | A | 107 |
| | B | 118, 148, 231 |
| | D | 747, 774 |
| James Taylor (Chertsey) Ltd, Bridge Wharf, Chertsey | B | 185, 205, 209, 442, 453, 570, 571, 576, 588, 906, 909, 922 |
| Thomson & Balfour, Victoria Saw Mills, Bo'ness | B | 240, 275, 444, 478, 494, 551 |
| | D | 641, 668, 694, 722, 734, 768, 791, 5011, 5029 |
| | MFV | 800, 802, 818, 819 |
| | H | 509, 524 |
| John I Thornycroft & Co Ltd, Woolston Works, Southampton | B | 158 |
| Tough Brothers Ltd, Teddington Wharf, Manor Road, Teddington | B | 113, 171, 199, 220, 228, 448 |
| | C | 316, 330, 331 |
| | D | 601, 603, 626, 644, 651, 673, 674, 703, 735, 736, 784, 792, 5022 |
| | HSL | 4429, 4430, 4433, 4434, 4435 |
| Kris Cruisers (1934) Ltd, Riverside Yard, Ferry Road, Isleworth | B | 165, 214 |
| | C | 323 |
| | D | 602, 632, 696, 780 |
| | F | 2001 |
| Lady Bee Ltd, Shoreham-by-Sea, Sussex | B | 117, 133, 202, 216, 299, 488, 496 |
| | C | 328 |
| | D | 654, 669, 692, 719, 733, 776, 5009 |
| | MFV | 809, 810, 825, 784, 785 |
| Alfred Lockhart (Marine) Ltd, Ferry Lane, Brentford, Middlesex | HSL | 4428 |
| | MFV | 776, 813 |
| Mashford Brothers, Chemyll Yard, Chemyll, Plymouth | B | 129, 141, 213, 255, 292, 452 |
| James N Miller & Sons Ltd, East Shore, St Monance, Fife | A | 108 |
| | B | 126, 159, 196, 203, 303, 346, 483, 489, 518, 529, 546, 552, 573, 574, 578, 579, 585, 586, 592, 598, 902, 904, 910, 914, 919, 924, 928 |
| | C | 313 |
| | MFV | 807, 808, 803, 804 |
| | HSL | 441150, 441155 |

| Builders | Type | Boat numbers |
|---|---|---|
| William Osbourne Ltd, Littlehampton, Sussex | A | 109 |
| | B | 174, 210, 219, 273, 291, 929 |
| | C | 320 |
| | D | 605, 616, 617, 634, 655, 663, 686, 700, 710, 728, 748, 749, 791, 796, 814, 815 |
| | MFV | 787, 795, 5005, 5020, 5026 |
| H T Percival, Yacht Station, Horning, Norfolk | B | 153, 193, 244, 283, 447, 470, 523, 531, 550, 567, 917 |
| | D | 765, 799 |
| | H | 253, 259, 537 |
| | MFV | 789, 790 |
| Risdon Beazley Ltd, Clausentum Yard, Northam Bridge, Southampton | B | 204, 208, 265, 338, 347, 467, 468, 498, 499 |
| | D | 646, 649, 676, 680, 705, 706, 738, 744, 772, 789, 5013, 5019, 5027 – cancelled |
| | C | 327 |
| | HSL | 441130, 441131, 441136, 441137, 441142, 441143, 441152, 441153, 441160, 441161 |
| Alex Robertson (Yachtbuilders) & Sons Ltd, Sandbank, Argyllshire | A | 106 |
| | B | 119, 136, 160, 197, 223, 238, 454 |
| | C | 315, 317 |
| | D | 625, 630, 637, 653, 661, 675, 691, 718, 731, 758, 793, 5018 |
| J W & A Upham, Brixham, Devon | B | 166, 167, 236, 237, 247, 309, 445, 511, 540 |
| | D | 628, 658, 701, 755 |
| Vosper Ltd, Portsmouth | B | 149 |
| Wallasea Bay Yacht Station Ltd, Wallasea Bay, Nr Rochford | B | 156, 177, 224, 249, 272, 289, 339 |
| | D | 606, 623, 640, 656, 670, 682, 698, 712, 724, 751, 766, 782, 5002, 5016, 5025 |
| | MFV | 780, 781, 797, 822, 823 |
| | HSL | 4431, 4432 |
| W Weatherhead & Sons, West Harbour, Cockenzie | B | 168, 213, 243, 269, 300, 455, 473, 495, 516, 535, 545, 561, 596, 599, 905, 912, 916, 921 |
| | H | 504, 517, 522, 530, 535, 540 |
| | MFV | 778, 779, 805, 806 |
| | HSL | 441134, 441135, 441144, 441145 |
| Woodnutt & Co Ltd, St Helens, Isle-of-Wight | A | 100, 102 |
| | B | 112, 155, 193, 931 |
| | C | 312, 324, 333 |
| | D | 610, 614, 643, 657, 684, 697, 715, 730, 759, 779, 5001, 5014, 5028 |
| | HSL | 441158, 441159, 441162, 441163 |
| Herbert Woods, Broads Haven, Potter Heigham, Great Yarmouth | B | 920 |
| | D | 739, 756, 794 |

HSL – Harbour Service Launch
MFV – Motor Fishing Vessel

# Fairmile production analysis *Oct 1939–Oct 1945*

**COASTAL FORCES, COMBINED OPERATIONS, RAF RESCUE CRAFT & WAR OFFICE HOSPITAL CRAFT ONLY**

## HOME PRODUCTION

| Class | No in Contract | First keel laid | Last keel laid | First boat completed | Last boat completed | Average building time | Approx average tonnage per boat | Total tonnage |
|---|---|---|---|---|---|---|---|---|
| A MLs | 12 | 29.10.39 | 14.2.40 | 21.3.40 | 6. 8.40 | 22 weeks | 62 tons | 744 tons |
| B " | 375 | 5. 3.40 | 23.6.44 | 12.8.40 | 15.12.44 | 24.8 " | 85 " | 31,875 " |
| B " (WO) | 13 | 18. 5.44 | 14.9.44 | 30.4.45 | 8. 9.45 | 44 " | 77 " | 1001 " |
| C MGBs | 24 | 1.12.40 | 10.5.41 | 24.5.41 | 21.11.41 | 29 " | 68 " | 1632 " |
| D MTBs | 209 | 23. 5.41 | 8.5.44 | 9.3.42 | 26. 7.45 | 43.3 " | 114 " | 23,826 " |
| D LRRC | 19 | 12. 1.44 | 6.7.44 | 16.3.45 | 30. 9.45 | 52 " | 111 " | 2109 " |
| F MGB | 1 | 6. 6.42 | — | 26.4.44 | — | 98 " | 99 " | 99 " |
| H LCI & LCS | 50 | 25. 8.42 | 3.9.43 | 24.2.43 | 14. 3.44 | 29 " | 107 " | 5350 " |
| | 703 | | | | | | | 66,636 |

## ANNUAL PRODUCTION

| | Keels laid | | | | | | | | | Boats completed | | | | | | | | | |
|---|---|---|---|---|---|---|---|---|---|---|---|---|---|---|---|---|---|---|---|
| Year | A | B | B(WO) | C | D | D(LRRC) | F | H | Total | A | B | B(WO) | C | D | D(LRRC) | F | H | Total | Tonnage |
| 1939 | 2 | — | — | — | — | — | — | — | 2 | — | — | — | — | — | — | — | — | — | — |
| 1940 | 10 | 145 | — | 8 | — | — | — | — | 163 | 12 | 42 | — | — | — | — | — | — | 54 | 4314 |
| 1941 | — | 125 | — | 16 | 35 | — | — | — | 176 | — | 178 | — | 24 | — | — | — | — | 202 | 16,752 |
| 1942 | — | 64 | — | — | 66 | — | 1 | 25 | 156 | — | 98 | — | — | 44 | — | — | — | 142 | 13,346 |
| 1943 | — | 28 | — | — | 91 | — | — | 25 | 144 | — | 32 | — | — | 72 | — | — | 42 | 146 | 15,422 |
| 1944 | — | 13 | 13 | — | 17 | 19 | — | — | 62 | — | 25 | — | — | 77 | — | 1 | 8 | 111 | 11,858 |
| 1945 | — | — | — | — | — | — | — | — | — | — | — | 13 | — | 16 | 19 | — | — | 48 | 4934 |
| Totals | 12 | 375 | 13 | 24 | 209 | 19 | 1 | 50 | 703 | 12 | 375 | 13 | 24 | 209 | 19 | 1 | 50 | 703 | 66,636 |

## MONTHLY COMPLETIONS

| Year | Jan | Feb | Mar | Apr | May | June | July | Aug | Sept | Oct | Nov | Dec | Total | Averages (per month) |
|---|---|---|---|---|---|---|---|---|---|---|---|---|---|---|
| 1939 | — | — | — | — | — | — | — | — | — | — | — | — | — | — |
| 1940 | — | — | 1 | — | — | 3 | 6 | 3 | 6 | 10 | 13 | 12 | 54 | 4.5 |
| 1941 | 16 | 20 | 15 | 14 | 20 | 15 | 20 | 16 | 17 | 24 | 13 | 12 | 202 | 16.38 |
| 1942 | 11 | 7 | 9 | 9 | 8 | 12 | 15 | 13 | 12 | 14 | 15 | 17 | 142 | 11,83 |
| 1943 | 11 | 10 | 8 | 17 | 20 | 9 | 23 | 11 | 8 | 9 | 13 | 7 | 146 | 12.16 |
| 1944 | 4 | 11 | 9 | 18 | 6 | 13 | 10 | 10 | 5 | 11 | 5 | 9 | 111 | 9.25 |
| 1945 | 3 | 1 | 11 | 4 | 5 | 3 | 16 | 3 | 2 | — | — | — | 48 | 5.33 |
| | | | | | | | | | | | | | 703 | |

## BOAT SETS OF PARTS SHIPPED ABROAD

| Egypt | Australia | Bermuda | Jamaica | Singapore | New Zealand | Hong Kong | Burma | Tanganyika | India | Rest of Africa |
|---|---|---|---|---|---|---|---|---|---|---|
| 56 | 20 | 2 | 8 | 14 | 12 | 4 | 2 | 4 | 24 | 34 |

Total 180

## TOTAL HOME AND EXPORT: 883 BOATS

*Key:* WO – War Office    LRRC – Long Range Rescue Craft    LCI – Landing Craft Infantry    LCS – Landing Craft Support

# Yard analysis

| Yard | A | B | Boats built | | | | | | Total | Boats per slip | Valuation (boats) A = .9 B = 1 C = 1.04 D = 1.67 H = 1.22 | C / A X B performance index figure (No of boats per slip per annum) | Order of merit |
|---|---|---|---|---|---|---|---|---|---|---|---|---|---|
| | Average number of slips | Period employed (years) | A | B | C | D | F | H | | | | | |
| Aldous | 2 | 4.5 | 1 | 11 | 2 | 2 | — | — | 16 | 8 | 17.32 | 1.92 | 26 |
| Austin | 1 | 4.75 | — | 10 | — | 4 | — | 4 | 18 | 18 | 21.56 | 4.53 | 1 |
| Boat Const | 2 | 5.25 | — | 10 | — | 11 | — | — | 21 | 10.5 | 28.37 | 2.7 | 14 |
| Brooke Marine | 5 | 5.16 | 1 | 15 | 1 | 10 | — | 8 | 35 | 7.0 | 43.40 | 1.68 | 32 |
| Cardnell | 1 | 4.66 | — | 7 | — | 3 | — | 2 | 12 | 12 | 14.45 | 3.1 | 6 |
| Collins | 1 | 5.00 | — | 8 | — | 2 | — | 2 | 12 | 12 | 13.78 | 2.75 | 13 |
| Curtis (Looe) | 5.5 | 4.6 | 1 | 41 | 1 | — | — | 8 | 51 | 9.27 | 52.70 | 2.08 | 22 |
| Curtis (Par) | 2 | 1.5 | — | 5 | — | — | — | — | 5 | 2.5 | 5 | 1.67 | 33 |
| Dickie (Bangor) | 3 | 5.33 | 1 | 9 | 4 | 14 | — | 1 | 29 | 9.7 | 38.66 | 2.41 | 19 |
| Dickie (Tarbert) | 2 | 4.84 | — | 6 | — | 8 | — | — | 14 | 7 | 19.36 | 2.00 | 24 |
| Diesel Oil | 1 | .83 | — | 1 | — | — | — | — | 1 | 1 | 1 | 1.2 | 37 |
| Doig (Grimsby) Ltd | 1 | 4.66 | — | 6 | — | 2 | — | 2 | 10 | 10 | 11.78 | 2.53 | 17 |
| Dorset | 3 | 5 | — | 10 | — | 13 | — | — | 23 | 7.6 | 31.71 | 2.11 | 21 |
| Hall Galmpton | 2 | 4.6 | — | 4 | — | 12 | — | — | 16 | 8 | 24.04 | 2.61 | 15 |
| Hampton | 1 | 1.4 | — | 4 | — | — | — | — | 4 | 4 | 4 | 2.86 | 10 |
| Harris | 2 | 4.83 | — | 8 | — | 10 | — | — | 18 | 9 | 24.7 | 2.55 | 16 |
| Itchenor | 1 | 4.66 | — | 8 | — | — | — | 1 | 9 | 9 | 9.22 | 1.98 | 25 |
| Johnson & Jago | 2 | 4.83 | — | 35 | — | — | — | — | 35 | 17.5 | 35 | 3.62 | 2 |
| King (Burnham on Crouch) | 1 | 4.90 | — | 4 | — | 7 | — | — | 11 | 11 | 15.69 | 3.2 | 5 |
| Kris Cruisers | 1 | 4.6 | — | 2 | 1 | 4 | 1 | — | 8 | 8 | 11.39 | 2.47 | 18 |
| Lady Bee Ltd | 2 | 5.16 | — | 7 | 1 | 7 | — | — | 15 | 7.5 | 19.73 | 1.9 | 27 |
| Mashford | 2 | 1.7 | — | 6 | — | — | — | — | 6 | 3 | 6 | 1.76 | 30 |
| Miller | 2 | 5.25 | 1 | 27 | 1 | — | — | — | 29 | 14.5 | 28.94 | 2.75 | 13 |
| Osborne | 2.5 | 5.25 | 1 | 6 | 1 | 17 | — | — | 25 | 10 | 36.33 | 2.77 | 12 |
| Percival | 2 | 5.25 | — | 11 | — | 2 | — | 3 | 16 | 8 | 18 | 1.7 | 31 |
| Risdon | 2 | 4.6 | — | 9 | 1 | 12 | — | — | 22 | 11 | 30.08 | 3.27 | 4 |
| Robertson | 3 | 5.4 | 1 | 7 | 2 | 12 | — | — | 22 | 7.3 | 30.02 | 1.85 | 28 |
| Robinson (Oulton) | 1 | 4.5 | — | 3 | — | 1 | — | 2 | 6 | 6 | 7.11 | 1.58 | 34 |
| Robinson (Tewkesbury) | 2 | 1.41 | — | 3 | — | — | — | — | 3 | 1.5 | 3.00 | 1.06 | 40 |
| Sadd | 1 | 4.16 | — | 6 | — | 2 | — | 2 | 10 | 10 | 11.78 | 2.83 | 11 |
| HM Dockyard (Sheerness) | 2 | 1.16 | — | 4 | — | — | — | — | 4 | 2 | 4 | 1.7 | 31 |
| Silver | 3 | 5.83 | 2 | 7 | 3 | 12 | — | — | 24 | 8 | 31.96 | 1.83 | 29 |
| Solent | 2 | 5.16 | — | 15 | — | 2 | — | 4 | 21 | 10.5 | 23.22 | 2.25 | 20 |
| Steam Joinery | 2 | 2.9 | — | 5 | — | — | — | 1 | 6 | 3 | 6.22 | 1.07 | 39 |
| Sussex | 2 | 3.5 | 1 | 3 | — | 2 | — | — | 6 | 3 | 7.24 | 1.03 | 41 |
| Taylor | 2 | 4.92 | — | 12 | — | — | — | — | 12 | 6 | 12 | 1.22 | 36 |
| Thompson & Balfour | 1.5 | 4.7 | — | 6 | — | 9 | — | 2 | 17 | 11.33 | 23.47 | 3.33 | 3 |
| Thornycroft (S'hampton) | 1 | 0.92 | — | 1 | — | — | — | — | 1 | 1 | 1 | 1.08 | 38 |
| Tough Bros | 2.25 | 5.00 | — | 6 | 3 | 13 | — | 2 | 24 | 10.66 | 33.27 | 2.96 | 9 |
| Upham (Brixham) | 1.75 | 4.25 | — | 9 | — | 4 | — | — | 13 | 7.4 | 15.68 | 2.11 | 21 |
| Vosper (Portsmouth) | 1 | 0.75 | — | 1 | — | — | — | — | 1 | 1 | 1 | 1.3 | 35 |
| Wallasea | 2 | 5.25 | — | 7 | — | 15 | — | — | 22 | 11 | 32.05 | 3.05 | 7 |
| Weatherhead | 2 | 4.25 | — | 18 | — | — | — | 6 | 24 | 12 | 25.32 | 2.98 | 8 |
| Woodnutt | 2 | 5.66 | 2 | 4 | 3 | 13 | — | — | 22 | 11 | 30.63 | 2.7 | 23 |
| Woods | 2 | 1.5 | — | 1 | — | 3 | — | — | 4 | 2 | 6.01 | 2.0 | 24 |
| Totals 45 | 87.5 | | 12 | 388 | 24 | 228 | 1 | 50 | 703 | | | | |

# Fairmile consumption of major materials

|  | Per boat | Total quantity (883 boats) |
|---|---|---|
| Timber | 2900cu ft | 2,560,700cu ft |
| Fastenings | 235,000 | 207,505,000 |
| Piping | 2500ft | 2,207,500ft (418 miles) |
| Wiring | 13,200ft | 11,655,600ft (2207 miles) |
| Paint | 350 gal | 309,050 gal |

# Area comparisons

YARDS AND NUMBERS OF BOATS

## SCOTLAND

| Yard | No of boats | Performance index figure |
|---|---|---|
| Thomson & Balfour | 17 | 3.33 |
| Weatherhead | 24 | 2.98 |
| Miller | 29 | 2.75 |
| Dickie (Tarbert) | 14 | 2.00 |
| Robertson | 22 | 1.84 |
| Silver | 24 | 1.83 |

Total boats 130

Total yards 6

Average per yard 21.66

## SOUTHERN

| Yard | No of boats | Performance index figure |
|---|---|---|
| Risdon | 22 | 3.27 |
| Osborne | 25 | 2.77 |
| Woodnutt | 22 | 2.70 |
| Solent | 21 | 2.29 |
| Dorset | 23 | 2.11 |
| Itchenor | 9 | 1.98 |
| Lady Bee | 15 | 1.90 |
| Vosper | 1 | 1.30 |
| Thornycroft | 1 | 1.08 |
| Steam J (S'hampton) | 6 | 1.07 |
| Sussex | 6 | 1.03 |

Total boats 15

Total yards 11

Average per yard 13.7

## EASTERN

| Yard | No of boats | Performance index figure |
|---|---|---|
| King | 11 | 3.20 |
| Cardnell | 12 | 3.10 |
| Wallasea | 22 | 3.05 |
| Sadd | 10 | 2.83 |
| Collins | 12 | 2.75 |
| Doig | 10 | 2.53 |
| Woods | 4 | 2.00 |
| Aldous | 16 | 1.92 |
| Percival | 16 | 1.7 |
| Brooke | 35 | 1.68 |
| Robinson | 6 | 1.59 |

Total boats 154

Total yards 11

Average per yard 14

## WESTERN

| Yard | No of boats | Performance index figure |
|---|---|---|
| Boat Const | 21 | 2.70 |
| Hall | 16 | 2.60 |
| Harris | 18 | 2.55 |
| Dickie (Bangor) | 29 | 2.41 |
| Upham | 13 | 2.11 |
| Curtis (Looe) | 51 | 2.08 |
| Curtis (Par) | 5 | 1.67 |
| Mashford | 6 | 1.76 |
| Robinson (Tewkesbury) | 3 | 1.06 |

Total boats 162

Total yards 9

Average per yard 18

## THAMES

| Yard | No of boats | Performance index figure |
|---|---|---|
| Austin | 18 | 4.53 |
| Johnson & Jago | 35 | 3.62 |
| Tough | 24 | 2.90 |
| Hampton L | 4 | 2.86 |
| Kris | 8 | 2.47 |
| Taylor | 12 | 1.22 |
| Diesel | 1 | 1.2 |

Total boats 102

Total yards 7

Average per yard 14.5

# Building times

| COMPARATIVE AVERAGES | | | | |
|---|---|---|---|---|
| **A CLASS** | **B CLASS** | **C CLASS** | **D CLASS** | **H CLASS** |

| A CLASS | | B CLASS | | C CLASS | | D CLASS | | H CLASS | |
|---|---|---|---|---|---|---|---|---|---|
| *Overall average – 22 weeks* | | *Overall average – 24.8 weeks* | | *Overall average – 29 weeks* | | *Overall average – 43.3 weeks* | | *Overall average – 29 weeks* | |
| *Below average yard* | *Average weeks* | *Below average yard* | *Average weeks* | *Below average yard* | *Average weeks* | *Below average yard* | *Average weeks* | *Below average yard* | *Average weeks* |
| Miller | 21 | Johnson & Jago | 16.9 | Tough | 20.5 | Risdon | 33 | Austin | 19.7 |
| Brooke | 21 | Thomson & Balfour | 17.5 | Kris | 22 | Austin | 35 | Weatherhead | 20.8 |
| Woodnutt | 21 | Miller | 17.9 | Dickie (Bangor) | 26 | Osborne | 35.4 | Collins | 22 |
| Sussex | 21 | King | 18.5 | Woodnutt | 26.3 | King | 38 | Curtis | 23.7 |
| Dickie (Bangor) | 22 | Austin | 19 | Risdon | 27 | Wallasea | 39 | Doig | 26 |
| Silver | 22 | Cardnell | 19 | Miller | 27 | Thomson & Balfour | 40.5 | Thomson & Balfour | 26.5 |
| Robertson | 22 | Tough | 19 | Silver | 27.5 | Sadd | 41 | Cardnell | 27 |
| | | Hampton LW | 20.2 | | | Woodnutt | 41.2 | | |
| | | Wallasea | 20.8 | | | Dickie (Bangor) | 41.3 | | |
| | | Weatherhead | 20.8 | | | Cardnell | 41.3 | | |
| | | Risdon | 21 | | | Tough Bros | 42.5 | | |
| | | Sadd | 21 | | | | | | |
| | | Hall | 21.7 | | | | | | |
| | | Kris | 22 | | | | | | |
| | | Collins | 22.8 | | | | | | |
| | | Dorset | 23.1 | | | | | | |
| | | Boat Const | 23.6 | | | | | | |
| | | Harris | 23.9 | | | | | | |
| | | Dickie (Bangor) | 24.2 | | | | | | |
| | | Silver | 24.8 | | | | | | |
| *Above average* | | *Above average* | | *Above average* | | *Above average* | | *Above average* | |
| Aldous | 23 | Doig | 25.5 | Aldous | 29.5 | Hall | 43.7 | Sadd | 30 |
| Curtis | 23 | Brooke | 25.7 | Curtis | 32 | Silver | 44 | Tough | 30 |
| Osborne | 24 | Osborne | 26 | Lady Bee | 32 | Dorset | 44.6 | Robinson | 33.5 |
| | | Curtis (Looe) | 27.6 | Robertson | 32 | Aldous | 45.5 | Dickie (Bangor) | 24 |
| | | Solent | 28 | Osborne | 35 | Lady Bee | 46.7 | Itchenor | 34 |
| | | Aldous | 28 | Brooke | 37 | Harris | 47.2 | Percival | 34 |
| | | Woodnutt | 28 | | | Woods | 47.3 | Steam Joinery | 34 |
| | | Dickie (Tarbert) | 28.3 | | | Dickie (Tarbert) | 47.4 | Solent | 37 |
| | | Lady Bee | 28.4 | | | Sussex | 49.5 | Brooke | 43.7 |
| | | Upham | 28.8 | | | Robertson | 50.5 | | |
| | | Mashford | 28.9 | | | Boat Const | 50.7 | | |
| | | Robertson | 29 | | | Doig | 52 | | |
| | | Sussex | 29 | | | Kris | 52.2 | | |
| | | Percival | 29.1 | | | Brooke | 52.5 | | |
| | | Itchenor | 29.8 | | | Upham | 54.5 | | |
| | | Curtis (Par) | 30.8 | | | Collins | 58 | | |
| | | Robinson (Oulton) | 32.7 | | | Percival | 58 | | |
| | | Sheerness DY | 34.5 | | | Robinson | 63 | | |
| | | Taylor | 35.4 | | | Solent | 69.5 | | |
| | | Steam Joinery | 39.2 | | | | | | |
| | | Vosper | 41 | | | | | | |
| | | Robinson (Tks'bury) | 42.7 | | | | | | |
| | | Diesel | 43 | | | | | | |
| | | Thornycroft (S'ton) | 48 | | | | | | |
| | | *Note*: The above figures do not include WOALs. | | | | *Note*: The above figures do not include LRRC. | | | |

# Provisions to be supplied to motor launches on commissioning

## REQUIREMENTS FOR 14 MEN FOR 14 DAYS

| Item | Quantity | Packages |
|------|----------|----------|
| Rum | 3 gal | 3 jars |
| Vinegar | 1 gal | 1 jar |
| Sugar | 50lb | 1 bag |
| Tea | 20lb | 1 box |
| Chocolate (Kye) | 25lb | 1 case |
| Milk | 48 tins | 1 case |
| Butter | 24lb | 1 case tin-lined |
| Corned beef, 12oz tins | 72lb | 2 cases |
| Biscuit | 84lb | 3 cases |
| Meat and vegetable rations | 36lb | 1 case |
| Tinned sausages, 2lb tins | 24 tins | 1 case |
| Sardines | 100 tins | 1 case |
| Tinned vegetables, 2½lb size | 48 tins | 2 cases |
| Currants | 14lb | 1 box |
| Baked beans | 48 tins | 1 case |
| Tinned fruits | 48 tins | 2 cases |
| Flour | 40lb | 1 bag |
| Marrowfat peas | 50lb | 1 bag |
| Rice | 20lb | |
| Suet, 1lb tins | 7lb | |
| Jam, 1lb tins | 12lb | |
| Marmalade, 1lb tins | 12lb | |
| Golden Syrup, 1lb tins | 7lb | To be packed |
| Pickles | 12lb | as convenient |
| Tinned tomatoes | 14 tins | |
| Coffee | 6lb | |
| Salt | 14lb | |
| Mustard, 1lb tins | 1lb | |
| Pepper, ½lb tins | 1lb | |
| Salmon | 24 tins | |
| Tinned herrings in tomato sauce | 24 tins | |
| Tinned bacon | 24 tins | |

# Fairmile designed classes – performance data

| Boat class | Fairmile B | Fairmile C | Fairmile D |
|------------|-----------|-----------|-----------|
| Size | 112ft 0in LOA | 110ft 0in LOA | 115ft 0in LOA |
| | 105ft 7in LWL | 108ft 0in LWL | 110ft 0in LWL |
| | 17ft 10in beam | 16ft 10in beam | 20ft 10in beam |
| | 4ft 10in draught | 5ft 10in draught | 4ft 9in draught |
| Type of hull | Displacement | Chine | Displacement chine |
| Displacement (designed) | 68 tons | 66½ tons | 85 tons |
| Displacement (actual) | 80 tons | 72 tons | 105 tons |
| Engines make and number | Hall-Scott Defender (2) | Hall-Scott Defender supercharged (3) | Packard model 4M-2500 (4) |
| Engines max bhp (total) | 1260bhp | 2700bhp | 5000bhp |
| Maximum continuous bhp (total) | 620bhp | 1800bhp | 3680bhp |
| Reduction gear | 2:1 | 2:1 | .444 and direct |
| Estimated maximum speed (designed) | 21 knots at 68 tons | 27 knots at 66½ tons | 34.5 knots at 85 tons |
| Continuous speed (designed) | 16 knots | — | 29.5 knots |
| Actual max. speed | 18.5 knots at 80 tons disp | 26.5 knots at 72 tons disp | 32 knots at 105 tons with reduction gear; 30 knots at 105 tons with direct drive |
| Actual continuous speed | 15 knots at 80 tons disp | 22 knots at 72 tons disp | 27 knots at 105 tons reduction gear; 26.5 knots at 105 tons direct drive |
| Fuel capacity (gallons) | 2185gal | 1800gal | 5200gal |
| Fuel capacity per hr/ max continuous speed | 47gal | 130gal | 278gal |
| Range at max continuous speed | 697 nautical miles | 305 nautical miles | 506 nautical miles |
| Silencers | Vortex Burgess Servars | Dumbflow | Dumbflow |
| Armament varies | | | |

Note: These are approx average figures from trial results of new craft, and allowance should be made for any variation of these conditions.

# Tough Brothers Limited – Production 1940–45

| Boats built | Commenced | Launched | Handed over | Remarks |
|---|---|---|---|---|
| **MTBs** | | | | |
| 601 | 1 June 1941 | 4 October 1941 | 20 February 1942 | (Prototype D); sunk after action off Dover 2/7/42 |
| 603 | 8 October 1941 | 5 March 1942 | 20 August 1942 | |
| 626 | 12 October 1941 | 16 May 1942 | — | R Nor N; sunk in harbour, 1943 |
| 644 | 8 February 1942 | 29 July 1942 | 16 October 1942 | Sunk 1943 |
| 651 | 7 March 1942 | 28 August 1942 | — | |
| 673 | 6 July 1942 | 22 January 1943 | 10 May 1943 | |
| 674 | 8 July 1942 | 5 March 1943 | 29 April 1943 | |
| 703 | 6 January 1943 | 19 July 1943 | — | |
| 735 | 2 June 1943 | 12 November 1943 | 6 March 1944 | Transferred to R Canadian Navy, 1944 |
| 736 | 2 June 1943 | 14 December 1943 | — | Transferred to R Canadian Navy, 1944 |
| 784 | 20 November 1943 | 26 April 1944 | 7 October 1944 | |
| 792 | 3 December 1943 | 23 May 1944 | 17 March 1945 | |
| 3022 | 5 May 1944 | 30 January 1945 | 20 March 1945 | Transferred to the RAF as ASRL 020 |
| **MGBs** | | | | |
| 316, 330 and 331 | | | | Built 1941, (all Fairmile C types) |
| **MLs** | | | | |
| 113 | January 1940 | | | |
| 171, 199, 220, 228 and 448 | 11 June 1941 | 8 October 1941 | 2 November 1941 | |
| **LCI (S)** | | | | |
| 501 | 28 August 1942 | 5 January 1943 | 12 May 1943 | |
| 525 | 6 January 1943 | 21 May 1943 | 27 July 1943 | |
| **MFVs** | *Parts arrived* | *Commenced* | *Handed over* | |
| 1 | 10 May 1944 | 20 June 1944 | 23 October 1944 | |
| 2 | 10 July 1944 | 8 September 1944 | — | |
| 3 | — | 24 September 1944 | — | |
| 4 | — | 2 November 1944 | — | Scrapped unfinished |
| 5 | — | 5 January 1945 | — | |
| 6 | — | 8 January 1945 | — | |

Fourteen 36ft harbour service launches were also built between 29 June 1944 and 20 October 1945.

These figures were kindly provided by Mr Robert Tough from the company's wartime records.

# Service summary – Norwegian-manned MTB 618

This craft was built by DK Harris & Sons Ltd of Appledore. Launched on 5 March 1942, she was commissioned on 18 June 1942 and allocated to the 30th (Norwegian) MTB Flotilla, based at Lerwick, Shetlands. This flotilla operated off the coast of Norway, and there is no evidence to suggest that it was ever in Iceland, as has sometimes been claimed. The flotilla took part in a number of attacks on the Norwegian coast in 1943–44 and those in which records show MTB 618 to have been involved are detailed below:

**23–24 Jan 1943**  MTBs 626, 627, 620, 631, 625 and 618 sailed in company to carry out various attacks along the Norwegian coast. 618 and 623 left the others and proceeded to attack Marstenen Island with gunfire, to which the enemy replied at a range of 500–600 yards. MTB 623 was hampered when her 2-pounder and Oerlikon guns jammed, but MTB 618 observed direct hits on at least four gun posts. 618 was hit twice below and twice above the waterline and peppered with machine gun bullet holes. A shell burst in an ammunition locker and started a fire, but this was promptly dealt with by two of the crew who threw the burning magazines overboard. MTB 623 was also damaged, but both craft returned safely to Lerwick. Two of 618's crew were wounded.

**22–23 Mar 1943**  MTBs 618 and 627 carried out a successful Commando raid on a bridge at Dragsund. Shots were exchanged with sentries and two Germans were believed killed. The MTBs withdrew without damage or casualties.

**3 April–26 June 1943**  Refitting at Inverness.

**10–11 Aug 1943**  MTBs 618 and 623 escorted three small Norwegian fishing vessels in approx position 62° 06'N, 33° 42'E. Attacked by two Arado 196 aircraft on return trip without damage or casualties.

**10–11 Sept 1943**  MTBs 618 and 627 attacked the 3811GRT merchant ship *Anke* off Kristiansund. At a range of 900 yards MTB 618 fired both torpedoes and struck the ship with one and possibly both. The ship stop-

ped and was then struck by at least one of 627's torpedoes. The MV appeared to break in two, but further observation was prevented by a cloud of dense smoke obscuring the target. Shore searchlights ranged on the MTBs and guns opened fire, but the MTBs escaped without casualties or damage.

**October 1943**  30th MTB Flotilla renamed 54th Flotilla.

**5–6 Feb 1944**  MTBs 618 and 619 engaged an enemy patrol vessel with gunfire in Sognesjoen and left it on fire. MTB 619 suffered two hits and five men were wounded.

**March 1944**  54th MTB Flotilla re-allocated to Nore Command, based at Great Yarmouth.

**10–11 April 1944**  MTBs 618, 623, 653 and 715, carrying out a sweep from Egmund to Texel, intercepted a convoy, but were unable to penetrate the E and R-boat screen. Three attacks were made on the escorts, one of which was set on fire. An R-boat which had apparently been hit by her own forces was attacked by the MTBs while enemy fire continued to be concentrated on it. The unit disengaged and returned to base. MTBs 618, 653 and 715 suffered superficial damage but no casualties.

**18 April**  Refitting at Oulton Broad, Norfolk.

**28 June–9 July 1944**  At Lowestoft for collision damage repairs.

Between 1 October 1944 and the end of the year the 54th MTB Flotilla, by then again based at Lerwick, had a number of successes against enemy shipping in the Norwegian leads, but the Naval Historical Branch records show no specific involvement by MTB 618. The boat paid off on 2 December 1944 and the Norwegian crew transferred to MTB 716. MTB 618 was sold to a private purchaser after the war.

This extract was prepared by the Naval Historical Branch, MoD, in October 1980. MTB 618 was then a houseboat moored at Shoreham-by-Sea, Sussex, and owned by Mr Kenneth Upperton.

# Engine trials of MTB 780, fitted with VP propellers

Date: 19/2/45
Time: 0910

MTB 780

Test Sheet No. 1

Displacement: 118 tons

Draught: Forward 4ft 6½ in
Aft: 5ft 4½ in

TRIAL: SCHEDULE PME/GCH.5/DE/29.9.44 No 3a

| | PO | PI | SI | SO | |
|---|---|---|---|---|---|
| RPM | 800 | 800 | 800 | 800 | Speed timed: 14.22 knots |
| Boost | –3 | –3 | –3 | –3 | Speed pito: 15.0 knots |
| Eng oil press | 95 | 95 | 80 | 85 | |
| Eng oil temp | 55 | 60 | 70 | 60 | |
| AIT Carb | — | 31 | — | — | Eng rm temp |
| | | | | | Eng rm depress 36 |
| | | | | | (inches Water) |
| VP propellers | | | | | PI exh back press |
| | | | | | (inches Mercury) |
| | | | | | PI accumulator press: |
| Pitch | 51 | 49 | 51 | 49 | Pump cut-in 540 |
| Oil press: fine | | 95 | | | Pump cut-out 780 |
| Oil press: coarse | | 40 | | | |
| | | | | | FUEL ON BOARD |
| | | | | | Total 4250 gal |
| Fuel: | | | | | |
| GPH | | | | | Barometric Press |
| Fuel consumption | 17 | 14.5 | 15 | 16 | 1030 Millibars |
| Total | 27 | 21 | 24 | 28 | |

*Remarks:* Engine room depression and exhaust back pressure gauges not fitted.
Pressures recorded in lb/sq in except as indicated.
Displacement, draught and fuel figures taken at beginning of trial.
All temperatures recorded in degrees Centigrade.

Date: 19/2/45
Time: 0930

MTB 780

Test Sheet No. 2

Displacement: tons

Draught: Forward ft in
Aft: ft in

TRIAL:

| | PO | PI | SI | SO | |
|---|---|---|---|---|---|
| RPM | 1200 | 1200 | 1200 | 1200 | Speed timed: 17.55 knots |
| Boost | –1½ | –1½ | –1½ | –1½ | Speed pito: 18.1 knots |
| Eng oil press | 100 | 100 | 95 | 105 | |
| Eng oil temp | 55 | 58 | 63 | 59 | |
| AIT Carb | | 32 | | | Eng rm temp |
| | | | | | Eng rm depress 35 |
| | | | | | (inches Water) |
| VP propellers | | | | | PI exh back press |
| | | | | | (inches Mercury) |
| | | | | | PI accumulator press: |
| Pitch | 43.5 | 42.5 | 44 | 41 | Pump cut-in |
| Oil press: fine | | 25 | | | Pump cut-out |
| Oil press: coarse | | 50 | | | |
| | | | | | FUEL ON BOARD |
| | | | | | Total gal |
| Fuel | | | | | |
| GPH | 33 | 30 | 30 | 31 | Barometric Press |
| Fuel consumption | 38 | 32 | 35 | 39 | 1030 Millibars |
| Total | | | | | |

*Remarks:* Engine room depression and exhaust back pressure gauges not fitted

Date: 19/2/45            Test Sheet No ___3___
Time: 0954          MTB 780

Displacement:    tons           Draught: Forward   ft   in
                                           Aft:   ft   in

TRIAL: SCH. No 3(a)

|  | PO | PI | SI | SO |  |
|---|---|---|---|---|---|
| RPM | 1600 | 1600 | 1600 | 1600 | Speed timed: 21.56 knots |
| Boost | +¾ | +¾ | +¾ | +¾ | Speed pito: 22.1 knots |
| Eng oil press | 100 | 100 | 95 | 105 |  |
| Eng oil temp | 55 | 60 | 62 | 69 |  |
| AIT Carb | — | 33 | — | — | Eng rm temp 35 |
|  |  |  |  |  | Eng rm depress |
|  |  |  |  |  | (inches Water) |
|  |  |  |  |  | PI exh back press |
| VP propellers |  |  |  |  | (inches Mercury) |
|  |  |  |  |  | PI accumulator press: |
| Pitch | 38 | 38.5 | 39 | 37 | Pump cut-in 540 |
| Oil press: fine |  | 20 |  |  | Pump cut-out 780 |
| Oil press: coarse |  | 70 |  |  |  |
|  |  |  |  |  | FUEL ON BOARD |
|  |  |  |  |  | Total ___ gal |
| Fuel: |  |  |  |  |  |
| GPH | 44 | 46 | 45 | 46 | Barometric Press |
| Fuel consumption | 52 | 46 | 49 | 54 | 1030 Millibars |
| Total |  |  |  |  |  |

*Remarks:* Engine room depression and exhaust back pressure gauges not fitted.

---

Date: 19/2/45            Test Sheet No ___4___
Time: 1018          MTB 780

Displacement:    tons           Draught: Forward   ft   in
                                           Aft:   ft   in

TRIAL: SCH No 3(a)

|  | PO | PI | SI | SO |  |
|---|---|---|---|---|---|
| RPM | 2000 | 2000 | 2000 | 2000 | Speed timed: 26.19 knots |
| Boost | +2¼ | +2¼ | +2¼ | +2¼ | Speed pito: 25.7 knots |
| Eng oil press | 92 | 98 | 80 | 97 |  |
| Eng oil temp | 58 | 60 | 78 | 60 |  |
| AIT Carb |  | 31 |  |  | Eng rm temp |
|  |  |  |  |  | Eng rm depress 34 |
|  |  |  |  |  | (inches Water) |
|  |  |  |  |  | PI exh back press |
| VP propellers |  |  |  |  | (inches Mercury) |
|  |  |  |  |  | PI accumulator press: |
| Pitch | 34 | 35 | 36 | 33 | Pump cut-in 540 |
| Oil press: fine |  | 20 |  |  | Pump cut-out 780 |
| Oil press: coarse |  | 65 |  |  |  |
|  |  |  |  |  | FUEL ON BOARD |
|  |  |  |  |  | Total ___ gal |
| Fuel: |  |  |  |  |  |
| GPH | 68 | 68 | 73 | 74 | Barometric Press |
| Fuel consumption | 75 | 68 | 73 | 78 | 1030 Millibars |
| Total |  |  |  |  |  |

*Remarks:* Engine room depression and exhaust back pressure gauges not fitted.
Timed and pitometer speeds shown above taken over six runs.
(1 5 10 10 5 1)

---

Date: 19/2/45            Test Sheet No ___5___
Time: 1132          MTB 780

Displacement:    tons           Draught: Forward   ft   in
                                           Aft:   ft   in

TRIAL: SCH No. 3a

|  | PO | PI | SI | SO |  |
|---|---|---|---|---|---|
| RPM | 2400 | 2400 | 2400 | 2400 | Speed timed: 29.46 knots |
| Boost | 6 | 6 | 6 | 6 | Speed pito: 29.45 knots |
| Eng oil press | 83 | 88 | 76 | 85 |  |
| Eng oil temp | 60 | 60 | 84 | 60 |  |
| AIT Carb | — | 32 | — | — | Eng rm temp |
|  |  |  |  |  | Eng rm depress 33 |
|  |  |  |  |  | (inches Water) |
|  |  |  |  |  | PI exh back press |
| VP propellers |  |  |  |  | (inches Mercury) |
|  |  |  |  |  | PI accumulator press: |
| Pitch | 32.3 | 32.3 | 33.3 | 31.7 | Pump cut-in 540 |
| Oil press: fine |  | 20 |  |  | Pump cut-out 780 |
| Oil press: coarse |  | 270 |  |  |  |
|  |  |  |  |  | FUEL ON BOARD |
|  |  |  |  |  | Total ___ gal |
| Fuel: |  |  |  |  |  |
| GPH | 110 | 113 | 115 | 112 | Barometric Press |
| Fuel consumption | 153 | 148 | 154 | 160 | 1030 Millibars |
| Total |  |  |  |  |  |

*Remarks:* Engine room depression and exhaust back pressure gauges not fitted.

---

Date: 20/2/45            Test Sheet No ___6 × 1___
Time: 1144          MTB 780

Displacement: 118 tons          Draught: Forward 4ft 7in
                                           Aft: 5ft 4in

TRIAL:

|  | PO | PI | SI | SO |  |
|---|---|---|---|---|---|
| RPM | 2200 | 2200 | 2200 | 2200 | Speed timed: 28.04 knots |
| Boost | +4½ | +4½ | +4½ | +4½ | Speed pito: 28.25 knots |
| Eng oil press | 92 | 98 | 83 | 93 |  |
| Eng oil temp | 59 | 60 | 78 | 60 |  |
| AIT Carb |  | 30 |  |  | Eng rm temp |
|  |  |  |  |  | Eng rm depress 35 |
|  |  |  |  |  | (inches Water) |
|  |  |  |  |  | PI exh back press |
| VP propellers |  |  |  |  | (inches Mercury) |
|  |  |  |  |  | PI accumulator press: |
| Pitch | 33.8 | 34.3 | 34.8 | 33.0 | Pump cut-in 560 |
| Oil press: fine |  | 20 |  |  | Pump cut-out 780 |
| Oil press: coarse |  | 205 |  |  |  |
|  |  |  |  |  | FUEL ON BOARD |
|  |  |  |  |  | Total 4045 gal |
| Fuel: |  |  |  |  |  |
| GPH | 88 | 90 | 98 | 90 | Barometric Press |
| Fuel consumption |  |  |  |  | 1033 Millibars |
| Total | 44 | 52 | 35 | 44 |  |

*Remarks:* Engine room depression and exhaust back pressure gauges not fitted.

Date: 20/2/45                    Test Sheet No ___2___
Time: 1202               MTB 780

Displacement:    tons            Draught: Forward  ft  in
                                          Aft:  ft  in

TRIAL: SCH No 3(a)

|  | PO | PI | SI | SO |  |
|---|---|---|---|---|---|
| RPM | 1800 | 1800 | 1800 | 1800 | Speed timed: 23.89 knots |
| Boost | +1½ | +1½ | +1½ | +1½ | Speed pito: 24.25 knots |
| Eng oil press | 98 | 100 | 82 | 98 |  |
| Eng oil temp | 59 | 60 | 79 | 60 |  |
| AIT Carb |  | 32 |  |  | Eng rm temp |
|  |  |  |  |  | Eng rm depress  35 |
|  |  |  |  |  | (inches Water) |
| VP propellers |  |  |  |  | PI exh back press |
|  |  |  |  |  | (inches Mercury) |
|  |  |  |  |  | PI accumulator press |
| Pitch | 36 | 37 | 37.2 | 35 | Pump cut-in  560 |
| Oil press: fine |  | 20 |  |  | Pump cut-out  780 |
| Oil press: coarse |  | 110 |  |  |  |
|  |  |  |  |  | FUEL ON BOARD |
|  |  |  |  |  | Total ___ gal |
| Fuel: |  |  |  |  |  |
| GPH | 51 | 55 | 58 | 56 | Barometric Press |
| Fuel consumption | 66 | 54 | 57 | 66 | 1033 Millibars |
| Total |  |  |  |  |  |

_Remarks_: Engine room depression and exhaust back pressure gauges not fitted.

---

Date: 20/2/45                    Test Sheet No ___3___
Time: 1221               MTB 780

Displacement:    tons            Draught: Forward  ft  in
                                          Aft:  ft  in

TRIAL: SCH No 3(a)

|  | PO | PI | SI | SO |  |
|---|---|---|---|---|---|
| RPM | 1400 | 1400 | 1400 | 1400 | Speed timed: 19.68 knots |
| Boost | −⅓ | −¼ | −¼ | −¼ | Speed pito: 20.35 knots |
| Eng oil press | 98 | 100 | 84 | 100 |  |
| Eng oil temp | 58 | 60 | 76 | 55 |  |
| AIT Carb |  | 34 |  |  | Eng rm temp  35 |
|  |  |  |  |  | Eng rm depress |
|  |  |  |  |  | (inches Water) |
| VP propellers |  |  |  |  | PI exh back press |
|  |  |  |  |  | (inches Mercury) |
|  |  |  |  |  | PI accumulator press |
| Pitch | 40.5 | 41.2 | 40.5 | 39 | Pump cut-in  560 |
| Oil press: fine |  | 40 |  |  | Pump cut-out  780 |
| Oil press: coarse |  | 55 |  |  |  |
|  |  |  |  |  | FUEL ON BOARD |
|  |  |  |  |  | Total ___ gal |
| Fuel: |  |  |  |  |  |
| GPH | 38 | 37 | 37 | 39 | Barometric Press |
| Fuel consumption | 81 | 70 | 73 | 82 | 1033 Millibars |
| Total |  |  |  |  |  |

_Remarks_: Engine room depression and exhaust back pressure gauges not fitted.

---

Date: 20/2/45                    Test Sheet No ___4___
Time: 1243               MTB 780

Displacement:    tons            Draught: Forward  ft  in
                                          Aft:  ft  in

TRIAL:

|  | PO | PI | SI | SO |  |
|---|---|---|---|---|---|
| RPM | 1000 | 1000 | 1000 | 1000 | Speed timed: 16.09 knots |
| Boost | −2 | −2 | −2 | −2 | Speed pito: 16.95 knots |
| Eng oil press | 97 | 105 | 84 | 92 |  |
| Eng oil temp | 56 | 60 | 67 | 59 |  |
| AIT Carb |  | 35 |  |  | Eng rm temp  39 |
|  |  |  |  |  | Eng rm depress |
|  |  |  |  |  | (inches Water) |
| VP propellers |  |  |  |  | PI exh back press |
|  |  |  |  |  | (inches Mercury) |
|  |  |  |  |  | PI accumulator press |
| Pitch | 47.2 | 46.5 | 47 | 45.5 | Pump cut-in  560 |
| Oil press: fine |  | 60 |  |  | Pump cut-out  780 |
| Oil press: coarse |  | 20 |  |  |  |
|  |  |  |  |  | FUEL ON BOARD |
|  |  |  |  |  | Total ___ gal |
| Fuel: |  |  |  |  |  |
| GPH | 24 | 24 | 24.5 | 24.8 | Barometric Press |
| Fuel consumption | 94 | 82 | 86 | 95 | 1033 Millibars |
| Total |  |  |  |  |  |

_Remarks_: Engine room depression and exhaust back pressure gauges not fitted.

# Service summary – HMIML 440

This abridged history of HMIML 440, which is typical of the work done by the number of MLs operating off the Burma coast between 1942 and 1945 in the campaign to clear the Japanese Army from Burma, has been compiled from information provided by Reg Pike (sometime Lieutenant R S Pike RINVR), who was her CO from 1942 to 1945.

HMIML 440 was a typical Indian-built Fairmile B type, constructed of Indian teak with copper sheathing below the waterline. Armament increased as the war progressed, and these boats finally mounted a 6-pounder (manual), a twin 20mm Oerlikon, a 40mm Bofors Mark III aft, two twin .303in machine guns on the bridge wings, smoke-making apparatus, a few depth charges and a rocket flare projector (in some, but not all units). They were manned by three or four officers and eighteen ratings, in extremely cramped accommodation, with no refrigeration or air-conditioning. They had paraffin cooking in the galleys and bunks for only sixteen persons.

The boats operated from shore bases and had access to a depot ship (HMIS *Barracuda*), but each unit was the only home for all its officers and crew, who lived, ate, slept and fought their war aboard for several months between visits to an Indian port for a rest and refit.

ML 440 was built in Bombay from local timber, with her main engines and electrical equipment shipped out from the UK. After fitting out, trials and training, she sailed around southern India for Chittagong, where she joined other units of the 55th Flotilla – MLs 438, 439, 440, 441, 474, 475, 476, 477 and one other.

Early duties consisted of patrols down the Arakan coast of Burma, seeking enemy supply lines and intercepting local fishing boats and small craft to gather information about enemy forces and their movements.

Early in 1943 an advance base was established at Tek Naaf on the Naaf River, some 100 miles to the south of Chittagong. Tek Naaf, about 8–10 miles up the river, provided a safe anchorage for the flotillas and enabled operations to be carried out much further down the Burma coastline. This advance base had limited facilities, but provided a welcome respite for craft returning from a 48- or 72-hour patrol to the south.

Monsoon conditions in the Bay of Bengal were far too severe to enable the MLs to operate successfully, so during the summer of 1943 they returned to Indian ports for rest, refit, re-equipping and retraining.

In March 1943 ML 440 met very severe conditions and her forward 6-pounder was carried away by the sea, and three depth charges with their racks were ripped out of the teak deck and washed overboard. The MLs would have stayed afloat during the monsoon, but apart from injury to the crew, they could not have fired their weapons with any accuracy. In the autumn the flotillas went back to the Arakan coast for further offensive patrols well to the south of Akyab and occasionally down to the mouth of the Bassein River.

Tragedy hit ML 440 while she was lying alongside a jetty in Calcutta in 1943. An accumulation of fumes from petrol in the engineroom bilges caused a violent explosion. The engineroom deckhead, together with the twin 20mm Oerlikon mounting, was blown clean over the side into the River Hoogly. The hull sides were considerably distorted and the petrol storage tanks crumpled, but did not themselves explode; two ratings were killed. Repairs were carried out and, after a seemingly endless round of delays,

ML 440 rejoined the rest of the flotilla at Chittagong, just in time for Christmas. Christmas was short that year, for on Boxing Day the flotilla sailed for further operations.

There were long patrols off the Burma coast with boats working singly or in pairs. These usually took the form of a long daytime cruise down the coast some 30 miles offshore and then a night landfall in the area of Ramree Island, Combermere Bay or the Cheduba Straight. Here the boats would lie to with sonar listening gear, trying to detect the movement of local supply craft, or would gently nose their way behind the islands, venturing up-river or crossing narrow creeks or chaungs. These expeditions, carried out at night with no navigation lights or other aids, called for the highest quality of navigation and some daring. Though these operations provided only limited success in the interception of enemy supply ships, occasional mortar fire was encountered and the presence of the boat in the area was frequently signalled by a type of green Very light fired from the cliffs and hillsides by Japanese lookouts. Shortly before dawn the boats would withdraw and commence their long return to base, ever on the lookout for attack by enemy aircraft.

There was no refrigeration and no facilities for carrying fresh meat, so it was quite customary to leave base with three or four live goats or sheep on deck, as it would be five or six days before further fresh meat supplies would be available. A small amount of hay might have been obtained from the stores, but on a number of occasions, at Tek Naaf, the animals were ferried ashore in the ship's dinghy to allow them to graze on the river bank. A rating would be left in charge as shepherd, to await the boat's return before nightfall or the next seagoing voyage. Animals were killed each morning and hung from the side of the bridge, to provide the day's meat supply for the ratings.

The officers' catering arrangements were independent of those for the crew and their live meat supply was normally in the form of chickens or ducks, also living on the upper deck. The chickens were not good travellers and died as frequently from natural as from unnatural causes, but the ducks were much hardier seafarers. On 440 a duck named Godfrey (so named after the then current Vice-Admiral of the RIN) survived for many months, saw much action and was indeed very closely guarded whenever the boat was tied up alongside any other vessel.

Together with other livestock on long-range patrols, pigeons were sometimes carried. This was not for food or to help find the way back, but was for their training as homing-pigeons, for they were used to carry messages from agents landed secretly on the enemy-occupied coast.

MLs carrying one or two agents would proceed for up to 200 miles along the coast into enemy-occupied territory, to land the agent at his pre-arranged dropping point. Exact navigation was essential as a landfall had to be made on moonless nights in complete darkness at a precise point, so that the agent could orient himself quickly, establish his local contacts and merge into the background as efficiently as possible. After a slow, cautious approach, the ML would be anchored lightly and the agent ferried ashore in the ship's dinghy or rubber inflatable. With the agent and his equipment safely landed, the crew member would return to the ML, which would quietly withdraw well out to sea before commencing its homeward journey.

The dropping of agents was comparatively straightforward, but their recovery was invariably a more hazardous operation. The ML would return a month or two later, on up to three consecutive nights. Lying some 200 yards offshore, the crew would flash a blue recognition signal and, on receiving the appropriate reply, send the dinghy inshore to retrieve the agent. Prudence was essential in case the agent had been compromised or captured, or was a double agent, and a Japanese 75mm gun was in position to welcome the boat. Each of those experiences were encountered by different boats of the flotillas, but the success rate was high and a great deal of valuable information was transmitted back to headquarters to enable the strategic and detailed planning of future operations.

With the development of Combined Operations landings it was desirable to keep the enemy guessing as to where such landings might take place. In January 1945 ML 440 was used on a diversionary exercise. At Tek Naaf a group of Army engineers and technical personnel were embarked, together with a load of equipment designed to simulate a landing some 50 miles along the coast. The exercise very nearly came to an abrupt, abortive end, for on approaching the mouth of the Naaf River the ship began to steer an erratic course and the coxswain reported with alarm that the compass was going round in circles. It was found that in the dark the Royal Engineers had clamped on to the sides of the wheelhouse two large loudspeakers, which seriously affected the magnetic compass. They were rapidly repositioned and, on approaching the appointed beach, switched on, broadcasting the loud noise of landing craft. Simultaneously the technicians dropped over the stern a series of floating, flashing buoys and occasional smoke incinerators, all intended to simulate an approaching landing force. As they moved nearer inshore, enemy guns in the hillsides started shelling the apparent invasion. Unknown to the crew of the ML, a British destroyer was lying a mile offshore, and to their surprise started its own bombardment of the enemy gun positions, which were soon silenced. Withdrawing with some satisfaction at a job well done, the ML returned quietly to its base.

Penetration and reconnaissance patrols carried on apace during late 1944 and early 1945. In January ML 440, in company with ML 441, was required to make a river penetration to the south of Ramree Island. A small Army group was aboard, and their objective was a bridge some 10 miles upstream. The ships had no river navigation charts, merely a crude map of the area, and the river was entered in the dark. Both units proceeded upstream cautiously, the leadsman taking continuous soundings. Enjoying readings of 'by the mark 2½', they had progressed some six miles upstream when 440, in the lead, suddenly hit a hard underwater obstruction, which severely damaged both propellers. Frantic signals were made to 441, to prevent her doing the same, while vibration on the quarterdeck of 440 was so strong that it was difficult for the crew to stand. The operation had to be abandoned and 441 took 440 in tow and beat a cautious retreat. The withdrawal downstream was accompanied by many green flares from the banks and hillsides, as well as some mortar fire, which fortunately was not accurate. Both units arrived back at Akyab and there the tow was transferred to another vessel, which took the crippled unit up to the mouth of the Hoogly, from where a tug took her on to Vizagpatam.

In less than two hours from arrival, 440 was hauled up the slipway and work on the replacement of propellers and shafts commenced immediately. Some 36 hours after her arrival at Vizag, she was repaired and refuelled and sailed directly across the Indian Ocean to rejoin her flotilla on the Burma coast.

The first major opposed Combined Operation landing took place in February 1945 at Kyaukpyu, when MLs of the Coastal Force Command played a major part in leading the landing craft on to the beaches. As dawn broke, MLs took position on the landward side of large troop-carrying merchant ships. The landing craft were lowered, filled with troops and then formed into columns, led and flanked by MLs, with 440 as leader of the starboard column. As the beaches were approached, shells from a battleship and two cruisers lying out to sea passed overhead. Just short of the breakers, the MLs turned aside and the landing craft surged ahead. As they went in, a South African ML struck a mine and was sunk.

As the build-up to forward operations continued, an increasing number of senior officers required transport from Chittagong to Akyab and other forward areas. Road communications were nonexistent and air transport facilities were limited, so MLs on passage to and from their bases frequently provided transport for a wide range of officers from all three services.

In July 1945 the flotilla moved southwards to Trincomalee in Ceylon (now Sri Lanka) to join the various ships and forces gathering for the Malayan invasion. Training exercises continued, but in that vast harbour there was no access to a shore depot and no base ship, so it was difficult to keep the crews physically fit and to maintain morale. During the next few weeks the flotilla sailed frequently out of Trincomalee harbour to one of the excellent beaches fringed with palms found in that part of the island. However, it was a period of hard training and practice drills designed to improve efficiency.

It was envisaged in the Malayan landing plans that the MLs would be used in two separate waves. The major group was to proceed across the Indian Ocean under their own power and then rest and recuperate. The other, smaller group of six MLs, with 440 as the leader, was to be embarked on two mobile floating docks which would carry them from Ceylon across the ocean and discharge them off the Malayan coastline. These units, fully fuelled and with fit and rested crews, would lead an assault up the Malayan rivers to capture vital bridges well inland. The attack, however, never took place, since the Japanese surrender intervened. VJ day was celebrated in some style.

During November 1945 the 55th Flotilla, led by ML 440, proceeded to Trombay, the Coastal Forces base in Bombay, and commenced the decommissioning process. By this time the Flotilla had been in existence for 3½ years, working for a great deal of the time in operational areas, with many crew changes.

In 1946, ML 440, with many other MLs, was tied up in a trot between buoys at Trombay. A cyclone hit Bombay, and ML 440 was lifted by a giant wave, broke loose from the buoys and landed on the power lines, putting half the city into darkness. Her end was thus every bit as spectacular as her service career.

# Bibliography

## Sources

ADM1/10241 Motor Launches (Fairmile Type):– from the Public Record Office, Kew. Light Coastal Craft operating in the North Sea & the English Channel. September '43.

B.R. 834:– a small identification booklet of British and Axis Coastal Forces Types. The Fairmile Motor Launch Engineering Handbook. February 1941.

The Instruction Manual for the Hall-Scott Defender as supplied on Lend-Lease – Contract No. 11933.

DEMS Pocket Book 1942 (Defensive Equipment of Merchant Ships). September 1942 – BR 282.

Technical History of British Minesweeping 1939–1945 (1, 2 and 3). Published 1947.

The Gunnery Pocket Book 1945 – BR 224/45.

Various official Gunnery Manuals from Priddy's Hard, the RN Naval Armament Museum, Gosport.

Official Fairmile Records – kindly provided by the late Fairmile Marine Company.

Official Records – kindly provided by Tough Brothers of Teddington, Middx.

## Other published material

Warship Supplement 59 – Winter 1979. MLs – HDMLs, etc. Lists and Data.

Warship Supplement 65 – Summer 1981. MTBs, MGBs, etc. Lists and Data

The Coastal Forces Veterans Association Newsletters.

The 56th MTB/MGB Flotilla, Coastal Forces Mediterranean 1943–45.

The Western Lady Ferry Service, by S A Armstrong – August 1988.

## Published books

Brown, DK *A Century of Naval Construction* Conway Maritime Press (1983)

Campbell, John *Naval Weapons of World War Two* Conway Maritime Press (1985)

Carter, Geoffrey *The Royal Navy at Portland Since 1845* Maritime Books (1987)

Cooper, Brian *The E-Boat Threat* Macdonald & Jane's (1976)

Cooper, Bryan *The Battle of the Torpedo Boats* Pan Books Ltd (1970)

Cooper, Bryan *The Buccaneers* (Weapons Book No 13) Purnell (1970)

Du Cane, Peter *High Speed Small Craft* Temple Press Books (1964)

Elliott, Peter *Allied Minesweeping in World War 2* Patrick Stephens Ltd (1979)

Fock, Harald *Fast Fighting Boats 1870–1945* Nautical Publishing Company Ltd (1978)

Friedman, Norman *Naval Radar* Conway Maritime Press (1981)

Friedman, Norman *US Naval Weapons* Naval Institute Press (1983)

Friedman, Norman *The Postwar Naval Revolution* Conway Maritime Press (1986)

Friedman, Norman *US Small Combatants* Naval Institute Press (1987)

Gillett, Ross *Fighting Ships of the Royal Australian Navy* Burgess Media Services Ltd (1983)

Goulden, OA *From Trombay to Changi . . . The Story of Arakan Coastal Forces* the Chameleon Press Ltd (1987)

Hackmann, Willem *Seek & Strike, Sonar, Anti-submarine Warfare and the Royal Navy 1914–54* HMSLO (1984)

Hampshire, A Cecil *The Secret Navies* Sphere Books Ltd (1980)

Howard, Grant *The Navy in New Zealand – An Illustrated History* Jane's Publishing (1981)

Lenton, HT and Colledge, JJ *British Warship Losses of World War II – British Fleet Losses* Ian Allan (1964)

Lenton HT and Colledge, JJ *Warships of World War II* Ian Allan (1973)

Macpherson, Ken *The Ships of Canada's Naval Forces 1910–1985* Collins (1985)

Meister, Jurg *Soviet Warships of the Second World War* ARCO Publishing Company (1977)

North, AJD *Royal Naval Coastal Forces 1939–45* Almark Publications (1972)

Phelan, Keiren and Brice, Martin H. *Fast Attack Craft* Macdonald & Jane's (1977)

Preston, Antony *Strike Craft* Bison Books Ltd (1982)

Reynolds, LC (Rover) *Gunboat 658* The New English Library (1974)

*Selected papers on British Warship Design in World War II* RINA (transactions of) Conway Maritime Press (1983)

Silverstone, Paul H *US Warships of World War Two* Ian Allan (1965)

Smith, Peter C *Hold the Narrow Sea* Moorland Publishing Co and Naval Institute Press (1984)

Stafford, Edward P *Subchaser* US Naval Institute Press (1988)
*Booklet of General Plans, SC1474–S1601–508774*
*Booklet of General Plans, SC676–S0107*
*Gun and Turret Catalog – 1945*
*Ships' Data – 1945*
*General Board Study 420–14 (Small Craft)*
*Naval Ordnance and Gunnery (Navpers 16116)* Bureau of Personnel Training Division (1944)

Waddington, CH *OR in World War 2: Operational Research against the U-Boat* Elek Science London (1973)

Watts, Anthony *The U-Boat Hunters* Purnell Book Services Ltd (1976)